Introduction to the Law of Corporations: Cases and Materials

9th Edition

Fall 2023

Introduction

This open-source casebook is the ninth edition of a casebook using the H2O/OpenCasebook platform of the Library Innovation Lab of the Harvard Library and the Berkman Center. This casebook and the H2O/OpenCasebook platform are part of an effort by educators to make high quality course materials and casebooks available to students at reasonable prices. Because this casebook is subject to a Creative Commons license and can be printed via Amazon/Kindle Direct Publishing, it is available to students at a very modest cost. Alternatively, students can access and read the cases and materials online via the H2O platform at opencasebook.org at no cost.

Although this course is called an *Introduction to the Law of Corporations*, it is better understood as a more general business organizations course. This casebook is intended to be used as the main casebook for this course. However, your learning during this semester-long course will not be limited to the corporate law. We will start the class with an online course covering the basic concepts of Agency. Agency is the single most important building block required to understand the corporate law. Agency is also an essential building block to understand the laws governing other forms of business organization.

During the course of this semester, you will also be introduced to other forms of business organization, including Partnerships, Limited Liability Companies, Nonprofit Corporations, and Public Benefit Corporations. Most of your introduction to these other forms will come through a series of online courses covering the basic concepts and rules for each of the forms. You should plan to complete all of these courses, including the accompanying quizzes in Canvas, by the dates set forth in the syllabus. While you are working on these online courses, in class we will focus on the corporate form, the Delaware corporate code, and the Delaware common law of corporations.

Because the corporate law is so much more extensive than the laws of other business forms, like for example the law governing LLCs, courts often lean heavily on the corporate law and apply it by analogy to other forms when they are in search of persuasive authority. By becoming expert in the corporate law, you will find it easy to translate that knowledge and apply it other business organizations.

Much of the work of the corporate lawyer starts with the code. As such, we will start with an in depth examination of the corporate code. Although we could study the Model Code or the Massachusetts code, for most corporate lawyers, the Delaware corporate law will be central to their practice. Sixty percent of all publicly traded corporations are Delaware corporations. With respect to private corporations, they are typically incorporated in the state in which they are physically located, or they are incorporated in Delaware.

Beyond the code, Delaware has a very deep corporate common law. It is in the corporate common law that the courts have developed the law of corporate fiduciary duties. It is through fiduciary duties that the corporate law attempts to regulate the relationship between stockholders and the corporation, between managers and the corporation, as well as the relationships of controlling stockholders and minority stockholders. Delaware's treatment of the corporate common law is so extensive that it is not at all uncommon at all for the courts of other states to refer to, or cite Delaware corporate law cases, when deciding questions involving their own corporate law. The Delaware corporate law is the closest we have to a lingua franca in the US for corporate law.

The fiduciary duties of corporate directors are tested most often in the context of corporate takeovers. The corporate takeover materials in this casebook attempt to highlight the most important issues in takeover situations as well as the court's doctrinal efforts to mitigate the transaction costs that arise in these situations.

Table of Contents

Before we dive into the corporate law, a quick word about what corporate law is and, perhaps more importantly, what it isn't. Many law students take corporate law thinking that it will equip them with enough business background, including finance and accounting, so that they can be successful in a corporate/transactional law practice. Unfortunately, if you're hoping that a course in the corporate law will substitute for an MBA, then you're mistaken. This course will focus on certain legal relationships that are central to the corporate form.

That said, a good corporate/transactional lawyer will be very conversant with the language of business and will understand what it is his or her clients are doing. If you wish to be an effective business lawyer, it is extremely important, therefore, to develop the vocabulary of business and some basic business skills while in law school or soon thereafter. Don't worry. Building this vocabulary can be easier than you might expect. First things first, you should begin to read the things that your clients will read. I recommend subscribing to the New York Times Dealbook newsletter delivered by email every day. If you begin to read it regularly, the business and legal issues that are central to your business clients will become apparent to you over time.

In addition to this informal education, you should take advantage of your time in law school to take at least one accounting/finance class at the business school. If you cannot enroll in courses at the business school, I recommend adding the <u>Wharton Foundation Series</u> (http://blog.coursera.org/post/60889088289/the-wharton-foundation-series) to your list of things to do before graduating or maybe in lieu of a bar trip after graduation. The foundation series is a series of four online courses available through Coursera and conducted by the faculty of the Wharton School at UPenn. The courses are as follows:

1. Introduction to Financial Accounting;
2. Introduction to Corporate Finance;
3. Introduction to Marketing; and
4. Introduction to Operations Management

Start with Financial Accounting and then Corporate Finance. Good luck!

Introduction to the Delaware Corporations Law   2.1

Although every state has its own corporate law, we
will focus on the Delaware General Corporation
Law. We do this for one very important reason: two-thirds of all
publicly-traded U.S. companies, including more than 60% of the
Fortune 500, and a significant number of private corporations are
incorporated in Delaware. A study by Robert Daines found that
when private companies are incorporated that there are only two
incorporation choices. First, they tend to incorporate in the state in
which they are headquartered and in which they do their business.
Second, they incorporate in Delaware.

You might well ask how is it possible that a corporation that is
headquartered in Massachusetts and does business in Massachusetts
should be governed by Delaware law? This seemingly odd result is a
function of a variety of factors, including historical developments as
well as our federal system.

In the earliest days of our Republic, the power to incorporate
corporations was reserved to the states. Prior to the adoption of
general incorporation statutes, the incorporation of a corporation
required state legislatures to adopt a law incorporating the entity.
These incorporation statutes laid out the powers and responsibilities
of the corporation, including the rights of corporate stockholders
with respect to the entity formed by the state legislature. It was not
uncommon at the time for the state grants of corporate charters to
reserve some monopoly power within the state to the corporation -
typically to facilitate the development of some critical infrastructure
like a canal, roadway, or railroad. Over time, the process of
incorporation was simplified as states adopted general incorporation
statutes, which took legislatures out of the business of incorporating
individual businesses. General incorporation statutes laid out default
powers and responsibilities of the corporation as well as describing

the default powers and rights of the corporation's stockholders vis a vis the corporation.

When one combines the power of states to incorporate businesses with constitutional prohibitions against states impeding interstate commerce and Article IV's full faith and credit clause (requiring each state to provide full faith and credit to public acts of every other state) with a state's power to incorporate, then one makes it possible for a corporation to be incorporated in one state and then do business in another.

Of course, a corporation's outward acts - acts other than those related to their relationships with their stockholders, for example with respect to employment law or the environment - are subject to the jurisdiction of the law in which the acts occur. However, the internal affairs of the corporation (relations among the stockholders, and managers with the corporation itself) are the stuff of the law of the state of incorporation. In a 1982 case, *Edgar v Mite Corp.* (457 US 624 (1982)) the US Supreme Court recognized the "internal affairs doctrine" as well settled law in the US:

> The internal affairs doctrine is a conflict of laws principle which recognizes that only one State should have the authority to regulate a corporation's internal affairs — matters peculiar to the relationships among or between the corporation and its current officers, directors, and shareholders — because otherwise a corporation could be faced with conflicting demands. See Restatement (Second) of Conflict of Laws § 302, Comment *b*, pp. 307-308 (1971).

But *Edgar* is not a unique application of the internal affairs doctrine by the US Supreme Court. In an earlier case, *Cort v. Ash* (422 US 66, 1975), the court described the doctrine and the primacy of state law in the following way:

> Corporations are creatures of state law, and investors commit their funds to corporate directors on the understanding that, except where federal law expressly requires certain responsibilities of directors with respect to stockholders, state law will govern the internal affairs of the corporation. If, for

example, state law permits corporations to use corporate funds as contributions in state elections, see *Miller, supra,* at 763 n. 4, shareholders are on notice that their funds may be so used and have no recourse under any federal statute.

The ability of entrepreneurs to elect to incorporate their businesses in one of any number of states gave way to something of a competition among states in the early 20th century for the revenue associated with incorporation of businesses. In corporate governance circles, this competitive environment was criticized as a "race to the bottom" with states competing with each other to reduce management accountability to its lowest possible level in order to attract incorporations. While this race to the bottom logic is by now slightly overblown, at one point in the past states aggressively competed for incorporations. Although some states occasionally attempt to revive their incorporation business, the age of active competition for incorporations is long since over with Delaware decisively winning. As Daines noted, the incorporation decision these days is more likely to be binary - incorporate where you do business or in Delaware.

Rather than see itself in competition against other state jurisdictions, Delaware sees itself in tension with the SEC and federal regulators for dominance in corporate governance. Delaware is protective of its position as a leader in the law of corporations. To the extent the SEC and federal regulators adopt, or threaten to adopt, rules that affect corporate governance, Delaware reacts. Over the course of this semester we will see various examples of federal movement in the corporate governance area along with reactions by the state of Delaware as it reacts to protect its position.

For now, though, we will focus on the basics of the Delaware corporate law, starting with formation.

Formation   2.2

The beginnings of incorporation

                                                                        2.2.1

Prior to the late 19th century, few states had general enabling laws with respect incorporations.

Incorporation was not a right, but rather a privilege granted by state governments on individual groups of promoters. At that time, the incorporation of a business required a legislative act by the state in which the corporation was to do its business. As a consequence, there were few corporations in the US. When legislatures granted incorporations, the majority of incorporations were limited to enterprises intended to engage in infrastructure development. The earliest corporations in the US were corporations formed to develop canals, turnpikes and bridges. It was not uncommon for state legislatures to grant monopoly rights to develop certain critical infrastructure. It was also not uncommon for states to invest in these enterprises by way of a contribution of land for the use of the infrastructure corporation.

By the early 20th century, general enabling laws, which granted everyone the right to incorporate, began to take hold in states across the country. One of the motivations for the switch to general enabling laws was a backlash to the high degree of corruption in state legislatures. Promoters seeking support for acts of incorporation often found that support the old-fashioned way - by means of a bribe. By turning the power dynamic on its head and making the act of incorporation ministerial rather than discretionary, state legislatures were robbed of an important motivation for corruption.

In his dissent in a 1933 case, Ligget v Lee (288, US 517), Justice Brandeis discussed the development of general enabling laws and the related concepts of "charter mongering" (or, competition amongst the states for incorporations in the period following adoption of the general enabling laws):

The prevalence of the corporation in America has led men of this generation to act, at times, as if the privilege of doing business in corporate form were inherent in the citizen; and has led them to accept the evils attendant upon the free and unrestricted use of the corporate mechanism as if these evils were the inescapable price of civilized life and, hence, to be borne with resignation. Throughout the greater part of our history a different view prevailed. Although the value of this instrumentality in commerce and industry was fully recognized, incorporation for business was commonly denied long after it had been freely granted for religious, educational and charitable purposes. It was denied because of fear. Fear of encroachment upon the liberties and opportunities of the individual. Fear of the subjection of labor to capital. Fear of monopoly. Fear that the absorption of capital by corporations, and their perpetual life, might bring evils similar to those which attended mortmain. There was a sense of some insidious menace inherent in large aggregations of capital, particularly when held by corporations. So, at first, the corporate privilege was granted sparingly; and only when the grant seemed necessary in order to procure for the community some specific benefit otherwise unattainable. The later enactment of general incorporation laws does not signify that the apprehension of corporate domination had been overcome. The desire for business expansion created an irresistible demand for more charters; and it was believed that under general laws embodying safeguards of universal application the scandals and favoritism incident to special incorporation could be avoided. The general laws, which long embodied severe restrictions upon size and upon the scope of corporate activity, were, in part, an expression of the desire for equality of opportunity.

(a) Limitation upon the amount of the authorized capital of business corporations was long universal. The maximum limit frequently varied with the kinds of business to be carried on, being dependent apparently upon the supposed requirements of the efficient unit. Although the statutory limits were changed from time to time this principle of limitation was long retained.

Thus in New York the limit was at first $100,000 for some businesses and as little as $50,000 for others. Until 1881 the maximum for business corporations in New York was $2,000,000; and until 1890, $5,000,000. In Massachusetts the limit was at first $200,000 for some businesses and as little as $5,000 for others. Until 1871 the maximum for mechanical and manufacturing corporations was $500,000; and until 1899, $1,000,000. The limit of $100,000 was retained for some businesses until 1903.

In many other states, including the leading ones in some industries, the removal of the limitations upon size was more recent. Pennsylvania did not remove the limits until 1905. Its first general act not having contained a maximum limit that of $500,000 was soon imposed. Later, it was raised to $1,000,000; and, for iron and steel companies, to $5,000,000. Vermont limited the maximum to $1,000,000 until 1911 when no amount over $10,000,000 was authorized if, in the opinion of a judge of the supreme court, such a capitalization would tend "to create a monopoly or result in restraining competition in trade." Maryland limited until 1918 the capital of mining companies to $3,000,000; and prohibited them from holding more than 500 acres of land (except in Allegany County, where 1,000 acres was allowed). New Hampshire did not remove the maximum limit until 1919. It had been $1,000,000 until 1907, when it was increased to $5,000,000. Michigan did not remove the maximum limit until 1921. The maximum, at first $100,000, had been gradually increased until in 1903 it became $10,000,000 for some corporations and $25,000,000 for others; and in 1917 became $50,000,000. Indiana did not remove until 1921 the maximum limit of $2,000,000 for petroleum and natural gas corporations. Missouri did not remove its maximum limit until 1927. Texas still has such a limit for certain corporations.

(b) Limitations upon the scope of a business corporation's powers and activity were also long universal. At first, corporations could be formed under the general laws only for a limited number of purposes — usually those which required a relatively large fixed capital, like transportation, banking, and insurance, and mechanical, mining, and manufacturing enterprises. Permission to incorporate for "any lawful purpose" was not common until 1875; and until that time the duration of corporate franchises was generally limited to a period of 20, 30, or 50 years. All, or a majority, of the incorporators or directors, or both, were required to be residents of the incorporating state. The powers which the corporation might exercise in carrying out its purposes were sparingly conferred and strictly construed. Severe limitations were imposed on the amount of indebtedness, bonded or otherwise. The power to hold stock in other corporations was not conferred or implied. The holding company was impossible.

(c) The removal by the leading industrial States of the limitations upon the size and powers of business corporations appears to have been due, not to their conviction that maintenance of the restrictions was undesirable in itself, but to the conviction that it was futile to insist upon them; because local restriction would be circumvented by foreign incorporation. Indeed, local restriction seemed worse than futile. Lesser States, eager for the revenue derived from the traffic in charters, had removed safeguards from their own incorporation laws. Companies were early formed to provide charters for corporations in states where the cost was lowest and the laws least restrictive. The states joined in advertising their wares. The race was one not of diligence but of laxity. Incorporation under such laws was possible; and the great industrial States yielded in order not to lose wholly the prospect of the revenue and the control incident to domestic incorporation.

The history of the changes made by New York is illustrative. The New York revision of 1890, which eliminated the maximum limitation on authorized capital, and permitted intercorporate stockholding in a limited class of cases, was passed after a migration of incorporation from New York, attracted by the more liberal incorporation laws of New Jersey. But the changes made by New York in 1890 were not sufficient to stem the tide. In 1892, the Governor of New York approved a special charter for the General Electric Company, modelled upon the New Jersey Act, on the ground that otherwise the enterprise would secure a New Jersey charter. Later in the same year the New York corporation law was again revised, allowing the holding of stock in other corporations. But the New Jersey law still continued to be more attractive to incorporators. By specifically providing that corporations might be formed in New Jersey to do all their business elsewhere, the state made its policy unmistakably clear. Of the seven largest trusts existing in 1904, with an aggregate capitalization of over two and a half billion dollars, all were organized under New Jersey law; and three of these were formed in 1899. During the first seven months of that year, 1336 corporations were organized under the laws of New Jersey, with an aggregate authorized capital of over two billion dollars. The Comptroller of New York, in his annual report for 1899, complained that "our tax list reflects little of the great wave of organization that has swept over the country during the past year and to which this state contributed more capital than any other state in the Union." "It is time," he declared, "that great corporations having their actual headquarters in this State and a nominal office elsewhere, doing nearly all of their business within our borders, should be brought within the jurisdiction of this State not only as to matters of taxation but in respect to other and equally important affairs." In 1901 the New York corporation law was again revised.

The history in other states was similar. Thus, the Massachusetts revision of 1903 was precipitated by the fact that "the possibilities of incorporation in other states have become well known, and have been availed of to the detriment of this Commonwealth."

... Able, discerning scholars have pictured for us the economic and social results of thus removing all limitations upon the size and activities of business corporations and of vesting in their managers vast powers once exercised by stockholders — results not designed by the States and long unsuspected. They show that size alone gives to giant corporations a social significance not attached ordinarily to smaller units of private enterprise. Through size, corporations, once merely an efficient tool employed by individuals in the conduct of private business, have become an institution — an institution which has brought such concentration of economic power that so-called private corporations are sometimes able to dominate the State. The typical business corporation of the last century, owned by a small group of individuals, managed by their owners, and limited in size by their personal wealth, is being supplanted by huge concerns in which the lives of tens or hundreds of thousands of employees and the property of tens or hundreds of thousands of investors are subjected, through the corporate mechanism, to the control of a few men. Ownership has been separated from control; and this separation has removed many of the checks which formerly operated to curb the misuse of wealth and power. And as ownership of the shares is becoming continually more dispersed, the power which formerly accompanied ownership is becoming increasingly concentrated in the hands of a few. The changes thereby wrought in the lives of the workers, of the owners and of the general public, are so fundamental and far-reaching as to lead these scholars to compare the evolving "corporate system" with the feudal system; and to lead other men of insight and experience to assert that this "master institution of civilised life" is committing it to the rule of a plutocracy.

Questions for discussion

1. Justice Brandeis observed that recently some had come to believe that the "privilege of doing business in the corporate form were inherent in the citizen." Should the people have the "right to incorporate" or should incorporation remain a "privilege?"

2. Why might a state engage in "charter mongering", otherwise known as the "race to the bottom?"

DGCL Sec. 101 - Formation 2.2.2

A certificate of incorporation is the functional equivalent of a corporation's constitution. The certificate goes by different names in different states. In other states it is known as the articles of incorporation or the corporate charter, or the articles of organization. All of these refer to the same document. As the corporation's constitution, the certificate may limit or define the power of the corporation and the corporation's board of directors. Drafters of certificates have a great deal of flexibility when drafting these documents. Although most certificates are "plain vanilla" certificates that rely almost entirely on the state corporate law default rules to define the power of the corporation and its directors as well as delineate the rights of stockholders. Of course, such a minimal approach to drafting corporate documents is not required. The corporate law is "enabling" in nature. Incorporators are free to tailor the internal governance of the corporation in any way they might like, provided it does not conflict with other provisions of the statute.

For example, some corporations, for example United Holdings, the parent corporation of United Airlines, have highly tailored certificates of incorporation. United's certificate, available in the appendix, regulates the relationships between stockholders and the corporation as well as among stockholders. In the case of United Airlines, the certificate limits the percentage of foreign stockholders to no more than 24.9% of the total stockholding. This limitation on foreign ownership is intended to facilitate compliance with federal law that prohibits the ownership of domestic airlines by foreign stockholders. In addition, as a result of negotiations with its unions over pay in the mid-1990s, unions were granted a special class of stock that accounts for 55% of the company's total stock in exchange for salary reductions. The results of this negotiation are reflected in the company's certificate of incorporation.

In addition to permitting the corporation's promoters a high degree of freedom in the design of their internal governance mechanisms, enabling statutes upend the 19th century view that a corporation is a special act of the state that requires legislative action. Rather, section 101 that follows below makes it clear that the filing of a certificate of incorporation is sufficient to form a corporation. This is the essence of an enabling statute.

This subtle, but important change, is more important than you might imagine at first glance. To the extent government control over decisions about who can form a corporation and under what circumstances gives rise to incentives for corruption and generally mucks up the business environment, the switch to a bottom-up incorporation regime can be seen as a valuable contribution of the Progressive Era.

§ 101. Incorporators; how corporation formed; purposes.

(a) Any person, partnership, association or corporation, singly or jointly with others, and without regard to such person's or entity's residence, domicile or state of incorporation, may incorporate or organize a corporation under this chapter by filing with the Division of Corporations in the Department of State a certificate of incorporation which shall be executed, acknowledged and filed in accordance with § 103 of this title.

(b) A corporation may be incorporated or organized under this chapter to conduct or promote any lawful business or purposes, except as may otherwise be provided by the Constitution or other law of this State.[...]

DGCL Sec. 102 - Contents of Certificate of Incorporation   2.2.3

The certificate of incorporation is the corporation's basic governing document. It lays out the basic understanding about governance of the corporation and the corporation's powers. It also limits the power and discretion of the corporation's board of directors in the management of the corporation. To the extent they comply with the requirements of the corporation law, the promoters of a corporation have the flexibility to tailor the internal governance of the corporation as well as to limit the powers of the board of directors. The certificate of incorporation is contractual in nature. Initial stockholders have the ability, at least in theory, to negotiate the terms of their relationship with the corporation. Later stockholders take their stock pursuant to the terms of the certificate of incorporation already in place.

DGCL §102 describes the contents of every corporation's certificate of incorporation. Section 102 has two basic components. First, §102(a) lays out the required elements of every certificate of incorporation. Many of the required elements relate to notice (e.g. how can the state contact responsible parties in the corporation). To the extent some of the required elements of §102 seem out of place (e.g. par value), remember they were first included in the code following the transition from discretionary charters to general enabling laws. Consequently, they may reflect a number of vestigial elements of the corporate law.

Second, §102(b) lays out the optional elements of every certificate of incorporation. Many of the optional elements in a certificate relate to corporate governance rights of stockholders and/or the board of directors. Section 102(b) does not generally limit promoters' ability to tailor governance structures, but it does often provide promoters with menus of options that they can choose from as they draft certificates.

§ 102. Contents of certificate of incorporation.

(a) The certificate of incorporation shall set forth:

(1) The name of the corporation, which (i) shall contain 1 of the words "association," "company," "corporation," "club," "foundation," "fund," "incorporated," "institute," "society," "union," "syndicate," or

"limited," (or abbreviations thereof, with or without punctuation), or words (or abbreviations thereof, with or without punctuation) of like import of foreign countries or jurisdictions (provided they are written in roman characters or letters); [...];

(2) The address (which shall be stated in accordance with § 131(c) of this title) of the corporation's registered office in this State, and the name of its registered agent at such address;

(3) The nature of the business or purposes to be conducted or promoted. It shall be sufficient to state, either alone or with other businesses or purposes, that the purpose of the corporation is to engage in any lawful act or activity for which corporations may be organized under the General Corporation Law of Delaware, and by such statement all lawful acts and activities shall be within the purposes of the corporation, except for express limitations, if any;

(4) If the corporation is to be authorized to issue only 1 class of stock, the total number of shares of stock which the corporation shall have authority to issue and the par value of each of such shares, or a statement that all such shares are to be without par value. If the corporation is to be authorized to issue more than 1 class of stock, the certificate of incorporation shall set forth the total number of shares of all classes of stock which the corporation shall have authority to issue and the number of shares of each class and shall specify each class the shares of which are to be without par value and each class the shares of which are to have par value and the par value of the shares of each such class. The certificate of incorporation shall also set forth a statement of the designations and the powers, preferences and rights, and the qualifications, limitations or restrictions thereof, which are permitted by § 151 of this title in respect of any class or classes of stock or any series of any class of stock of the corporation and the fixing of which by the certificate of incorporation is desired, and an express grant of such authority as it may then be desired to grant to the board of directors to fix by resolution or resolutions any thereof that may be desired but which shall not be fixed by the certificate of incorporation. [...];

(5) The name and mailing address of the incorporator or incorporators;

(6) If the powers of the incorporator or incorporators are to terminate upon the filing of the certificate of incorporation, the names and mailing addresses of the persons who are to serve as directors until the first annual meeting of stockholders or until their successors are elected and qualify.

(b) In addition to the matters required to be set forth in the certificate of incorporation by subsection (a) of this section, the certificate of incorporation may also contain any or all of the following matters:

(1) Any provision for the management of the business and for the conduct of the affairs of the corporation, and any provision creating, defining, limiting and regulating the powers of the corporation, the directors, and the stockholders, or any class of the stockholders, or the governing body, members, or any class or group of members of a nonstock corporation; if such provisions are not contrary to the laws of this State. Any provision which is required or permitted by any section of this chapter to be stated in the bylaws may instead be stated in the certificate of incorporation; [...]

(3) Such provisions as may be desired granting to the holders of the stock of the corporation, or the holders of any class or series of a class thereof, the preemptive right to subscribe to any or all additional issues of stock of the corporation of any or all classes or series thereof, or to any securities of the corporation convertible into such stock. No stockholder shall have any preemptive right to subscribe to an additional issue of stock or to any security convertible into such stock unless, and except to the extent that, such right is expressly granted to such stockholder in the certificate of incorporation. [...];

(4) Provisions requiring for any corporate action, the vote of a larger portion of the stock or of any class or series thereof, or of any other securities having voting power, or a larger number of the directors, than is required by this chapter;

(5) A provision limiting the duration of the corporation's existence to a specified date; otherwise, the corporation shall have perpetual existence;

(6) A provision imposing personal liability for the debts of the corporation on its stockholders to a specified extent and upon specified conditions; otherwise, the stockholders of a corporation shall not be personally liable for the payment of the corporation's debts except as they may be liable by reason of their own conduct or acts;

(7) A provision eliminating or limiting the personal liability of a director or officer to the corporation or its stockholders for monetary damages for breach of fiduciary duty as a director or officer, provided that such provision shall not eliminate or limit the liability of: (i) a director or officer for any breach of the director's or officer's duty of loyalty to the corporation or its stockholders; (ii) a director or officer for acts or omissions not in good faith or which involve intentional misconduct or a knowing violation of law; (iii) a director under § 174 of this title; or (iv) a director or officer for any transaction from which the director or officer 16 derived an improper personal benefit; or (v) an officer in any action by or in the right of the corporation. No such provision shall eliminate or limit the liability of a director or officer for any act or omission occurring prior to the date when such provision becomes effective. An amendment, repeal or elimination of such a provision shall not affect its application with respect to an act or omission by a director or officer occurring before such amendment, repeal or elimination unless the provision provides otherwise at the time of such act or omission.

All references in this paragraph to a director shall also be deemed to refer to such other person or persons, if any, who, pursuant to a provision of the certificate of incorporation in accordance with § 141(a) of this title, exercise or perform any of the powers or duties otherwise conferred or imposed upon the board of directors by this title.

All references in this paragraph to an officer shall mean only a person who at the time of an act or omission as to which liability is asserted is deemed to have consented to service by the delivery of process to the registered agent of the corporation pursuant to § 3114(b) of Title 10 (for purposes of this sentence only, treating

residents of this State as if they were nonresidents to apply §
3114(b) of Title 10 to this sentence).

(c) It shall not be necessary to set forth in the certificate of
incorporation any of the powers conferred on corporations by this
chapter.

(d) Except for provisions included pursuant to paragraphs (a)(1),
(a)(2), (a)(5), (a)(6), (b)(2), (b)(5), (b)(7) of this section, and
provisions included pursuant to paragraph (a)(4) of this section
specifying the classes, number of shares, and par value of shares a
corporation other than a nonstock corporation is authorized to
issue, any provision of the certificate of incorporation may be made
dependent upon facts ascertainable outside such instrument,
provided that the manner in which such facts shall operate upon the
provision is clearly and explicitly set forth therein. The term "facts,"
as used in this subsection, includes, but is not limited to, the
occurrence of any event, including a determination or action by any
person or body, including the corporation.[...]

Note on Exculpation Provisions   2.2.4

Section 102(b)(7)

Section 102(b)(7) was added to the statute in 1985 following *Smith v
Van Gorkom* where directors were found liable for monetary
damages for violating their fiduciary duty of care to the corporation.
Although §102(b)(7) appears to provide blanket exculpation from
monetary liability for any violation of fiduciary duties, it carves out
various flavors of loyalty violations. In effect, §102(b)(7) provides
that where such a provision is present in a certificate of
incorporation, directors will face no monetary liability to
stockholders for any violations of their duty of care while remaining
liable for monetary damages for violations of the duty of loyalty.

Although a §102(b)(7) exculpation provision is an optional provision, the protection granted to directors of §102(b)(7) is so powerful that this provision is ubiquitous in corporate charters.

The original §102(b)(7) provision exculpated *directors*. For many years there was a question whether corporate officers, like the CEO or the CFO, were also protected by §102(b)(7). In fact, the exclusion of officers from §102(b)(7)'s protection was a deliberate policy choice. The thought, at the time, was the to the extent officers remained liable, this would create an incentive for officers to bring matters to the board for resolution. Over time, it became apparent that the liability gap created an avenue for sometimes less-than-meritorious litigation against officers to proceed against officers for no reason other than there was potential for monetary liability and thus such litigation had settlement value without regard to the merits of the underlying claims. During the Summer of 2022 the Delaware legislature effectively closed this "loophole" and §102(b)(7) was amended to extend exculpation to officer of the corporation. This places the attention back on the board of directors as the statutory locus for corporate power and accountability.

You should keep in mind that exculpation provisions are different in kind and character from indemnification provisions, which are provided for under §145. Exculpation provisions limit or eliminate monetary of directors for violations of the duty of care. Indemnification provisions reimburse indemnified persons for certain costs associated with litigation.

DGCL Sec. 103 - Filing requirements   2.2.5

Section 103 describes the requirements for filing corporate documents, where to file, what to file, and who has to sign which documents. Although this section may seem boring, it is actually an important one for practicing attorneys. As we work our way through the code, you will notice that some provisions will require documents be filed with the state in order for them to take effect. All such documents, including the certificate of incorporation, must be filed in compliance with §103. You should familiarize yourself with §103's requirements.

§103. Execution, acknowledgment, filing, recording and effective date of original certificate of incorporation and other instruments; exceptions.

(a) Whenever any instrument is to be filed with the Secretary of State or in accordance with this section or chapter, such instrument shall be executed as follows:

(1) The certificate of incorporation, and any other instrument to be filed before the election of the initial board of directors if the initial directors were not named in the certificate of incorporation, shall be signed by the incorporator or incorporators[...]

(2) All other instruments shall be signed:

a. By any authorized officer of the corporation; or

b. If it shall appear from the instrument that there are no such officers, then by a majority of the directors or by such directors as may be designated by the board; or

c. If it shall appear from the instrument that there are no such officers or directors, then by the holders of record, or such of them as may be designated by the holders of record, of a majority of all outstanding shares of stock; or

d. By the holders of record of all outstanding shares of stock.

(b) Whenever this chapter requires any instrument to be acknowledged, such requirement is satisfied by either:

(1) The formal acknowledgment by the person or 1 of the persons signing the instrument that it is such person's act and deed or the act and deed of the corporation, and that the facts stated therein are true. [...]

(2) The signature, without more, of the person or persons signing the instrument, in which case such signature or signatures shall

constitute the affirmation or acknowledgment of the signatory, under penalties of perjury, that the instrument is such person's act and deed or the act and deed of the corporation, and that the facts stated therein are true shall be true at the time such instrument becomes effective in accordance with this chapter.

(c) Whenever any instrument is to be filed with the Secretary of State or in accordance with this section or chapter, such requirement means that:

(1) The signed instrument shall be delivered to the office of the Secretary of State;

(2) All taxes and fees authorized by law to be collected by the Secretary of State in connection with the filing of the instrument shall be tendered to the Secretary of State; and

(3) Upon delivery of the instrument, the Secretary of State shall record the date and time of its delivery. Upon such delivery and tender of the required taxes and fees, the Secretary of State shall certify that the instrument has been filed in the Secretary of State's office by endorsing upon the signed instrument the word "Filed", and the date and time of its filing. This endorsement is the "filing date" of the instrument, and is conclusive of the date and time of its filing in the absence of actual fraud. [...]

(4) Upon request made upon or prior to delivery, the Secretary of State may, to the extent deemed practicable, establish as the filing date of an instrument a date and time after its delivery. If the Secretary of State refuses to file any instrument due to an error, omission or other imperfection, the Secretary of State may hold such instrument in suspension, and in such event, upon delivery of a replacement instrument in proper form for filing and tender of the required taxes and fees within 5 business days after notice of such suspension is given to the filer, the Secretary of State shall establish as the filing date of such instrument the date and time that would have been the filing date of the rejected instrument had it been accepted for filing. [...]

(h) Any signature on any instrument authorized to be filed with the Secretary of State under this title may be a facsimile, a conformed signature or an electronically transmitted signature.

DGCL Sec. 107 - Powers of Incorporators   2.2.6

Corporations cannot incorporate themselves. The parties who incorporate a business are known as "incorporators" or "promoters". An incorporator need not be a person. An incorporator may also be another corporation.

Typically, the incorporator names the initial board of directors of the corporation immediately as part of the incorporation process, but if not, the incorporator has plenary power to manage the corporation until such time as the incorporator appoints the initial board of directors. [...]

§ 107. Powers of incorporators.

If the persons who are to serve as directors until the first annual meeting of stockholders have not been named in the certificate of incorporation, the incorporator or incorporators, until the directors are elected, shall manage the affairs of the corporation and may do whatever is necessary and proper to perfect the organization of the corporation, including the adoption of the original bylaws of the corporation and the election of directors.

DGCL Sec. 108 - Organization Meeting   2.2.7

Once a corporation is incorporated, a formal organization meeting of the initial board of directors is required to adopt corporate bylaws, and ratify any actions taken by the incorporator. This organizational meeting may be in person, or as is often the case, undertaken by relying on written consent of the directors.

]

§ 108. Organization meeting of incorporators or directors named in certificate of incorporation.

(a) After the filing of the certificate of incorporation an organization meeting of the incorporator or incorporators, or of the board of directors if the initial directors were named in the certificate of incorporation, shall be held, either within or without this State, at the call of a majority of the incorporators or directors, as the case may be, for the purposes of adopting bylaws, electing directors (if the meeting is of the incorporators) to serve or hold office until the first annual meeting of stockholders or until their successors are elected and qualify, electing officers if the meeting is of the directors, doing any other or further acts to perfect the organization of the corporation, and transacting such other business as may come before the meeting.[...]

(c) Any action permitted to be taken at the organization meeting of the incorporators or directors, as the case may be, may be taken without a meeting if each incorporator or director, where there is more than 1, or the sole incorporator or director where there is only 1, signs an instrument which states the action so taken. [...]

Amendment of Certificate of Incorporation   2.2.8

Like a constitution, a corporation's certificate of incorporation may be amended at any point in the future. It is not a "forever" contract. A board of directors together with the corporation's stockholders can amend a certificate of incorporation. Section 242 outlines the procedures for amending a certificate.

DGCL Sec. 242 - Amendments to Certificate   2.2.8.1

There are two features of the amendment process that are worth pointing out. First, any amendment to a corporation's certificate of incorporation must be initiated by the corporation's board of directors and requires the board's assent. A certificate amendment may not be initiated by stockholders. A certificate may not be amended against the will of the board of directors. Second, any amendments recommended by the board of directors must be approved by a vote of a majority of the outstanding shares of the corporation. A certificate may not be amended against the will of the majority of the stockholders. These dual requirements can make the process of amending a certificate of incorporation difficult. Thus, the limitations placed on a board or a corporation's stockholders by the certificate of incorporation are effective constraints.

Although any portion of the certificate may be amended, the most common amendment to certificates of incorporation involves increases to the number of authorized shares. Such amendments are usually, but not always, noncontroversial.

§ 242. Amendment of certificate of incorporation after receipt of payment for stock; nonstock corporations

(a) After a corporation has received payment for any of its capital stock, or after a nonstock corporation has members, it may amend its certificate of incorporation, from time to time, in any and as many respects as may be desired, so long as its certificate of incorporation as amended would contain only such provisions as it would be lawful and proper to insert in an original certificate of incorporation filed at the time of the filing of the amendment; and, if a change in stock or the rights of stockholders, or an exchange, reclassification, subdivision, combination or cancellation of stock or rights of stockholders is to be made, such provisions as may be necessary to effect such change, exchange, reclassification, subdivision, combination or cancellation. In particular, and without limitation upon such general power of amendment, a corporation may amend its certificate of incorporation, from time to time, so as:

(1) To change its corporate name; or

(2) To change, substitute, enlarge or diminish the nature of its business or its corporate powers and purposes; or

(3) To increase or decrease its authorized capital stock or to reclassify the same, by changing the number, par value, designations, preferences, or relative, participating, optional, or other special rights of the shares, or the qualifications, limitations or restrictions of such rights, or by changing shares with par value into shares without par value, or shares without par value into shares with par value either with or without increasing or decreasing the number of shares, or by subdividing or combining the outstanding shares of any class or series of a class of shares into a greater or lesser number of outstanding shares; or

(4) To cancel or otherwise affect the right of the holders of the shares of any class to receive dividends which have accrued but have not been declared; or

(5) To create new classes of stock having rights and preferences either prior and superior or subordinate and inferior to the stock of any class then authorized, whether issued or unissued; or

(6) To change the period of its duration; or

(7) To delete:

a. Such provisions of the original certificate of incorporation which named the incorporator or incorporators, the initial board of directors and the original subscribers for shares; and

b. Such provisions contained in any amendment to the certificate of incorporation as were necessary to effect a change, exchange, reclassification, subdivision, combination or cancellation of stock, if such change, exchange, reclassification, subdivision, combination or cancellation has become effective.

Any or all such changes or alterations may be effected by 1 certificate of amendment.

(b) Every amendment authorized by subsection (a) of this section shall be made and effected in the following manner:

(1) If the corporation has capital stock, its board of directors shall adopt a resolution setting forth the amendment proposed, declaring its advisability, and either calling a special meeting of the stockholders entitled to vote in respect thereof for the consideration of such amendment or directing that the amendment proposed be considered at the next annual meeting of the stockholders; provided, however, that unless otherwise expressly required by the certificate of incorporation, no meeting or vote of stockholders shall be required to adopt an amendment that effects only changes described in paragraph (a)(1) or (7) of this section. [...]If no vote of stockholders is required to effect such amendment, or if a majority of the outstanding stock entitled to vote thereon, and a majority of the outstanding stock of each class entitled to vote thereon as a class has been voted in favor of the amendment, a certificate setting forth the amendment and certifying that such amendment has been duly adopted in accordance with this section shall be executed, acknowledged and filed and shall become effective in accordance with § 103 of this title.

(2) The holders of the outstanding shares of a class shall be entitled to vote as a class upon a proposed amendment, whether or not entitled to vote thereon by the certificate of incorporation, if the amendment would increase or decrease the aggregate number of authorized shares of such class, increase or decrease the par value of the shares of such class, or alter or change the powers, preferences, or special rights of the shares of such class so as to affect them adversely. If any proposed amendment would alter or change the powers, preferences, or special rights of 1 or more series of any class so as to affect them adversely, but shall not so affect the entire class, then only the shares of the series so affected by the amendment shall be considered a separate class for the purposes of this paragraph. The number of authorized shares of any such class or classes of stock may be increased or decreased (but not below the number of shares thereof then outstanding) by the affirmative vote of the holders of a majority of the stock of the corporation entitled to vote irrespective of this subsection, if so provided in the original certificate of incorporation, in any amendment thereto which created such class or classes of stock or which was adopted prior to the issuance of any shares of such class or classes of stock, or in any

amendment thereto which was authorized by a resolution or resolutions adopted by the affirmative vote of the holders of a majority of such class or classes of stock. [...]

(c) The resolution authorizing a proposed amendment to the certificate of incorporation may provide that at any time prior to the effectiveness of the filing of the amendment with the Secretary of State, notwithstanding authorization of the proposed amendment by the stockholders of the corporation or by the members of a nonstock corporation, the board of directors or governing body may abandon such proposed amendment without further action by the stockholders or members.

DGCL Sec. 245 - Restating the Certificate   2.2.8.2

When certificates are amended, the amendments are simply "stapled" to the back of the original certificate. The result is often a document that is cumbersome to read. Rather than rely on a potentially confusing set of documents, a certificate may be "restated" in its entirety reading all the amendments into the certificate so that the document is easier to read and more understandable. Section 245 lays out the process by which a certificate may be restated.

§ 245. Restated certificate of incorporation.

(a) A corporation may, whenever desired, integrate into a single instrument all of the provisions of its certificate of incorporation which are then in effect and operative as a result of there having theretofore been filed with the Secretary of State 1 or more certificates or other instruments pursuant to any of the sections referred to in § 104 of this title, and it may at the same time also further amend its certificate of incorporation by adopting a restated certificate of incorporation.

(b) If the restated certificate of incorporation merely restates and integrates but does not further amend the certificate of incorporation, as theretofore amended or supplemented by any instrument that was filed pursuant to any of the sections mentioned in § 104 of this title, it may be adopted by the board of directors without a vote of the stockholders[...]. If the restated certificate of incorporation restates and integrates and also further amends in any respect the certificate of incorporation, as theretofore amended or supplemented, it shall be proposed by the directors and adopted by the stockholders in the manner and by the vote prescribed by § 242 of this title or, if the corporation has not received any payment for any of its stock, in the manner and by the vote prescribed by § 241 of this title.

(c) A restated certificate of incorporation shall be specifically designated as such in its heading. It shall state, either in its heading or in an introductory paragraph, the corporation's present name, and, if it has been changed, the name under which it was originally incorporated, and the date of filing of its original certificate of incorporation with the Secretary of State. A restated certificate shall also state that it was duly adopted in accordance with this section. If it was adopted by the board of directors without a vote of the stockholders (unless it was adopted pursuant to § 241 of this title or without a vote of members pursuant to § 242(b)(3) of this title), it shall state that it only restates and integrates and does not further amend the provisions of the corporation's certificate of incorporation as theretofore amended or supplemented, and that there is no discrepancy between those provisions and the provisions of the restated certificate. A restated certificate of incorporation may omit (a) such provisions of the original certificate of incorporation which named the incorporator or incorporators, the initial board of directors and the original subscribers for shares, and (b) such provisions contained in any amendment to the certificate of incorporation as were necessary to effect a change, exchange, reclassification, subdivision, combination or cancellation of stock, if such change, exchange, reclassification, subdivision, combination or cancellation has become effective. Any such omissions shall not be deemed a further amendment.

(d) A restated certificate of incorporation shall be executed, acknowledged and filed in accordance with § 103 of this title. [...]

Piercing the Corporate Veil   2.2.9

Legal personality and limited liability are two critical
features of the modern corporate structure.
Although these two features are often described as
different, they are in fact two sides of the same coin.
The "coin" in this case is the principle of separateness. Legal
personality means that the corporate entity stands on its own,
independent of its stockholders, such that the debts and other
liabilities of the stockholders of the corporation are not the debts or
liabilities of the corporation.

Equally important, limited liability (the default rule, provided under
102(b)(6)) means that the debts and other liabilities of the
corporation are the debts and liabilities of the corporation and not
the stockholders. The separate life of the corporation and the power
of limited liability are extremely powerful policy choices that have
implications for third parties as well as for corporate decision-
makers.

Businesses can, and do, fail. When they do, limited liability means
that the costs of that failure will mostly be borne by third party
creditors of the firm and not by the directors or the stockholders of
the firm. This may create incentives for third parties to careful when
dealing with corporations. Before agreeing to a contract with a
corporation, it is not uncommon for counterparties to engage in
some "due diligence" to investigate the capabilities of the
corporation. But, limited liability also creates incentives that
improve the liquidity of capital markets and encourage corporate
risk-taking - a stockholder can feel free to invest in a risky business,
like a start-up, safe in the knowledge that should it fail, the
stockholder will not be risking all of her assets, including the college
fund she has saved for her kids.

"Piercing the corporate veil" is an equitable doctrine that is the
exception to the limited liability rule. In extreme cases, courts may
look through the protective barrier of limited liability and assign the

corporation's liabilities to the stockholders. The following cases raise of the issues common in veil piercing cases.

Although the concept of corporate separateness is well understood at the state level, in recent years a series of First Amendment cases have provided the US Supreme Court the opportunity to give its own view on the traditional state law question of corporate separateness. Unlike state level courts, the US Supreme Court has taken a much more malleable view towards the doctrine of corporate separateness as that concept relates to the First Amendment.

Walkovszky v. Carlton   2.2.9.1

The default rule for the corporation is that stockholders face limited liability for the debts of the corporation. The liability of stockholders is limited to the capital they contributed to the corporation. For instance, if a stockholder contributes $100 in equity capital to the corporation by buying stock from the corporation for $100 (assume this represents all the equity capital available to the corporation), and if the corporation has $150 in debts, the corporation may be required to pay all of its equity capital (i.e. $100) to settle the corporation's debts. In most circumstances, stockholders will not be liable for the balance of the corporation's debt of $50. The liability of stockholders is thus limited to only their capital contributions.

Although limited liability as described above is the default rule, in extreme cases courts may look through the corporate form, or "pierce the corporate veil", and assign liability for corporate debts to stockholders.

The following case is paradigmatic. The owner of the corporation has obviously established the corporations in question specifically to limit his exposure to debts of each of the corporations he controls. In deciding whether the stockholder should receive the benefit of corporate limited liability, the court lays out an equitable test to determine whether it should look through the veil of limited liability protection and find the shareholders liable for the debts of the corporation.

If the corporation is a mere "alter ego" of the stockholders (e.g. if the corporation is operated without formality and for mere convenience of its stockholders) and the stockholder used the corporate form to engage in some injustice, it is more likely, though not certain, that a court will look through the corporate form and assign corporate liabilities to stockholders in order to prevent a fraud or inequitable result.

WALKOVSKY V. CARLTON
18 N.Y.2d 414 (1966)

This case involves what appears to be a rather common practice in the taxicab industry of vesting the ownership of a taxi fleet in many corporations, each owning only one or two cabs.

The complaint alleges that the plaintiff was severely injured four years ago in New York City when he was run down by a taxicab owned by the defendant Seon Cab Corporation and negligently operated at the time by the defendant Marchese. The individual defendant, Carlton, is claimed to be a stockholder of 10 corporations, including Seon, each of which has but two cabs registered in its name, and it is implied that only the minimum automobile liability insurance required by law (in the amount of $10,000) is carried on any one cab. Although seemingly independent of one another, these corporations are alleged to be "operated * * * as a single entity, unit and enterprise" with regard to financing, supplies, repairs, employees and garaging, and all are named as defendants.[III] The plaintiff asserts that he is also entitled to hold their stockholders personally liable for the damages sought because the multiple corporate structure constitutes an unlawful attempt "to defraud members of the general public" who might be injured by the cabs. [...]

The law permits the incorporation of a business for the very purpose of enabling its proprietors to escape personal liability [...] but, manifestly, the privilege is not without its limits. Broadly speaking, the courts will disregard the corporate form, or, to use accepted terminology, "pierce the corporate veil", whenever necessary "to prevent fraud or to achieve equity". [...] In determining whether liability should be extended to reach assets beyond those belonging to the corporation, we are guided, as Judge CARDOZO noted, by "general rules of agency". [...] In other words, whenever anyone uses control of the corporation to further his own rather than the corporation's business, he will be liable for the corporation's acts "upon the principle of *respondeat superior* applicable even where the agent is a natural person". [...]

In the case before us, the plaintiff has explicitly alleged that none of the corporations "had a separate existence of their own" and, as indicated above, all are named as defendants. However, it is one thing to assert that a corporation is a fragment of a larger corporate combine which actually conducts the business. [...] It is quite another to claim that the corporation is a "dummy" for its individual stockholders who are in reality carrying on the business in their personal capacities for purely personal rather than corporate ends. [...] Either circumstance would justify treating the corporation as an agent and piercing the corporate veil to reach the principal but a different result would follow in each case. In the first, only a larger *corporate* entity would be held financially responsible [...] while, in the other, the stockholder would be personally liable. [...] Either the stockholder is conducting the business in his individual capacity or he is not. If he is, he will be liable; if he is not, then, it does not matter — insofar as his personal liability is concerned — that the enterprise is actually being carried on by a larger "enterprise entity". [...]

Reading the complaint in this case most favorably and liberally, we do not believe that there can be gathered from its averments the allegations required to spell out a valid cause of action against the defendant Carlton.

The individual defendant is charged with having "organized, managed, dominated and controlled" a fragmented corporate entity but there are no allegations that he was conducting business in his individual capacity. Had the taxicab fleet been owned by a single corporation, it would be readily apparent that the plaintiff would face formidable barriers in attempting to establish personal liability on the part of the corporation's stockholders. The fact that the fleet ownership has been deliberately split up among many corporations does not ease the plaintiff's burden in that respect. The corporate form may not be disregarded merely because the assets of the corporation, together with the mandatory insurance coverage of the vehicle which struck the plaintiff, are insufficient to assure him the recovery sought. If Carlton were to be held individually liable on those facts alone, the decision would apply equally to the thousands of cabs which are owned by their individual drivers who conduct their businesses through corporations organized pursuant to section 401 of the Business Corporation Law and carry the minimum insurance required by subdivision 1 (par. [a]) of section 370 of the Vehicle and Traffic Law. These [420] taxi owner-operators are entitled to form such corporations (cf. *Elenkrieg v. Siebrecht*, 238 N.Y. 254), and we agree with the court at Special Term that, if the insurance coverage required by statute "is inadequate for the protection of the public, the remedy lies not with the courts but with the Legislature." It may very well be sound policy to require that certain corporations must take out liability insurance which will afford adequate compensation to their potential tort victims. However, the responsibility for imposing conditions on the privilege of incorporation has been committed by the Constitution to the Legislature (N. Y. Const., art. X, § 1) and it may not be fairly implied, from any statute, that the Legislature intended, without the slightest discussion or debate, to require of taxi corporations that they carry automobile liability insurance over and above that mandated by the Vehicle and Traffic Law.[2]

This is not to say that it is impossible for the plaintiff to state a valid cause of action against the defendant Carlton. However, the simple fact is that the plaintiff has just not done so here. While the complaint alleges that the separate corporations were undercapitalized and that their assets have been intermingled, it is barren of any "sufficiently particular[ized] statements" [...] that the defendant Carlton and his associates are actually doing business in their individual capacities, shuttling their personal funds in and out of the corporations "without regard to formality and to suit their immediate convenience." [...]Such a "perversion of the privilege to do business in a corporate form" [...] would justify imposing personal liability on the individual stockholders. [...]Nothing of the sort has in fact been charged, and it cannot reasonably or logically be inferred from the happenstance that the business of Seon [...] Cab Corporation may actually be carried on by a larger corporate entity composed of many corporations which, under general principles of agency, would be liable to each other's creditors in contract and in tort.[3]

In point of fact, the principle relied upon in the complaint to sustain the imposition of personal liability is not agency but fraud. Such a cause of action cannot withstand analysis. If it is not fraudulent for the owner-operator of a single cab corporation to take out only the minimum required liability insurance, the enterprise does not become either illicit or fraudulent merely because it consists of many such corporations. The plaintiff's injuries are the same regardless of whether the cab which strikes him is owned by a single corporation or part of a fleet with ownership fragmented among many corporations. Whatever rights he may be able to assert against parties other than the registered owner of the vehicle come into being not because he has been defrauded but because, under the principle of *respondeat superior*, he is entitled to hold the whole enterprise responsible for the acts of its agents.

In sum, then, the complaint falls short of adequately stating a cause of action against the defendant Carlton in his individual capacity.

The order of the Appellate Division should be reversed, with costs in this court and in the Appellate Division, the certified question answered in the negative and the order of the Supreme Court, Richmond County, reinstated, with leave to serve an amended complaint.

KEATING, J. (dissenting).

The defendant Carlton, the shareholder here sought to be held for the negligence of the driver of a taxicab, was a principal shareholder and organizer of the defendant corporation which owned the taxicab. The corporation was one of 10 organized by the defendant, each containing [422] two cabs and each cab having the "minimum liability" insurance coverage mandated by section 370 of the Vehicle and Traffic Law. The sole assets of these operating corporations are the vehicles themselves and they are apparently subject to mortgages.[1]

From their inception these corporations were intentionally undercapitalized for the purpose of avoiding responsibility for acts which were bound to arise as a result of the operation of a large taxi fleet having cars out on the street 24 hours a day and engaged in public transportation. And during the course of the corporations' existence all income was continually drained out of the corporations for the same purpose.

The issue presented by this action is whether the policy of this State, which affords those desiring to engage in a business enterprise the privilege of limited liability through the use of the corporate device, is so strong that it will permit that privilege to continue no matter how much it is abused, no matter how irresponsibly the corporation is operated, no matter what the cost to the public. I do not believe that it is.

Under the circumstances of this case the shareholders should all be held individually liable to this plaintiff for the injuries he suffered. [...] At least, the matter should not be disposed of on the pleadings by a dismissal of the complaint. "If a corporation is organized and carries on business without substantial capital in such a way that the corporation is likely to have no sufficient assets available to meet its debts, it is inequitable that shareholders should set up such a flimsy organization to escape personal liability. The attempt to do corporate business without providing any sufficient basis of financial responsibility to creditors is an abuse of the separate entity and will be ineffectual to exempt the shareholders from corporate debts. It is coming to be recognized as the policy of law that shareholders should in good faith put at the risk of the business unincumbered capital reasonably adequate for its prospective liabilities. If capital is illusory or trifling compared with the business to be done and the risks [423] of loss, this is a ground for denying the separate entity privilege." (Ballantine, Corporations [rev. ed., 1946], § 129, pp. 302-303.)

In *Minton v. Cavaney* (56 Cal. 2d 576) the Supreme Court of California had occasion to discuss this problem in a negligence case. The corporation of which the defendant was an organizer, director and officer operated a public swimming pool. One afternoon the plaintiffs' daughter drowned in the pool as a result of the alleged negligence of the corporation.

Justice ROGER TRAYNOR, speaking for the court, outlined the applicable law in this area. "The figurative terminology `alter ego' and `disregard of the corporate entity'", he wrote, "is generally used to refer to the various situations that are an abuse of the corporate privilege * * * The equitable owners of a corporation, for example, are personally liable when they treat the assets of the corporation as their own and add or withdraw capital from the corporation at will * * *; when they hold themselves out as being personally liable for the debts of the corporation * * *; *or when they provide inadequate capitalization and actively participate in the conduct of corporate affairs*". (56 Cal. 2d, p. 579; italics supplied.)

Examining the facts of the case in light of the legal principles just enumerated, he found that "[it was] undisputed that there was no attempt to provide adequate capitalization. [The corporation] never had any substantial assets. It leased the pool that it operated, and the lease was forfeited for failure to pay the rent. Its capital was `trifling compared with the business to be done and the risks of loss'". (56 Cal. 2d, p. 580.)

It seems obvious that one of "the risks of loss" referred to was the possibility of drownings due to the negligence of the corporation. And the defendant's failure to provide such assets or any fund for recovery resulted in his being held personally liable.

In *Anderson v. Abbott* (321 U. S. 349) the defendant shareholders had organized a holding company and transferred to that company shares which they held in various national banks in return for shares in the holding company. The holding company did not have sufficient assets to meet the double liability requirements of the governing Federal statutes which provided that the owners of shares in national [424] banks were personally liable for corporate obligations "to the extent of the amount of their stock therein, at the par value thereof, in addition to the amount invested in such shares" (U. S. Code, tit. 12, former § 63).

The court had found that these transfers were made in good faith, that other defendant shareholders who had purchased shares in the holding company had done so in good faith and that the organization of such a holding company was entirely legal. Despite this finding, the Supreme Court, speaking through Mr. Justice DOUGLAS, pierced the corporate veil of the holding company and held all the shareholders, even those who had no part in the organization of the corporation, individually responsible for the corporate obligations as mandated by the statute.

"Limited liability", he wrote, "is the rule, not the exception; and on that assumption large undertakings are rested, vast enterprises are launched, and huge sums of capital attracted. But there are occasions when the limited liability sought to be obtained through the corporation will be qualified or denied. Mr. Justice CARDOZO stated that a surrender of that principle of limited liability would be made `when the sacrifice is essential to the end that some accepted public policy may be defended or upheld.' * * * The cases of fraud make up part of that exception * * * But they do not exhaust it. *An obvious inadequacy of capital, measured by the nature and magnitude of the corporate undertaking, has frequently been an important factor in cases denying stockholders their defense of limited liability * * * That rule has been invoked even in absence of a legislative policy which undercapitalization would defeat.* It becomes more important in a case such as the present one where the statutory policy of double liability will be defeated if impecunious bank-stock holding companies are allowed to be interposed as non-conductors of liability. *It has often been held that the interposition of a corporation will not be allowed to defeat a legislative policy, whether that was the aim or only the result of the arrangement* * * * `the courts will not permit themselves to be blinded or deceived by mere forms of law' but will deal `with the substance of the transaction involved as if the corporate agency did not exist and as the justice of the case may require.'" (321 U. S., pp. 362-363; emphasis added.)

[425] The policy of this State has always been to provide and facilitate recovery for those injured through the negligence of others. The automobile, by its very nature, is capable of causing severe and costly injuries when not operated in a proper manner. The great increase in the number of automobile accidents combined with the frequent financial irresponsibility of the individual driving the car led to the adoption of section 388 of the Vehicle and Traffic Law which had the effect of imposing upon the owner of the vehicle the responsibility for its negligent operation. It is upon this very statute that the cause of action against both the corporation and the individual defendant is predicated.

In addition the Legislature, still concerned with the financial irresponsibility of those who owned and operated motor vehicles, enacted a statute requiring minimum liability coverage for all owners of automobiles. The important public policy represented by both these statutes is outlined in section 310 of the Vehicle and Traffic Law. That section provides that: "The legislature is concerned over the rising toll of motor vehicle accidents and the suffering and loss thereby inflicted. The legislature determines that it is a matter of grave concern that motorists shall be financially able to respond in damages for their negligent acts, so that innocent victims of motor vehicle accidents may be recompensed for the injury and financial loss inflicted upon them."

The defendant Carlton claims that, because the minimum amount of insurance required by the statute was obtained, the corporate veil cannot and should not be pierced despite the fact that the assets of the corporation which owned the cab were "trifling compared with the business to be done and the risks of loss" which were certain to be encountered. I do not agree.

The Legislature in requiring minimum liability insurance of $10,000, no doubt, intended to provide at least some small fund for recovery against those individuals and corporations who just did not have and were not able to raise or accumulate assets sufficient to satisfy the claims of those who were injured as a result of their negligence. It certainly could not have intended to shield those individuals who organized corporations, with the specific intent of avoiding responsibility to the public, where the operation of the corporate enterprise yielded profits sufficient to purchase additional insurance. Moreover, it is reasonable [426] to assume that the Legislature believed that those individuals and corporations having substantial assets would take out insurance far in excess of the minimum in order to protect those assets from depletion. Given the costs of hospital care and treatment and the nature of injuries sustained in auto collisions, it would be unreasonable to assume that the Legislature believed that the minimum provided in the statute would in and of itself be sufficient to recompense "innocent victims of motor vehicle accidents * * * for the injury and financial loss inflicted upon them".

The defendant, however, argues that the failure of the Legislature to increase the minimum insurance requirements indicates legislative acquiescence in this scheme to avoid liability and responsibility to the public. In the absence of a clear legislative statement, approval of a scheme having such serious consequences is not to be so lightly inferred.

The defendant contends that the court will be encroaching upon the legislative domain by ignoring the corporate veil and holding the individual shareholder. This argument was answered by Mr. Justice DOUGLAS in *Anderson v. Abbot* (*supra*, pp. 366-367) where he wrote that: "In the field in which we are presently concerned, judicial power hardly oversteps the bounds when it refuses to lend its aid to a promotional project which would circumvent or undermine a legislative policy. To deny it that function would be to make it impotent in situations where historically it has made some of its most notable contributions. If the judicial power is helpless to protect a legislative program from schemes for easy avoidance, then indeed it has become a handy implement of high finance. *Judicial interference to cripple or defeat a legislative policy is one thing; judicial interference with the plans of those whose corporate or other devices would circumvent that policy is quite another.* Once the purpose or effect of the scheme is clear, once the legislative policy is plain, we would indeed forsake a great tradition to say we were helpless to fashion the instruments for appropriate relief." (Emphasis added.)

The defendant contends that a decision holding him personally liable would discourage people from engaging in corporate enterprise.

What I would merely hold is that a participating shareholder of a corporation vested with a public interest, organized with capital insufficient to meet liabilities which are certain to arise in the ordinary course of the corporation's business, may be held personally responsible for such liabilities. Where corporate income is not sufficient to cover the cost of insurance premiums above the statutory minimum or where initially adequate finances dwindle under the pressure of competition, bad times or extraordinary and unexpected liability, obviously the shareholder will not be held liable (Henn, Corporations, p. 208, n. 7).

The only types of corporate enterprises that will be discouraged as a result of a decision allowing the individual shareholder to be sued will be those such as the one in question, designed solely to abuse the corporate privilege at the expense of the public interest.

For these reasons I would vote to affirm the order of the Appellate Division.

Order reversed, etc.

Footnotes

[1] The corporate owner of a garage is also included as a defendant.

[2] There is no merit to the contention that the ownership and operation of the taxi fleet "constituted a breach of hack owners regulations as promulgated by [the] Police Department of the City of New York". Those regulations are clearly applicable to individual owner-operators and fleet owners alike. They were not intended to prevent either incorporation of a single-vehicle taxi business or multiple incorporation of a taxi fleet.

[3] In his affidavit in opposition to the motion to dismiss, the plaintiff's counsel claimed that corporate assets had been "milked out" of, and "siphoned off" from the enterprise. Quite apart from the

fact that these allegations are far too vague and conclusory, the charge is premature. If the plaintiff succeeds in his action and becomes a judgment creditor of the corporation, he may then sue and attempt to hold the individual defendants accountable for any dividends and property that were wrongfully distributed (Business Corporation Law, §§ 510, 719, 720).

[*] It appears that the medallions, which are of considerable value, are judgment proof. (Administrative Code of City of New York, § 436-2.0.)

Kinney Shoe Corp. v. Polan   2.2.9.2

Courts have long recognized that a corporation is an entity, separate and distinct from its officers and stockholders, and the individual stockholders are not responsible for the debts of the corporation.

In the following case, a Federal court lays out its approach to the question of whether a court should depart from the limited liability norm and "pierce the corporate veil" thus making stockholders liable for the debts of the corporation. The approach taken by the Federal court here differs only slightly from the approach to piercing taken by various state courts, including *Walkovszky*.

Central to a court's inquiry will be whether the stockholders treated the corporation as a separate entity with respect for the formalities due to a separate entity such that a court should also respect the corporation's limited liability.

Although the court in this case provides us with a convenient "test" it is worth remembering that piercing the corporate veil is an equitable remedy, therefore courts can – at times – appear to be inconsistent in their application of these tests. Success will usually require highly idiosyncratic facts and very sympathetic plaintiffs. In the most general terms, piercing the corporate veil is never going to be a court's first instinct.

KINNEY SHOE CORP. V POLAN
939 F.2d 209 (1991)

CHAPMAN, Senior Circuit Judge:

Plaintiff-appellant Kinney Shoe Corporation ("Kinney") brought this action in the United States District Court for the Southern District of West Virginia against Lincoln M. Polan ("Polan") seeking to recover money owed on a sublease between Kinney and Industrial Realty Company ("Industrial"). Polan is the sole shareholder of Industrial. The district court found that Polan was not personally liable on the lease between Kinney and Industrial. Kinney appeals asserting that the corporate veil should be pierced, and we agree. [...]

In 1984 Polan formed two corporations, Industrial and Polan Industries, Inc., for the purpose of re-establishing an industrial manufacturing business. [...] Polan was the owner of both corporations. Although certificates of incorporation were issued, no organizational meetings were held, and no officers were elected.

In November 1984 Polan and Kinney began negotiating the sublease of a building in which Kinney held a leasehold interest. [...]

The term of the sublease from Kinney to Industrial commenced in December 1984, even though the written lease was not signed by the parties until April 5, 1985. On April 15, 1985, Industrial subleased part of the building to Polan Industries for fifty percent of the rental amount due Kinney. Polan signed both subleases on behalf of the respective companies.

Other than the sublease with Kinney, Industrial had no assets, no income and no bank account. Industrial issued no stock certificates because nothing was ever paid in to this corporation. Industrial's only income was from its sublease to Polan Industries, Inc. The first rental payment to Kinney was made out of Polan's personal funds, and no further payments were made by Polan or by Polan Industries, Inc. to either Industrial or to Kinney.

Kinney filed suit against Industrial for unpaid rent and obtained a judgment in the amount of $166,400.00 on June 19, 1987. [...] Kinney then filed this action against Polan individually to collect the amount owed by Industrial to Kinney. Since the amount to which Kinney is entitled is undisputed, the only issue is whether Kinney can pierce the [211] corporate veil and hold Polan personally liable. [...]

II.

We have long recognized that a corporation is an entity, separate and distinct from its officers and stockholders, and the individual stockholders are not responsible for the debts of the corporation. [...] This concept, however, is a fiction of the law "` and it is now well settled, as a general principle, that the fiction should be disregarded when it is urged with an intent not within its reason and purpose, and in such a way that its retention would produce injustices or inequitable consequences.'" *Laya v. Erin Homes, Inc.,* 352 S.E.2d 93, 97-98 (W.Va.1986).

Piercing the corporate veil is an equitable remedy, and the burden rests with the party asserting such claim. *DeWitt Truck Brokers,* 540 F.2d at 683. A totality of the circumstances test is used in determining whether to pierce the corporate veil, and each case must be decided on its own facts. The district court's findings of facts may be overturned only if clearly erroneous. *Id.*

Kinney seeks to pierce the corporate veil of Industrial so as to hold Polan personally liable on the sublease debt. The Supreme Court of Appeals of West Virginia has set forth a two prong test to be used in determining whether to pierce a corporate veil in a breach of contract case. This test raises two issues: first, is the unity of interest and ownership such that the separate personalities of the corporation and the individual shareholder no longer exist; and second, would an equitable result occur if the acts are treated as those of the corporation alone. [...]Numerous factors have been identified as relevant in making this determination.[iii][...]

It is undisputed that Industrial was not adequately capitalized. Actually, it had no paid in capital. Polan had put nothing into this corporation, and it did not observe any corporate formalities. As the West Virginia court stated in *Laya,* "`[i]ndividuals who wish to enjoy limited personal liability for business activities under a corporate umbrella should be expected to adhere to the relatively simple formalities of creating and maintaining a corporate entity.'" [ ... ] This, the court stated, is "`a relatively small price to pay for limited liability.'" *Id.* Another important factor is adequate capitalization. "[G]rossly inadequate capitalization combined with disregard of corporate formalities, causing basic unfairness, are sufficient to pierce the corporate veil in order to hold the shareholder(s) actively participating in the operation of the business personally liable for a breach of contract to the party who entered into the contract with the corporation." [...]

In this case, Polan bought no stock, made no capital contribution, kept no minutes, and elected no officers for Industrial. In addition, Polan attempted to protect his assets by placing them in Polan Industries, Inc. and interposing Industrial between Polan Industries, Inc. and Kinney so as to prevent Kinney from going against the corporation with assets. Polan gave no explanation or justification for the existence of Industrial as the intermediary between Polan Industries, Inc. and Kinney. Polan was obviously trying to limit his liability and the liability of Polan Industries, Inc. by setting up a paper curtain constructed of nothing more than Industrial's certificate of incorporation. These facts present the classic scenario for an action to pierce the corporate veil so as to reach the responsible party and produce an equitable result. Accordingly, we hold that the district court correctly found that the two prong test in *Laya* had been satisfied. [...]

III.

For the foregoing reasons, we hold that Polan is personally liable for the debt of Industrial.

Footnotes

[1] The following factors were identified in *Laya:*

(1) commingling of funds and other assets of the corporation with those of the individual shareholders;

(2) diversion of the corporation's funds or assets to noncorporate uses (to the personal uses of the corporation's shareholders);

(3) failure to maintain the corporate formalities necessary for the issuance of or subscription to the corporation's stock, such as formal approval of the stock issue by the board of directors;

(4) an individual shareholder representing to persons outside the corporation that he or she is personally liable for the debts or other obligations of the corporation;

(5) failure to maintain corporate minutes or adequate corporate records;

(6) identical equitable ownership in two entities;

(7) identity of the directors and officers of two entities who are responsible for supervision and management (a partnership or sole proprietorship and a corporation owned and managed by the same parties);

(8) failure to adequately capitalize a corporation for the reasonable risks of the corporate undertaking;

(9) absence of separately held corporate assets;

(10) use of a corporation as a mere shell or conduit to operate a single venture or some particular aspect of the business of an individual or another corporation;

(11) sole ownership of all the stock by one individual or members of a single family;

(12) use of the same office or business location by the corporation and its individual shareholder(s);

(13) employment of the same employees or attorney by the corporation and its shareholder(s);

(14) concealment or misrepresentation of the identity of the ownership, management or financial interests in the corporation, and concealment of personal business activities of the shareholders (sole shareholders do not reveal the association with a corporation, which makes loans to them without adequate security);

(15) disregard of legal formalities and failure to maintain proper arm's length relationships among related entities;

(16) use of a corporate entity as a conduit to procure labor, services or merchandise for another person or entity;

(17) diversion of corporate assets from the corporation by or to a stockholder or other person or entity to the detriment of creditors, or the manipulation of assets and liabilities between entities to concentrate the assets in one and the liabilities in another;

(18) contracting by the corporation with another person with the intent to avoid risk of nonperformance by use of the corporate entity; or the use of a corporation as a subterfuge for illegal transactions;

(19) the formation and use of the corporation to assume the existing liabilities of another person or entity.

Laya, 352 S.E.2d at 98-99

Fletcher v. Atex Inc.   2.2.9.3

A subsidiary corporation is a corporation whose shares are owned entirely (or mostly) by another corporation. As between parent corporations and their subsidiaries, the default rule of limited liability still applies. A parent corporation will not normally be held liable for the debts of its subsidiary corporations.

In *Fletcher*, tort victims are asking the court to pierce the corporate veil of one of its defunct subsidiaries in order to make Kodak liable for the subsidiary's debts that resulted from an alleged product defect that caused repetitive stress disorders in customers.

The *Fletcher* court uses two different theories to test whether it should pierce the corporate veil and make Kodak, the sole stockholder of Atex, liable for the damages caused by Atex. The first theory is the same two prong test applied in other piercing the corporate veil cases. The second theory relies on more straightforward concepts of agency law. These theories are not necessarily mutually exclusive.

FLETCHER V. ATEX
68 F.3d 1451 (1995)

JOSÉ A. CABRANES, Circuit Judge:

The plaintiffs-appellants filed suit against Atex, Inc. ("Atex") and its parent, Eastman Kodak Company ("Kodak"), to recover for repetitive stress injuries that they claim were caused by their use of computer keyboards manufactured by Atex. [...]

I. BACKGROUND

The *Fletcher* and *Hermanson* plaintiffs filed their respective complaints on December 4, 1992, and February 25, 1994, seeking recovery from Atex and Kodak, among others, for repetitive stress injuries that they claim were caused by their use of Atex computer keyboards. From 1981 until December 1992, Atex was a wholly-owned subsidiary of Kodak. In 1987, Atex's name was changed to Electronic Pre-Press Systems, Inc., ("EPPS"), but its name was changed back to Atex in 1990. In December 1992, Atex sold substantially all of its assets to an independent third party and again changed its name to 805 Middlesex Corp., which holds the proceeds from the sale. Kodak continues to be the sole shareholder of 805 Middlesex Corp.

After extensive discovery, Kodak moved for summary judgment in *Fletcher* on April 21, 1994, and in *Hermanson* on April 28, 1994. The plaintiffs opposed Kodak's motion, arguing that genuine issues of material fact existed as to Kodak's liability under any number of theories, including (1) that Atex was merely Kodak's alter ego or instrumentality; (2) that Atex was Kodak's agent in the manufacture and marketing of the keyboards; (3) that Kodak was the "apparent manufacturer" of the Atex keyboards;[...]

B. Theories of Liability

1. Alter Ego Liability

The plaintiffs claim that the district court erred in granting Kodak's motion for summary judgment on their alter ego theory of liability. [...]

The district court correctly noted that "[u]nder New York choice of law principles, `[t]he law of the state of incorporation determines when the corporate form will be disregarded and liability will be imposed on shareholders.'" [...]Because Atex was a Delaware corporation, Delaware law determines whether the corporate veil can be pierced in this instance.

[1457] Delaware law permits a court to pierce the corporate veil of a company "where there is fraud or where [it] is in fact a mere instrumentality or alter ego of its owner." [...] Although the Delaware Supreme Court has never explicitly adopted an alter ego theory of parent liability for its subsidiaries, lower Delaware courts have applied the doctrine on several occasions, as has the United

States District Court for the District of Delaware. [...] Thus, under an alter ego theory, there is no requirement of a showing of fraud. *Id.* at 1085. To prevail on an alter ego claim under Delaware law, a plaintiff must show (1) that the parent and the subsidiary "operated as a single economic entity" and (2) that an "overall element of injustice or unfairness ... [is] present." [...]

In the New York state action of *King v. Eastman,* the court granted Kodak's motion for summary judgment, relying on an erroneous interpretation of Delaware's alter ego doctrine. The court noted that although the plaintiffs had raised "ample questions of fact regarding the first element of the piercing theory — domination," they made "no showing that Kodak used whatever dominance it had over Atex to perpetrate a fraud or other wrong that proximately cause[d] injury to them." This was an error; under Delaware law, the alter ego theory of liability does not require any showing of fraud. [...]

To prevail on an alter ego theory of liability, a plaintiff must show that the two corporations "`operated as a single economic entity such that it would be inequitable ... to uphold a legal distinction between them.'" [...] Among the factors to be considered in determining whether a subsidiary and parent operate as a "single economic entity" are:

> "[W]hether the corporation was adequately capitalized for the corporate undertaking; whether the corporation was solvent; whether dividends were paid, corporate records kept, officers and directors functioned properly, and other corporate formalities were observed; whether the dominant shareholder siphoned corporate funds; and whether, in general, the corporation simply functioned as a facade for the dominant shareholder."

[...] As noted above, a showing of fraud or wrongdoing is not necessary under an alter ego theory, but the plaintiff must demonstrate an overall element of injustice or unfairness. [...]

A plaintiff seeking to persuade a Delaware court to disregard the corporate structure faces "a difficult task." [...] Courts have made it clear that "[t]he legal entity of a corporation will not be disturbed until sufficient reason appears." [...] Although the question of domination is generally one of fact, courts have granted motions to dismiss as well as motions for summary judgment in favor of defendant parent companies where there has been a lack of sufficient evidence to place the alter ego issue in dispute. [...]

Kodak has shown that Atex followed corporate formalities, and the plaintiffs have offered no evidence to the contrary. Significantly, the plaintiffs have not challenged Kodak's assertions that Atex's board of directors held regular meetings, that minutes from those meetings were routinely prepared and maintained in corporate minute books, that appropriate financial records and other files were maintained by Atex, that Atex filed its own tax returns and paid its own taxes, and that Atex had its own employees and management executives who were responsible for the corporation's day-to-day business. The plaintiffs' primary arguments regarding domination concern (1) the defendant's use of a cash management system; (2) Kodak's exertion of control over Atex's major expenditures, stock sales, and the sale of Atex's assets to a third party; (3) Kodak's "dominating presence" on Atex's board of directors; (4) descriptions of the relationship between Atex and Kodak in the corporations' advertising, promotional literature, and annual reports; and (5) Atex's assignment of one of its former officer's mortgage to Kodak in order to close Atex's asset-purchase agreement with a third party. The plaintiffs argue that each of these raises a genuine issue of material fact about Kodak's domination of Atex, and that the district court therefore erred in granting summary judgment to Kodak on the plaintiffs' alter ego theory. We find that the district court correctly held that, in light of the undisputed factors of independence cited by Kodak, "the elements identified by the plaintiffs ... [were] insufficient as a matter of law to establish the degree of domination necessary to disregard Atex's corporate identity." [...]

First, the district court correctly held that "Atex's participation in Kodak's cash management system is consistent with sound business practice and does not show undue domination or control." [...] The parties do not dispute the mechanics of Kodak's cash management system. Essentially, all of Kodak's domestic subsidiaries participate in the system and maintain zero-balance bank accounts. All funds transferred from the subsidiary accounts are recorded as credits to the subsidiary, and when a subsidiary is in need of funds, a transfer is made. At all times, a strict accounting is kept of each subsidiary's funds.

Courts have generally declined to find alter ego liability based on a parent corporation's use of a cash management system. *See, e.g., In re Acushnet River & New Bedford Harbor Proceedings,* 675 F.Supp. 22, 34 (D.Mass.1987) (Without "considerably more," "a centralized cash management system ... where the accounting records always reflect the indebtedness of one entity to another, is not the equivalent of intermingling funds" and is insufficient to justify disregarding the corporate form.); [...] The plaintiffs offer no facts to support their speculation that Kodak's centralized cash management system was actually a "complete commingling" of funds or a means by which Kodak sought to "siphon[] all of Atex's revenues into its own account."

Second, the district court correctly concluded that it could find no domination based on the plaintiffs' evidence that Kodak's approval was required for Atex's real estate leases, major capital expenditures, negotiations for a sale of minority stock ownership to IBM, or the fact that Kodak played a significant role in the ultimate sale of Atex's assets to a third party. Again, the parties do not dispute that Kodak required Atex to seek its approval and/or participation for the above transactions. However, this evidence, viewed in the light most favorable to the plaintiffs, does not raise an issue of material fact about whether the two corporations constituted "a single economic entity."[...] In *Akzona,* the Delaware district court noted that a parent's "general executive responsibilities" for its subsidiary's operations included approval over major policy decisions and guaranteeing bank loans, and that that type of oversight was insufficient to demonstrate domination and control. [...]

The plaintiffs' third argument, that Kodak dominated the Atex board of directors, also fails. Although a number of Kodak employees have sat on the Atex board, it is undisputed that between 1981 and 1988, only one director of Atex was also a director of Kodak. Between 1989 and 1992, Atex and Kodak had no directors in common. Parents and subsidiaries frequently have overlapping boards of directors while maintaining separate business operations. In *Japan Petroleum,* the Delaware district court held that the fact that a parent and a subsidiary have common officers and directors does not necessarily demonstrate that the parent corporation dominates the activities of the subsidiary. [...]Since the overlap is negligible here, we find this evidence to be entirely insufficient to raise a question of fact on the issue of domination. [...]

Finally, even if the plaintiffs did raise a factual question about Kodak's domination of Atex, summary judgment would still be appropriate because the plaintiffs offer no evidence on the second prong of the alter ego analysis. The plaintiffs have failed to present evidence of an "overall element of injustice or unfairness" that would result from respecting the two companies' corporate separateness. *See Harper,* 743 F.Supp. at 1085 (holding that plaintiff cannot prevail on alter ego theory "because he has failed to allege any unfairness or injustice which would justify the court in disregarding the [companies'] separate legal existences"). In the instant case, the plaintiffs offer nothing more than the bare assertion that Kodak "exploited" Atex "to generate profits but not to safeguard safety." There is no indication that Kodak sought to defraud creditors and consumers or to siphon funds from its subsidiary. The plaintiffs' conclusory assertions, without more, are not evidence, [...] and are completely inadequate to support a finding that it would be unjust to respect Atex's corporate form.

2. Agency Liability

The plaintiffs next contend that a genuine issue of fact was raised as to whether Kodak could be held liable on an agency theory — that is, whether Kodak, as principal, could be liable for the tortious acts of Atex, its agent. The plaintiffs rely on statements in Atex/ EPPS literature to support their theory: (1) the statement in the Atex document "Setting Up TPE 6000 on the Sun 3 Workstation" that "Atex is an unincorporated division of Electronic Pre-Press Systems, Inc., a Kodak company"; and (2) the statements in the EPPS promotional pamphlet that "EPPS serves as Kodak's primary agent to supply electronic pre-press products" and that "Atex is the largest of the EPPS business units." In granting Kodak's motion for summary judgment, the district court rejected the plaintiffs' agency theory of liability, finding that there was no evidence that Kodak authorized the statements. [...]

The plaintiffs contend that the fact that Kodak permitted the use of its logo on these documents raises a question of fact as to whether Kodak authorized or appeared to authorize the references to Atex/EPPS as its agent. First, the plaintiffs' argument fails under a theory of actual authority. The Restatement (Second) of Agency states: "Authority is the power of the agent to affect the legal relations of the principal by acts done in accordance with the principal's manifestations of consent to him." RESTATEMENT (SECOND) OF AGENCY § 7 (1958). "Manifestation of consent" is "the expression of the will to another as distinguished from the undisclosed purpose or intention." [...] A close reading of the record reveals no evidence that Kodak conferred actual authority upon Atex to act on its behalf. The plaintiffs have offered no evidence that either document was produced by Kodak; in fact, it appears that Atex and EPPS published and disseminated the documents at issue. The presence of a parent's logo on documents created and distributed by a subsidiary, standing alone, does not confer authority [1462] upon the subsidiary to act as an agent.

For similar reasons, plaintiffs' arguments fail under a theory of apparent authority. New York's Court of Appeals has made it clear that "apparent authority is dependent upon verbal or other acts *by a principal* which reasonably give an appearance of authority to conduct the transaction." [...]"Key to the creation of apparent authority," the court continued, "is that the third person, accepting the appearance of authority as true, has relied upon it." *Id.* The plaintiffs offer no evidence that Kodak authorized or gave the appearance of having authorized the statements in the Atex/EPPS documents. Atex's/EPPS's use of the Kodak logo is not a "verbal or other act by a *principal,"* but rather, an act by the purported agent. Furthermore, the record contains no evidence that the plaintiffs relied on the documents at issue. If there were evidence that the plaintiffs relied on these documents and if there were evidence that Kodak uttered or authorized them, then there would be an issue of material fact as to the existence of apparent authority. However, there is neither. We affirm the district court's order granting summary judgment to the defendant on the plaintiffs' agency theory of liability. [...]

III. CONCLUSION

To summarize:

We affirm the district court's order granting summary judgment for the defendant on each of the plaintiffs' four theories of liability.

1. We agree with the district court's conclusion that the defendant was entitled to summary judgment on the plaintiffs' alter ego theory of liability. The collateral estoppel doctrine does not preclude relitigation of the question of Kodak's domination over Atex because the state court's finding of material facts in dispute was not essential to its judgment and because the defendant did not have a full and fair opportunity to litigate the issue. The elements identified by the plaintiffs were insufficient to raise a material issue of fact regarding domination, and further, the plaintiffs failed to offer evidence of injustice that would justify disregarding Atex's corporate form.

2. We affirm the district court's conclusion that the defendant was entitled to summary judgment on the plaintiffs' agency theory of liability because the plaintiffs offered no evidence that Kodak authorized or appeared to authorize Atex to act on its behalf in the manufacturing and marketing of keyboards or that the plaintiffs relied on the documents in question. [...]

Delaware's Veil Piercing Standard   2.2.9.4

In *SARN Energy LLC v. Tatra Defence Vehicles AS* (Del. Super. Ct. 2018) the court described the two prongs of Delaware's veil piercing standard. Delaware's standard is similar to those in other jurisdictions. It requires that the plaintiff demonstrate that the corporation is the mere alter ego of the stockholder (lack of attention to corporate formalities, etc.), and that failure to pierce would result in a fraud or injustice:

Alter-ego liability is analogous to veil piercing. Therefore, it requires that the corporate structure cause fraud or similar injustice. The injustice must be more than a breach of contract or an unsatisfied judgment. Generally, this requires the plaintiff to show that the defendant is involved in an elaborate shell game or is otherwise abusing the corporate form to affect a fraud. Mere dominion and control of the parent over the subsidiary will not support alter ego liability. Rather, the degree of control required is exclusive domination and contract . . . to the point that the subsidiary no longer has legal or independent significance of its own.

This standard applies also where the corporation in question is a subsidiary of a parent corporation. A subsidiary's unsatisfied judgment or a breach of contract by the subsidiary will not be sufficient to justify piercing the limited liability protection of the corporate subsidiary, more will be required.

Of course, this does not mean that parent corporations are entirely protected from liability when dealing through subsidiaries. Especially in the context of a subsidiary's contractual relations, counterparties can, and do, regularly seek to have parent corporations guarantee subsidiary contractual obligations. This is, obviously, less true when one is dealing with creditors and nonvoluntary liabilities of subsidiary corporations (e.g. tort liabilities).

First Amendment, the Corporation, and "Reverse Veil Piercing"   2.2.9.5

In recent years, the US Supreme Court has pursued an aggressive expansion of First Amendment rights for corporations. Underlying all of the court's opinions in this area is the proposition that a corporation's rights under the First Amendment are derived from the rights of the corporation's stockholders and that there is no separation between stockholders and the corporation for purposes of the First Amendment and regulation of corporate speech. It is important to recognize that this view of the corporation - as one and the same with its stockholders - is at odds with state corporate law where the default is legal separation between the existence of the corporation and its stockholders. This default rule is also known as the "doctrine of corporate separateness."

In arriving at its present view of the First Amendment rights for corporations, the Roberts Court has had to basically ignore this doctrine. If one were to arrive at where the Roberts Court presently is, and still comport with basic conceptions of the corporate law and the doctrine of corporate separateness, one would first have to develop a theory of "reverse veil piercing". In neither of the two landmark First Amendment cases in recent years in which the court has imputed the First Amendment rights of stockholders, managers and employees to the corporation has the court done so through a reverse veil piercing theory.

First Amendment and Corporation

In *Citizens United*, the court protected speech rights of corporations by analogizing that corporations are nothing more than "associations of citizens." Let us leave to the side the court's assumption that corporations are associations of "citizens", which clearly they are not. It is well established that corporations can hold stock in other corporations. There is also no statutory requirement that limits stock ownership in corporations to citizens versus say, non-resident aliens. Nevertheless, the *Citizens United* court would not sanction government restrictions on corporate speech because "citizens" had decided associate themselves together in the corporate form. The court reasoned that since citizens had decided to associate in the form of a corporation that government cannot restrict speech of such persons under the constitution. Thus, corporations have speech rights derivative of the citizen stockholders associated with the corporation, even if the stockholders are not, in fact, citizens.

In *Hobby Lobby*, the Roberts Court extended the court's corporate First Amendment jurisprudence by imputing the religious views of its citizen stockholders to the corporation. Much like in *Citizens United*, Justice Alito rationalized extending constitutional rights to corporations because of the people associated with the corporation. Justice Alito was, however, more expansive in his derivation of corporate rights:

> A corporation is simply a form of organization used by human beings to achieve desired ends. An established body of law specifies the rights and obligations of the *people* (including shareholders, officers, and employees) who are associated with a corporation in one way or another. When rights, whether constitutional or statutory, are extended to corporations, the purpose is to protect the rights of these people.

In the view of Justice Alito in *Hobby Lobby*, the motivation for extension of the First Amendment to the corporation is to protect the right of a various constituents of the incorporation, specifically including "shareholders, officers, and employees" of the corporation. The court in *Hobby Lobby* used this rationale to impute the religious views of Hobby Lobby's shareholders onto the corporation itself. Nowhere in the court's opinion did the court attempt to describe how the court balanced the diverse religious views of Hobby Lobby's thousands of employees against the religious views of its shareholders or officers, not to mention the corporation's board of directors.

In another recent high-profile case involving the First Amendment and the corporate form, *Masterpiece Cakeshop Ltd v. Colorado Civil Rights Commission* (2018), the Roberts Court ignored the doctrine of corporate separateness entirely. Throughout the opinion, which was decided on other grounds, the majority equated the controlling shareholder of Masterpiece Cakeshop Ltd with the corporation. Indeed, the opinion mostly ignored the fact that the Masterpiece Cakeshop, the named party in the litigation, had an existence separate and distinct from its shareholders. Whether this was by accident or design is unclear. One thing is clear: if this case were about piercing the corporate veil to assign the financial liabilities of the corporation to its shareholders, the court would have been much less cavalier about separate existence of the corporation.

Citizens United, Hobby Lobby, and *Masterpiece Cakeshop* represent a distinct departure from earlier cases where the Supreme Court expressed a high degree of deference to the corporate form and the doctrine of corporate separateness. Take, for example *Domino's Pizza v. McDonald* (546 US 470, 2006). In *Domino's,* John W. McDonald, the sole shareholder and employee of JWM, Inc., brought a civil rights claim against Domino's. McDonald argued that Domino's discriminated against JWM, Inc. (a Domino's vendor) because McDonald himself was African-American. In that case, the Supreme Court had no problem in seeing a clear difference between the sole shareholder and the corporation and dismissed McDonald's claim for lack of standing. Justice Scalia reasoned that because McDonald had signed the contracts in his capacity as an officer of JWM, Inc. and *not* in his personal capacity, he had no standing to sue in his personal capacity:

> McDonald's complaint does identify a contractual relationship, the one between Domino's and JWM. But it is fundamental corporation and agency law—indeed, it can be said to be the whole purpose of corporation and agency law—that the shareholder and contracting officer of a corporation has no rights and is exposed to no liability under the corporation's contracts. McDonald now makes light of the law of corporations and of agency—arguing, for instance, that because he "negotiated, signed, performed, and sought to enforce the contract," Domino's was wrong to "insist that [the contract] somehow was not his 'own.'" Brief for Respondent 4. This novel approach to the law contradicts McDonald's own experience. Domino's filed a proof of claim against JWM during its corporate bankruptcy; it did *not* proceed against McDonald personally. The corporate form and the rules of agency protected his personal assets, even though he "negotiated, signed, performed, and sought to enforce" contracts for JWM. The corporate form and the rules of agency similarly deny him rights under those contracts.

On the one hand, the court is happy to look through the corporate form in order to impute shareholders' religious views onto the legal fiction we call the corporation. On the other hand, when shareholders seek to asserts civil rights claims on behalf of the corporation, the court refuses to impute the rights of the shareholders to corporation. If it seems hard to make sense of the Robert Court's approach to the corporate form that is because, frankly, it does not make much sense.

Reverse Veil Piercing Theory

If one were to create a doctrinally sound path for a court to impute the constitutional rights of stockholders to the corporation, one would have to do much more work than the Roberts Court has done in preparing the way. One would have to "pierce the corporate veil" but in reverse.

Remember, in the context of traditional veil piercing, courts will rely on a two prong test to overcome the partition between stockholders and the corporation. First, stockholders must have operated the corporation as an "alter ego." In practice, that means stockholders must have disregarded the simple corporate formalities required by the statute that give a separate life to the corporation: articles of incorporation, bylaws, meetings of a board of directors, etc. Second, the court must determine that not piercing the corporate veil of limited liability would result in some inequity or injustice.

Any theory of looking through the corporate form and pierce the corporate veil in reverse, as the Supreme Court would have us do, must require a test that is an analogue of the traditional veil piercing test: a unity of interest between the corporation and the corporation and whether not permitting a reverse veil piercing would result in some injustice to the stockholders.

Where stockholders treat the corporation as no more than their alter ego (due to lack of formality, etc.) and where the failure of the court to impute the constitutional rights of the stockholders to the corporation would result in some inequity or injustice, then a court would be right to impute the constitutional rights of the shareholder to the corporation. Of course, application of this reverse veil piercing standard to corporations would be a two-edge sword for the corporations that avail themselves of this. Corporations seeking to disregard the doctrine of corporate separateness for the purposes of imputing the constitutional rights of stockholders to the corporation would also give up, in effect, the benefits of limited liability.

In Manichean Cap., LLC. v. Exela Techs., Inc. (Del. Ch. May 25, 2021), the Chancery Court laid out a rule for reverse veil piercing. Like traditional veil piercing, the court emphasized a reverse veil piercing doctrine should be used only in exceptional circumstances: "Only in cases alleging egregious facts, coupled with the lack of real and substantial prejudice to third parties, should the court even consider utilizing the reverse veil-piercing doctrine."

Having sufficiently limited any expectation of the use of reverse veil piercing, Vice Chancellor Slights then laid out a framework for pursuing a reverse veil piercing claim:

The natural starting place when reviewing a claim for reverse veil-piercing are the traditional factors Delaware courts consider when reviewing a traditional veil-piercing claim—the so-called 'alter ego' factors that include insolvency, undercapitalization, commingling of corporate and personal funds, the absence of corporate formalities, and whether the subsidiary is simply a facade for the owner. The court should then ask whether the owner is utilizing the corporate form to perpetuate fraud or an injustice. This inquiry should focus on additional factors, including (1) the degree to which allowing a reverse pierce would impair the legitimate expectations of any adversely affected shareholders who are not responsible for the conduct of the insider that gave rise to the reverse pierce claim, and the degree to which allowing a reverse pierce would establish a precedent troubling to shareholders generally; (2) the degree to which the corporate entity whose disregard is sought has exercised dominion and control over the insider who is subject to the claim by the party seeking a reverse pierce; (3) the degree to which the injury alleged by the person seeking a reverse pierce is related to the corporate entity's dominion and control of the insider, or to that person's reasonable reliance upon a lack of separate entity status between the insider and the corporate entity; (4) the degree to which the public convenience, as articulated by [the Delaware General Corporation Law and Delaware's common law], would be served by allowing a reverse pierce; (5) the extent and severity of the wrongful conduct, if any, engaged in by the corporate entity whose disregard is sought by the insider; (6) the possibility that the person seeking the reverse pierce is himself guilty of wrongful conduct sufficient to bar him from obtaining equitable relief; (7) the extent to which the reverse pierce will harm innocent third-party creditors of the entity the plaintiff seeks to reach; and (8) the extent to which other claims or remedies are practically available to the creditor at law or in equity to recover the debt.

* ** ***

Question for Discussion

If the Supreme Court were to apply state-level veil piercing doctrines to the question of imputing a group of stockholders' religious views to the corporation, what might that "reverse veil piercing" doctrine look like? In that case, what would have to be true before the court might impute the religious views of stockholders to the corporation?

Corporate Powers   **2.3**

Prior to the passage of general enabling laws, the explication of corporate power through the corporate charter was extremely important. State legislatures could tailor corporate charters to provide corporations significant powers, including monopoly rights over markets or territories. Although states no longer grant corporations such unique powers, explication of corporate powers (e.g. right to own property, right sue and be sued, etc.) nevertheless remains important in establishing a corporation's legal personality.

Sections 121 and 122 are authorizing provisions that grant corporate entities both explicit and implicit authority to act and conduct business. While §122 provides explicit authority for certain activities of the corporation, §121 is a catch-all provision that provides implied authority to the corporation to undertake all other actions required to conduct business. Taken together, the corporation has a great deal of flexibility to act. Section 123 gives corporations the power to own and vote shares of other corporations. While it might seem like a simple thing, §123 is the basis for the modern holding company.

DGCL Sec. 121 - General Powers   2.3.1

Section 121 provides for the general powers of a corporation. The corporation has implied authority to undertake all actions required in order to conduct its business as determined by the board of directors and as limited by the corporation's certificate of incorporation and the statute.

§ 121. General powers.

(a) In addition to the powers enumerated in § 122 of this title, every corporation, its officers, directors and stockholders shall possess and may exercise all the powers and privileges granted by this chapter or by any other law or by its certificate of incorporation, together with any powers incidental thereto, so far as such powers and privileges are necessary or convenient to the conduct, promotion or attainment of the business or purposes set forth in its certificate of incorporation.

(b) Every corporation shall be governed by the provisions and be subject to the restrictions and liabilities contained in this chapter.

DGCL Sec. 122 - Specific Powers   2.3.2

In addition to a corporation's general powers, the statute lays out a series of specific powers available to every corporation. Many of these specific powers are critical to the life of a corporation. These specific powers under §122 were once controversial, but by now are almost taken for granted.

For example, the corporate power to make charitable donations is one such specific corporate power that was once controversial. In the early years of the corporate form, donations to charitable causes were deemed to be *ultra vires* – or beyond the power of boards of directors. Through a series of changes – in the code and the common law – charitable contributions are now permissible. The power to make charitable contributions is intertwined with the current "ESG" discussion. Critics argue that corporate attention to social causes is in conflict with corporate purposes. However, it has been clear since at least the middle of the last century that corporations have the power, and perhaps even a fiduciary duty, to engage in "ESG" conversations.

Section 122 grants the corporation other specific powers, all of which are calculated to facilitating the ability of the corporation to act in its own behalf as a corporate person separate from its stockholders.

§ 122. Specific powers.

Every corporation created under this chapter shall have power to:

(1) Have perpetual succession by its corporate name, unless a limited period of duration is stated in its certificate of incorporation;

(2) Sue and be sued in all courts and participate, as a party or otherwise, in any judicial, administrative, arbitrative or other proceeding, in its corporate name;

(3) Have a corporate seal, which may be altered at pleasure, and use the same by causing it or a facsimile thereof, to be impressed or affixed or in any other manner reproduced;

(4) Purchase, receive, take by grant, gift, devise, bequest or otherwise, lease, or otherwise acquire, own, hold, improve, employ, use and otherwise deal in and with real or personal property, or any

interest therein, wherever situated, and to sell, convey, lease, exchange, transfer or otherwise dispose of, or mortgage or pledge, all or any of its property and assets, or any interest therein, wherever situated;

(5) Appoint such officers and agents as the business of the corporation requires and to pay or otherwise provide for them suitable compensation;

(6) Adopt, amend and repeal bylaws;

(7) Wind up and dissolve itself in the manner provided in this chapter;

(8) Conduct its business, carry on its operations and have offices and exercise its powers within or without this State;

(9) Make donations for the public welfare or for charitable, scientific or educational purposes, and in time of war or other national emergency in aid thereof;

(10) Be an incorporator, promoter or manager of other corporations of any type or kind;

(11) Participate with others in any corporation, partnership, limited partnership, joint venture or other association of any kind, or in any transaction, undertaking or arrangement which the participating corporation would have power to conduct by itself, whether or not such participation involves sharing or delegation of control with or to others;

(12) Transact any lawful business which the corporation's board of directors shall find to be in aid of governmental authority;

(13) Make contracts, including contracts of guaranty and suretyship, incur liabilities, borrow money at such rates of interest as the corporation may determine, issue its notes, bonds and other obligations, and secure any of its obligations by mortgage, pledge or other encumbrance of all or any of its property, franchises and income, and make contracts of guaranty and suretyship which are necessary or convenient to the conduct, promotion or attainment of the business of (a) a corporation all of the outstanding stock of

which is owned, directly or indirectly, by the contracting corporation, or (b) a corporation which owns, directly or indirectly, all of the outstanding stock of the contracting corporation, or (c) a corporation all of the outstanding stock of which is owned, directly or indirectly, by a corporation which owns, directly or indirectly, all of the outstanding stock of the contracting corporation, which contracts of guaranty and suretyship shall be deemed to be necessary or convenient to the conduct, promotion or attainment of the business of the contracting corporation, and make other contracts of guaranty and suretyship which are necessary or convenient to the conduct, promotion or attainment of the business of the contracting corporation;

(14) Lend money for its corporate purposes, invest and reinvest its funds, and take, hold and deal with real and personal property as security for the payment of funds so loaned or invested;

(15) Pay pensions and establish and carry out pension, profit sharing, stock option, stock purchase, stock bonus, retirement, benefit, incentive and compensation plans, trusts and provisions for any or all of its directors, officers and employees, and for any or all of the directors, officers and employees of its subsidiaries;

(16) Provide insurance for its benefit on the life of any of its directors, officers or employees, or on the life of any stockholder for the purpose of acquiring at such stockholder's death shares of its stock owned by such stockholder.

(17) Renounce, in its certificate of incorporation or by action of its board of directors, any interest or expectancy of the corporation in, or in being offered an opportunity to participate in, specified business opportunities or specified classes or categories of business opportunities that are presented to the corporation or 1 or more of its officers, directors or stockholders.

Theodora Holding Corp. v. Henderson   2.3.3

Theodora deals with the issue of corporate charity.
Until the post-World War II period, there was some
question whether a corporation had the power to make donations to
charity. On the one hand, there were those who felt that a board's
sole duty was to maximize profits for stockholders and that absent
express authority to make corporate charitable contributions in the
corporation's certificate of incorporation, that a board does not have
the authority to make such contributions. On the other hand, there
were those who recognized corporations had – even back to the pre-
enabling laws period – a broader social role beyond maximizing
profit for stockholders in the short run.

Eventually, states legislatures put this question to rest by amending
their corporate statutes to recognize the power of boards to make
charitable corporate gifts. A series of court cases, including
Theodora, reinforced the importance of corporate charitable
contributions and the role of corporate charitable contributions in
reinforcing the social compact that makes corporate form possible.

The power of a corporation to make charitable contributions is not
unlimited, however. *Theodora* and *AP Smith* [cited in *Theodora*]
hint at the limits to corporate largesse.

The debate about the extent of corporate power to make charitable
donations runs parallel to a modern debate about corporate
purpose. On the one side, there are those who argue that boards
should be focused exclusively on maximizing stockholder value. On
the other are those who argue that corporations have responsibilities
to a broader group of stakeholders. Managing the tension that is
reflected in this ongoing debate is central to understanding the
corporate law and how modern boards make decisions.

THEODORA HOLDING CORP. V. HENDERSON
257 A. 2D 398 (1969)

MARVEL, Vice Chancellor:

Plaintiff, which was formed in May of 1967 by the defendant Girard B. Henderson's former wife, Theodora G. Henderson, is the holder of record of 11,000 of the 40,500 issued and outstanding shares of common stock of the defendant Alexander Dawson, Inc. It sues derivatively as well as on its own behalf for an accounting by the individual defendants for the losses allegedly sustained by the corporate defendant and the concomitant improper gains allegedly received by the individual defendants as a result of certain transactions of which plaintiff complains. [...]

As of September 30, 1968, Theodora G. Henderson, in addition to her interest in [400] the plaintiff corporation, was the holder of the following shares of preferred stock of the corporate defendant, namely, 3,000 of first preferred, 12,000 of second preferred, and 22,000 of third preferred. She continues to receive dividends on such shares. Prior to plaintiff's formation in 1967 Mrs. Henderson had received dividends on both common and preferred shares of the corporate defendant until she transferred her 11,000 shares of the common stock of said company to plaintiff during the year 1967. Corporate dividends paid to Mrs. Henderson in recent years and now to plaintiff and Mrs. Henderson have increased substantially in recent years. As of December 3, 1968, dividends paid to plaintiff and Mrs. Henderson in that year totalled $385,240. In 1966, Mrs. Henderson had received dividends in the amount of $292,840, and in 1967, a year in which Alexander Dawson, Inc., made a controversial charitable contribution having a value of $528,000, the combined dividends of plaintiff and Mrs. Henderson totalled $286,240.

In January of 1955, the defendant Girard B. Henderson and his then wife, Theodora G. Henderson, had entered into a separation agreement looking towards a divorce, at which time Mrs. Henderson's dividends from the corporate defendant totalled approximately $50,000 per annum. Under the terms of such agreement Mrs. Henderson acknowledged that she had received from her then husband the shares of common stock of Alexander Dawson, Inc., here in issue as well as a number of shares of preferred stock of such corporation. Upon plaintiff's organization, it became the owner of Mrs. Henderson's 11,000 shares of common stock[1] on May 3, 1967. As of April 30, 1967, the shares of Alexander Dawson, Inc., to be turned over to the plaintiff corporation had a fair market value of $15,675,000 and an underlying net asset value of $28,996,000. [...]

The individual defendant Henderson by reason of the extent of his combined majority holdings of common and preferred stock of Alexander Dawson, Inc., each class of which has voting rights, exercises effective control over the affairs of such corporation, the net worth of the assets of which, at the time of the filing of this suit, was approximately $150,000,000.

It is claimed and the evidence supports such contention that on December 8, 1967, the defendant Girard B. Henderson, by virtue of his voting control over the affairs of Alexander Dawson, Inc., caused the board of directors of such corporation to be reduced in number from eight to three persons, namely himself, the defendant Bengt Ljunggren,[2] an employee of the corporate defendant, and Mr. Henderson's daughter, Theodora H. Ives. It is alleged that thereafter the defendant Girard B. Henderson (over the objection of the director, Mrs. Ives) caused the board and the majority of the voting stock of Alexander [401] Dawson, Inc., improperly to contribute stock held by it in the approximate value of $550,000 to the Alexander Dawson Foundation, a charitable trust, the affairs of which were then controlled and continue to be controlled by Mr. Henderson. [...]

Alexander Dawson, Inc. has functioned as a personal holding company since 1935 when Mr. Henderson's mother exchanged a substantial number of shares held by her in a company which later became Avon Products, Inc., for all of the shares of her own company known as Alexander Dawson, Inc. Mr. Henderson and a brother later succeeded to their mother's interest in Alexander Dawson, Inc., the brother thereafter permitting his shares to be redeemed by the corporation. As noted earlier, Mr. Henderson, by reason of his combined holdings of common and preferred stock of the corporate defendant, is in clear control of the affairs of such corporation, which, for the most part, has been operated informally by Mr. Henderson with scant regard for the views of other board members. Some seventy-five percent of its assets consist of shares of Avon Products, Inc. stock, there having been some diversification, particularly in 1967, largely through the urging of officers of the United States Trust Company of New York who have served as advisors. Through exercise of such control, Mr. Henderson has, since 1957, [402] caused the corporate defendant to donate varying amounts to a charitable trust organized in that year by Mr. Henderson, namely the Alexander Dawson Foundation. In 1957, $10,610 was donated to such trust. From 1960 to 1966 (except for the year 1965) gifts were in the range of approximately $63,000 to $70,000 or higher in each year other than 1963 when $27,923 was donated. In 1966, however, a gift in the form of a large tract of land in Colorado, having a value of some $467,750, was made.[3] All of these gifts through 1966 were unanimously approved by all of the stockholders of Alexander Dawson, Inc., including Mrs. Theodora G. Henderson. The gift now under attack, namely one of the shares of stock of the corporate defendant having a value of some $528,000, was made to the Alexander Dawson Foundation in December of 1967. Such gift was first proposed by Mr. Henderson in April, 1967 before the board of the corporate defendant was reduced in number from eight to three. However, director reaction was thereafter confused, one of the directors, Mrs. Henderson's daughter, Theodora H. Ives, having expressed a desire that a corporate gift also be made to her own charitable corporation and that of her mother, Theodora G. Henderson. Accordingly, the matter was not pressed by Mr. Henderson until late December when the reduced board had taken over management of the corporate defendant. It is claimed and admitted that such gift had an effect on the equity and dividends of shareholders of the corporate defendant although the tax consequences of such gift clearly soften the apparent impact of such transaction. It is significant, however, as noted above, that the 1966 corporate gift, consisting of a ranch located in Colorado, had been approved by all of the directors and stockholders of the corporate defendant, and that the gift here under attack was apparently intended to be a step towards consummation of the purpose behind such grant of land, namely to provide a fund for the financing of a western camp for under privileged boys, particularly members of the George Junior Republic, a self-governing institution which has served the public interest for some seventy-five years at a school near Freeville, New York. Thus, in the summer of 1967, a small group of under privileged children had enjoyed the advantages of such camp in a test of the feasibility of such an institution. However, it is apparently Mr. Henderson's intention to continue and expand his interest in such camp where he maintains an underground home which he occupies at a $6,000 rental per annum, such house being occupied by him during some three months of the year. Plaintiff initially attacked such use. However, [...] plaintiff seeks no accounting from the individual defendants[...], plaintiff asks that all actions undertaken by Mr. Henderson which demonstrate a course of irresponsible corporate conduct as well as misuse of corporate power and assets should be considered by the Court in reaching an ultimate decision on the question of whether or not a liquidating receiver for Alexander Dawson, Inc., should be appointed. [...]

The next matter to be considered is the propriety of the December 1967 gift made by Alexander Dawson, Inc. to the Alexander Dawson Foundation of shares of stock of the corporate defendant having a value in excess of $525,000, an amount within the limits of the provisions of the federal tax law having to do with deductible corporate gifts, Internal Revenue Code of 1954 §§ 170(b) (2), 545(b) (2).

Title 8 Del.C. § 122 provides as follows:

"Every corporation created under this chapter shall have power to —

* * * * * *

(9) Make donations for the public welfare or for charitable, scientific or educational purposes, and in time of war or other national emergency in aid thereof."

There is no doubt but that the Alexander Dawson Foundation is recognized as a legitimate charitable trust by the Department of Internal Revenue. It is also clear that it is authorized to operate exclusively in the fields of "* * * religious, charitable, scientific, literary, or educational purposes, or for the prevention of cruelty to children or animals * * *". Furthermore, contemporary courts recognize that unless corporations carry an increasing share of the burden of supporting charitable and educational causes that the business advantages now reposed in corporations by law may well prove to be unacceptable to the representatives of an aroused public. The recognized obligation of corporations towards philanthropic, educational and artistic causes is reflected in the statutory law of all of the states, other than the states of Arizona and Idaho.

In A. P. Smith Mfg. Co. v. Barlow, 13 N.J. 145, 98 A.2d 681, 39 A.L.R.2d 1179, appeal dismissed, 346 U.S. 861, 74 S.Ct. 107, 98 L.Ed. 373, a case in which the corporate donor had been organized long before the adoption of a statute authorizing corporate gifts to charitable or educational institutions, the Supreme Court of New Jersey upheld a gift of $1500 by the plaintiff corporation to Princeton University, being of the opinion that the trend towards the transfer of wealth from private industrial entrepreneurs to corporate institutions, the increase of taxes on individual income, coupled with steadily increasing philanthropic needs, necessitate corporate giving for educational needs even were there no statute permitting such gifts, and this was held to be the case apart from the question of the reserved power of the state to amend corporate charters. The court also noted that the gift tended to bolster the free enterprise system and the general social climate in which plaintiff was nurtured. And while the court pointed out that there was no showing that the gift in question was made indiscriminately or to a pet charity in furtherance of personal rather than corporate ends, the actual holding of the opinion appears to be that a corporate charitable or educational gift to be valid must merely be within reasonable limits both as to amount and purpose. Compare Union Pacific R. R. v. Trustees, Inc., 8 Utah 2d 101, 329 P.2d 398.

The New Jersey statute in force and effect at the time of the Smith case gift provided that directors might cause their corporation to contribute for charitable and educational purposes and the like "* * such reasonable sum or sums as they may determine * * *" provided, however, that such contributions might not be made in situations where the proposed donee owned more than 10% of the voting stock of the donor and provided further that such gifts be limited to 5% of capital and surplus unless "* * * authorized by the stockholders."

[405] Whether or not these statutory limitations on corporate giving were the source of the limiting language of the New Jersey Supreme Court is not clear, the point being that the Delaware statute contains no such limiting language and therefor must, in my opinion, be construed to authorize any reasonable corporate gift of a charitable or educational nature. Significantly, Alexander Dawson, Inc. was incorporated in Delaware in 1958 after 8 Del.C. § 122(9) was cast in its present form, therefor no constitutional problem arising out of the effect on a stockholder's property rights of the State's reserved power to amend corporate charters is presented.

I conclude that the test to be applied in passing on the validity of a gift such as the one here in issue is that of reasonableness, a test in which the provisions of the Internal Revenue Code pertaining to charitable gifts by corporations furnish a helpful guide. The gift here under attack was made from gross income and had a value as of the time of giving of $528,000 in a year in which Alexander Dawson, Inc.'s total income was $19,144,229.06, or well within the federal tax deduction limitation of 5% of such income. The contribution under attack can be said to have "cost" all of the stockholders of Alexander Dawson, Inc. including plaintiff, less than $80,000, or some fifteen cents per dollar of contribution, taking into consideration the federal tax provisions applicable to holding companies as well as the provisions for compulsory distribution of dividends received by such a corporation. In addition, the gift, by reducing Alexander Dawson, Inc.'s reserve for unrealized capital gains taxes by some $130,000, increased the balance sheet net worth of stockholders of the corporate defendant by such amount. It is accordingly obvious, in my opinion, that the relatively small loss of immediate income otherwise payable to plaintiff and the corporate defendant's other stockholders, had it not been for the gift in question, is far outweighed by the overall benefits flowing from the placing of such gift in channels where it serves to benefit those in need of philanthropic or educational support, thus providing justification for large private holdings, thereby benefiting plaintiff in the long run. Finally, the fact that the interests of the Alexander Dawson Foundation appear to be increasingly directed towards the rehabilitation and education of deprived but deserving young people is peculiarly appropriate in an age when a large segment of youth is alienated even from parents who are not entirely satisfied with our present social and economic system.

DGCL Sec. 123 - Ownership of securities

2.3.4

Prior to the adoption of general incorporation statutes, corporations were regularly prohibited from owning stock or securities of other corporations. By specifically permitting a corporation to own and vote the stock of another corporation, §123 makes possible the "holding company" structure.

A holding company is a corporation that has no operations but holds assets in the form of stock of subsidiary operating corporations. This hierarchical business structure is now quite common in the US and has a number of obvious benefits. First and foremost, the holding company structure permits the parent corporation to hold risky assets at arm's length, utilizing the subsidiary's limited liability shield to prevent an adverse risk in one business unit from affecting the entire business operation. The holding company structure also makes it easier to buy and sell corporate assets. Rather than engage in a corporate level merger or sale, the board of directors of a holding company can buy or sell divisions by simply transferring the shares of the division to or from a buyer. For these reasons, and others, the holding company structure has become ubiquitous.

§ 123. Powers respecting securities of other corporations or entities.

Any corporation organized under the laws of this State may
guarantee, purchase, take, receive, subscribe for or otherwise
acquire; own, hold, use or otherwise employ; sell, lease, exchange,
transfer or otherwise dispose of; mortgage, lend, pledge or
otherwise deal in and with, bonds and other obligations of, or shares
or other securities or interests in, or issued by, any other domestic
or foreign corporation, partnership, association or individual, or by
any government or agency or instrumentality thereof. A corporation
while owner of any such securities may exercise all the rights,
powers and privileges of ownership, including the right to vote.

Public Benefit Corporations   2.3.5

The development of corporate social responsibility
and social entrepreneurship has given rise to
demand for a different kind of corporate form, the
"public benefit corporation". The public benefit corporation is a
for-profit corporation established with a specific public purpose.
The certificate of incorporation of a public benefit corporation
requires that incorporators specify some public benefit against
which the pecuniary interests of the corporation's business must be
balanced. Public benefit corporations as a specific form are a
relatively new addition to corporate laws of states in response to a
growing desire by promoters to have a corporate form that
outwardly signals a credible commitment by managers to a more
publicly-minded business. Although the form is relatively new, there
is very little in the public benefit form that could not also be
accomplished using a regular corporation.

In recent years, there has been a proliferation of public benefit corporations. For example, Ello, a Delaware public benefit corporation (social networking site), specifies as its public benefit that it will not share the private information of its customers with third parties. Plum Organics, another Delaware public benefit corporation (a baby food manufacturer), specifies that its public benefit includes "the delivery of nourishing, organic food to the nation's little ones." Finally, Lemonade, PBC, a publicly-traded, Delaware public benefit corporation, specifies that its public benefit is to "harness novel business models, technologies and private-nonprofit partnerships to deliver insurance products where charitable giving is a core feature, for the benefit of communities and their common cause."

As you work through the provisions of the public benefit corporation statute, notice that while the statute permits directors to explicitly work to further the corporation's stated public benefit, it does not permit beneficiaries of the stated public benefit to sue to enforce the benefit. So, where Plum Organics creates a stated benefit of "providing nourishing, organic food to the nation's little ones," the nation's little ones have no standing when it comes to enforcing that benefit.

Public Benefit Corporations   2.3.5.1

Sections 361-368

The following amendments to the Delaware corporation code were adopted in 2013 and provide for the establishment of public benefit corporations under the Delaware General Corporation Law. The main difference between a public benefit corporation and the traditional for profit corporation is the requirement that the public benefit identify some public benefit and then manage the corporation in a manner that balances profit with the best interests of those affected by the corporation's conduct as well as the specific public benefit identified in the certificate of incorporation.

An existing for profit corporation may convert to a public benefit corporation by amending its certificate of incorporation, in accordance with § 242 so that it comports with the requirements of § 362.

Subchapter XV. Public Benefit Corporations

§ 362. Public benefit corporation defined; contents of certificate of incorporation.

(a) A "public benefit corporation" is a for-profit corporation organized under and subject to the requirements of this chapter that is intended to produce a public benefit or public benefits and to operate in a responsible and sustainable manner. To that end, a public benefit corporation shall be managed in a manner that balances the stockholders' pecuniary interests, the best interests of those materially affected by the corporation's conduct, and the public benefit or public benefits identified in its certificate of incorporation. In the certificate of incorporation, a public benefit corporation shall:

(1) Identify within its statement of business or purpose pursuant to §102(a)(3) of this title one or more specific public benefits to be promoted by the corporation; and

(2) State within its heading that it is a public benefit corporation.

(b) "Public benefit" means a positive effect (or reduction of negative effects) on 1 or more categories of persons, entities, communities or interests (other than stockholders in their capacities as stockholders) including, but not limited to, effects of an artistic, charitable, cultural, economic, educational, environmental, literary, medical, religious, scientific or technological nature. "Public benefit provisions" means the provisions of a certificate of incorporation contemplated by this subchapter.

(c) The name of the public benefit corporation may contain the words "public benefit corporation," or the abbreviation "P.B.C.," or the designation "PBC," which shall be deemed to satisfy the requirements of § 102(a)(1)(i) of this title. ...

§ 365. Duties of directors.

(a) The board of directors shall manage or direct the business and affairs of the public benefit corporation in a manner that balances the pecuniary interests of the stockholders, the best interests of those materially affected by the corporation's conduct, and the specific public benefit or public benefits identified in its certificate of incorporation.

(b) A director of a public benefit corporation shall not, by virtue of the public benefit provisions or § 362(a) of this title, have any duty to any person on account of any interest of such person in the public benefit or public benefits identified in the certificate of incorporation or on account of any interest materially affected by the corporation's conduct and, with respect to a decision implicating the balance requirement in subsection (a) of this section, will be deemed to satisfy such director's fiduciary duties to stockholders and the corporation if such director's decision is both informed and disinterested and not such that no person of ordinary, sound judgment would approve.

(c) A director's ownership of or other interest in the stock of the public benefit corporation shall not alone, for the purposes of this section, create a conflict of interest on the part of the director with respect to the director's decision implicating the balancing requirement in subsection (a) of this section, except to the extent that such ownership or interest would create a conflict of interest if the corporation were not a public benefit corporation. In the absence of a conflict of interest, no failure to satisfy that balancing requirement shall, for the purposes of § 102(b)(7) or § 145 of this title, constitute an act or omission not in good faith, or a breach of the duty of loyalty, unless the certificate of incorporation so provides.

§ 366. Periodic statements and third-party certification.

(a) A public benefit corporation shall include in every notice of a meeting of stockholders a statement to the effect that it is a public benefit corporation formed pursuant to this subchapter.

(b) A public benefit corporation shall no less than biennially provide its stockholders with a statement as to the corporation's promotion of the public benefit or public benefits identified in the certificate of incorporation and of the best interests of those materially affected by the corporation's conduct. The statement shall include:

(1) The objectives the board of directors has established to promote such public benefit or public benefits and interests;

(2) The standards the board of directors has adopted to measure the corporation's progress in promoting such public benefit or public benefits and interests;

(3) Objective factual information based on those standards regarding the corporation's success in meeting the objectives for promoting such public benefit or public benefits and interests; and

(4) An assessment of the corporation's success in meeting the objectives and promoting such public benefit or public benefits and interests.

(c) The certificate of incorporation or bylaws of a public benefit corporation may require that the corporation:

(1) Provide the statement described in subsection (b) of this section more frequently than biennially;

(2) Make the statement described in subsection (b) of this section available to the public; and/or

(3) Use a third-party standard in connection with and/or attain a periodic third-party certification addressing the corporation's promotion of the public benefit or public benefits identified in the certificate of incorporation and/or the best interests of those materially affected by the corporation's conduct.

§ 367. Suits to enforce the requirements of § 365(a) of this title.

Any action to enforce the balancing requirement of § 365(a) of this title, including any individual, derivative or any other type of action, may not be brought unless the plaintiffs in such action own individually or collectively, as of the date of instituting such action, at least 2% of the corporation's outstanding shares or, in the case of a corporation with shares listed on a national securities exchange, the lesser of such percentage or shares of the corporation with a market value of at least $2,000,000 as of the date the action is instituted. This section shall not relieve the plaintiffs from complying with any other conditions applicable to filing a derivative action including § 327 of this title and any rules of the court in which the action is filed. ...

Bylaws 2.4

The corporate bylaws, in addition to the certificate of incorporation, make up the core of any corporation's governance documents. Whereas the subject matter of the certificate of incorporation deals with the basic relationships between stockholders and the corporation, the substance of corporate bylaws is typically limited to issue of governance process within the corporation. Bylaws typically do not contain substantive mandates, but direct how the corporation, the board, and its stockholders may take certain actions.

The corporate bylaws are subordinate to the certificate of incorporation. To the extent bylaws and the certificate or the DGCL are in conflict, the certificate and/or the DGCL will take precedence over the bylaws. Because they are subordinate, corporate bylaws are also easier to amend. Typically, corporate bylaws may be amended by a corporation's board of directors or its stockholders. When stockholders amend the bylaws, they need only achieve a majority of a quorum rather than the more exacting majority of the outstanding shares as is the case in an amendment to the corporation's certificate of incorporation.

Whereas the certificate of incorporation must be filed with the state, a corporation is not required to file its bylaws with any state authority.

DGCL Sec. 109   2.4.1

This provision authorizes the corporation to adopt bylaws governing the conduct of the affairs of the corporation. The provision provides that the power to adopt and amend bylaws lies with the stockholders. However, if a corporation provides for such in its certificate of incorporation - as most corporate certificates do - then the board of directors may also amend the bylaws. As you might guess, issues may arise when stockholders and directors adopt conflicting bylaws.

§ 109. Bylaws.

(a) The original or other bylaws of a corporation may be adopted, amended or repealed by the incorporators, by the initial directors of a corporation [...] if they were named in the certificate of incorporation, or, before a corporation [...] has received any payment for any of its stock, by its board of directors. After a corporation [...]has received any payment for any of its stock, the power to adopt, amend or repeal bylaws shall be in the stockholders entitled to vote. [...] Notwithstanding the foregoing, any corporation may, in its certificate of incorporation, confer the power to adopt, amend or repeal bylaws upon the directors[...]. The fact that such power has been so conferred upon the directors or governing body, as the case may be, shall not divest the stockholders or members of the power, nor limit their power to adopt, amend or repeal bylaws.

(b) The bylaws may contain any provision, not inconsistent with law or with the certificate of incorporation, relating to the business of the corporation, the conduct of its affairs, and its rights or powers or the rights or powers of its stockholders, directors, officers or employees.

Boilermakers Local 154 v. Chevron Corp.   **2.4.2**

In *Boilermakers*, the court answers the question
whether directors can unilaterally adopt bylaws to restrict the rights
of stockholders. The bylaw in question is an 'exclusive forum
provision' bylaw that purports to limit the rights of stockholders to
bring certain kinds of litigation against the corporation and its board
to courts in Delaware. Forum selection provisions are common in
commercial contracts.

In this case, the board – and not the stockholders – adopted an
exclusive forum bylaw. This case raises important questions about
the ability of directors to act unilaterally in the context of corporate
bylaws as well as the nature of the "corporate contract" that
stockholders enter into when they purchase shares of any
corporation.

This case also reviews the standards of review a court will apply to
judicial challenges to bylaws as well as the typical subject matter
appropriate for bylaws.

BOILERMAKERS LOCAL 154 V. CHEVRON
Del: Court of Chancery 2013

STRINE, Chancellor.

I. Introduction

The board of Chevron, the oil and gas major, has adopted a bylaw
providing that litigation relating to Chevron's internal affairs should
be conducted in Delaware, the state where Chevron is
incorporated and whose substantive law Chevron's stockholders

know governs the corporation's internal affairs. The board of the logistics company FedEx, which is also incorporated in Delaware and whose internal affairs are also therefore governed by Delaware law, has adopted a similar bylaw providing that the forum for litigation related to FedEx's internal affairs should be the Delaware Court of Chancery. The boards of both companies have been empowered in their certificates of incorporation to adopt bylaws under 8 *Del. C.* § 109(a).[1]

The plaintiffs, stockholders in Chevron and FedEx, have sued the boards for adopting these "forum selection bylaws." The plaintiffs' complaints are nearly identical and were filed only a few days apart by clients of the same law firm. In Count I, the plaintiffs claim that the bylaws are statutorily invalid because they are beyond the board's authority under the Delaware General Corporation Law ("DGCL"). In Count IV, the plaintiffs allege that the bylaws are contractually invalid, and therefore cannot be enforced like other contractual forum selection clauses under the test adopted by the Supreme Court of the United States in *The Bremen v. Zapata Offshore Co.,*[2] because they were unilaterally adopted by the Chevron and FedEx boards using their power to make bylaws. [...]

In this opinion, the court resolves the defendants' motion for judgment on the pleadings on the counts relating to the statutory and contractual validity of the bylaws. Because the two bylaws are similar, present common legal issues, and are the target of near-identical complaints, the court decided to address them together. This is efficient, and is also in the interests of the parties, because a decision on the legal validity of the bylaws under the DGCL will moot the plaintiffs' other challenges if the bylaws are found to be invalid. And, it also aids the administration of justice, because a foreign court that respects the internal affairs doctrine, as it must,[3] when faced with a motion to enforce the bylaws will consider, as a first order issue, whether the bylaws are valid under the "chartering jurisdiction's domestic law."[4] Furthermore, the plaintiffs' facial statutory invalidity claim and their related contention that, as a matter of law, the bylaws are not contractually enforceable, have cast a cloud over the defendants' bylaws and those of other corporations. A decision as to the basic legal questions presented by the plaintiffs' complaints will provide efficiency benefits to not only the defendants and their stockholders, but to other corporations and their investors. [...]

II. Background And Procedural Posture

A. The Chevron And FedEx Forum Selection Bylaws

Critical to the resolution of this motion is an understanding of who has the power to adopt, amend, and repeal the bylaws, and what subjects the bylaws may address under the DGCL. 8 *Del. C.* § 109(a) identifies who has the power to adopt, amend, and repeal the bylaws:

> [T]he power to adopt, amend or repeal bylaws shall be in the stockholders entitled to vote . . . . Notwithstanding the foregoing, any corporation may, in its certificate of incorporation, confer the power to adopt, amend or repeal bylaws upon the directors . . . . The fact that such power has been so conferred upon the directors . . . shall not divest the stockholders . . . of the power, nor limit their power to adopt, amend or repeal bylaws.

8 *Del. C.* § 109(b) states the subject matter the bylaws may address:

> The bylaws may contain any provision, not inconsistent with law or with the certificate of incorporation, relating to the business of the corporation, the conduct of its affairs, and its rights or powers or the rights or powers of its stockholders, directors, officers or employees.

Both Chevron's and FedEx's certificates of incorporation conferred on the boards the power to adopt bylaws under 8 *Del. C.* § 109(a). Thus, all investors who bought stock in the corporations whose forum selection bylaws are at stake knew that (i) the DGCL allows for bylaws to address the subjects identified in 8 *Del. C.* § 109(b), (ii) the DGCL permits the certificate of incorporation to contain a provision allowing directors to adopt bylaws unilaterally, and (iii) the certificates of incorporation of Chevron and FedEx contained a provision conferring this power on the boards.

Acting consistent with the power conferred to the board in Chevron's certificate of incorporation, the board amended the bylaws and adopted a forum selection bylaw. Generally speaking, a forum selection bylaw is a provision in a corporation's bylaws that designates a forum as the exclusive venue for certain stockholder suits against the corporation, either as an actual or nominal defendant, and its directors and employees. On September 29, 2010, the board of Chevron, a Delaware corporation headquartered in California, adopted a forum selection bylaw that provided:

> Unless the Corporation consents in writing to the selection of an alternative forum, the Court of Chancery of the State of Delaware shall be the sole and exclusive forum for (i) any derivative action or proceeding brought on behalf of the Corporation, (ii) any action asserting a claim of breach of a fiduciary duty owed by any director, officer or other employee of the Corporation to the Corporation or the Corporation's stockholders, (iii) any action asserting a claim arising pursuant to any provision of the Delaware General Corporation Law, or (iv) any action asserting a claim governed by the internal affairs doctrine. Any person or entity purchasing or otherwise acquiring any interest in shares of capital stock of the Corporation shall be deemed to have notice of and consented to the provisions of this [bylaw].[19]

Several months later, on March 14, 2011, the board of FedEx, a Delaware corporation headquartered in Tennessee, adopted a forum selection bylaw identical to Chevron's.[1-1]

In their briefing, the boards of Chevron and FedEx state that the forum selection bylaws are intended to cover four types of suit, all relating to internal corporate governance:

- *Derivative suits.* The issue of whether a derivative plaintiff is qualified to sue on behalf of the corporation and whether that derivative plaintiff has or is excused from making demand on the board is a matter of corporate governance, because it goes to the very nature of who may speak for the corporation.

- *Fiduciary duty suits.* The law of fiduciary duties regulates the relationships between directors, officers, the corporation, and its stockholders.

- *D.G.C.L. suits.* The Delaware General Corporation Law provides the underpinning framework for all Delaware corporations. That statute goes to the core of how such corporations are governed.

- *Internal affairs suits.* As the U.S. Supreme Court has explained, "internal affairs," in the context of corporate law, are those "matters peculiar to the relationships among or between the corporation and its current officers, directors, and shareholders."[23]

That is, the description of the forum selection bylaws by the Chevron and FedEx boards is consistent with what the plain language of the bylaws suggests: that these bylaws are not intended to regulate *what* suits may be brought against the corporations, only *where* internal governance suits may be brought.[24]

B. The Defendant Boards Have Identified Multiforum Litigation Over Single Corporate Transactions Or Decisions As The Reason Why They Adopted The Bylaws

The Chevron and FedEx boards say that they have adopted forum selection bylaws in response to corporations being subject to litigation over a single transaction or a board decision in more than one forum simultaneously, so-called "multiforum litigation."[25] The defendants' opening brief argues that the boards adopted the forum selection bylaws to address what they perceive to be the inefficient costs of defending against the same claim in multiple courts at one time.[26] The brief describes how, for jurisdictional purposes, a corporation is a citizen both of the state where it is incorporated and of the state where it has its principal place of business.[27]

Because a corporation need not be, and frequently is not, headquartered in the state where it is incorporated, a corporation may be subject to personal jurisdiction as a defendant in a suit involving corporate governance matters in two states.[28] Therefore, any act that the corporation or its directors undertake is potentially subject to litigation in at least two states.[29] Furthermore, both state and federal courts may have jurisdiction over the claims against the corporation. The result is that any act that the corporation or its directors undertake may be challenged in various forums within those states simultaneously.[30] The boards of Chevron and FedEx argue that multiforum litigation, when it is brought by dispersed stockholders in different forums, directly or derivatively, to challenge a single corporate action, imposes high costs on the corporations and hurts investors by causing needless costs that are ultimately born by stockholders, and that these costs are not justified by rational benefits for stockholders from multiforum filings.[31]

III. The Standard Of Review

As our Supreme Court held in the *Frantz Manufacturing* case, "[t]he bylaws of a corporation are presumed to be valid, and the courts will construe the bylaws in a manner consistent with the law rather than strike down the bylaws."[54] Thus, the plaintiffs' burden on this motion challenging the facial statutory and contractual validity of the bylaws is a difficult one: they must show that the bylaws cannot operate lawfully or equitably *under any circumstances.*[55] So, the plaintiffs must show that the bylaws do not address proper subject matters of bylaws as defined by the DGCL in 8 *Del. C.* § 109(b), and can never operate consistently with law.[56] The plaintiffs voluntarily assumed this burden by making a facial validity challenge,[57] and cannot satisfy it by pointing to some future hypothetical application of the bylaws that might be impermissible.[--]
[...]

IV. Legal Analysis

A. The Board-Adopted Forum Selection Bylaws Are Statutorily Valid

Given this procedural context, the court structures its analysis to mirror the two facial claims of invalidity as they have been presented in the complaints. First, the court looks at Count I's challenge that the "bylaw[s are] invalid because [they are] beyond the authority granted in 8 *Del. C.* § 109(b)."[163] As to that claim, the court must determine whether the adoption of the forum selection bylaws was beyond the board's authority in the sense that they do not address a proper subject matter under 8 *Del. C.* § 109(b), which provides that:

> The bylaws may contain any provision, not inconsistent with law or with the certificate of incorporation, relating to the business of the corporation, the conduct of its affairs, and its rights or powers or the rights or powers of its stockholders, directors, officers or employees.

Thus, the court must decide if the bylaws are facially invalid under the DGCL because they do not relate to the business of the corporations, the conduct of their affairs, or the rights of the stockholders.

After first making that determination, the court then addresses Count IV's challenge that "the bylaw[s are] not a valid and enforceable forum selection provision."[164] That is, even if forum selection bylaws regulate proper subject matter under 8 *Del. C.* § 109(b), the plaintiffs allege that forum selection bylaws are contractually invalid because they have been unilaterally adopted by the board.[1~1]

1. The Forum Selection Bylaws Regulate A Proper Subject Matter Under 8 *Del. C.* § 109(b)

As a matter of easy linguistics, the forum selection bylaws address the "rights" of the stockholders, because they regulate where stockholders can exercise their right to bring certain internal affairs claims against the corporation and its directors and officers.[168] They also plainly relate to the conduct of the corporation by channeling internal affairs cases into the courts of the state of incorporation, providing for the opportunity to have internal affairs cases resolved authoritatively by our Supreme Court if any party wishes to take an appeal.[69] That is, because the forum selection bylaws address internal affairs claims, the subject matter of the actions the bylaws govern relates quintessentially to "the corporation's business, the conduct of its affairs, and the rights of its stockholders [*qua* stockholders]."[...]

The bylaws of Delaware corporations have a "procedural, process-oriented nature."[74] It is doubtless true that our courts have said that bylaws typically do not contain substantive mandates, but direct how the corporation, the board, and its stockholders may take certain actions.[75] 8 *Del. C.* § 109(b) has long been understood to allow the corporation to set "self-imposed rules and regulations [that are] deemed expedient for its convenient functioning."[76] The forum selection bylaws here fit this description. They are process-oriented, because they regulate *where* stockholders may file suit, not *whether* the stockholder may file suit or the kind of remedy that the stockholder may obtain on behalf of herself or the corporation. The bylaws also clearly address cases of the kind that address "the business of the corporation, the conduct of its affairs, and . . . the rights or powers of its stockholders, directors, officers or employees," because they govern where internal affairs cases governed by state corporate law may be heard.[77] These are the kind of claims most central to the relationship between those who manage the corporation and the corporation's stockholders. [...]

Nor is it novel for bylaws to regulate how stockholders may exercise their rights as stockholders. For example, an advance notice bylaw "requires stockholders wishing to make nominations or proposals at a corporation's annual meeting to give notice of their intention in advance of so doing."[79] Like such bylaws, which help organize what could otherwise be a chaotic stockholder meeting, the forum selection bylaws are designed to bring order to what the boards of Chevron and FedEx say they perceive to be a chaotic filing of duplicative and inefficient derivative and corporate suits against the directors and the corporations. The similar purpose of the advance notice bylaws and the forum selection bylaws reinforce that forum selection bylaws have a proper relationship to the business of the corporation and the conduct of its affairs under 8 *Del. C.* § 109(b).[1-1]

The plaintiffs' argument, then, reduces to the claim that the bylaws do not speak to a "traditional" subject matter, and should be ruled invalid for that reason alone. For starters, the factual premise of this argument is not convincing. The bylaws cannot fairly be argued to regulate a novel subject matter: the plaintiffs ignore that, in the analogous contexts of LLC agreements and stockholder agreements, the Supreme Court and this court have held that forum selection clauses are valid.[1-1] But in any case, the Supreme Court long ago rejected the position that board action should be invalidated or enjoined simply because it involves a novel use of statutory authority. [...]Merely because the General Corporation Law is silent as to a specific matter does not mean that it is prohibited."[184][...]

Therefore, the court concludes that forum selection bylaws are statutorily valid under Delaware law, and Count I of the plaintiffs' complaints is dismissed. The court now considers whether a forum selection bylaw is contractually invalid when adopted by the board unilaterally.

2. The Board-Adopted Bylaws Are Not Contractually Invalid As Forum Selection Clauses Because They Were Adopted Unilaterally By The Board

Despite the contractual nature of the stockholders' relationship with the corporation under our law, the plaintiffs argue, in Count IV of their complaints, that the forum selection bylaws by their nature are different and cannot be adopted by the board unilaterally. The plaintiffs' argument is grounded in the contention that a board-adopted forum selection bylaw cannot be a *contractual* forum selection clause because the stockholders do not vote in advance of its adoption to approve it.[1-1]The plaintiffs acknowledge that contractual forum selection clauses are "prima facie valid" under *The Bremen v. Zapata Off-Shore Co.* and *Ingres Corp. v. CA, Inc.,* and that they are presumptively enforceable.[92] But, the plaintiffs say, the forum selection bylaws are contractually invalid in this case, because they were adopted by a board, rather than by Chevron's and FedEx's dispersed stockholders. The plaintiffs argue that this method of adopting a forum selection clause is invalid as a matter of contract law, because it does not require the assent of the stockholders who will be affected by it. Thus, in the plaintiffs' view, there are two types of bylaws: (i) contractually binding bylaws that are adopted by stockholders; (ii) non-contractually binding bylaws that are adopted by boards using their statutory authority conferred by the certificate of incorporation.[93]

By this artificial bifurcation, the plaintiffs misapprehend fundamental principles of Delaware corporate law. Our corporate law has long rejected the so-called "vested rights" doctrine.[94] That vested rights view, which the plaintiffs have adopted as their own, "asserts that boards cannot modify bylaws in a manner that arguably diminishes or divests pre-existing shareholder rights absent stockholder consent."[95] As then-Vice Chancellor, now Justice, Jacobs explained in the *Kidsco* case, under Delaware law, where a corporation's articles or bylaws "put all on notice that the by-laws may be amended at any time, *no vested rights can arise that would contractually prohibit an amendment.*"[96]

In an unbroken line of decisions dating back several generations, our Supreme Court has made clear that the bylaws constitute a binding part of the contract between a Delaware corporation and its stockholders.[97] Stockholders are on notice that, as to those subjects that are subject of regulation by bylaw under 8 *Del. C.* § 109(b), the board itself may act unilaterally to adopt bylaws addressing those subjects.[98] Such a change by the board is not extra-contractual simply because the board acts unilaterally; rather it is the kind of change that the overarching statutory and contractual regime the stockholders buy into explicitly allows the board to make on its own.[99] Therefore, when stockholders have authorized a board to unilaterally adopt bylaws, it follows that the bylaws are not contractually invalid simply because the board-adopted bylaw lacks the contemporaneous assent of the stockholders.[100]

Even so, the statutory regime provides protections for the stockholders, through the indefeasible right of the stockholders to adopt and amend bylaws themselves. "[B]y its terms Section 109(a) vests in the shareholders a power to adopt, amend or repeal bylaws that is legally sacrosanct, *i.e.,* the power cannot be non-consensually eliminated or limited by anyone other than the legislature itself."[1104] Thus, even though a board may, as is the case here, be granted authority to adopt bylaws, stockholders can check that authority by repealing board-adopted bylaws. And, of course, because the DGCL gives stockholders an annual opportunity to elect directors,[1105] stockholders have a potent tool to discipline boards who refuse to accede to a stockholder vote repealing a forum selection clause.[1106] Thus, a corporation's bylaws are part of an inherently flexible contract between the stockholders and the corporation under which the stockholders have powerful rights they can use to protect themselves if they do not want board-adopted forum selection bylaws to be part of the contract between themselves and the corporation. [...]

In sum, stockholders contractually assent to be bound by bylaws that are valid under the DGCL—that is an essential part of the contract agreed to when an investor buys stock in a Delaware corporation. Where, as here, the certificate of incorporation has conferred on the board the power to adopt bylaws, and the board has adopted a bylaw consistent with 8 *Del. C.* § 109(b), the stockholders have assented to that new bylaw being contractually binding. Thus, Count IV of the complaints cannot survive and the bylaws are contractually valid as a facial matter.

DGCL Section 115 - Forum Selection Bylaw Provision   2.4.3

Subsequent to Boilermakers, the Delaware legislature adopted section 115, which specifically permits corporations to adopt bylaws specifying a forum for the dispute of intra-stockholder disputes, including stockholder fiduciary duty suits.

§ 115. Forum selection provisions.

The certificate of incorporation or the bylaws may require, consistent with applicable jurisdictional requirements, that any or all internal corporate claims shall be brought solely and exclusively in any or all of the courts in this State, and no provision of the certificate of incorporation or the bylaws may prohibit bringing such claims in the courts of this State. "Internal corporate claims" means claims, including claims in the right of the corporation, (i) that are based upon a violation of a duty by a current or former director or officer or stockholder in such capacity, or (ii) as to which this title confers jurisdiction upon the Court of Chancery.

Board of Directors   2.5

Stockholders – as we will see later – have a number of rights with respect to the corporation. However, one right that stockholders do not have is the right to directly manage the day-to-day operations of the business. The general corporation law, as well as the common law, vests exclusive responsibility for corporate management and decisionmaking not with the stockholders, but rather with the corporation's board of directors.

We might like to think that shareholders own and run the business, but they do not. The authority to manage and oversee the operation of the business on a day to day basis is vested exclusively with the board. To the extent stockholders have rights to oversee the operations of the business, those rights are attenuated. Perhaps the most important provision of the Delaware corporate law is §141. Delaware is by no means unique; *every state* has its equivalent to §141. Section 141 centralizes decisionmaking authority to the board.

The statutory authority granted to the board by §141 lies at the heart of the business judgment presumption, or the "business judgment rule." The business judgment presumption is judicial presumption that exists as an acknowledgment of the statutory authority vested in boards, and not shareholders, to run the corporation. The effect of this judicial presumption is to cause courts to defer to decisions of the board in most matters when those decisions are challenged by stockholders.

This presumption is quite powerful and have effects beyond the courtroom. Because courts will generally abstain from intervening in disputes between stockholders and boards about most business decisions, boards will feel a great deal of latitude and independence in their decision making process. The insulation from stockholders afforded by this judicial presumption encourages boards to take business risk.

DGCL Sec. 141 - Board of directors

Section 141 deals with the power and the structure of the board of directors. Of all the provisions in the corporate law, §141(a) is perhaps the single most important. Section 141(a) grants plenary power over the management of the corporation – not the stockholders – but to the board of directors. Among other things, §141(a) provides the statutory basis for the business judgment presumption.

Sections 141(b) & (f) describe the requirements for the conduct of regular business at board meetings or actions by the board without a meeting. Under §141(c), a board is authorized to delegate almost all of its authority to committees of directors. Section 141(d) permits the creation of staggered, or classified, board structures.

Section 141(e) creates a safe harbor from liability for boards that reasonably rely on experts when making decisions. Section 141(h) provides boards the statutory authority to set their own compensation, while §141(k) describes the circumstances under which stockholders may dismiss a director.

§ 141. Board of directors; powers; number, qualifications, terms and quorum; committees; classes of directors; nonstock corporations; reliance upon books; action without meeting; removal.

(a) The business and affairs of every corporation organized under this chapter shall be managed by or under the direction of a board of directors, except as may be otherwise provided in this chapter or in its certificate of incorporation. If any such provision is made in the certificate of incorporation, the powers and duties conferred or imposed upon the board of directors by this chapter shall be exercised or performed to such extent and by such person or persons as shall be provided in the certificate of incorporation.

(b) The board of directors of a corporation shall consist of 1 or more members, each of whom shall be a natural person. The number of directors shall be fixed by, or in the manner provided in, the bylaws, unless the certificate of incorporation fixes the number of directors, in which case a change in the number of directors shall be made only by amendment of the certificate. Directors need not be stockholders unless so required by the certificate of incorporation or the bylaws. The certificate of incorporation or bylaws may prescribe other qualifications for directors. Each director shall hold office until such director's successor is elected and qualified or until such director's earlier resignation or removal. Any director may resign at any time upon notice given in writing or by electronic transmission to the corporation. A resignation is effective when the resignation is delivered unless the resignation specifies a later effective date or an effective date determined upon the happening of an event or events. A resignation which is conditioned upon the director failing to receive a specified vote for reelection as a director may provide that it is irrevocable. A majority of the total number of directors shall constitute a quorum for the transaction of business unless the certificate of incorporation or the bylaws require a greater number. Unless the certificate of incorporation provides otherwise, the bylaws may provide that a number less than a majority shall constitute a quorum which in no case shall be less than 1/3 of the total number of directors except that when a board of 1 director is authorized under this section, then 1 director shall constitute a quorum. The vote of the majority of the directors present at a meeting at which a quorum is present shall be the act of the board of directors unless the certificate of incorporation or the bylaws shall require a vote of a greater number.

(c)[...]

(2) The board of directors may designate 1 or more committees, each committee to consist of 1 or more of the directors of the corporation. The board may designate 1 or more directors as alternate members of any committee, who may replace any absent or disqualified member at any meeting of the committee. [...] Any such committee, to the extent provided in the resolution of the board of directors, or in the bylaws of the corporation, shall have and may exercise all the powers and authority of the board of directors in the management of the business and affairs of the corporation, and may authorize the seal of the corporation to be affixed to all papers which may require it; but no such committee shall have the power or authority in reference to the following matter: (i) approving or adopting, or recommending to the stockholders, any action or matter (other than the election or removal of directors) expressly required by this chapter to be submitted to stockholders for approval or (ii) adopting, amending or repealing any bylaw of the corporation.

(3) Unless otherwise provided in the certificate of incorporation, the bylaws or the resolution of the board of directors designating the committee, a committee may create 1 or more subcommittees, each subcommittee to consist of 1 or more members of the committee, and delegate to a subcommittee any or all of the powers and authority of the committee.

(d) The directors of any corporation organized under this chapter may, by the certificate of incorporation or by an initial bylaw, or by a bylaw adopted by a vote of the stockholders, be divided into 1, 2 or 3 classes; the term of office of those of the first class to expire at the first annual meeting held after such classification becomes effective; of the second class 1 year thereafter; of the third class 2 years thereafter; and at each annual election held after such classification becomes effective, directors shall be chosen for a full term, as the case may be, to succeed those whose terms expire. The certificate of incorporation or bylaw provision dividing the directors into classes may authorize the board of directors to assign members of the board already in office to such classes at the time such classification becomes effective. The certificate of incorporation may confer upon holders of any class or series of stock the right to elect 1 or more directors who shall serve for such term, and have such voting powers as shall be stated in the certificate of incorporation. The terms of office and voting powers of the directors elected separately by the holders of any class or series of stock may be greater than or less than those of any other director or class of directors. In addition, the certificate of incorporation may confer upon 1 or more directors, whether or not elected separately by the holders of any class or series of stock, voting powers greater than or less than those of other directors. Any such provision conferring greater or lesser voting power shall apply to voting in any committee or subcommittee, unless otherwise provided in the certificate of incorporation or bylaws. If the certificate of incorporation provides that 1 or more directors shall have more or less than 1 vote per director on any matter, every reference in this chapter to a majority or other proportion of the directors shall refer to a majority or other proportion of the votes of the directors.

(e) A member of the board of directors, or a member of any committee designated by the board of directors, shall, in the performance of such member's duties, be fully protected in relying in good faith upon the records of the corporation and upon such information, opinions, reports or statements presented to the corporation by any of the corporation's officers or employees, or committees of the board of directors, or by any other person as to matters the member reasonably believes are within such other person's professional or expert competence and who has been selected with reasonable care by or on behalf of the corporation.

(f) Unless otherwise restricted by the certificate of incorporation or bylaws, any action required or permitted to be taken at any meeting of the board of directors or of any committee thereof may be taken without a meeting if all members of the board or committee, as the case may be, consent thereto in writing, or by electronic transmission and the writing or writings or electronic transmission or transmissions are filed with the minutes of proceedings of the board, or committee. Such filing shall be in paper form if the minutes are maintained in paper form and shall be in electronic form if the minutes are maintained in electronic form.

(g) Unless otherwise restricted by the certificate of incorporation or bylaws, the board of directors of any corporation organized under this chapter may hold its meetings, and have an office or offices, outside of this State.

(h) Unless otherwise restricted by the certificate of incorporation or bylaws, [...]

otherwise restricted by the certificate of incorporation or bylaws, members of the board of directors of any corporation, or any committee designated by the board, may participate in a meeting of such board, or committee by means of conference telephone or other communications equipment by means of which all persons participating in the meeting can hear each other, and participation in a meeting pursuant to this subsection shall constitute presence in person at the meeting. [...]

(k) Any director or the entire board of directors may be removed, with or without cause, by the holders of a majority of the shares then entitled to vote at an election of directors, except as follows:

(1) Unless the certificate of incorporation otherwise provides, in the case of a corporation whose board is classified as provided in subsection (d) of this section, stockholders may effect such removal only for cause; or

(2) In the case of a corporation having cumulative voting, if less than the entire board is to be removed, no director may be removed without cause if the votes cast against such director's removal would be sufficient to elect such director if then cumulatively voted at an election of the entire board of directors, or, if there be classes of directors, at an election of the class of directors of which such director is a part.

Whenever the holders of any class or series are entitled to elect 1 or more directors by the certificate of incorporation, this subsection shall apply, in respect to the removal without cause of a director or directors so elected, to the vote of the holders of the outstanding shares of that class or series and not to the vote of the outstanding shares as a whole.

The Nature of the Board of Directors 2.5.2

Corporations are managed by boards of directors.
It's important to note that no director, acting individually, is empowered to speak or act on behalf of the corporation. Individual directors, in that sense, are not agents of the corporation, nor are they principals. The board of directors - as group - is the only party statutorily authorized to manage the corporation.

Individual directors have no authority to speak on behalf of the corporation unless they have been specifically delegated such authority by the board. Along the same lines, unless otherwise outlined in the certificate of incorporation, no director is superior or has more rights than any other director. Each member of a corporate board has the right to consultation with the others and has the right to be heard upon all questions considered by the board. Absent a governance agreement to the contrary, each director is entitled to receive the same information furnished to his or her fellow board members.

While stockholders are permitted to act at a stockholders meeting by "proxy" - that is they need not be present, but may authorize someone else to act on their behalf pursuant to instructions - directors are not permitted to delegate their proxy to another at a board meeting. If a director is not present at a meeting, that director's vote may not be counted. There are important reasons for not permitting directors to act by proxy. A director cannot authorize anyone to act for her, because her associates are entitled to their own judgment, experience and business ability, just as her associates cannot deprive her of her rights and powers as director.

Delaware corporate law embraces a "board-centric" model of governance. This model expects that all directors - and not their proxies - will participate in a collective and deliberative decision-making process.

Given that the DGCL allocates fundamental decision-making power to the board as a whole, and not to any individual director *qua* director, all directors must have an equal opportunity to participate meaningfully in any matter brought before the board and to discharge their oversight responsibilities. In more granular terms, directors must be afforded, at a minimum, (i) proper notice of all board meetings, (ii) the opportunity to attend and to express their views at board meetings, and (iii) access to all information that is necessary or appropriate to discharge their fiduciary duties, including the opportunity to consult with officers, employees, and other agents of the corporation. *OptimisCorp v Waite* (Del. Sup. Ct., April 20, 2016) at Footnote 9.

The Delaware corporate law does not generally follow a rule that permits "super directors": the size of a director's stock ownership does not convey additional powers. However, consistent with the enabling nature of the statute and pursuant to Section 141(d), the certificate of incorporation may confer upon 1 or more directors, voting powers greater than or less than those of other directors. Any such provision conferring greater or lesser voting power shall apply to voting in any committee, unless otherwise provided in the certificate of incorporation or bylaws.

DGCL Sec. 216 - Director elections   2.5.3

One of the most important rights a stockholder has
is the right to vote for directors of the corporation.
The default rule for voting for directors is "first past the post", or
plurality voting. In a competitive election, votes in favor of a

director are counted and directors with the most votes fill seats until there are no more seats available. Since majority voting is not the default rule, in non-competitive (or even in competitive) elections, it is very possible for a director to win a seat on the board without gaining a majority of votes.

Section 141(b) makes it possible to jerry-rig a majority voting requirement by permitting board members to submit irrevocable letters of resignation conditioned on not receiving a specified vote for reelection (typically >50%).

In addition to the default "first past the post" voting rule, corporations may opt to permit cumulative voting, allowed for by §214.

§ 216 Quorum and required vote for stock corporations.

In the absence of such specification in the certificate of incorporation or bylaws of the corporation: ...

(3) Directors shall be elected by a plurality of the votes of the shares present in person or represented by proxy at the meeting and entitled to vote on the election of directors...

DGCL Sec. 214 - Cumulative voting option for directors

2.5.4

Although plurality voting is the default rule for the election of directors under §216, a corporation may, in its certificate of incorporation, opt into a cumulative voting structure. The cumulative voting structure gives minority blockholders the power to elect representatives to the board in a manner that would be impossible under plurality voting. It does so by permitting stockholders to accumulate all their votes into a single (or multiple) block and then allocate that block of votes to a single candidate.

For example, if the election is for four directors and the stockholder has 500 shares, under the default plurality voting regime, the stockholder can vote a maximum of 500 shares for each one candidate. Under a cumulative voting regime, the stockholder has that number of votes equal to the number of shares owned by the stockholder multiplied by the number of available board seats in the election. In this case: 500 * 4 = 2,000 votes. The stockholder is then free to allocate those votes in any many she pleases, for example all 2,000 votes on candidate A, splitting her votes 1,000 each between candidate A and B while giving no votes to candidates C and D.

Under §141(k), the director removal provision, a director may be removed under cumulative voting, however, removal of a director may be blocked by minority stockholders. Under §141(k), no director in a cumulative voting regime may be removed when the votes cast against removal would be sufficient to elect the director if voted cumulatively at an election where all memberships entitled to vote were voted.

§ 214. Cumulative voting.

The certificate of incorporation of any corporation may provide that at all elections of directors of the corporation, or at elections held under specified circumstances, each holder of stock or of any class or classes or of a series or series thereof shall be entitled to as many votes as shall equal the number of votes which (except for such provision as to cumulative voting) such holder would be entitled to cast for the election of directors with respect to such holder's shares of stock multiplied by the number of directors to be elected by such holder, and that such holder may cast all of such votes for a single director or may distribute them among the number to be voted for, or for any 2 or more of them as such holder may see fit.

Shlensky v. Wrigley   2.5.5

In this iconic case, a stockholder challenges a
decision of the board of directors of the Chicago
Cubs not to install lights at the field and to only play
games during daylight hours.

For many years, the Chicago Cubs, a Delaware corporation, were
controlled by Philip K. Wrigley – also known for his success as a
chewing gum manufacturer. In many respects, Wrigley was an
innovative businessman. During World War II he founded the All
American Girls Baseball League to fill the void created when many
professional baseball players went to war. The film, *A League of
Their Own*, was a fictionalized account of the experiences of the
AAGBL. In addition, Wrigley made a decision to increase the value
of the Cubs brand by effectively giving away the rights to radio
broadcasts of Cubs games.

In *Shlensky v Wrigley*, a stockholder sued the board of the Cubs,
including Philip Wrigley, for the board's decision not to install lights
and refusal to play night games at Wrigley Field. The stockholder
alleged that the board's decision to only play day games at Wrigley
caused the corporation to make less money than had the board
installed lights and permitted the team to play night games.

This case highlights a very typical board decision and a common
tension between the managers of the corporation and its
stockholders. In this case we also see the degree of deference that
courts will pay to a board's business judgment when that decision is
made in an informed manner at arm's length.

SHLENSKY V. WRIGLEY
237 NE 2d 776

This is an appeal from a dismissal of plaintiff's amended complaint
on motion of the defendants. [...]

Plaintiff is a minority stockholder of defendant corporation,
Chicago National League Ball Club (Inc.), a Delaware corporation
with its principal place of business in Chicago, Illinois. [...] The

individual defendants are directors of the Cubs and have served for varying periods of years. Defendant Philip K. Wrigley is also president of the corporation and owner of approximately 80% of the stock therein.

Plaintiff alleges that since night baseball was first played in 1935 nineteen of the twenty major league teams have scheduled night games. In 1966, out of a total of 1,620 games in the major leagues, 932 were played at night. Plaintiff alleges that every member of the major leagues, other than the Cubs, scheduled substantially all of its home games in 1966 at night, exclusive of opening days, Saturdays, Sundays, holidays and days prohibited by league rules. Allegedly this has been done for the specific purpose of maximizing attendance and thereby maximizing revenue and income.

The Cubs, in the years 1961-65, sustained operating losses from its direct baseball operations. Plaintiff attributes those losses to inadequate attendance at Cubs' home games. He concludes that if the directors continue to refuse to install lights at Wrigley Field and schedule [176] night baseball games, the Cubs will continue to sustain comparable losses and its financial condition will continue to deteriorate.

Plaintiff alleges that, except for the year 1963, attendance at Cubs' home games has been substantially below that at their road games, many of which were played at night.

Plaintiff compares attendance at Clubs' games with that of the Chicago White Sox, an American League club, whose weekday games were generally played at night. The weekend attendance figures for the two teams were similar; however, the White Sox week-night games drew many more patrons than did the Cubs' weekday games.

Plaintiff alleges that the funds for the installation of lights can be readily obtained through financing and the cost of installation would be far more than offset and recaptured by increased revenues and incomes resulting from the increased attendance.

Plaintiff further alleges that defendant Wrigley has refused to install lights, not because of interest in the welfare of the corporation but because of his personal opinions "that baseball is a `daytime sport' and that the installation of lights and night baseball games will have a deteriorating effect upon the surrounding neighborhood." It is alleged that he has admitted that he is not interested in whether the Cubs would benefit financially from such action because of his concern for the neighborhood, and that he would be willing for the team to play night games if a new stadium were built in Chicago. [...]

The question on appeal is whether plaintiff's amended complaint states a cause of action. It is plaintiff's position that fraud, illegality and conflict of interest are not the only bases for a stockholder's derivative action against the directors. Contrariwise, defendants argue that the courts will not step in and interfere with honest business judgment of the directors unless there is a showing of fraud, illegality or conflict of interest. [...]

The standards set in Delaware are [...] clearly stated in the cases[...]:

"We have then a conflict in view between the responsible managers of a corporation and an overwhelming majority of its stockholders on the one hand and a dissenting minority on the other — a conflict touching matters of business policy, such as has occasioned innumerable applications to courts to intervene and determine which of the two conflicting views should prevail. The response which courts make to such applications is that it is not their function to resolve for corporations questions of policy and business management. The directors are chosen to pass upon such questions and their judgment *unless shown to be tainted with fraud* is accepted as final. The judgment of the directors of corporations enjoys the benefit of a presumption that it was formed in good faith and was designed to promote the best interests of the corporation they serve." (Emphasis supplied.)

Similarly, the court in Toebelman v. Missouri-Kansas Pipe Line Co., 41 F Supp 334, said at page 339:

[179] "The general legal principle involved is familiar. [...] Reference may be made to the statement of the rule in Helfman v. American Light & Traction Company, 121 NJ Eq 1, 187 A 540, 550, in which the Court stated the law as follows: `In a purely business corporation ... the authority of the directors in the conduct of the business of the corporation must be regarded as absolute when they act within the law, and the court is without authority to substitute its judgment for that of the directors.'" [...]

Plaintiff in the instant case argues that the directors are acting for reasons unrelated to the financial interest and welfare of the Cubs. However, we are not satisfied that the motives assigned to Philip K. Wrigley, and through him to the other directors, are contrary to the best interests of the corporation and the stockholders. For example, it appears to us that the effect on the surrounding neighborhood might well be considered by a [181] director who was considering the patrons who would or would not attend the games if the park were in a poor neighborhood. Furthermore, the long run interest of the corporation in its property value at Wrigley Field might demand all efforts to keep the neighborhood from deteriorating. By these thoughts we do not mean to say that we have decided that the decision of the directors was a correct one. That is beyond our jurisdiction and ability. We are merely saying that the decision is one properly before directors and the motives alleged in the amended complaint showed no fraud, illegality or conflict of interest in their making of that decision. [...]

There is no allegation that the night games played by the other nineteen teams enhanced their financial position or that the profits, if any, of those teams were directly related to the number of night games scheduled. There is an allegation that the installation of lights and [182] scheduling of night games in Wrigley Field would have resulted in large amounts of additional revenues and incomes from increased attendance and related sources of income. Further, the cost of installation of lights, funds for which are allegedly readily available by financing, would be more than offset and recaptured by increased revenues. However, no allegation is made that there will be a net benefit to the corporation from such action, considering all increased costs.

Plaintiff claims that the losses of defendant corporation are due to poor attendance at home games. However, it appears from the amended complaint, taken as a whole, that factors other than attendance affect the net earnings or losses. For example, in 1962, attendance at home and road games decreased appreciably as compared with 1961, and yet the loss from direct baseball operation and of the whole corporation was considerably less.

The record shows that plaintiff did not feel he could allege that the increased revenues would be sufficient to cure the corporate deficit. The only cost plaintiff was at all concerned with was that of installation of lights. No mention was made of operation and maintenance of the lights or other possible increases in operating costs of night games and we cannot speculate as to what other factors might influence the increase or decrease of profits if the Cubs were to play night home games. [...]

[6, 7] Finally, we do not agree with plaintiff's contention that failure to follow the example of the other major league clubs in scheduling night games constituted negligence. Plaintiff made no allegation that these teams' night schedules were profitable or that the purpose for which night baseball had been undertaken was fulfilled. Furthermore, it cannot be said that directors, even those of corporations that are losing money, must follow the lead of the other corporations in the field. Directors are elected for their business capabilities and judgment and the courts cannot require them to forego their judgment because of the decisions of directors of other companies. Courts may not decide these questions in the absence of a clear showing of dereliction of duty on the part of the specific directors and mere failure to "follow the crowd" is not such a dereliction.

For the foregoing reasons the order of dismissal entered by the trial court is affirmed.

Aronson v. Lewis   2.5.6

Business Judgment Presumption

In Shlensky, the court described its policy of deferring to the decisions of the board of directors absent some evidence of fraud or wrongdoing. Aronson is the leading case for the restatement of the principle highlighted in Shlensky: the business judgment presumption, or the business judgment rule. This presumption, which is rooted in §141(a)'s allocation of exclusive management authority to the board of directors, requires that court leave board decisions undisturbed unless complaining stockholders present some evidence that the board made the challenged decisions in an uninformed manner, or in a manner not in good faith, or for reasons otherwise not in the best interests of the corporation (e.g. board self-dealing).

Note that the pleading burden is on the complaining stockholders. In the absence of facts to undermine the business judgment presumption, courts will leave board decisions, even bad ones, in place.

ARONSON V. LEWIS
473 A.2d 805

A.

A cardinal precept of the General Corporation Law of the State of Delaware is that directors, rather than shareholders, manage the business and affairs of the corporation. 8 *Del.C.* § 141(a). Section 141(a) states in pertinent part:

> "The *business and affairs* of a corporation organized under this chapter *shall be managed by or under the direction* of a board of directors except as may be otherwise provided in this chapter or in its certificate of incorporation."

8 *Del.C.* § 141(a) (Emphasis added). The existence and exercise of this power carries with it certain fundamental fiduciary obligations to the corporation and its shareholders.[1-1]

The business judgment rule is an acknowledgment of the managerial prerogatives of Delaware directors under Section 141(a). [...] It is a presumption that in making a business decision the directors of a corporation acted on an informed basis, in good faith and in the honest belief that the action taken was in the best interests of the company. [...] The burden is on the party challenging the decision to establish facts rebutting the presumption. [...]

First, its protections can only be claimed by disinterested directors whose conduct otherwise meets the tests of business judgment. From the standpoint of interest, this means that directors can neither appear on both sides of a transaction nor expect to derive any personal financial benefit from it in the sense of self-dealing, as opposed to a benefit which devolves upon the corporation or all stockholders generally. [...]

Second, to invoke the rule's protection directors have a duty to inform themselves, prior to making a business decision, of all material information reasonably available to them. Having become so informed, they must then act with requisite care in the discharge of their duties. While the Delaware cases use a variety of terms to describe the applicable standard of care, our analysis satisfies us that under the business judgment rule director liability is predicated upon concepts of gross negligence.[1-1]

However, it should be noted that the business judgment rule operates only in the context of director action. Technically speaking, it has no role where directors have either abdicated their functions, or absent a conscious decision, failed to act.[2] But it also follows that under applicable principles, a conscious decision to refrain from acting may nonetheless be a valid exercise of business judgment and enjoy the protections of the rule. [...]

Gagliardi v. TriFoods International, Inc.   2.5.7

In this case, a stockholder brings suit to challenge a
series of what turned out ultimately to be ill-advised board
decisions. As in Shlensky, we see the degree of deference that
courts will pay to a board's business judgment. The court in
Gagliardi also offers up a rationale for why a high degree of
deference for disinterested board decisions might generally be good
policy.

GAGLIARDI V. TRIFOODS INTERNATIONAL, INC.
683 A. 2d 1049

ALLEN, Chancellor.

Plaintiff, Eugene Gagliardi, is the founder of the TriFoods, Inc. and
in 1990 he induced certain persons to invest in the company by
buying its stock. In 1993 he was removed as Chairman of the board
and his employment with the company terminated. He continues to
own approximately 13% of the company's common stock. The
business of the company has, according to the allegations of the
complaint, deteriorated very badly since Mr. Gagliardi's ouster.

The suit asserts that defendants are liable to the corporation and to
plaintiff individually on a host of theories, most importantly for
mismanagement. [...]

Count IV: Negligent Mismanagement:

This count, which is asserted against all defendants, alleges that
"implementation of their grandiose scheme for TriFoods' future
growth ... in only eighteen months destroyed TriFoods." Plaintiff
asserts that the facts alleged, which sketch that "scheme" and those
results, constitute mismanagement and waste.

The allegations of Count IV are detailed.

They assert most centrally that prior to his dismissal Gagliardi disagreed with Hart concerning the wisdom of TriFoods manufacturing its products itself and disagreed strongly that the company should buy a plant in Pomfret, Connecticut and move its operations to that state. Plaintiff thought it foolish (and he alleges that it was negligent judgment) to borrow funds from CDA for that purpose. ¶¶ 71-74; 77-81.

Plaintiff also alleges that Hart caused the company to acquire and fit-out a research or new product facility in Chadds Ford Pennsylvania, which "duplicated one already available and under lease to Designer Foods [the predecessor name of TriFoods], and which was therefore, a further waste of corporate assets." ¶ 76.

Next, it is alleged that "defendants either acquiesced in or approved a reckless or grossly negligent sales commission to build volume." ¶ 82.

Next, it is alleged that "Hart and the other defendants caused TriFoods to purchase [the exclusive rights to produce and sell a food product known as] Steak-umms from Heinz in April 1994." ¶ 85. The price paid compared unfavorably with a transaction in 1980 in which this product had been sold and which earlier terms are detailed. ¶ 86. "Defendants recklessly caused TriFoods to pay $15 million for Steak-umms alone (no plant, no equipment, etc) which was then doing annual sales of only $28 million." *Id.*

Next, it is alleged that "Hart caused TriFoods... to pay $125,000 to a consultant for its new name, logo and packaging." ¶ 87.

Next, it is alleged that Hart destroyed customer relationships by supplying inferior products. ¶¶ 88-91.

Next, it is alleged that "Hart refused to pay key manufacturers and suppliers ... thus injuring TriFoods' trade relations." ¶ 92.

Next, it is alleged that "defendants entered into a transaction whereby TriFoods was to acquire "Lloyd's Ribs" at a grossly excessive price, knowing (or recklessly not knowing) that the Company could not afford the transaction." [...]

Do these allegations of Count IV state a claim upon which relief may be granted? In addressing that question, I start with what I take to be an elementary precept of corporation law: in the absence of facts showing self-dealing or improper motive, a corporate officer or director is not legally responsible to the corporation for losses that may be suffered as a result of a decision that an officer made or that directors authorized in good faith.[12] [...] Thus, to allege that a corporation has suffered a loss as a result of a lawful transaction, within the corporation's powers, authorized by a corporate fiduciary *acting in a good faith pursuit of corporate purposes,* does not state a claim for relief against that fiduciary no matter how foolish the investment may appear in retrospect.

The rule could rationally be no different. Shareholders can diversify the risks of their corporate investments. Thus, it is in their economic interest for the corporation to accept in rank order all positive net present value investment projects available to the corporation, starting with the *highest risk adjusted rate of return first.* Shareholders don't want (or shouldn't rationally want) directors to be risk averse. Shareholders' investment interests, across the full range of their diversifiable equity investments, will be maximized if corporate directors and managers honestly assess risk and reward and accept for the corporation the highest risk adjusted returns available that are above the firm's cost of capital.

But directors will tend to deviate from this rational acceptance of corporate risk *if* in authorizing the corporation to undertake a risky investment, the directors must assume some degree of personal risk relating to *ex post facto* claims of derivative liability for any resulting corporate loss.

Corporate directors of public companies typically have a very small proportionate ownership interest in their corporations and little or no incentive compensation. Thus, they enjoy (as residual owners) only a very small proportion of any "upside" gains earned by the corporation on risky investment projects. If, however, corporate directors were to be found liable for a corporate loss from a risky project on the ground that the investment was too risky (foolishly risky! stupidly risky! egregiously risky! — you supply the adverb), their liability would be joint and several for the whole loss (with I suppose a right of contribution). Given the scale of operation of modern public corporations, this stupefying disjunction between risk and reward for corporate directors threatens undesirable effects. Given this disjunction, only a very small probability of director liability based on "negligence", "inattention", "waste", etc., could induce a board to avoid authorizing risky investment projects to any extent! Obviously, it is in the shareholders' economic interest to offer sufficient protection to directors from liability for negligence, etc., to allow directors to conclude that, as a practical matter, there is no risk that, if they act in good faith and meet minimal proceduralist standards of attention, they can face liability as a result of a business loss.

The law *protects shareholder investment interests* against the uneconomic consequences that the presence of such second-guessing risk would have on director action and shareholder wealth in a number of ways. It authorizes corporations to pay for director and officer liability insurance and authorizes corporate indemnification in a broad range of cases, for example. But the first protection against a threat of sub-optimal risk acceptance is the so-called business judgment rule. That "rule" in effect provides that where a [1053] director is independent and disinterested, there can be no liability for corporate loss, unless the facts are such that no person could possibly authorize such a transaction if he or she were attempting in good faith to meet their duty. [...]

Thus, for example it does not state a claim to allege that: (1) Hart caused the corporation to pay $125,000 to a consultant for the design of a new logo and packaging. On what possible basis might a corporate officer or director be put to the expense of defending such a claim? Nothing is alleged except that an expenditure of corporate funds for a corporate purpose was made. Whether that expenditure was wise or foolish, low risk or high risk is of no concern to this Court. [...] (2) Nor does an allegation that defendants acquiesced in a reckless commission structure "in order to build volume" state a claim; it alleges no conflicting interest or improper motivation[...]. It alleges only an ordinary business decision with a pejorative characterization added. (3) The allegation of "duplication" of existing product research facilities similarly simply states a matter that falls within ordinary business judgment; that plaintiff regards the decision as unwise, foolish, or even stupid in the circumstances is not legally significant; indeed that others may look back on it and agree that it was stupid is legally unimportant, in my opinion. (4) That the terms of the purchase of "Steak-umms" seem to plaintiff unwise (especially when compared to the terms of a 1980 transaction involving that product) again fail utterly to state any legal claim. No self-interest, nor facts possibly disclosing improper motive or judgment satisfying the waste standard are alleged. Similarly, (5) the allegations of corporate loss resulting from harm to customer relations by delivery of poor product and (6) harm to supplier relations by poor payment practices, again state nothing that constitutes a legal claim. Certainly these allegations state facts that, if true, constitute either mistakes, poor judgment, or reflect hard choices facing a cash-pressed company, but where is the allegation of conflicting interest or suspect motivation? [...]There are none. Nothing is alleged other than poor business practices. To permit the possibility of director liability on that basis would be very destructive of shareholder welfare in the long-term.

A similar analysis holds for the allegations concerning a contract to acquire the product "Lloyd's Ribs" (7); nothing is alleged other than that the price was excessive and the directors knew (or recklessly didn't know) that "the company could not afford such a transaction." More importantly, the complaint does not allege that the contract was ever closed! Indeed in Count V it is alleged that certain defendants diverted the opportunity to acquire Lloyd's Ribs from TriFoods! Thus, with respect to this possible transaction, not only does the amended complaint contain no allegation of conflict of interest or improper motivation in TriFoods' acquiring "Lloyd's Ribs," but it contains no allegation that a transaction involving the company ever occurred.

Finally, (8) there is the allegation that despite warnings from plaintiff and despite the alleged fact that the Pomfret facility "was not reasonably fit" for the purpose, the directors authorized the purchase of the facility at a "grossly excessive" price in order to implement a business plan that would have the company manufacture some or all of its food products and that defendants caused the company to borrow substantial funds to accomplish that task. Once more there is no allegation of conflict of interest with respect to this transaction[14], nor is there any allegation [1054] of improper motivation in authorizing the transactions. There is, in effect, only an allegation that plaintiff believes the transaction represents poor business judgment and the conclusion that "no reasonable business person would have engaged in it." [...]

For the foregoing reason Count IV of the amended complaint will be dismissed.

DGCL Sec. 145 - Indemnification   2.5.8

As we learned in the Agency Course, agents acting within the scope of their agency have a common law right of indemnification. Section 145 authorizes the corporation to indemnify agents of the corporation (including directors, officers, and other agents) under certain conditions.

Section 145(a) gives the corporation the power to indemnify agents of the corporation in suits by third parties. In such suits, the corporation may pay any judgments, fines or settlements that result from the agents actions with respect to third parties. Section 145(b) empowers the corporation to indemnify agents of the corporation in derivative suits. In the context of derivative suits, a corporation does not have the power to indemnify agents for any judgments, fines or settlements except upon application to the Chancery Court where there has not been an adjudication of liability. Under Section 145(c), where the corporate agent has successfully defended an action, the corporation is required to indemnify the agent.

The statute envisions that directors seeking indemnification under (a) or (b) may well create conflicts as directors seek the approval of their fellow directors for indemnification. Consequently, the statute requires specific procedures prior to board approval of any such payments. These procedures attempt to mimic an arm's length approval of such payments by enlisting independent directors and/or unaffiliated stockholders. Note the analogue between an approval for purposes of §145 and agency law's approach to approving conflicted agent transactions.

§ 145. Indemnification of officers, directors, employees and agents; insurance.

(a) A corporation shall have power to indemnify any person who was or is a party or is threatened to be made a party to any threatened, pending or completed action, suit or proceeding, whether civil, criminal, administrative or investigative (other than an action by or in the right of the corporation) by reason of the fact that the person is or was a director, officer, employee or agent of the corporation, or is or was serving at the request of the corporation as a director, officer, employee or agent of another corporation, partnership, joint venture, trust or other enterprise, against expenses (including attorneys' fees), judgments, fines and amounts paid in settlement actually and reasonably incurred by the person in connection with such action, suit or proceeding if the person acted in good faith and in a manner the person reasonably believed to be in or not opposed to the best interests of the corporation, and, with respect to any criminal action or proceeding, had no reasonable cause to believe the person's conduct was unlawful. The termination of any action, suit or proceeding by judgment, order, settlement, conviction, or upon a plea of nolo contendere or its equivalent, shall not, of itself, create a presumption that the person did not act in good faith and in a manner which the person reasonably believed to be in or not opposed to the best interests of the corporation, and, with respect to any criminal action or proceeding, had reasonable cause to believe that the person's conduct was unlawful.

(b) A corporation shall have power to indemnify any person who was or is a party or is threatened to be made a party to any threatened, pending or completed action or suit by or in the right of the corporation to procure a judgment in its favor by reason of the fact that the person is or was a director, officer, employee or agent of the corporation, or is or was serving at the request of the corporation as a director, officer, employee or agent of another corporation, partnership, joint venture, trust or other enterprise against expenses (including attorneys' fees) actually and reasonably incurred by the person in connection with the defense or settlement of such action or suit if the person acted in good faith and in a manner the person reasonably believed to be in or not opposed to the best interests of the corporation and except that no indemnification shall be made in respect of any claim, issue or matter as to which such person shall have been adjudged to be liable to the corporation unless and only to the extent that the Court of Chancery or the court in which such action or suit was brought shall determine upon application that, despite the adjudication of liability but in view of all the circumstances of the case, such person is fairly and reasonably entitled to indemnity for such expenses which the Court of Chancery or such other court shall deem proper.

(c) To the extent that a present or former director or officer of a corporation has been successful on the merits or otherwise in defense of any action, suit or proceeding referred to in subsections (a) and (b) of this section, or in defense of any claim, issue or matter therein, such person shall be indemnified against expenses (including attorneys' fees) actually and reasonably incurred by such person in connection therewith.

(d) Any indemnification under subsections (a) and (b) of this section (unless ordered by a court) shall be made by the corporation only as authorized in the specific case upon a determination that indemnification of the present or former director, officer, employee or agent is proper in the circumstances because the person has met the applicable standard of conduct set forth in subsections (a) and (b) of this section. Such determination shall be made, with respect to a person who is a director or officer of the corporation at the time of such determination:

(1) By a majority vote of the directors who are not parties to such action, suit or proceeding, even though less than a quorum; or

(2) By a committee of such directors designated by majority vote of such directors, even though less than a quorum; or

(3) If there are no such directors, or if such directors so direct, by independent legal counsel in a written opinion; or

(4) By the stockholders.

(e) Expenses (including attorneys' fees) incurred by an officer or director of the corporation in defending any civil, criminal, administrative or investigative action,[...]including attorneys' fees) incurred by former directors and officers or other employees and agents of the corporation or by persons serving at the request of the corporation as directors, officers, employees or agents of another corporation, partnership, joint venture, trust or other enterprise may be so paid upon such terms and conditions, if any, as the corporation deems appropriate.

(f) The indemnification and advancement of expenses provided by, or granted pursuant to, the other subsections of this section shall not be deemed exclusive of any other rights to which those seeking indemnification or advancement of expenses may be entitled under any bylaw, agreement, vote of stockholders or disinterested directors or otherwise, both as to action in such person's official capacity and as to action in another capacity while holding such office. A right to indemnification or to advancement of expenses arising under a provision of the certificate of incorporation or a bylaw shall not be eliminated or impaired by an amendment to the certificate of incorporation or the bylaws after the occurrence of the act or omission that is the subject of the civil, criminal, administrative or investigative action, suit or proceeding for which indemnification or advancement of expenses is sought, unless the provision in effect at the time of such act or omission explicitly authorizes such elimination or impairment after such action or omission has occurred.

(g) A corporation shall have power to purchase and maintain insurance on behalf of any person who is or was a director, officer, employee or agent of the corporation, or is or was serving at the request of the corporation as a director, officer, employee or agent of another corporation, partnership, joint venture, trust or other enterprise against any liability asserted against such person and incurred by such person in any such capacity, or arising out of such person's status as such, whether or not the corporation would have the power to indemnify such person against such liability under this section.

(h) For purposes of this section, references to "the corporation" shall include, in addition to the resulting corporation, any constituent corporation (including any constituent of a constituent) absorbed in a consolidation or merger which, if its separate existence had continued, would have had power and authority to indemnify its directors, officers, and employees or agents, so that any person who is or was a director, officer, employee or agent of such constituent corporation, or is or was serving at the request of such constituent corporation as a director, officer, employee or agent of another corporation, partnership, joint venture, trust or other enterprise, shall stand in the same position under this section with respect to the resulting or surviving corporation as such person would have with respect to such constituent corporation if its separate existence had continued.

Stock and Dividends   2.6

The following provisions of the corporate law are enabling provisions related the corporation's stock. In general terms, a corporation may issue shares with a variety of rights and powers. Unless the certificate reserves to the board of directors the right designate stock rights, such rights must be stipulated in the corporation's certificate of incorporation.

Where the certificate has reserved to the board the power to designate rights, when a board issues shares it may designate special rights, including voting power and dividend rights, for the stock it issues. Boards have used this power to create high vote shares and other types of stock with preferences and rights. This power to tailor the rights of stock is central to the board's ability to adopt "poison pills", also known as shareholder rights plans.

A common right built in a share of stock is the "liquidation preference". In firms funded by venture capital, venture capitalists will often demand that the shares they are issued come with liquidation preferences. A liquidation preference is a right that grants certain preferential payments to stockholder in the event the corporation undertakes any one of a series of different liquidation events (e.g. a merger, sale of the corporation, or a dissolution). Below is an example of a liquidation preference that might appear in a certificate of incorporation of venture backed start up firm:

- Upon the occurrence of a Liquidation, the holders of the Preferred Stock shall be entitled to receive, prior and in preference to any distribution of any of the assets or surplus funds of the Corporation to the holders of the Common Stock by reason of their ownership thereof, the amount of $5 per share (as adjusted for any stock dividends, combinations or splits with respect to such shares) plus all declared or accumulated but unpaid dividends on such share for each share of Preferred Stock then held by them.

This preference ensures that in the event of a liquidation event like a sale of the corporation, the venture investor receives $5 per share of the transaction consideration before any other stockholder is paid. Once the preference is paid, then stockholders share the balance of the transaction proceeds ratably.

When a board issues shares, this chapter of the code also permits boards to restrict the ability of stockholders to buy and sell shares of the corporation – making such shares subject to redemption rights, rights of first offer, and also prohibiting in some circumstances interested stockholder transactions.

With respect to dividends, the provisions in this chapter makes it clear that decisions with respect to the declaration of dividends are ones that lie wholly within the discretion of the board of directors and are not the realm of stockholder action.

DGCL Sec. 151 - Classes and series of stock   2.6.1

A corporation may issue shares in more than one
class, with each class having separate rights and
powers. In addition to the liquidation preference, discussed
previously, a board can use §151 to issue shares with variable voting
rights. For example, Facebook, Google, Twitter and other tech
firms have used §151 to issue shares classes of stock to founders
with 10 votes per share. Stock issued to the public have 1 vote per
share, or in some cases, no votes at all.

Shares issued by the corporation, may also be subject to redemption
should that right be stipulated in the certificate of incorporation or
the certificate of designation. In a redemption, the board may at any
time make a "call" on the stock and can redeem the stock for a
price determined in the certificate. A redemption differs from a
stock repurchase in a number of ways. First, a stock repurchase
involves a decision by the stockholder to sell their stock. Absent
consent of the stockholder, no one can force a stockholder to sell
into a stock repurchase. A redemption can lack a certain degree of
voluntariness. Stockholders take the stock knowing that the board
has the power to redeem stock against the will of stockholders.
Second, the stock repurchase can be done at any price. Presumably,
the board will want a sufficient number of stockholders to
voluntarily tender their shares, consequently the repurchase is
typically done a premium to the market price. In a redemption, the
redemption price, or at least a formula to calculate the price is set in
the certificate of incorporation.

§ 151. Classes and series of stock; redemption; rights.

(a) Every corporation may issue 1 or more classes of stock or 1 or
more series of stock within any class thereof, any or all of which
classes may be of stock with par value or stock without par value
and which classes or series may have such voting powers, full or
limited, or no voting powers, and such designations, preferences
and relative, participating, optional or other special rights, and

qualifications, limitations or restrictions thereof, as shall be stated and expressed in the certificate of incorporation or of any amendment thereto, or in the resolution or resolutions providing for the issue of such stock adopted by the board of directors pursuant to authority expressly vested in it by the provisions of its certificate of incorporation. Any of the voting powers, designations, preferences, rights and qualifications, limitations or restrictions of any such class or series of stock may be made dependent upon facts ascertainable outside the certificate of incorporation or of any amendment thereto, or outside the resolution or resolutions providing for the issue of such stock adopted by the board of directors pursuant to authority expressly vested in it by its certificate of incorporation, provided that the manner in which such facts shall operate upon the voting powers, designations, preferences, rights and qualifications, limitations or restrictions of such class or series of stock is clearly and expressly set forth in the certificate of incorporation or in the resolution or resolutions providing for the issue of such stock adopted by the board of directors. The term "facts," as used in this subsection, includes, but is not limited to, the occurrence of any event, including a determination or action by any person or body, including the corporation. The power to increase or decrease or otherwise adjust the capital stock as provided in this chapter shall apply to all or any such classes of stock.

(b) Any stock of any class or series may be made subject to redemption by the corporation at its option or at the option of the holders of such stock or upon the happening of a specified event; provided however, that immediately following any such redemption the corporation shall have outstanding 1 or more shares of 1 or more classes or series of stock, which share, or shares together, shall have full voting powers. [...]

Any stock which may be made redeemable under this section may be redeemed for cash, property or rights, including securities of the same or another corporation, at such time or times, price or prices, or rate or rates, and with such adjustments, as shall be stated in the certificate of incorporation or in the resolution or resolutions providing for the issue of such stock adopted by the board of directors pursuant to subsection (a) of this section.

(c) The holders of preferred or special stock of any class or of any series thereof shall be entitled to receive dividends at such rates, on such conditions and at such times as shall be stated in the certificate of incorporation or in the resolution or resolutions providing for the issue of such stock adopted by the board of directors as hereinabove provided, payable in preference to, or in such relation to, the dividends payable on any other class or classes or of any other series of stock, and cumulative or noncumulative as shall be so stated and expressed. [...]

(d) The holders of the preferred or special stock of any class or of any series thereof shall be entitled to such rights upon the dissolution of, or upon any distribution of the assets of, the corporation as shall be stated in the certificate of incorporation or in the resolution or resolutions providing for the issue of such stock adopted by the board of directors as hereinabove provided.

(e) Any stock of any class or of any series thereof may be made convertible into, or exchangeable for, at the option of either the holder or the corporation or upon the happening of a specified event, shares of any other class or classes or any other series of the same or any other class or classes of stock of the corporation, at such price or prices or at such rate or rates of exchange and with such adjustments as shall be stated in the certificate of incorporation or in the resolution or resolutions providing for the issue of such stock adopted by the board of directors as hereinabove provided. [...]

DGCL Sec. 157 - Rights and options   2.6.2

By now, stock options have become well known as a device for employee compensation in corporations. A stock option provides the holder with the right to purchase a share of the corporation at a stated price. When this "strike price" is below the price of the shares trading in the stock market, the options are considered "in the money" and the optionholder has an economic incentive to exercise the stock option. When the strike price is above the market price for the stock, the optionholder does not have an incentive to exercise the options.

Because stock options increase in value with an increase in the stock price, options are thought to be reasonably efficient incentive mechanisms, delivering value to employees when the firm succeeds. Because stock options issued to employees also vest over time, the existence of unvested options as part of an employee's compensation package creates a bonding mechanism between the corporation and the employee.

§ 157. Rights and options respecting stock.

(a) Subject to any provisions in the certificate of incorporation, every corporation may create and issue, whether or not in connection with the issue and sale of any shares of stock or other securities of the corporation, rights or options entitling the holders thereof to acquire from the corporation any shares of its capital stock of any class or classes, such rights or options to be evidenced by or in such instrument or instruments as shall be approved by the board of directors.

(b) The terms upon which, including the time or times which may be limited or unlimited in duration, at or within which, and the consideration (including a formula by which such consideration may be determined) for which any such shares may be acquired from the corporation upon the exercise of any such right or option, shall be such as shall be stated in the certificate of incorporation, or in a resolution adopted by the board of directors providing for the creation and issue of such rights or options, and, in every case, shall be set forth or incorporated by reference in the instrument or instruments evidencing such rights or options.[...]

DGCL Sec. 160 - Corporate ownership of its own stock   2.6.3

Corporations, as entities separate from their stockholders, are empowered by the statute to hold and maintain all sorts of assets, including holding stock of other corporations (making the holding company possible). But can a corporation own its own stock? And, if it does, what are the implications?

The short answer is that a corporation can indeed buy and own its own stock. However, the implications of the corporation buying its own stock are significant. When a corporation buys or redeems its own stock that stock is deemed to be "treasury stock" and is no longer outstanding stock. Treasury stock may not be voted and does not count towards determining a quorum at stockholder meetings.

Any corporation stock held by wholly-owned subsidiary of the corporation is also deemed treasury stock. However, corporation stock held by the corporation in a fiduciary capacity (corporation stock held as part of an employee retirement plan managed by the corporation, for example), is not deemed to be treasury stock.

§ 160. Corporation's powers respecting ownership, voting, etc., of its own stock; rights of stock called for redemption.

(a) Every corporation may purchase, redeem, receive, take or otherwise acquire, own and hold, sell, lend, exchange, transfer or otherwise dispose of, pledge, use and otherwise deal in and with its own shares; provided, however, that no corporation shall: [...]

(2) Purchase, for more than the price at which they may then be redeemed, any of its shares which are redeemable at the option of the corporation; or [...]

(c) Shares of its own capital stock belonging to the corporation or to another corporation, if a majority of the shares entitled to vote in the election of directors of such other corporation is held, directly or indirectly, by the corporation, shall neither be entitled to vote nor be counted for quorum purposes. Nothing in this section shall be construed as limiting the right of any corporation to vote stock, including but not limited to its own stock, held by it in a fiduciary capacity.

(d) Shares which have been called for redemption shall not be deemed to be outstanding shares for the purpose of voting or determining the total number of shares entitled to vote on any matter on and after the date on which written notice of redemption has been sent to holders thereof and a sum sufficient to redeem such shares has been irrevocably deposited or set aside to pay the redemption price to the holders of the shares upon surrender of certificates therefor.

DGCL Sec. 161 - Issuance of stock

2.6.4

The board of directors has the authority to issuance of new shares of the corporation. Provided the shares have been authorized in the certificate of incorporation, the board need not seek stockholder approval prior to issuing such shares.

§ 161. Issuance of additional stock; when and by whom.

The directors may, at any time and from time to time, if all of the shares of capital stock which the corporation is authorized by its certificate of incorporation to issue have not been issued, subscribed for, or otherwise committed to be issued, issue or take subscriptions for additional shares of its capital stock up to the amount authorized in its certificate of incorporation.

DGCL Sec. 170 - Dividends

2.6.5

When a corporation has profits, it may distribute those profits back to stockholders. These profit distributions back to stockholders are known as "dividends".

The decision whether or not to issue dividends to stockholders lies wholly within the discretion of the board of directors. Unless the certificate of incorporation states otherwise, stockholders have no right to corporate dividends.

Some old-line corporations, like G.E. are well-known for a long-standing board policy of making dividend payments to their stockholders. Other corporations, like start-up corporations or corporations in high-growth stages of development, have the exact opposite policy. Companies like Alphabet or Facebook have board policies against making dividend payments to stockholders, opting to reinvest all their profits into the company.

§ 170. Dividends; payment; wasting asset corporations.

(a) The directors of every corporation, subject to any restrictions contained in its certificate of incorporation, may declare and pay dividends upon the shares of its capital stock either:

(1) Out of its surplus, as defined in and computed in accordance with §§ 154 and 244 of this title; or

(2) In case there shall be no such surplus, out of its net profits for the fiscal year in which the dividend is declared and/or the preceding fiscal year.

If the capital of the corporation, computed in accordance with §§ 154 and 244 of this title, shall have been diminished by depreciation in the value of its property, or by losses, or otherwise, to an amount less than the aggregate amount of the capital represented by the issued and outstanding stock of all classes having a preference upon the distribution of assets, the directors of such corporation shall not declare and pay out of such net profits any dividends upon any shares of any classes of its capital stock until the deficiency in the amount of capital represented by the issued and outstanding stock of all classes having a preference upon the distribution of assets shall have been repaired. [...]

DGCL Sec. 202 - Restrictions on transfer of stock 2.6.6

When a board issues new shares, in addition
assigning voting rights to the shares, the board may
also, pursuant to §202, place restrictions on the ability of
stockholders to transfer or sell such shares. Requirements for such
restrictions to be valid require, first, actual knowledge by the
stockholder of such restrictions (conspicuously noting the
restrictions on the stock certificate will be sufficient evidence of
actual knowledge) and, second, that the restrictions on ownership or
transfer are 'reasonable'. Violations of such restrictions will result in
the transferee having no legal or equitable title to the stock.

Restrictions on stock ownership are common in private companies.
There are a variety of common restrictions that are often included
in the private company context, including rights of first refusal, buy-
sell agreements, or automatic sales/transfers. All of these restrictions
have the effect of controlling access to ownership of a corporation's
stock.

Under §202(c)(5), the certificate may restrict designated persons or
classes of persons from owning shares. This kind of restriction is
common in closely held private companies where the intention is to
ensure control of the company's stock is maintained by a family.
Additionally, corporations operating in some business areas (eg.
national security, media) may be under legal requirements to ensure
the domestic citizenship or residency of stockholders.
Consequently, citizenship requirements on the ownership of stock
are not unreasonable for some businesses. For example, United
Airlines (see Apppendix) limits ownership of its stock by non-
citizens to no more than 24.9% in order to comply with federal law
that limits foreign ownership of domestic U.S. airlines. Another
common restriction prevents accumulation of shares by any one
stockholder. For example, a corporation may, through its certificate
of incorporation, limit the stockholding of any single stockholder to
no more than 5% in order to assure that no single stockholder can
dominate the corporation.

The ability of boards to design restrictions on the transfer of stock is fairly broad. Of course, this power is not without limits. Such restrictions are subject to 'reasonableness' limitations. Restrictions against selling stock to based on racial or gender categories run afoul of Federal law and thus would not be 'reasonable.'

§ 202. Restrictions on transfer and ownership of securities.

(a) A written restriction or restrictions on the transfer or registration of transfer of a security of a corporation, or on the amount of the corporation's securities that may be owned by any person or group of persons, if permitted by this section and noted conspicuously on the certificate or certificates representing the security or securities so restricted [...] may be enforced against the holder of the restricted security or securities or any successor or transferee of the holder including an executor, administrator, trustee, guardian or other fiduciary entrusted with like responsibility for the person or estate of the holder. Unless noted conspicuously on the certificate or certificates representing the security or securities so restricted [...], a restriction, even though permitted by this section, is ineffective except against a person with actual knowledge of the restriction.

(b) A restriction on the transfer or registration of transfer of securities of a corporation, or on the amount of a corporation's securities that may be owned by any person or group of persons, may be imposed by the certificate of incorporation or by the bylaws or by an agreement among any number of security holders or among such holders and the corporation. No restrictions so imposed shall be binding with respect to securities issued prior to the adoption of the restriction unless the holders of the securities are parties to an agreement or voted in favor of the restriction.

(c) A restriction on the transfer or registration of transfer of securities of a corporation or on the amount of such securities that may be owned by any person or group of persons is permitted by this section if it:

(1) Obligates the holder of the restricted securities to offer to the corporation or to any other holders of securities of the corporation or to any other person or to any combination of the foregoing, a prior opportunity, to be exercised within a reasonable time, to acquire the restricted securities; or

(2) Obligates the corporation or any holder of securities of the corporation or any other person or any combination of the foregoing, to purchase the securities which are the subject of an agreement respecting the purchase and sale of the restricted securities; or

(3) Requires the corporation or the holders of any class or series of securities of the corporation to consent to any proposed transfer of the restricted securities or to approve the proposed transferee of the restricted securities, or to approve the amount of securities of the corporation that may be owned by any person or group of persons; or

(4) Obligates the holder of the restricted securities to sell or transfer an amount of restricted securities to the corporation or to any other holders of securities of the corporation or to any other person or to any combination of the foregoing, or causes or results in the automatic sale or transfer of an amount of restricted securities to the corporation or to any other holders of securities of the corporation or to any other person or to any combination of the foregoing; or

(5) Prohibits or restricts the transfer of the restricted securities to, or the ownership of restricted securities by, designated persons or classes of persons or groups of persons, and such designation is not manifestly unreasonable.

(d) Any restriction on the transfer or the registration of transfer of the securities of a corporation, or on the amount of securities of a corporation that may be owned by a person or group of persons, for any of the following purposes shall be conclusively presumed to be for a reasonable purpose:

(1) Maintaining any local, state, federal or foreign tax advantage to the corporation or its stockholders, including without limitation:

a. Maintaining the corporation's status as an electing small business corporation under subchapter S of the United States Internal Revenue Code [26 U.S.C. § 1371 et seq.], or

b. Maintaining or preserving any tax attribute (including without limitation net operating losses), or

c. Qualifying or maintaining the qualification of the corporation as a real estate investment trust pursuant to the United States Internal Revenue Code[...], or

(2) Maintaining any statutory or regulatory advantage or complying with any statutory or regulatory requirements under applicable local, state, federal or foreign law.

(e) Any other lawful restriction on transfer or registration of transfer of securities, or on the amount of securities that may be owned by any person or group of persons, is permitted by this section.

DGCL Sec. 203 - State anti-takeover legislation   2.6.7

Section 203 is an example of state anti-takeover legislation. Section 203 is a flavor of the kinds of restrictions on stock transfer as we saw in §202. In §203 restrictions a board may prohibit a stockholder from purchasing additional shares in the corporation for a period of time once they have completed a transaction that gives them control of the corporation. The restrictions described in §203 are intended to delay the ability of a hostile acquirer to quickly complete a hostile acquisition of the corporation unless the target corporation's board consents. Note that the requirements of §203 can be waived by a resolution of the target corporation's board.

§ 203. Business combinations with interested stockholders.

(a) Notwithstanding any other provisions of this chapter, a corporation shall not engage in any business combination with any interested stockholder for a period of 3 years following the time that such stockholder became an interested stockholder, unless:

(1) Prior to such time the board of directors of the corporation approved either the business combination or the transaction which resulted in the stockholder becoming an interested stockholder;

(2) Upon consummation of the transaction which resulted in the stockholder becoming an interested stockholder, the interested stockholder owned at least 85% of the voting stock of the corporation outstanding at the time the transaction commenced, excluding for purposes of determining the voting stock outstanding (but not the outstanding voting stock owned by the interested stockholder) those shares owned (i) by persons who are directors and also officers and (ii) employee stock plans in which employee participants do not have the right to determine confidentially whether shares held subject to the plan will be tendered in a tender or exchange offer; or

(3) At or subsequent to such time the business combination is approved by the board of directors and authorized at an annual or special meeting of stockholders, and not by written consent, by the affirmative vote of at least 66 2/3% of the outstanding voting stock which is not owned by the interested stockholder.

(b) The restrictions contained in this section shall not apply if:

(1) The corporation's original certificate of incorporation contains a provision expressly electing not to be governed by this section; [...]

(c) As used in this section only, the term: [...]

(3) "Business combination," when used in reference to any corporation and any interested stockholder of such corporation, means:

(i) Any merger or consolidation of the corporation or any direct or indirect majority-owned subsidiary of the corporation with (A) the interested stockholder, or (B) with any other corporation, partnership, unincorporated association or other entity if the merger or consolidation is caused by the interested stockholder and as a result of such merger or consolidation subsection (a) of this section is not applicable to the surviving entity;

(ii) Any sale, lease, exchange, mortgage, pledge, transfer or other disposition (in 1 transaction or a series of transactions), except proportionately as a stockholder of such corporation, to or with the interested stockholder, whether as part of a dissolution or otherwise, of assets of the corporation or of any direct or indirect majority-owned subsidiary of the corporation which assets have an aggregate market value equal to 10% or more of either the aggregate market value of all the assets of the corporation determined on a consolidated basis or the aggregate market value of all the outstanding stock of the corporation; [...]

Stockholder Meetings and Voting for Directors 2.7

Stockholders do not have a general right to manage the business and affairs of the corporation. Nor do they have a general right to vote on matters related to the operation of the corporation's business. The principle power of stockholders is the power to vote for directors and certain corporate transactions which for which there is a statutory stockholder vote required. Stockholders who disagree with the strategy or direction of the corporation have generally have two choices: vote in favor of a different board and thus change the composition of the board of directors; or sell their shares. In many cases, institutional stockholders or indexed stockholders will not be in a position to sell their shares. Thus, the corporate ballot box becomes a fulcrum to affect a change in corporate strategy.

Nominations for membership on the board of directors are typically made by the board itself through a nominations and governance committee of the board created for that purpose. Stockholder activists will often use the threat of a contested election in which they nominate their own directors to sway incumbent directors with respect to corporate strategy. In that sense, stockholder control over corporations can be better described as a "bank shot" (to use a basketball description). While stockholders cannot dictate business decisions to boards of directors, when a board feels sufficiently vulnerable to expulsion at the ballot box, boards will become more amenable to activists' suggestions about the strategic direction of the business.

The importance of the stockholder franchise and votes for control over the board of directors are the central tension in modern corporate governance. Boards are free to manage corporations in any manner they see fit, subject to regular votes of confidence by stockholders. To the extent boards stray far from the interests of stockholders, boards are vulnerable to replacement through regular stockholder votes.

The following provisions lay out the requirements for stockholder meetings as well as stockholder voting at these meetings.

DGCL Sec. 211 - Stockholder meetings   2.7.1

The following provision lays out the requirements for a corporation to hold a meeting of the stockholders. There are two types of meetings of stockholders: annual meetings and special meetings. The principle business of any corporation's annual meeting is the election of the directors. It is through the annual election of directors that stockholders have their biggest voice and influence in the running of the corporation's business and affairs. Special meetings may be called by the board of directors or any person specified by the certificate or bylaws (typically the chair of the board and/or large stockholders) at any time with sufficient notice. Special meetings can be called for any reason. Usually, boards will call special meetings to ask for stockholders to vote on statutory transactions, like mergers or a corporate dissolution.

§ 211. Meetings of stockholders.

(a)(1) Meetings of stockholders may be held at such place, either within or without this State as may be designated by or in the manner provided in the certificate of incorporation or bylaws, or if not so designated, as determined by the board of directors.[...]

(b) Unless directors are elected by written consent in lieu of an annual meeting as permitted by this subsection, an annual meeting of stockholders shall be held for the election of directors on a date and at a time designated by or in the manner provided in the bylaws. [...]

(c) A failure to hold the annual meeting at the designated time or to elect a sufficient number of directors to conduct the business of the corporation shall not affect otherwise valid corporate acts or work a forfeiture or dissolution of the corporation except as may be otherwise specifically provided in this chapter. If the annual meeting for election of directors is not held on the date designated therefor or action by written consent to elect directors in lieu of an annual meeting has not been taken, the directors shall cause the meeting to be held as soon as is convenient. If there be a failure to hold the annual meeting or to take action by written consent to elect directors in lieu of an annual meeting for a period of 30 days after the date designated for the annual meeting, or if no date has been designated, for a period of 13 months after the latest to occur of the organization of the corporation, its last annual meeting or the last action by written consent to elect directors in lieu of an annual meeting, the Court of Chancery may summarily order a meeting to be held upon the application of any stockholder or director. The shares of stock represented at such meeting, either in person or by proxy, and entitled to vote thereat, shall constitute a quorum for the purpose of such meeting, notwithstanding any provision of the certificate of incorporation or bylaws to the contrary. The Court of Chancery may issue such orders as may be appropriate, including, without limitation, orders designating the time and place of such meeting, the record date or dates for determination of stockholders entitled to notice of the meeting and to vote thereat, and the form of notice of such meeting.

(d) Special meetings of the stockholders may be called by the board of directors or by such person or persons as may be authorized by the certificate of incorporation or by the bylaws.

(e) All elections of directors shall be by written ballot unless otherwise provided in the certificate of incorporation; [...]

DGCL. Sec. 228 - Action by written consent 2.7.2

Stockholders may act by providing their written consent rather than at a meeting. Taking action by written consent rather than at a formal meeting may be preferrable in corporations, like start-up companies, where the number of stockholders is relatively small and easily identifiable. Any action that can be taken at a meeting of the stockholders can also be accomplished by written consent of the majority of the outstanding shares.

This default right to act by written consent can be stripped from stockholders. It is not uncommon for larger, publicly-traded corporations to include a prohibition against acting by written consent in the corporation's certificate of incorporation. By requiring stockholders to act only at a meeting - the time and place of which is controlled by the board of directors - managers of the corporation make it difficult for stockholder activists or for potential hostile acquirers of the corporation to organize stockholders against the incumbent board of directors and managers.

§ 228. Consent of stockholders or members in lieu of meeting.

(a) Unless otherwise provided in the certificate of incorporation, any action required by this chapter to be taken at any annual or special meeting of stockholders of a corporation, or any action which may be taken at any annual or special meeting of such stockholders, may be taken without a meeting, without prior notice and without a vote, if a consent or consents in writing, setting forth the action so taken, shall be signed by the holders of outstanding stock having not less than the minimum number of votes that would be necessary to authorize or take such action at a meeting at which all shares entitled to vote thereon were present and voted and shall be delivered to the corporation by delivery to its registered office in this State, its principal place of business or an officer or agent of the corporation having custody of the book in which proceedings of meetings of stockholders are recorded. [...]

(c) Every written consent shall bear the date of signature of each stockholder or member who signs the consent, and no written consent shall be effective to take the corporate action referred to therein unless, within 60 days of the earliest dated consent delivered in the manner required by this section to the corporation[...]

(e) Prompt notice of the taking of the corporate action without a meeting by less than unanimous written consent shall be given to those stockholders or members who have not consented in writing and who, if the action had been taken at a meeting, would have been entitled to notice of the meeting if the record date for notice of such meeting had been the date that written consents signed by a sufficient number of holders or members to take the action were delivered to the corporation as provided in subsection (c) of this section. [...]

DGCL Sec. 212 - Stockholder voting rights   2.7.3

The default rule is that each share of stock gets one vote unless the certificate of incorporation provides otherwise. A stockholder may vote in person, or may delegate authority to another person to vote as their proxy.

You will often hear reference to a "proxy statement". The proxy statement is a federally-mandated information disclosure filed on Form 14A that publicly-traded corporations are required to send to stockholders in advance of a stockholder meeting. The proxy statement includes all the material information required by the

Securities Exchange Act of 1934 that stockholders will need in advance of their votes for directors and any other business put to the stockholders for a vote. The proxy statement will also include a stockholder ballot.

§ 212. Voting rights of stockholders; proxies; limitations.

(a) Unless otherwise provided in the certificate of incorporation and subject to § 213 of this title, each stockholder shall be entitled to 1 vote for each share of capital stock held by such stockholder. If the certificate of incorporation provides for more or less than 1 vote for any share, on any matter, every reference in this chapter to a majority or other proportion of stock, voting stock or shares shall refer to such majority or other proportion of the votes of such stock, voting stock or shares.

(b) Each stockholder entitled to vote at a meeting of stockholders or to express consent or dissent to corporate action in writing without a meeting may authorize another person or persons to act for such stockholder by proxy, [...]

Stock with Multiple Voting Classes   2.7.4

According to §212, the default is that every share of stock has one vote. However, because the corporate code provides for parties to tailor their arrangements, it is possible for boards to issue different classes or series of stock with different rights. The most common, though certainly not the only, customization of stock in recent years is the creation of multiple classes of stock with different voting power. In recent years, multiple class voting structures have become popular with founder-led tech companies when they go public. For example, corporations like Alphabet (Google), Facebook, Twitter, and Snap, among others, all have multiple classes of stock, each with different voting rights. High vote stock, held by the controlling stockholders in these corporations, typically have ten votes per share, while stock held by the public has stock with a lower number of votes per share.

Alphabet (Google) has a relative complex share structure. Alphabet's Class A shares are the shares commonly held by the public. These shares have one vote each. Alphabet's Class B shares are high vote shares held by the founders. These shares have 10 votes each. The final Class of shares in Alphabet at no-vote Class C shares. Class C shares do not have the right to vote. Alphabet uses these shares as acquisition currency. Class C shares permit the founders to purchase other companies for using Alphabet stock as the currency without risking reduction in the voting power of the founders. By holding high vote Class B shares, Google's founders can control the outcome of stockholder votes without holding an equivalent economic interest in the corporation.

Snap went public in 2017 with its own version of multiple classes of shares. In Snap's case, the company has three classes of common stock: Class A, Class B, and Class C. Holders of Snap's Class A common stock are not entitled to vote on matters submitted to the stockholders. Holders of Snap's Class B common stock (mostly made up of employees and venture investors) are entitled to one vote per share. And holders of Snap's Class C common stock (held by Snap's founders: Evan Spiegal and Robert Murphy) and are entitled to ten votes per share. Holders of shares of Class B common stock and Class C common stock will vote together as a single class on all matters (including the election of directors) submitted to a vote of stockholders. As a result of this voting structure founders Evan Spiegel and Robert Murphy are able to exercise voting rights with respect to approximately 88.5% of the voting power of Snap's outstanding capital stock.

Pursuant to Section 212(a), where a corporation has multiple classes of stock with different voting power, then the entire code should be re-read and where the code calls for *"share"* (with respect to required votes or quorum, etc) that must be read to read *"votes"*.

DGCL Sec. 213 - Record dates   2.7.5

Prior to any stockholder meeting, the board must set a "record date" for determining who are the stockholders of the corporation who have the right to vote at the meeting.

Determining who is a stockholder for the purposes of notice and the right to vote at a meeting can be more complex than you might initially think. In a private corporation, like a start-up, determining who are the record stockholders entitled to notice and to vote at a meeting is, typically, a simple matter. Shares of a private corporation are not transferrable and are held by a relatively small number of easily identifiable persons. One need only refer to the corporation's stock ledger (usually an Excel spreadsheet) to determine who are the stockholders.

On the other hand, determining who is a stockholder in a modern publicly-traded corporation is an altogether different matter. In publicly-traded corporations, there are potentially millions of stockholders and the demographic of the stockholding base turns over regularly as traders in the market buy and sell shares of the corporation. Determining who is a stockholder for purposes of receiving notice of a meeting and then being entitled to vote at that meeting is difficult. For one thing, a stockholder who is given notice today may very well not be a stockholder of the corporation 45 days later when the meeting is actually held.

Later, when we discuss stockholder lists and §219, you will be introduced to the complexities of the system that has been gerry-rigged to try to deal with the question of "record ownership" and "beneficial ownership" in a fast-paced trading environment. For now, though, note that §213 tries to deal with some obvious issues.

By permitting a board to separate a stockholder's right to receive notice of a meeting and the identification of stockholders entitled to vote at a meeting, §213 acknowledges the reality that in many corporations there will be significant turnover in the stockholding demographic between notice and the meeting. Consequently, a board may, pursuant to §213, elect to fix a date for providing stockholder notice for a meeting that that is different from the date to determine which stockholders have the actual right to vote. For purposes of providing notice, a board may select a day between 10-60 days in advance of a meeting. For purposes of deciding who actually gets to vote, the board may select any day as late as the last day preceding the meeting. By permitting a board to identify stockholders entitled to vote at a point in time much closer to the meeting day, drafters of the statute hope the actual stockholding demographic more closely resembles those who have been identified as having the right to vote at a meeting.

§ 213. Fixing date for determination of stockholders of record.

(a) In order that the corporation may determine the stockholders entitled to notice of any meeting of stockholders or any adjournment thereof, the board of directors may fix a record date, which record date shall not precede the date upon which the resolution fixing the record date is adopted by the board of directors, and which record date shall not be more than 60 nor less than 10 days before the date of such meeting. If the board of directors so fixes a date, such date shall also be the record date for determining the stockholders entitled to vote at such meeting unless the board of directors determines, at the time it fixes such record date, that a later date on or before the date of the meeting shall be the date for making such determination. If no record date is fixed by the board of directors, the record date for determining stockholders entitled to notice of and to vote at a meeting of stockholders shall be at the close of business on the day next preceding the day on which notice is given, or, if notice is waived, at the close of business on the day next preceding the day on which the meeting is held. A determination of stockholders of record entitled to notice of or to vote at a meeting of stockholders shall apply to any adjournment of the meeting; provided, however, that the board of directors may fix a new record date for determination of stockholders entitled to vote at the adjourned meeting, and in such case shall also fix as the record date for stockholders entitled to notice of such adjourned meeting the same or an earlier date as that fixed for determination of stockholders entitled to vote in accordance with the foregoing provisions of this subsection (a) at the adjourned meeting.

If no record date has been fixed by the board of directors, the record date for determining stockholders entitled to consent to corporate action in writing without a meeting, when no prior action by the board of directors is required by this chapter, shall be the first date on which a signed written consent setting forth the action taken or proposed to be taken is delivered to the corporation by delivery to its registered office in this State, its principal place of business or an officer or agent of the corporation having custody of the book in which proceedings of meetings of stockholders are recorded. [...] If no record date has been fixed by the board of directors and prior action by the board of directors is required by this chapter, the record date for determining stockholders entitled to consent to corporate action in writing without a meeting shall be at the close of business on the day on which the board of directors adopts the resolution taking such prior action.

DGCL Sec. 222 - Notice of meetings   2.7.6

A meeting may not be called unless all stockholders of record have received adequate notice under the provisions of the statute. Section 222 below outlines the notice requirements for stockholder meetings and should be read in conjunction with §213, which provides for fixing the record date for determining who are the stockholders of record for purposes of notice and voting.

§ 222. Notice of meetings and adjourned meetings.

(a) Whenever stockholders are required or permitted to take any action at a meeting, a written notice of the meeting shall be given which shall state the place, if any, date and hour of the meeting, the means of remote communications, if any, by which stockholders and proxy holders may be deemed to be present in person and vote at such meeting, the record date for determining the stockholders entitled to vote at the meeting, if such date is different from the record date for determining stockholders entitled to notice of the meeting, and, in the case of a special meeting, the purpose or purposes for which the meeting is called.

(b) Unless otherwise provided in this chapter, the written notice of any meeting shall be given not less than 10 nor more than 60 days before the date of the meeting to each stockholder entitled to vote at such meeting as of the record date for determining the stockholders entitled to notice of the meeting. [...]

(c) When a meeting is adjourned to another time or place, unless the bylaws otherwise require, notice need not be given of the adjourned meeting if the time, place, if any, thereof, and the means of remote communications, if any, by which stockholders and proxy holders may be deemed to be present in person and vote at such adjourned meeting are announced at the meeting at which the adjournment is taken. [...] If the adjournment is for more than 30 days, a notice of the adjourned meeting shall be given to each stockholder of record entitled to vote at the meeting. If after the adjournment a new record date for stockholders entitled to vote is fixed for the adjourned meeting, the board of directors shall fix a new record date for notice of such adjourned meeting in accordance with § 213(a) of this title, and shall give notice of the adjourned meeting to each stockholder of record entitled to vote at such adjourned meeting as of the record date fixed for notice of such adjourned meeting.[...]

DGCL Sec. 216 - Quorum and required votes   2.7.7

For any stockholder meeting to be a valid meeting, there must be sufficient representation of the corporation's underlying stockholder base. Quorum requirements exist to ensure that when a corporation's stockholders meet they are sufficiently representative such that their votes reflect the will of the stockholders as a whole.

This §216 also sets out the default rules for voting for directors.

§ 216. Quorum and required vote for stock corporations.

Subject to this chapter in respect of the vote that shall be required for a specified action, the certificate of incorporation or bylaws of any corporation authorized to issue stock may specify the number of shares and/or the amount of other securities having voting power the holders of which shall be present or represented by proxy at any meeting in order to constitute a quorum for, and the votes that shall be necessary for, the transaction of any business, but in no event shall a quorum consist of less than 1/3 of the shares entitled to vote at the meeting, except that, where a separate vote by a class or series or classes or series is required, a quorum shall consist of no less than 1/3 of the shares of such class or series or classes or series. In the absence of such specification in the certificate of incorporation or bylaws of the corporation:

(1) A majority of the shares entitled to vote, present in person or represented by proxy, shall constitute a quorum at a meeting of stockholders;

(2) In all matters other than the election of directors, the affirmative vote of the majority of shares present in person or represented by proxy at the meeting and entitled to vote on the subject matter shall be the act of the stockholders;

(3) Directors shall be elected by a plurality of the votes of the shares present in person or represented by proxy at the meeting and entitled to vote on the election of directors; and

(4) Where a separate vote by a class or series or classes or series is required, a majority of the outstanding shares of such class or series or classes or series, present in person or represented by proxy, shall constitute a quorum entitled to take action with respect to that vote on that matter and, in all matters other than the election of directors, the affirmative vote of the majority of shares of such class or series or classes or series present in person or represented by proxy at the meeting shall be the act of such class or series or classes or series.

A bylaw amendment adopted by stockholders which specifies the votes that shall be necessary for the election of directors shall not be further amended or repealed by the board of directors. [...]

Who Gets to Vote and Lists of Record Shareholders   2.7.8

In advance of a meeting, stockholders have the right to seek a list of fellow stockholders of record for the purpose of communicating with them about the upcoming meeting. In the typical private corporation, identifying the stockholders of record is a relatively simple matter: every time the corporation issues a share, the corporate secretary records the name of the stockholder into the corporation's stock ledger. In order to determine the stockholders of record, one need only refer to the stock ledger.

This exercise is more complex when one wishes to determine the stockholders of record of a corporation which has its stock trading on the public markets, like the NASDAQ or the NYSE. In the *Dell* case that follows, Vice Chancellor Laster provides an overview of the US system of recording beneficial and record stockholders for public corporations.

DGCL Sec. 219 - Stockholder lists   2.7.8.1

Stockholders of a corporation have a right to access
the list of stockholders in anticipation of a
stockholder meeting. A corporation that wishes to prevent a
stockholder from inspecting this list bears a burden of proving to
the court why it should not be required to permit inspection.

§ 219. List of stockholders entitled to vote; penalty for refusal to produce; stock ledger.

(a) The officer who has charge of the stock ledger of a corporation
shall prepare and make, at least 10 days before every meeting of
stockholders, a complete list of the stockholders entitled to vote at
the meeting; provided, however, if the record date for determining
the stockholders entitled to vote is less than 10 days before the
meeting date, the list shall reflect the stockholders entitled to vote as
of the tenth day before the meeting date, arranged in alphabetical
order, and showing the address of each stockholder and the number
of shares registered in the name of each stockholder. [...] Such list
shall be open to the examination of any stockholder for any purpose
germane to the meeting for a period of at least 10 days prior to the
meeting: [...]

(b) If the corporation, or an officer or agent thereof, refuses to
permit examination of the list by a stockholder, such stockholder
may apply to the Court of Chancery for an order to compel the
corporation to permit such examination. The burden of proof shall
be on the corporation to establish that the examination such
stockholder seeks is for a purpose not germane to the meeting. The
Court may summarily order the corporation to permit examination
of the list upon such conditions as the Court may deem appropriate,
and may make such additional orders as may be appropriate,
including, without limitation, postponing the meeting or voiding the
results of the meeting.

(c) The stock ledger shall be the only evidence as to who are the
stockholders entitled by this section to examine the list required by
this section or to vote in person or by proxy at any meeting of
stockholders. [...]

In re Appraisal of Dell Inc. 2.7.8.2

In this appraisal opinion, Vice Chancellor Laster
provides an overview and history of stockholder
record keeping for public companies. The excerpted opinion is a
useful introduction to the distinctions between beneficial and record
stockholders.

LASTER, Vice Chancellor.

The petitioners are five institutions[1] who owned common stock of
Dell, Inc. They sought appraisal after Dell announced a going-
private merger. Dell contends that they did not hold their shares
continuously through the effective date of the merger and therefore
lost their appraisal rights.

The Funds held their shares through custodial banks. By virtue of
this relationship, the Funds did not have legal title to the shares;
they were beneficial owners. But the custodial banks did not have
legal title either. The shares they held were registered in the name
of Cede & Co., which is the nominee of the Depository Trust
Company ("DTC").[2]

DTC's place in the ownership structure results from the federal
response to a paperwork crisis on Wall Street during the late 1960s
and early 1970s. Increased trading volume in the securities markets
overwhelmed the back offices of brokerage firms and the
capabilities of transfer agents. No one could cope with the burdens
of documenting stock trades using paper certificates. The markets
were forced to declare trading holidays so administrators could
catch up. With trading volumes continuing to climb, it was obvious
that reform was needed. Congress directed the SEC to evaluate
alternatives that would facilitate trading.

After studying the issue, the SEC adopted a national policy of share immobilization. To carry out its policy, the SEC placed a new entity—the depository institution—at the bottom the ownership chain. DTC emerged as the only domestic depository. Over 800 custodial banks and brokers are participating members of DTC and maintain accounts with that institution. DTC holds shares on their behalf in fungible bulk, meaning that none of the shares are issued in the names of DTC's participants. Instead, all of the shares are issued in the name of Cede. Through a Fast Automated Securities Transfer account (the "FAST Account"), DTC uses an electronic book entry system to track the number of shares of stock that each participant holds.

By adding DTC to the bottom of the ownership chain, the SEC eliminated the need for the overwhelming majority of legal transfers. Before share immobilization, custodial banks and brokers held shares through their own nominees, so new certificates had to be issued frequently when shares traded. With share immobilization, legal title remains with Cede. No new certificates are required. [...]

A. The Funds' Ownership Of Dell Shares

On February 5, 2013, Dell agreed to a merger in which each publicly held share of Dell common stock would be converted into the right to receive $13.75 in cash, subject to the right of stockholders to seek appraisal. The Funds held at least 922,975 shares of Dell common stock. Like most investors, the Funds did not hold legal title to their shares. The Funds owned the shares indirectly through accounts at custodial banks. Two of the Funds used J.P. Morgan Chase ("JP Morgan") as their custodian. The others used The Bank of New York Mellon ("BONY").

The custodial banks did not own record title either. JP Morgan and BONY are two of more than 800 custodial banks and brokers who are participating members of DTC.

> The vast majority of publicly traded shares in the United States are registered on the companies' books not in the name of beneficial owners— i.e., those investors who paid for, and have

the right to vote and dispose of, the shares—but rather in the name of "Cede & Co.," the name used by The Depository Trust Company ("DTC").

Shares registered in this manner are commonly referred to as being held in "street name." . . . DTC holds the shares on behalf of banks and brokers, which in turn hold on behalf of their clients (who are the underlying beneficial owners or other intermediaries).

John C. Wilcox, John J. Purcell III, & Hye-Won Choi, *"Street Name" Registration & The Proxy Solicitation Process, in A Practical Guide to SEC Proxy and Compensation Rules* 10-3, 10-3 (Amy Goodman et al. eds., 4th ed. 2007 & 2008 Supp.) [hereinafter *Street Name*] (footnote omitted).

The history of how we arrived at this ownership structure is important and informative.[1]

Prior to 1970, negotiation was the most common method used to transfer stock in the United States. The owner would endorse the physical certificate to the name of the assignee on the back of the certificate. This endorsement instruct[ed] the corporation, upon notification, [about] the change in ownership of the shares on its corporate books. If the parties used the services of a broker, the seller would transfer the certificate to his brokerage firm. The brokerage firm representing the customer buying the security would receive the physical certificate and transfer it to the buyer as the new record owner of the security. Occasionally, the new owner might request that the physical certificate remain at the street address of the brokerage firm to facilitate the transfer of the certificate in a subsequent sale.

Wolfe, *supra,* at 180 (footnotes omitted).

Transfer of securities in the traditional certificate-based system was a complicated, labor-intensive process. Each time securities were traded, the physical certificates had to be delivered from the seller to the buyer, and in the case of registered securities the certificates had to be surrendered to the issuer or its transfer agent for registration of transfer.

Prefatory Note at 2.

By the late 1960s, increased trading rendered the certificate system obsolete. The paperwork burden reached "crisis proportions." *Id.*

> Stock certificates and related documents were piled "halfway to the ceiling" in some offices; clerical personnel were working overtime, six and seven days a week, with some firms using a second or even a third shift to process each day's transaction. Hours of trading on the exchange and over the counter were curtailed to give back offices additional time after the closing bell. Deliveries to customers and similar activities dropped seriously behind, and the number of errors in brokers' records, as well as the time to trace and correct these errors, exacerbated the crisis.

Wolfe, *supra,* at 181 n.49 (quoting *SEC Study* at 219 n.1). "The difficulty that brokers and dealers experienced in keeping their records due to the volume of transactions and their thin capitalization caused many brokerage firms to declare bankruptcy and many investors to realize losses." *Id.* at 182.

Congress responded by passing the Securities Investor Protection Act of 1970, which directed the SEC to study the practices leading to the growing crisis in securities transfer. 15 U.S.C. § 78kkk(g). The SEC recommended discontinuing the physical movement of certificates and adopting a depository system. Wolfe, *supra,* at 182 n.58 (citing *SEC Study* at 13). Congress then passed the Securities Acts Amendments of 1975, which directed the SEC to "use its authority under this chapter to end the physical movement of securities certificates in connection with the settlement among brokers and dealers of transactions in securities consummated by means of the mails or any means or instrumentalities of interstate commerce." 15 U.S.C. § 78q-1(e). In a resulting report, the SEC found that "registering securities in other than the name of the beneficial owner" was essential to establishing "a national system for the prompt and accurate clearance and settlement of securities transactions." Kahan & Rock, *supra,* at 1237 n.49.

Thus was born the federal policy of immobilizing share certificates through a depository system. "Congress called for a more efficient process for comparison, clearing, and settlement in a national market system, and for the end of the physical movement of securities certificates in connection with the settlement of transactions among brokers and dealers." Egon Guttman, *Transfer of Securities: State and Federal Interaction,* 12 Cardozo L. Rev. 437, 447 (1990); *accord* S. REP. NO. 94-75 at 5 (1975) ("A national clearance and settlement system is clearly needed."). To comply, "[b]rokerages and banks created [depositories] to allow them to deposit certificates centrally (so-called `jumbo certificates,' often representing tens or hundreds of thousands of shares) and leave them at rest." Larry T. Garvin, *The Changed (And Changing?) Uniform Commercial Code,* 26 Fla. St. U. L. Rev. 285, 315 (1999).

In 1973, just after the paperwork crisis and with the federal writing on the wall, the members of the New York Stock Exchange created DTC to serve as a depository and clearing agency. Originally there were three regional depositories in addition to DTC: the Midwest Securities Depository Trust Company, which held through its nominee, Kray & Co.; the Pacific Securities Depository Trust Company, which held through its nominee, Pacific & Co; and the Philadelphia Depository Trust Company, which held through its nominee, Philadep & Co. "[I]n the 1990's DTC . . . assumed the activities of the [other] depositories." Carnell & Hanks, *supra,* at 26. Today DTC is the world's largest securities depository and the only domestic depository. Kahan & Rock, *supra,* at 1238 n.50. "DTC is owned by its `participants,' which are the member organizations of the various national stock exchanges (*e.g.,* State Street Bank, Merrill Lynch, Goldman Sachs & Co.)." *Street Name* at 10-6 to 10-7.

DTC has been estimated to hold "about three-quarters of [the] shares in publicly traded companies." Garvin, *supra,* at 315; *accord* Kahan & Rock, *supra,* at 1236; *Street Name* at 10-4 n.2. "The shares of each company held by DTC are typically represented by only one or more `immobilized' jumbo stock certificates held in DTC's vaults." *Street Name* at 10-7. "The immobilized jumbo certificates are the direct result of Section 17A(e) of the Exchange Act, in which Congress instructed the SEC to `use its authority . . . to end the physical movement of securities certificates. . . .'" *Id.* at 10-7 n.10.

The depository system is what enables public trading of securities to take place. In 2014, the NYSE reported average *daily* volume of approximately 1 *billion* shares and approximately 4 *million* separate trades. *See* NYSE Factbook, http://www.nysedata.com/factbook (last visited June 19, 2015). The failure of the certificate-based system to keep up with much lower trading volumes in the 1960s demonstrates that it cannot meet current demand. *Prefatory Note* at 2. Without immobilization and DTC, "implementing a system to settle securities within five business days (T+5), much less today's norm of T+3 or the current goals of T+1 or T+0, would simply be impossible." Kahan & Rock, *supra,* at 1238. Trading at current levels is only possible because of share immobilization and DTC. *Street Name* at 10-7; *accord* Garvin, *supra,* at 315-16; *Prefatory Note* at 2-3.

Because of the federal policy of share immobilization, it is now Cede—not the ultimate beneficial owner and not the DTC-participant banks and brokers—that appears on the stock ledger of a Delaware corporation. Cede is typically the largest holder on the stock ledger of most publicly traded Delaware corporations. *Street Name* at 10-6. To preserve the pre-immobilization status quo—at least at the federal level—the SEC provided that for purposes of federal law, the custodial banks and brokers remain the record holders. Depositories are defined as "clearing agencies." 15 U.S.C. § 78c(23)(A). The term "record holder" is defined as "any broker, dealer, voting trustee, bank, association or other entity that exercises fiduciary powers which holds securities of record in nominee name or otherwise or as a participant in a clearing agency registered pursuant to section 17A of the Act." 17 C.F.R. § 240.14c-1(i). The term "entity that exercises fiduciary powers" is similarly defined as "any entity that holds securities in nominee name or otherwise on behalf of a beneficial owner but does not include a clearing agency registered pursuant to section 17A of the Act or a broker or a dealer." *Id.* § 240.14c-1(c). Federal law thus looks through DTC when determining a corporation's record holders. For example, when determining whether an issuer has 500 or more record holders of a class of its equity securities such that it must register under 15 U.S.C. § 781(g), DTC does not count as a single holder of record. Each DTC participant member counts as a holder of record. Michael K. Molitor, *Will More Sunlight Fade The Pink Sheets?*, 39 Ind. L. Rev. 309, 315-16 (2006) (citing SEC interpretive releases).

The federal regulations also ensure that a corporation can easily find out the identities of the banks and brokers who hold shares through DTC. Federal regulations require that DTC "furnish a securities position listing promptly to each issuer whose securities are held in the name of the clearing agency or its nominee." 17 C.F.R. § 240.17Ad-8(b). The participant listing is known colloquially as the "Cede breakdown," and it identifies for a particular date the custodial banks and brokers that hold shares in fungible bulk as of that date along with the number of shares held. A Delaware corporation can obtain a Cede breakdown with ease. In 1981, this court noted that a Cede breakdown could be obtained in a matter of minutes. *Hatleigh Corp. v. Lane Bryant, Inc.,* 428 A.2d 350, 354 (Del. Ch. 1981). A Cede breakdown can now be obtained through DTC's website or by calling the DTC "Proxy Services Hotline." Issuers use the Cede breakdown to understand their stockholder profile, and proxy solicitors use it when advising clients. Commentary regards the information as reliable. *Handbook for the Conduct of Shareholders' Meetings* 40 (ABA Business Law Section, Corporate Governance Committee ed., 2000) (identifying the "lists of holders obtained from depositories" as one of the documents that can be relied on in "determining the shares entitled to vote and tabulating the vote").

A publicly traded corporation cannot avoid going through DTC. Federal law requires that when submitting a matter for a stockholder vote, an issuer must send a broker search card at least twenty business days prior to the record date to any "broker, dealer, voting trustee, bank, association, or other entity that exercises fiduciary powers in nominee name" that the company "knows" is holding shares for beneficial owners. 17 C.F.R. § 240.14a-13(a). Rule 14a-13 provides that "[i]f the registrant's list of security holders indicates that some of its securities are registered in the name of a clearing agency registered pursuant to Section 17A of the Act (e.g., `Cede & Co.,' nominee for Depository Trust Company), the registrant *shall make* appropriate inquiry of the clearing agency and thereafter of the participants in such clearing agency." *Id.* § 240.14a-13(a) n.1 (emphasis added). An issuer cannot look only at its own records and treat Cede as a single, monolithic owner.

Shareholder Proposals   2.7.9

At the annual stockholder meeting, directors ask stockholders to vote on certain matters, including the election of directors and other matters, like the ratification of the board's selection of a corporate auditor. But, directors do not have exclusive control over the agenda at a stockholder meeting. Stockholders also have the right to put proposals and questions before the meeting. Some matters that are proposed by stockholders, including amendments to bylaws are expressly permitted by the state corporate law. Others are governed by bylaws, for example stockholder nomination of candidates for the position of director.

For publicly-traded corporations, the process by which a stockholder can get access to the company's proxy statement to put a question before the shareholders at a meeting is governed by SEC regulation. The SEC's 14a-8 rules have been developed to govern when a board is required to put a shareholder proposal on the corporate proxy statement, or to be more precise rules governing when a board is permitted to exclude a shareholder proposal from the corporation's proxy materials sent to stockholders.

Although many shareholder proposals are focused on traditional corporate governance issues, there is a long history of social activists, especially faith-based groups like the Interfaith Center on Corporate Responsibility, using the shareholder proposal process to put important social issues on the agendas of corporate America. For example, during the 1970s, shareholders used the shareholder proposal process to raise questions about corporate support for the war in Vietnam. In the 1980s, the anti-Apartheid movement used the shareholder proposal process to raise awareness of the evils of Apartheid in South Africa.

14a-8 Shareholder Proposals   2.7.9.1

A "proxy statement" is a required disclosure
document that publicly traded companies must send
to all beneficial stockholders prior to any meeting of the
stockholders. The proxy statement describes for beneficial
stockholders the business of the upcoming meeting and include a
voting proxy that a beneficial stockholder can return to the record
holder. The most common business at a meeting is the annual
election of directors. However, a board can bring any business or
question to the stockholders for consideration and a vote.

The contents of this document are laid out in a series of rules under the '34 Act. The rules governing how a stockholder can get access to a corporation's proxy statement for the purpose of presenting proposals to fellow shareholders for their consideration at annual shareholder meetings are presented below in a unique FAQ format.

The default rule is that any proposal put forward by an eligible stockholder in a timely manner must be included in the corporate proxy. However, the board is not required to include all proposals in the proxy. There are a number of very important exceptions to the inclusion requirement, and they are laid out in the 14a-8 rules that follow.

§ 240.14a-8   Shareholder proposals.

This section addresses when a company must include a shareholder's proposal in its proxy statement and identify the proposal in its form of proxy when the company holds an annual or special meeting of shareholders. In summary, in order to have your shareholder proposal included on a company's proxy card, and included along with any supporting statement in its proxy statement, you must be eligible and follow certain procedures. Under a few specific circumstances, the company is permitted to exclude your proposal, but only after submitting its reasons to the Commission. We structured this section in a question-and-answer format so that it is easier to understand. The references to "you" are to a shareholder seeking to submit the proposal.

(a) Question 1: What is a proposal? A shareholder proposal is your recommendation or requirement that the company and/or its board of directors take action, which you intend to present at a meeting of the company's shareholders. Your proposal should state as clearly as possible the course of action that you believe the company should follow. If your proposal is placed on the company's proxy card, the company must also provide in the form of proxy means for shareholders to specify by boxes a choice between approval or disapproval, or abstention. Unless otherwise indicated, the word "proposal" as used in this section refers both to your proposal, and to your corresponding statement in support of your proposal (if any).

(b) [To be eligible to submit a proposal, you must satisfy the following requirements:

(i) You must have continuously held:

(A) At least $2,000 in market value of the company's securities entitled to vote on the proposal for at least three years; or

(B) At least $15,000 in market value of the company's securities entitled to vote on the proposal for at least two years; or

(C) At least $25,000 in market value of the company's securities entitled to vote on the proposal for at least one year; or

(D) The amounts specified in paragraph (b)(3) of this section. This paragraph (b)(1)(i)(D) will expire on the same date that §240.14a-8(b)(3) expires; and

(ii) You must provide the company with a written statement that you intend to continue to hold the requisite amount of securities, determined in accordance with paragraph (b)(1)(i)(A) through (C) of this section, through the date of the shareholders' meeting for which the proposal is submitted; and

(iii) You must provide the company with a written statement that you are able to meet with the company in person or via teleconference no less than 10 calendar days, nor more than 30 calendar days, after submission of the shareholder proposal. You must include your contact information as well as business days and specific times that you are available to discuss the proposal with the company. You must identify times that are within the regular business hours of the company's principal executive offices. If these hours are not disclosed in the company's proxy statement for the prior year's annual meeting, you must identify times that are between 9 a.m. and 5:30 p.m. in the time zone of the company's principal executive offices. If you elect to co-file a proposal, all co-filers must either:

(A) Agree to the same dates and times of availability, or

(B) Identify a single lead filer who will provide dates and times of the lead filer's availability to engage on behalf of all co-filers; and

(iv) If you use a representative to submit a shareholder proposal on your behalf, you must provide the company with written documentation that:

(A) Identifies the company to which the proposal is directed;

(B) Identifies the annual or special meeting for which the proposal is submitted;

(C) Identifies you as the proponent and identifies the person acting on your behalf as your representative;

(D) Includes your statement authorizing the designated representative to submit the proposal and otherwise act on your behalf;

(E) Identifies the specific topic of the proposal to be submitted;

(F) Includes your statement supporting the proposal; and

(G) Is signed and dated by you.

(v) The requirements of paragraph (b)(1)(iv) of this section shall not apply to shareholders that are entities so long as the representative's authority to act on the shareholder's behalf is apparent and self-evident such that a reasonable person would understand that the agent has authority to submit the proposal and otherwise act on the shareholder's behalf.

(vi) For purposes of paragraph (b)(1)(i) of this section, you may not aggregate your holdings with those of another shareholder or group of shareholders to meet the requisite amount of securities necessary to be eligible to submit a proposal.

(2) One of the following methods must be used to demonstrate your eligibility to submit a proposal:

(i) If you are the registered holder of your securities, which means that your name appears in the company's records as a shareholder, the company can verify your eligibility on its own, although you will still have to provide the company with a written statement that you intend to continue to hold the requisite amount of securities, determined in accordance with paragraph (b)(1)(i)(A) through (C) of this section, through the date of the meeting of shareholders.

(ii) If, like many shareholders, you are not a registered holder, the company likely does not know that you are a shareholder, or how many shares you own. In this case, at the time you submit your proposal, you must prove your eligibility to the company in one of two ways:

(A) The first way is to submit to the company a written statement from the "record" holder of your securities (usually a broker or bank) verifying that, at the time you submitted your proposal, you continuously held at least $2,000, $15,000, or $25,000 in market value of the company's securities entitled to vote on the proposal for at least three years, two years, or one year, respectively. ...;]

(c) [Question 3: How many proposals may I submit? Each person may submit no more than one proposal, directly or indirectly, to a company for a particular shareholders' meeting. A person may not rely on the securities holdings of another person for the purpose of meeting the eligibility requirements and submitting multiple proposals for a particular shareholders' meeting.]

(d) Question 4: How long can my proposal be? The proposal, including any accompanying supporting statement, may not exceed 500 words.

(e) Question 5: What is the deadline for submitting a proposal? (1) If you are submitting your proposal for the company's annual meeting, you can in most cases find the deadline in last year's proxy statement. However, if the company did not hold an annual meeting last year, or has changed the date of its meeting for this year more than 30 days from last year's meeting, you can usually find the deadline in one of the company's quarterly reports on Form 10-Q (§ 249.308a of this chapter), or in shareholder reports of investment companies under § 270.30d-1 of this chapter of the Investment Company Act of 1940. In order to avoid controversy, shareholders should submit their proposals by means, including electronic means, that permit them to prove the date of delivery.

(2) The deadline is calculated in the following manner if the proposal is submitted for a regularly scheduled annual meeting. The proposal must be received at the company's principal executive offices not less than 120 calendar days before the date of the company's proxy statement released to shareholders in connection with the previous year's annual meeting. However, if the company did not hold an annual meeting the previous year, or if the date of this year's annual meeting has been changed by more than 30 days from the date of the previous year's meeting, then the deadline is a reasonable time before the company begins to print and send its proxy materials.

(3) If you are submitting your proposal for a meeting of shareholders other than a regularly scheduled annual meeting, the deadline is a reasonable time before the company begins to print and send its proxy materials.

(f) Question 6: What if I fail to follow one of the eligibility or procedural requirements explained in answers to Questions 1 through 4 of this section? (1) The company may exclude your proposal, but only after it has notified you of the problem, and you have failed adequately to correct it. Within 14 calendar days of receiving your proposal, the company must notify you in writing of any procedural or eligibility deficiencies, as well as of the time frame for your response. Your response must be postmarked, or transmitted electronically, no later than 14 days from the date you received the company's notification. A company need not provide you such notice of a deficiency if the deficiency cannot be remedied, such as if you fail to submit a proposal by the company's properly determined deadline. If the company intends to exclude the proposal, it will later have to make a submission under § 240.14a-8 and provide you with a copy under Question 10 below, § 240.14a-8(j).

(2) If you fail in your promise to hold the required number of securities through the date of the meeting of shareholders, then the company will be permitted to exclude all of your proposals from its proxy materials for any meeting held in the following two calendar years.

(g) Question 7: Who has the burden of persuading the Commission or its staff that my proposal can be excluded? Except as otherwise noted, the burden is on the company to demonstrate that it is entitled to exclude a proposal.

(h) Question 8: Must I appear personally at the shareholders' meeting to present the proposal? (1) Either you, or your representative who is qualified under state law to present the proposal on your behalf, must attend the meeting to present the proposal. Whether you attend the meeting yourself or send a qualified representative to the meeting in your place, you should make sure that you, or your representative, follow the proper state law procedures for attending the meeting and/or presenting your proposal.

(2) If the company holds its shareholder meeting in whole or in part via electronic media, and the company permits you or your representative to present your proposal via such media, then you

may appear through electronic media rather than traveling to the meeting to appear in person.

(3) If you or your qualified representative fail to appear and present the proposal, without good cause, the company will be permitted to exclude all of your proposals from its proxy materials for any meetings held in the following two calendar years.

(i) Question 9: If I have complied with the procedural requirements, on what other bases may a company rely to exclude my proposal?
(1) Improper under state law: If the proposal is not a proper subject for action by shareholders under the laws of the jurisdiction of the company's organization;

Note to paragraph (i)(1): Depending on the subject matter, some proposals are not considered proper under state law if they would be binding on the company if approved by shareholders. In our experience, most proposals that are cast as recommendations or requests that the board of directors take specified action are proper under state law. Accordingly, we will assume that a proposal drafted as a recommendation or suggestion is proper unless the company demonstrates otherwise.

(2) Violation of law: If the proposal would, if implemented, cause the company to violate any state, federal, or foreign law to which it is subject;

Note to paragraph (i)(2): We will not apply this basis for exclusion to permit exclusion of a proposal on grounds that it would violate foreign law if compliance with the foreign law would result in a violation of any state or federal law.

(3) Violation of proxy rules: If the proposal or supporting statement is contrary to any of the Commission's proxy rules, including § 240.14a-9, which prohibits materially false or misleading statements in proxy soliciting materials;

(4) Personal grievance; special interest: If the proposal relates to the redress of a personal claim or grievance against the company or any other person, or if it is designed to result in a benefit to you, or to

further a personal interest, which is not shared by the other shareholders at large;

(5) Relevance: If the proposal relates to operations which account for less than 5 percent of the company's total assets at the end of its most recent fiscal year, and for less than 5 percent of its net earnings and gross sales for its most recent fiscal year, and is not otherwise significantly related to the company's business;

(6) Absence of power/authority: If the company would lack the power or authority to implement the proposal;

(7) Management functions: If the proposal deals with a matter relating to the company's ordinary business operations;

(8) Director elections: If the proposal:

(i) Would disqualify a nominee who is standing for election;

(ii) Would remove a director from office before his or her term expired;

(iii) Questions the competence, business judgment, or character of one or more nominees or directors;

(iv) Seeks to include a specific individual in the company's proxy materials for election to the board of directors; or

(v) Otherwise could affect the outcome of the upcoming election of directors.

(9) Conflicts with company's proposal: If the proposal directly conflicts with one of the company's own proposals to be submitted to shareholders at the same meeting;

Note to paragraph (i)(9): A company's submission to the Commission under this section should specify the points of conflict with the company's proposal.

(10) Substantially implemented: If the company has already substantially implemented the proposal;

Note to paragraph (i)(10): A company may exclude a shareholder proposal that would provide an advisory vote or seek future advisory votes to approve the compensation of executives as disclosed pursuant to Item 402 of Regulation S-K (§ 229.402 of this chapter) or any successor to Item 402 (a "say-on-pay vote") or that relates to the frequency of say-on-pay votes, provided that in the most recent shareholder vote required by § 240.14a-21(b) of this chapter a single year (i.e., one, two, or three years) received approval of a majority of votes cast on the matter and the company has adopted a policy on the frequency of say-on-pay votes that is consistent with the choice of the majority of votes cast in the most recent shareholder vote required by § 240.14a-21(b) of this chapter.

(11) Duplication: If the proposal substantially duplicates another proposal previously submitted to the company by another proponent that will be included in the company's proxy materials for the same meeting;

(12) [Resubmissions. If the proposal addresses substantially the same subject matter as a proposal, or proposals, previously included in the company's proxy materials within the preceding five calendar years if the most recent vote occurred within the preceding three calendar years and the most recent vote was:

(i) Less than 5 percent of the votes cast if previously voted on once;

(ii) Less than 15 percent of the votes cast if previously voted on twice; or

(iii) Less than 25 percent of the votes cast if previously voted on three or more times.; and]

(13) Specific amount of dividends: If the proposal relates to specific amounts of cash or stock dividends.

(j) Question 10: What procedures must the company follow if it intends to exclude my proposal? (1) If the company intends to exclude a proposal from its proxy materials, it must file its reasons with the Commission no later than 80 calendar days before it files its definitive proxy statement and form of proxy with the Commission. The company must simultaneously provide you with a copy of its submission. The Commission staff may permit the company to make its submission later than 80 days before the company files its definitive proxy statement and form of proxy, if the company demonstrates good cause for missing the deadline.

(2) The company must file six paper copies of the following:

(i) The proposal;

(ii) An explanation of why the company believes that it may exclude the proposal, which should, if possible, refer to the most recent applicable authority, such as prior Division letters issued under the rule; and

(iii) A supporting opinion of counsel when such reasons are based on matters of state or foreign law.

(k) Question 11: May I submit my own statement to the Commission responding to the company's arguments?

Yes, you may submit a response, but it is not required. You should try to submit any response to us, with a copy to the company, as soon as possible after the company makes its submission. This way, the Commission staff will have time to consider fully your submission before it issues its response. You should submit six paper copies of your response.

(l) Question 12: If the company includes my shareholder proposal in its proxy materials, what information about me must it include along with the proposal itself?

(1) The company's proxy statement must include your name and address, as well as the number of the company's voting securities that you hold. However, instead of providing that information, the company may instead include a statement that it will provide the information to shareholders promptly upon receiving an oral or written request.

(2) The company is not responsible for the contents of your proposal or supporting statement.

(m) Question 13: What can I do if the company includes in its proxy statement reasons why it believes shareholders should not vote in favor of my proposal, and I disagree with some of its statements?

(1) The company may elect to include in its proxy statement reasons why it believes shareholders should vote against your proposal. The company is allowed to make arguments reflecting its own point of view, just as you may express your own point of view in your proposal's supporting statement.

(2) However, if you believe that the company's opposition to your proposal contains materially false or misleading statements that may violate our anti-fraud rule, § 240.14a-9, you should promptly send to the Commission staff and the company a letter explaining the reasons for your view, along with a copy of the company's statements opposing your proposal. To the extent possible, your letter should include specific factual information demonstrating the inaccuracy of the company's claims. Time permitting, you may wish to try to work out your differences with the company by yourself before contacting the Commission staff.

(3) We require the company to send you a copy of its statements opposing your proposal before it sends its proxy materials, so that you may bring to our attention any materially false or misleading statements, under the following timeframes:

(i) If our no-action response requires that you make revisions to your proposal or supporting statement as a condition to requiring the company to include it in its proxy materials, then the company must provide you with a copy of its opposition statements no later than 5 calendar days after the company receives a copy of your revised proposal; or

(ii) In all other cases, the company must provide you with a copy of its opposition statements no later than 30 calendar days before its files definitive copies of its proxy statement and form of proxy under § 240.14a-6. [...]

New York City Employees' Retirement System v.   2.7.9.2
Dole Food Co.

NYC EMPLOYEES RETIREMENT SYSTEM V. DOLE FOOD CO.
795 F. Supp. 95 (1992)

NYCERS is a public pension fund that owns approximately 164,841 shares of common stock in Dole Food Company, Inc. ("Dole"). Affidavit of Elizabeth Holtzman Dated April 8, 1992 ("Holtzman Afft.") ¶ 3. On December 12, 1991, New York City Comptroller Elizabeth Holtzman, in her capacity as the custodian of NYCERS' assets, wrote to the executive vice president of Dole, requesting Dole to include the following proposal ("the NYCERS proposal") in its proxy statement prior to its annual meeting:

NEW YORK CITY EMPLOYEE'S [sic.] RETIREMENT SYSTEM

SHAREHOLDER RESOLUTION ON HEALTH CARE

TO DOLE FOOD COMPANY, INC.

WHEREAS: The Dole Food Company is concerned with remaining competitive in the domestic and world marketplace, acknowledging the positive relationship between the health and well being of its employees and productivity, and the resulting effect on corporate growth and financial stability; and

WHEREAS: Sustained double-digit increases in health care costs have put severe financial pressure on a company attempting to continue to provide adequate health care for its employees and their dependents; and

WHEREAS: The company has a societal obligation to conduct its affairs in a way which promotes the health and well being of all;

BE IT THEREFORE RESOLVED: That the shareholders request the Board of Directors to establish a committee of the Board consisting of outside and independent directors for the purpose of evaluating the impact of a representative cross section of the various health care reform proposals being considered by national policy makers on the company and

their [sic.] competitive standing in domestic and international markets. These various proposals can be grouped in three generic categories; the single pay- or model (as in the Canadian plan), the limited payor (as in the Pepper Commission Report) and the employer mandated (as in the Kennedy-Waxman legislation).

Further, the aforementioned committee should be directed to prepare a report of its findings. The report should be prepared in a reasonable time, at a reasonable cost and should be made available to any shareholder upon written request.

SUPPORTING STATEMENT

Our nation is now at a crossroads on health care. Because of cutbacks in public programs, jobs that offer no benefits and efforts by employers to shift health care costs to workers, 50 million Americans have health care coverage that is inadequate to meet their needs and another 37 million have no protection at all.

The United States spends $2 billion a day, or eleven percent of its gross national product, on health care. As insurance premiums increase 18 to 30 percent a year, basic health care has moved well beyond the reach of a growing number of working families. This increase also places heavy pressure on employer labor costs. There is no end in sight to this trend.

As a result and because of the significant social and public policy issues attendant to operations involving health care, we urge shareholders to SUPPORT the resolution. Holtzman Afft., Exhibit B (emphasis in original).

On January 16, 1992, J. Brett Tibbitts, deputy general counsel of Dole Food Company, Inc., wrote to the office of chief counsel of the Securities & Exchange Commission's ("SEC") division of corporation finance and stated Dole's position that Dole could exclude the NYCERS proposal from its proxy statement because the proposal concerned employee benefits, an assertedly "ordinary business operation," and both SEC regulations and the law of the Dole's state of incorporation relegate such ordinary business operations to management, not shareholder, control.

On February 10, 1992, John Brousseau, special counsel to the SEC's division of corporation finance, responded to Tibbitts' letter with the following written statement:

> The proposal relates to the preparation of a report by a Committee of the Company's Board of Directors to evaluate various health-care proposals being considered by national policy makers.

> There appears to be some basis for your view that the proposal may be excluded pursuant to rule 14a-8(c)(7) because the proposal is directed at involving the Company in the political or legislative process relating to an aspect of the Company's operations. Accordingly, we will not recommend enforcement action to the Commission if the proposal is omitted from the Company's proxy materials. In reaching a position, the staff has not found it necessary to address the alternative basis for omission on which the Company relies. Holtzman Afft., Exhibit D.

On March 19, 1992, Brousseau reported to NYCERS that the SEC had denied NY-CERS' request for the SEC to review the SEC staff determination on the NYCERS proposal. Holtzman Afft., Exhibit E. On April 9,1992, NYCERS brought the instant action. [...]

II. *Discussion*

A party seeking a preliminary injunction must normally establish a) irreparable harm and b) either a substantial likelihood of success on the merits, or sufficiently serious questions on the merits to make them fair grounds for litigation with a balance of hardships tipping decidedly toward the moving party. *Abdul Wali v. Coughlin*, 754 F.2d 1015, 1025 (2d Cir.1985). In this case, NYCERS must prove a substantial likelihood of success on the merits because NYCERS requests a so-called mandatory injunction, *i.e.,* one that disturbs the *status quo,* and the relief that NYCERS seeks from the preliminary injunction is identical to that sought as the ultimate relief in the action. *Abdul Wali*, 754 F.2d at 1025-26.

A. Substantial Likelihood of Success on the Merits

The federal securities regulation that governs proposals of securities holders is 17 CFR § 240.14a-8 ("Rule 14a-8"). Rule 14(a)-8(a) states in pertinent part:

> If any security holder of a registrant notifies the registrant of his intention to present a proposal for action at a forthcoming meeting of the registrant's security holders, the registrant shall set forth the proposal in its proxy statement....

However, Rule 14(a)-8(c) allows a corporation to omit a shareholder proposal from its proxy statement because of certain enumerated circumstances. In substance, Dole argues that the instant matter fits within the "ordinary business operations," "insignificant relation," and "beyond power to effectuate" exceptions enumerated in Rule *14(a)-8(c)* .

The corporation has the burden to show that a proposal fits within an exception to Rule 14(a)-8(a). [...]

On April 16, this Court held a hearing pursuant to NYCERS' request for a mandatory injunction. At the hearing, counsel for both parties elaborated on the legal arguments that they had submitted in their papers, but neither party produced any witnesses, or any proof by affidavit of the nature of Dole's employee health care programs, coverage, costs, union agreements or insurance contracts. Indeed, the argument and the parties' briefs were largely abstract in nature. Nevertheless, for the reasons stated below, we find that NY-CERS has met its burden of showing that it is substantially likely that Dole would fail to show on the merits that the proposal falls within one of the enumerated exceptions.

1. *Rule 14a-8(c)(7): "Ordinary Business Operations"*

Rule 14a-8(c)(7) states that a corporation may exclude a shareholder proposal from a proxy statement

> [i]f the proposal deals with a matter relating to the conduct of the ordinary business operations of the registrant.

The term "ordinary business operations" is neither self-explanatory nor easy to explain. The exception does not elaborate on whether "business operations" encompass merely certain routine internal functions or whether they can extend to cost-benefit analyses or profit-making activity. The SEC's commentary on the current version of the "ordinary business operations" exception states, "[W]here proposals involve business matters that are mundane in nature *and* do not involve any substantial policy or other considerations, the sub-paragraph may be relied upon to omit them." Adoption of Amendments Relating to Proposals by Security Holders, 41 Fed.Reg. 52,994, 52,998 (1976) (emphasis added). This commentary indicates that even if the proposal touches on the way daily business matters are conducted, the statement may not be excluded if it involves a significant strategic decision as to those daily business matters, *i.e.,* one that will significantly affect the manner in which a company does business. One Court has held that the purpose of the "ordinary business exception" is to prevent shareholders from seeking to "assert the power to dictate the minutiae of daily business decisions." *Grimes v. Centerior Energy Corp.,* 909 F.2d 529, 531 (D.C.Cir.1990)[...].

While we give due deference to the SEC staff opinion letter in this case and other similar cases, we find that NYCERS has shown under that the proposal does not relate to "ordinary business operations." If one aspect of "ordinary business operations" is certain, it is that the outcome of close cases such as the instant one are largely fact-dependent. Nevertheless, Dole has not provided the Court with any information on (1) whether Dole has a health insurance program; (2) if such a program exists at Dole, how it operates; and (3) the amount of corporate financial resources that Dole devotes to health insurance. Instead, Dole argues, "To the extent [the NYCER proposal] relates to Dole's business at all, it relates to its employee relations and health care benefits, a matter traditionally within the "ordinary business" category. [...] In support of its position, Dole cites several SEC "No-Action" letters relating to proposals similar to the instant one. However, the SEC "No-Action" letters contain scarcely any analysis, and, while they are entitled to defer ence, they do not bind this Court. We note that the SEC itself has changed its reasoning as to why proposals relating to national employee health insurance relate to "ordinary business relations." The SEC has shifted rationales for rejecting proposals such as this one, initially stressing the "employee relations" aspect of national health insurance and then emphasizing its "political [and] legislative" dimensions.

We further find that the principal cases relied upon by Dole are distinguishable from the instant case. *Austin v. Consolidated Edison Co. of New York,* 788 F.Supp. 192 (S.D.N.Y.1992) involved an internal, relatively mundane plan to change the eligibility criteria of a company's specific retirement benefits policy, a subject of union collective bargaining. *Austin,* at 198. As Professor Marmor's affidavit demonstrates, however, the proposals in the instant case relate to a strategic policy choice as to the prospect of a major outlay to the federal treasury, as well as possible internal changes that may affect the entire scope of Dole's employee health insurance policy. [...] The question of which plan, if any, that Dole should support, and how Dole would choose to function under the plans *(e.g.,* "pay or play") could have large financial consequences on Dole. [...]

The proposed report primarily relates to Dole's policy making on an issue of social significance that, while not relating to a specific health care policy at Dole, nevertheless relates to a distinct type of operations that Dole has undoubtedly grappled with in the past. *See e.g. Pacific Telesis Group,* 1989 WL 245523, 1989 SEC No-Act. LEXIS 104, *supra,* at note 6. Accordingly, we do not find that the instant proposal relates to "ordinary business operations."

2. Rule 14a-8(c)(5): "Insignificant Relationship" Exception

Rule 14a-8(c)(5) states that a corporation may exclude a shareholder proposal from a proxy statement

> [i]f the proposal relates to operations which account for less than 5 percent of the registrant's total assets at the end of its most recent fiscal year, and for less than 5 percent of its net earnings and gross sales for its most recent fiscal year, *and* is not otherwise significantly related to the registrant's business, (emphasis supplied).

Dole does not dispute that the clear language of the NYCERS proposal in large part relates to national health insurance's impact on Dole. Without specific reference to Rule 14a-8(c)(5), Dole argues that the NYCERS proposal lacked a discrete nexus to Dole's distinct line of business, presumably the manufacture of food products. Dole's argument is essentially made under the exception referred to in the last phrase of Rule 14a-8(c)(5), *i.e.,* that the proposal is "not otherwise significantly related to the registrant's business." [...]

We need not address Dole's "nexus" argument because we find the activity addressed by the NYCERS proposal relates to activities that likely occupy outlays more than five percent of Dole's income. It is substantially likely that Dole's health insurance outlays constitute more than five percent of its income. Dole has offered no information on the percentage of its income that it devotes to employee health insurance. In his affidavit, Professor Mar-mor stated that nationwide, 1989 health care expenditures represented 56 percent of pre-tax company profits. Mar mor Afft. ¶ 5. We find it substantially likely that this figure applies to Dole to a greater or lesser extent. Because the subject of the proposed study likely relates to a significant aspect of Dole's business, we find that the proposal does not fall within the exception stated in Rule 14(a) — 8(c)(5).

3. *Rule H(a)-8(c)(6): "Beyond Power to Effectuate" Exception*

Rule 14(a)-8(c)(6) states that a corporation need not include a shareholder proposal on a proxy statement

[i]f the proposal deals with a matter beyond the registrant's power to effectuate....

Dole argues, "The NYCERS proposal requests the analysis of, and implicitly suggests that Dole should attempt to influence the selection of, national health care re form proposals." Dole Supplemental Memo at 8. However, Dole does not point to any language that suggests that a necessary consequence of the proposal is political lobbying. While couched in language that clearly supports a national solution to the problems of growing health insurance costs, the NYCERS proposal merely calls for the commission of a research report on national health insurance proposals and their impact on Dole's competitive standing. Moreover, we fail to see why such a study necessarily "deals with a matter beyond the registrant's power to effectuate." For example, a decision that Dole's interests mandate a choice to "pay" rather than "play" under two of the three major proposals would clearly be within Dole's power to effectuate if these proposals are enacted. Moreover, Dole might conceivably find that it is in its interests to draft such a proposal and lobby for its enactment. For the reasons stated above, we disagree with Dole's argument that the political aspect of this proposal means that it does not relate to Dole's business in a substantial way.

B. Irreparable Harm

The exclusion of the NYCERS proposal from the upcoming annual shareholder vote would mean that NYCERS would not be able to bring its proposal to Dole shareholders for another year. We find that Dole has established the required element of irreparable harm.[...]

Having found that the required showing has been met, this Court directs Dole to include in its proxy materials for its June 4, 1992 annual meeting NYCERS' shareholder proposal submitted to Dole by letter dated December 12, 1991.

Say on Pay Vote [Frank-Dodd, Sec 951] 2.7.9.3

In the wake of the Financial Crisis of 2008, Congress adopted the Frank-Dodd bill. Section 951 of Frank-Dodd requires regular votes by shareholders to approve executive compensation. Note that the structure and effect of the vote are sensitive to the 14a-8 process and comport with what one might expect of other shareholder proposals. When approving the "say on pay" votes, Congress was sensitive to the traditional preeminance of the state corporate law. Consequently, "say on pay" votes are precatory in nature.

SEC. 951. SHAREHOLDER VOTE ON EXECUTIVE COMPENSATION DISCLOSURES.

The Securities Exchange Act of 1934 (15 U.S.C. 78a et seq.) is amended by inserting after section 14 (15 U.S.C. 78n) the following:

SHAREHOLDER APPROVAL OF EXECUTIVE COMPENSATION.

`` (a) <<NOTE: Deadlines.>> Separate Resolution Required.--

`` (1) In general.--Not less frequently than once every 3 years, a proxy or consent or authorization for an annual or other meeting of the shareholders for which the proxy solicitation rules of the Commission require compensation disclosure shall include a separate resolution subject to shareholder vote to approve the compensation of executives, as disclosed pursuant to section 229.402 of title 17, Code of Federal Regulations, or any successor thereto.

`` (2) Frequency of vote.--Not less frequently than once every 6 years, a proxy or consent or authorization for an annual or other meeting of the shareholders for which the proxy solicitation rules of the Commission require compensation disclosure shall include a separate resolution subject to shareholder vote to determine whether votes on the resolutions required under paragraph (1) will occur every 1, 2, or 3 years.

``(b) Shareholder Approval of Golden Parachute Compensation.--

``(1) Disclosure.--... at which shareholders are asked to approve an acquisition, merger, consolidation, or proposed sale or other disposition of all or substantially all the assets of an issuer, the person making such solicitation shall disclose in the proxy or consent solicitation material, in a clear and simple form in accordance with regulations to be promulgated by the Commission, any agreements or understandings that such person has with any named executive officers of such issuer (or of the acquiring issuer, if such issuer is not the acquiring issuer) concerning any type of compensation (whether present, deferred, or contingent) that is based on or otherwise relates to the acquisition, merger, consolidation, sale, or other disposition of all or substantially all of the assets of the issuer and the aggregate total of all such compensation that may (and the conditions upon which it may) be paid or become payable to or on behalf of such executive officer.

``(2) Shareholder approval.--Any proxy or consent or authorization relating to the proxy or consent solicitation material containing the disclosure required by paragraph (1) shall include a separate resolution subject to shareholder vote to approve such agreements or understandings and compensation as disclosed, unless such agreements or understandings have been subject to a shareholder vote under subsection (a).

``(c) Rule of Construction.--The shareholder vote referred to in subsections (a) and (b) shall not be binding on the issuer or the board of directors of an issuer, and may not be construed--

``(1) as overruling a decision by such issuer or board of directors;

``(2) to create or imply any change to the fiduciary duties of such issuer or board of directors;

``(3) to create or imply any additional fiduciary duties for such issuer or board of directors; or

``(4) to restrict or limit the ability of shareholders to make proposals for inclusion in proxy materials related to executive compensation.

Stockholder Litigation   3

Before we turn to too much more case law, it is important to understand the particular procedural aspects of the stockholder litigation that we will be reading. Because the litigation involves stockholders, directors, and the corporation, it is procedurally different than litigation you may have seen until now in law school.

The source of these differences is often a question about who gets to speak for and vindicate the rights of the corporation - the board or the stockholder. Resolution of this question is especially important when it is the board itself that is accused of wrong-doing against the corporation.

Direct and Derivative Suits

3.1

Officers and directors of Delaware corporations are
subject to the jurisdiction of Delaware courts under
Delaware's long-arm statute for lawsuits related to
the corporation and their duties as directors and
officers of the corporation. By virtue of incorporating in Delaware
and maintaining an agent in Delaware for service of process,
directors of a Delaware corporation, no matter where they are, can
be served by making service on the corporation's agent as listed in
the corporation's certificate of incorporation.

Stockholders may bring different kinds of litigation against the
corporation. **Direct suits** are brought on behalf of the stockholder in
the stockholder's capacity as a stockholder and seek to vindicate the
rights of the stockholder. **Derivative suits** are brought by
stockholders on behalf of the corporation and seek to vindicate the
rights of the corporation. Stockholders seeking to bring a derivative
action on behalf of the corporation must comply with the
requirements of Chancery Rule 23.1.

Many times the most important question in stockholder litigation
turns on the type of litigation that is at issue. Stockholders may
attempt to characterize the litigation as direct in order to maintain
control, while boards may attempt to characterize the question
before the court as derivative in order to assert control over the
litigation and end it. Understanding the distinction between direct
and derivative suits can be confusing. However, there is a coherent
test (Tooley) for determining which is which.

Historical Development of Derivative Litigation

3.1.1

It is black-letter law that the board of directors of a
Delaware corporation exercises all corporate powers
and manages, or directs others in the management
of, the business and affairs of the corporation. One corporate power

exercised by the board of directors is the conduct of litigation that seeks to redress harm inflicted upon the corporation, including harm inflicted upon the corporation by its officers or directors from a breach of fiduciary duty owed to the corporation and its shareholders. Recognizing, however, that directors and officers of a corporation may not hold themselves accountable to the corporation for their own wrongdoing, courts of equity have created an ingenious device to police the activities of corporate fiduciaries: the shareholder's derivative suit. Chancellor Wolcott described this device:

Generally a cause of action belonging to a corporation can be asserted only by the corporation. However, whenever a corporation possesses a cause of action which it either refuses to assert or, by reason of circumstances, is unable to assert, equity will permit a stockholder to sue in his own name for the benefit of the corporation solely for the purpose of preventing injustice when it is apparent that the corporation's rights would not be protected otherwise.

As the above description reveals, a derivative action may not be pursued if the corporation is willing and able to assert the suit on its own behalf, *i.e.,* the complaining shareholder must give the board of directors the opportunity to manage the litigation to its satisfaction or the board of directors must for some reason be incapable of pursuing the litigation.

The requirement that shareholders exhaust their remedies within the corporation before pursuing derivative litigation is found in Court of Chancery Rule 23.1. Rule 23.1 requires that the complaint in a derivative action "allege with particularity the efforts, if any, made by the plaintiff to obtain the action the plaintiff desires from the directors or comparable authority and the reasons for the plaintiff's failure to obtain the action or for not making the effort." Even if attempting to obtain the action that the plaintiff desires from the board of directors would be futile because a majority of the directors suffer some disabling interest, the board may appoint a special litigation committee of disinterested directors that may recommend dismissal of the derivative action after a reasonable investigation. Rule 23.1 also requires, as does Section 327 of the

Delaware General Corporation Law, that the complaint allege that "the plaintiff was a stockholder of the corporation at the time of the transaction." Rule 23.1 further provides that a derivative action generally may not be dismissed or settled without approval of this Court and notice to other shareholders. The requirements of Rule 23.1, while burdensome to the equitable device created by the courts to remedy harm inflicted upon a corporation, are necessary to prevent the potentially disruptive effects of derivative litigation on the ability of a board of directors to direct the business and affairs of a corporation. The prerequisites to a derivative action, developed over time, have attempted to balance the Delaware prerogative that directors manage the affairs of a corporation with the realization that shareholder policing, via derivative actions, is a necessary check on the behavior of directors that serve in a fiduciary capacity to shareholders.

The exacting procedural prerequisites to the prosecution of a derivative action create incentives for plaintiffs to characterize their claims as "direct" or "individual" in the sense that they seek recovery not for harm done to the corporation, but for harm done to them. A decision finding that a complaint alleges direct claims allows plaintiffs to bypass the ability of the corporation's board to decide, in the best interests of the corporation, how to proceed with the litigation. In clear-cut cases, where the corporation has not been harmed by the conduct at issue in the litigation but the plaintiff has suffered injury, bypassing the board's involvement in the litigation is of little concern. In fact, it seems wholly inappropriate to allow a board of directors to control litigation where the corporation's concerns are only tangential to the claim and where the corporation would not share any eventual recovery.

Delaware long arm statute

3.1.2

You might wonder how it is the case that a corporate director sitting in New York or Massachusetts could be subject to the jurisdiction of the courts of Delaware. The short answer is that all persons who agree to become corporate directors also consent to jurisdiction of the Delaware courts under Delaware's "long arm statute."

§ 3114 Service of process on nonresident directors, trustees, members of the governing body or officers of Delaware corporations. [...]

(b) Every nonresident of this State who after January 1, 2004, accepts election or appointment as an officer of a corporation organized under the laws of this State, or who after such date serves in such capacity, and every resident of this State who so accepts election or appointment or serves in such capacity and thereafter removes residence from this State shall, by such acceptance or by such service, be deemed thereby to have consented to the appointment of the registered agent of such corporation (or, if there is none, the Secretary of State) as an agent upon whom service of process may be made in all civil actions or proceedings brought in this State, by or on behalf of, or against such corporation, in which such officer is a necessary or proper party, or in any action or proceeding against such officer for violation of a duty in such capacity, whether or not the person continues to serve as such officer at the time suit is commenced. Such acceptance or service as such officer shall be a signification of the consent of such officer that any process when so served shall be of the same legal force and validity as if served upon such officer within this State and such appointment of the registered agent (or, if there is none, the Secretary of State) shall be irrevocable. [...]

DGCL § 321 - Service of process

Certificates of incorporation all require the corporation to name a registered agent, along with an address in the state of Delaware where the agent may be contacted. The registered agent plays an important role in ensuring corporate officers and directors (their principles) are subject to the jurisdiction of the Delaware courts for the purpose of stockholder litigation and other litigation related to the corporation.

§ 321 Service of process on corporations.

(a) Service of legal process upon any corporation of this State shall be made by delivering a copy personally to any officer or director of the corporation in this State, or the registered agent of the corporation in this State, or by leaving it at the dwelling house or usual place of abode in this State of any officer, director or registered agent (if the registered agent be an individual), or at the registered office or other place of business of the corporation in this State.[...]

(b) In case the officer whose duty it is to serve legal process cannot by due diligence serve the process in any manner provided for by subsection (a) of this section, it shall be lawful to serve the process against the corporation upon the Secretary of State, and such service shall be as effectual for all intents and purposes as if made in any of the ways provided for in subsection (a) of this section.[...]

DGCL Sec. 327 - Derivative actions

3
.
1
4

In order to have standing in derivative litigation, a stockholder must have already been a stockholder at the time of the bad act that gave rise to the litigation.
This requirement prevents people from observing some bad act and then buying into a lawsuit.

§ 327. Stockholder's derivative action; allegation of stock ownership.

In any derivative suit instituted by a stockholder of a corporation, it shall be averred in the complaint that the plaintiff was a stockholder of the corporation at the time of the transaction of which such stockholder complains or that such stockholder's stock thereafter devolved upon such stockholder by operation of law.

Delaware Rules of Civil Procedure, Rule 23.1   3.1.5

The Delaware Rules of Civil Procedure lay out rules for bringing and maintaining a stockholder derivative action. Compliance with these rules is necessary in order for a claim to stay in court. Often times, defendants will move to dismiss a plaintiff's claim for failure to comply with the requirements of Rule 23.1.

The Rule 23.1 Motion to Dismiss often revolves around the characterization of the claim (direct v. derivative) and the independence of the directors (demand required/demand futility).

Rule 23.1. Derivative actions by shareholders.

(a) In a derivative action brought by one or more shareholders or members to enforce a right of a corporation or of an unincorporated association, the corporation or association having failed to enforce a right which may properly be asserted by it, the complaint shall allege that the plaintiff was a shareholder or member at the time of the transaction of which the plaintiff complains or that the plaintiff's share or membership thereafter devolved on the plaintiff by operation of law. The complaint shall also allege with particularity the efforts, if any, made by the plaintiff to obtain the action the plaintiff desires from the directors or comparable authority and the reasons for the plaintiff's failure to obtain the action or for not making the effort.

(b) Each person seeking to serve as a representative plaintiff on behalf of a corporation or unincorporated association pursuant to this Rule shall file with the Register in Chancery an affidavit stating that the person has not received, been promised or offered and will not accept any form of compensation, directly or indirectly, for prosecuting or serving as a representative party in the derivative action in which the person or entity is a named party except (i) such fees, costs or other payments as the Court expressly approves to be paid to or on behalf of such person, or (ii) reimbursement, paid by such person's attorneys, of actual and reasonable out-of pocket expenditures incurred directly in connection with the prosecution of the action. The affidavit required by this subpart shall be filed within 10 days after the earliest of the affiant filing the complaint, filing a motion to intervene in the action or filing a motion seeking appointment as a representative party in the action. An affidavit provided pursuant to this subpart shall not be construed to be a waiver of the attorney-client privilege.

(c) The action shall not be dismissed or compromised without the approval of the Court, and notice by mail, publication or otherwise of the proposed dismissal or compromise shall be given to shareholders or members in such manner as the Court directs; except that if the dismissal is to be without prejudice or with prejudice to the plaintiff only, then such dismissal shall be ordered without notice thereof if there is a showing that no compensation in any form has passed directly or indirectly from any of the defendants to the plaintiff or plaintiff's attorney and that no promise to give any such compensation has been made. At the time that any party moves or otherwise applies to the Court for approval of a compromise of all or any part of a derivative action, each representative plaintiff in such action shall file with the Register in Chancery a further affidavit in the form required by subpart (b) of this rule.

Tooley v. Donaldson Lufkin, & Jenrette, Inc.   316

In Tooley, the court was asked to determine whether shareholder litigation is direct or derivative. Rather than rely on a more traditional, and cumbersome, "special injury" test, the court in Tooley announced a new, simpler test for determining whether a stockholder action is direct or derivative. Since Tooley other jurisdictions, like New York, have abandoned their own versions of the special injury in favor of specifically adopting Delaware's Tooley standard.

Tooley v. DLJ

Delaware Supreme Court

845 A.2d 1031 (2004)

VEASEY, Chief Justice:

Plaintiff-stockholders brought a purported class action in the Court of Chancery, alleging that the members of the board of directors of their corporation breached their fiduciary duties by agreeing to a 22-day delay in closing a proposed merger. Plaintiffs contend that the delay harmed them due to the lost time-value of the cash paid for their shares. The Court of Chancery granted the defendants' motion to dismiss on the sole ground that the claims were, "at most," claims of the corporation being asserted derivatively. They were, thus, held not to be direct claims of the stockholders, individually. Thereupon, the Court held that the plaintiffs lost their standing to bring this action when they tendered their shares in connection with the merger.

Although the trial court's legal analysis of whether the complaint alleges a direct or derivative claim reflects some concepts in our prior jurisprudence, we believe those concepts are not helpful and should be regarded as erroneous. We set forth in this Opinion the law to be applied henceforth in determining whether a stockholder's claim is derivative or direct. That issue must turn *solely* on the following questions: (1) who suffered the alleged harm (the corporation or the suing stock-holders, individually); and (2) who would receive the benefit of any recovery or other remedy (the corporation or the stock-holders, individually)? [...]

Facts

Patrick Tooley and Kevin Lewis are former minority stockholders of Donaldson, Lufkin & Jenrette, Inc. (DLJ), a Delaware corporation engaged in investment banking. DLJ was acquired by Credit Suisse Group (Credit Suisse) in the Fall of 2000. Before that acquisition, AXA Financial, Inc.(AXA), which owned 71% of DLJ stock, controlled DLJ. Pursuant to a stockholder agreement between AXA and Credit Suisse, AXA agreed to exchange with Credit Suisse its DLJ stockholdings for a mix of stock and cash. The consideration [1034] received by AXA consisted primarily of stock. Cash made up one-third of the purchase price. Credit Suisse intended to acquire the remaining minority interests of publicly-held DLJ stock through a cash tender offer, followed by a merger of DLJ into a Credit Suisse subsidiary.

The tender offer price was set at $90 per share in cash. The tender offer was to expire 20 days after its commencement. The merger agreement, however, authorized two types of extensions. First, Credit Suisse could unilaterally extend the tender offer if certain conditions were not met, such as SEC regulatory approvals or certain payment obligations. Alternatively, DLJ and Credit Suisse could agree to postpone acceptance by Credit Suisse of DLJ stock tendered by the minority stockholders.

Credit Suisse availed itself of both types of extensions to postpone the closing of the tender offer. The tender offer was initially set to expire on October 5, 2000, but Credit Suisse invoked the five-day unilateral extension provided in the agreement. Later, by agreement between DLJ and Credit Suisse, it postponed the merger a second time so that it was then set to close on November 2, 2000.

Plaintiffs challenge the second extension that resulted in a 22-day delay. They contend that this delay was not properly authorized and harmed minority stockholders while improperly benefitting AXA. They claim damages representing the time-value of money lost through the delay. [...]

The ruling before us on appeal is that the plaintiffs' claim is derivative, purportedly brought on behalf of DLJ. The Court of Chancery, relying upon our confusing jurisprudence on the direct/derivative dichotomy, based its dismissal on the following ground: "Because this delay affected all DLJ shareholders equally, plaintiffs' injury was not a special injury, and this action is, thus, a derivative action, at most."[131]

Plaintiffs argue that they have suffered a "special injury" because they had an alleged contractual right to receive the merger consideration of $90 per share without suffering the 22-day delay arising out of the extensions under the merger agreement. But the trial court's opinion convincingly demonstrates that plaintiffs had no such contractual right that had ripened at the time the extensions were entered into:

> *Here, it is clear that plaintiffs have no separate contractual right to bring a direct claim, and they do not assert contractual rights under the merger agreement.* First, the merger agreement specifically disclaims any persons as being third party beneficiaries to the contract. Second, any contractual shareholder right to payment of the merger consideration did not ripen until the conditions of the agreement were met. The agreement stated that Credit Suisse Group was not required to accept any shares for tender, or could extend the offer, under certain conditions — one condition of which included an extension or termination by agreement between [1035] Credit Suisse Group and DLJ. *Because Credit Suisse Group and DLJ did in fact agree to extend the tender offer period, any right to payment plaintiffs could have did not ripen until this newly negotiated period was over. The merger agreement only became binding and mutually enforceable at the time the tendered shares ultimately were accepted for payment by Credit Suisse Group.* It is at that moment in time, November 3, 2000, that the company became bound to purchase the tendered shares, making the contract mutually enforceable. *DLJ stockholders had no individual contractual right to payment until November 3, 2000, when their tendered shares were accepted for payment.* Thus, they have no contractual basis to challenge a delay in the closing of the tender offer up until November 3. *Because this is the date the tendered shares were accepted for payment, the contract was not breached and plaintiffs do not have a contractual basis to bring a direct suit.*[14]

Moreover, no other individual right of these stockholder-plaintiffs was alleged to have been violated by the extensions.

That conclusion could have ended the case because it portended a definitive ruling that plaintiffs have no claim whatsoever on the facts alleged. But the defendants chose to argue, and the trial court chose to decide, the standing issue, which is predicated on an assertion that this claim is a derivative one asserted on behalf of the corporation, DLJ.

The Court of Chancery correctly noted that "[t]he Court will independently examine the nature of the wrong alleged and any potential relief to make its own determination of the suit's classification.... Plaintiffs' classification of the suit is not binding."[5] The trial court's analysis was hindered, however, because it focused on the confusing concept of "special injury" as the test for determining whether a claim is derivative or direct. The trial court's premise was as follows:

> In order to bring a *direct* claim, a plaintiff must have experienced some "special injury." [citing *Lipton v. News Int'l,* 514 A.2d 1075, 1079 (Del.1986)]. A special injury is a wrong that "is separate and distinct from that suffered by other shareholders, ... or a wrong involving a contractual right of a shareholder, such as the right to vote, or to assert majority control, which exists independently of any right of the corporation." [citing *Moran v. Household Int'l. Inc.,* 490 A.2d 1059, 1070 (Del.Ch.1985), *aff'd* 500 A.2d 1346 (Del.1986 [1985])].[6]

In our view, the concept of "special injury" that appears in some Supreme Court and Court of Chancery cases is not helpful to a proper analytical distinction between direct and derivative actions. We now disapprove the use of the concept of "special injury" as a tool in that analysis.

The Proper Analysis to Distinguish Between Direct and Derivative Actions

The analysis must be based solely on the following questions: Who suffered the alleged harm — the corporation or the suing stockholder individually — and who would receive the benefit of the recovery or other remedy? This simple analysis is well imbedded in our jurisprudence,[7] but some cases have complicated it by injection of the amorphous and confusing concept of "special injury." [...]

A Brief History of Our Jurisprudence

The derivative suit has been generally described as "one of the most interesting and ingenious of accountability mechanisms for large formal organizations."[10] It enables a stockholder to bring suit on behalf of the corporation for harm done to the corporation.[11] Because a derivative suit is being brought on behalf of the corporation, the recovery, if any, must go to the corporation. A stockholder who is directly injured, however, does retain the right to bring an individual action for injuries affecting his or her legal rights as a stockholder. Such a claim is distinct from an injury caused to the corporation alone. In such individual suits, the recovery or other relief flows directly to the stockholders, not to the corporation.

Determining whether an action is derivative or direct is sometimes difficult and has many legal consequences, some of which may have an expensive impact on the parties to the action.[12] For example, if an action is derivative, the plaintiffs are then required to comply with the requirements of Court of Chancery Rule 23.1, that the stockholder: (a) retain ownership of the shares throughout the litigation; (b) make presuit demand on the board; and (c) obtain court approval of any settlement. Further, the recovery, if any, flows only to the corporation. The decision whether a suit is direct or derivative may be out-come-determinative. Therefore, it is necessary that a standard to distinguish such actions be clear, simple and consistently articulated and applied by our courts. [...]

Thus, two confusing propositions have encumbered our caselaw governing the direct/derivative distinction. The "special injury" concept[...] can be confusing in identifying the nature of the action. The same is true of the proposition [...] that an action cannot be direct if all stockholders are equally affected or unless the [1039] stockholder's injury is separate and distinct from that suffered by other stockholders. The proper analysis has been and should remain that [...]a court should look to the nature of the wrong and to whom the relief should go. The stockholder's claimed direct injury must be independent of any alleged injury to the corporation. The stockholder must demonstrate that the duty breached was owed to the stockholder and that he or she can prevail without showing an injury to the corporation.

Standard to Be Applied in This Case

In this case it cannot be concluded that the complaint alleges a derivative claim. There is no derivative claim asserting injury to the corporate entity. There is no relief that would go the corporation. Accordingly, there is no basis to hold that the complaint states a derivative claim.

But, it does not necessarily follow that the complaint states a direct, individual claim. While the complaint purports to set forth a direct claim, in reality, it states no claim at all. The trial court analyzed the complaint and correctly concluded that it does not claim that the plaintiffs have any rights that have been injured.[27] Their rights have not yet ripened. The contractual claim is nonexistent until it is ripe, and that claim will not be ripe until the terms of the merger are fulfilled, including the extensions of the closing at issue here. Therefore, there is no direct claim stated in the complaint before us.

Accordingly, the complaint was properly dismissed. But, due to the reliance on the concept of "special injury" by the Court of Chancery, the ground set forth for the dismissal is erroneous, there being no derivative claim. That error is harmless, however, because, in our view, there is no direct claim either.

Conclusion

For purposes of distinguishing between derivative and direct claims, we expressly disapprove both the concept of "special injury" and the concept that a claim is necessarily derivative if it affects all stockholders equally. In our view, the tests going forward should rest on those set forth in this opinion. [...]

Note on characterization of direct and derivative claims

Tooley's simpler inquiry ("Who has been harmed and to whom will a remedy flow?") makes it easier for litigants and courts to determine the nature of the claims being brought. Where the corporation has been harmed by the actions of the board and where the remedy flows back to the corporation, such claims are derivative in nature. For example, a decision by the board of directors results in a fall or a drop in the stock price, the corporation has been harmed. To the extent there is a remedy available in that case, it would flow back to the corporation (e.g. damages paid by the board back to the corporation). Consequently, such stock drop cases are derivative. Other typical derivative claims are claims against the board for engaging in self-dealing transactions or other transactions that result in harm to the corporation.

In another example, if the board took an action to restrict the rights of stockholders to vote in an annual meeting, claims challenging the board's action would be direct. The stockholder has been harmed because their votes have been compromised and any remedy (restoring their right to vote) would flow back to the stockholder. Other typical direct claims where stockholder rights are directly implicated include (but are not limited to) challenges to restrictions under the certificate of incorporation or bylaws.

Demand and Demand Futility

3.2

As we know, the corporate law places the board of directors in a central place with respect to the management of the corporation. Section 141(a) and its mandate that the board manage the business and affairs of the corporation extends naturally to control over any legal claims that the corporation may have. Claims of the corporation against third parties are relatively simple to deal with. Stockholders have little reason to worry that a board might not pursue claims against third parties. Legal claims against the corporation's own board of directors or the corporation's own agents, on the other hand, are more troublesome.

It may not be realistic to expect the board to pursue potential legal claims owned by the corporation against themselves. The derivative action permits stockholders in certain circumstances to stand in the shoes of the corporation to vindicate rights of the corporation that its own directors will not pursue.

The ability of stockholders to take up litigation on behalf of the corporation is not unlimited.

In order to preserve the central importance of the board in the management of the corporation, courts will require shareholders who wish to sue on behalf the corporation to jump through certain procedural hoops.

Consequently, procedure plays an extremely important role in derivative litigation. This section provides an overview to procedural requirements in derivative cases. In particular, Rule 23.1 requires that in any complaint, a statement that the stockholder made a "demand" to the corporation or if they did not why such a demand would have been "futile". Many cases will be resolved on a Rule 23.1 Motion to Dismiss for failure of the stockholder to make a demand when a demand was required.

Demand Futility Standards   3.2.1

UFCWU v. Zuckerberg

For many years, Delaware had two different demand
futility standards (Aronson & Rales). Application of   3.2.2
the standards depended on the facts presented in
the complaint and they could sometimes be
confusing. In Zuckerberg the Chancery Court

undertook to simplify, without overturning, application of these standards. The Chancery Court's approach was endorsed by the Delaware Supreme Court in this opinion. It's worth keeping in mind that the old standards (Aronson & Rales) are still good law and have not be overruled. Rather, the court has created a new, unified application of those standards that is intended to simplify and improve pleading.

UNITED FOOD AND COMMERCIAL WORKERS UNION AND PARTICIPATING FOOD INDUSTRY EMPLOYERS TRI-STATE PENSION FUND
V.
MARK ZUCKERBERG, ET AL

Supreme Court of Delaware.
September 23, 2021.

MONTGOMERY-REEVES, Justice:

In 2016, the board of directors of Facebook, Inc. ("Facebook") voted in favor of a stock reclassification (the "Reclassification") that would allow Mark Zuckerberg— Facebook's controller, chairman, and chief executive officer—to sell most of his Facebook stock while maintaining voting control of the company. Zuckerberg proposed the Reclassification to allow him and his wife to fulfill a pledge to donate most of their wealth to philanthropic causes. With Zuckerberg casting the deciding votes, Facebook's stockholders approved the Reclassification.

Not long after, numerous stockholders filed lawsuits in the Court of Chancery, alleging that Facebook's board of directors violated their fiduciary duties by negotiating and approving a purportedly one-sided deal that put Zuckerberg's interests ahead of the company's interests. The trial court consolidated more than a dozen of these lawsuits into a single class action. At Zuckerberg's request and shortly before trial, Facebook withdrew the Reclassification and mooted the fiduciary-duty class action. Facebook spent more than $20 million defending against the class action and paid plaintiffs' counsel more than $68 million in attorneys' fees under the corporate benefit doctrine.

Following the settlement, another Facebook stockholder—the United Food and Commercial Workers Union and Participating Food Industry Employers Tri-State Pension Fund ("Tri-State")—filed a derivative complaint in the Court of Chancery. This new action rehashed many of the allegations made in the prior class action but sought compensation for the money Facebook spent in connection with the prior class action.

Tri-State did not make a litigation demand on Facebook's board. Instead, Tri-State pleaded that demand was futile because the board's negotiation and approval of the Reclassification was not a valid exercise of its business judgment and because a majority of the directors were beholden to Zuckerberg. Facebook and the other defendants moved to dismiss Tri-State's complaint under Court of Chancery Rule 23.1, arguing that Tri-State did not make demand or prove that demand was futile. Both sides agreed that the demand futility test established in *Aronson v. Lewis* applied to Tri-State's complaint.

In October 2020, the Court of Chancery dismissed Tri-State's complaint under Rule 23.1. The court held that *exculpated* care claims do not excuse demand under *Aronson's* second prong because they do not expose directors to a substantial likelihood of liability. The court also held that the complaint failed to raise a reasonable doubt that a majority of the demand board lacked independence from Zuckerberg. In reaching these conclusions, the Court of Chancery applied a three-part test for demand futility that blended the *Aronson* test with the test articulated in *Rales v. Blasband.*

Tri-State has appealed the Court of Chancery's judgment. For the reasons provided below, this Court affirms the Court of Chancery's judgment. The second prong of *Aronson* focuses on whether the derivative claims would expose directors to a substantial likelihood of liability. Exculpated claims do not satisfy that standard because they do not expose directors to a substantial likelihood of liability. Further, the complaint does not plead with particularity that a majority of the demand board lacked independence. Thus, the Court of Chancery properly dismissed Tri-State's complaint for failing to make a demand on the board.

Additionally, this Opinion adopts the Court of Chancery's three-part test for demand futility. When the Court decided *Aronson,* raising a reasonable doubt that the business judgment standard of review would apply exposed directors to a substantial likelihood of liability for care violations. The General Assembly's enactment of Section 102(b)(7) and other developments in corporate law have weakened the connection between rebutting the business judgment standard and exposing directors to a risk that would sterilize their judgment with respect to a litigation demand. Further, the *Aronson* test has proved difficult to apply in many contexts, such as where there is turnover on a corporation's board. The Court of Chancery's refined articulation of the *Aronson* standard helps to address these issues. Nonetheless, this refined standard is consistent with *Aronson, Rales,* and their progeny. Thus, cases properly applying those holdings remain good law.

1. **RELEVANT FACTS AND PROCEDURAL BACKGROUND**

2. **The Parties and Relevant Non-Parties**

Appellee Facebook is a Delaware corporation with its principal place of business in California. Facebook is the world's largest social media and networking service and one of the ten largest companies by market capitalization.

Appellant Tri-State has continuously owned stock in Facebook since September 2013.

Appellee Mark Zuckerberg founded Facebook and has served as its chief executive officer since July 2014. Zuckerberg controls a majority of Facebook's voting power and has been the chairman of Facebook's board of directors since January 2012.

Appellee Marc Andreessen has served as a Facebook director since June 2008. Andreessen was a member of the special committee that negotiated and recommended that the full board approve the

Reclassification. In addition to his work as a Facebook director, Andreessen is a cofounder and general partner of the venture capital firm Andreessen Horowitz.

Appellee Peter Thiel has served as a Facebook director since April 2005. Thiel voted in favor of the Reclassification. In addition to his work as a Facebook director, Thiel is a partner at the venture capital firm Founders Firm.

Appellee Reed Hastings began serving as a Facebook director in June 2011 and was still a director when Tri-State filed its complaint. Hastings voted in favor of the Reclassification. In addition to his work as a Facebook director, Hastings founded and serves as the chief executive officer and chairman of Netflix, Inc. ("Netflix").

Appellee Erskine B. Bowles began serving as a Facebook director in September 2011 and was still a director when Tri-State filed its complaint. Bowles was a member of the special committee that negotiated and recommended that the full board approve the Reclassification.

Appellee Susan D. Desmond-Hellman began serving as a Facebook director in March 2013 and was still a director when Tri-State filed its complaint. Desmond-Hellman was the chair of the special committee that negotiated and recommended that the full board approve the Reclassification. In addition to her work as a Facebook director, Desmond-Hellman served as the chief executive officer of the Bill and Melinda Gates Foundation (the "Gates Foundation") during the events relevant to this appeal.

Sheryl Sandberg has been Facebook's chief operating officer since March 2018 and has served as a Facebook director since January 2012.

Kenneth I. Chenault began serving as a Facebook director in February 2018 and was still a director when Tri-State filed its complaint. Chenault was not a director when Facebook's board voted in favor of the Reclassification in 2016.

Jeffery Zients began serving as a Facebook director in May 2018 and was still a director when Tri-State filed its complaint. Zients was not a director when Facebook's board voted in favor of the Reclassification in 2016.

1. Zuckerberg Takes the Giving Pledge

According to the allegations in the complaint, in December 2010, Zuckerberg took the Giving Pledge, a movement championed by Bill Gates and Warren Buffet that challenged wealthy business leaders to donate a majority of their wealth to philanthropic causes. Zuckerberg communicated widely that he had taken the pledge and intended to start his philanthropy at an early age.

In March 2015, Zuckerberg began working on an accelerated plan to complete the Giving Pledge by making annual donations of $2 to $3 billion worth of Facebook stock. Zuckerberg asked Facebook's general counsel to look into the plan. Facebook's legal team cautioned Zuckerberg that he could only sell a small portion of his stock—$3 to $4 billion based on the market price—without dipping below majority voting control. To avoid this problem, the general counsel suggested that Facebook could follow the "Google playbook" and issue a new class of non-voting stock that Zuckerberg could sell without significantly diminishing his voting power. The legal team recommended that the board form a special committee of independent directors to review and approve the plan and noted that litigation involving Google's reclassification resulted in a $522 million settlement. Zuckerberg instructed Facebook's legal team to "start figuring out how to make this happen."

1. The Special Committee Approves the Reclassification

At an August 20, 2015 meeting of Facebook's board, Zuckerberg formally proposed that Facebook issue a new class of non-voting shares, which would allow him to sell a substantial amount of stock without losing control of the company. Zuckerberg also disclosed that he had hired Simpson Thacher & Bartlett LLP ("Simpson Thacher") to give him personal legal advice about "what creating a new class of stock might look like."

A couple of days later, Facebook established a special committee, which was composed of three purportedly-independent directors: Andreessen, Bowles, and Desmond-Hellman (the "Special

Committee"). The board charged the Special Committee with evaluating the Reclassification, considering alternatives, and making a recommendation to the full board. The board also authorized the Special Committee to retain legal counsel, financial advisors, and other experts.

Facebook management recommended and the Special Committee hired Wachtell, Lipton, Rosen & Katz ("Wachtell") as the committee's legal advisor. Before meeting with the Special Committee, Wachtell called Zuckerberg's contacts at Simpson Thacher to discuss the potential terms of the Reclassification. Simpson Thacher rejected as non-starters several features from the Google playbook, such as a stapling provision that would have required Zuckerberg to sell a share of his voting stock each time that he sold a share of the non-voting stock, and a true-up payment that would compensate Facebook's other stockholders for the dilution of their voting power. By the time Wachtell first met with the Special Committee, the key contours of the Reclassification were already taking shape, and the Special Committee anticipated that the Reclassification would occur. Thus, the Special Committee focused on suggesting changes to the Reclassification rather than considering alternatives or threatening to reject the plan. ...

As the negotiations progressed, the Special Committee largely agreed to give Zuckerberg the terms that he wanted and did not consider alternatives or demand meaningful concessions. ...

A few weeks later, Zuckerberg published a post on his Facebook page announcing that he planned to begin making large donations of his Facebook stock. The post noted that Zuckerberg intended to "remain Facebook's CEO for many, many years to come" and did not mention that his plan hinged on the Special Committee's approval of the Reclassification. The Special Committee did not try to use the public announcement as leverage to extract more concessions from Zuckerberg. ...

On April 13, 2016, the Special Committee recommend that the full board approve the Reclassification. The next day, Facebook's full board accepted the Special Committee's recommendation and voted to approve the Reclassification. Zuckerberg and Sandberg abstained from voting on the Reclassification.

1. Facebook Settles a Class Action Challenging the Reclassification

On April 27, 2016, Facebook revealed the Reclassification to the public. ... On April 29, 2016, the first class action was filed in the Court of Chancery challenging the Reclassification. Several more similar complaints were filed, and in May 2016 the Court of Chancery consolidated thirteen cases into a single class action (the "Reclassification Class Action"). ...

On June 24, 2016, Facebook agreed that it would not go forward with the Reclassification while the Reclassification Class Action was pending. The Court of Chancery certified the Reclassification Class Action in April 2017 and tentatively scheduled the trial for September 26, 2017. About a week before the trial was scheduled to begin, Zuckerberg asked the board to abandon the Reclassification. The board agreed, and the next day Facebook filed a Form 8-K with the Securities and Exchange Commission disclosing that the company had abandoned the Reclassification and mooted the Class Action. The Form-8K also disclosed that despite abandoning the Reclassification, Zuckerberg planned to sell a substantial number of shares over the coming 18 months. ...

1. Tri-State Files a Class Action Seeking to Recoup the Money that Facebook Spent Defending and Settling the Reclassification Class Action

Facebook spent about $21.8 million defending the Reclassification Class Action, including more than $17 million on attorneys' fees. Additionally, Facebook paid $68.7 million to the plaintiff's attorneys in the Reclassification Class Action to settle a claim under the corporate benefit doctrine.

On September 12, 2018, Tri-State filed a derivative action in the Court of Chancery seeking to recoup the money that Facebook spent defending and settling the Reclassification Class Action. ...

The complaint alleged that demand was excused as futile under Court of Chancery Rule 23.1 because "the Reclassification was not the product of a valid exercise of business judgment" and because "a majority of the Board face[d] a substantial likelihood of liability[] and/or lack[ed] independence." ...

Tri-State appeals the Court of Chancery's judgment dismissing the derivative complaint under Rule 23.1 for failing to make a demand on the board or plead with particularity facts establishing that demand would be futile.

1. STANDARD OF REVIEW

"A cardinal precept" of Delaware law is "that directors, rather than shareholders, manage the business and affairs of the corporation." This precept is reflected in Section 141(a) of the Delaware General Corporation Law ("DGCL"), which provides that "[t]he business and affairs of every corporation organized under this chapter *shall be managed by or under the direction of a board of directors* except as may be otherwise provided in this chapter or in [a corporation's] certificate of incorporation." The board's authority to govern corporate affairs extends to decisions about what remedial actions a corporation should take after being harmed, including whether the corporation should file a lawsuit against its directors, its officers, its controller, or an outsider.

"In a derivative suit, a stockholder seeks to displace the board's [decision-making] authority over a litigation asset and assert the corporation's claim." Thus, "[b]y its very nature[,] the derivative action" encroaches "on the managerial freedom of directors" by seeking to deprive the board of control over a corporation's litigation asset. "In order for a stockholder to divest the directors of their authority to control the litigation asset and bring a derivative action on behalf of the corporation, the stockholder must" (1) make a demand on the company's board of directors or (2) show that demand would be futile. The demand requirement is a substantive requirement that "`[e]nsure[s] that a stockholder exhausts his intracorporate remedies,' `provide[s] a safeguard against strike suits,' and `assure[s] that the stockholder affords the corporation the opportunity to address an alleged wrong without litigation and to control any litigation which does occur.'"

Court of Chancery Rule 23.1 implements the substantive demand requirement at the pleading stage by mandating that derivative complaints "allege with particularity the efforts, if any, made by the plaintiff to obtain the action the plaintiff desires from the directors or comparable authority and the reasons for the plaintiff's failure to obtain the action or for not making the effort." To comply with Rule 23.1, the plaintiff must meet "stringent requirements of factual particularity that differ substantially from . . . permissive notice pleadings." When considering a motion to dismiss a complaint for failing to comply with Rule 23.1, the Court does not weigh the evidence, must accept as true all of the complaint's particularized and well-pleaded allegations, and must draw all reasonable inferences in the plaintiff's favor.

The plaintiff in this action did not make a pre-suit demand. Thus, the question before the Court is whether demand is excused as futile. This Court has articulated two tests to determine whether the demand requirement should be excused as futile: the *Aronson* test and the *Rales* test. The *Aronson* test applies where the complaint challenges a decision made by the same board that would consider a litigation demand. Under *Aronson,* demand is excused as futile if the complaint alleges particularized facts that raise a reasonable doubt that "(1) the directors are disinterested and independent[,] [or] (2) the challenged transaction was otherwise the product of a valid business judgment." This reflects the "rule . . . that where officers and directors are under an influence which sterilizes their discretion, they cannot be considered proper persons to conduct litigation on behalf of the corporation. Thus, demand would be futile."

The *Rales* test applies in all other circumstances. Under *Rales,* demand is excused as futile if the complaint alleges particularized facts creating a "reasonable doubt that, as of the time the complaint is filed," a majority of the demand board "could have properly exercised its independent and disinterested business judgment in responding to a demand." "Fundamentally, *Aronson* and *Rales* both `address the same question of whether the board can exercise its business judgment on the corporat[ion]'s behalf" in considering demand." For this reason, the Court of Chancery has recognized that the broader reasoning of *Rales* encompasses *Aronson,* and therefore the *Aronson* test is best understood as a special application of the *Rales* test.

While Delaware law recognizes that there are circumstances where making a demand would be futile because a majority of the directors "are under an influence which sterilizes their discretion" and "cannot be considered proper persons to conduct litigation on behalf of the corporation," the demand requirement is not excused lightly because derivative litigation upsets the balance of power that the DGCL establishes between a corporation's directors and its stockholders. Thus, the demand-futility analysis provides an important doctrinal check that ensures the board is not improperly deprived of its decision-making authority, while at the same time leaving a path for stockholders to file a derivative action where there is reason to doubt that the board could bring its impartial business judgment to bear on a litigation demand.

In this case, Tri-State alleged that demand was excused as futile for several reasons, including that the board's negotiation and approval of the Reclassification would not be "protected by the business judgment rule" because "[t]heir approval was not fully informed" or "duly considered," and that a majority of the directors on the Demand Board lacked independence from Zuckerberg. The Court of Chancery held that Tri-State failed to plead with particularity facts establishing that demand was futile and dismissed the complaint because it did not comply with Court of Chancery Rule 23.1.

On appeal, Tri-State raises two issues with the Court of Chancery's demand-futility analysis. First, Tri-State argues that the Court of Chancery erred by holding that exculpated care violations do not satisfy the second prong of the *Aronson* test. Second, Tri-State argues that its complaint contained particularized allegations establishing that a majority of the directors on the Demand Board were beholden to Zuckerberg. ...

3.   This Court adopts the Court of Chancery's three-part test for demand futility

This [first] issue raises one more question—whether the three-part test for demand futility the Court of Chancery applied below is consistent with *Aronson, Rales,* and their progeny. The Court of Chancery noted that turnover on Facebook's board, along with a director's decision to abstain from voting on the Reclassification, made it difficult to apply the *Aronson* test to the facts of this case:

The composition of the Board in this case exemplifies the difficulties that the *Aronson* test struggles to overcome. The Board has nine members, six of whom served on the Board when it approved the Reclassification. Under a strict reading of *Rales,* because the Board does not have a new majority of directors, *Aronson* provides the governing test. But one of those six directors abstained from the vote on the Reclassification, meaning that the *Aronson* analysis only has traction for five of the nine. *Aronson* does not provide guidance about what to do with either the director who abstained or the two directors who joined the Board later. The director who abstained from voting on the Reclassification suffers from other conflicts that renders her incapable of considering a demand, yet a strict reading of *Aronson* only focuses on the challenged decision and therefore would not account for those conflicts. Similarly, the plaintiff alleges that one of the directors who subsequently joined the Board has conflicts that render him incapable of considering a demand, but a strict reading of *Aronson* would not account for that either. Precedent thus calls for applying *Aronson,* but its analytical framework is not up to the task. The *Rales* test, by contrast, can accommodate all of these considerations.

The court also suggested that in light of the developments discussed above, "*Aronson* is broken in its own right because subsequent jurisprudential developments have rendered non-viable the core premise on which *Aronson* depends—the notion that an elevated standard of review standing alone results in a substantial likelihood of liability sufficient to excuse demand. Perhaps the time has come to move on from *Aronson* entirely."

To address these concerns, the Court of Chancery applied the following three-part test on a director-by-director basis to determine whether demand should be excused as futile:

(i) whether the director received a material personal benefit from the alleged misconduct that is the subject of the litigation demand;

(ii) whether the director would face a substantial likelihood of liability on any of the claims that are the subject of the litigation demand; and

(iii) whether the director lacks independence from someone who received a material personal benefit from the alleged misconduct that is the subject of the litigation demand or who would face a substantial likelihood of liability on any of the claims that are the subject of the litigation demand.

This approach treated "*Rales* as the general demand futility test," while "draw[ing] upon *Aronson*-like principles when evaluating whether particular directors face a substantial likelihood of liability as a result of having participated in the decision to approve the Reclassification."

This Court adopts the Court of Chancery's three-part test as the universal test for assessing whether demand should be excused as futile. When the Court decided *Aronson,* it made sense to use the standard of review to assess whether directors were subject to an influence that would sterilize their discretion with respect to a litigation demand. Subsequent changes in the law have eroded the ground upon which that framework rested. Those changes cannot be ignored, and it is both appropriate and necessary that the common law evolve in an orderly fashion to incorporate those developments. The Court of Chancery's three-part test achieves that important goal. Blending the *Aronson* test with the *Rales* test is appropriate because "both `address the same question of whether the board can exercise its business judgment on the corporat[ion]'s behalf' in considering demand"; and the refined test does not change the result of demand-futility analysis.

Further, the refined test "refocuses the inquiry on the decision regarding the litigation demand, rather than the decision being challenged." Notwithstanding text focusing on the propriety of the challenged transaction, this approach is consistent with the overarching concern that *Aronson* identified: whether the directors on the demand board "cannot be considered proper persons to conduct litigation on behalf of the corporation" because they "are under an influence which sterilizes their discretion." The purpose of the demand-futility analysis is to assess whether the board should be deprived of its decision-making authority because there is reason to doubt that the directors would be able to bring their impartial business judgment to bear on a litigation demand. That is a different consideration than whether the derivative claim is strong or weak because the challenged transaction is likely to pass or fail the applicable standard of review. It is helpful to keep those inquiries separate. And the Court of Chancery's three-part test is particularly helpful where, like here, board turnover and director abstention make it difficult to apply the *Aronson* test as written.

Finally, because the three-part test is consistent with and enhances *Aronson, Rales,* and their progeny, the Court need not overrule *Aronson* to adopt this refined test, and cases properly construing *Aronson, Rales,* and their progeny remain good law.

Accordingly, from this point forward, courts should ask the following three questions on a director-by-director basis when evaluating allegations of demand futility:

(i) whether the director received a material personal benefit from the alleged misconduct that is the subject of the litigation demand;

(ii) whether the director faces a substantial likelihood of liability on any of the claims that would be the subject of the litigation demand; and

(iii) whether the director lacks independence from someone who received a material personal benefit from the alleged misconduct that would be the subject of the litigation demand or who would face a substantial likelihood of liability on any of the claims that are the subject of the litigation demand.

If the answer to any of the questions is "yes" for at least half of the members of the demand board, then demand is excused as futile. It is no longer necessary to determine whether the *Aronson* test or the *Rales* test governs a complaint's demand-futility allegations.

...

The Demand Board was composed of nine directors. Tri-State concedes on appeal that two of those directors, Chenault and Zients, could have impartially considered a litigation demand. And Facebook does not argue on appeal that Zuckerberg, Sandberg, or Andreessen could have impartially considered a litigation demand. Thus, in order to show that demand is futile, Tri-State must sufficiently allege that two of the following directors could not impartially consider demand: Thiel, Hastings, Bowles, and Desmond-Hellmann.

1. Hastings

The complaint does not raise a reasonable doubt that Hastings lacked independence from Zuckerberg. According to the complaint, Hastings was not independent because:

- "Netflix purchased advertisements from Facebook at relevant times," and maintains "ongoing and potential future business relationships with" Facebook.

- According to an article published by *The New York Times,*Facebook gave to Netflix and several other technology companies "more intrusive access to users' personal data than it ha[d] disclosed, effectively exempting those partners from privacy rules."

- "Hastings (as a Netflix founder) is biased in favor of founders maintaining control of their companies."

- "Hastings has . . . publicly supported large philanthropic donations by founders during their lifetimes. Indeed, both Hastings and Zuckerberg have been significant contributors . . . [to] a well-known foundation known for soliciting and obtaining large contributions from company founders and

206

> which manages donor funds for both Hastings . . . and
> Zuckerberg . . . ."

These allegations do not raise a reasonable doubt that Hastings was beholden to Zuckerberg. Even if Netflix purchased advertisements from Facebook, the complaint does not allege that those purchases were material to Netflix or that Netflix received anything other than arm's length terms under those agreements. Similarly, the complaint does not make any particularized allegations explaining how obtaining special access to Facebook user data was material to Netflix's business interests, or that Netflix used its special access to user data to obtain any concrete benefits in its own business.

Further, having a bias in favor of founder-control does not mean that Hastings lacks independence from Zuckerberg. Hastings might have a good-faith belief that founder control maximizes a corporation's value over the long-haul. If so, that good-faith belief would play a valid role in Hasting's exercise of his impartial business judgment.

Finally, alleging that Hastings and Zuckerberg have a track record of donating to similar causes falls short of showing that Hastings is beholden to Zuckerberg. As the Court of Chancery noted below, "[t]here is no logical reason to think that a shared interest in philanthropy would undercut Hastings' independence. Nor is it apparent how donating to the same charitable fund would result in Hastings feeling obligated to serve Zuckerberg's interests." Accordingly, the Court affirms the Court of Chancery's holding that the complaint does not raise a reasonable doubt about Hastings's independence.

2. Thiel

The complaint does not raise a reasonable doubt that Thiel lacked independence from Zuckerberg. According to the complaint, Thiel was not independent because:

- "Thiel was one of the early investors in Facebook," is "its longest-tenured board member besides Zuckerberg," and "has . . . been instrumental to Facebook's business strategy and direction over the years."

- "Thiel has a personal bias in favor of keeping founders in control of the companies they created ..."

- The venture capital firm at which Thiel is a partner, Founders Fund, "gets `good deal flow'" from its "high-profile association with Facebook."

- "According to Facebook's 2018 Proxy Statement, the Facebook shares owned by the Founders Fund (*i.e.,*by Thiel and Andreessen) will be released from escrow in connection with" an acquisition.

- "Thiel is Zuckerberg's close friend and mentor."

- In October 2016, Thiel made a $1 million donation to an "organization that paid [a substantial sum to] Cambridge Analytica" and "cofounded the Cambridge Analytica-linked data firm Palantir." Even though "[t]he Cambridge Analytica scandal has exposed Facebook to regulatory investigations" and litigation, Zuckerberg did not try to remove Thiel from the board.

- Similarly, Thiel's "acknowledge[ment] that he secretly funded various lawsuits aimed at bankrupting [the] news website Gawker Media" lead to "widespread calls for Zuckerberg to remove Thiel from Facebook's Board given Thiel's apparent antagonism toward a free press." Zuckerberg ignored those calls and did not seek to remove Thiel from Facebook's board.

These allegations do not raise a reasonable doubt that Thiel is beholden to Zuckerberg. The complaint does not explain why Thiel's status as a long-serving board member, early investor, or his contributions to Facebook's business strategy make him beholden to Zuckerberg. And for the same reasons provided above, a director's good faith belief that founder controller maximizes value does not raise a reasonable doubt that the director lacks independence from a corporation's founder.

While the complaint alleges that Founders Fund "gets `good deal flow'" from Thiel's "high-profile association with Facebook," the complaint does not identify a single deal that flowed to—or is expected to flow to—Founders Fund through this association, let alone any deals that would be material to Thiel's interests. The complaint also fails to draw any connection between Thiel's continued status as a director and the vesting of Facebook stock related to the acquisition. And alleging that Thiel is a personal friend of Zuckerberg is insufficient to establish a lack of independence.

The final pair of allegations suggest that because "Zuckerberg stood by Thiel" in the face of public scandals, "Thiel feels a sense of obligation to Zuckerberg." These allegations can only raise a reasonable doubt about Thiel's independence if remaining a Facebook director was financially or personally material to Thiel. As the Court of Chancery noted below, given Thiel's wealth and stature, "[t]he complaint does not support an inference that Thiel's service on the Board is financially material to him. Nor does the complaint sufficiently allege that serving as a Facebook director confers such cachet that Thiel's independence is compromised." Accordingly, this Court affirms the Court of Chancery's holding that the complaint does not raise a reasonable doubt about Thiel's independence.

3. Bowles

The complaint does not raise a reasonable doubt that Bowles lacked independence from Zuckerberg. According to the complaint, Thiel was not independent because:

- "Bowles is beholden to the entire board" because it granted "a waiver of the mandatory retirement age for directors set forth in Facebook's Corporate Governance Guidelines," allowing "Bowles to stand for reelection despite having reached 70 years old before" the May 2018 annual meeting.

- "Morgan Stanley—a company for which [Bowles] . . . served as a longstanding board member at the time (2005-2017)—directly benefited by receiving over $2 million in fees for its work . . . in connection with the Reclassification . . . ."

- Bowles "ensured that Evercore and his close friend Altman financially benefitted from the Special Committee's engagement" without properly vetting Evercore's competency or considering alternatives.

These allegations do not raise a reasonable doubt that Bowles is beholden to Zuckerberg or the other members of the Demand Board. The complaint does not make any particularized allegation explaining why the board's decision to grant Bowles a waiver from the mandatory retirement age would compromise his ability to impartially consider a litigation demand or engender a sense of debt to the other directors. For example, the complaint does not allege that Bowles was expected to do anything in exchange for the waiver, or that remaining a director was financially or personally material to Bowles.

The complaint's allegations regarding Bowles's links to financial advisors are similarly ill-supported. None of these allegations suggest that Bowles received a personal benefit from the Reclassification, or that Bowles's ties to these advisors made him beholden to Zuckerberg as a condition of sending business to Morgan Stanley, Evercore, or his "close friend Altman." Accordingly, this Court affirms the Court of Chancery's holding that the complaint does not raise a reasonable doubt about Bowles's independence. ...

For the reasons provided above, the Court of Chancery's judgment is affirmed.

Evaluating Demand Futility   3.2.3

In re Kraft Heinz Co. Deriv. Litig.

Application of the Zuckerberg standard in response to a 23.1 Motion to Dismiss requires the court to go through a "head counting" exercise in order to determine whether a majority of the board could   3.2.3.1

have properly considered a demand. If the answer is yes, then the litigation will be dismissed for failure to make demand. If the answer to that question is no, then the stockholders will be permitted to pursue the litigation and temporarily stand in the shoes of the corporation to vindicate the corporation's rights.

IN RE KRAFT HEINZ COMPANY DERIVATIVE LITIGATION.
C.A. No. 2019-0587 (2021)
Court of Chancery of Delaware.

WILL, Vice Chancellor.

This stockholder derivative action arises from 3G Capital, Inc's sale of 7% of its then-24% stake in The Kraft Heinz Company. The sale was followed by Kraft Heinz disclosing disappointing financial results and its stock price dropping significantly. 3G's proceeds from the sale exceeded $1.2 billion.

In this litigation, the plaintiffs contend that defendants 3G, entities affiliated with it, and certain dual fiduciaries of 3G and Kraft Heinz breached their fiduciary duties to Kraft Heinz stockholders. The plaintiffs' claims are based on allegations that the defendants either approved 3G's stock sale based on adverse material nonpublic information or allowed 3G to effectuate the sale to the detriment of Kraft Heinz and its non-3G stockholders.

As with every stockholder derivative action, the plaintiffs must adhere to Court of Chancery Rule 23.1 by making a demand on the board of directors or demonstrating that a demand would have been futile. The plaintiffs did not make a demand on the Kraft Heinz board and maintain that demand should be excused because a majority of the board is not independent of 3G. ...

The Kraft Heinz Company Is Formed.

The Kraft Heinz Company is a publicly traded Delaware corporation that describes itself as "one of the largest global food and beverage companies." Kraft Heinz was formed in 2015 when

Kraft Food Groups, Inc. ("Kraft") merged with The H.J. Heinz Company ("Heinz").

Heinz was jointly purchased by global investment firm 3G Capital, Inc. and Berkshire Hathaway Inc. in 2013. 3G and Berkshire each took a 50% stake in the company and contributed $4 billion in capital as part of the deal. 3G was charged with managing the day-to-day operations of Heinz. 3G partners (and defendants) Bernando Hees and Paulo Basilio were named CEO and CFO, respectively.

3G—founded by defendants Jorge Paulo Lemann, Alexandre Behring, and Marcel Herrmann Telles, among others—had previously and successfully rolled up brand-name companies in the food and beverage and hospitality sectors. For example, 3G was involved in the creation of Anheuser-Busch InBev ("AB InBev"), in which Berkshire once held a large stake. Berkshire also invested alongside 3G in Burger King's 2014 acquisition of Canadian fast food chain Tim Hortons.

On March 24, 2015, Heinz entered into an Agreement and Plan of Merger with Kraft to form Kraft Heinz. Kraft stockholders approved the merger agreement on July 1, 2015 and the merger closed the next day. Post-closing, 3G and Berkshire together owned roughly 51% of Kraft Heinz, with 3G holding 24.2% and Berkshire holding 26.8%. Legacy Kraft stockholders owned the remaining 49% of the company.

Under the Merger Agreement, Kraft Heinz's eleven-member board of directors (the "Board") was composed of five former Kraft directors, three 3G designees, and three Berkshire designees. 3G appointed Behring, Lemann, and Telles to the Board. Berkshire appointed Gregory Abel, Warren Buffett, and Tracy Britt Cool. John T. Cahill, the former CEO and chairman of Kraft, was among the five former Kraft directors who completed the original Board. 3G's Hees and Basilio became the CEO and CFO of Kraft Heinz. Basilio was later replaced by another 3G partner, defendant David Knopf.

The day the merger closed, 3G and Berkshire entered into a Shareholders' Agreement. The Shareholders' Agreement required Berkshire and 3G to vote their shares in favor of each other's Board nominees. 3G and Berkshire also agreed not to take any action "to effect, encourage, or facilitate" the removal of the other's director designees. Kraft Heinz's March 3, 2016 proxy statement explained that "Berkshire Hathaway, Mr. Buffett and the 3G Funds may be deemed to be a group for purposes of Section 13(d) of the Exchange Act."

3G Sells $1.2 Billion of Kraft Heinz Stock.

On August 2, 2018, Hees, Knopf, and Kraft Heinz's then-Executive Vice President (and defendant) Eduardo Pelleissone informed the Board that Kraft Heinz was unlikely to achieve its EBITDA target for the first half of 2018 and was expected to miss its 2018 full year target by over $700 million. The news came after Kraft Heinz had already missed its 2017 EBITDA target of $8.5 billion by $440 million, missed its target for the first quarter of 2018, and reduced its 2018 full year EBITDA projections from $8.4 billion to $8 billion. Behring, Lemann, Telles, and Basilio (in addition to Hees and Knopf) were present at the meeting. The Audit Committee and Knopf had previously been informed that Kraft Heinz's goodwill and intangible asset valuations were largely driven by Kraft Heinz management's revenue and cash flow forecasts.

Four days after the Board meeting, on August 7, 2018, 3G sold 7% of its stake in Kraft Heinz for proceeds of over $1.2 billion. The trade was made possible by Kraft Heinz removing the shares' restrictive legends. Before their removal, a 3G partner had provided Kraft Heinz's counsel with a statement that 3G "is not in possession of any material, non-public information." Pelleissone personally sold about $2.3 million of his Kraft Heinz shares on the same day.

Kraft Heinz Announces Poor Financial Results and an Accounting Impairment.

A pair of financial announcements followed by significant one-day price drops came next. On November 1, 2018, Kraft Heinz reported its third quarter 2018 financial results—it had missed its EBITDA target for the quarter by $232 million. Kraft Heinz's stock price fell nearly 10% from close on November 1 to close on November 2, 2018. On February 21, 2019, Kraft Heinz reported its fourth quarter and full year 2018 financial results, again missing internal targets by hundreds of millions of dollars. It also disclosed an adjustment to its goodwill and intangible assets resulting in a non-cash impairment charge of $15.4 billion. Kraft Heinz's stock price fell roughly 27.5% from close on February 21 to close on February 22, 2019.

Litigation followed. ...

This Litigation

The Complaint advances three counts on behalf of Kraft Heinz. Count I alleges breaches of fiduciary duty under *Brophy v. Cities Service Company* for either approving 3G's August 7, 2018 block sale of Kraft Heinz stock based on adverse material nonpublic information or allowing the sale to the detriment of Kraft Heinz's non-3G stockholders. Count II seeks contribution and indemnification from the defendants for allegedly causing Kraft Heinz to issue false and misleading statements in violation of federal securities laws. Count III brings aiding and abetting claims against several 3G entity defendants that were "the mechanisms through which 3G accomplished" the sale. ...

LEGAL ANALYSIS

The defendants have moved to dismiss the Complaint under Court of Chancery Rule 23.1 for failure to make a demand on the Kraft Heinz Board and under Court of Chancery Rule 12(b)(6) for failure to state a claim for relief. ...

As with all derivative cases, demand excusal is a threshold issue. My analysis begins and ends there. After conducting a demand futility analysis on a director-by-director basis, I conclude that a majority of the Board was disinterested and independent. Demand is therefore not excused, and the plaintiffs lack standing to press this derivative action.

The Demand Futility Standard

Under Court of Chancery Rule 23.1, a stockholder who seeks to displace the board's authority by asserting a derivative claim on behalf of a corporation must "allege with particularity the efforts, if any, made by the plaintiff to obtain the action the plaintiff desires from the directors or comparable authority and the reasons for the plaintiff's failure to obtain the action or for not making the effort." This requirement is rooted in the "basic principle of the Delaware General Corporation Law . . . that the directors, and not the stockholders, manage the business and affairs of the corporation." "It is designed to give a corporation, on whose behalf a derivative suit is brought, the opportunity to rectify the alleged wrong without suit and to control any litigation brought for its benefit."

Stockholders who forego a demand must "comply with stringent requirements of factual particularity" when alleging why demand should be excused. "Rule 23.1 is not satisfied by conclusory statements or mere notice pleading." Instead, "[w]hat the pleader must set forth are particularized factual statements that are essential to the claim."

The court is confined to the well-pleaded allegations in the Complaint, the documents incorporated into the Complaint by reference, and facts subject to judicial notice while conducting a Rule 23.1 analysis. All reasonable inferences from the particularized allegations in the Complaint must be drawn in the plaintiffs' favor. Under the heightened pleading requirement of Rule 23.1, "conclus[ory] allegations of fact or law not supported by the allegations of specific fact may not be taken as true."

The Delaware Supreme Court recently established a three-part, "universal test" for assessing demand futility in *United Food & Commercial Workers Union v. Zuckerberg.* The test is "consistent with and enhances" the standards articulated in *Aronson, Rales,* and their progeny, which "remain good law." Under *Zuckerberg,* this court must consider, director-by-director:

(i) whether the director received a material personal benefit from the alleged misconduct that is the subject of the litigation demand;

(ii) whether the director faces a substantial likelihood of liability on any of the claims that would be the subject of the litigation demand; and

(iii) whether the director lacks independence from someone who received a material personal benefit from the alleged misconduct that would be the subject of the litigation demand or who would face a substantial likelihood of liability on any of the claims that are the subject of the litigation demand.

If "the answer to any of these three questions is `yes' for at least half of the members of [a] demand board," demand is excused as futile.

The Demand Futility Analysis in This Case

"The court 'counts heads' of the members of a board to determine whether a majority of its members are disinterested and independent for demand futility purposes." The Board in place when this litigation was first filed on July 30, 2019 had eleven members: (1) defendant Lemann; (2) defendant Behring; (3) non-party Joao M. Castro-Neves, a 3G partner; (4) non-party Abel, a Berkshire designee; (5) non-party Cool, a Berkshire designee; (6) non-party Cahill, a former Kraft Heinz consultant and the former CEO of Kraft; (7) non-party Zoghbi, a former Kraft Heinz executive and current consultant; (8) non-party Alexandre Van Damme, a director of AB InBev; (9) non-party Feroz Dewan, who joined the Board in 2016; (10) non-party Jeanne P. Jackson, a former Kraft director; and (11) non-party John C. Pope, a former Kraft director. This decision refers to those eleven directors as the "Demand Board."

The defendants concede that the three 3G-affiliated directors— Lemann, Behring, and Castro-Neves—could not exercise impartial judgment regarding a demand. The plaintiffs, for their part, concede that Jackson and Pope are independent and disinterested for purposes of a demand futility analysis.

That leaves six directors for consideration: Dewan, Abel, Cool, Cahill, Zoghbi, and Van Damme. Only the third prong of the *Zuckerberg* test is relevant to that assessment. None of these directors are alleged to have sold Kraft Heinz stock during the relevant period or personally benefited from 3G's sale. These non-party directors would not face a substantial likelihood of liability, even if were assumed that the court might find in the plaintiffs' favor after trial. The demand futility analysis hinges entirely on whether the directors had disabling connections to 3G. If four of these six directors could exercise their independent and disinterested judgment regarding a demand to sue 3G, Rule 23.1 mandates dismissal.

The Plaintiffs' Control Allegations

The plaintiffs contend that the "demand futility analysis is strengthened by 3G's status as a controlling stockholder." "[T]he presence and influence of a controller is an important factor that should be considered in the director-based focus of the demand futility inquiry . . . particularly on the issue of independence." As Chancellor Chandler explained in *Orman v. Cullman,* an independence inquiry focuses on whether a director's decision would "result[] from that director being *controlled* by another," meaning that the director was dominated by or beholden to "the allegedly controlling entity."

3G is not Kraft Heinz's largest stockholder. At the filing of this litigation (post-sale), 3G owned approximately 22% of Kraft Heinz's stock. 3G had the right to appoint three of the Board's 11 members under the Shareholders' Agreement. Berkshire—which was disinterested in the stock sale—beneficially owned about 27% of Kraft Heinz and could also designate three directors under the Shareholders' Agreement.

The plaintiffs maintain that 3G and Berkshire should be viewed as a "control group" because they are bound together in a legally significant way based on the Shareholders' Agreement. ...

Whether 3G should be deemed a controlling stockholder (on its own or together with Berkshire) does not, however, "change[] the director-based focus of the demand futility inquiry." As the Delaware Supreme Court explained in *Aronson,* even "proof of majority ownership of a company does not strip the directors of the presumption of independence" in the demand context. Instead, "[t]here must be coupled with the allegation of control such facts as would demonstrate that through personal or other relationships the directors are beholden to the controlling person." Regardless of whether 3G controlled Kraft Heinz together with Berkshire, the plaintiffs cannot overcome the presumption of independence for a majority of the Demand Board.

The Demand Board's Independence from 3G

As discussed above, demand futility will be determined by whether at least four of Dewan, Abel, Cool, Cahill, Zoghbi, and Van Damme could have independently considered a demand to sue 3G. At the motion to dismiss stage, "a lack of independence turns on 'whether the plaintiffs have pled facts from which the director's ability to act impartially on a matter important to the interested party can be doubted because that director may feel either subject to the interested party's dominion or beholden to that interested party.'"

When assessing independence, "our law cannot ignore the social nature of humans or that they are motivated by things other than money, such as love, friendship, and collegiality." The court must "consider all the particularized facts pled by the plaintiffs about the relationships between the director and the interested party in their totality and not in isolation from each other, and draw all reasonable inferences from the totality of those facts in favor of the plaintiffs."

After doing so, I conclude that the plaintiffs have not pleaded particularized facts sufficient to create reasonable doubt about the independence of Dewan, Abel, Cool, and Cahill. Because they join the concededly independent and disinterested Jackson and Pope to form a majority of the Demand Board, demand is not excused under Rule 23.1.

Dewan

Feroz Dewan has served on the Board since October 2016. The plaintiffs assert that he is beholden to 3G but do not plead any particularized facts undermining his independence. The only grounds provided to question Dewan's independence are (1) that Dewan's private foundation held more than 12% of its investment portfolio in a 3G fund as of 2016, and (2) that Dewan chairs a non-profit that receives donations from organizations including 3G-controlled Restaurant Brands International ("RBI"). No further context is provided, including whether Dewan's foundation remained invested in a 3G fund when this litigation was filed, whether 3G had a role in RBI's donation, and whether RBI's donation was material to the charity. Without that information, it is not possible to infer that Dewan lacks independence from 3G.

Abel and Cool

Gregory Abel previously served on the Heinz board and has served as a Berkshire designee on the Board since the merger. He is a member of Berkshire's board of directors and its Vice Chairman of Non-Insurance Business Operations. The plaintiffs allege that he "lacks independence given Berkshire's close co-investing relationship with 3G and Buffett's close friendship with Lemann."

Tracy Britt Cool also served on the Heinz board and served as a Berkshire Board designee after the merger until January 2020. Cool joined Berkshire in 2009 as a financial assistant to Buffett and has served as a director of several Berkshire companies and as the CEO of a Berkshire subsidiary. She allegedly has a close relationship with Buffett, who "walked Cool down the aisle at her wedding in 2013." The plaintiffs aver that she lacks independence "by virtue of her personal relationship with Buffett and her career as a longtime Berkshire executive."

The parties' arguments with regard to the independence of Abel and Cool are substantively identical. Considered in their totality, the plaintiffs' allegations provide no reason to doubt that either director could not exercise disinterested and independent judgment regarding a demand.

Berkshire's Relationship with 3G

Neither Abel nor Cool has any direct relationships with 3G or its defendant partners. Rather, Abel and Cool are allegedly not independent of 3G because they are beholden to Berkshire and Buffett who, in turn, are beholden to 3G and its partners. This transitive theory of independence does not impugn Abel or Cool's independence for several reasons.

First, the plaintiffs assert that Abel and Cool's employment and potential for promotion at Berkshire "would be jeopardized by causing [Kraft Heinz] to sue 3G or Lemann." This argument ties back, in some respects, to the plaintiffs' allegation that Berkshire and 3G are a control group. Delaware courts have recognized that when a controller is interested in a transaction, directors may seek to "preserve their positions and align themselves with the controller" by declining to initiate litigation against it. That logic might apply if Abel and Cool were asked to consider pursuing litigation against Berkshire. But Berkshire is not a defendant. It was uninvolved in the challenged stock sale and is not alleged to have received any benefit from it.

The plaintiffs argue that Abel and Cool could not impartially sue 3G because of Berkshire and 3G's history of co-investment, totaling $25 billion since 2013. The vast majority of those investments are Kraft Heinz related: $12.4 billion from the Heinz acquisition and $10 billion from the Kraft Heinz merger. The only other co-investment specified in the Complaint is Berkshire's 2014 $3 billion investment in Burger King's acquisition of Tim Horton's. It cannot be reasonably inferred from these allegations that Berkshire—which had nearly $447 billion in total assets as of December 31, 2019— relies on 3G to gain access to investments. Even if it could, the necessary link to Abel and Cool is missing. There are no particularized allegations supporting a conclusion that Abel or Cool felt subject to 3G's dominion or beholden to 3G based on those investments.

The plaintiffs further allege that Abel and Cool's independence was compromised given Buffett's "close relationship" with 3G co-founder Lemann. According to the plaintiffs, Buffett has described Lemann as a friend, views him favorably as a business partner, attended one of his birthday parties, and joined him for three professional workshops. Those facts (if true) would hardly be sufficient to show that Buffett lacks independence. His relationship with Lemann is not "suggestive of the type of very close personal relationship that, like family ties, one would expect to heavily influence a human's ability to exercise impartial judgment." Allegations that individuals "moved in the same social circles," "developed business relationships before joining the board," or described each other as "friends" are insufficient, without more, to rebut the presumption of independence. And one step removed from Abel and Cool, these allegations are of little consequence.

Shareholder's Agreement

The plaintiffs also maintain that the Shareholders' Agreement would prevent Abel and Cool from exercising their independent judgment regarding a demand. According to the Complaint, the Shareholders' Agreement "prevents any of Berkshire's designees from voting to cause [Kraft Heinz] to sue 3G's designees." Section 2.1(c)(ii) of the Shareholders' Agreement provides that "Berkshire . . . agrees it will not vote its Shares or take any other action to effect, encourage or facilitate the removal of any 3G Designee elected to the Board therefrom . . . without the consent of . . . 3G." The plaintiffs' theory is that pursuing litigation against 3G on behalf of Kraft Heinz could "`effect, encourage or facilitate the removal' of the 3G-designated directors from the Board" under 8 *Del. C.* § 225(c).

The plaintiffs seemingly waived any argument about the effect of the Shareholders' Agreement on Abel and Cool's independence after failing to advance it in their briefing. In any event, the Shareholders' Agreement has little bearing on the demand futility analysis for several reasons. It did not bind Abel and Cool, who are not parties to it. The plain language of Section 2(c)(ii) would only cause Berkshire to prevent an "Affiliate" that "hold[s] shares" from acting to facilitate the removal of a 3G Board designee. Neither Abel nor Cool fit that definition. And pursuing litigation against 3G is not equivalent to automatic removal from the Board under Section 225(c). More fundamentally, there are no particularized allegations indicating that Abel or Cool would have been guided by the Shareholders' Agreement in assessing a demand to sue 3G.

Taken together, the plaintiffs' allegations are insufficient. Even when viewed in the context of the Shareholders' Agreement, Berkshire's ties to 3G cannot support a reasonable inference that either Abel or Cool is personally beholden to 3G.

Cahill

John T. Cahill has served as Vice Chairman of the Board since the merger. He previously served as the CEO of Kraft and, after the merger, worked as a consultant to Kraft Heinz. The plaintiffs assert that Cahill lacks independence from 3G because of (1) his consulting relationship and director compensation, (2) his status as not "independent" under Nasdaq listing standards in Kraft Heinz's 2019 proxy, and (3) his son's employment at AB InBev. Taken together, these allegations do not impugn Cahill's ability to impartially consider a demand.

First, the plaintiffs allege that Cahill lacks independence from 3G because his prior consulting compensation of $500,000 per year, coupled with his director compensation of about $235,000 per year, constituted more than half of Cahill's publicly reported income in 2018. Cahill's consulting agreement with Kraft Heinz terminated on July 1, 2019—before this action was filed. There are no facts alleged indicating that Cahill expected his consulting arrangement to resume.

At the time the Complaint was filed, Cahill's income from Kraft Heinz was limited to standard director compensation. That compensation accounted for roughly 17% of his publicly reported income. "[D]irector compensation alone cannot create a reasonable basis to doubt a director's impartiality." [*Citing* Robotti & Co., LLC v. Liddell, 2010 WL 157474, at *15 (Del. Ch. Jan. 14, 2010); see also In re Oracle Corp. Deriv. Litig., 2018 WL 1381331, at *18 (Del. Ch. Mar. 19, 2018) (noting that "even this lucrative compensation [of $548,005] would form insufficient cause to doubt [a director's] impartiality" because "[t]here [we]re no allegations that the director compensation . . . is material to [the director]").]

Even if the court were to infer that Cahill's past consulting and director fees were material to him at that time, it is not clear why they would create a sense of "owingness" to 3G. Cahill had no relationship with 3G before Kraft was merged with Heinz. The Complaint lacks any particularized allegations supporting a pleading-stage inference that 3G was responsible for his directorship or consulting arrangement with Kraft Heinz or had the power to strip him of potential future consulting fees or his Board position.

The fact that Kraft Heinz's 2019 proxy stated that the Board does not consider Cahill independent from Kraft Heinz for Nasdaq listing purposes does not change that conclusion. The Delaware Supreme Court has held that "the criteria NASDAQ has articulated as bearing on independence are relevant under Delaware law," but do not "perfectly marry with the standards" applicable under Rule 23.1. An independence determination under stock exchange rules "is qualitatively different from, and thus does not operate as a surrogate for, this Court's analysis of independence under Delaware law for demand futility purposes." Delaware courts recognize that exchange rules, such as the criteria Nasdaq has articulated as bearing on independence, should be considered as part of a holistic demand futility analysis. But the determination of whether Cahill is independent under Nasdaq rules concerns his independence from Kraft Heinz—not from 3G. In my view, that determination carries little weight given the dearth of particularized allegations suggesting that Cahill is beholden to 3G.

The plaintiffs' final attempt to impugn Cahill's independence concerns his son's employment as a District Sales Manager at AB InBev following his completion of its "highly selective management trainee program." The plaintiffs assert that those who complete the program "*can* maintain a direct relationship with 3G founding partner Telles." That allegation is conclusory. There are no particularized allegations tying Cahill's son's employment to 3G or suggesting that he, in fact, had a "direct relationship" with Telles. Thus, there is no well-pleaded basis from which to infer that Cahill's son's employment at AB InBev would bear on Cahill's ability to assess a demand.

The allegations regarding Cahill's son are insufficient to overcome his presumed independence, even when viewed holistically with the plaintiffs' other allegations. It would not be reasonable to infer that Cahill is so beholden to 3G that he would be motivated to cover up insider trading.

Zoghbi and Van Damme

George Zoghbi has served on the Board since April 2018. He was Kraft Heinz's Chief Operating Officer from the time of the merger until October 2017, when he became a Special Advisor. The plaintiffs' arguments about Zoghbi largely overlap with those about

Cahill, except that he is alleged to have received a larger consulting fee, which was ongoing as of July 2019 and accounts for a comparatively greater percentage of his income. Whether Zoghbi is independent of 3G is therefore a closer call than Cahill.

Alexandre Van Damme has also served on the Board since April 2018. The Complaint describes Van Damme as immersed in an "intricate web of personal, professional and financial ties to 3G and its principals." The particularized allegations that make up that web, taken as true and in their totality, come closest to supporting a reasonable doubt about a non-3G director's ability to objectively consider a demand.

Because this decision has already found that six of the Demand Board's eleven directors were able to consider a demand impartially, I need not resolve whether Zoghbi or Van Damme are independent.

CONCLUSION

The plaintiffs have failed to plead particularized facts creating a reasonable doubt that six of the eleven Demand Board members lack independence from 3G or its defendant partners. The plaintiffs have conceded the independence of Jackson and Pope. Abel and Cool do not lack independence from 3G based on their ties to Berkshire. And the plaintiff's allegations about Cahill and Dewan do not, in totality, impugn their independence from 3G. Accordingly, demand is not excused.

The defendants' motions to dismiss the Complaint pursuant to Rule 23.1 are granted. The Complaint is dismissed with prejudice in its entirety.

In Re The Goldman Sachs Group, Inc. Shareholder Litigation　　　　3.2.3.2

In the case that follows, the Chancery Court considers the defendant's Rule 23.1 motion to dismiss. In a 23.1 motion, the defendant argues that the complaint should be dismissed for lack of standing. The defendant argues that the plaintiff lacks standing because it did not comply with the requirements of 23.1, typically failure to make demand when demand is not futile.

As is required in such cases, the court reviews the interestedness and independence of each director in order to determine whether demand was futile. Remember, in making a ruling on a 23.1 motion to dismiss, the court must go through the exercise of assessing each director's interestedness and independence pursuant to either *Aronson* or *Rales* and not the underlying merits of the claim. In this particular case, the court applies both *Aronson* and *Rales* to each of the directors on the Goldman Sachs board. As you work through the opinion, consider how a court would apply the newer *Zuckerberg* standard to each director.

IN RE THE GOLDMAN SACHS GROUP, INC. SHAREHOLDER LITIGATION.
Del Ct of Chancery (2011)

GLASSCOCK, Vice Chancellor.

The Delaware General Corporation Law is, for the most part, enabling in nature. It provides corporate directors and officers with broad discretion to act as they find appropriate in the conduct of corporate affairs. It is therefore left to Delaware case law to set a boundary on that otherwise unconstrained realm of action. The restrictions imposed by Delaware case law set this boundary by requiring corporate officers and directors to act as faithful fiduciaries to the corporation and its stockholders. Should these corporate actors perform in such a way that they are violating their fiduciary obligations—their core duties of care or loyalty—their faithless acts properly become the subject of judicial action in vindication of the rights of the stockholders. Within the boundary of fiduciary duty, however, these corporate actors are free to pursue corporate opportunities in any way that, in the exercise of their business judgment on behalf of the corporation, they see fit. It is this broad freedom to pursue opportunity on behalf of the corporation, in the myriad ways that may be revealed to creative human minds, that has made the corporate structure a supremely effective engine for the production of wealth. Exercising that freedom is precisely what directors and officers are elected by their shareholders to do. So long as such individuals act within the boundaries of their fiduciary duties, judges are ill-suited by training (and should be disinclined by temperament) to second-guess the business decisions of those chosen by the stockholders to fulfill precisely that function. This case, as in so many corporate matters considered by this Court, involves whether actions taken by certain director defendants fall outside of the fiduciary boundaries existing under Delaware case law—and are therefore subject to judicial oversight—or whether the acts complained of are within those broad boundaries, where a law-trained judge should refrain from acting.

This matter is before me on a motion to dismiss, pursuant to Court of Chancery Rule 23.1, for failure to make a pre-suit demand upon the board, and Court of Chancery Rule 12(b)(6) for failure to state a claim. The Plaintiffs contend that Goldman's compensation structure created a divergence of interest between Goldman's management and its stockholders. The Plaintiffs allege that because Goldman's directors have consistently based compensation for the firm's management on a percentage of net revenue, Goldman's employees had a motivation to grow net revenue at any cost and without regard to risk.

The Plaintiffs allege that under this compensation structure, Goldman's employees would attempt to maximize short-term profits, thus increasing their bonuses at the expense of stockholders' interests. The Plaintiffs contend that Goldman's employees would do this by engaging in highly risky trading practices and by over-leveraging the company's assets. If these practices turned a profit, Goldman's employees would receive a windfall; however, losses would fall on the stockholders.

The Plaintiffs allege that the Director Defendants breached their fiduciary duties by approving the compensation structure discussed above. [...]

I. FACTS

Defendant Goldman is a global financial services firm which provides investment banking, securities, and investment management services to consumers, businesses, and governments. Goldman is a Delaware corporation with its principal executive offices in New York, NY.

The complaint also names fourteen individual current and former directors and officers of Goldman as defendants: Lloyd C. Blankfein, Gary D. Cohn, John H. Bryan, Claes Dahlback, Stephen Friedman, William W. George, Rajat K. Gupta, James A. Johnson, Lois D. Juliber, Lakshmi N. Mittal, James J. Schiro, Ruth J. Simmons, David A. Viniar, and J. Michael Evans (together with Goldman, "the Defendants"). [...]

B. Background

Goldman engages in three principal business segments: investment banking, asset management and securities services, and trading and principal investments. The majority of Goldman's revenue comes from the trading and principal investment segment.[2] In that segment Goldman engages in market making, structuring and entering into a variety of derivative transactions, and the proprietary trading of financial instruments.[-]

As the revenue generated by the trading and principal investment segment grew, so did the trading department's stature within Goldman. The traders "became wealthier and more powerful in the bank."[9] The Plaintiffs allege that the compensation for these traders was not based on performance and was unjustifiable because Goldman was doing "nothing more than compensat[ing] employees for results produced by the vast amounts of shareholder equity that Goldman ha[d] available to be deployed."[10]

C. Compensation

Goldman employed a "pay for performance" philosophy linking the total compensation of its employees to the company's performance.[11] Goldman has used a Compensation Committee since at least 2006 to oversee the development and implementation of its compensation scheme.[12] The Compensation Committee was responsible for reviewing and approving the Goldman executives' annual compensation.[13] To fulfill their charge, the Compensation Committee consulted with senior management about management's projections of net revenues and the proper ratio of compensation and benefits expenses to net revenues (the "compensation ratio").[14] Additionally, the Compensation Committee compared Goldman's compensation ratio to that of Goldman's competitors such as Bear Stearns, Lehman Brothers, Merrill Lynch, and Morgan Stanley. The Compensation Committee would then approve a ratio and structure that Goldman would use to govern Goldman's compensation to its employees.[15]

The Plaintiffs allege that from 2007 through 2009, the Director Defendants approved a management-proposed compensation structure that caused management's interests to diverge from those of the stockholders.[16] According to the Plaintiffs, in each year since 2006 the Compensation Committee approved the management-determined compensation ratio, which governed "the total amount of funds available to compensate all employees including senior executives," without any analysis.[17] Although the total compensation paid by Goldman varied significantly each year, total compensation as a percentage of net revenue remained relatively constant.[18] Because management was awarded a relatively constant percentage of total revenue, management could maximize their compensation by increasing Goldman's total net revenue and total stockholder equity.[19] The Plaintiffs contend that this compensation structure led management to pursue a highly risky business strategy that emphasized short term profits in order to increase their yearly bonuses.[20]

D. Business Risk

The Plaintiffs allege that management achieved Goldman's growth "through extreme leverage and significant uncontrolled exposure to risky loans and credit risks."[41] The trading and principal investment segment is the largest contributor to Goldman's total revenues; it is also the segment to which Goldman commits the largest amount of capital.[42] The Plaintiffs argue that this was a risky use of Goldman's assets, pointing out that Goldman's Value at Risk (VAR) increased between 2007 and 2009, and that in 2007 Goldman had a leverage ratio of 25 to 1, exceeding that of its peers.[43]

The Plaintiffs charge that this business strategy was not in the best interest of the stockholders, in part, because the stockholders did not benefit to the same degree that management did. Stockholders received roughly 2% of the revenue generated in the form of dividends—but if the investment went south, it was the stockholders' equity at risk, not that of the traders. [...]

E. The Plaintiffs' Claims

The Plaintiffs allege that the Director Defendants breached their fiduciary duties by (1) failing to properly analyze and rationally set compensation levels for Goldman's employees and (2) committing waste by "approving a compensation ratio to Goldman employees in an amount so disproportionately large to the contribution of management, as opposed to capital as to be unconscionable."[50]

The Plaintiffs also allege that the Director Defendants violated their fiduciary duties by failing to adequately monitor Goldman's operations and by "allowing the Firm to manage and conduct the Firm's trading in a grossly unethical manner."[51]

II. LEGAL STANDARDS

The Plaintiffs have brought this action derivatively on behalf of Goldman "to redress the breaches of fiduciary duty and other violations of law by [the] Defendants."[52] The Defendants have moved to dismiss, pursuant to Court of Chancery Rule 23.1, for failure to make a pre-suit demand upon the board[...].

"[T]he pleading burden imposed by Rule 23.1 . . . is more onerous than that demanded by Rule 12(b)(6)."[57] Though a complaint may plead a "conceivable" allegation that would survive a motion to dismiss under Rule 12(b)(6), "vague allegations are . . . insufficient to withstand a motion to dismiss pursuant to Rule 23.1."[58] This difference reflects the divergent reasons for the two rules: Rule 12(b)(6) is designed to ensure a decision on the merits of any potentially valid claim, excluding only clearly meritless claims; Rule 23.1 is designed to vindicate the authority of the corporate board, except in those cases where the board will not or (because of conflicts) cannot exercise its judgment in the interest of the corporation. Rule 23.1 requires that "a plaintiff shareholder . . . make a demand upon the corporation's current board to pursue derivative claims owned by the corporation before a shareholder is permitted to pursue legal action on the corporation's behalf."[59] Demand is required because "[t]he decision whether to initiate or pursue a lawsuit on behalf of the corporation is generally within the power and responsibility of the board of directors."[60] Accordingly, the complaint must allege "with particularity the efforts, if any, made by the plaintiff to obtain the action the plaintiff desires from the directors or comparable authority and the reasons for the plaintiff's failure to obtain the action or for not making the effort."[61]

C. Demand Futility

If, as here, a stockholder does not first demand that the directors pursue the alleged cause of action, he must establish that demand is excused by satisfying "stringent [pleading] requirements of factual particularity" by "set[ting] forth particularized factual statements that are essential to the claim" in order to demonstrate that making demand would be futile.[62] Pre-suit demand is futile if a corporation's board is "deemed incapable of making an impartial decision regarding the pursuit of the litigation."[63]

Under the two-pronged test, first explicated in *Aronson,* when a plaintiff challenges a conscious decision of the board, a plaintiff can show demand futility by alleging particularized facts that create a reasonable doubt that either (1) the directors are disinterested and independent or (2) "the challenged transaction was otherwise the product of a valid exercise of business judgment."[64]

On the other hand, when a plaintiff complains of board *inaction,* "there is no `challenged transaction,' and the ordinary *Aronson* analysis does not apply."[65] Instead, the board's inaction is analyzed under *Rales v. Blasband.*[66] Under the *Rales* test, a plaintiff must plead particularized facts that "create a reasonable doubt that, as of the time the complaint [was] filed, the board of directors could have properly exercised its independent and disinterested business judgment in responding to a demand."[67]

Here, the Plaintiffs concede that they have not made demand upon Goldman's board of directors, but they assert that such demand would be futile for numerous reasons. First, they argue that Goldman's board of directors is interested or lacks independence because of financial ties between the Director Defendants and Goldman.[68] Next, they allege that there is a reasonable doubt as to whether the board's compensation structure was the product of a valid exercise of business judgment.[69] The Plaintiffs further assert that there is a substantial likelihood that the Director Defendants will face personal liability for the dereliction of their duty to oversee Goldman's operations.[70]

I evaluate the Plaintiffs' claims involving active decisions by the board under *Aronson.* I evaluate the Plaintiffs' oversight claims against the Director Defendants for the failure to monitor Goldman's operations under *Rales.*

III. ANALYSIS

A. Approval of the Compensation Scheme

The Plaintiffs challenge the Goldman board's approval of the company's compensation scheme on three grounds. They allege (1) that the majority of the board was interested or lacked independence when it approved the compensation scheme, (2) the board did not otherwise validly exercise its business judgment, and

(3) the board's approval of the compensation scheme constituted waste. Because the approval of the compensation scheme was a conscious decision by the board, the Plaintiffs must satisfy the *Aronson* test to successfully plead demand futility. I find that under all three of their challenges to the board's approval of the compensation scheme, the Plaintiffs have failed to adequately plead demand futility.

1. Independence and Disinterestedness of the Board

A plaintiff successfully pleads demand futility under the first prong of *Aronson* when he alleges particularized facts that create a reasonable doubt that "a `majority' of the directors could [have] impartially consider[ed] a demand" either because they were interested or lacked independence, as of the time that suit was filed.[71] Generally, "[a] director's interest may be shown by demonstrating a potential personal benefit or detriment to the director as a result of the decision."[72] A director is independent if the "director's decision is based on the corporate merits of the subject before the board rather than extraneous considerations or influences."[73]

When the complaint was originally filed, Goldman's board had 12 directors: Blankfein, Cohn, Bryan, Dahlback, Friedman, George, Gupta, Johnson, Juliber, Mittal, Schiro, and Simmons.[74] The Plaintiffs fail to allege that George and Schiro were interested or lacked independence. It can be assumed that Blankfein and Cohn, as officials of Goldman, would be found to be interested or lack independence. Therefore, the Plaintiffs must satisfy *Aronson* with respect to at least four of the remaining eight directors.[75]

The Plaintiffs argue that demand is excused because a majority of the Director Defendants lacked independence or were interested as a result of significant financial relationships with Goldman. The Plaintiffs contend that directors Bryan, Friedman, Gupta, Johnson, Juliber, and Simmons were interested because the private Goldman Sachs Foundation ("the Goldman Foundation") has made contributions to charitable organizations that the directors were affiliated with.[76] The Plaintiffs assert that directors Dahlback,

Friedman, and Mittal were interested because of financial interactions with Goldman.

Below I provide the specific allegations found in the complaint about the Director Defendants. Since the Plaintiffs do not allege that the Director Defendants (aside from Blankfein and Cohn) were interested in the compensation decisions, I analyze whether the director lacks independence.

a. Directors and Charitable Contributions.

i. John H. Bryan

Bryan has served as a Goldman director since 1999.[77] He was also a member of Goldman's Audit Committee and Goldman's Compensation Committee.[78] His charitable works included chairing a successful campaign to raise $100 million for the renovation of the Chicago Lyric Opera House and Orchestra Hall, and acting as a life trustee of the University of Chicago.[79] The Plaintiffs state that part of Bryan's responsibility, as a trustee, was to raise money for the University. The Plaintiffs note that Goldman has made "substantial contributions"[80] to the campaign to renovate the Chicago Lyric Opera House and Orchestra Hall and that the Goldman Foundation donated $200,000 to the University in 2006 and allocated an additional $200,000 in 2007.[81]

The Plaintiffs allege that because Goldman and the Goldman Foundation have assisted Bryan in his fund raising responsibilities, Bryan lacks independence.[82]

This Court has previously addressed directorial independence and charitable contributions. *Hallmark*[83] involved a special committee member who served on a variety of charitable boards where the charity received donations from the defendant corporation. The *Hallmark* Court noted that, even though part of the member's role was to act as a fund raiser, the member did not receive a salary for his work and did not actively solicit donations from the defendant corporation; therefore, the plaintiff failed to sufficiently show that the member was incapable of "exercising independent judgment."[84]

This Court also addressed charitable contributions in *J.P. Morgan*.[85] In that case, the plaintiff challenged the independence of a director who was the President and a trustee of the American Natural History Museum, another director who was a trustee of the American Natural History Museum, and a director who was the President and CEO of the United Negro College Fund.[86] The plaintiff alleged that because the defendant corporation made donations to these organizations and was a significant benefactor, the directors lacked independence.[87] The Court decided that without additional facts showing, for instance, how the donations would affect the decision making of the directors or what percentage of the overall contribution was represented by the corporation's donations, the plaintiff had failed to demonstrate that the directors were not independent.[88]

In the case at bar, nothing more can be inferred from the complaint than the facts that the Goldman Foundation made donations to a charity that Bryan served as trustee, that part of Bryan's role as a trustee was to raise money, and that Goldman made donations to another charity where Bryan chaired a renovation campaign. The Plaintiffs do not allege that Bryan received a salary for either of his philanthropic roles, that the donations made by the Goldman Foundation or Goldman were the result of active solicitation by Bryan, or that Bryan had other substantial dealings with Goldman or the Goldman Foundation. The Plaintiffs do not provide the ratios of the amounts donated by Goldman, or the Goldman Foundation, to overall donations, or any other information demonstrating that the amount would be material to the charity. Crucially, the Plaintiffs fail to provide any information on how the amounts given influenced Bryan's decision-making process.[89] Because the complaint lacks such particularized details, the Plaintiffs have failed to create a reasonable doubt as to Bryan's independence.

ii. Rajat K. Gupta

Gupta has served as a Goldman director since 2006.[90] He was also a member of Goldman's Audit Committee and Goldman's Compensation Committee.[91] Gupta is chairman of the board of the Indian School of Business, to which the Goldman Foundation has donated $1.6 million since 2002.[92] Gupta is also a member of the dean's advisory board of Tsinghua University School of Economics and Management, to which the Foundation has donated at least $3.5 million since 2002.[93] Finally, Gupta is a member of the United Nations Commission on the Private Sector and Development and he is a special advisor to the UN Secretary General on UN Reform.[94] Since 2002, the Foundation has donated around $1.6 million to the Model UN program.[95] The Plaintiffs allege that as "a member of these boards and commission, it is part of Gupta's job to raise money."[96]

The Plaintiffs challenge to Gupta's independence fails for reasons similar to Bryan's. The Plaintiffs allegations only provide information that shows that Gupta was engaged in philanthropic activities and that the Goldman foundation made donations to charities to which Gupta had ties. The Plaintiffs do not mention the materiality of the donations to the charities or any solicitation on the part of Gupta. The Plaintiffs do not state how Gupta's decision-making was altered by the donations. Without such particularized allegations, the Plaintiffs fail to raise a reasonable doubt that Gupta was independent.

iii. James A. Johnson

Again the Plaintiffs fail to provide any information other than that a director was affiliated with a charity and the Goldman Foundation made a donation to that charity. Without more, the Plaintiffs fail to provide particularized factual allegations that create a reasonable doubt in regards to Johnson's independence.

iv. Lois D. Juliber

For the same reasons that the Plaintiffs' allegations fall short for directors Bryan, Gupta, and Johnson, the Plaintiffs' allegations fall short here. The Plaintiffs do not plead facts sufficient to create a reasonable doubt whether Juliber was independent.

v. Ruth J. Simmons

Simmons has served as a Goldman director since 2000.[1105] She was also a member of Goldman's Compensation Committee.[1106] Simmons is President of Brown University, and the Plaintiffs allege that part of her job is to raise money for the University.[1107] The Plaintiffs note that "[t]he [Goldman] Foundation has pledged funding in an undisclosed amount to share in the support of a position of Program Director at The Swearer Center for Public Service at Brown University," and so far $200,000 has been allocated to this project.[1108]

Simmons differs from the other directors in that, rather than sitting on a charitable board, as the other defendants do, Simmons livelihood as President of Brown University does directly depend on her fundraising abilities;[1109] however, the Plaintiffs fail to allege particularized factual allegations that create a reasonable doubt that Simmons was independent.

The Plaintiffs provide the amount donated to Brown University, but do not give any additional information showing the materiality of the donation to Brown University. The Plaintiffs do not provide the percentage this amount represented of the total amount raised by Brown, or even how this amount was material to the Swearer Center. Additionally, the Plaintiffs' allegations do not provide information that Simmons actively solicited this amount or how this or potential future donations would affect Simmons. The facts pled are insufficient to raise the inference that Simmons feels obligated to the foundation or Goldman management. Consequently, the factual allegations pled by the Plaintiffs fail to raise a reasonable doubt that, despite Simmons's position as President of Brown University, she remained independent.

b. Directors with Other Alleged Interests.

The Plaintiffs allege that three directors have, in addition (in the case of Mr. Friedman) to charitable connections to Goldman or the Goldman Foundation, business dealings with Goldman that render them dependent for purposes of the first prong of the *Aronson* analysis. Having already found that a majority of the Goldman board was independent, I could simply omit analysis of the independence of these directors under *Aronson.* I will briefly address the Plaintiffs contentions with respect to the directors below.

i. Stephen Friedman

The Plaintiffs allege that Friedman lacks independence for two reasons. First, the Plaintiffs allege that Friedman is not independent because of his philanthropic work and Goldman's advancement thereof. Second, the Plaintiffs allege that Friedman is not independent due to his business dealings with Goldman.[...]

Taken by themselves, the facts pled, concerning Friedman's charitable connection to the Goldman Foundation, are insufficient to create a reasonable doubt that Friedman was independent. [...]

Besides their allegations concerning Friedman's charitable endeavors, the Plaintiffs also allege that Goldman "*has* invested at least $670 million in funds managed by Friedman."[1141] This is the entirety of the pleadings regarding Friedman's business involvement with Goldman. Contrary to the contentions in the Plaintiffs' Answering Brief, the complaint does not allege that Friedman relies on the management of these funds for his livelihood; that contention, if buttressed by factual allegations in the complaint, might reasonably demonstrate lack of independence. The complaint is insufficient, as written, for that purpose.

ii. Claes Dahlback

Besides serving on Goldman's board, Dahlback is a senior advisor to an entity described in the complaint as "Investor AB."[1117] The Plaintiffs note that Goldman has invested more than $600 million in funds to which Dahlback is an adviser (presumably, but not explicitly, Investor AB).[1118] The Plaintiffs contend that because Dahlback had substantial financial relationships with Goldman, he lacked independence.

The Plaintiffs' allegations regarding Dahlback are sparse and tenuous. "[T]he complaint contains no allegations of fact tending to show that [any] fees paid were material to [Dahlback]."[1119] The Plaintiffs only note that Dahlback is an advisor to Investor AB, and that Goldman has invested more than $600 million in funds with an entity to which Dahlback is an advisor. Contrary to the statements by the Plaintiffs in the answering brief, the complaint does not allege that Dahlback's "livelihood depends on his full-time job as an advisor." The Plaintiffs fail to allege that Dahlback derives a substantial benefit from being an advisor to Investor AB, that Dahlback solicited funds from Goldman, that Investor AB received funds because of Dahlback's involvement, or any other fact that would tend to raise a reasonable doubt that Dahlback's future employment with Investor AB is independent of Goldman's investment. As with defendant Friedman, the pleadings are insufficient to raise a reasonable doubt as to Dahlback's independence.

iii. Lakshmi N. Mittal

Mittal is the chairman and CEO of ArcelorMittal.[1122] The Plaintiffs allege that "Goldman has arranged or provided billions of euros in financing to his company" and that "[d]uring 2007 and 2008 alone, the Company had made loans to AcelorMittal [sic] in the aggregate amount of 464 million euros."[1123]

Goldman is an investment bank. The fact "[t]hat it provided financing to large . . . companies should come as no shock to anyone. Yet this is all that the plaintiffs allege."[1124] The Plaintiffs fail to plead facts that show anything other than a series of market transactions occurred between ArcelorMittal and Goldman. For instance, the Plaintiffs have not alleged that ArcelorMittal is receiving a discounted interest rate on the loans from Goldman, that Mittal was unable to receive financing from any other lender, or that loans from Goldman compose a substantial part of ArcelorMittal's funding.[125] The pleadings fail to raise a reasonable doubt as to the independence of Mittal.

1. Good Faith

"[A] failure to act in good faith requires conduct that is qualitatively different from, and more culpable than, the conduct giving rise to a violation of the fiduciary duty of care (i.e., gross negligence)."[131] Examples of this include situations where the fiduciary intentionally breaks the law, "where the fiduciary intentionally acts with a purpose other than that of advancing the best interests of the corporation," or "where the fiduciary intentionally fails to act in the face of a known duty to act, demonstrating a conscious disregard for his duties."[132] While this is not an exclusive list, "these three are the most salient."[133]

The third category above falls between "conduct motivated by subjective bad intent," and "conduct resulting from gross negligence."[134] "Conscious disregard" involves an "intentional dereliction of duty" which is "more culpable than simple inattention or failure to be informed of all facts material to the decision."[135]

The Plaintiffs' main contention is that Goldman's compensation scheme itself was approved in bad faith. The Plaintiffs allege that "[n]o person acting in good faith on behalf of Goldman consistently could approve the payment of between 44% and 48% of net revenues to Goldman's employees year in and year out"[...]

[...]

The decision as to how much compensation is appropriate to retain and incentivize employees, both individually and in the aggregate, is a core function of a board of directors exercising its business judgment. The Plaintiffs' pleadings fall short of creating a reasonable doubt that the Directors Defendants have failed to exercise that judgment here. The Plaintiffs acknowledge that the compensation plan authorized by Goldman's board, which links compensation to revenue produced, was intended to align employee interests with those of the stockholders and incentivize the production of wealth. To an extent, it does so: extra effort by employees to raise corporate revenue, if successful, is rewarded. The Plaintiffs' allegations mainly propose that the compensation scheme implemented by the board does not perfectly align these interests; and that, in fact, it may encourage employee behavior incongruent with the stockholders' interest. This may be correct, but it is irrelevant. The fact that the Plaintiffs may desire a different compensation scheme does not indicate that equitable relief is warranted. Such changes may be accomplished through directorial elections, but not, absent a showing unmet here, through this Court. [...]

The Plaintiffs argue that there was an intentional dereliction of duty or a conscious disregard by the Director Defendants in setting compensation levels; however, the Plaintiffs fail to plead with particularity that any of the Director Defendants had the scienter necessary to give rise to a violation of the duty of loyalty.[1140] The Plaintiffs do not allege that the board failed to employ a metric to set compensation levels; rather, they merely argue that a different metric, such as comparing Goldman's compensation to that of hedge fund managers rather than to compensation at other investment banks, would have yielded a better result.[1141] But this observance does not make the board's decision self-evidently wrong, and it does not raise a reasonable doubt that the board approved Goldman's compensation structure in good faith.

2. Adequately Informed

The Plaintiffs also contend that the board was uninformed in making its compensation decision. "Pre-suit demand will be excused in a derivative suit only if the . . . particularized facts in the complaint create a reasonable doubt that the informational component of the directors' decisionmaking process, *measured by concepts of gross negligence,* included consideration of all material information reasonably available."[1142] Here, Goldman's charter has a

8 *Del. C.* § 102(b)(7) provision, so gross negligence, by itself, is insufficient basis upon which to impose liability. The Plaintiffs must allege particularized facts creating a reasonable doubt that the directors acted in good faith. [...]

Rather than suggesting that the Director Defendants acted on an uninformed basis, the Plaintiffs' pleadings indicate that the board adequately informed itself before making a decision on compensation. The Director Defendants considered other investment bank comparables, varied the total percent and the total dollar amount awarded as compensation, and changed the total amount of compensation in response to changing public opinion.[150] None of the Plaintiffs' allegations suggests gross negligence on the part of the Director Defendants, and the conduct described in the Plaintiffs' allegations certainly does not rise to the level of bad faith such that the Director Defendants would lose the protection of an 8 *Del. C.* § 102(b)(7) exculpatory provision.

At most, the Plaintiffs' allegations suggest that there were other metrics not considered by the board that might have produced better results. The business judgment rule, however, only requires the board to *reasonably* inform itself; it does not require perfection or the consideration of every conceivable alternative.[151] The factual allegations pled by the Plaintiffs, therefore, do not raise a reasonable doubt that the board was informed when it approved Goldman's compensation scheme.

D. The Plaintiffs' Caremark Claim

In addition to the claims addressed above, the Plaintiffs assert that the board breached its duty to monitor the company as required under *Caremark*.[170] Because this claim attacks a failure to act, rather than a specific transaction, the *Rales* standard applies.[171] The *Rales* standard addresses whether the "board that would be addressing the demand can impartially consider its merits without being influenced by improper considerations."[172] To properly plead demand futility under *Rales,* a plaintiff must allege particularized facts which create a reasonable doubt that "the board of directors could have properly exercised its independent and disinterested business judgment in responding to a demand."[1173]

"Under *Rales,* defendant directors who face a *substantial* likelihood of personal liability are deemed interested in the transaction and thus cannot make an impartial decision."[1174] A simple allegation of potential directorial liability is insufficient to excuse demand, else the demand requirement itself would be rendered toothless, and directorial control over corporate litigation would be lost. The likelihood of directors' liability is significantly lessened where, as here, the corporate charter exculpates the directors from liability to the extent authorized by 8 *Del. C.* § 102(b)(7).[1175] Because Goldman's charter contains such a provision, shielding directors from liability for breaches of the duty of care (absent bad faith) "a serious threat of liability may only be found to exist if the plaintiff pleads a *non-exculpated* claim against the directors based on particularized facts."[1176] This means that "plaintiffs must plead particularized facts showing bad faith in order to establish a substantial likelihood of personal directorial liability."[1177]

The Plaintiffs' contentions that the Director Defendants face a substantial likelihood of personal liability are based on oversight liability, as articulated by then-Chancellor Allen in *Caremark.* In *Caremark,* Chancellor Allen held that a company's board of directors could not "satisfy [its] obligation to be reasonably informed . . . without assuring [itself] that information and reporting systems exist[ed] in the organization."[1178] These systems are needed to provide the board with accurate information so that the board may reach "informed judgments concerning both the corporation's compliance with law and its business performance."[1179] A breach of oversight responsibilities is a breach of the duty of loyalty, and thus not exculpated under section 102(b)(7).

To face a substantial likelihood of oversight liability for a *Caremark* claim, the Director Defendants must have "(a) . . . utterly failed to implement any reporting or information system or controls" (which the Plaintiffs concede is not the case here); "*or* (b) having implemented such a system or controls, consciously failed to monitor or oversee its operations thus disabling themselves from being informed of risks or problems requiring their attention."[1180]

Furthermore, "where a claim of directorial liability for corporate loss is predicated upon ignorance of liability creating activities within the corporation . . . only a sustained or systematic failure of the board to exercise oversight—such as an utter failure to attempt to assure a reasonable information and reporting system [exists] —will establish the lack of good faith that is a necessary condition to liability."[181]

The Plaintiffs specifically contend that the Director Defendants created a compensation structure that caused management's interests to diverge from the stockholders' interests. As a result, management took risks which eventually led to unethical behavior and illegal conduct that exposed Goldman to financial liability. According to the Plaintiffs, after the Director Defendants created Goldman's compensation structure, they had a duty to ensure protection from abuses by management, which were allegedly made more likely due to the form of that structure. Instead of overseeing management, however, the Director Defendants abdicated their oversight responsibilities.[182]

Unlike the original and most subsequent *Caremark* claims, where plaintiffs alleged that liability was predicated on a failure to oversee corporate conduct leading to violations of law,[183] the Plaintiffs here argue that the Director Defendants are also liable for oversight failure relating to Goldman's business performance.[184] [...]

Part of the Plaintiffs' *Caremark* claim stems from the Director Defendants' oversight of Goldman's business practices. As a preliminary matter, this Court has not definitively stated whether a board's *Caremark* duties include a duty to monitor business risk. In *Citigroup,* then-Chancellor Chandler posited that "it may be possible for a plaintiff to meet the burden under some set of facts."[208] Indeed, the *Caremark* court seemed to suggest the possibility of such a claim:

> [I]t would . . . be a mistake to conclude that . . . corporate boards may satisfy their obligation to be reasonably informed concerning the corporation without assuring themselves that information and reporting systems exist in the organization that are reasonably designed to provide to senior management and to the board itself timely, accurate information sufficient to

allow management and the board, each within its scope, to reach informed judgments concerning both the corporation's compliance with law *and its business performance.*[209]

As was the case in *Citigroup,* however, the facts pled here do not give rise to a claim under *Caremark,* and thus I do not need to reach the issue of whether the duty of oversight includes the duty to monitor business risk.

As the Court observed in *Citigroup,* "imposing *Caremark*-type duties on directors to monitor business risk is fundamentally different" from imposing on directors a duty to monitor fraud and illegal activity.[210] Risk is "the chance that a return on an investment will be different than expected."[211] Consistent with this, "a company or investor that is willing to take on more risk can earn a higher return."[212] The manner in which a company "evaluate[s] the trade-off between risk and return" is "[t]he essence of . . . business judgment."[213] The Plaintiffs here allege that Goldman was over-leveraged, engaged in risky business practices, and did not set enough money aside for future losses.[214] As a result, the Plaintiffs assert, Goldman was undercapitalized, forcing it to become a bank holding company and to take on an onerous loan from Warren Buffet.[215]

Although the Plaintiffs have molded their claims with an eye to the language of *Caremark,* the essence of their complaint is that I should hold the Director Defendants "personally liable for making (or allowing to be made) business decisions that, in hindsight, turned out poorly for the Company."[216] If an actionable duty to monitor business risk exists, it cannot encompass any substantive evaluation by a court of a board's determination of the appropriate amount of risk. Such decisions plainly involve business judgment.[217]

The Plaintiffs' remaining allegations in essence seek to hold the Director Defendants "personally liable to the Company because they failed to fully recognize the risk posed by subprime securities."[218] The Plaintiffs charge that the entire board was aware of, or should have been aware of, "the details of the trading business of Goldman and failed to take appropriate action."[219] The Plaintiffs note that "[a]s the housing market began to fracture in early 2007, a committee of senior Goldman executives . . . including Defendants Viniar, Cohn, and Blankfein and those helping to manage Goldman's mortgage, credit and legal operations, took an active role in overseeing the mortgage unit."[1220] "[This] committee's job was to vet potential new products and transactions, being wary of deals that exposed Goldman to too much risk."[1221] This committee eventually decided that housing prices would decline and decided to take a short position in the mortgage market.[1222] The Plaintiffs contend that the Director Defendants were "fully aware of the extent of Goldman's RMBS and CDO securities market activities."[1223] The Plaintiffs point out that the Director Defendants were informed about the business decisions Goldman made during the year including an "intensive effort to not only reduce its mortgage risk exposure, but profit from high risk RMBS and CDO Securities incurring losses."[1224] The Plaintiffs further allege that because of this the Director Defendants "understood that these efforts involved very large amounts of Goldman's capital that exceeded the Company's Value-at-Risk measures."[1225] Finally, the Plaintiffs allege that the practices allowed by the board, including transactions in which Goldman's risk was hedged, imposed reputational risk upon the corporation.[1226]

Thus, the Plaintiffs do not plead with particularity anything that suggests that the Director Defendants acted in bad faith or otherwise consciously disregarded their *oversight* responsibilities in regards to Goldman's business risk. Goldman had an Audit Committee in place that was "charged with assisting the Board in its oversight of the Company's management of market, credit liquidity and other financial and operational risks."[1227] The Director Defendants exercised their business judgment in choosing and implementing a risk management system that they presumably believed would keep them reasonably informed of the company's business risks. As described in detail above, the Plaintiffs admit that the Director Defendants were "fully aware of the extent of Goldman's RMBS and CDO securities market activities."[1228] [...]

Goldman's board and management made decisions to hedge exposure during the deterioration of the housing market, decisions that have been roundly criticized in Congress and elsewhere. Those decisions involved taking objectively large risks, including particularly reputational risks. The outcome of that risk-taking may prove ultimately costly to the corporation. The Plaintiffs, however, have failed to plead with particularity that the Director Defendants consciously and in bad faith disregarded these risks; to the contrary, the facts pled indicate that the board kept itself informed of the risks involved. The Plaintiffs have failed to plead facts showing a substantial likelihood of liability on the part of the Director Defendants[...].

IV. CONCLUSION

The Delaware General Corporation law affords directors and officers broad discretion to exercise their business judgment in the fulfillment of their obligations to the corporation. Consequently, Delaware's case law imposes fiduciary duties on directors and officers to ensure their loyalty and care toward the corporation. When an individual breaches these duties, it is the proper function of this Court to step in and enforce those fiduciary obligations.

Here, the Plaintiffs [...] have failed to allege facts sufficient to demonstrate that the directors were unable to properly exercise this judgment in deciding whether to bring these claims. Since the Plaintiffs have failed to make a demand upon the Corporation, this matter must be dismissed; therefore, I need not reach the Defendant's motion to dismiss under Rule 12 (b)(6).

For the foregoing reasons, the Defendants' motion to dismiss is granted, and the Plaintiffs' claims are dismissed with prejudice. [...]

A Note on Interestedness and Independence   3.2.3.3

In the context of the corporate law, "interest" is a bit of jargon. "A director is considered interested where he or she will receive a personal financial benefit from a transaction that is not equally shared by the stockholders." *Aronson*. The mere fact that a director participated in approving a challenged transaction, without more, is never going to be sufficient to establish interestedness for purposes of establishing demand futility. Plaintiffs will have to plead facts that the director is engaging in self-dealing of some sort.

"Directorial interest also exists where a corporate decision [to pursue litigation or not] will have a materially detrimental impact on a director, but not on the corporation and the stockholders." *Rales*. Where a director faces potential monetary liability as a result of litigation that potential liability may cause the director to be considered "interested." Merely being named a defendant in a lawsuit will not be sufficient to establish director interestedness, however. The potential liability has to be more than a "mere threat" and has to rise to the level of a "substantial likelihood" of liability before a director can be considered interested for demand purposes.

For purposes of demand futility analysis, the income a director receives from her membership on the board of directors will not render a director "interested." Rather, to the extent director income is subjectively material to the director in question it is relevant to an analysis of the director's independence, but only in a certain subset of cases. The mere fact that director income is material to a director, without more, will not be sufficient to establish that a director lacks independence. Remember under Aronson, a director must lack independence *from* an interested party in order to lack independence.

In order to show a lack of independence, a plaintiff must create a reasonable doubt that a director is so "beholden" to an interested director that her "discretion would be sterilized." *Beam*. The axiomatic example is a director on a controlled corporation, where the controller who is interested in the challenged transaction has the power to appoint or remove directors. In that situation, if the director's compensation is subjectively material to the director, then it can be reasonably pleaded that the director lacks independence from the interested party. For example, a director whose only source of income comes from her position as director might be deemed to lack independence from an interested party if that party has the power to remove the director from the board and the director income is material to the director. Where the income is not material to the director (because the director is independently wealthy or has other substantial sources of income), the mere fact that the interested party has the power to remove a director from the board will not likely be enough to create a reasonable doubt as to a director's independence.

The same analysis is true of an employee-director. Directors who happen to be employees do not lose the presumption of disinterestedness and independence merely because they happen to receive a paycheck from the company. That said, where the interested party has control over the employee-director's employment with the company, a plaintiff can reasonably allege that the employee-director lacks independence from the interested party for purposes of demand futility. Take for example an allegation that the Company A engaged in self-dealing with an entity controlled by the CEO. In that instance, the CEO of Company A is the interested person. If the CFO of Company A is on Company A's board, then because the CFO-board member is reliant on the goodwill of the CEO to maintain her employment, she will lack independence from the interested CEO. Conversely, if the CFO of Company A is the interested party in a challenged transaction, the CEO is not presumed to lack independence from her subordinate.

Effect of Refusal of Demand	3.2.4

Spiegel v. Buntrock

If a board receives and then refuses demand, the stockholder may not bring a derivative claim on behalf of the corporation. Of course, if a board could just refuse demand without regard to the merits of the demand, the demand requirement would devolve into a toothless exercise. Consequently, when a board refuses demand, the	3.2.4.1

248

good faith and reasonableness of the board's refusal may still be examined by the courts.

However, a board's decision to refuse demand is a business decision, like any other. As a result, such decisions receive the protection of the business judgment presumption. In challenging a demand refusal, a stockholder will have to plead particularized facts with respect to the board's decision to refuse demand as to overcome the business judgment presumption.

SPIEGEL V. BUNTROCK
571 A.2d 767

HOLLAND, Justice:

This is an appeal from an order of the Court of Chancery dismissing a derivative action filed by the plaintiff-appellant, Ted Spiegel ("Spiegel"), a shareholder of Waste Management, Inc. ("Waste Management"). In his complaint, Spiegel alleged that Dean L. Buntrock ("Buntrock"), Chairman of the Board of Directors and Chief Executive Officer of Waste Management; Jerry E. Dempsey ("Dempsey"), Vice Chairman; Peter H. Huizenga ("Huizenga"), Vice President and Secretary; and James E. Koenig ("Koenig"), Staff Vice President[1] (collectively "management defendants"), improperly acquired stock in ChemLawn Corporation ("ChemLawn"), based upon inside information, during the two years immediately preceding Waste Management's tender [770] offer for ChemLawn. [...]

The underlying issue in this controversy is the often debated subject of when the requirement that a stockholder make demand on a board of directors, prior to filing a derivative lawsuit for the benefit of a corporation, is excused and when a demand, which has been made, is properly refused. Superimposed upon the "demand excused/demand refused" debate[2] are additional issues relating to the use of a special litigation committee by the Board of Waste Management, and the propriety of continuing to argue that demand was excused, after a demand has been made. All of the issues raised implicate the proper standard of judicial review.

[...]Spiegel contended that demand was excused. However, when his failure to make a pre-suit demand was raised by the Board of Waste Management ("Board") as a defense, Spiegel responded by filing a demand. The Board contended that demand was required, because it was disinterested and capable of responding to Spiegel's request for legal action. However, when a demand for such action was made by Spiegel, the Board responded by appointing a special litigation committee with complete authority to review and act upon Spiegel's request. Ultimately, each party used their opponent's legal sword as their own legal shield. Spiegel argued that by appointing a special litigation committee, the Board conceded that demand was excused and the Board argued that by filing a demand Spiegel had admitted that one was required.

The Court of Chancery carefully reviewed the allegations in Spiegel's complaint and found that demand was not excused. Thereafter, the Court of Chancery proceeded to examine the post-suit demand for legal action, which was sent to the Board by Spiegel, and the decision to refuse that demand. The Court of Chancery held that the decision to refuse Spiegel's demand was subject to review according to the traditional business judgment rule, notwithstanding the fact that the Board had delegated its authority to act on Spiegel's demand to a special litigation committee. Applying the traditional business judgment rule, the Court of Chancery held that Spiegel's demand, for the Board to take legal action on behalf of Waste Management, was properly refused.

On appeal, Spiegel contends that, even though he made a demand, given the facts of this case, demand was excused nevertheless. [...]

Facts

Waste Management is a Delaware corporation headquartered in Oak Brook, Illinois. It provides domestic and international waste removal and disposal services. In the spring of 1984, Waste

Management decided to diversify its operations by expanding into new service areas. [...]

Waste Management's interest in Chem-Lawn gradually intensified until on February 26, 1987, it launched a cash tender offer for ChemLawn at $27.00 per share.[4] The tender offer included a disclosure that the management defendants owned shares of ChemLawn stock, which they had acquired during the prior two years.[5] Waste Management's tender offer proved to be unsuccessful.

ChemLawn was purchased by EcoLab, Inc. for $36.50 per share. On March 30, 1987, the *Wall Street Journal* carried an article entitled "ChemLawn's Sale Could Yield $1 Million In Profit for Officials of Thwarted Suitor."[6] That same day, Spiegel filed the action against Waste Management, and its directors, that is the subject of this appeal.

On April 30, 1987, the Board filed a motion to dismiss Spiegel's complaint pursuant to Court of Chancery Rule 23.1. The basis for that motion was that Spiegel had failed to make a demand upon the Board prior to instituting his derivative suit and had failed to allege with particularity facts demonstrating that such a demand would have been futile. [...]

Spiegel did not immediately contest the Board's motion to dismiss in the Court of Chancery.[8] Instead, Spiegel responded by making a demand to the Board in a letter which stated:

> [772] On behalf of Ted Spiegel, a shareholder of Waste Management, Inc., we hereby formally demand that the Board of Directors take all appropriate action to redress the wrongs as alleged in the enclosed complaint.

In response to Spiegel's demand letter, the Board established a special litigation committee of outside directors (the "Committee") "for the purpose of conducting an independent review of the transactions in the common stock of ChemLawn Corporation by officers of the Company."[...]

The Committee conducted an investigation into Spiegel's allegations that spanned over five months. The Committee was represented by its own independent counsel, a Washington, D.C.[...]The Committee interviewed a great many people, both within and without Waste Management.[110] It also reviewed volumes of documents.

[...]On the basis of its investigation, and its analysis of the applicable law, the Committee concluded that it would not be in the best interests of Waste Management and its stockholders to pursue Spiegel's derivative action. [...]

Consequently, the Committee, acting for the Board, filed a motion on behalf of Waste Management, in the Court of Chancery to dismiss or, alternatively, for summary judgment, along with the affidavits of the Committee members and the entire report which summarized its findings and analysis.

Derivative Action/Demand Requirement

A basic principle of the General Corporation Law of the State of Delaware is that directors, rather than shareholders, [773] manage the business and affairs of the corporation.[...] The decision to bring a law suit or to refrain from litigating a claim on behalf of a corporation is a decision concerning the management of the corporation. [...]Consequently, such decisions are part of the responsibility of the board of directors. 8 *Del.C.* § 141(a).[111]

Nevertheless, a shareholder may file a derivative action to redress an alleged harm to the corporation. The nature of the derivative action is two-fold.

> First, it is the equivalent of a suit by the shareholders to compel the corporation to sue. Second, it is a suit by the corporation, asserted by the shareholders on its behalf, against those liable to it. [...]

"Because the shareholders' ability to institute an action on behalf of the corporation inherently impinges upon the directors' power to

manage the affairs of the corporation the law imposes certain
prerequisites on a stockholder's right to sue derivatively." [...]
Chancery Court Rule 23.1 requires that shareholders seeking to
assert a claim on behalf of the corporation must first exhaust
intracorporate remedies by making a demand on the directors to
obtain the action desired, or to plead with particularity why demand
is excused. Ch. Ct.R. 23.1; [...]

The purpose of pre-suit demand is to assure that the stockholder
affords the corporation the opportunity to address an alleged wrong
without litigation, to decide whether to invest the resources of the
corporation in litigation, and to control any litigation which does
occur. [...] "[B]y promoting this form of alternate dispute
resolution, rather than immediate recourse to litigation, the demand
requirement is a recognition of the fundamental precept that
directors manage the business and affairs of corporations." [...]

Standard Of Review Demand Excused/Demand Refused

Since a conscious decision by a board of directors to refrain from
acting [774] may be a valid exercise of business judgment, "where
demand on a board has been made and refused, [courts] apply the
business judgment rule in reviewing the board's refusal to act
pursuant to a stockholder's demand" to file a lawsuit. [...] The
business judgment rule is a presumption that in making a business
decision, not involving self-interest, the directors of a corporation
acted on an informed basis, in good faith and in the honest belief
that the action taken was in the best interests of the company. [...]
"The burden is on the party challenging the decision to establish
facts rebutting th[is] presumption." [...] Thus, the business
judgment rule operates as a judicial acknowledgement of a board of
directors' managerial prerogatives. [...]

Demand Made/Futility Waived

Spiegel filed a derivative action on behalf of Waste Management,
alleging that a presuit demand on the Board was excused, i.e., would

have been a futile gesture. However, Spiegel then filed a demand with the Board to take legal action and "redress the wrongs" set forth in his complaint. Spiegel alleges that he was entitled to simultaneously argue these inconsistent arguments. The Board argues that when Spiegel filed his demand, he waived his right to continue asserting that demand was excused. The Court of Chancery gave implicit recognition to the validity of Spiegel's position by examining the merits of both of his arguments.[-1]

"When deciding a motion to dismiss for failure to make a demand under Chancery Rule 23.1 the record before the court must be restricted to the allegations of the complaint." [...] In determining demand futility, the Court of Chancery must decide whether, under the particularized facts alleged in the complaint:

> [A] reasonable doubt is created that: (1) the directors are disinterested and independent and (2) the challenged transaction was otherwise the product of a valid exercise of business judgment.

Aronson v. Lewis, 473 A.2d at 814. In this case, the Court of Chancery concluded that the facts alleged in Spiegel's complaint did not raise a reasonable doubt that the Board was disabled from responding to Spiegel's demand and passing upon whether it was in Waste Management's interest to pursue Spiegel's claims.

Spiegel argues that, even though he made a demand, the Court of Chancery properly reviewed the merits of his complaint, which alleged that demand was excused. Spiegel submits that demand [775] should be encouraged by permitting a demand to be made, while at the same time permitting the argument, that demand was excused, to be preserved. Spiegel finds some support for his position in other jurisdictions. [...]However, this Court has held that by making a demand, a shareholder thereby makes his original contention, that demand was excused, moot. [...]

This Court has recently held that when a board of directors is confronted with a derivative action asserted on its behalf, it cannot stand neutral. [...] The Board "must affirmatively object to or support the continuation of the [derivative] litigation." [...]

Similarly, a stockholder who asserts a derivative claim cannot stand neutral, in effect, with respect to the board of directors' ability to respond to a request to take legal action, by simultaneously making a demand for such action *and* continuing to argue that demand is excused.

By making a demand, a stockholder tacitly acknowledges the absence of facts to support a finding of futility. [...] Thus, when a demand is made, the question of whether demand was excused is moot. [...] Therefore, we hold once Spiegel made a demand, it was unnecessary for the Court of Chancery to consider the merits of Spiegel's argument that demand was excused. [...]

A shareholder who makes a demand can no longer argue that demand is excused. [...] The effect of a demand is to place control of the derivative litigation in the hands of the board of directors. [...] Consequently, stockholders who, [776] like Spiegel, make a demand which is refused, subject the board's decision to judicial review according to the traditional business judgment rule. [...]

Standard Of Review Demand Refused/Motion To Dismiss

Whenever any action or inaction by a board of directors is subject to review according to the traditional business judgment rule, the issues before the Court are independence, the reasonableness of its investigation and good faith. By electing to make a demand, a shareholder plaintiff tacitly concedes the independence of a majority of the board to respond. Therefore, when a board refuses a demand, the only issues to be examined are the good faith and reasonableness of its investigation.

Absent an abuse of discretion, if the requirements of the traditional business judgment rule are met, the board of directors' decision not to pursue the derivative claim will be respected by the courts. [...]In such cases, a board of directors' motion to dismiss an action filed by a shareholder, whose demand has been rejected, must be granted.[20] "If Courts would not respect [778] the directors' decision not to file suit, then demand would be an empty formality." [...]

Conclusion

For the reasons stated in this opinion, the ultimate decision of the Court of Chancery, dismissing Spiegel's complaint is AFFIRMED.

Solak v. Welch

SOLAK V. WELCH
C.A. No. 2018-0810-KSJM
2019 WL 5588877

McCORMICK, V.C.

As interpreted by the Delaware Supreme Court in *Spiegel v. Buntrock*, Court of Chancery Rule 23.1 gives a stockholder wishing to file a derivative lawsuit two mutually exclusive options. The stockholder may either make a pre-suit demand on the board or plead with particularity the reasons it would have been futile to do so. If a stockholder elects to make a pre-suit demand, then the stockholder may not allege that demand would have been futile in a subsequent complaint concerning the subject matter of the demand. Rather, the stockholder is limited to making the more difficult claim that the board wrongfully refused the demand. Making a pre-suit demand, therefore, carries significant downsides affecting the viability of a derivative claim.

The parties in this case dispute whether a pre-suit communication constitutes a pre-suit demand for purposes of Rule 23.1. Before commencing this litigation, the plaintiff-stockholder sent a letter requesting that the defendant-company's board of directors take remedial action to address allegedly excessive non-employee director compensation. This lawsuit ensued after the board rejected the letter's request. The plaintiff portrays the letter as no more than an informal, good faith attempt to educate the board and encourage it to make changes to the company's compensation policies. He argues that demand futility is the appropriate standard and that the complaint demonstrates that demand is excused. The defendants have moved to dismiss the complaint under Rule 23.1. They argue that the letter constitutes a pre-suit demand and that the plaintiff failed to plead wrongful demand refusal.

Revealing the proverbial wolf in sheep's clothing, this decision finds that what the plaintiff describes as a harmless letter seeking prospective board action is something with far more legal bite—a pre-suit demand. Because the plaintiff fails to allege wrongful demand refusal, the action is dismissed.

I. FACTUAL BACKGROUND

The facts are drawn from the Complaint, documents it incorporates by reference, and relevant pre-suit communications.

Plaintiff John Solak ("Plaintiff") is a current stockholder of Ultragenyx Pharmaceutical Inc. ("Ultragenyx" or the "Company"), a biopharmaceutical company incorporated under Delaware law and headquartered in Novato, California. In June 2018, Plaintiff's counsel sent a letter on his behalf (the "Letter") addressed to the Ultragenyx Board of Directors (the "Board").

The Letter states that its purpose is "to suggest that the [Board] take corrective action to address excessive director compensation as well as compensation practices and policies pertaining to directors." The Letter focuses on the Company's updated compensation policy disclosed in its Definitive Proxy Statement filed with the United States Securities and Exchange Commission on April 27, 2018 (the "Compensation Policy"), which "the Board approved" and in which all non-employee directors participate.

According to the Letter, non-employee directors have been "compensated at an extraordinarily high level – averaging in excess of $400,000 per annum each since 2014" under the Compensation Policy. The Letter compares the median compensation for non-employee directors at the "Top 200" companies in the S&P 500 against the median total compensation for non-employee directors at Ultragenyx, describing the latter as comparatively excessive.

The Letter references *In re Investors Bancorp, Inc. Stockholder Litigation,* in which the Delaware Supreme Court revived claims challenging director compensation decisions a board made pursuant to a stockholder-approved, discretionary equity incentive plan. In reversing the Court of Chancery decision dismissing those claims, the Delaware Supreme Court held: "[W]hen it comes to the discretion directors exercise following stockholder approval of an equity incentive plan, ratification cannot be used to foreclose the Court of Chancery from reviewing those further discretionary actions when a breach of fiduciary duty claim has been properly alleged." Citing *Investors Bancorp,* the Letter states: "The Compensation Policy lacks any meaningful limitations with regard to cash and equity awards, allows for too much discretion by the Board, and ... is not subject to shareholder approval." The Letter then warns: "The Company is more susceptible than ever to shareholder challenges unless it revises or amends its director compensation practices and policies."

The Letter concludes by "suggesting" that the Board "take[ ] immediate remedial measures to address these issues, including, but not limited to, reducing retainer fees, reducing the awards of options and restricted stock units, moving to full-value equity grants, adopting mandatory stock-ownership guidelines, and setting meaningful limits or targets for overall compensation." The Letter does not expressly request that the Board initiate any litigation, but it states that if the Board did not respond within thirty days, Plaintiff would consider "all available shareholder remedies."

The Letter includes the following footnote:

> Please be advised that nothing contained herein shall be construed as a pre-suit litigation demand under Delaware Chancery Rule 23.1. This letter is intended only as a good-faith attempt to encourage corrective action by the Board. We do not seek or expect the Board to initiate any legal action against its members. Further, any rights and/or remedies our client or any other Ultragenyx shareholder may have are specifically reserved and nothing contained herein shall be deemed a waiver of those rights and/or remedies.

In October 2018, the Board responded to the Letter through counsel (the "Response"). The Response first states that the Board viewed Plaintiff's Letter as a demand pursuant to Rule 23.1. It then explains that the Board conducted an investigation with the assistance of counsel, which included a review of public and private documents, as well as interviews with the Chairman of the Compensation Committee and the Compensation Committee's independent compensation consultant. The Response also describes the approach used to set Ultragenyx's compensation policies and explains that "the Board unanimously resolved that it would be in the best interests of the Company to not authorize commencement of a civil action or further changes to the Compensation Policy in response to the Demand."

Plaintiff commenced this derivative action on November 7, 2018, asserting claims stemming from the Board's allegedly excessive non-employee director compensation practices. The Complaint names as defendants the eight individual directors who served on the Board at the time the Complaint was filed (the "Defendants"). The Complaint asserts three causes of action against Defendants: breach of fiduciary duty, unjust enrichment, and corporate waste. Defendants moved to dismiss the Complaint on December 26, 2018. The parties fully briefed the motion by April 8, 2019, and the Court heard oral argument on August 1, 2019.

II. LEGAL ANALYSIS

Defendants have moved to dismiss the Complaint pursuant to Rule 23.1(a), which derives from the bedrock principle that directors, rather than stockholders, manage the business and affairs of the corporation. "By its very nature the derivative action impinges on the managerial freedom of directors," whose authority includes decisions to pursue or refrain from pursuing litigation on behalf of the corporation.

As part of this board-centric model, Rule 23.1 requires that a stockholder wishing to bring a derivative action first demand that the board of directors take action. If a stockholder chooses not to make pre-suit demand, the stockholder must plead with particularity the reasons it would have been futile to present the matter to the board such that pre-suit demand should be excused. This requirement "exists at the threshold, first to insure that a stockholder exhausts his intracorporate remedies, and then to provide a safeguard against strike suits."

Of the two potential routes presented by Rule 23.1—pleading demand futility with particularity or making pre-suit demand—the former is a steep road, but the latter is "steeper yet." The Delaware Supreme Court steepened this incline in *Spiegel* by holding that a stockholder who makes pre-suit demand "tacitly concedes" that the board was able to properly consider that demand. The board's affirmative decision to refuse the demand, therefore, is subject to the business judgment rule.

A stockholder's options under Rule 23.1 are mutually exclusive. As explained in *Spiegel*, after making pre-suit demand, a stockholder plaintiff may not pursue claims challenging the subject matter of that demand. Rather, the stockholder is limited to a claim that the board wrongfully refused the demand. Put differently, a stockholder may not pursue demand refusal and demand excusal strategies simultaneously in order to "cover all the bases." The Delaware Supreme Court has broadly interpreted this limitation to apply to all derivative claims arising from the subject matter of the demand, even legal theories not expressly identified by the stockholder or considered by the board. In light of these principles, "a judicial determination that a plaintiff has made a demand carries with it significant legal consequences."

In this case, the parties dispute whether Plaintiff, in fact, made a pre-suit demand on the Board. Defendants construe the Letter as a pre-suit demand and argue that the demand refusal analysis applies. Plaintiff responds that the Letter does not constitute a pre-suit demand and argues that the demand excusal analysis applies. This decision first confronts this gating issue before applying the relevant standard.

A. The Letter Constitutes a Pre-Suit Demand Under Rule 23.1.

The burden of demonstrating that a pre-suit stockholder communication qualifies as a demand under Rule 23.1 lies with the party asserting as much—here, Defendants. There are no " 'magic words' establishing that a communication is a demand." Nor is there an "all-inclusive legal formula" serving such a purpose. Rather, "[t]hat determination is essentially fact-driven." In *Yaw*, then-Vice Chancellor (later Justice) Jacobs helpfully distilled a series of decisions to three criteria for determining whether a pre-suit communication constitutes a pre-suit demand. Under *Yaw*, a pre-suit communication is a demand for purposes of Rule 23.1 if it provides "(i) the identity of the alleged wrongdoers, (ii) the wrongdoing they allegedly perpetrated and the resultant injury to the corporation, and (iii) the legal action the shareholder wants the board to take on the corporation's behalf."

Plaintiff first argues that this Court need not review the substance of the Letter under *Yaw* because of the Letter's footnote disclaimer, which states: "nothing contained herein shall be construed as a pre-suit demand under Delaware Chancery Rule 23.1." Vice Chancellor Glasscock has coined this argument the "Magritte defense," a term referencing a 1929 painting by surrealist artist René Magritte titled "The Treachery of Images." That painting portrays a smoking pipe, but it bears the caption: "This is not a pipe."[FN 42]

Plaintiff's footnote disclaimer does not obviate the Court's review of the Letter's substance for obvious reasons, namely that "Delaware law is quite strict as to the application of Chancery Rule 23.1." As discussed above, Delaware law prohibits a stockholder from both making a demand and pleading demand futility "to, in essence, cover all the bases." That prohibition would become a virtual nullity if a stockholder could avoid a judicial determination that pre-suit demand was made by simply stating "this is not a demand" in his pre-suit communication. For this reason, the test for determining whether a pre-suit communication constitutes a demand under Rule 23.1 cannot look to the subjective intent of the sender. Rather, in applying the three *Yaw* criteria, the Court must evaluate the substance of the communication objectively to determine whether it would place a recipient "on notice of possible wrongdoing" in a manner that would enable that person to take "corrective intracorporate action."

Turning to an application of *Yaw* in this case, the parties' dispute concerns whether the Letter satisfies the third criterion, which requires that the communication identify the legal action the stockholder wants the board to take on the company's behalf. Plaintiff's argument is straightforward: because the Letter does not expressly demand that Defendants commence litigation, it cannot be construed as a pre-suit litigation demand for purposes of Rule 23.1.

Delaware law does not construe the third *Yaw* criterion as narrowly as Plaintiff suggests, and this Court has deemed pre-suit communications that do not expressly demand litigation sufficient to constitute pre-suit demand. On this point, two cases are instructive. In *In re Riverstone National, Inc. Stockholder Litigation*, the Court held that a pre-suit communication constituted demand even though it did not "specifically request that the board commence litigation" because it asked the board to transfer equity owned by the company's officers, directors, and employees back to the company itself. The Court reasoned that by "clearly articulat[ing] the remedial action to be taken by the board," the letter met the third *Yaw* criterion. Similarly, in *Herd v. Major Realty Corp.*, the Court considered two pre-suit communications: one demanding termination of a merger agreement and another demanding that the board postpone the stockholders' meeting at which the merger was to be considered. The Court concluded that the letters "clearly demanded corporate action" sufficient to satisfy Rule 23.1, despite the fact that they did not demand that the board pursue litigation on behalf of the company.

Similar to the pre-suit communications in *Riverstone* and *Herd*, although the Letter avoids expressly demanding that the Board commence litigation, the Letter clearly articulates the need for "immediate remedial measures," proposes remedial action, and requests that the Board take such action. The Letter further states that "the Company is more susceptible than ever to shareholder challenges unless it revises or amends its director compensation practices and policies," identifies the legal basis for such challenges, and warns that, absent a response from the Board within thirty days,

Plaintiff would "consider all available shareholder remedies." Although Plaintiff says "this is not a demand," these strong overtures of litigation very much make it look like one. Thus, the Letter satisfies the third criterion of *Yaw*.

Beyond a mechanical application of *Yaw*, numerous other observations inform this Court's conclusion that the Letter constitutes a pre-suit demand. For starters, the Letter reads like a complaint. In fact, the Complaint in this action is nearly a carbon copy of the Letter. Not only does the Complaint allege the same wrongdoing using similar verbiage as the Letter, but it also adopts the Letter's method of illustrating the alleged wrongdoing by drawing comparisons between the Company's compensation levels and those of other companies. The similarities between the Letter and the Complaint are relevant because a pre-suit demand is supposed to fulfill a notice function—notifying a board of the alleged wrongs to be corrected through litigation. Thus, the more closely a complaint tracks the pre-suit communication in question, the more likely the communication will have provided the notice required of a pre-suit demand. The similarities between the Letter and the Complaint in this case therefore weigh in favor of deeming the Letter a pre-suit demand.

In the same vein, the remedial measures requested in the Letter support a determination that the Letter is a demand. The Letter seeks relief that would benefit Ultragenyx stockholders and the Company as a whole, rather than just Plaintiff personally. And the Letter's requested remedial measures resemble therapeutic benefits commonly achieved in derivative lawsuits challenging non-employee director compensation. Where a communication demands action that stockholders commonly achieve through derivative litigation challenging similar conduct, it is more likely that the communication will be construed as a demand for the purposes of Rule 23.1. ...

B. The Complaint Does Not Adequately Plead Wrongful Demand Refusal.

"[A] conscious decision by a board of directors to refrain from acting may be a valid exercise of business judgment," and where, as here, " 'demand on a board has been made and refused, [courts] apply the business judgment rule in reviewing the board's refusal to act pursuant to a stockholder's demand' to file a lawsuit." Because the business judgment rule is the operative standard, a plaintiff stockholder asserting wrongful refusal of a demand must allege with particularity "facts that give rise to a reasonable doubt as to the good faith or reasonableness of [the Board's] investigation" and deliberations. To do so, the plaintiff must plead particularized facts to support an inference that the board of directors committed gross negligence or acted in bad faith in rendering a decision to refuse a demand.

The Complaint fails to allege any facts supporting an inference that the Board wrongfully rejected the demand. Indeed, the Complaint fails to acknowledge even the Letter or the Response, much less explain how the Response was wrongful. And the content of the Response chafes against Plaintiff's argument. As explained in its Response, the Board, "[w]ith the aid of counsel," conducted an investigation, which included, among other things, "a review of pertinent documents (including publicly available documents and confidential Company documents), as well as interviews of the Chairman of the Compensation Committee and the Compensation Committee's independent compensation consultant, Radford." The Response also sets forth the substantive reasons underlying the Board's decision with respect to the demand. Finally, the Response describes other considerations affecting the Board's decision to refuse the demand, including the claims' likelihood of success on the merits and the costs of pursuing litigation.

For these reasons, the Complaint fails to allege particularized facts showing that the Board wrongfully refused Plaintiff's pre-suit demand.

III. CONCLUSION

For the foregoing reasons, Defendants' motion to dismiss the Complaint is GRANTED.

IT IS SO ORDERED.

* * *

Footnote

FN42. René Magritte, *La Trahison des images (Ceci n'est pas une pipe)* (1929). "Magritte's word-image paintings are treatises on the impossibility of reconciling words, images, and objects. La Trahison des images challenges the linguistic convention of identifying an image of something as the thing itself." *The Treachery of Images (This is Not a Pipe) (La trahison des images [Ceci n'est pas une pipe]),* L.A. County Museum of Art, https://collections.lacma.org/node/239578 (last visited Oct. 29, 2019).

Special Litigation Committees 3.3

In situations where demand is futile, stockholders can file derivative litigation without making demand. Does that mean that boards have forever lost control over the derivative litigation? In some circumstances the answer is no.

The following cases lay out the doctrine with respect to how a board can retake control over derivative litigation in later stages of litigation. The board through an independent committee, often known as a special litigation committee, may file a pretrial motion to retake control and then dismiss the derivative litigation. The Special Committee must be prepared to meet the burden under Rule 56 (Summary Judgment) that there is no genuine issue as to any material fact and that the moving party is entitled to dismiss as a matter of law.

Remember, unlike in the case of demand and demand futility, at this stage of the litigation, boards bear the burden of proving that notwithstanding the fact that demand was previously futile, the board is now in a position to fairly consider the facts of the complaint. As you will see, this is a heavy burden for a board to bear.

Zapata v. Maldonado

Zapata is the leading case on the legal standard a court will apply to a special litigation committee's motion to take control over derivative litigation following the 23.1 motion to dismiss and prior to going to trial. Look at the facts related to the interestedness and independence of directors on the special litigation committee. Consider whether under these same facts demand would have been deemed futile with respect to these directors at the 23.1 motion to dismiss stage.

ZAPATA V. MALDONADO
Delaware Supreme Court
430 A.2d 779

QUILLEN, Justice:

In June, 1975, William Maldonado, a stockholder of Zapata, instituted a derivative action in the Court of Chancery on behalf of Zapata against ten officers and/or directors of Zapata, alleging, essentially, breaches of fiduciary duty. Maldonado did not first demand that the board bring this action, stating instead such demand's futility because all directors were named as defendants and allegedly participated in the acts specified.[1]

[781] By June, 1979, four of the defendant-directors were no longer on the board, and the remaining directors appointed two new outside directors to the board. The board then created an "Independent Investigation Committee" (Committee), composed solely of the two new directors, to investigate Maldonado's actions, as well as a similar derivative action then pending in Texas, and to

determine whether the corporation should continue any or all of the litigation. The Committee's determination was stated to be "final, ... not ... subject to review by the Board of Directors and ... in all respects ... binding upon the Corporation."

Following an investigation, the Committee concluded, in September, 1979, that each action should "be dismissed forthwith as their continued maintenance is inimical to the Company's best interests...." Consequently, Zapata moved for dismissal or summary judgment in the three derivative actions. [...]

On March 18, 1980, the Court of Chancery, in a reported opinion, the basis for the order of April 9, 1980, denied Zapata's motions, holding that Delaware law does not sanction this means of dismissal. More specifically, it held that the "business judgment" rule is not a grant of authority to dismiss derivative actions and that a stockholder has an individual right to maintain derivative actions in certain instances. [...]

We limit our review in this interlocutory appeal to whether the Committee has the power to cause the present action to be dismissed.

We begin with an examination of the carefully considered opinion of the Vice Chancellor which states, in part, that the "business judgment" rule does not confer power "to a corporate board of directors to terminate a derivative suit", 413 A.2d at 1257. His conclusion is particularly pertinent because several federal courts, applying Delaware law, have held that the business judgment rule enables boards (or their committees) to terminate derivative suits, decisions now in conflict with the holding below.[4]

[782] As the term is most commonly used, and given the disposition below, we can understand the Vice Chancellor's comment that "the business judgment rule is irrelevant to the question of whether the Committee has the authority to compel the dismissal of this suit". 413 A.2d at 1257. Corporations, existing because of legislative grace, possess authority as granted by the legislature. Directors of Delaware corporations derive their managerial decision making power, which encompasses decisions whether to initiate, or refrain from entering, litigation,[5] from 8 *Del.C.* § 141 (a).[6] This statute is

267

the fount of directorial powers. The "business judgment" rule is a judicial creation that presumes propriety, under certain circumstances, in a board's decision.[7] Viewed defensively, it does not create authority. In this sense the "business judgment" rule is not relevant in corporate decision making until after a decision is made. It is generally used as a defense to an attack on the decision's soundness. The board's managerial decision making power, however, comes from § 141(a). The judicial creation and legislative grant are related because the "business judgment" rule evolved to give recognition and deference to directors' business expertise when exercising their managerial power under § 141(a).

In the case before us, although the corporation's decision to move to dismiss or for summary judgment was, literally, a decision resulting from an exercise of the directors' (as delegated to the Committee) business judgment, the question of "business judgment", in a defensive sense, would not become relevant until and unless the decision to seek termination of the derivative lawsuit was attacked as improper. [...]

Thus, the focus in this case is on the power to speak for the corporation as to whether the lawsuit should be continued or terminated.[...]

Accordingly, we turn first to the Court of Chancery's conclusions concerning the right of a plaintiff stockholder in a derivative action. We find that its determination that a stockholder, once demand is made and refused, possesses an independent, individual right to continue a derivative suit for breaches of fiduciary duty over objection by the corporation,[...]as an absolute rule, is erroneous. [...]

McKee v. Rogers[...] stated "as a general rule" that "a stockholder cannot be permitted... to invade the discretionary field committed to the judgment of the directors and sue in the corporation's behalf when the managing body refuses. This rule is a well settled one." [...][9]

The *McKee* rule, of course, should not be read so broadly that the board's refusal will be determinative in every instance. Board members, owing a well-established fiduciary duty to the corporation, will not be allowed to cause a derivative suit to be dismissed when it would be a breach of their fiduciary duty. Generally [784] disputes pertaining to control of the suit arise in two contexts.

Consistent with the purpose of requiring a demand, a board decision to cause a derivative suit to be dismissed as detrimental to the company, after demand has been made and refused, will be respected unless it was wrongful.[1-1]A claim of a wrongful decision not to sue is thus the first exception and the first context of dispute. Absent a wrongful refusal, the stockholder in such a situation simply lacks legal managerial power. [...]

But it cannot be implied that, absent a wrongful board refusal, a stockholder can never have an individual right to initiate an action. [...]

A demand, when required and refused (if not wrongful), terminates a stockholder's legal ability to initiate a derivative action.[12] But where demand is properly excused, the stockholder does possess the ability to initiate the action on his corporation's behalf.

These conclusions, however, do not determine the question before us. Rather, they merely bring us to the question to be decided. It is here that we part company with the Court below. Derivative suits enforce corporate rights and any recovery obtained goes to the corporation. [...] We see no inherent reason why the "two phases" of a derivative suit, the stockholder's suit to compel the corporation to sue and the corporation's suit (see 413 A.2d at 1261-62), should automatically result in the placement in the hands of the [785] litigating stockholder sole control of the corporate right throughout the litigation. To the contrary, it seems to us that such an inflexible rule would recognize the interest of one person or group to the exclusion of all others within the corporate entity. Thus, we reject the view of the Vice Chancellor as to the first aspect of the issue on appeal.

The question to be decided becomes: When, if at all, should an authorized board committee be permitted to cause litigation, properly initiated by a derivative stockholder in his own right, to be dismissed? As noted above, a board has the power to choose not to pursue litigation when demand is made upon it, so long as the decision is not wrongful. If the board determines that a suit would be detrimental to the company, the board's determination prevails. Even when demand is excusable, circumstances may arise when continuation of the litigation would not be in the corporation's best interests. Our inquiry is whether, under such circumstances, there is a permissible procedure under § 141(a) by which a corporation can rid itself of detrimental litigation. If there is not, a single stockholder in an extreme case might control the destiny of the entire corporation[...]: "To allow one shareholder to incapacitate an entire board of directors merely by leveling charges against them gives too much leverage to dissident shareholders." But, when examining the means, including the committee mechanism examined in this case, potentials for abuse must be recognized. This takes us to the second and third aspects of the issue on appeal.

Before we pass to equitable considerations as to the mechanism at issue here, it must be clear that an independent committee possesses the corporate power to seek the termination of a derivative suit. Section 141(c) allows a board to delegate all of its authority to a committee.[13] Accordingly, a committee with properly delegated authority would have the power to move for dismissal or summary judgment if the entire board did.

Even though demand was not made in this case and the initial decision of whether to litigate was not placed before the board, Zapata's board, it seems to us, retained all of its corporate power concerning litigation decisions. If Maldonado had made demand on the board in this case, it could have refused to bring suit. Maldonado could then have asserted that the decision not to sue was wrongful and, if correct, would have been allowed to maintain the suit. The board, however, never would have lost its statutory managerial authority. The demand requirement itself evidences that the managerial power is retained [786] by the board. When a derivative plaintiff is allowed to bring suit after a wrongful refusal, the board's authority to choose whether to pursue the litigation is not challenged although its conclusion — reached through the exercise of that authority — is not respected since it is wrongful. Similarly, Rule 23.1, by excusing demand in certain instances, does not strip the board of its corporate power. It merely saves the plaintiff the expense and delay of making a futile demand resulting in a probable tainted exercise of that authority in a refusal by the board or in giving control of litigation to the opposing side. But the board entity remains empowered under § 141(a) to make decisions regarding corporate litigation. The problem is one of member disqualification, not the absence of power in the board.

The corporate power inquiry then focuses on whether the board, tainted by the self-interest of a majority of its members, can legally delegate its authority to a committee of two disinterested directors. We find our statute clearly requires an affirmative answer to this question. [...]

We do not think that the interest taint of the board majority is per se a legal bar to the delegation of the board's power to an independent committee composed of disinterested board members. The committee can properly act for the corporation to move to dismiss derivative litigation that is believed to be detrimental to the corporation's best interest.

Our focus now switches to the Court of Chancery which is faced with a stockholder assertion that a derivative suit, properly instituted, should continue for the benefit of the corporation and a corporate assertion, properly made by a board committee acting with board authority, that the same derivative suit should be dismissed as inimical to the best interests of the corporation.

At the risk of stating the obvious, the problem is relatively simple. If, on the one hand, corporations can consistently wrest bona fide derivative actions away from well-meaning derivative plaintiffs through the use of the committee mechanism, the derivative suit will lose much, if not all, of its generally-recognized effectiveness as an intra-corporate means of policing boards of directors. [...]If, on the other hand, corporations are unable to rid themselves of meritless or harmful litigation [787] and strike suits, the derivative action, created to benefit the corporation, will produce the opposite, unintended result. [...] It thus appears desirable to us to find a balancing point where bona fide stockholder power to bring corporate causes of action cannot be unfairly trampled on by the board of directors, but the corporation can rid itself of detrimental litigation.

As we noted, the question has been treated by other courts as one of the "business judgment" of the board committee. If a "committee, composed of independent and disinterested directors, conducted a proper review of the matters before it, considered a variety of factors and reached, in good faith, a business judgment that [the] action was not in the best interest of [the corporation]", the action must be dismissed. [...] The issues become solely independence, good faith, and reasonable investigation. The ultimate conclusion of the committee, under that view, is not subject to judicial review. [...]

The context here is a suit against directors where demand on the board is excused. We think some tribute must be paid to the fact that the lawsuit was properly initiated. It is not a board refusal case. Moreover, this complaint was filed in June of 1975 and, while the parties undoubtedly would take differing views on the degree of litigation activity, we have to be concerned about the creation of an "Independent Investigation Committee" four years later, after the election of two new outside directors. Situations could develop where such motions could be filed after years of vigorous litigation for reasons unconnected with the merits of the lawsuit.

Moreover, notwithstanding our conviction that Delaware law entrusts the corporate power to a properly authorized committee, we must be mindful that directors are passing judgment on fellow directors in the same corporation and fellow directors, in this instance, who designated them to serve both as directors and committee members. The question naturally arises whether a "there but for the grace of God go I" empathy might not play a role. And the further question arises whether inquiry as to independence, good faith and reasonable investigation is sufficient safeguard against abuse, perhaps subconscious abuse. [...]

Whether the Court of Chancery will be persuaded by the exercise of a committee power resulting in a summary motion for dismissal of a derivative action, where a demand has not been initially made, should rest, in our judgment, in the independent discretion of the

Court of Chancery. We thus steer a middle course between those cases which yield to the independent business judgment of a board committee and this case as determined below which would yield to unbridled plaintiff stockholder control. [...]

After an objective and thorough investigation of a derivative suit, an independent committee may cause its corporation to file a pretrial motion to dismiss in the Court of Chancery. The basis of the motion is the best interests of the corporation, as determined by the committee. The motion should include a thorough written record of the investigation and its findings and recommendations. Under appropriate Court supervision, akin to proceedings on summary judgment, each side should have an opportunity to make a record on the motion. As to the limited issues presented by the motion noted below, the moving party should be prepared to meet the normal burden under Rule 56 that there is no genuine issue as to any material fact and that the moving party is entitled to dismiss as a matter of law.[15] The Court should apply a two-step test to the motion.

First, the Court should inquire into the independence and good faith of the committee and the bases supporting its conclusions. Limited discovery may be ordered to facilitate such inquiries.[16] The corporation should have the burden of proving independence, good faith and a reasonable investigation, rather than presuming independence, good faith and reasonableness.[17] [789] If the Court determines either that the committee is not independent or has not shown reasonable bases for its conclusions, or, if the Court is not satisfied for other reasons relating to the process, including but not limited to the good faith of the committee, the Court shall deny the corporation's motion. If, however, the Court is satisfied under Rule 56 standards that the committee was independent and showed reasonable bases for good faith findings and recommendations, the Court may proceed, in its discretion, to the next step.

The second step provides, we believe, the essential key in striking the balance between legitimate corporate claims as expressed in a derivative stockholder suit and a corporation's best interests as expressed by an independent investigating committee. The Court should determine, applying its own independent business judgment, whether the motion should be granted.[18] This means, of course, that instances could arise where a committee can establish its independence and sound bases for its good faith decisions and still have the corporation's motion denied. The second step is intended to thwart instances where corporate actions meet the criteria of step one, but the result does not appear to satisfy its spirit, or where corporate actions would simply prematurely terminate a stockholder grievance deserving of further consideration in the corporation's interest. The Court of Chancery of course must carefully consider and weigh how compelling the corporate interest in dismissal is when faced with a non-frivolous lawsuit. The Court of Chancery should, when appropriate, give special consideration to matters of law and public policy in addition to the corporation's best interests.

If the Court's independent business judgment is satisfied, the Court may proceed to grant the motion, subject, of course, to any equitable terms or conditions the Court finds necessary or desirable.

The interlocutory order of the Court of Chancery is reversed and the cause is remanded for further proceedings consistent with this opinion. [...]

In re Oracle Corp. Derivative Litigation   3.3.2

At the later stages of stockholder litigation, a board may use a special litigation committee to attempt to take control of litigation back from stockholders. However, at that time the burden of proof with respect to the independence of the board and its special committee have shifted. The special committee bears the burden of proving its independence. At this stage, facts that might not have been troublesome at the 23.1 stage take on a different light. Oracle puts a spotlight on the difference the procedural posture makes when assessing social relationships amongst directors.

IN RE ORACLE CORP. DERIVATIVE LITIGATION
824 A. 2d 917

STRINE, Vice Chancellor.

In this opinion, I address the motion of the special litigation committee ("SLC") of Oracle Corporation to terminate this action, "the Delaware Derivative Action," and other such actions pending in the name of Oracle against certain Oracle directors and officers. These actions allege that these Oracle directors engaged in insider trading while in possession of material, non-public information showing that Oracle would not meet the earnings guidance it gave to the market for the third quarter of Oracle's fiscal year 2001. The SLC bears the burden of persuasion on this motion and must convince me that there is no material issue of fact calling into doubt its independence. This requirement is set forth in *Zapata Corp. v. Maldonado*[1] and its progeny.[2]

The question of independence "turns on whether a director is, *for any substantial reason,* incapable of making a decision with only the best interests of the corporation in mind."[3] That is, the independence test ultimately "focus[es] on impartiality and objectivity."[4] In this case, the SLC has failed to demonstrate that no material factual question exists regarding its independence.

During discovery, it emerged that the two SLC members — both of whom are professors at Stanford University — are being asked to investigate fellow Oracle directors who have important ties to Stanford, too. Among the directors who are accused by the derivative plaintiffs of insider trading are: (1) another Stanford professor, who taught one of the SLC members when the SLC member was a Ph.D. candidate and who serves as a senior fellow and a steering committee member alongside that SLC member at the Stanford Institute for Economic Policy Research or "SIEPR"; (2) a Stanford alumnus who has directed millions of dollars of contributions to Stanford during recent years, serves as Chair of SIEPR's Advisory Board and has a conference center named for him at SIEPR's facility, and has contributed nearly $600,000 to

SIEPR and the Stanford Law School, both parts of Stanford with which one of the SLC members is closely affiliated; and (3) Oracle's CEO, who has made millions of dollars in donations to Stanford through a personal [921] foundation and large donations indirectly through Oracle, and who was considering making donations of his $100 million house and $170 million for a scholarship program as late as August 2001, at around the same time period the SLC members were added to the Oracle board. Taken together, these and other facts cause me to harbor a reasonable doubt about the impartiality of the SLC.

It is no easy task to decide whether to accuse a fellow director of insider trading. For Oracle to compound that difficulty by requiring SLC members to consider accusing a fellow professor and two large benefactors of their university of conduct that is rightly considered a violation of criminal law was unnecessary and inconsistent with the concept of independence recognized by our law. The possibility that these extraneous considerations biased the inquiry of the SLC is too substantial for this court to ignore. I therefore deny the SLC's motion to terminate.

[...]

A. *Summary of the Plaintiffs' Allegations*

The Delaware Derivative Complaint centers on alleged insider trading by four members of Oracle's board of directors — Lawrence Ellison, Jeffrey Henley, Donald Lucas, and Michael Boskin (collectively, the "Trading Defendants"). Each of the Trading Defendants had a very different role at Oracle.

Ellison is Oracle's Chairman, Chief Executive Officer, and its largest stockholder, owning nearly twenty-five percent of Oracle's voting shares. By virtue of his ownership position, Ellison is one of the wealthiest men in America. By virtue of his managerial position, Ellison has regular access to a great deal of information about how Oracle is performing on a week-to-week basis.

Henley is Oracle's Chief Financial Officer, Executive Vice President, and a director of the corporation. Like Ellison, Henley has his finger on the pulse of Oracle's performance constantly.

Lucas is a director who chairs Oracle's Executive Committee and its Finance and Audit Committee. Although the plaintiffs allege that Lucas's positions gave him access to material, non-public information about the company, they do so cursorily. On the present record, it appears that Lucas did not receive copies of week-to-week projections or reports of actual results for the quarter to date. Rather, his committees primarily received historical financial data.

Boskin is a director, Chairman of the Compensation Committee, and a member of the Finance and Audit Committee. As with Lucas, Boskin's access to information was limited mostly to historical financials and did not include the week-to-week internal projections and revenue results that Ellison and Henley received.

According to the plaintiffs, each of these Trading Defendants possessed material, non-public information demonstrating that Oracle would fail to meet the earnings and revenue guidance it had provided to the market in December 2000. [...]

In addition, the plaintiffs contend more generally that the Trading Defendants received material, non-public information that the sales growth for Oracle's other products was slowing in a significant way, which made the attainment of the earnings and revenue guidance extremely difficult. [...]

During the time when these disturbing signals were allegedly being sent, the Trading Defendants engaged in the following trades:

- On January 3, 2001, Lucas sold 150,000 shares of Oracle common stock at $30 per share, reaping proceeds of over $4.6 million. These sales constituted 17% of Lucas's Oracle holdings.

- On January 4, 2001, Henley sold one million shares of Oracle stock at approximately $32 per share, yielding over $32.3 million. These sales represented 7% of Henley's Oracle holdings.

- On January 17, 2001, Boskin sold 150,000 shares of Oracle stock at over $33 per share, generating in excess of $5 million. These sales were 16% of Boskin's Oracle holdings.

- From January 22 to January 31, 2001, Ellison sold over 29 million shares at prices above $30 per share, producing over $894 million. Despite the huge proceeds generated by these sales, they constituted the sale of only 2% of Ellison's Oracle holdings.

[...]

First, the plaintiffs allege that the Trading Defendants breached their duty of loyalty by misappropriating inside information and using it as the basis for trading decisions. This claim rests its legal basis on the venerable case of *Brophy v. Cities Service Co.*[5] Its factual foundation is that the Trading Defendants were aware (or at least possessed information that should have made them aware) that the company would miss its December guidance by a wide margin and used that information to their advantage in selling at artificially inflated prices. [...]

D. *The Formation of the Special Litigation Committee*

On February 1, 2002, Oracle formed the SLC in order to investigate the Delaware Derivative Action and to determine whether Oracle should press the claims raised by the plaintiffs, settle the case, or terminate it. Soon after its formation, the SLC's charge was broadened to give it the same mandate as to all the pending derivative actions, wherever they were filed.

The SLC was granted full authority to decide these matters without the need for approval by the other members of the Oracle board.

E. *The Members of the Special Litigation Committee*

Two Oracle board members were named to the SLC. Both of them joined the Oracle board on October 15, 2001, more than a half a year after Oracle's 3Q FY 2001 closed. The SLC members also share something else: both are tenured professors at Stanford University.

Professor Hector Garcia-Molina is Chairman of the Computer Science Department at Stanford and holds the Leonard Bosack and Sandra Lerner Professorship in the Computer Science and Electrical Engineering Departments at Stanford. [...]

The other SLC member, Professor Joseph Grundfest, is the W.A. Franke Professor of Law and Business at Stanford University. [...]

As will be discussed more specifically later, Grundfest also serves as a steering committee member and a senior fellow of the Stanford Institute for Economic Policy Research, and releases working papers under the "SIEPR" banner.

For their services, the SLC members were paid $250 an hour, a rate below that which they could command for other activities, such as consulting or expert witness testimony. Nonetheless, during the course of their work, the SLC members became concerned that (arguably scandal-driven) developments in the evolving area of corporate governance as well as the decision in *Telxon v. Meyerson*,[9] might render the amount of their compensation so high as to be an argument against their independence. Therefore, Garcia-Molina and Grundfest agreed to give up any SLC-related compensation if their compensation was deemed by this court to impair their impartiality. [...]

The SLC members were recruited to the board primarily by defendant Lucas, with help from defendant Boskin.[10] The wooing of them began in the summer of 2001. Before deciding to join the Oracle board, Grundfest, in particular, did a good deal of due diligence. His review included reading publicly available information, among other things, the then-current complaint in the Federal Class Action.

Grundfest then met with defendants Ellison and Henley, among others, and asked them some questions about the Federal Class Action. The claims in the Federal Class Action are predicated on facts that are substantively identical to those on which the claims in

the Delaware Derivative Action are based. Grundfest received
answers that were consistent enough with what he called the
"exogenous" information about the case to form sufficient
confidence to at least join the Oracle board. Grundfest testified that
this did not mean that he had concluded that the claims in the
Federal Class Action had no merit, only that Ellison's and Henley's
explanations of their conduct were plausible. Grundfest did,
however, conclude that these were reputable businessmen with
whom he felt comfortable serving as a fellow director, and that
Henley had given very impressive answers to difficult questions
regarding the way Oracle conducted its financial reporting
operations.[111][...]

H. *The SLC's Investigation and Report*

The SLC's investigation was, by any objective measure, extensive.
The SLC reviewed an enormous amount of paper and electronic
records. SLC counsel interviewed seventy witnesses, some of them
twice. SLC members participated in several key interviews,
including the interviews of the Trading Defendants.

Importantly, the interviewees included all the senior members of
Oracle's management most involved in its projection and
monitoring of the company's financial performance, including its
sales and revenue growth. These interviews combined with a special
focus on the documents at the company bearing on these subjects,
including e-mail communications.

The SLC also asked the plaintiffs in the various actions to identify
witnesses the Committee should interview. The Federal Class
Action plaintiffs identified ten such persons and the Committee
interviewed all but one, who refused to cooperate. The Delaware
Derivative Action plaintiffs and the other derivative plaintiffs
declined to provide the SLC with any witness list or to meet with the
SLC.

During the course of the investigation, the SLC met with its counsel
thirty-five times for a total of eighty hours. In addition to that, the

SLC members, particularly Professor Grundfest, devoted many more hours to the investigation.

In the end, the SLC produced an extremely lengthy Report totaling 1,110 pages (excluding appendices and exhibits) that concluded that Oracle should not pursue the plaintiffs' claims against the Trading Defendants or any of the other Oracle directors serving during the 3Q FY 2001. [...]

II. *The SLC Moves to Terminate*

Consistent with its Report, the SLC moved to terminate this litigation. The plaintiffs were granted discovery focusing on three primary topics: the independence of the SLC, the good faith of its investigative efforts, and the reasonableness of the bases for its conclusion that the lawsuit should be terminated. Additionally, the plaintiffs received a large volume of documents comprising the materials that the SLC relied upon in preparing its Report.

III. *The Applicable Procedural Standard*

In order to prevail on its motion to terminate the Delaware Derivative Action, the SLC must persuade me that: (1) its members were independent; (2) that they acted in good faith; and (3) that they had reasonable bases for their recommendations.[117] If the SLC meets that burden, I am free to grant its motion or may, in my discretion, undertake my own examination of whether Oracle should terminate and permit the suit to proceed if I, in my oxymoronic judicial "business judgment," conclude that procession is in the best interests of the company.[118] This two-step analysis comes, of course, from *Zapata*. [...]

IV. *Is the SLC Independent?*

A. *The Facts Disclosed in the Report*

In its Report, the SLC took the position that its members were independent. In support of that position, the Report noted several factors including:

- the fact that neither Grundfest nor Garcia-Molina received compensation from Oracle other than as directors;

- the fact that neither Grundfest nor Garcia-Molina were on the Oracle board at the time of the alleged wrongdoing;

- the fact that both Grundfest and Garcia-Molina were willing to return their compensation as SLC members if necessary to preserve their status as independent;

- the absence of any other material ties between Oracle, the Trading Defendants, and any of the other defendants, on the one hand, and Grundfest and Garcia-Molina, on the other; and

- the absence of any material ties between Oracle, the Trading Defendants, and any of the other defendants, on the one hand, and the SLC's advisors, on the other.

Noticeably absent from the SLC Report was any disclosure of several significant ties between Oracle or the Trading Defendants and Stanford University, the university that employs both members of the SLC. In the Report, it was only disclosed that:

- defendant Boskin was a Stanford professor;

- the SLC members were aware that Lucas had made certain donations to Stanford; and

- among the contributions was a donation of $50,000 worth of stock that Lucas donated to Stanford Law School after Grundfest delivered a speech to a venture capital fund meeting in response to Lucas's request. It happens that Lucas's son is a partner in the fund and that approximately half the donation was allocated for use by Grundfest in his personal research.

B. *The "Stanford" Facts that Emerged During Discovery*

In view of the modesty of these disclosed ties, it was with some shock that a series of other ties among Stanford, Oracle, and the Trading Defendants emerged during discovery. [...]

I begin to discuss the specific ties that allegedly compromise the SLC's independence, beginning with those involving Professor Boskin.

1. *Boskin*

Defendant Michael J. Boskin is the T.M. Friedman Professor of Economics at Stanford University. [...]

During the 1970s, Boskin taught Grundfest when Grundfest was a Ph.D. candidate. Although Boskin was not Grundfest's advisor and although they do not socialize, the two have remained in contact over the years, speaking occasionally about matters of public policy.

Furthermore, both Boskin and Grundfest are senior fellows and steering committee members at the Stanford Institute for Economic Policy Research, which was previously defined as "SIEPR." [...]

Likewise, the SLC contends that Grundfest went MIA as a steering committee member, having failed to attend a meeting since 1997. The SIEPR web site, however, identifies its steering committee as having the role of "advising the director [of SIEPR] and guiding [SIEPR] on matters pertaining to research and academics."[123] Because Grundfest allegedly did not attend to these duties, his service alongside Boskin in that capacity is, the SLC contends, not relevant to his independence. [...]

But Lucas's ties with Stanford are far, far richer than the SLC Report lets on. To begin, Lucas is a Stanford alumnus, having obtained both his undergraduate and graduate degrees there. By any measure, he has been a very loyal alumnus.

[...] The Richard M. Lucas Foundation has given $11.7 million to Stanford since its 1981 founding. Among its notable contributions, the Foundation funded the establishment of the Richard M. Lucas

Center [932] for Magnetic Resonance Spectroscopy and Imaging at Stanford's Medical School. Donald Lucas was a founding member and lead director of the Center.

The SLC Report did not mention the Richard M. Lucas Foundation or its grants to Stanford. In its briefs on this motion, the SLC has pointed out that Donald Lucas is one of nine directors at the Foundation and does not serve on its Grant Review Committee. Nonetheless, the SLC does not deny that Lucas is Chairman of the board of the Foundation and that the board approves all grants. [...]

From these undisputed facts, it is inarguable that Lucas is a very important alumnus of Stanford and a generous contributor to not one, but two, parts of Stanford important to Grundfest: the Law School and SIEPR.

With these facts in mind, it remains to enrich the factual stew further, by considering defendant Ellison's ties to Stanford.

3. *Ellison*

There can be little doubt that Ellison is a major figure in the community in which Stanford is located. [...] Silicon Valley has generated many success stories, among the greatest of which is that of Oracle and its leader, Ellison. One of the wealthiest men in America, Ellison is a major figure in the nation's increasingly important information technology industry. Given his wealth, Ellison is also in a position to make — and, in fact, he has made — major charitable contributions. [...]

Although it is not represented on the Scientific Advisory Board, Stanford has nonetheless been the beneficiary of grants from the Ellison Medical Foundation — to the tune of nearly $10 million in paid or pledged funds. [...]

During the time Ellison has been CEO of Oracle, the company itself has also made over $300,000 in donations to Stanford. Not only that, when Oracle established a generously endowed educational foundation — the Oracle Help Us Help Foundation —

to help further the deployment of educational technology in schools serving disadvantaged populations, it named Stanford as the "appointing authority," which gave Stanford the right to name four of the Foundation's seven directors[...]

Beginning in the year 2000 and continuing well into 2001 — the same year that Ellison made the trades the plaintiffs contend were suspicious and the same year the SLC members were asked to join the Oracle board — Ellison and Stanford discussed a much more lucrative donation. The idea Stanford proposed for discussion was the creation of an Ellison Scholars Program modeled on the Rhodes Scholarship at Oxford. The proposed budget for Stanford's answer to Oxford: $170 million. The Ellison Scholars were to be drawn from around the world and were to come to Stanford to take a two-year interdisciplinary graduate program in economics, political science, and computer technology. During the summer between the two academic years, participants would work in internships at, among other companies, Oracle.

[...]

As part of his proposal for the Ellison Scholars Program, Shoven suggested that three of the four Trading Defendants — Ellison, Lucas, and Boskin — be on the Program board. In the hypothetical curriculum that Shoven presented to Ellison, he included a course entitled "Legal Institutions and the Modern Economy" to be taught by Grundfest. [...]

Ultimately, it appears that Ellison decided to abandon the idea of making a major donation on the Rhodes Scholarship model to Stanford or any other institution. At least, that is what he now says by affidavit. According to Shoven of SIEPR, the Ellison Scholars Program idea is going nowhere now, and all talks with Ellison have ceased on that front.

Given the nature of this case, it is natural that there must be yet another curious [935] fact to add to the mix. This is that Ellison told the *Washington Post* in an October 30, 2000 article that he intended to leave his Woodside, California home — which is worth over $100 million — to Stanford upon his death.[131] In an affidavit, Ellison does not deny making this rather splashy public statement.

But, he now (again, rather conveniently) says that he has changed his testamentary intent. Ellison denies having "bequeathed, donated or otherwise conveyed the Woodside property (or any other real property that I own) to Stanford University."[34] And, in the same affidavit, Ellison states unequivocally that he has no intention of ever giving his Woodside compound (or any other real property) to Stanford.[35] Shortly before his deposition in this case, Grundfest asked Ellison about the Woodside property and certain news reports to the effect that he was planning to give it to Stanford. According to Grundfest, Ellison's reaction to his inquiry was one of "surprise."[36] Ellison admitted to Grundfest that he said something of that sort, but contended that whatever he said was merely a "passing" comment.[37] Plus, Ellison said, Stanford would, of course, not want his $100 million home unless it came with a "dowry" — *i.e.,* an endowment to support what is sure to be a costly maintenance budget.[̶]

In order to buttress the argument that Stanford did not feel beholden to him, Ellison shared with the court the (otherwise private) fact that one of his children had applied to Stanford in October 2000 and was not admitted.[40] If Stanford felt comfortable rejecting Ellison's child, the SLC contends, why should the SLC members hesitate before recommending that Oracle press insider trading-based fiduciary duty claims against Ellison?[41] [...]

C. *The SLC's Argument*

The SLC contends that even together, these facts regarding the ties among Oracle, the Trading Defendants, Stanford, and the SLC members do not impair the SLC's independence. In so arguing, the SLC places great weight on the fact that none [936] of the Trading Defendants have the practical ability to deprive either Grundfest or Garcia-Molina of their current positions at Stanford. Nor, given their tenure, does Stanford itself have any practical ability to punish them for taking action adverse to Boskin, Lucas, or Ellison — each of whom, as we have seen, has contributed (in one way or another) great value to Stanford as an institution. As important, neither Garcia-Molina nor Grundfest are part of the official fundraising apparatus at Stanford; thus, it is not their on-the-job duty to be solicitous of contributors, and fundraising success does not factor into their treatment as professors. [...]

More subtly, the SLC argues that university professors simply are not inhibited types, unwilling to make tough decisions even as to fellow professors and large contributors. What is tenure about if not to provide professors with intellectual freedom, even in non-traditional roles such as special litigation committee members? No less ardently — but with no record evidence that reliably supports its ultimate point — the SLC contends that Garcia-Molina and Grundfest are extremely distinguished in their fields and were not, in fact, influenced by the facts identified heretofore. Indeed, the SLC argues, how could they have been influenced by many of these facts when they did not learn them until the post-Report discovery process? If it boils down to the simple fact that both share with Boskin the status of a Stanford professor, how material can this be when there are 1,700 others who also occupy the same position?

E. *The Court's Analysis of the SLC's Independence*

Having framed the competing views of the parties, it is now time to decide.

I begin with an important reminder: the SLC bears the burden of proving its independence. It must convince me.

But of what? According to the SLC, its members are independent unless they are essentially subservient to the Trading Defendants — *i.e.,* they are under the "domination and control" of the interested parties.[145] If the SLC is correct and this is the central inquiry in the independence determination, they would win. Nothing in the record suggests to me that either Garcia-Molina or Grundfest are dominated and controlled by any of the Trading Defendants, by Oracle, or even by Stanford.[146]

But, in my view, an emphasis on "domination and control" would serve only to fetishize much-parroted language, at the cost of denuding the independence inquiry of its intellectual integrity. Take an easy example. Imagine if two brothers were on a corporate board, each successful in different businesses and not dependent in any way on the other's beneficence in order to be wealthy. The brothers are brothers, they stay in touch and consider each other family, but each is opinionated and strong-willed. A derivative action is filed targeting a transaction involving one of the brothers. The other brother is put [938] on a special litigation committee to investigate the case. If the test is domination and control, then one brother could investigate the other. Does any sensible person think that is our law? I do not think it is.

And it should not be our law. Delaware law should not be based on a reductionist view of human nature that simplifies human motivations on the lines of the least sophisticated notions of the law and economics movement. *Homo sapiens* is not merely *homo economicus.* We may be thankful that an array of other motivations exist that influence human behavior; not all are any better than greed or avarice, think of envy, to name just one. But also think of motives like love, friendship, and collegiality, think of those among us who direct their behavior as best they can on a guiding creed or set of moral values.[47]

Nor should our law ignore the social nature of humans. To be direct, corporate directors are generally the sort of people deeply enmeshed in social institutions. Such institutions have norms, expectations that, explicitly and implicitly, influence and channel the behavior of those who participate in their operation.[48] Some things are "just not done," or only at a cost, which might not be so severe as a loss of position, but may involve a loss of standing in the institution. In being appropriately sensitive to this factor, our law also cannot assume — absent some proof of the point — that corporate directors are, as a general matter, persons of unusual social bravery, who operate heedless to the inhibitions that social norms generate for ordinary folk. [...]

In examining whether the SLC has met its burden to demonstrate that there is no material dispute of fact regarding its independence, the court must bear in mind the function of special litigation committees under our jurisprudence. Under Delaware law, the primary means by which corporate defendants may obtain a dismissal of a derivative suit is by showing that the plaintiffs have not met their pleading burden under the test of *Aronson v. Lewis,*[156] or the related standard set forth in *Rales v. Blasband.*[157] In simple terms, these tests permit a corporation to terminate a derivative suit if its board is comprised of directors who can impartially consider a demand.[158]

Special litigation committees are permitted as a last chance for a corporation to control a derivative claim in circumstances when a majority of its directors cannot [940] impartially consider a demand. By vesting the power of the board to determine what to do with the suit in a committee of independent directors, a corporation may retain control over whether the suit will proceed, so long as the committee meets the standard set forth in *Zapata.* [...]

Thus, in assessing the independence of the Oracle SLC, I necessarily examine the question of whether the SLC can independently make the difficult decision entrusted to it: to determine whether the Trading Defendants should face suit for insider trading-based allegations of breach of fiduciary duty. An affirmative answer by the SLC to that question would have potentially huge negative consequences [941] for the Trading Defendants, not only by exposing them to the possibility of a large damage award but also by subjecting them to great reputational harm. To have Professors Grundfest and Garcia-Molina declare that Oracle should press insider trading claims against the Trading Defendants would have been, to put it mildly, "news." Relatedly, it is reasonable to think that an SLC determination that the Trading Defendants had likely engaged in insider trading would have been accompanied by a recommendation that they step down as fiduciaries until their ultimate culpability was decided.

[...]

2. *The SLC Has Not Met Its Burden to Demonstrate the Absence of a Material Dispute of Fact About Its Independence*

Using the contextual approach I have described, I conclude that the SLC has not met its burden to show the absence of a material factual question about its independence. I find this to be the case because the ties among the SLC, the Trading Defendants, and Stanford are so substantial that they cause reasonable doubt about the SLC's ability to impartially consider whether the Trading Defendants should face suit. The concern that arises from these ties can be stated fairly simply, focusing on defendants Boskin, Lucas, and Ellison in that order, and then collectively.

As SLC members, Grundfest and Garcia-Molina were already being asked to consider whether the company should level extremely serious accusations of wrongdoing against fellow board members. As to Boskin, both SLC members faced another layer of complexity: the determination of whether to have Oracle press insider trading claims against a fellow professor at their university. Even though Boskin was in a different academic department from either SLC member, it is reasonable to assume that the fact that Boskin was also on faculty would — to persons possessing typical sensibilities and institutional loyalty — be a matter of more than trivial concern. Universities are obviously places of at-times intense debate, but they also see themselves as communities. In fact, Stanford refers to itself as a "community of scholars."[641] To accuse a fellow professor — whom one might see at the faculty club or at inter-disciplinary presentations of academic papers — of insider trading cannot be a small thing — even for the most callous of academics.

As to Boskin, Grundfest faced an even more complex challenge than Garcia-Molina. Boskin was a professor who had taught him and with whom he had maintained contact over the years. [...] Having these ties, Grundfest [943] (I infer) would have more difficulty objectively determining whether Boskin engaged in improper insider trading than would a person who was not a fellow professor, had not been a student of Boskin, had not kept in touch with Boskin over the years, and who was not a senior fellow and steering committee member at SIEPR.

In so concluding, I necessarily draw on a general sense of human nature. It may be that Grundfest is a very special person who is capable of putting these kinds of things totally aside. But the SLC has not provided evidence that that is the case. In this respect, it is critical to note that I do not infer that Grundfest would be less likely to recommend suit against Boskin than someone without these ties. Human nature being what it is, it is entirely possible that Grundfest would in fact be tougher on Boskin than the would on someone with whom he did not have such connections. The inference I draw is subtly, but importantly, different. What I infer is that a person in Grundfest's position would find it difficult to assess Boskin's conduct without pondering his own association with Boskin and their mutual affiliations. Although these connections might produce bias in either a tougher or laxer direction, the key inference is that these connections would be on the mind of a person in Grundfest's position, putting him in the position of either causing serious legal action to be brought against a person with whom he shares several connections (an awkward thing) or not doing so (and risking being seen as having engaged in favoritism toward his old professor and SIEPR colleague).

The same concerns also exist as to Lucas. For Grundfest to vote to accuse Lucas of insider trading would require him to accuse SIEPR's Advisory Board Chair and major benefactor of serious wrongdoing — of conduct that violates federal securities laws. Such action would also require Grundfest to make charges against a man who recently donated $50,000 to Stanford Law School after Grundfest made a speech at his request.[1651][...]

In view of the ties involving Boskin and Lucas alone, I would conclude that the SLC has failed to meet its burden on the independence question. The tantalizing facts about Ellison merely reinforce this conclusion. The SLC, of course, argues that Ellison is not a large benefactor of Stanford personally, that Stanford has demonstrated its independence of him by rejecting his child for admission, and that, in any event, the SLC was ignorant of any negotiations between Ellison and Stanford about a large contribution. For these reasons, the SLC says, its ability to act independently of Ellison is clear.

I find differently. The notion that anyone in Palo Alto can accuse Ellison of insider trading without harboring some fear of social awkwardness seems a stretch. That being said, I do not mean to imply that the mere fact that Ellison is worth tens of billions of dollars and is the key force behind a very important social institution in Silicon Valley disqualifies all persons who live there from being independent of him. Rather, it is merely an acknowledgement of the simple fact that accusing such a significant person in that community of such serious wrongdoing is no small thing.

Given that general context, Ellison's relationship to Stanford itself contributes to my overall doubt, when heaped on top of the ties involving Boskin and Lucas. During the period when Grundfest and Garcia-Molina were being added to the Oracle board, Ellison was publicly considering making extremely large contributions to Stanford. Although the SLC denies [946] knowledge of these public statements, Grundfest claims to have done a fair amount of research before joining the board, giving me doubt that he was not somewhat aware of the possibility that Ellison might bestow large blessings on Stanford. This is especially so when I cannot rule out the possibility that Grundfest had been told by Lucas about, but has now honestly forgotten, the negotiations over the Ellison Scholars Program. [...]

Of course, the SLC says these facts are meaningless because Stanford rejected Ellison's child for admission. I am not sure what to make of this fact, but it surely cannot bear the heavy weight the SLC gives it. The aftermath of denying Ellison's child admission might, after all, as likely manifest itself in a desire on the part of the Stanford community never to offend Ellison again, lest he permanently write off Stanford as a possible object of his charitable aims — as the sort of thing that acts as not one, but two strikes, leading the batter to choke up on the bat so as to be even more careful not to miss the next pitch. Suffice to say that after the rejection took place, it did not keep Ellison from making public statements in *Fortune* magazine on August 13, 2001 about his consideration of making a huge donation to Stanford, at the same time when the two SLC members were being courted to join the Oracle board. [...]

Whether the SLC members had precise knowledge of all the facts that have emerged is not essential, what is important is that by any measure this was a social atmosphere painted in too much vivid Stanford Cardinal red for the SLC members to have reasonably ignored it. Summarized fairly, two Stanford professors were recruited to the Oracle board in summer 2001 and soon asked to investigate a fellow professor and two benefactors of the University. On Grundfest's part, the facts are more substantial, because his connections — through his personal experiences, SIEPR, and the Law School — to Boskin and to Lucas run deeper. [...]

Rather than form an SLC whose membership was free from bias-creating relationships, Oracle formed a committee fraught with them. As a result, the SLC has failed to meet its *Zapata* burden, and its motion to terminate must be denied. Because of this reality, I do not burden the reader with an examination of the other *Zapata* factors. In the absence of a finding that the SLC was independent, its subjective good faith and the reasonableness of its conclusions would not be sufficient to justify termination. Without confidence that the SLC was impartial, its findings do not provide the assurance our law requires for the dismissal of a derivative suit without a merits inquiry.

220 Actions and Tools at Hand   3.4

Stockholders have a statutory right to access the books and records of the corporation. This power is an extremely important tool for stockholders to monitor the actions the board of directors and to root wrong-doing or malfeasance. However, the right to monitor a corporation's books and records is also subject to limitations.

Courts – as in *Beam v. Stewart* – regularly exhort plaintiffs to use § 220 to seek out books and records prior to filing derivative complaints. However, the § 220 process can be lengthy. Consequently, the economics of plaintiff litigation make it difficult for plaintiffs to both pursue § 220 litigation and also maintain control positions in early filed derivative litigation. This challenge makes § 220 actions a less than perfect vehicle for curbing the excesses of the litigation industrial complex.

The § 220 online course module will allow you to work through § 220 and the various judicial standards related to plaintiffs seeking access to book and records of the corporation.

DGCL Sec. 220 - Inspection of books and records 3
.
Stockholders who comply with the requirements of 4
§220 can access the books and records of the .
corporation. 1

§ 220. Inspection of books and records.

(a) As used in this section:

(1) "Stockholder" means a holder of record of stock in a stock corporation, or a person who is the beneficial owner of shares of such stock held either in a voting trust or by a nominee on behalf of such person. [...]

(b) Any stockholder, in person or by attorney or other agent, shall, upon written demand under oath stating the purpose thereof, have the right during the usual hours for business to inspect for any proper purpose, and to make copies and extracts from:

(1) The corporation's stock ledger, a list of its stockholders, and its other books and records; and

(2) A subsidiary's books and records, to the extent that:

a. The corporation has actual possession and control of such records of such subsidiary; or

b. The corporation could obtain such records through the exercise of control over such subsidiary, provided that as of the date of the making of the demand:

1. The stockholder inspection of such books and records of the subsidiary would not constitute a breach of an agreement between the corporation or the subsidiary and a person or persons not affiliated with the corporation; and

2. The subsidiary would not have the right under the law applicable to it to deny the corporation access to such books and records upon demand by the corporation.

In every instance where the stockholder is other than a record holder of stock in a stock corporation, or a member of a nonstock corporation, the demand under oath shall state the person's status as a stockholder, be accompanied by documentary evidence of beneficial ownership of the stock, and state that such documentary evidence is a true and correct copy of what it purports to be. A proper purpose shall mean a purpose reasonably related to such person's interest as a stockholder. [...]The demand under oath shall be directed to the corporation at its registered office in this State or at its principal place of business.

(c) If the corporation, or an officer or agent thereof, refuses to permit an inspection sought by a stockholder or attorney or other agent acting for the stockholder pursuant to subsection (b) of this section or does not reply to the demand within 5 business days after the demand has been made, the stockholder may apply to the Court of Chancery for an order to compel such inspection. The Court of Chancery is hereby vested with exclusive jurisdiction to determine whether or not the person seeking inspection is entitled to the inspection sought. The Court may summarily order the corporation to permit the stockholder to inspect the corporation's stock ledger, an existing list of stockholders, and its other books and records, and to make copies or extracts therefrom; or the Court may order the corporation to furnish to the stockholder a list of its stockholders as of a specific date on condition that the stockholder first pay to the corporation the reasonable cost of obtaining and furnishing such list and on such other conditions as the Court deems appropriate. Where the stockholder seeks to inspect the corporation's books and records, other than its stock ledger or list of stockholders, such stockholder shall first establish that:

(1) Such stockholder is a stockholder;

(2) Such stockholder has complied with this section respecting the form and manner of making demand for inspection of such documents; and

(3) The inspection such stockholder seeks is for a proper purpose.

Where the stockholder seeks to inspect the corporation's stock ledger or list of stockholders and establishes that such stockholder is a stockholder and has complied with this section respecting the form and manner of making demand for inspection of such documents, the burden of proof shall be upon the corporation to establish that the inspection such stockholder seeks is for an improper purpose. The Court may, in its discretion, prescribe any limitations or conditions with reference to the inspection, or award such other or further relief as the Court may deem just and proper. The Court may order books, documents and records, pertinent extracts therefrom, or duly authenticated copies thereof, to be brought within this State and kept in this State upon such terms and conditions as the order may prescribe.

(d) Any director shall have the right to examine the corporation's stock ledger, a list of its stockholders and its other books and records for a purpose reasonably related to the director's position as a director. The Court of Chancery is hereby vested with the exclusive jurisdiction to determine whether a director is entitled to the inspection sought. The Court may summarily order the corporation to permit the director to inspect any and all books and records, the stock ledger and the list of stockholders and to make copies or extracts therefrom. The burden of proof shall be upon the corporation to establish that the inspection such director seeks is for an improper purpose. The Court may, in its discretion, prescribe any limitations or conditions with reference to the inspection, or award such other and further relief as the Court may deem just and proper.

Fiduciary Duties of Directors   4

Although the Delaware code - and the corporate codes
of all the other states for that matter - do a good job of
describing the corporate form and the mechanics of operating this
form, with the exception of perhaps §144, the code says precious
little about the standards to which boards of directors who are
managing the corporation will be held. This is so because corporate
fiduciary duties are a product of the common law and not statute. In
the following sections we examine the various core duties of
corporate directors. These duties are entirely consistent with the
fiduciary obligations of agents, which you studied in a previous
module in this course.

In Basho Technologies v. Georgetown Basho Investors (2018), Vice
Chancellor Glasscock described claims for breaches of fiduciary
duty as equitable torts in the following manner:

The basic elements of a common law tort claim are well known:
The plaintiff must prove existence of a duty, a breach of that duty,
injury, and a causal connection between the breach and injury that is
sufficient to warrant a remedy, such as compensatory damages.

The equitable tort for breach of fiduciary duty has only two formal
elements: (i) the existence of a fiduciary duty and (ii) a breach of
that duty. The first element closely resembles the corresponding
aspect of a common law tort claim: the plaintiff must prove by a
preponderance of the evidence that the defendant was a fiduciary
and owed duties to the plaintiff. The second element departs from
the common law model in significant respects. For the traditional
common law tort, the court analyzes the question of breach using
the standard of conduct that the defendant director was expected to
follow.

For the equitable tort, the court evaluates the question of breach
through the lens of one of several possible standards of review. In
each manifestation, the standard of review is more forgiving of
[defendant fiduciaries] and more onerous for [the] plaintiffs than
the standard of conduct.

The following section describes the difference between the standard of conduct for corporate directors and the various standards of review that a court will deploy when evaluating a fiduciary duty claim.

Standards of Conduct and Standards of Review 4.1

Directors of corporations owe fiduciary duties of
care and loyalty to the corporation and its residual
claimants (stockholders). The duty of care generally requires a
director to use the care that a reasonably prudent person in like
position would reasonably believe appropriate under the
circumstances. The duty of loyalty generally requires a director to
discharge her duties in good faith and with the reasonable belief that
her actions are in the best interests of the corporation and the
residual claimants.

When a court is asked to judge director actions against the
obligations the directors owe, the court deploys one of several
standards of review depending on the circumstances and the duty
being questioned. The excerpt from *In re Trados S'holder
Litigation* provides a broad overview of how courts approach the
question of evaluating director conduct against the appropriate
standard of review.

IN RE TRADOS INC. SHAREHOLDER LITIGATION
73 A. 3d 17, 35
Del: Court of Chancery 2013

... When determining whether directors have breached their
fiduciary duties, Delaware corporate law distinguishes between the
standard of conduct and the standard of review. *See* William T.
Allen, Jack B. Jacobs, & Leo E. Strine, Jr., *Realigning the Standard
of Review of Director Due Care with Delaware Public Policy: A
Critique of Van Gorkom and its Progeny as a Standard of Review
Problem,* 96 Nw. U.L.Rev. 449, 451-52 (2002)
[hereinafter *Realigning the Standard*]. The standard of conduct
describes what directors are expected to do and is defined by the

content of the duties of loyalty and care. The standard of review is the test that a court applies when evaluating whether directors have met the standard of conduct. It describes what a plaintiff must first plead and later prove to prevail.

Under Delaware law, the standard of review depends initially on whether the board members (i) were disinterested and independent (the business judgment rule), (ii) faced potential conflicts of interest because of the decisional dynamics present in particular recurring and recognizable situations (enhanced scrutiny), or (iii) confronted actual conflicts of interest such that the directors making the decision did not comprise a disinterested and independent board majority (entire fairness). The standard of review may change further depending on whether the directors took steps to address the potential or actual conflict, such as by creating an independent committee, conditioning the transaction on approval by disinterested stockholders, or both. Regardless, in every situation, the standard of review is more forgiving of directors and more onerous for stockholder plaintiffs than the standard of conduct. This divergence is warranted for diverse policy reasons typically cited as justifications for the business judgment rule. *See, e.g., Brehm v. Eisner,* 746 A.2d 244, 263 (Del.2000) (explaining justifications for business judgment rule).

The Standard Of Conduct

Delaware corporate law starts from the bedrock principle that "[t]he business and affairs of every corporation ... shall be managed by or under the direction of a board of directors." 8 *Del. C.* § 141(a). When exercising their statutory responsibility, the standard of conduct requires that directors seek "to promote the value of the corporation for the benefit of its stockholders."

"It is, of course, accepted that a corporation may take steps, such as giving charitable contributions or paying higher wages, that do not maximize profits currently. They may do so, however, because such activities are rationalized as producing greater profits over the long-term." Leo E. Strine, Jr., *Our Continuing Struggle with the Idea that For-Profit Corporations Seek Profit,* 47 Wake Forest L.Rev. 135,

147 n. 34 (2012) [hereinafter *For-Profit Corporations*]. Decisions of this nature benefit the corporation as a whole, and by increasing the value of the corporation, the directors increase the share of value available for the residual claimants. Judicial opinions therefore often refer to directors owing fiduciary duties "to the corporation and its shareholders."*Gheewalla*, 930 A.2d at 99; *accord Mills Acq. Co. v. Macmillan, Inc.*, 559 A.2d 1261, 1280 (Del.1989) ("[D]irectors owe fiduciary duties of care and loyalty to the corporation and its shareholders ...."); *Polk v. Good*, 507 A.2d 531, 536 (Del.1986) ("In performing their duties the directors owe fundamental fiduciary duties of loyalty and care to the corporation and its shareholders."). This formulation captures the foundational relationship in which directors owe duties to the corporation for the ultimate benefit of the entity's residual claimants. Nevertheless, "stockholders' best interest must always, within legal limits, be the end. Other constituencies may be considered only instrumentally to advance that end." *For-Profit Corporations, supra,* at 147 n. 34.

A Delaware corporation, by default, has a perpetual existence. 8 *Del. C.* §§ 102(b)(5), 122(1). Equity capital, by default, is permanent capital. In terms of the standard of conduct, the duty of loyalty therefore mandates that directors maximize the value of the corporation over the long-term for the benefit of the providers of equity capital, as warranted for an entity with perpetual life in which the residual claimants have locked in their investment. When deciding whether to pursue a strategic alternative that would end or fundamentally alter the stockholders' ongoing investment in the corporation, the loyalty-based standard of conduct requires that the alternative yield value exceeding what the corporation otherwise would generate for stockholders over the long-term. Value, of course, does not just mean cash. It could mean an ownership interest in an entity, a package of other securities, or some combination, with or without cash, that will deliver greater value over the anticipated investment horizon. *See QVC*, 637 A.2d at 44 (describing how directors should approach consideration of non-cash or mixed consideration).

The duty to act for the ultimate benefit of stockholders does not require that directors fulfill the wishes of a particular subset of the stockholder base. *See In re Lear Corp. S'holder Litig.*, 967 A.2d 640, 655 (Del.Ch.2008) ("Directors are not thermometers, existing to register the ever-changing sentiments of stockholders.... During their term of office, directors may take good faith actions that they believe will benefit stockholders, even if they realize that the stockholders do not agree with them."); *Paramount Commc'ns Inc. v. Time Inc.*, 1989 WL 79880, at *30 (Del.Ch. July 14, 1989) ("The corporation law does not operate on the theory that directors, in exercising their powers to manage the firm, are obligated to follow the wishes of a majority of shares. In fact, directors, not shareholders, are charged with the duty to manage the firm."), *aff'd in pertinent part, Time*, 571 A.2d at 1150; *TW Servs.*, 1989 WL 20290, at *8 n. 14 ("While corporate democracy is a pertinent concept, a corporation is not a New England town meeting; directors, not shareholders, have responsibilities to manage the business and affairs of the corporation, subject however to a fiduciary obligation."). Stockholders may have idiosyncratic reasons for preferring decisions that misallocate capital. Directors must exercise their independent fiduciary judgment; they need not cater to stockholder whim. *See Time*, 571 A.2d at 1154 ("Delaware law confers the management of the corporate enterprise to the stockholders' duly elected board representatives. The fiduciary duty to manage a corporate enterprise includes the selection of a time frame for achievement of corporate goals. That duty may not be delegated to the stockholders." (citations omitted)).

More pertinent to the current case, a particular class or series of stock may hold contractual rights against the corporation and desire outcomes that maximize the value of those rights. *See MCG Capital Corp. v. Maginn*, 2010 WL 1782271, at *6 (Del.Ch. May 5, 2010) (noting that preferential contract rights may appear in "the articles of incorporation, the preferred share designations, or some other appropriate document" such as a registration rights agreement, investor rights agreement, or stockholder agreement). By default, "all stock is created equal." *Id.* Unless a corporation's certificate of incorporation provides otherwise, each share of stock is common stock. If the certificate of incorporation grants a particular class or series of stock special "voting powers, ... designations, preferences and relative, participating, optional or other special rights" superior to the common stock, then the class or series holding the rights is known as preferred stock. 8 *Del. C.* § 151(a); *see Starring v. Am. Hair & Felt Co.,*191 A. 887, 890 (Del.Ch.1937) (Wolcott, C.) ("The term `preferred stock' is of fairly definite import. There is no difficulty in understanding its general concept. [It] is of course a stock which in relation to other classes enjoys certain defined rights and privileges."), *aff'd,* 2 A.2d 249 (Del.1937). If the certificate of incorporation is silent on a particular issue, then as to that issue the preferred stock and the common stock have the same rights. Consequently, as a general matter, "the rights and preferences of preferred stock are contractual in nature." *Trados I,* 2009 WL 2225958, at *7; *accord Judah v. Del. Trust Co.,* 378 A.2d 624, 628 (Del.1977) ("Generally, the provisions of the certificate of incorporation govern the rights of preferred shareholders, the certificate of incorporation being interpreted in accordance with the law of contracts, with only those rights which are embodied in the certificate granted to preferred shareholders.").

A board does not owe fiduciary duties to preferred stockholders when considering whether or not to take corporate action that might trigger or circumvent the preferred stockholders' contractual rights. Preferred stockholders are owed fiduciary duties only when they do not invoke their special contractual rights and rely on a right shared equally with the common stock. Under those circumstances, "the existence of such right and the correlative duty may be measured by equitable as well as legal standards." Thus, for example, just as common stockholders can challenge a disproportionate allocation of merger consideration, so too can preferred stockholders who do not possess and are not limited by a contractual entitlement. Under those circumstances, the decision to allocate different consideration is a discretionary, fiduciary determination that must pass muster under the appropriate standard of review, and the degree to which directors own different classes or series of stock may affect the standard of review.

To reiterate, the standard of conduct for directors requires that they strive in good faith and on an informed basis to maximize the value of the corporation for the benefit of its residual claimants, the ultimate beneficiaries of the firm's value, not for the benefit of its contractual claimants. In light of this obligation, "it is the duty of directors to pursue the best interests of the corporation and its common stockholders, if that can be done faithfully with the contractual promises owed to the preferred." _LC Capital,_ 990 A.2d at 452. Put differently, "generally it will be the duty of the board, where discretionary judgment is to be exercised, to prefer the interests of the common stock — as the good faith judgment of the board sees them to be — to the interests created by the special rights, preferences, _etc_.... of preferred stock." _Equity-Linked,_ 705 A.2d at 1042. This principle is not unique to preferred stock; it applies equally to other holders of contract rights against the corporation. Consequently, as this court observed at the motion to dismiss stage, "in circumstances where the interests of the common stockholders diverge from those of the preferred stockholders, it is _possible_ that a director could breach her duty by improperly favoring the interests of the preferred stockholders over those of the common stockholders." _Trados I,_ 2009 WL 2225958, at *7; _accord LC Capital,_ 990 A.2d at 447 (quoting _Trados I_ and remarking that it "summarized the weight of authority very well"). ...

The Standards Of Review

To determine whether directors have met their fiduciary obligations, Delaware courts evaluate the challenged decision through the lens of a standard of review. In this case, the Board lacked a majority of disinterested and independent directors, making entire fairness the applicable standard.

"Delaware has three tiers of review for evaluating director decision-making: the business judgment rule, enhanced scrutiny, and entire fairness." _Reis v. Hazelett Strip-Casting Corp.,_ 28 A.3d 442, 457 (Del.Ch.2011). Delaware's default standard of review is the business judgment rule. The rule presumes that "in making a business decision the directors of a corporation acted on an informed basis, in good faith and in the honest belief that the action taken was in the best interests of the company." This standard of review "reflects and promotes the role of the board of directors as the proper body to manage the business and affairs of the corporation." _Trados_

I, 2009 WL 2225958, at *6. Unless one of its elements is rebutted, "the court merely looks to see whether the business decision made was rational in the sense of being one logical approach to advancing the corporation's objectives." *In re Dollar Thrifty S'holder Litig.,* 14 A.3d 573, 598 (Del.Ch. 2010). Only when a decision lacks any rationally conceivable basis will a court infer bad faith and a breach of duty.

Enhanced scrutiny is Delaware's intermediate standard of review. Framed generally, it requires that the defendant fiduciaries "bear the burden of persuasion to show that their motivations were proper and not selfish" and that "their actions were reasonable in relation to their legitimate objective." *Mercier v. Inter-Tel (Del.), Inc.,* 929 A.2d 786, 810 (Del.Ch. 2007). Enhanced scrutiny applies to specific, recurring, and readily identifiable situations involving potential conflicts of interest where the realities of the decisionmaking context can subtly undermine the decisions of even independent and disinterested directors. In *Unocal,* the Delaware Supreme Court created enhanced scrutiny to address the potential conflicts of interest faced by a board of directors when resisting a hostile takeover, namely the "omnipresent specter" that target directors may be influenced by and act to further their own interests or those of incumbent management, "rather than those of the corporation and its shareholders." 493 A.2d at 954. Tailored for this context, enhanced scrutiny requires that directors who take defensive action against a hostile takeover show (i) that "they had reasonable grounds for believing that a danger to corporate policy and effectiveness existed," and (ii) that the response selected was "reasonable in relation to the threat posed." *Id.* at 955.

In *Revlon,* the Delaware Supreme Court extended the new intermediate standard to the sale of a corporation. *See* 506 A.2d at 180-82 (expressly applying *Unocal* test). Here too, enhanced scrutiny applies because of the potential conflicts of interest that fiduciaries must confront. "[T]he potential sale of a corporation has enormous implications for corporate managers and advisors, and a range of human motivations, including but by no means limited to greed, can inspire fiduciaries and their advisors to be less than faithful." *In re El Paso Corp. S'holders Litig.,* 41 A.3d 432, 439

(Del.Ch.2012). These potential conflicts warrant a more searching standard of review than the business judgment rule:

> The heightened scrutiny that applies in the *Revlon* (and *Unocal*) contexts are, in large measure, rooted in a concern that the board might harbor personal motivations in the sale context that differ from what is best for the corporation and its stockholders. Most traditionally, there is the danger that top corporate managers will resist a sale that might cost them their managerial posts, or prefer a sale to one industry rival rather than another for reasons having more to do with personal ego than with what is best for stockholders.

Dollar Thrifty, 14 A.3d at 597 (footnote omitted). Consequently, "the predicate question of what the board's true motivation was comes into play," and "[t]he court must take a nuanced and realistic look at the possibility that personal interests short of pure self-dealing have influenced the board ...." *Id.* at 598. Tailored to the sale context, enhanced scrutiny requires that the defendant fiduciaries show that they acted reasonably to obtain for their beneficiaries the best value reasonably available under the circumstances, which may be no transaction at all. *See QVC,* 637 A.2d at 48-49.

Entire fairness, Delaware's most onerous standard, applies when the board labors under actual conflicts of interest. Once entire fairness applies, the defendants must establish "to the court's satisfaction that the transaction was the product of both fair dealing *and* fair price." *Cinerama, Inc. v. Technicolor, Inc. (Technicolor III),* 663 A.2d 1156, 1163 (Del. 1995) (internal quotation marks omitted). "Not even an honest belief that the transaction was entirely fair will be sufficient to establish entire fairness. Rather, the transaction itself must be objectively fair, independent of the board's beliefs." *Gesoff v. IIC Indus., Inc.,* 902 A.2d 1130, 1145 (Del.Ch.2006).

To obtain review under the entire fairness test, the stockholder plaintiff must prove that there were not enough independent and disinterested individuals among the directors making the challenged decision to comprise a board majority. *See Aronson,* 473 A.2d at 812 (noting that if "the transaction is not approved by a majority consisting of the disinterested directors, then the business judgment rule has no application"). To determine whether the directors approving the transaction comprised a disinterested and independent board majority, the court conducts a director-by-director analysis.

Duty of Care 4.2

Aronson v. Lewis

In an earlier case (*Shlensky v Wrigley*) you were introduced the business judgment presumption. Remember that in *Shlensky*, the court ruled that absent some act of fraud or gross negligence that it would not second guess business decisions of a board of directors. This general deference to the board's statutory role is known as the business judgment presumption and it plays out most commonly in cases where stockholders bring claims that boards have somehow violated their duty of care to the corporation. The case that follows, *Aronson*, is the leading restatement of the business judgment presumption.

4.2.1

ARONSON V. LEWIS
473 A.2d 805

MOORE, Justice:

A.

A cardinal precept of the General Corporation Law of the State of Delaware is that directors, rather than shareholders, manage the business and affairs of the corporation. 8 *Del.C.* § 141(a). Section 141(a) states in pertinent part:

> "The *business and affairs* of a corporation organized under this chapter *shall be managed by or under the direction* of a board of directors except as may be otherwise provided in this chapter or in its certificate of incorporation."

8 *Del.C.* § 141(a) (Emphasis added). The existence and exercise of this power carries with it certain fundamental fiduciary obligations to the corporation and its shareholders.[—]

The business judgment rule is an acknowledgment of the managerial prerogatives of Delaware directors under Section 141(a).[...] It is a presumption that in making a business decision the directors of a corporation acted on an informed basis, in good faith and in the honest belief that the action taken was in the best interests of the company. [...] The burden is on the party challenging the decision to establish facts rebutting the presumption. [...]

First, its protections can only be claimed by disinterested directors whose conduct otherwise meets the tests of business judgment. From the standpoint of interest, this means that directors can neither appear on both sides of a transaction nor expect to derive any personal financial benefit from it in the sense of self-dealing, as opposed to a benefit which devolves upon the corporation or all stockholders generally. [...]

Second, to invoke the rule's protection directors have a duty to inform themselves, prior to making a business decision, of all material information reasonably available to them. Having become so informed, they must then act with requisite care in the discharge of their duties. While the Delaware cases use a variety of terms to describe the applicable standard of care, our analysis satisfies us that under the business judgment rule director liability is predicated upon concepts of gross negligence.[—]

However, it should be noted that the business judgment rule operates only in the context of director action. Technically speaking, it has no role where directors have either abdicated their functions, or absent a conscious decision, failed to act.[7] But it also follows that under applicable principles, a conscious decision to refrain from acting may nonetheless be a valid exercise of business judgment and enjoy the protections of the rule.

Smith v. Van Gorkom   4.2.2

Van Gorkom is a controversial case of the duty of care in the context of a corporate acquisition. In *Van Gorkom*, the court found that the board had violated its duty of care to the corporation and awarded damages to stockholders. *Van Gorkom* was the impetus for the adoption of the § 102(b)(7)'s exculpation provision. Consequently, the result in *Van Gorkom* is unlikely to occur again. However, the *Van Gorkom* case is worth reading because it demonstrates the kinds of director failures that may well rise to the level of a violation of the duty of care.

SMITH V. VAN GORKOM
488 A.2d 858

HORSEY, Justice (for the majority):

This appeal from the Court of Chancery involves a class action brought by shareholders of the defendant Trans Union Corporation ("Trans Union" or "the Company"), originally seeking rescission of a cash-out merger of Trans Union into the defendant New T Company ("New T"), a wholly-owned subsidiary of the defendant, Marmon Group, Inc. ("Marmon"). Alternate relief in the form of damages is sought against the defendant members of the Board of Directors of Trans Union, [864] New T, and Jay A. Pritzker and Robert A. Pritzker, owners of Marmon.[1]

Following trial, the former Chancellor granted judgment for the defendant directors by unreported letter opinion dated July 6, 1982.[2] Judgment was based on two findings: (1) that the Board of

Directors had acted in an informed manner so as to be entitled to protection of the business judgment rule in approving the cash-out merger; and (2) that the shareholder vote approving the merger should not be set aside because the stockholders had been "fairly informed" by the Board of Directors before voting thereon. The plaintiffs appeal. [...]

We hold: (1) that the Board's decision, reached September 20, 1980, to approve the proposed cash-out merger was not the product of an informed business judgment; (2) that the Board's subsequent efforts to amend the Merger Agreement and take other curative action were ineffectual, both legally and factually; and (3) that the Board did not deal with complete candor with the stockholders by failing to disclose all material facts, which they knew or should have known, before securing the stockholders' approval of the merger. [...]

Trans Union was a publicly-traded, diversified holding company, the principal earnings of which were generated by its railcar leasing business. During the period here involved, the Company had a cash flow of hundreds of millions of dollars annually. However, the Company had difficulty in generating sufficient taxable income to offset increasingly large investment tax credits (ITCs). [...]

Beginning in the late 1960's, and continuing through the 1970's, Trans Union pursued a program of acquiring small companies in order to increase available taxable income. In July 1980, Trans Union Management prepared the annual revision of the Company's Five Year Forecast. This report [...] referred to the ITC situation as a "nagging problem" and, given that problem, the leasing company "would still appear to be constrained to a tax breakeven." The report then listed four alternative uses of the projected 1982-1985 equity surplus: (1) stock repurchase; (2) dividend increases; (3) a major acquisition program; and (4) combinations of the above. The sale of Trans Union was not among the alternatives. The report emphasized that, despite the overall surplus, the operation of the Company would consume all available equity for the next several years, and concluded: "As a result, we have sufficient time to fully develop our course of action."

-B-

On August 27, 1980, Van Gorkom met with Senior Management of Trans Union. Van Gorkom reported on his lobbying efforts in Washington and his desire to find a solution to the tax credit problem more permanent than a continued program of acquisitions. Various alternatives were suggested and discussed preliminarily, including the sale of Trans Union to a company with a large amount of taxable income.

Donald Romans, Chief Financial Officer of Trans Union, stated that his department had done a "very brief bit of work on the possibility of a leveraged buy-out." This work had been prompted by a media article which Romans had seen regarding a leveraged buy-out by management. The work consisted of a "preliminary study" of the cash which could be generated by the Company if it participated in a leveraged buyout. As Romans stated, this analysis "was very first and rough cut at seeing whether a cash flow would support what might be considered a high price for this type of transaction."

On September 5, at another Senior Management meeting which Van Gorkom attended, Romans again brought up the idea of a leveraged buy-out as a "possible strategic alternative" to the Company's acquisition program. [...]According to Romans: They did not "come up" with a price for the Company. They merely "ran the numbers" at $50 a share and at $60 a share with the "rough form" of their cash figures at the time. Their "figures indicated that $50 would be very easy to do but $60 would be very difficult to do under those figures." This work did not purport to establish a fair price for either the Company or 100% of the stock. It was intended to determine the cash flow needed to service the debt that would "probably" be incurred in a leveraged buyout, based on "rough calculations" without "any benefit of experts to identify what the limits were to that, and so forth." [...]

At this meeting, Van Gorkom stated that he would be willing to take $55 per share for his own 75,000 shares. He vetoed the suggestion of a leveraged buy-out by Management, however, as involving a potential conflict of interest for Management. Van Gorkom, a certified public accountant and lawyer, had been an officer of Trans

311

Union [866] for 24 years, its Chief Executive Officer for more than 17 years, and Chairman of its Board for 2 years. It is noteworthy in this connection that he was then approaching 65 years of age and mandatory retirement.

For several days following the September 5 meeting, Van Gorkom pondered the idea of a sale[...]

Van Gorkom decided to meet with Jay A. Pritzker, a well-known corporate takeover specialist and a social acquaintance. However, rather than approaching Pritzker simply to determine his interest in acquiring Trans Union, Van Gorkom assembled a proposed per share price for sale of the Company and a financing structure by which to accomplish the sale. Van Gorkom did so without consulting either his Board or any members of Senior Management except one: Carl Peterson, Trans Union's Controller. Telling Peterson that he wanted no other person on his staff to know what he was doing, but without telling him why, Van Gorkom directed Peterson to calculate the feasibility of a leveraged buy-out at an assumed price per share of $55. Apart from the Company's historic stock market price,[5] and Van Gorkom's long association with Trans Union, the record is devoid of any competent evidence that $55 represented the per share intrinsic value of the Company.

Having thus chosen the $55 figure, based solely on the availability of a leveraged buy-out, Van Gorkom multiplied the price per share by the number of shares outstanding to reach a total value of the Company of $690 million. Van Gorkom told Peterson to use this $690 million figure and to assume a $200 million equity contribution by the buyer. Based on these assumptions, Van Gorkom directed Peterson to determine whether the debt portion of the purchase price could be paid off in five years or less if financed by Trans Union's cash flow as projected in the Five Year Forecast, and by the sale of certain weaker divisions identified in a study done for Trans Union by the Boston Consulting Group ("BCG study"). Peterson reported that, of the purchase price, approximately $50-80 million would remain outstanding after five years. Van Gorkom was disappointed, but decided to meet with Pritzker nevertheless.

Van Gorkom arranged a meeting with Pritzker at the latter's home on Saturday, September 13, 1980. Van Gorkom prefaced his presentation by stating to Pritzker: "Now as far as you are concerned, I can, I think, show how you can pay a substantial premium over the present stock price and pay off most of the loan in the first five years. * * * If you could pay $55 for this Company, here is a way in which I think it can be financed."

Van Gorkom then reviewed with Pritzker his calculations based upon his proposed price of $55 per share. Although Pritzker mentioned $50 as a more attractive figure, no other price was mentioned. However, Van Gorkom stated that to be sure that $55 was the best price obtainable, Trans Union should be free to accept any better offer. Pritzker demurred, stating that his organization would serve as a "stalking horse" for an "auction contest" only if Trans Union would permit Pritzker to buy 1,750,000 shares of Trans Union stock at market price which Pritzker could then sell to any higher bidder. After further discussion on this point, Pritzker told Van Gorkom that he would give him a more definite reaction soon.

[...] Monday, September 15, Pritzker advised Van Gorkom that he was interested in the $55 cash-out merger proposal and requested more information on Trans Union. Van Gorkom agreed to meet privately with Pritzker, accompanied by Peterson, Chelberg, and Michael Carpenter, Trans Union's consultant from the Boston Consulting Group. The meetings took place on September 16 and 17. Van Gorkom was "astounded that events were moving with such amazing rapidity."

On Thursday, September 18, Van Gorkom met again with Pritzker. At that time, Van Gorkom knew that Pritzker intended to make a cash-out merger offer at Van Gorkom's proposed $55 per share. Pritzker instructed his attorney, a merger and acquisition specialist, to begin drafting merger documents. There was no further discussion of the $55 price. However, the number of shares of Trans Union's treasury stock to be offered to Pritzker was negotiated down to one million shares; the price was set at $38-75 cents above the per share price at the close of the market on September 19. At this point, Pritzker insisted that the Trans Union

Board act on his merger proposal within the next three days, stating to Van Gorkom: "We have to have a decision by no later than Sunday [evening, September 21] [...]

Van Gorkom retained James Brennan, Esquire, to advise Trans Union on the legal aspects of the merger. Van Gorkom did not consult with William Browder, a Vice-President and director of Trans Union and former head of its legal department, or with William Moore, then the head of Trans Union's legal staff.

On Friday, September 19, Van Gorkom called a special meeting of the Trans Union Board for noon the following day. He also called a meeting of the Company's Senior Management to convene at 11:00 a.m., prior to the meeting of the Board. No one, except Chelberg and Peterson, was told the purpose of the meetings. Van Gorkom did not invite Trans Union's investment banker, Salomon Brothers or its Chicago-based partner, to attend.

Of those present at the Senior Management meeting on September 20, only Chelberg and Peterson had prior knowledge of Pritzker's offer. Van Gorkom disclosed the offer and described its terms, but he furnished no copies of the proposed Merger Agreement. Romans announced that his department had done a second study which showed that, for a leveraged buy-out, the price range for Trans Union stock was between $55 and $65 per share. Van Gorkom neither saw the study nor asked Romans to make it available for the Board meeting.

Senior Management's reaction to the Pritzker proposal was completely negative. [...]Romans objected to the price as being too low;[6] he was critical of the timing and suggested that consideration should be given to the adverse tax consequences of an all-cash deal for low-basis shareholders; and he took the position that the agreement to sell Pritzker one million newly-issued shares at market price would inhibit other offers, as would the prohibitions against soliciting bids and furnishing inside information [868] to other bidders. Romans argued that the Pritzker proposal was a "lock up" and amounted to "an agreed merger as opposed to an offer." Nevertheless, Van Gorkom proceeded to the Board meeting as scheduled without further delay.

[...] Chelberg, and Van Gorkom) and five outside (defendants Wallis, Johnson, Lanterman, Morgan and Reneker). All directors were present at the meeting, except O'Boyle who was ill. [...]

Van Gorkom began the Special Meeting of the Board with a twenty-minute oral presentation. Copies of the proposed Merger Agreement were delivered too late for study before or during the meeting.[17] He reviewed the Company's ITC and depreciation problems and the efforts theretofore made to solve them. He discussed his initial meeting with Pritzker and his motivation in arranging that meeting. Van Gorkom did not disclose to the Board, however, the methodology by which he alone had arrived at the $55 figure, or the fact that he first proposed the $55 price in his negotiations with Pritzker.

Van Gorkom outlined the terms of the Pritzker offer as follows: Pritzker would pay $55 in cash for all outstanding shares of Trans Union stock upon completion of which Trans Union would be merged into New T Company, a subsidiary wholly-owned by Pritzker and formed to implement the merger; for a period of 90 days, Trans Union could receive, but could not actively solicit, competing offers; the offer had to be acted on by the next evening, Sunday, September 21[...].

Van Gorkom took the position that putting Trans Union "up for auction" through a 90-day market test would validate a decision by the Board that $55 was a fair price. He told the Board that the "free market will have an opportunity to judge whether $55 is a fair price." Van Gorkom framed the decision before the Board not as whether $55 per share was the highest price that could be obtained, but as whether the $55 price was a fair price that the stockholders should be given the opportunity to accept or reject.[18]

Attorney Brennan advised the members of the Board that they might be sued if they failed to accept the offer and that a fairness opinion was not required as a matter of law.

Romans attended the meeting as chief financial officer of the Company. He told the Board that he had not been involved in the negotiations with Pritzker and knew nothing about the merger proposal until [869] the morning of the meeting; [...] Romans testified:

> I told the Board that the study ran the numbers at 50 and 60, and then the subsequent study at 55 and 65, and that was not the same thing as saying that I have a valuation of the company at X dollars. But it was a way — a first step towards reaching that conclusion.

Romans told the Board that, in his opinion, $55 was "in the range of a fair price," but "at the beginning of the range." [...]

The Board meeting of September 20 lasted about two hours. Based solely upon Van Gorkom's oral presentation, Chelberg's supporting representations, Romans' oral statement, Brennan's legal advice, and their knowledge of the market history of the Company's stock,[19] the directors approved the proposed Merger Agreement. [...]

The Merger Agreement was executed by Van Gorkom during the evening of September 20 at a formal social event that he hosted for the opening of the Chicago Lyric Opera. Neither he nor any other director read the agreement prior to its signing and delivery to Pritzker. [...]

On Monday, September 22, the Company issued a press release announcing that Trans Union had entered into a "definitive" Merger Agreement with an affiliate of the Marmon Group, Inc., a Pritzker holding company. Within 10 days of the public announcement, dissent among Senior Management over the merger had become widespread. Faced with threatened resignations of key officers, Van Gorkom met with Pritzker who agreed to several modifications of the Agreement. [...]

Van Gorkom reconvened the Board on October 8 and secured the directors' approval of the proposed amendments — sight unseen. The Board also authorized the employment of Salomon Brothers, its investment [870] banker, to solicit other offers for Trans Union during the proposed "market test" period.

The next day, October 9, Trans Union issued a press release announcing: (1) that Pritzker had obtained "the financing commitments necessary to consummate" the merger with Trans Union; (2) that Pritzker had acquired one million shares of Trans Union common stock at $38 per share; (3) that Trans Union was now permitted to actively seek other offers and had retained Salomon Brothers for that purpose; and (4) that if a more favorable offer were not received before February 1, 1981, Trans Union's shareholders would thereafter meet to vote on the Pritzker proposal.

It was not until the following day, October 10, that the actual amendments to the Merger Agreement were prepared by Pritzker and delivered to Van Gorkom for execution. As will be seen, the amendments were considerably at variance with Van Gorkom's representations of the amendments to the Board on October 8; and the amendments placed serious constraints on Trans Union's ability to negotiate a better deal and withdraw from the Pritzker agreement. Nevertheless, Van Gorkom proceeded to execute what became the October 10 amendments to the Merger Agreement without conferring further with the Board members and apparently without comprehending the actual implications of the amendments. [...]

On February 10, the stockholders of Trans Union approved the Pritzker merger proposal. Of the outstanding shares, 69.9% were voted in favor of the merger; 7.25% were voted against the merger; and 22.85% were not voted.

II.

We turn to the issue of the application of the business judgment rule to the September 20 meeting of the Board. [...]

Under Delaware law, the business judgment rule is the offspring of the fundamental principle, codified in 8 *Del.C.* § 141(a), that the business and affairs of a Delaware corporation are managed by or under its board of directors.[1-1] In carrying out their managerial roles, directors are charged with an unyielding fiduciary duty to the corporation and its shareholders. [...] The business judgment rule exists to protect and promote the full and free exercise of the managerial power granted to Delaware directors. [...]The rule itself "is a presumption that in making a business decision, the directors of a corporation acted on an informed basis, in good faith and in the honest belief that the action taken was in the best interests of the company." *Aronson, supra* at 812. Thus, the party attacking a board decision as uninformed must rebut the presumption that its business judgment was an informed one. *Id.*

The determination of whether a business judgment is an informed one turns on whether the directors have informed themselves "prior to making a business decision, of all material information reasonably available to them." *Id.*[12]

Under the business judgment rule there is no protection for directors who have made "an unintelligent or unadvised judgment." [...] A director's duty to inform himself in preparation for a decision derives from the fiduciary capacity in which he serves the corporation and its stockholders. [...] Since a director is vested with the responsibility for the management of the affairs of the corporation, he must execute that duty with the recognition that he acts on behalf of others. Such obligation does not tolerate faithlessness or self-dealing. But fulfillment of the fiduciary function requires more than the mere absence of bad faith or fraud. Representation of the financial interests of others imposes on a director an affirmative duty to protect those interests and to proceed with a critical eye in assessing information of the type and under the circumstances present here. [...]

Thus, a director's duty to exercise an informed business judgment is in [873] the nature of a duty of care, as distinguished from a duty of loyalty. Here, there were no allegations of fraud, bad faith, or self-dealing, or proof thereof. Hence, it is presumed that the directors reached their business judgment in good faith[...].

The standard of care applicable to a director's duty of care has also been recently restated by this Court. In *Aronson, supra,* we stated:

> While the Delaware cases use a variety of terms to describe the applicable standard of care, our analysis satisfies us that under the business judgment rule director liability is predicated upon concepts of gross negligence. [...]

We again confirm that view. We think the concept of gross negligence is also the proper standard for determining whether a business judgment reached by a board of directors was an informed one.[13]

In the specific context of a proposed merger of domestic corporations, a director has a duty under 8 *Del.C.* 251(b),[14] along with his fellow directors, to act in an informed and deliberate manner in determining whether to approve an agreement of merger before submitting the proposal to the stockholders. Certainly in the merger context, a director may not abdicate that duty by leaving to the shareholders alone the decision to approve or disapprove the agreement. [...]

It is against those standards that the conduct of the directors of Trans Union must be tested, as a matter of law and as a matter of fact, regarding their exercise of an informed business judgment in voting to approve the Pritzker merger proposal.

III.

The defendants argue that the determination of whether their decision to accept $55 per share for Trans Union represented an informed business judgment requires consideration, not only of that which they knew and learned on September 20, but also of that which they subsequently learned and did over the following four-month [874] period before the shareholders met to vote on the proposal in February, 1981. The defendants thereby seek to reduce the significance of their action on September 20 and to widen the time frame for determining whether their decision to accept the Pritzker proposal was an informed one. Thus, the defendants contend that what the directors did and learned subsequent to September 20 and through January 26, 1981, was properly taken into account by the Trial Court in determining whether the Board's judgment was an informed one. We disagree with this *post hoc* approach.

The issue of whether the directors reached an informed decision to "sell" the Company on September 20, 1980 must be determined

319

only upon the basis of the information then reasonably available to the directors and relevant to their decision to accept the Pritzker merger proposal. This is not to say that the directors were precluded from altering their original plan of action, had they done so in an informed manner. What we do say is that the question of whether the directors reached an informed business judgment in agreeing to sell the Company, pursuant to the terms of the September 20 Agreement presents, in reality, two questions: (A) whether the directors reached an informed business judgment on September 20, 1980; and (B) if they did not, whether the directors' actions taken subsequent to September 20 were adequate to cure any infirmity in their action taken on September 20. We first consider the directors' September 20 action in terms of their reaching an informed business judgment.

-A-

On the record before us, we must conclude that the Board of Directors did not reach an informed business judgment on September 20, 1980 in voting to "sell" the Company for $55 per share pursuant to the Pritzker cash-out merger proposal. Our reasons, in summary, are as follows:

The directors (1) did not adequately inform themselves as to Van Gorkom's role in forcing the "sale" of the Company and in establishing the per share purchase price; (2) were uninformed as to the intrinsic value of the Company; and (3) given these circumstances, at a minimum, were grossly negligent in approving the "sale" of the Company upon two hours' consideration, without prior notice, and without the exigency of a crisis or emergency.

As has been noted, the Board based its September 20 decision to approve the cash-out merger primarily on Van Gorkom's representations. None of the directors, other than Van Gorkom and Chelberg, had any prior knowledge that the purpose of the meeting was to propose a cash-out merger of Trans Union. No members of Senior Management were present, other than Chelberg, Romans and Peterson; and the latter two had only learned of the proposed sale an hour earlier. Both general counsel Moore and former general counsel Browder attended the meeting, but were equally uninformed as to the purpose of the meeting and the documents to be acted upon.

Without any documents before them concerning the proposed transaction, the members of the Board were required to rely entirely upon Van Gorkom's 20-minute oral presentation of the proposal. No written summary of the terms of the merger was presented; the directors were given no documentation to support the adequacy of $55 price per share for sale of the Company; and the Board had before it nothing more than Van Gorkom's statement of his understanding of the substance of an agreement which he admittedly had never read, nor which any member of the Board had ever seen.

Under 8 *Del.C.* § 141(e),[15] "directors are fully protected in relying in [875] good faith on reports made by officers." [...] The term "report" has been liberally construed to include reports of informal personal investigations by corporate officers, [...] However, there is no evidence that any "report," as defined under § 141(e), concerning the Pritzker proposal, was presented to the Board on September 20.[16] Van Gorkom's oral presentation of his understanding of the terms of the proposed Merger Agreement, which he had not seen, and Romans' brief oral statement of his preliminary study regarding the feasibility of a leveraged buy-out of Trans Union do not qualify as § 141(e) "reports" for these reasons: The former lacked substance because Van Gorkom was basically uninformed as to the essential provisions of the very document about which he was talking. Romans' statement was irrelevant to the issues before the Board since it did not purport to be a valuation study. At a minimum for a report to enjoy the status conferred by § 141(e), it must be pertinent to the subject matter upon which a board is called to act, and otherwise be entitled to good faith, not blind, reliance. Considering all of the surrounding circumstances — hastily calling the meeting without prior notice of its subject matter, the proposed sale of the Company without any prior consideration of the issue or necessity therefor, the urgent time constraints imposed by Pritzker, and the total absence of any documentation whatsoever — the directors were duty bound to make reasonable inquiry of Van Gorkom and

Romans, and if they had done so, the inadequacy of that upon which they now claim to have relied would have been apparent.

The defendants rely on the following factors to sustain the Trial Court's finding that the Board's decision was an informed one: (1) the magnitude of the premium or spread between the $55 Pritzker offering price and Trans Union's current market price of $38 per share; (2) the amendment of the Agreement as submitted on September 20 to permit the Board to accept any better offer during the "market test" period; (3) the collective experience and expertise of the Board's "inside" and "outside" directors;[17] and (4) their reliance on Brennan's legal advice that the directors might be sued if they rejected the Pritzker proposal. [...]

(1)

A substantial premium may provide one reason to recommend a merger, but in the absence of other sound valuation information, the fact of a premium alone does not provide an adequate basis upon which to assess the fairness of an offering price. Here, the judgment reached as to the adequacy of the premium was based on a comparison between the historically depressed Trans Union market price and the amount of the Pritzker offer. Using market price as a basis for concluding that the premium adequately reflected the true value [876] of the Company was a clearly faulty, indeed fallacious, premise, as the defendants' own evidence demonstrates.

The record is clear that before September 20, Van Gorkom and other members of Trans Union's Board knew that the market had consistently undervalued the worth of Trans Union's stock, despite steady increases in the Company's operating income in the seven years preceding the merger. [...]

In the Proxy Statement, however, the directors reversed their position. There, they stated that, although the earnings prospects for Trans Union were "excellent," they found no basis for believing that this would be reflected in future stock prices. With regard to past trading, the Board stated that the prices at which the Company's common stock had traded in recent years did not reflect the "inherent" value of the Company. But having referred to the "inherent" value of Trans Union, the directors ascribed no number to it. Moreover, nowhere did they disclose that they had no basis on which to fix "inherent" worth beyond an impressionistic reaction to the premium over market and an unsubstantiated belief that the value of the assets was "significantly greater" than book value. By their own admission they could not rely on the stock price as an accurate measure of value. Yet, also by their own admission, the Board members assumed that Trans Union's market price was adequate to serve as a basis upon which to assess the adequacy of the premium for purposes of the September 20 meeting. [...]

Indeed, as of September 20, the Board had no other information on which to base a determination of the intrinsic value of Trans Union as a going concern. As of September 20, the Board had made no evaluation of the Company designed to value the entire enterprise, nor had the Board ever previously considered selling the Company or consenting to a buy-out merger. Thus, the adequacy of a premium is indeterminate unless it is assessed in terms of other competent and sound valuation information that reflects the value of the particular business. [...]

We do not imply that an outside valuation study is essential to support an informed business judgment; nor do we state that fairness opinions by independent investment bankers are required as a matter of law. Often insiders familiar with the business of a going concern are in a better position than are outsiders to gather relevant information; and under appropriate circumstances, such directors may be fully protected in relying in good faith upon the valuation reports of their management. [...]

Here, the record establishes that the Board did not request its Chief Financial Officer, Romans, to make any valuation study or review of the proposal to determine the adequacy of $55 per share for sale of the Company. On the record before us: The Board rested on Romans' elicited response that the $55 figure was within a "fair price range" within the context of a leveraged buy-out. No director sought any further information from Romans. No director asked him why he put $55 at the bottom of his range. No director asked Romans for any details as to his study, the reason why it had been undertaken or its depth. No director asked to see the study; and no director asked Romans whether Trans Union's finance department could do a fairness study within the remaining 36-hour[118] period available under the Pritzker offer. [...]

Thus, the record compels the conclusion that on September 20 the Board lacked valuation information adequate to reach an informed business judgment as to the fairness of $55 per share for sale of the Company.[20]

(2)

This brings us to the post-September 20 "market test" upon which the defendants ultimately rely to confirm the reasonableness of their September 20 decision to accept the Pritzker proposal. In this connection, the directors present a two-part argument: (a) that by making a "market test" of Pritzker's $55 per share offer a condition of their September 20 decision to accept his offer, they cannot be found to have acted impulsively or in an uninformed manner on September 20; and (b) that the adequacy of the $17 premium for sale of the Company was conclusively established over the following 90 to 120 days by the most reliable evidence available — the marketplace. Thus, the defendants impliedly contend that the "market test" eliminated the need for the Board to perform any other form of fairness test either on September 20, or thereafter.

Again, the facts of record do not support the defendants' argument. There is no evidence: (a) that the Merger Agreement was effectively amended to give the Board freedom to put Trans Union up for auction sale to the highest bidder; or (b) that a public auction was in fact permitted to occur[...]:

The Merger Agreement, specifically identified as that originally presented to the Board on September 20, has never been produced by the defendants, notwithstanding the plaintiffs' several demands for production before as well as during trial. No acceptable explanation of this failure to produce documents has been given to either the Trial Court or this Court. Significantly, neither the defendants nor their counsel have made the affirmative representation that this critical document has been produced. Thus, the Court is deprived of the best evidence on which to judge the merits of the defendants' position as to the care and attention which they gave to the terms of the Agreement on September 20.

[...] Van Gorkom, conceding that he never read the Agreement, stated that he was relying upon his understanding that, under corporate law, directors always have an inherent right, as well as a fiduciary duty, to accept a better offer notwithstanding an existing contractual commitment by the Board. [...]

Several of Trans Union's outside directors resolutely maintained that the Agreement as submitted was approved on the understanding that, "if we got a better deal, we had a right to take it." Director Johnson so testified; but he then added, "And if they didn't put that in the agreement, then the management did not carry out the conclusion of the Board. And I just don't know whether they did or not." The only clause in the Agreement as finally executed to which the defendants can point as "keeping the door open" is the following underlined statement found in subparagraph (a) of section 2.03 of the Merger Agreement as executed:

> The Board of Directors shall recommend to the stockholders of Trans Union that they approve and adopt the Merger Agreement ('the stockholders' approval') and to use its best efforts to obtain the requisite votes therefor. *GL acknowledges that Trans Union directors may have a competing fiduciary obligation to the shareholders under certain circumstances.*

Clearly, this language on its face cannot be construed as incorporating either of the two "conditions" described above: either the right to accept a better offer or the right to distribute proprietary information to third parties. The logical witness for the defendants to call to confirm their construction of this clause of the Agreement would have been Trans Union's outside attorney, James Brennan. The defendants' failure, without explanation, to call this witness again permits the logical inference that his testimony would not have been helpful to them. The further fact that the directors adjourned, rather than recessed, the meeting without incorporating in the

Agreement these important "conditions" further weakens the defendants' position. As has been noted, nothing in the Board's Minutes supports these claims. No reference to either of the so-called "conditions" or of Trans Union's reserved right to test the market appears in any notes of the Board meeting or in the Board Resolution accepting the Pritzker offer or in the Minutes of the meeting itself. That evening, in the midst of a formal party which he hosted for the opening of the Chicago Lyric Opera, Van Gorkom executed the Merger Agreement without he or any other member of the Board having read the instruments. [...]

(3)

The directors' unfounded reliance on both the premium and the market test as the basis for accepting the Pritzker proposal undermines the defendants' remaining contention that the Board's collective experience and sophistication was a sufficient basis for finding that it reached its September 20 decision with informed, reasonable deliberation.[...]

(4)

Part of the defense is based on a claim that the directors relied on legal advice rendered at the September 20 meeting by James Brennan, Esquire, who was present at Van Gorkom's request. Unfortunately, Brennan did not appear and testify at trial even though his firm participated in the defense of this action. [...]

-B-

We now examine the Board's post-September 20 conduct for the purpose of determining first, whether it was informed and not grossly negligent; and second, if informed, whether it was sufficient to legally rectify and cure the Board's derelictions of September 20.[23]

[...]

The press release made no reference to provisions allegedly reserving to the Board the rights to perform a "market test" and to withdraw from the Pritzker Agreement if Trans Union received a better offer before the shareholder meeting. The defendants also concede that Trans Union never made a subsequent public announcement stating that it had in fact reserved the right to accept alternate offers, the Agreement notwithstanding.

The public announcement of the Pritzker merger resulted in an "en masse" revolt of Trans Union's Senior Management. [...]

Van Gorkom then advised Senior Management that the Agreement would be amended to give Trans Union the right to solicit competing offers through January, 1981, if they would agree to remain with Trans Union. Senior Management was temporarily mollified; and Van Gorkom then called a special meeting of Trans Union's Board for October 8.

Thus, the primary purpose of the October 8 Board meeting was to amend the Merger Agreement, in a manner agreeable to Pritzker, to permit Trans Union to conduct a "market test."[1-1] Van Gorkom presumably so represented the amendments to Trans Union's Board members on October 8. In a brief session, the directors approved Van Gorkom's oral presentation of the substance of the proposed amendments, [883] the terms of which were not reduced to writing until October 10. But rather than waiting to review the amendments, the Board again approved them sight unseen and adjourned, giving Van Gorkom authority to execute the papers when he received them.[25][...]

The next day, October 9, and before the Agreement was amended, Pritzker moved swiftly to off-set the proposed market test amendment. First, Pritzker informed Trans Union that he had completed arrangements for financing its acquisition and that the parties were thereby mutually bound to a firm purchase and sale arrangement. Second, Pritzker announced the exercise of his option to purchase one million shares of Trans Union's treasury stock at $38 per share — 75 cents above the current market price.[...]

The next day, October 10, Pritzker delivered to Trans Union the proposed amendments to the September 20 Merger Agreement. Van Gorkom promptly proceeded to countersign all the instruments on behalf of Trans Union without reviewing the instruments to determine if they were consistent with the authority previously granted him by the Board. The amending documents were apparently not approved by Trans Union's Board until a much later date, December 2. The record does not affirmatively establish that Trans Union's directors ever read the October 10 amendments.[26]

The October 10 amendments to the Merger Agreement did authorize Trans Union to solicit competing offers, but the amendments had more far-reaching effects.[...] Under the October 10 amendments, a better *offer* was no longer sufficient to permit Trans Union's withdrawal. Trans Union was now permitted to terminate the Pritzker Agreement and abandon the merger only if, prior to February 10, 1981, Trans Union had either consummated a merger (or sale of assets) with a third party or had entered into a "definitive" merger agreement more favorable than Pritzker's and for a greater consideration — subject only to stockholder approval. Further, the "extension" of the market test period to February 10, 1981 was circumscribed by other amendments which required Trans Union to file its preliminary proxy statement on the Pritzker merger proposal by December 5, 1980 and use its best efforts to mail the statement to its shareholders by January 5, 1981. Thus, the market test period was effectively reduced, not extended. [...]

In our view, the record compels the conclusion that the directors' conduct on October [884] 8 exhibited the same deficiencies as did their conduct on September 20. [...]

Section 102(b)(7)   4.2.3

The Delaware Supreme Court's decision in *Van Gorkom* was highly controversial at the time - and even now. The imposition of monetary liability for directors' lack of care, while not unheard of, was not a common occurrence. The court's opinion was a divided 3-2 decision. The Delaware Supreme Court has a norm of unanimity, and it is highly unusual for the court - particularly with respect to the corporate law - to issue divided opinions. This gives you a sense how controversial this opinion was at the time.

The decision has been variously derided by observers as a "comedy of errors", a "serious mistake", "dumbfounding", and "surely one of the worst decisions in the history of corporate law." Nevertheless, *Van Gorkom* has endured over the years. In part, that may be because a combination of statutory responses and subsequent developments in the common law have robbed *Van Gorkom* of much of its bite. In the wake of *Van Gorkom*, there was a public outcry by groups and associations representing the interests of corporate directors. They argued loudly that the real - albeit remote - prospect of directors facing monetary liability for violations of their duty of care would open the floodgates to litigation and cause otherwise qualified directors to retreat from the service on boards of directors. In the alternative, directors who remained on boards would face sky-rocketing insurance premiums for D&O insurance, making American businesses uncompetitive on the global stage.

In response to *Van Gorkom* and the public outcry that followed it, the Delaware legislature (as well soon thereafter the legislatures in all 50 states, DC, and Puerto Rico) adopted exculpation provisions, which exculpate from liability for monetary damages violations by directors of their duty of care, as well as reliance provisions like §141(e).

The text of §102(b)(7), which you've seen earlier in this course, follows below.

One can reasonably disagree with the policy of insulating directors from monetary liability for violations of their duty of care. Indeed, other countries impose liability on corporate directors for care violations.

§ 102. Contents of certificate of incorporation.

(b) In addition to the matters required to be set forth in the certificate of incorporation by subsection (a) of this section, the certificate of incorporation may also contain any or all of the following matters: ... **(7)** A provision eliminating or limiting the personal liability of a director or officer to the corporation or its stockholders for monetary damages for breach of fiduciary duty as a director or officer, provided that such provision shall not eliminate or limit the liability of: (i) a director or officer for any breach of the director's or officer's duty of loyalty to the corporation or its stockholders; (ii) a director or officer for acts or omissions not in good faith or which involve intentional misconduct or a knowing violation of law; (iii) a director under § 174 of this title; or (iv) a director or officer for any transaction from which the director or officer 16 derived an improper personal benefit; or (v) an officer in any action by or in the right of the corporation. No such provision shall eliminate or limit the liability of a director or officer for any act or omission occurring prior to the date when such provision becomes effective. An amendment, repeal or elimination of such a provision shall not affect its application with respect to an act or omission by a director or officer occurring before such amendment, repeal or elimination unless the provision provides otherwise at the time of such act or omission.

All references in this paragraph to a director shall also be deemed to refer to such other person or persons, if any, who, pursuant to a provision of the certificate of incorporation in accordance with § 141(a) of this title, exercise or perform any of the powers or duties otherwise conferred or imposed upon the board of directors by this title.

All references in this paragraph to an officer shall mean only a person who at the time of an act or omission as to which liability is asserted is deemed to have consented to service by the delivery of process to the registered agent of the corporation pursuant to § 3114(b) of Title 10 (for purposes of this sentence only, treating residents of this State as if they were nonresidents to apply § 3114(b) of Title 10 to this sentence).

* * * * * * * * *

Question for Discussion

Given the elimination of monetary liability, what incentives are there for directors and officers to do a good job? Is potential monetary liability required in order to assure directors and officers live up to the standard of care?

In Re Cornerstone Therapeutics, Inc. 4.2.4

Following Van Gorkom, Delaware adopted its exculpation statute: §102(b)(7). The effect of §102(b)(7) provisions on litigation is significant. Exculpation provisions eliminate the monetary liability of directors for violations of their duty of care. Consequently, if a plaintiffs alleges only that directors violated their duty of care and that caused them some damage, there is no remedy available at law for these plaintiffs. In *Malpiede v Townson*, the Delaware courts encountered such a situation. In *Malpiede*, stockholders alleged that directors violated their duty of care to the corporation resulting in an injury to the corporation and its stockholders that could only be remedied with cash damages. The *Malpiede* court considered the effect of an exculpation provision in the corporate charter on the litigation and held that where the plaintiff pleads only a violation of the duty of care, and where the plaintiff is seeking only cash damages, and, finally, where the corporation has a §102(b)(7) provision in its certificate of incorporation, that the court will be unable to provide a remedy. Consequently, judicial economy requires that such a case be dismissed upon a 12(b)(6) motion to dismiss and that the defendant need not file an answer to the complaint.

In many cases, the entire board is not guilty of a violation of the duty of loyalty. Rather, only one or two directors may have been alleged to have engaged in bad acts. Nevertheless, plaintiffs will often sue the entire board of directors. The question then arises whether when a plaintiff challenges an interested transaction that is presumptively subject to entire fairness review, must the plaintiff plead a non-exculpated claim against the disinterested, independent directors to survive a motion to dismiss by those directors? Or must those directors remain in the suit. The *Cornerstone* opinion applies the principles of *Malpiede* provides some guidance on this question.

As you read the *Cornerstone* opinion consider the effect of the holding in *Cornerstone* on questions of demand futility and the *Zuckerberg* standard.

In Re Cornerstone Therapeutics
115 A. 3d 1173

STRINE, Chief Justice:

I. INTRODUCTION

These appeals were scheduled for argument on the same day because they turn on a single legal question: in an action for damages against corporate fiduciaries, where the plaintiff challenges an interested transaction that is presumptively subject to entire fairness review, must the plaintiff plead a non-exculpated claim against the disinterested, independent directors to survive a motion to dismiss by those directors?[2] We answer that question in the affirmative. A plaintiff seeking only monetary damages must plead non-exculpated claims against a director who is protected by an exculpatory charter provision to survive a motion to dismiss, regardless of the underlying standard of review for the board's conduct—be it *Revlon,*[3] [1176] *Unocal,*[4] the entire fairness standard, or the business judgment rule. [...]

In this decision, we hold that even if a plaintiff has pled facts that, if true, would require the transaction to be subject to the entire fairness standard of review, and the interested parties to face a claim for breach of their duty of loyalty, the independent directors do not automatically have to remain defendants. When the independent directors are protected by an exculpatory charter provision and the plaintiffs are unable to plead a non-exculpated claim against them, those directors are entitled to have the claims against them dismissed, in keeping with this Court's opinion in *Malpiede v. Townson*[5] and cases following that decision.[6] [...]

II. BACKGROUND

These appeals both involve damages actions by stockholder plaintiffs arising out of mergers in which the controlling stockholder, who had representatives on the board of directors, acquired the remainder of the shares that it did not own in a Delaware public corporation.[7] Both mergers [1177] were negotiated by special committees of independent directors, were ultimately approved by a majority of the minority stockholders, and were at substantial premiums to the pre-announcement market price.[8] Nonetheless, the plaintiffs filed suit in the Court of Chancery in each case, contending that the directors had breached their fiduciary duty by approving transactions that were unfair to the minority stockholders.

[...] In both cases, the defendant directors were insulated from liability for monetary damages for breaches of the fiduciary duty of care by an exculpatory charter provision adopted in accordance with 8 *Del. C.* § 102(b)(7). Despite that provision, the plaintiffs in each case not only sued the controlling stockholders and their affiliated directors, but also sued the independent directors who had negotiated and approved the mergers.

In the first of these cases to be decided, *In re Cornerstone Therapeutics Inc. Stockholder Litigation,* the independent director defendants moved to dismiss on the grounds that the plaintiffs had failed to plead any non-exculpated claim against them.[11] The independent directors argued that although the entire fairness standard applied to the Court of Chancery's review of the underlying transaction, and thus the controlling stockholder and its affiliated directors were at risk of being found liable for breaches of the duty of loyalty, the plaintiffs still bore the burden to plead non-exculpated claims against the independent directors.[12] The independent directors noted that this Court held in *Malpiede v. Townson* that, in the analogous context of review under the *Revlon* standard, plaintiffs seeking damages must plead non-exculpated claims against each individual director or risk dismissal.[13] [...]

In response, the plaintiffs argued that the Court of Chancery could not grant the independent directors' motion to dismiss, regardless of whether they had sufficiently pled non-exculpated claims.[15] Under their reading of language in two of the four decisions issued by this Court in the extensive *Emerald Partners* litigation,[16] the plaintiffs contended that they could defeat the independent directors' motions to dismiss solely by establishing that the underlying transaction was subject to the entire fairness standard.[--]

In *In re Zhongpin Stockholders Litigation,* the independent director defendants also argued that the claims against them should be dismissed because the plaintiffs had failed to plead any non-exculpated claims.[23] The Court of Chancery in *Zhongpin* deferred to *Cornerstone*'s interpretation of precedent[24] and held that the claims against the independent directors survived their motion to dismiss "regardless of whether the Complaint state[d] a non-exculpated claim" because the transaction was subject to entire fairness review.[25]

In each case, the Court of Chancery did not analyze the plaintiffs' duty of loyalty claims against the independent directors because it determined that it was required to deny their motions to dismiss regardless of whether such claims had been sufficiently pled.[26] But, recognizing the important and uncertain issue of corporate law at stake, the Court of Chancery in each case recommended certification of an interlocutory appeal to this Court to determine whether its reading of precedent was correct.

III. ANALYSIS

In answering the legal question raised by these appeals, we acknowledge that the body of law relevant to these disputes presents a debate between two competing but colorable views of the law. These cases thus exemplify a benefit of careful employment of the interlocutory appeal process: to enable this Court to clarify precedent that could arguably be read in two different ways before litigants incur avoidable costs.

We now resolve the question presented by these cases by determining that plaintiffs must plead a non-exculpated claim for breach of fiduciary duty against an independent director protected by an exculpatory charter provision, or that director will be entitled to be dismissed from the suit. That rule applies regardless of the underlying standard of review for the transaction. When a director is protected by an exculpatory charter provision, a plaintiff can survive a motion to dismiss by that director defendant by pleading facts supporting a rational inference that the [1180] director harbored self-interest adverse to the stockholders' interests, acted to advance the self-interest of an interested party from whom they could not be presumed to act independently, or acted in bad faith.[27] But the mere fact that a plaintiff is able to plead facts supporting the application of the entire fairness standard to the transaction, and can thus state a duty of loyalty claim against the interested fiduciaries, does not relieve the plaintiff of the responsibility to plead a non-exculpated claim against each director who moves for dismissal.[28]

No doubt, the invocation of the entire fairness standard has a powerful pro-plaintiff effect against interested parties.[29] When that standard is invoked at the pleading stage, the plaintiffs will be able to survive a motion to dismiss by interested parties regardless of the presence of an exculpatory charter provision because their conflicts of interest support a pleading-stage [1181] inference of disloyalty.[30] Indeed, as to the interested party itself, a finding of unfairness after trial will subject it to liability for breach of the duty of loyalty regardless of its subjective bad faith.[31]

The stringency of after-the-fact entire fairness review by the court intentionally puts strong pressure on the interested party and its affiliates to deal fairly before-the-fact when negotiating an interested transaction. To accomplish this, the burden of proving entire fairness in an interested merger falls on the "the controlling or dominating shareholder proponent of the transaction."[32] But applying the entire fairness standard against interested parties does not relieve plaintiffs seeking damages of the obligation to plead non-exculpated claims against each of the defendant directors.[33]

In *Malpiede,* this Court analyzed the effect of a Section 102(b)(7) provision on a due care claim against directors who approved a transaction which the plaintiffs argued should be subject to review under the *Revlon* standard. This Court noted that although "plaintiffs are entitled to all reasonable inferences flowing from their pleadings, ... if those inferences do not support a valid legal claim, the complaint should be dismissed."[134] Because a director will only be liable for monetary damages if she has breached a non-exculpated duty, a plaintiff who pleads only a due care claim against that director has not set forth any grounds for relief. In such a case, "*as a matter of law* [] then Section 102(b)(7) would bar the claim."[135]

Nevertheless, the plaintiffs in each of these cases contend that their exculpated claims against the independent directors cannot be dismissed solely because the transaction at issue is subject to entire fairness review. The plaintiffs argue that they should be entitled to an automatic inference that a director facilitating an interested transaction is disloyal because the possibility of conflicted loyalties is heightened in controller transactions, and the facts that give rise to a duty of loyalty breach may be unknowable at the pleading stage.[136] But there are several problems with such an inference: to require independent directors to remain defendants solely because the plaintiffs stated a non-exculpated claim against the controller and its affiliates would be inconsistent with Delaware law and would also increase costs for disinterested directors, corporations, and stockholders, without providing a corresponding benefit.

First, this Court and the Court of Chancery have emphasized that each director has a right to be considered individually when the directors face claims for damages in a suit challenging board action.[137] And under Delaware corporate law, that individualized consideration does not start with the assumption that each director was disloyal; rather, "independent [1183] directors are presumed to be motivated to do their duty with fidelity."[138] Thus, in *Aronson v. Lewis,* this Court emphasized that the mere fact that a director serves on the board of a corporation with a controlling stockholder does not automatically make that director not independent.[139] This Court has similarly refused to presume that an independent director is not entitled to the protection of the business judgment rule solely because the controlling stockholder may itself be subject to liability for breach of the duty of loyalty if the transaction was not entirely fair to the minority stockholders.[40]

Adopting the plaintiffs' approach would not only be inconsistent with these basic tenets of Delaware law, it would likely create more harm than benefit for minority stockholders in practice.[41] Our common law of corporations has rightly emphasized [1184] the need for independent directors to be willing to say no to interested transactions proposed by controlling stockholders.[42] For that reason, our law has long inquired into the practical negotiating power given to independent directors in conflicted transactions.[43] Although it is wise for our law to focus on whether the independent directors can say no, it does not follow that it is prudent to create an invariable rule that any independent director who says yes to an interested transaction subject to entire fairness review must remain as a defendant until the end of the litigation, regardless of the absence of any evidence suggesting that the director acted for an improper motive.

For more than a generation, our law has recognized that the negotiating efforts of independent directors can help to secure transactions with controlling stockholders that are favorable to the minority.[44] Indeed, respected scholars have found evidence that interested transactions subject to special committee approval are often priced on terms that are attractive to minority stockholders.[45] We decline to adopt an approach that would create incentives for independent directors to avoid serving as special committee members, or to reject transactions solely because their role in negotiating on behalf of the stockholders would cause them to remain as defendants until the end of any litigation challenging the transaction.[46]

As is well understood, the fear that directors who faced personal liability for potentially value-maximizing business decisions might be dissuaded from making such decisions is why Section 102(b)(7) was adopted in the first place. As this Court explained in *Malpiede,* "Section 102(b)(7) was adopted by the Delaware General Assembly in 1986 following a directors and officers insurance liability crisis and the 1985 Delaware Supreme Court decision in *Smith v. Van*

Gorkom."[147] Because of that "crisis," the General Assembly feared that directors would not be willing to make decisions that would benefit stockholders if they faced personal liability for making them. The purpose of Section 102(b)(7) was to "free[] up directors to take business risks without worrying about negligence lawsuits."[148] Establishing a rule that all directors must remain as parties in litigation involving a transaction with a controlling stockholder would thus reduce the benefits that the General Assembly anticipated in adopting Section 102(b)(7).

We understand that the plaintiffs, and certain members of the Court of Chancery, have read the decisions this Court issued in the complex circumstances of the *Emerald Partners* litigation to support a different conclusion than we reach here. But the Court in *Emerald Partners* was focused on a separate question; namely, whether courts can consider the effect of a Section 102(b)(7) provision before trial when the plaintiffs have pled facts supporting the inference not only that each director breached not just his duty of care, but also his duty of loyalty, when the applicable standard of review of the underlying transaction is entire fairness.[149] In that circumstance, the Court held that the [1186] determination of whether any failure of the putatively independent directors was the result of disloyalty or a lapse in care was best determined after a trial, because the substantive fairness inquiry would shed light on why the directors acted as they did.[150] The sentence in *Emerald II* that the plaintiffs claim is dispositive here must be understood in that context, as referring to a case where there was a viable, non-exculpated loyalty claim against each putatively independent director. The *Emerald Partners* litigation thus did not answer the specific question at issue in these appeals, whether the application of the entire fairness standard requires the Court of Chancery to deny a motion to dismiss by independent directors even when the plaintiffs may not have sufficiently pled a non-exculpated claim against those directors. Indeed, much of the language in the *Emerald Partners* decisions issued by this Court is consistent with the answer we reach here. For example, this Court observed in *Emerald II* that:

The rationale of *Malpiede* constitutes judicial cognizance of a practical reality: unless there is a violation of the duty of loyalty or the duty of good faith, a trial on the issue of entire fairness is unnecessary because a Section 102(b)(7) provision will exculpate director defendants from paying monetary damages that are exclusively attributable to a violation of the duty of care. The effect of our holding in *Malpiede* is that, in actions against the directors of Delaware corporations with a Section 102(b)(7) charter provision, a shareholder's complaint must allege well-pled facts that, if true, implicate breaches of loyalty or good faith.[51]

Thus, to the extent that other isolated statements in *Emerald Partners* could be interpreted as inconsistent with the result we reach today, we clarify that the *Emerald Partners* decisions should be read in their case-specific context and not for the broad proposition that the plaintiffs advocate. The reading of the *Emerald Partners* decisions we embrace is also the one adopted by the Court of Chancery itself in *DiRienzo v. Lichtenstein.*[52] In that case, the Court of Chancery recognized that the *Emerald Partners* decisions had to be read in the context of their facts, where there was sufficient record evidence to attribute any lack of effectiveness in the putatively independent directors' handling of the transaction to either a breach of the duty of loyalty (*e.g.,* as the result of bad faith) or a lack of care. The Court of Chancery thus observed that "the directors in *Emerald Partners* were precluded from relying on a 102(b)(7) charter provision by virtue of their conduct, not because the transaction was subject to entire fairness review for other reasons."[53] In other words, *DiRienzo* interpreted the *Emerald Partners* decisions as standing for the mundane proposition that a defendant cannot obtain dismissal on the basis of an exculpatory provision when there is evidence that he committed a non-exculpated breach of fiduciary duty.[54]

Thus, when a complaint pleads facts creating an inference that seemingly [1187] independent directors approved a conflicted transaction for improper reasons, and thus, those directors may have breached their duty of loyalty, the pro-plaintiff inferences that must be drawn on a motion to dismiss counsels for resolution of that question of fact only after discovery.[55] By contrast, when the plaintiffs have pled no facts to support an inference that any of the independent directors breached their duty of loyalty, fidelity to the purpose of Section 102(b)(7) requires dismissal of the complaint against those directors. Accordingly, we reverse the judgments of the Court of Chancery denying the independent directors' motions to dismiss, and remand each case for the Court of Chancery to determine if the plaintiffs have sufficiently pled facts suggesting that the independent directors committed a non-exculpated breach of their fiduciary duty. [...]

Orman v. Cullman   4.2.5

In Orman v. Cullman (794 A2d 5, 2002), the Chancery Court considered the pleading requirements to overcome the business judgment presumption. Importantly, in the absence of a controlling shareholder, plaintiffs must plead facts sufficient to call into question the ability of a majority of the board to act in the best interests of the corporation. In the absence of such disability on behalf of a majority of the board, the court will presume that the board, as a whole, was capable of making a disinterested decision.

As a general matter, the business judgment rule presumption that a board acted loyally can be rebutted by alleging facts which, if accepted as true, establish that the *board* was either interested in the outcome of the transaction or lacked the independence to consider objectively whether the transaction was in the best interest of its company and all of its shareholders. To establish that a *board* was interested or lacked independence, a plaintiff must allege facts as to the interest and lack of independence of the *individual members* of that board. To rebut successfully business judgment presumptions in this manner, thereby leading to the application of the entire fairness standard, a plaintiff must normally plead facts demonstrating "that a *majority* of the director defendants have a financial interest in the transaction or were dominated or controlled by a materially interested director."

I recognize situations can exist when the material interest of a number of directors *less* than a majority may rebut the business judgment presumption and lead to an entire fairness review. That is when an "`interested director *fail[ed] to disclose his interest* in the transaction to the board *and* a reasonable board member would have regarded the existence of the material interest as a significant fact in the evaluation of the proposed transaction."

Orman v. Cullman, 794 A.2d 5, 22-23 (2002)

Duty of Loyalty   4.3

The business judgment presumption presumes, among other things, that directors act "in the best interests of the corporation." When a plaintiff can plead facts to suggest that director does not act in the best interests of the corporation, then the defendant director will lose the deferential business judgment presumption and will be required to prove at trial that notwithstanding the facts pleaded by the plaintiff that the challenged decision was nevertheless entirely fair to the corporation (the entire fairness standard).

Factual situations that commonly call into question whether a director acted in the best interests of the corporation include some of the following factual scenarios:

1. A director engages in a commercial transaction with the corporation (a director is "on both sides" of a transaction with the corporation).

2. A director uses his or her position to obtain a benefit for the director rather that the corporation.

3. A director acts secretly acts as an adverse party or in competition with the corporation.

4. A director gets a material personal benefit from a third party in connection with a transaction between the corporation and third party.

In each of these factual situations, a plaintiff can reasonably plead that a director's decision was not in the best interests of the corporation and the director can lose the presumption of business judgment.

Unlike violations of the duty of care, violations of the duty of loyalty are not exculpable. That is to say, if a director violates her duty of loyalty to the corporation, the director may be personally liable to the corporation and its stockholders for damages. Violations of the duty of care, as you will remember, are exculpable. The availability of a monetary remedy consequently draws the attention of plaintiffs' counsel who can be expected to engage in a high degree of scrutiny of interested director transactions.

Dweck v. Nasser   4.3.1

Consider the facts in the following case. Do the agents of the corporation and the corporate directors appear to comport themselves as loyal agents of the corporation? If not, how do their actions fall short of the standard of conduct expected of corporate fiduciaries?

DWECK V. NASSER AND KIDS INTERNATIONAL CORPORATION
DEL. CT. OF CHANCERY (2012)

LASTER, Vice Chancellor.

In 2005, after thirteen years in business together, Gila Dweck and Albert Nasser parted ways. Their messy split spawned nearly seven years of litigation.

Before the split, Dweck was the CEO, a director, and 30% stockholder in Kids International Corporation ("Kids"). Both before and after the split, Nasser was the Chairman and controlling stockholder of Kids. Dweck and Nasser accused each other of breaching their fiduciary duties, and Nasser asserted third-party claims for breach of fiduciary duty against Dweck's colleagues Kevin Taxin, Kids' President, and Bruce Fine, Kids' CFO and corporate secretary. [...]

In this post-trial decision, I find that Dweck and Taxin breached their fiduciary duties to Kids by establishing competing companies that usurped Kids' corporate opportunities and converted Kids' resources to the point of literally using Kids' own employees, office space, letters of credit, customer relationships, and goodwill to conduct their operations. Dweck further breached her fiduciary duties by causing Kids to reimburse her for hundreds of thousands of dollars of personal expenses. Fine breached his fiduciary duties by abdicating his responsibility to review Dweck's expenses and signing off on them wholesale. In the months leading up to the final split, Dweck, Taxin, and Fine again breached their duties by transferring Kids' customer relationships and business expectancies to their competing companies, packing up Kids' documents and other property and moving them to the competing companies, and organizing a mass employee departure that left Kids crippled. Dweck, Taxin, and Fine are liable to Kids for the damages caused by their breaches of duty.[...]

Having weighed the parties' testimony, evaluated their demeanor, and considered the evidence as a whole, I make the following factual findings. [...]

Morris Dabah had three sons: Haim, Ezra, and Isaac.[iii] Morris and his sons founded the Gitano Group, a large, multi-division apparel wholesaler.

Morris' fourth and youngest child was a daughter: Gila Dweck. While still in college, Dweck began working at Gitano as a receptionist. After graduating, Dweck joined the childrenswear division, known as EJ Gitano, as a salesperson. She rose rapidly through the ranks to become President of EJ Gitano.

In 1993, Haim and Isaac pleaded guilty to criminal violations of United States customs regulations and spent time under house arrest. Wal-Mart, Gitano's largest customer, refused to continue selling Gitano's lines of clothing. Gitano defaulted on its debt and teetered on the verge of bankruptcy.

In the debacle, Dweck saw opportunity. She suggested to Haim that they purchase EJ Gitano. It was profitable, and Dweck thought the existing pipeline of orders made the purchase "essentially risk free." Tr. 448.

But there was a problem. Because of Gitano's default, its lender had the right to veto any sale of assets, and the bank would not approve a sale of EJ Gitano to the Dabah family. Dweck needed a third party.

Enter Albert Nasser, a successful entrepreneur with numerous holdings in the apparel sector. Nasser was a cousin of Dweck's mother, and despite maintaining his primary residence in Switzerland, he moved within the same tightly-knit New York community as the Dabah family. [...]

In September 1993, Dweck, Haim, and Nasser purchased the assets of EJ Gitano. The basic deal was straightforward. Nasser agreed to provide 100% of the funding, comprising $8.2 million for acquisition financing plus $1 million in start-up capital. In return, Nasser originally would own 100% of the new company's equity. Once Nasser received payments equal to his original investment plus 10% interest, Nasser would transfer 50% of the equity to Dweck and Haim. Nasser would serve as Chairman of the Board; Dweck and Haim would be in charge of day-to-day management. [...]

EJ Gitano's trademarks were acquired separately. For this part of the transaction, Woodsford advanced $4.2 million to Hocalar B.V. ("Hocalar"), a Netherlands corporation. Hocalar then paid the money to Gitano for a perpetual license to the Gitano trademarks. Hocalar immediately sub-licensed the trademarks to Kids in return for a 5% royalty on Kids' sales of Gitano products (the "License Agreement"). [...] [...]

Kids was profitable from day one. Although the transaction closed at the end of September 1993, the sale was effective as of June and included EJ Gitano's substantial order base from the pre-closing period. Nasser agreed to indemnify EJ Gitano's lender for its letters of credit, which enabled Kids to take the profits on the existing orders. The new company continued selling Gitano-branded products, primarily jeans. Kids also continued as a major supplier of private label (non-branded) childrenswear for Wal-Mart, which originally comprised approximately 90-95% of Kids' business. In the private label business, a retailer like Wal-Mart outsources to a manufacturer like Kids the work of producing a house brand owned by Wal-Mart and sold only in Wal-Mart's stores. [...]

Because of its significant sales, Kids was able to distribute substantial amounts via the License Agreement in addition to the interest-only payments on the Maubi Loan. By 1998, Nasser had received back his original investment plus 10% interest, and it was time for Dweck and Haim to receive equity in Kids. Dweck and Haim were issued 45% of Kids' outstanding equity, paid for out of the corporation's retained earnings. The original deal had been 50%, but it turned out that Nasser had issued a warrant to Shiboleth for 5% of the equity as compensation for his role in setting up Kids. Dweck and Haim acquiesced to the new arrangement, and Nasser left it to Dweck and Haim to divvy up their shares. Dweck received 27.5% of Kids' stock, which she held individually and through trusts for the benefit of her children. Haim received the remaining 17.5%. Around the same time, Taxin was promoted to President of Kids. [...]

With Kids enjoying continued success under her management, Dweck began to feel exploited. Despite receiving stock in 1998, Dweck believed she was doing all of the work for less than a third of the profits. To Dweck's further frustration, Nasser decided in 1996 that Kids was a *de facto* partnership, that partners should not receive salaries, and that Dweck's salary as Kids' CEO should be deemed a distribution of profits. [...]

Dweck felt she should own a percentage of Kids equity that more fairly represented her responsibility for Kids' success. She complained to Nasser and Haim, but to no avail. Nasser would not give Dweck any more equity, nor would he sell her any of his shares. [...]

Unable to gain a greater share of Kids' profits, Dweck decided to bypass Kids by starting a new company into which she would channel "new opportunities." Tr. 461. As she admitted on cross-examination, she decided to compete "because it was [her] only way to . . . receive more income." Tr. 469.

In October 2001, Dweck formed Success Apparel LLC ("Success"), a New York limited liability company, to operate as a wholesaler of children's clothing. The impetus to form Success came from Taxin, who also had grown dissatisfied with his remuneration. Taxin felt that he was primarily responsible for Kids' success and deserved a share of Kids' profits. He asked Dweck repeatedly for equity, but she consistently turned him down on the grounds that Nasser "only takes in family." Tr. 259. When the President of Bugle Boy, Mary Gleason, offered Taxin the opportunity to purchase the Bugle Boy license in 2001, Taxin decided he was "only interested in doing the opportunity with [Dweck], not Kids . . . ." Tr. 258. Taxin made the decision despite meeting with Gleason in his capacity as President of Kids, and even though Gleason did not restrict the opportunity or indicate that Kids could not pursue it. Taxin discussed the matter with Dweck, and they decided to take it for themselves. Dweck granted Taxin a 20% membership interest in Success and retained 80% for herself.

From 2001 until 2005, Success operated out of Kids' premises using Kids' employees. Success drew on Kids' letters of credit, sold products under Kids' vendor agreements, used Kids' vendor numbers, and capitalized on Kids' relationships. Ostensibly to compensate Kids, Dweck decided that Success would pay an administrative fee equal to 1% of total sales. Dweck selected the 1% figure unilaterally without disclosure to or consultation with Nasser. The only mention of the fee was an opaque entry on Kids' financial statements entitled "Due from affiliates." *See, e.g.,* JX 783. The identity of the affiliates was not specified, and Fine never discussed it with Nasser. The 1% fee appears to have been grossly inadequate.

Success also reimbursed Kids for the salaries of certain employees (but not for their benefits) and for a portion of Kids' rent. The only employees were those Dweck deemed to be working exclusively for Success. Dweck admitted that most Kids employees performed some work for Success. No effort was made to compensate Kids for their services. Taxin estimated at trial that he spent approximately 20% of his time on Success, which likely was a self-interestedly conservative figure. Numerous other Kids employees performed work for Success without reimbursement, including Pauline Pei, Mark Simonetti, Stanley Bernstein, Joseph Ezraty, Steve Golub, Leah Justice, and Kim Epps. Taxin estimated (doubtless conservatively) that these employees spent approximately 10-20% of their time on Success. Success also used Kids' overseas quality control inspectors and internal quality control employees. The rental reimbursements further illustrate the inadequacy of Success' payments to Kids. In 2004, for example, Dweck's companies reimbursed Kids for rent of $14,594. In 2005, after obtaining space of its own, Dweck's companies paid $437,689 for rent.

In its first three years of operation, Success signed license agreements to manufacture and distribute a number of brands, including Bugle Boy, Everlast, and John Deere. In the pitches to obtain the licenses, Success used marketing materials that listed the logos of Kids and Success side by side, cited industry awards won by Kids, and touted Kids' lengthy record in the apparel business. This resulted in confusion amongst the licensors. John Deere originally drafted their license agreement with Kids as the licensee, and the document was only changed to name Success at Dweck's request. The draft agreement for a license to the Mack brand was also prepared in Kids' name. A press release issued by Everlast described its licensee as "Success Apparel Group LLC, also known as Kids International . . . ." JX 531.

Inside Kids' offices, Success and Kids operated so seamlessly that many of the Kids employees who routinely worked for Success never suspected that Success was a separate company or had different ownership from Kids. Kids and Success used the same showroom and displayed their brands in the same space. There were no references to Success, and nothing suggested that the brands were not all owned by Kids. The only name on the door was Kids.

[...]

In June 2004, Dweck founded Premium Apparel Brands LLC ("Premium"), a New York limited liability company. Like Success, Premium was a clothing wholesaler, operated out of Kids' premises, and used Kids' employees and resources. Dweck owned 100% of Premium and served as its CEO. Taxin had no equity stake in Premium.

Dweck founded Premium to serve as licensee and manufacturer for the Gloria Vanderbilt brand. When Dweck originally negotiated the Gloria Vanderbilt license, the owner of the brand, Jones Apparel, understood that the license could be with Kids. Dweck switched the agreement to Premium. [...]

Not content with her compensation from Kids and the profits from her parasitic companies, Dweck billed Kids for a luxurious lifestyle. Between 2002 and 2005, Dweck charged at least $466,948 in expenses to Kids. At trial, she admitted that at least $171,966 was for personal expenses, including Club Med vacations and assorted luxury goods from Armani, Prada, Gucci, and Bergdorf Goodman. Dweck could not determine whether another $170,400 was for business or personal expenses. She asserted that the remaining $124,582 was for legitimate business expenses. During the same period, Dweck was being paid $850,000 to $1.3 million per year in salary. [...]

During 2004, Kids stopped sending Nasser quarterly financial reports. Nasser repeatedly requested the reports, but Dweck and Fine ignored him. In November 2004, Lidia Lozovsky, a secretary at Kids who worked for Nasser, Dweck, and Fine, mentioned to Nasser that Dweck appeared to be handling a Gloria Vanderbilt line. In December, Lozovsky warned Nasser in stronger terms that there was "something going on" at Kids and that "there were other companies" operating out of Kids' offices. [...]

To get a handle on what was going on, Nasser had Shiboleth notice formal meetings of the board and stockholders for January 5, 2005. They were the first formal meetings in Kids' history. In advance of the meetings, Dweck and Fine told Nasser that Kids would book $115 million in sales for 2004. Days later, they lowered the sales figure to $95 million. During the January 5 board meeting, Dweck and Fine revealed that the actual sales figure was $72 million, a decline of roughly $18 million from the previous year. Nasser testified that after hearing the sales figure, "everybody looked at each other. And we knew that something [was] wrong because we were not told the truth at the beginning." [...]

Because of his growing suspicions, Nasser came to the January 5 meetings ready to take action. Nasser elected Lozovsky and his nephew, Itzhak Djemal, as directors of Kids. He appointed Djemal to the position of Vice Chairman and gave him authority equal to Dweck's: Djemal would handle production and corporate finances while Dweck would handle sales and design. Nasser privately tasked Djemal with uncovering what was going on at Kids.

Dweck was extremely unhappy with Djemal's appointment. [...]

Dweck promptly met with Taxin and discussed the prospect of leaving Kids. With Taxin and Fine's assistance, she located separate office space for Success and Premium. More importantly, Dweck and Taxin organized a campaign to divert Kids' future orders to Success. Over the next three months, Kids employees carried out the campaign by contacting Kids' customers on behalf of Success. [...]

In early 2005, Kids was working to fill orders for the Fall 2005 season and had started product development and design work for the Holiday 2005 and Spring 2006 seasons. At the direction of Dweck and Taxin, Kids employees systematically switched the vendor information and customer contacts from Kids to Success, thereby ensuring that when the orders came in, they came to Success. Taxin instructed Paul Cohn, the Kids salesperson for Wal-Mart, to switch the Wal-Mart orders. Taxin instructed Pat Zobel, the Kids salesperson for Target, to switch the Target orders. At the time he gave these instructions, Taxin was President of Kids. Taxin also communicated directly with Wal-Mart and Target about switching purchases from Kids to Success.

H. The March 11, 2005 Meetings

Despite active resistance from Dweck, Djemal soon found evidence that Dweck was operating her own businesses from Kids' premises. When pressed for information, Dweck admitted it but insisted that she had Nasser's permission. Djemal reported his findings to Nasser.

Because Dweck disputed whether the January meetings were properly noticed, Nasser had Shiboleth notice a second round of board and stockholder meetings for March 11, 2005. [...]

Shiboleth noticed the meetings to be held at Kids' offices. After arriving at Kids, Nasser and Shiboleth were asked to wait in a conference room. Samples for Gloria Vanderbilt and other brands handled by Success and Premium covered the walls. Meanwhile, Haim, Dweck, and Dweck's counsel, Barry Slotnick, showed up at Shiboleth's office. After learning that Nasser and Shiboleth were at Kids, Dweck told Nasser and Shiboleth that they would be right over. She then instructed one of her employees to remove the samples. As Nasser and Shiboleth waited, an employee entered and removed the samples without explanation. It was a less-than-adroit maneuver, but consistent with Dweck's efforts to conceal her activities.

When the stockholder meeting convened, Shiboleth proposed that Dweck stand for re-election as a director. Dweck's lawyer, Slotnick, then announced that Dweck could not serve as a director because she had a conflict of interest as a result of operating competing businesses. Nasser and Shiboleth were nonplussed. Shiboleth assumed Slotnick made a mistake, so he suggested that he and Dweck consult privately. When they returned after fifteen minutes, Slotnick reiterated that Dweck declined to serve as a director because of a potential claim of a conflict of interest from selling competitive product from Kids' premises. All eyes turned to Dweck, who admitted that she was selling "overlapping product" from Kids' premises. Tr. 567. Nasser and Shiboleth were shocked: it was the first time Dweck had indicated that she was competing with Kids from Kids' premises. During the board meeting convened immediately after the stockholder meeting, Nasser observed that Dweck should not be an officer if she declined to serve as a director. The board formally elected a slate of officers that excluded Dweck, with Djemal as President and CEO.

[...]Dweck, Taxin, And Fine Destroy Kids' Business.

Although no longer employed by Kids after the March 11 meetings, Dweck worked out of Kids' offices until April 11, 2005. Dweck and Taxin continued their campaign to divert Kids' business to Success, and they succeeded in transferring all of the Wal-Mart and Target business from the Holiday 2005 season onward. Kids did not receive any orders after May 2005.

Dweck and Taxin also arranged for Kids' employees to join Success. In early May 2005, Dweck and Taxin met with Kids' managers to inform them that Dweck would be operating her own companies separately from Kids and to offer them positions at her companies. Dweck told the managers to make the same offer to the employees under their supervision. She indicated that if they chose to accept her offer, "they would receive word to pack shortly." JX 636. Taxin later met with Kids' managers, reiterated the plan to leave Kids, and promised them jobs at Success. Fine met with at least one Kids employee and offered him a job at Success.

On May 17, 2005, Taxin informed the employees that May 18 was departure day. In the early morning of May 18, Kids employees began loading a moving truck with roughly 100 boxes of Kids' documents and materials. Fine supervised the process and attempted to conceal the move from Nasser and Djemal. Nasser, however, was tipped by a Kids employee the day before, and he arranged for Djemal and Lozovsky to arrive early at Kids' offices. Lozovsky found the move already underway and Kids' materials loaded in the moving truck. Lozovsky called Nasser, who demanded to speak to the driver. Fine took the phone, claimed that he was a driver named "Gregory," and listened while Nasser threatened to

351

summon the police. Djemal arrived at Kids' offices just in time to stop the truck. He could not stop many of the former employees from taking boxes with them. A computer consultant whom Djemal hired later determined that a number of the hard drives from Kids' computers had been wiped clean.

As part of the May 18 mass departure, Taxin resigned to join Dweck at Success. Fine remained at Kids until May 25, 2005, when he too joined Dweck. [...]

On May 20, Dweck and Taxin flew to Wal-Mart's headquarters in Bentonville, Arkansas to meet with more senior Wal-Mart managers. After the meeting, Wal-Mart recognized Success as its existing supplier and no longer recognized Kids. Dweck and Taxin then met with Target managers and achieved the same transition.

To protect their customer relationships, Dweck and Taxin made sure that a handful of employees remained at Kids to fill the Fall 2005 orders. Dweck and Taxin oversaw their efforts, effectively running Kids from afar. [...]

J. Nasser And Djemal Fail To Revive Kids.

Having lost nearly all its employees and with its pipeline diverted to Success, Kids had to start over from scratch. Djemal began hiring new employees and attempted to solicit orders from the retail giants that had been Kids' customer base. He immediately encountered difficulties. The Hong Kong factory that Kids relied on for samples was working for Success and would not return his calls. The manufacturing facilities Kids used also would not respond. When Djemal visited Wal-Mart headquarters with a new line of samples, Wal-Mart told him that Success was the recognized supplier and that Djemal would have to reestablish Kids as a new vendor. When he met with Target, the representative told Djemal that she only gave him an appointment because "`I thought you were Success.'" Tr. 1081. [...]

A. Success And Premium

Dweck and Taxin formed Success and Premium, took Kids' business opportunities for their new entities, competed directly with Kids, ran their businesses out of Kids' premises, used Kids' employees, and appropriated Kids' resources. In doing so, Dweck and Taxin breached their duty of loyalty to Kids.

1. The Nature Of The Breach

"The essence of a duty of loyalty claim is the assertion that a corporate officer or director has misused power over corporate property or processes in order to benefit himself rather than advance corporate purposes." *Steiner v. Meyerson,* 1995 WL 441999, at *2 (Del. Ch. July 19, 1995) (Allen, C.). "At the core of the fiduciary duty is the notion of loyalty—the equitable requirement that, with respect to the property subject to the duty, a fiduciary always must act in a good faith effort to advance the interests of his beneficiary." *US W., Inc. v. Time Warner Inc.,* 1996 WL 307445, at *21 (Del. Ch. June 6, 1996) (Allen, C.). "Most basically, the duty of loyalty proscribes a fiduciary from any means of misappropriation of assets entrusted to his management and supervision." *Id.* "The doctrine of corporate opportunity represents . . . one species of the broad fiduciary duties assumed by a corporate director or officer." *Broz v. Cellular Info. Sys., Inc.,* 673 A.2d 148, 154 (Del. 1996). The doctrine "holds that a corporate officer or director may not take a business opportunity for his own if: (1) the corporation is financially able to exploit the opportunity; (2) the opportunity is within the corporation's line of business; (3) the corporation has an interest or expectancy in the opportunity; and (4) by taking the opportunity for his own, the corporate fiduciary will thereby be placed in a position inimicable to his duties to the corporation." *Id.* at 154-55.

Dweck was a director and officer of Kids. Taxin was an officer of Kids. In these capacities, they owed a duty of loyalty to Kids. *Gantler v. Stephens,* 965 A.2d 695, 708-09 (Del. 2009). Dweck and Taxin breached their duty of loyalty by diverting what they decided were "new opportunities" to Success and Premium, including license agreements with Bugle Boy, Everlast, John Deere, and Gloria

Vanderbilt, Wal-Mart private label business, and Target direct import business. Kids was a profitable enterprise with the financial capability to exploit each of these opportunities. Indeed, Dweck and Taxin used Kids' personnel and resources to pursue each opportunity, demonstrating that Kids just as easily could have pursued the opportunities in its own name. After appropriating the opportunities, Dweck and Taxin operated Success and Premium as if the companies were divisions of Kids, but kept the resulting profits for themselves. By doing so, Dweck and Taxin placed themselves "in a position inimicable to [their] duties to [Kids]." *Broz,* 673 A.2d at 155.

Dweck and Taxin's conduct bears a striking resemblance to the continuing exploitation of corporate resources in *Guth v. Loft, Inc.,* 5 A.2d 503 (Del. 1939), the seminal corporate opportunity case in Delaware jurisprudence. In *Guth,* a director and the President of Loft Incorporated, Charles Guth, appropriated for himself the opportunity to purchase the secret formula and trademark for Pepsi-Cola from then-bankrupt National Pepsi-Cola Company. *Guth,* 5 A.2d at 505-06. Guth then operated Pepsi-Cola as a division of Loft, secretly using its employees and resources but keeping all the profits for himself. *Id.* at 507. The Delaware Supreme Court agreed that Guth breached his duty of loyalty and affirmed that Guth was required to disgorge all profits and equity from the venture to Loft. *Id.* at 515. Like Guth, Dweck and Taxin established a competing company into which they channeled new opportunities, then used Kids' "materials, credit, executives and employees as [they] willed." *Id.* at 506. [...]

To defend their actions, Dweck and Taxin tried to distinguish between the private label clothing business and the branded clothing business, then argued that Kids only operated in the private label business. Supposedly this distinction left them free to take the branded business. To the contrary, Kids had an interest in the branded business.

When determining whether a corporation has an interest in a line of business, the nature of the corporation's business should be broadly interpreted. "[...]

It is abundantly clear that Kids could have capitalized on each of the branded opportunities taken by Success and Premium. At trial, Taxin conceded that Kids could have handled the Bugle Boy and John Deere business. Moreover, Success and Premium did not in fact limit themselves to branded opportunities; they also appropriated private label opportunities. When Wal-Mart approached Kids about manufacturing men's clothing for the Wal-Mart private label called No Boundaries, Dweck and Taxin decided it was a "new opportunity" in which Kids had no expectancy. Manufacturing Wal-Mart private label brands had long been Kids' core business, and Kids had manufactured No Boundaries girls' clothing since 2000. At trial, Taxin admitted that Kids could have taken this opportunity. [...] When Target offered Kids the opportunity to engage in "direct importing," a process by which a company would have clothing manufactured overseas and shipped directly to Target, Dweck and Taxin again decided to take the opportunity for Success. Taxin obtained the opportunity while visiting Target's headquarters as Kids' President on a business trip for Kids. At trial, Taxin admitted that Kids could have handled the Target direct business. [...]

3. The Consent Defense

As their next defense, Dweck and her colleagues claimed that Nasser gave Dweck permission to compete. According to Dweck, she approached Nasser before forming Success and disclosed that she was planning to start a company that would compete with Kids. In her direct testimony, she claimed to remember "very vividly" a meeting with Nasser in February 2002, at his offices, when she sat with him at "a little round table by the window." [...]She recalled telling Nasser that "I'm not motivated to kill myself, continue to work, you know, so many hours a day and weekends, and therefore I would take any new opportunities outside of Kids." Tr. 461. She asserted that Nasser encouraged her to start her own business, declaring "` I'm not standing in your way for improving yourself.'" Tr. 495. According to Dweck, this statement gave her the go-ahead to use Kids' employees and Kids' resources to run a business out of Kids' offices that competed directly with Kids.

[...] On cross-examination, Dweck admitted that [...]Nasser was out of the country, likely in Tel Aviv. She admitted never discussing with Nasser what new opportunities she might pursue. She admitted never suggesting to Nasser that she would take opportunities from Wal-Mart or Target, Kids' largest customers. She admitted never mentioning that her business would operate from Kids' premises, use Kids' resources, or compete with Kids.

Nasser did not recall any meeting or conversation with Dweck. Instead, he remembered a call from Shiboleth, who told him that Dweck wanted to start her own business. After Nasser expressed concern that Dweck's new venture would compete with Kids, Shiboleth assured him that Dweck planned to operate in the upscale department store market. This would have differentiated Dweck's new company from Kids, which sold almost exclusively to discount retailers. Having been assured that Dweck's business would not compete with Kids, Nasser offered to help Dweck and told Shiboleth to advise her on how to set up the business. [...]

Having considered the witnesses' testimony and demeanor, I reject Dweck's version of events. [...]

Nasser never consented to Dweck competing directly with Kids, using Kids' employees and resources, and operating out of Kids' premises. In a real sense, that was not competition at all. It was conversion and theft. Regardless, Dweck and Taxin cannot rely on Nasser's purported consent to justify their conduct. [...]

6. The Remedy

As damages for usurping Kids' corporate opportunities, Dweck, Taxin, Success, and Premium are jointly and severally liable to Kids for the lost profits Kids would have generated from business diverted to Success and Premium. [...]

Dweck, Taxin, Success, and Premium also are jointly and severally liable for profits generated by Success and Premium after May 18, 2005 for the duration of the license agreements then in effect, including any rights of renewal or extension. If Dweck and Taxin had been faithful fiduciaries, those license agreements would have been in Kids' name, and Kids could have continued to perform under the agreements together with any renewals or extensions contemplated by the then-existing contracts. [...]

B. The Mass Departure And The Taking Of Kids' Property And Business Expectancies

Dweck, Taxin, and Fine breached their fiduciary duties by directing Kids employees to transfer Kids' expected orders and customer accounts to Success, taking Kids' property and files, and arranging a mass employee departure on May 18, 2005. "A breach of fiduciary duty occurs when a fiduciary commits an unfair, fraudulent, or wrongful act, including . . . misuse of confidential information, solicitation of employer's customers before cessation of employment, conspiracy to bring about mass resignation of an employer's key employees, or usurpation of the employer's business opportunity." *[...]*. Dweck cannot limit her liability by citing the termination of her relationship with Kids on March 11. Before that point, Dweck breached her own duties as a fiduciary. After that point, Dweck actively conspired with Taxin and Fine, thereby aiding and abetting Taxin and Fine's breaches of fiduciary duty. [...]

In my view, Kids' remedy for the departure-related breaches of fiduciary duty should be limited to the damages Kids suffered over and above where Kids would have been had Dweck and Taxin resigned in an appropriate manner. To approximate this loss, I award Kids the profits generated by Success in its non-branded business for the Holiday 2005 and Spring 2006 seasons. In May 2005, Kids was hard at work on the Fall 2005 season and had started preparing for the Holiday 2005 and Spring 2006 seasons. Kids' designers already had been traveling and shopping internationally to develop ideas for the Spring 2006 season, and they had a good understanding about what Wal-Mart and Target's Spring 2006 needs would be. During their departure from Kids, Dweck and Taxin took this business. I award it to Kids and hold Dweck, Taxin, Success, and Premium liable for the profits that Success and Premium earned from these seasons. [...]

C. Dweck's Personal Expenses

Between 2002 and 2005, Dweck caused Kids to reimburse her $466,948 in personal and business expenses. Dweck conceded that $171,966 were personal expenses that she wrongfully charged to Kids. She claimed she could not determine whether $170,400 were business or personal, but nevertheless asserted that she should not be ordered to repay that amount to Kids. She testified that $124,582 corresponded to legitimate Kids' business expenses.

> Under Delaware law, fiduciaries have a duty to account to their beneficiaries for their disposition of all assets that they manage in a fiduciary capacity. That duty carries with it the burden of proving that the disposition was proper. . . . [I]ncluded within the duty to account is a duty to maintain records that will discharge the fiduciaries' burden, and . . . if that duty is not observed, every presumption will be made against the fiduciaries.

Technicorp Int'l II, Inc. v. Johnston, 2000 WL 713750, at *2 (Del. Ch. May 31, 2000). "If corporate fiduciaries divert corporate assets to themselves for non-corporate purposes, they are liable for the amounts wrongfully diverted." *Id.* at *45.

As a Kids fiduciary, Dweck bore the burden at trial of proving that the challenged expenses were legitimate. Dweck failed to meet her burden. Instead, Dweck testified that she "didn't think Mr. Nasser would mind." Tr. 519. She later explained: "I felt that [the expense reimbursement] was part of, really, part of my compensation. In retrospect, I'm sorry I did it and I made a mistake." Tr. 521.

Dweck accordingly is liable to Kids for a total of $342,366 in expenses, comprising both the $171,966 of admittedly personal expenses and the $170,400 of indeterminate expenses. [...]

Entire Fairness   4.3.2

When fiduciaries of the corporation lose the business judgment presumption, they will have to justify to the court that their actions were entirely fair to the corporation. A defendant director who bears the burden of proving its actions were entirely fair to the corporation has to bear a heavy burden. The entire fairness standard as described in Weinberger has two components: fair dealing and fair price.

Unlike the business judgment presumption, which can a defendant can rely on to have a claim dismissed on the pleadings, when a defendant must bear the burden of proving the entire fairness, the defendant can only do that after a full trial. Consequently, losing the business judgment presumption and being forced to prove at trial that the actions of the defendants were entirely fair to the corporation is often outcome determinative. Defendant directors will often seek to settle litigation rather than go to trial under the entire fairness standard.

In older cases, the "entire fairness" standard is also known as the "intrinsic fairness" standard or the "inherent fairness" standard.

Weinberger v. UOP, Inc.   4.3.2.1

In Weinberger, the court deals with a common loyalty problem. What are the fiduciary duties of a controlling stockholder in dealing with minority stockholders. In such situations, the controlling stockholder, because of her ability to control and direct management decisions of the corporation, has fiduciary obligations to deal with minority stockholders fairly. Transactions between the controller and the corporation will not receive the protection of the business judgment presumption.

Rather, the controlling stockholder bears the burden of proving the fairness of its dealings with the corporation. The entire fairness standard requires the court to examine two aspects of the board's dealings with the corporation: whether the board dealt fairly with the corporation and whether the challenged transaction was at a fair price to the corporation.

As you read Weinberger, consider the facts and ask yourself if you were advising the controller how, if they were able to do things all over again, they might change things to make sure the actions of the controller and the board comported with the entire fairness standard as described by the court.

WEINBERGER v. UOP, INC.
457 A.2d 701 (1983)

MOORE, Justice:

Signal is a diversified, technically based company operating through various subsidiaries. Its stock is publicly traded on the New York, Philadelphia and Pacific Stock Exchanges. UOP, formerly known as Universal Oil Products Company, was a diversified industrial company engaged in various lines of business, including petroleum and petro-chemical services and related products, construction, fabricated metal products, transportation equipment products, chemicals and plastics, and other products and services including land development, lumber products and waste disposal. Its stock was publicly held and listed on the New York Stock Exchange.

In 1974 Signal sold one of its wholly-owned subsidiaries for $420,000,000 in cash. [...]While looking to invest this cash surplus, Signal became interested in UOP as a possible acquisition. Friendly negotiations ensued, and Signal proposed to acquire a controlling interest in UOP at a price of $19 per share. UOP's representatives sought $25 per share. In the arm's length bargaining that followed, an understanding was reached whereby Signal agreed to purchase from UOP 1,500,000 shares of UOP's authorized but unissued stock at $21 per share. [...]

The negotiations between Signal and UOP occurred during April 1975, and the resulting tender offer was greatly oversubscribed.

However, Signal limited its total purchase of the tendered shares so that, when coupled with the stock bought from UOP, it had achieved its goal of becoming a 50.5% shareholder of UOP.

Although UOP's board consisted of thirteen directors, Signal nominated and elected only six. Of these, five were either directors or employees of Signal. The sixth, a partner in the banking firm of Lazard Freres & Co., had been one of Signal's representatives in the negotiations and bargaining with UOP concerning the tender offer and purchase price of the UOP shares.

[...] However, the president and chief executive officer of UOP retired during 1975, and Signal caused him to be replaced by James V. Crawford, a long-time employee and senior executive vice president of one of Signal's wholly-owned subsidiaries. [...]

By the end of 1977 Signal basically was unsuccessful in finding other suitable investment candidates for its excess cash, and by February 1978 considered that it had no other realistic acquisitions available to it on a friendly basis. Once again its attention turned to UOP.

The trial court found that at the instigation of certain Signal management personnel, including William W. Walkup, its board chairman, [...] a feasibility study was made concerning the possible acquisition of the balance of UOP's outstanding shares. This study was performed by two Signal officers, Charles S. Arledge, [...]Arledge and Chitiea were all directors of UOP in addition to their membership on the Signal board.

Arledge and Chitiea concluded that it would be a good investment for Signal to acquire the remaining 49.5% of UOP shares at any price up to $24 each. Their report was discussed between Walkup and Shumway who, along with Arledge, Chitiea and Brewster L. Arms, internal counsel for Signal, constituted Signal's senior management. [...] It was ultimately agreed that a meeting of Signal's executive committee would be called to propose that Signal acquire the remaining outstanding stock of UOP through a cash-out merger in the range of $20 to $21 per share.

The executive committee meeting was set for February 28, 1978. As a courtesy, UOP's president, Crawford, was invited to attend, although he was not a member of Signal's executive committee. On his arrival, and prior to the meeting, Crawford was asked to meet privately with Walkup and Shumway. He was then told of Signal's plan to acquire full ownership of UOP and was asked for his reaction to the proposed price range of $20 to $21 per share. Crawford said he thought such a price would be "generous", and that it was certainly one which should be submitted to UOP's minority shareholders for their ultimate consideration. [...]

Thus, it was the consensus that a price of $20 to $21 per share would be fair to both Signal and the minority shareholders of UOP. Signal's executive committee authorized [706] its management "to negotiate" with UOP "for a cash acquisition of the minority ownership in UOP, Inc., with the intention of presenting a proposal to [Signal's] board of directors ... on March 6, 1978". Immediately after this February 28, 1978 meeting, Signal issued a press release stating:

> The Signal Companies, Inc. and UOP, Inc. are conducting negotiations for the acquisition for cash by Signal of the 49.5 per cent of UOP which it does not presently own, announced Forrest N. Shumway, president and chief executive officer of Signal, and James V. Crawford, UOP president.

> Price and other terms of the proposed transaction have not yet been finalized and would be subject to approval of the boards of directors of Signal and UOP, scheduled to meet early next week, the stockholders of UOP and certain federal agencies.

The announcement also referred to the fact that the closing price of UOP's common stock on that day was $14.50 per share.

Two days later, on March 2, 1978, Signal issued a second press release stating that its management would recommend a price in the range of $20 to $21 per share for UOP's 49.5% minority interest. [...]

Between Tuesday, February 28, 1978 and Monday, March 6, 1978, a total of four business days, Crawford spoke by telephone with all of UOP's non-Signal, i.e., outside, directors. Also during that period, Crawford retained Lehman Brothers to render a fairness opinion as to the price offered the minority for its stock. He gave two reasons for this choice. First, the time schedule between the announcement and the board meetings was short (by then only three business days) and since Lehman Brothers had been acting as UOP's investment banker for many years, Crawford felt that it would be in the best position to respond on such brief notice. Second, James W. Glanville, a long-time director of UOP and a partner in Lehman Brothers, had acted as a financial advisor to UOP for many years. Crawford believed that Glanville's familiarity with UOP, as a member of its board, would also be of assistance in enabling Lehman Brothers to render a fairness opinion within the existing time constraints. [...]

Glanville assembled a three-man Lehman Brothers team to do the work on the fairness opinion. These persons examined relevant documents and information concerning UOP, including its annual reports and its Securities and Exchange Commission filings from 1973 through 1976, as well as its audited financial statements for 1977, its interim reports to shareholders, and its recent and historical market prices and trading volumes. In addition, on Friday, March 3, 1978, two members of the Lehman Brothers team flew to UOP's headquarters in Des Plaines, Illinois, to perform a "due diligence" visit, during the course of which they interviewed Crawford as well as UOP's general counsel, its chief financial officer, and other key executives and personnel.

[707] As a result, the Lehman Brothers team concluded that "the price of either $20 or $21 would be a fair price for the remaining shares of UOP". They telephoned this impression to Glanville, who was spending the weekend in Vermont.

On Monday morning, March 6, 1978, Glanville and the senior member of the Lehman Brothers team flew to Des Plaines to attend the scheduled UOP directors meeting. Glanville looked over the assembled information during the flight. The two had with them the draft of a "fairness opinion letter" in which the price had been left blank. Either during or immediately prior to the directors' meeting, the two-page "fairness opinion letter" was typed in final form and the price of $21 per share was inserted. [...]

A primary issue mandating reversal is the preparation by two UOP directors, Arledge and Chitiea, of their feasibility study for the exclusive use and benefit of Signal. This document was of obvious significance to both Signal and UOP. Using UOP data, it described the advantages to Signal of ousting the minority at a price range of $21-$24 per share. [...]

it is clear from the record that neither Arledge nor Chitiea shared this report with their fellow directors of UOP. We are satisfied that no one else did either. This conduct hardly meets the fiduciary standards applicable to such a transaction. [...] Mr. Shumway, Signal's president, testified that he made sure the Signal outside directors had this report prior to the March 6, 1978 Signal board meeting, but he did not testify that the Arledge-Chitiea report was also sent to UOP's outside directors. [...]

C.

The concept of fairness has two basic aspects: fair dealing and fair price. The former embraces questions of when the transaction was timed, how it was initiated, structured, negotiated, disclosed to the directors, and how the approvals of the directors and the stockholders were obtained. The latter aspect of fairness relates to the economic and financial considerations of the proposed merger, including all relevant factors: assets, market value, earnings, future prospects, and any other elements that affect the intrinsic or inherent value of a company's stock. [...] However, the test for fairness is not a bifurcated one as between fair dealing and price. All aspects of the issue must be examined as a whole since the question is one of entire fairness. However, in a non-fraudulent transaction we recognize that price may be the preponderant consideration outweighing other features of the merger. Here, we address the two basic aspects of fairness separately because we find reversible error as to both. [...]

Part of fair dealing is the obvious duty of candor[...], one possessing superior knowledge may not mislead any stockholder by use of corporate information to which the latter is not privy. [...] With the well-established Delaware law on the subject, and the

Court of Chancery's findings of fact here, it is inevitable that the obvious conflicts posed by Arledge and Chitiea's preparation of their "feasibility study", derived from UOP information, for the sole use and benefit of Signal, cannot pass muster.

The Arledge-Chitiea report is but one aspect of the element of fair dealing. How did this merger evolve? It is clear that it was entirely initiated by Signal. The serious time constraints under which the principals acted were all set by Signal. It had not found a suitable outlet for its excess cash and considered UOP a desirable investment, particularly since it was now in a position to acquire the whole company for itself. For whatever reasons, and they were only Signal's, the entire transaction was presented to and approved by UOP's board within four business days. Standing alone, this is not necessarily indicative of any lack of fairness by a majority shareholder. It was what occurred, or more properly, what did not occur, during this brief period that makes the time constraints imposed by Signal relevant to the issue of fairness.

The structure of the transaction, again, was Signal's doing. So far as negotiations were concerned, it is clear that they were modest at best. Crawford, Signal's man at UOP, never really talked price with Signal, except to accede to its management's statements on the subject, and to convey to Signal the UOP outside directors' view that as between the $20-$21 range under consideration, it would have to be $21. The latter is not a surprising outcome, but hardly arm's length negotiations. [...]

As we have noted, the matter of disclosure to the UOP directors was wholly flawed by the conflicts of interest raised by the Arledge-Chitiea report. All of those conflicts were resolved by Signal in its own favor without divulging any aspect of them to UOP.

This cannot but undermine a conclusion that this merger meets any reasonable test of fairness. The outside UOP directors lacked one material piece of information generated by two of their colleagues, but shared only with Signal. True, the UOP board had the Lehman Brothers' fairness opinion, but that firm has been blamed by the plaintiff for the hurried task it performed, when more properly the responsibility for this lies with Signal. There was no disclosure of the circumstances surrounding the rather cursory preparation of the Lehman Brothers' fairness opinion. Instead, the impression was given UOP's minority that a careful study had been made, when in fact speed was the hallmark[...]. Yet, none of this was disclosed to UOP's minority.

Finally, the minority stockholders were denied the critical information that Signal considered a price of $24 to be a good investment. Since this would have meant over $17,000,000 more to the minority, we cannot conclude that the shareholder vote was an informed one. Under the circumstances, an approval by a majority of the minority was meaningless. [...]

Given these particulars and the Delaware law on the subject, the record does not establish that this transaction satisfies any reasonable concept of fair dealing[...].

E.

Turning to the matter of price, plaintiff also challenges its fairness. [...]

In this breach of fiduciary duty case, the Chancellor perceived that the approach to valuation was the same as that in an appraisal proceeding. Consistent with precedent, he rejected plaintiff's method of proof and accepted defendants' evidence of value as being in accord with practice under prior case law. This means that the so-called "Delaware block" or weighted average method was employed wherein the elements of value, i.e., assets, market price, earnings, etc., were assigned a particular weight and the resulting amounts added to determine the value per share. This procedure has been in use for decades. [...]However, to the extent it excludes other generally accepted techniques used in the financial community and the courts, it is now clearly outmoded. It is time we recognize this in appraisal and other stock valuation proceedings and bring our law current on the subject.

While the Chancellor rejected plaintiff's discounted cash flow method of valuing UOP's stock, as not corresponding with "either logic or the existing law" [...], it is significant that this was essentially the focus, i.e., earnings potential of UOP, of Messrs. Arledge and Chitiea in their evaluation of the merger. Accordingly, the standard "Delaware block" or weighted average method of valuation, formerly [713] employed in appraisal and other stock valuation cases, shall no longer exclusively control such proceedings. We believe that a more liberal approach must include proof of value by any techniques or methods which are generally considered acceptable in the financial community and otherwise admissible in court, subject only to our interpretation of 8 *Del.C.* § 262(h)[...]. This will obviate the very structured and mechanistic procedure that has heretofore governed such matters. [...]

Fair price obviously requires consideration of all relevant factors involving the value of a company. [...]

While a plaintiff's monetary remedy ordinarily should be confined to the more liberalized appraisal proceeding herein established, we do not intend any limitation on the historic powers of the Chancellor to grant such other relief as the facts of a particular case may dictate. The appraisal remedy we approve may not be adequate in certain cases, particularly where fraud, misrepresentation, self-dealing, deliberate waste of corporate assets, or gross and palpable overreaching are involved. [...] Under such circumstances, the Chancellor's powers are complete to fashion any form of equitable and monetary relief as may be appropriate, including rescissory damages. Since it is apparent that this long completed transaction is too involved to undo, and in view of the Chancellor's discretion, the award, if any, should be in the form of monetary damages based upon entire fairness standards, i.e., fair dealing and fair price.

Who is a controlling stockholder? 4.3.2.2

Typically stockholders owe no fiduciary duties to other stockholders or the corporation. However, where a stockholder controls the corporation, the stockholder will stand in fiduciary relation to the corporation and other stockholders.

In *Sinclair v. Levien* where Sinclair Oil Corp owned 97% of the shares in its subsidiary, Sinclair Venezuelan Oil Company, there really was no question that Sinclair was a controlling stockholder with fiduciary obligations to the minority stockholders. However, it is not always so obvious that a stockholder is a controlling stockholder with fiduciary obligations.

In *Kahn v. Lynch Communications Systems, Inc.*, the Supreme Court observed that Delaware courts will deem a stockholder a "controlling stockholder" when the stockholder: (1) owns more than 50% of the voting power of a corporation *or* (2) owns less than 50% of the voting power of the corporation but "exercises control over the business affairs of the corporation."

Blocks of 50% more of the voting power obviously create the ability to control the corporation. A 50%+ stockholder has the power to unilaterally replace the board of directors and can thus guide decision-making in the corporation.

That a 50% blockholder is a controller is hardly news. The more interesting question is whether a minority blockholder where the stockholder holds a block of less than 50% can also be deemed a controller. The answer to that question is obviously "yes". For example, a 48% blockholder holds less than majority voting control, but in a world where meeting participation and voting is not universal, 48% will usually be enough to determine the result of contested director elections.

For the court to reach a determination that a minority blockholder is a controller, the minority blockholder must exercise *actual* control over the business affairs of the corporation. In *Tesla Stockholder Litigation*, plaintiffs argued that Elon Musk, a 22.1% stockholder in Tesla had actual control of the corporation notwithstanding his minority position. The court required plaintiffs to demonstrate that Musk "exercised actual domination and control over . . . [the] directors." In this regard, his power must be "so potent that independent directors . . . [could not] freely exercise their judgment."

The court laid out the challenge for plaintiffs in demonstrating control thusly: "The requisite degree of control can be shown to exist generally or 'with regard to the particular transaction that is being challenged.'" Stated differently, when pleading that a minority blockholder is a controlling stockholder, the plaintiff may plead either (or both) of the following: (1) that the minority blockholder actually dominated and controlled the corporation, its board or the deciding committee with respect to the challenged transaction or (2) that the minority blockholder actually dominated and controlled the majority of the board generally. "[W]hether a large blockholder is so powerful as to have obtained the status of a 'controlling stockholder' is intensely factual [and] it is a difficult [question] to resolve on the pleadings. In the case of Tesla, the court reached a determination that with his 22.1% block and control of the board that plaintiffs had demonstrated Musk was the controlling stockholder of Tesla.

Sinclair Oil Corp. v. Levien   4.3.2.3

Stockholders do not normally have fiduciary duties with respect to other stockholders. This principle makes sense for a number of reasons. Stockholders with small stakes have no ability to influence the board of directors and therefore should be free from restrictions in their dealings with other stockholders. However, this principle is subject to an exception. When stockholders can, through their ownership position influence and control the direction of the corporation, then those stockholders have fiduciary obligations with respect to minority stockholders. As a result, in such circumstances, controlling stockholders will bear the burden of proving entire fairness when they engage in self-dealing with the corporation.

SINCLAIR OIL CORP. V LEVIEN
280 A.2d 717 (1971)

WOLCOTT, Chief Justice.

This is an appeal by the defendant, Sinclair Oil Corporation (hereafter Sinclair), from an order of the Court of Chancery, 261 A.2d 911 in a derivative action requiring Sinclair to account for damages sustained by its subsidiary, Sinclair Venezuelan Oil Company (hereafter Sinven), organized by Sinclair for the purpose of operating in Venezuela, as a result of dividends paid by Sinven, the denial to Sinven of industrial development, and a breach of contract between Sinclair's wholly-owned subsidiary, Sinclair International Oil Company, and Sinven.

Sinclair, operating primarily as a holding company, is in the business of exploring for oil and of producing and marketing crude oil and oil products. At all times relevant to this litigation, it owned about 97% of Sinven's stock. The plaintiff owns about 3000 of 120,000 publicly held shares of Sinven. Sinven, incorporated in 1922, has been engaged in petroleum operations primarily in Venezuela and since 1959 has operated exclusively in Venezuela.

Sinclair nominates all members of Sinven's board of directors. The Chancellor found as a fact that the directors were not independent of Sinclair. Almost without exception, they were officers, directors, or employees of corporations in the Sinclair complex. By reason of Sinclair's domination, it is clear that Sinclair owed Sinven a fiduciary duty. [...]

The Chancellor held that because of Sinclair's fiduciary duty and its control over Sinven, its relationship with Sinven must meet the test of intrinsic fairness. The [720] standard of intrinsic fairness involves both a high degree of fairness and a shift in the burden of proof. Under this standard the burden is on Sinclair to prove, subject to careful judicial scrutiny, that its transactions with Sinven were objectively fair. [...]

Sinclair argues that the transactions between it and Sinven should be tested, not by the test of intrinsic fairness with the accompanying shift of the burden of proof, but by the business judgment rule

370

under which a court will not interfere with the judgment of a board of directors unless there is a showing of gross and palpable overreaching. [...]

We think, however, that Sinclair's argument in this respect is misconceived. When the situation involves a parent and a subsidiary, with the parent controlling the transaction and fixing the terms, the test of intrinsic fairness, with its resulting shifting of the burden of proof, is applied. [...] The basic situation for the application of the rule is the one in which the parent has received a benefit to the exclusion and at the expense of the subsidiary. [...]

A parent does indeed owe a fiduciary duty to its subsidiary when there are parent-subsidiary dealings. However, this alone will not evoke the intrinsic fairness standard. This standard will be applied only when the fiduciary duty is accompanied by self-dealing — the situation when a parent is on both sides of a transaction with its subsidiary. Self-dealing occurs when the parent, by virtue of its domination of the subsidiary, causes the subsidiary to act in such a way that the parent receives something from the subsidiary to the exclusion of, and detriment to, the minority stockholders of the subsidiary.

We turn now to the facts. The plaintiff argues that, from 1960 through 1966, Sinclair caused Sinven to pay out such excessive dividends that the industrial development of Sinven was effectively prevented, and it became in reality a corporation in dissolution.

From 1960 through 1966, Sinven paid out $108,000,000 in dividends ($38,000,000 [721] in excess of Sinven's earnings during the same period). The Chancellor held that Sinclair caused these dividends to be paid during a period when it had a need for large amounts of cash. Although the dividends paid exceeded earnings, the plaintiff concedes that the payments were made in compliance with 8 Del.C. § 170, authorizing payment of dividends out of surplus or net profits. However, the plaintiff attacks these dividends on the ground that they resulted from an improper motive — Sinclair's need for cash. The Chancellor, applying the intrinsic fairness standard, held that Sinclair did not sustain its burden of proving that these dividends were intrinsically fair to the minority stockholders of Sinven.

Since it is admitted that the dividends were paid in strict compliance with 8 Del.C. § 170, the alleged excessiveness of the payments alone would not state a cause of action. Nevertheless, compliance with the applicable statute may not, under all circumstances, justify all dividend payments. If a plaintiff can meet his burden of proving that a dividend cannot be grounded on any reasonable business objective, then the courts can and will interfere with the board's decision to pay the dividend.

Sinclair contends that it is improper to apply the intrinsic fairness standard to dividend payments even when the board which voted for the dividends is completely dominated. [...]

We do not accept the argument that the intrinsic fairness test can never be applied to a dividend declaration by a dominated board, although a dividend declaration by a dominated board will not inevitably demand the application of the intrinsic fairness standard. [...] If such a dividend is in essence self-dealing by the parent, then the intrinsic fairness standard is the proper standard. For example, suppose a parent dominates a subsidiary and its board of directors. The subsidiary has outstanding two classes of stock, X and Y. Class X is owned by the parent and Class Y is owned by minority stockholders of the subsidiary. If the subsidiary, at the direction of the parent, declares a dividend on its Class X stock only, this might well be self-dealing by the parent. It would be receiving something from the subsidiary to the exclusion of and detrimental to its minority stockholders. This self-dealing, coupled with the parent's fiduciary duty, would make intrinsic fairness the proper standard by which to evaluate the dividend payments.

Consequently it must be determined whether the dividend payments by Sinven were, in essence, self-dealing by Sinclair. The dividends resulted in great sums of money being transferred from Sinven to Sinclair. However, a proportionate share of this money was received by the minority shareholders of Sinven. Sinclair received nothing from Sinven to the exclusion of its [722] minority stockholders. As such, these dividends were not self-dealing. We hold therefore that

372

the Chancellor erred in applying the intrinsic fairness test as to these dividend payments. The business judgment standard should have been applied.

We conclude that the facts demonstrate that the dividend payments complied with the business judgment standard and with 8 Del.C. § 170. The motives for causing the declaration of dividends are immaterial unless the plaintiff can show that the dividend payments resulted from improper motives and amounted to waste. The plaintiff contends only that the dividend payments drained Sinven of cash to such an extent that it was prevented from expanding.

The plaintiff proved no business opportunities which came to Sinven independently and which Sinclair either took to itself or denied to Sinven. As a matter of fact, with two minor exceptions which resulted in losses, all of Sinven's operations have been conducted in Venezuela, and Sinclair had a policy of exploiting its oil properties located in different countries by subsidiaries located in the particular countries.

From 1960 to 1966 Sinclair purchased or developed oil fields in Alaska, Canada, Paraguay, and other places around the world. The plaintiff contends that these were all opportunities which could have been taken by Sinven. The Chancellor concluded that Sinclair had not proved that its denial of expansion opportunities to Sinven was intrinsically fair. He based this conclusion on the following findings of fact. Sinclair made no real effort to expand Sinven. The excessive dividends paid by Sinven resulted in so great a cash drain as to effectively deny to Sinven any ability to expand. During this same period Sinclair actively pursued a company-wide policy of developing through its subsidiaries new sources of revenue, but Sinven was not permitted to participate and was confined in its activities to Venezuela.

However, the plaintiff could point to no opportunities which came to Sinven. Therefore, Sinclair usurped no business opportunity belonging to Sinven. Since Sinclair received nothing from Sinven to the exclusion of and detriment to Sinven's minority stockholders, there was no self-dealing. Therefore, business judgment is the proper standard by which to evaluate Sinclair's expansion policies.

Since there is no proof of self-dealing on the part of Sinclair, it follows that the expansion policy of Sinclair and the methods used to achieve the desired result must, as far as Sinclair's treatment of Sinven is concerned, be tested by the standards of the business judgment rule. Accordingly, Sinclair's decision, absent fraud or gross overreaching, to achieve expansion through the medium of its subsidiaries, other than Sinven, must be upheld.

Even if Sinclair was wrong in developing these opportunities as it did, the question arises, with which subsidiaries should these opportunities have been shared? No evidence indicates a unique need or ability of Sinven to develop these opportunities. The decision of which subsidiaries would be used to implement Sinclair's expansion policy was one of business judgment with which a court will not interfere absent a showing of gross and palpable overreaching.[...] No such showing has been made here.

Next, Sinclair argues that the Chancellor committed error when he held it liable to Sinven for breach of contract.

In 1961 Sinclair created Sinclair International Oil Company (hereafter International), a wholly owned subsidiary used for the purpose of coordinating all of Sinclair's foreign operations. All crude purchases by Sinclair were made thereafter through International.

On September 28, 1961, Sinclair caused Sinven to contract with International whereby Sinven agreed to sell all of its [723] crude oil and refined products to International at specified prices. The contract provided for minimum and maximum quantities and prices. The plaintiff contends that Sinclair caused this contract to be breached in two respects. Although the contract called for payment on receipt, International's payments lagged as much as 30 days after receipt. Also, the contract required International to purchase at least a fixed minimum amount of crude and refined products from Sinven. International did not comply with this requirement.

Clearly, Sinclair's act of contracting with its dominated subsidiary was self-dealing. Under the contract Sinclair received the products produced by Sinven, and of course the minority shareholders of Sinven were not able to share in the receipt of these products. If the contract was breached, then Sinclair received these products to the detriment of Sinven's minority shareholders. We agree with the Chancellor's finding that the contract was breached by Sinclair, both as to the time of payments and the amounts purchased.

Although a parent need not bind itself by a contract with its dominated subsidiary, Sinclair chose to operate in this manner. As Sinclair has received the benefits of this contract, so must it comply with the contractual duties.

Under the intrinsic fairness standard, Sinclair must prove that its causing Sinven not to enforce the contract was intrinsically fair to the minority shareholders of Sinven. Sinclair has failed to meet this burden. Late payments were clearly breaches for which Sinven should have sought and received adequate damages. As to the quantities purchased, Sinclair argues that it purchased all the products produced by Sinven. This, however, does not satisfy the standard of intrinsic fairness. Sinclair has failed to prove that Sinven could not possibly have produced or someway have obtained the contract minimums. As such, Sinclair must account on this claim.

Finally, Sinclair argues that the Chancellor committed error in refusing to allow it a credit or setoff of all benefits provided by it to Sinven with respect to all the alleged damages. The Chancellor held that setoff should be allowed on specific transactions, e. g., benefits to Sinven under the contract with International, but denied an over all setoff against all damages claimed. We agree with the Chancellor, although the point may well be moot in view of our holding that Sinclair is not required to account for the alleged excessiveness of the dividend payments.

We will therefore reverse that part of the Chancellor's order that requires Sinclair to account to Sinven for damages sustained as a result of dividends paid between 1960 and 1966, and by reason of the denial to Sinven of expansion during that period. We will affirm the remaining portion of that order and remand the cause for further proceedings.

Corporate Opportunity Doctrine 4.3.3

Remember that directors have an obligation to act in the best interests of the corporation. However, that charge can sometimes be difficult for even well-meaning directors to operationalize. For example, directors are often experienced business-people with their own relationships and their own business ventures. A common challenge facing directors comes in the form of business opportunities that come to them while they are directors. Which of the opportunities that come to directors properly belong to the corporation and which of them properly belongs to the director can be a vexing question.

If the director gets the answer to that question wrong, she may well find herself on the wrong end of a lawsuit alleging violations of the duty of loyalty for wrongfully benefitting from an opportunity that properly belonged to the corporation. On the other hand, the director may also mistakenly forego personal business opportunities for fear that her duty to the corporation prohibited her from pursuing them.

The corporate opportunity doctrine provides directors an affirmative defense to claims against them for taking a corporate opportunity. If a director can establish that the opportunity offered her was not properly an opportunity for the corporation, then the court will deem the director to have dealt fairly with the corporation.

Personal Touch Corp. v. Glaubach 4.3.3.1

PERSONAL TOUCH HOLDING CORP. v. GLAUBACH, D.D.S.,
February 25, 2019

This action involves a series of disputes between Personal Touch Holding Corp., a provider of home healthcare services, and one of its co-founders, Felix Glaubach. In April 2015, after tensions had been mounting between Glaubach and his fellow directors for some time over the company's management, Glaubach announced to the company's board of directors that he had purchased a building the company was interested in acquiring (the "AAA Building") and then offered to lease the building to the company. [...]

I. BACKGROUND

A. The Parties and Relevant Non-Parties

In 1974, Felix Glaubach, an orthodontist, and non-party Robert Marx, a lawyer, co-founded the organization that later became Personal Touch Holding Corp. ("Personal Touch" or the "Company").1 In the beginning, Glaubach became involved in Personal Touch's business and continued his orthodontic practice part-time, while Marx devoted most of his time to his law practice and his investments.2 They later became equal partners in the business.

Personal Touch is a Delaware corporation with its principal place of business in Lake Success, New York.3 The Company provides home healthcare services, including nursing, physical therapy, and long-term care. It currently operates through various subsidiaries with locations in seven different states.4

Glaubach served as President of the Company from December 13, 2010 until June 24, 2015, when he was terminated from that position.5 Glaubach, together with his wife and family trusts, currently holds approximately 27% of the Company's outstanding common stock.6 At the time of trial, Glaubach was about eighty-eight years old, and had been married to his wife for over fifty-eight years.7

*2 Glaubach and Marx currently serve as special directors of the Company's board of directors (the "Board"), entitling them to three votes each.8 The Board has four other members, each of whom is entitled to one vote.9 They are: John L. Miscione, John D. Calabro, Lawrence J. Waldman, and Robert E. Goff (collectively, the "Outside Directors").10 Marx is Chairman of the Board and the Company's Senior Legal Officer.11

Two other individuals prominent in this action are David Slifkin and his wife, Dr. Trudy Balk.12 Slifkin joined the Company in 1990 and served as its CEO from January 31, 2011 until December 7, 2015.13 Slifkin resigned as CEO on the heels of an internal investigation that uncovered his central role in a tax evasion scheme involving many Company employees. Balk joined the Company in 1980 and was its Vice President of Operations when she left the Company in July 2014. [...]

D. The AAA Building Becomes Available to Purchase

On or about February 28, 2013, Jim Clifford, the Director of Management Services at AAA New York ("AAA"), informed Mike Macagnone, the Director of Employee Services at the Company, that the building located next door to one of the Company's subsidiaries in Jamaica, New York (as defined above, the "AAA Building") was for sale. The Company had been seeking additional office space in Jamaica, New York for several years and was especially interested in the AAA Building due to its location.34 Management believed that the AAA Building could be used to relocate the Company's corporate offices, to expand the Company's operations in the area, as additional office space for one of the Company's subsidiaries, or as storage.35

On March 4, 2013, Slifkin emailed Marx and Glaubach stating that the AAA Building "is up for sale and the asking price seems reasonable."36 Two days later, Marx, Glaubach, and Macagnone met with Clifford to see the building and discuss a price.37 Marx told Clifford that the Company was "very interested" in the property but that the asking price of $ 1,200,000 was "a little high."38 Marx then offered Clifford $ 1 million in cash for the building.39 A few days later, Clifford responded that AAA was concerned about the tax implications of the sale, which prompted Marx to offer to pay AAA's tax obligation as part of the transaction.40

Less than one month later, Clifford informed Marx that AAA could not proceed with a sale at that time because its relocation plans had fallen through.41 Marx continued to inquire with Clifford about the AAA Building for several months.42 During one of those inquiries,

Clifford told Marx that AAA wants "to move and we'll call you as soon as we have anything." [...]

F. Glaubach Hires Reich and Pursues the AAA Building for Himself

On or around January 1, 2014, Glaubach hired David Reich as "Assistant to the President" with a salary of $ 100,000 per year.[51] Glaubach asserts he hired Reich primarily to assist him in exposing fraud that he suspected was occurring within the Company.[52] Reich was an employee of the Company from January 8, 2014 until April 15, 2015, during which time he was paid a total of approximately $ 209,440.[53] Also during this time period, Reich assisted Glaubach in acquiring the AAA Building for himself.

In 2014, Glaubach instructed Reich to contact Clifford to see whether AAA was ready to sell the AAA Building.[54] Reich and Clifford discussed the sale of the building during the summer of 2014. Both were under the impression at the time that they were negotiating the sale of the building to the Company.[55] Clifford continued to have this impression until September 24, 2014.

At some point before September 24, Glaubach told Reich that he wanted to buy the AAA Building himself in order to develop it or sell it for a profit.[57] Glaubach did not want anyone at the Company to know about his negotiations regarding the AAA Building and made efforts to keep them secret.[58] Reich thus stopped using his Company email account and began using a personal one in his communications about the AAA Building.[59] Reich also suggested meeting with Clifford in a conference room in Reich's temple rather than on Company grounds because there were "a lot of blabbermouths" in the Company's offices. [...]

I. The Board Suspends Glaubach

Later on November 25, 2014, all the Board members except Glaubach held an emergency phone conference during which they unanimously agreed to suspend Glaubach with pay pending further Board action.[...]

J. The Board Begins to Investigate Glaubach's Allegations of Tax Fraud While Glaubach Purchases the AAA Building

On February 10, 2015, during a regularly scheduled meeting, the Board ratified its decision to suspend Glaubach with pay and extended his suspension for thirty days.111 The Board also adopted resolutions (i) to create an audit committee (the "Audit Committee"), a corporate governance committee, and a compliance committee; [...]

*8 During the February 10 Board meeting, Marx "reported on ... conversations that he had ongoing with the owners of the AAA Building."113 Glaubach attended the meeting with his personal counsel but remained silent when Marx mentioned the AAA Building.114 The next day, on February 11, 2015, Glaubach closed on his purchase of the AAA Building for $ 1.8 million plus six months' free rent for AAA.115 Glaubach personally paid Reich $ 25,000 for his work on the deal. [...]

On April 29, 2015, the Board held what turned out to be a highly contentious meeting. Glaubach, represented by his personal counsel, asserted that he was being denied access to Company information. [...]

During the April 29 Board meeting, Glaubach announced that he had purchased the AAA Building and then offered to lease it to the Company.125 This "surprised" Goff because the Company previously had been negotiating to purchase the AAA Building.126 Months later, in a letter to Marx dated August 11, 2015, Glaubach again offered to lease the AAA Building to the Company.127 Marx replied ten days later, asserting that Glaubach's purchase of the property "constituted a breach of your fiduciary duties as a director of the Company."

L. Glaubach Is Terminated as President

On May 27, 2015, the Board created another special committee (the "Second Special Committee") that was empowered to decide all matters on which the Company or the Board may be adverse to Glaubach.129 [...]

*9 On June 22, 2015, the Second Special Committee voted to terminate Glaubach as President of Personal Touch.131 The Company sent an official termination letter two days later, on June 24, which specified, among other reasons for the decision, that Glaubach had [...] interfered with the Company's purchase of the AAA Building, and misappropriated Company assets by having Reich work on personal matters and hiring a personal driver.132 [...]

III. ANALYSIS

A. Glaubach Usurped a Corporate Opportunity by Secretly Acquiring the AAA Building for Himself

The Company contends that Glaubach breached his fiduciary duty of loyalty by usurping the corporate opportunity of acquiring the AAA Building for himself. I agree for the reasons explained below.

Eighty years ago, in its seminal decision of Guth v. Loft, Inc., our Supreme Court described the corporate opportunity doctrine as follows:

> [I]f there is presented to a corporate officer or director a business opportunity which the corporation is financially able to undertake, is, from its nature, in the line of the corporation's business and is of practical advantage to it, is one in which the corporation has an interest or a reasonable expectancy, and, by embracing the opportunity, the self-interest of the officer or director will be brought into conflict with that of his corporation, the law will not permit him to seize the opportunity for himself.189

The high court explained that the question of whether a usurpation of a corporate opportunity has occurred "is not one to be decided on narrow or technical grounds, but upon broad considerations of corporate duty and loyalty."190 The corporate opportunity doctrine is therefore rightly considered "a subspecies of the fiduciary duty of loyalty."191 That "duty has been consistently defined as 'broad and encompassing,' demanding of a director 'the most scrupulous observance.' "192

In Broz v. Cellular Information Systems, Inc., our Supreme Court more recently explained that:

> The corporate opportunity doctrine, as delineated by Guth and its progeny, holds that a corporate officer or director may not take a business opportunity for his own if: (1) the corporation is financially able to exploit the opportunity; (2) the opportunity is within the corporation's line of business; (3) the corporation has an interest or expectancy in the opportunity; and (4) by taking the opportunity for his own, the corporate fiduciary will thereby be placed in a position inimicable to his duties to the corporation.193

*14 Although these four factors are articulated in the conjunctive, the Supreme Court in Broz emphasized "that the tests enunciated in Guth and subsequent cases provide guidelines to be considered by a reviewing court in balancing the equities of an individual case" and that "[n]o one factor is dispositive and all factors must be taken into account insofar as they are applicable."194 Consistent with this approach, the Supreme Court previously referred to the "line of business" and "interest or expectancy" factors in the disjunctive, suggesting that proof of either factor could sustain a corporate opportunity claim,195 and this court has decided the viability of corporate opportunity claims by weighing the four Broz factors in a holistic fashion.196 With the above principles in mind, the court next considers each of the Broz factors based on the trial record.

1. The Company Was Financially Able to Acquire the AAA Building

Although Delaware courts have not delineated a clear standard for determining whether a corporation is financially able to avail itself of a corporate opportunity, our Supreme Court has opined (albeit in dictum) that this court may consider "a number of options and standards for determining financial inability, including but not limited to, a balancing standard, temporary insolvency standard, or practical insolvency standard."197 Since then, this court has applied various standards, "including the 'insolvency-in-fact' test, as well as considering whether the corporation is in a position to commit capital, notwithstanding the fact that the corporation is actually solvent."198

Glaubach purchased the AAA Building for $ 1.8 million in February 2015 and gave AAA six months of free rent as part of the transaction. This equates, at most, to an acquisition price of approximately $ 2.4 million, as discussed below.199 Applying any reasonable standard of financial ability, I am convinced that the Company was financially able to acquire the AAA Building in this price range during the time period when purchase discussions were occurring with AAA.

Marx and Goff (an Outside Director) both testified that they believed the Company could afford to purchase the AAA Building, with Goff explaining that Slifkin, the Company's CEO at the time, reported at a February 2015 Board meeting that the Company "could easily finance the acquisition of the AAA Building."200 Their views are substantiated by evidence that the Company generated well over $ 300 million in revenues and earned approximately $ 15 million in EBITDAE in 2014, had cash on hand of approximately $ 30.4 million as of December 31, 2014, and that its annualized EBITDAE for "2015 and beyond" was expected as of April 2015 to increase from approximately $ 15 million to approximately $ 20 million after a planned acquisition.201 On the other side of the ledger, the record is devoid of any evidence indicating that the Company's financial position was precarious when the AAA Building was purchased, and Glaubach offered no evidence suggesting that the Company was not financially able to purchase it for what he paid.

2. The Company Had a Clear Interest and Expectancy in Acquiring the AAA Building

With respect to the third Broz factor, I find that the Company clearly had an interest and expectancy in acquiring the AAA Building. It is stipulated that the Company "had been seeking additional office space in the Jamaica, New York area for years and was particularly interested in the AAA Building because it was located next door to the offices of one of the Company's key operating subsidiaries" and "could be used to relocate the Company's corporate offices, for expansion of the Company's Jamaica operations, as offices for the Company's other subsidiaries and for storage."202

The Company's general interest in acquiring the AAA Building became an actual opportunity in March 2013, when Slifkin learned that the AAA Building was for sale.203 On March 4, 2013, Slifkin reported this news to Marx and Glaubach in an email, explaining that the "asking price seems reasonable" and discussing several ways the Company could use the property.204 Two days later, Marx and Glaubach met with Clifford of AAA to inspect the building and negotiate a price for the Company to purchase it.205 Glaubach understood at the time that it was the Company that was the intended purchaser of the building.206 Marx's negotiations with Clifford stalled not because the Company lost interest in the property, but because AAA's plans to move to a different location fell through for a time.207> Clifford reassured Marx, however, that "we want to move and we'll call you as soon as we have anything."208

While the Company was waiting to hear back from AAA, Glaubach stepped in to take the opportunity for himself by instructing his assistant (Reich) to contact Clifford to see whether AAA was ready to sell the building.209 Tellingly, when Reich and Clifford were engaged in discussions during the summer of 2014, they were both under the impression that the Company was to be the purchaser of the building.210 And when Reich learned later that Glaubach wanted the building for himself, he took steps at Glaubach's direction to conceal his negotiations with AAA from others at the Company.211

The Company's interest in acquiring the AAA Building continued right up to the time Glaubach closed on his own purchase. As Goff testified, Marx updated the Board about "conversations that he had ongoing with the owners of the AAA Building" at a Board meeting on February 10, 2015—the day before Glaubach closed on the property.212

Glaubach's assertion that the Company lost interest in acquiring the AAA Building is not supported by the record. To the contrary, after Marx initiated a dialogue with AAA to acquire the building, AAA's representative expressly told him that he would contact Marx when AAA was ready to move forward. Glaubach used that opening to hijack the negotiations for his own benefit while concealing from AAA that he was acting on his own behalf (instead of the Company's) and while concealing from the Board his interactions with AAA up to the very end, including at the February 2015 Board meeting. In sum, the record clearly supports the conclusion that the Company was keenly interested in, and had a reasonable expectation of, acquiring the AAA Building at all relevant times.

3. The Line of Business Inquiry

*16 The second Broz factor asks whether the opportunity to acquire the AAA Building was within Personal Touch's line of business. Noting that the Company historically had leased office space and that it had owned a piece of real estate only once before, Glaubach argues that owning real estate is not in the Company's line of business.213 Quoting the Company's own brief, Glaubach contends that the Company's "two main lines of business " consist of "(i) a managed long-term healthcare program that provides home-based services to patients who would otherwise be in nursing homes; and (ii) a more traditional home care operation, which is in seven states and provides home healthcare aides, nurses, physical therapy and other home-based healthcare services."214

The Company counters that the Company's past practice of leasing office space, including from Marx and/or Glaubach,215 rather than owning it does not matter because the "line of business" inquiry should be construed broadly based "on the current needs of the Company, not on past practices."216 According to Personal Touch, "the Company had significantly changed following the ESOP transaction, because it was no longer controlled by Marx and Glaubach alone."217

Consistent with its doctrinal moorings in the duty of loyalty, the "line of business" concept was intended to be applied flexibly. In Guth, the Supreme Court stated that "[t]he phrase is not within the field of precise definition, nor is it one that can be bounded by a set formula."218 Rather, "[i]t has a flexible meaning, which is to be applied reasonably and sensibly to the facts and circumstances of the particular case," and "latitude should be allowed for development and expansion."219 Delaware courts accordingly have "broadly interpreted" the "nature of the corporation's business" when "determining whether a corporation has an interest in a line of business."220

In my opinion, Glaubach takes a crabbed view of the line of business inquiry that misses the central point of the corporate opportunity doctrine. Although the record bears out that the Company historically did not purchase real estate to house its operations, the Company has never been engaged in the business of purchasing and leasing real estate. Personal Touch is a healthcare provider, not a commercial real estate venture. Applying the line of business concept flexibly, the sensible way to consider the issue in the context of this case is that, irrespective of its past practice of leasing office space, the Company was presented with a rare opportunity to acquire a building with a highly desirable location that it could use to relocate or expand its healthcare operations. In that sense, the opportunity to acquire the AAA Building fit within the Company's existing line of business.

An equally sensible way to consider the issue is that the line of business test is simply not relevant here, where (i) the Company had a clear interest and expectancy in acquiring the AAA Building for the reasons explained previously, and (ii) the opportunity presented concerns an operational decision about how to manage or expand an existing business—i.e., whether it is better to buy or lease office space—as opposed to the opportunity to acquire a new business.221 Vice Chancellor Lamb's decision in Kohls v. Duthie222 exemplifies this approach.

*17 In Kohls, the court found that stockholders of Kenetech Corporation stated a derivative claim for usurpation of a corporate opportunity where one of the corporation's directors purchased a block of the corporation's stock from its largest stockholder for a nominal price.223 The court noted that "because corporate opportunity cases arise in widely varying factual contexts, '[h]ard and fast rules are not easily crafted to deal with such an array of complex situations.' "224 The court then rejected the argument that the offer to purchase the stock "did not constitute an opportunity in the company's line of business" given that the corporation "did not have in place any policy or plan for repurchasing its stock" and "had no share repurchase program in effect."225 It was sufficient, the court concluded, that the corporation logically would have an "expectancy in being presented with an opportunity to repurchase a large block of its own stock for little or no consideration."226

I agree with this reasoning. Even if the opportunity to acquire the AAA Building could be said not to fall within the Company's existing line of business under a strict interpretation of that concept, that is not fatal to the Company's claim. To the contrary, it is sufficient that the Company had a clear interest and expectancy in the property at the time the opportunity to acquire it arose.

4. Glaubach Acted Inimicably to His Fiduciary Duties

The fourth Broz factor prohibits a corporate officer or director from taking an opportunity for his own if "the corporate fiduciary will thereby be placed in a position inimicable to his duties to the corporation."227 Elaborating on this factor, the Supreme Court explained that "the corporate opportunity doctrine is implicated only in cases where the fiduciary's seizure of an opportunity results in a conflict between the fiduciary's duties to the corporation and the self-interest of the director as actualized by the exploitation of the opportunity."228 That is what occurred here.

After learning about the opportunity to purchase the AAA Building from Slifkin, Glaubach attended the initial meeting with Marx and Clifford in March 2013 and knew full well that the Company was interested in purchasing it. Putting his self-interest above his duty of loyalty to Personal Touch, Glaubach chose to compete directly with the Company to acquire for himself an admittedly "vital property" while making concerted efforts to conceal his activities from the Company until after he had closed on the deal.229 Indeed, Glaubach did not disclose to his fellow directors his efforts to buy the building for himself even when Marx was updating the Board about his efforts to purchase the property for the Company in Glaubach's presence.230

Removing any doubt about the importance of the building to the Company and the conflicted nature of what Glaubach did, Glaubach sought to lease the building to the Company almost immediately after he purchased it.231 In short, Glaubach was acutely aware of the value the opportunity to acquire the AAA Building presented to the Company because of the building's unique location and, instead of looking out for the interests of Personal Touch, he secretly thwarted its ability to take advantage of that opportunity so that he could profit personally by acquiring the building for himself.

Finally, I reject Glaubach's contention that he "did not place himself in a position 'inimical' to his corporate duties by purchasing the building" based on Section 2.2 of his Employment Agreement.232 That provision states simply that "[t]he Company acknowledges that [Glaubach] has business interests outside of the Company and will continue to devote a material portion of his business time, attention and affairs to such other business interests."233 Nothing in this provision allows Glaubach to compete with the Company for opportunities in which it has an interest or expectancy. Indeed, the preceding sentence in Section 2.2 states that Glaubach "shall not engage, directly or indirectly, in any other business, employment or occupation which is competitive with the business of the Company."

* * * * *

For the reasons explained above, balancing each of the Broz factors and considering them in a holistic fashion, the court concludes that Glaubach breached his fiduciary duty of loyalty by usurping the opportunity to purchase the AAA Building. [...]

Corporate Opportunity "Safe Harbor" 4.3.3.2

Although formal presentation of the corporate opportunity to the board of directors is not required, by presenting it and receiving the assent of disinterested directors the director who takes a corporate opportunity has created a "safe harbor".

In *Broz v. Celluar* (673 A2d 148), the Delaware Supreme Court had an opportunity to apply the corporate opportunity doctrine and then comment on the corporate opportunity "safe harbor" that comes from disclosure of corporate opportunities and then approval from disinterested directors:

> The classic statement of the doctrine is derived from the venerable case of *Guth v. Loft, Inc.* In *Guth,* this Court held that:
>
> if there is presented to a corporate officer or director a business opportunity which the corporation is financially able to undertake, is, from its nature, in the line of the corporation's business and is of practical advantage to it, is one in which the corporation has an interest or a reasonable expectancy, and, by embracing the opportunity, the self-interest of the officer or director will be brought into conflict with that of the corporation, the law will not permit him to seize the opportunity for himself.
>
> *Guth,* 5 A.2d at 510-11.
>
> The corporate opportunity doctrine, as delineated by *Guth* and its progeny, holds that a corporate officer or director may not take a business opportunity for his own if: (1) the corporation is financially able to exploit the opportunity; (2) the opportunity is within the corporation's line of business; (3) the corporation has an interest or expectancy in the opportunity; and (4) by taking the opportunity for his own, the corporate fiduciary will thereby be placed in a position inimicable to his duties to the corporation. The Court in *Guth* also derived a corollary which states that a director or officer *may* take a corporate opportunity if: (1) the opportunity is presented to the director or officer in his individual and not his corporate capacity; (2) the opportunity is not essential to the corporation; (3) the corporation holds no

interest or expectancy in the opportunity; and (4) the director or officer has not wrongfully employed the resources of the corporation in pursuing or exploiting the opportunity. *Guth, 5 A.2d at 509.*

Thus, the contours of this doctrine are well established. It is important to note, however, that the tests enunciated in *Guth* and subsequent cases provide guidelines to be considered by a reviewing court in balancing the equities of an individual case. No one factor is dispositive and all factors must be taken into account insofar as they are applicable. Cases involving a claim of usurpation of a corporate opportunity range over a multitude of factual settings. Hard and fast rules are not easily crafted to deal with such an array of complex situations. The determination of "[w]hether or not a director has appropriated for himself something that in fairness should belong to the corporation is `a factual question to be decided by reasonable inference from objective facts.'" [citations ommitted].

In applying the doctrine to the facts before it, the Delaware Supreme Court rejected the court below's seeming requirement that a director must always present a potential opportunity to disinterested directors, but highlighted the potential value of doing so:

> [I]n concluding that Broz had usurped a corporate opportunity, the Court of Chancery placed great emphasis on the fact that Broz had not formally presented the matter to the board. ... In so holding, the trial court erroneously grafted a new requirement onto the law of corporate opportunity, *viz.,* the requirement of formal presentation under circumstances where the corporation does not have an interest, expectancy or financial ability.

The teaching of *Guth* and its progeny is that the director or officer must analyze the situation *ex ante* to determine whether the opportunity is one rightfully belonging to the corporation. If the director or officer believes, based on one of the factors articulated above, that the corporation is not entitled to the opportunity, then he may take it for himself. Of course, presenting the opportunity to the board creates a kind of "safe harbor" for the director, which removes the specter of a *post hoc* judicial determination that the director or officer has improperly usurped a corporate opportunity. Thus, presentation avoids the possibility that an error in the fiduciary's assessment of the situation will create future liability for breach of fiduciary duty. It is not the law of Delaware that presentation to the board is a necessary prerequisite to a finding that a corporate opportunity has not been usurped.

Other cases, such as *Kaplan v. Fenton,* Del.Supr., 278 A.2d 834 (1971), have found no violation of the corporate opportunity doctrine where the director determined that the corporation was not interested in the opportunity, but never made formal presentation to the board. The director in *Kaplan* asked the CEO and another board member if the corporation would be interested in the opportunity and whether he should present the opportunity to the board. These questions were answered in the negative and the director then acquired the opportunity for himself. The *Kaplan* Court found no breach of the doctrine, despite the absence of formal presentation.

Sec. 144 Safe Harbor and Interested Director Transactions   4.3.4

During the 19th century, transactions between the corporation and its directors were commonplace. Such transactions often worked to the advantage of the interested director at the expense of the stockholder. The pernicious effect of such transactions caused legislatures to strictly regulate relationships between corporations and their directors. Through the early 20th century, transactions between a corporation and a director were considered **void**.

Over the years, courts adopted common law exceptions to the per se policy against interested director transactions. These common law exceptions relied, in part, on devices that resembled common law ratification doctrines, including disclosure of the interested transaction followed by consent. Although public policy with respect to interested director transactions has loosened over the years, such transactions are still, rightly, looked at with suspicion. Section 144 provides for a statutory safe harbor for interested director transactions. Interested director transactions that comply with the requirements of Section 144 will not be considered **void** or **voidable**.

While compliance with the requirements of Section 144 provides a board with a safe harbor against attacks for **voidability**, interested director transactions are still subject to attack for potential violations of the duty of loyalty. So, while the challenged transaction might not be void, it could still be unfair to the corporation, consequently boards may be required to defend the transaction on another basis.

The procedures for insulating interested director transactions from attack rely heavily on two principles: disclosure and then uncoerced approval. As you will see disclosure of one's interest coupled with the consent of disinterested directors or stockholders has a very powerful cleansing effect.

Where a transaction has been cleansed pursuant to the requirements of the statute, then it will not be vulnerable to subsequent attack solely because of a director's interest. However, it is still vulnerable to attack for lack of fairness.

The overlap between cleansing pursuant to Section 144 and the common law ratification doctrine is extensive, but not complete. We will compare the two in a subsequent section.

DGCL Sec. 144

4.3.4.1

The following provision of the statute provides a safe harbor for interested director transactions. If the requirements of the safe harbor are complied with then an interested director transaction will not be void or voidable because of the participation of the director. This statutory safe harbor essentially mimics the common law standard developed for saving interested director transactions from voidability challenges through the mid-Twentieth century.

§ 144. Interested directors; quorum.

(a) No contract or transaction between a corporation and 1 or more of its directors or officers, or between a corporation and any other corporation, partnership, association, or other organization in which 1 or more of its directors or officers, are directors or officers, or have a financial interest, shall be void or voidable solely for this reason, or solely because the director or officer is present at or participates in the meeting of the board or committee which authorizes the contract or transaction, or solely because any such director's or officer's votes are counted for such purpose, if:

(1) The material facts as to the director's or officer's relationship or interest and as to the contract or transaction are disclosed or are known to the board of directors or the committee, and the board or committee in good faith authorizes the contract or transaction by the affirmative votes of a majority of the disinterested directors, even though the disinterested directors be less than a quorum; or

(2) The material facts as to the director's or officer's relationship or interest and as to the contract or transaction are disclosed or are known to the stockholders entitled to vote thereon, and the contract or transaction is specifically approved in good faith by vote of the stockholders; or

(3) The contract or transaction is fair as to the corporation as of the time it is authorized, approved or ratified, by the board of directors, a committee or the stockholders.

(b) Common or interested directors may be counted in determining the presence of a quorum at a meeting of the board of directors or of a committee which authorizes the contract or transaction.

Benihana of Tokyo Inc. v. Benihana Inc.   4.3.4.2

Section 144(a)(1) provides that when a board member's interest is disclosed to or is known by disinterested directors and a majority of the disinterested directors approve the challenged transaction, the board's decision to enter into the transaction will receive the benefit of the §144 safe harbor protection from challenges for voidness and voidability.

Benihana raises a couple of important issues. First, does the disclosure of the director's interest need to be accomplished formally? Or, is it sufficient that the director's interest be common knowledge to the disinterested directors? Second, to the extent a majority of disinterested directors approve the transaction does such an approval provide the interested director and the transaction any additional protection beyond merely protection against the transaction being deemed void or voidable? If a transaction is approved by a majority of disinterested directors who are fully informed about the transaction should that transaction get the protection of the business judgment presumption?

BENIHANA OF TOKYO, INC. V. BENIHANA, INC.

906 A.2d 114 (2006)

BERGER, Justice:

Rocky Aoki founded Benihana of Tokyo, Inc. (BOT), and its subsidiary, Benihana, which own and operate Benihana restaurants in the United States and other countries. Aoki owned 100% of BOT until 1998, when he pled guilty to insider trading charges. In order to avoid licensing problems created by his status as a convicted felon, Aoki transferred his stock to the Benihana Protective Trust. The trustees of the Trust were Aoki's three children (Kana Aoki Nootenboom, Kyle Aoki and Kevin Aoki) and Darwin Dornbush (who was then the family's attorney, a Benihana director, and, effectively, the company's general counsel).

Benihana, a Delaware corporation, has two classes of common stock. There are approximately 6 million shares of Class A common stock outstanding. Each share has 1/10 vote and the holders of Class A common are entitled to elect 25% of the directors. There are approximately 3 million shares of Common stock outstanding. Each share of Common has one vote and the holders of Common stock are entitled to elect the remaining 75% of Benihana's directors. Before the transaction at issue, BOT owned 50.9% of the Common stock and 2% of the Class A stock. The nine member board of directors is classified and the directors serve three-year terms.[1]

In 2003, shortly after Aoki married Keiko Aoki, conflicts arose between Aoki and his children. In August, the children were upset to learn that Aoki had changed his will to give Keiko control over BOT. Joel Schwartz, Benihana's president and chief executive officer, also was concerned about this change in control. He discussed the situation with Dornbush, and they briefly considered various options, including the issuance of sufficient Class A stock to trigger a provision in the certificate of incorporation that would allow the Common and Class A to vote together for 75% of the directors.[2]

The Aoki family's turmoil came at a time when Benihana also was facing challenges. Many of its restaurants were old and outmoded. Benihana hired WD Partners to evaluate its facilities and to plan and design appropriate renovations. The resulting Construction and Renovation Plan anticipated that the project would take at least five years and cost $56 million or more. Wachovia offered to provide Benihana a $60 million line of credit for the Construction and

Renovation Plan, but the restrictions Wachovia imposed made it unlikely that Benihana would be able to borrow the full amount.[3] Because the Wachovia line of credit did not assure that Benihana would have the capital it needed, the company retained Morgan Joseph & Co. to develop other financing options.

On January 9, 2004, after evaluating Benihana's financial situation and needs, Fred Joseph, of Morgan Joseph, met with Schwartz, Dornbush and John E. Abdo, the board's executive committee. Joseph expressed concern that Benihana would not have sufficient available capital to complete the Construction and Renovation Plan and pursue appropriate acquisitions. Benihana was conservatively leveraged, and Joseph discussed various financing alternatives, including bank debt, high yield debt, convertible debt or preferred stock, equity and sale/leaseback options.

The full board met with Joseph on January 29, 2004. He reviewed all the financing alternatives that he had discussed with the executive committee, and recommended that Benihana issue convertible preferred stock.[4] Joseph explained that the preferred stock would provide the funds needed for the Construction and Renovation Plan and also put the company in a better negotiating position if it sought additional financing from Wachovia.

The board met again on February 17, 2004, to review the terms of the Transaction. The directors discussed Benihana's preferences and Joseph predicted what a buyer likely would expect or require. [...]

Shortly after the February meeting, Abdo contacted Joseph and told him that BFC Financial Corporation was interested in buying the new convertible stock.[5] In April 2005, Joseph sent BFC a private placement memorandum. Abdo negotiated with Joseph for several weeks.[6] They agreed to the Transaction on the following basic terms: (i) $20 million issuance in two tranches of $10 million each, with the second tranche to be issued one to three years after the first; (ii) BFC obtained one seat on the board, and one additional seat if Benihana failed to pay dividends for two consecutive quarters; (iii) BFC obtained preemptive rights on any new voting securities; (iv) 5% dividend; (v) 15% conversion premium; (vi) BFC had the right to force Benihana to redeem the preferred stock in full after ten years; and (vii) the stock would have immediate "as if converted" voting rights. Joseph testified that he was satisfied with the negotiations, as he had obtained what he wanted with respect to the most important points.

On April 22, 2004, Abdo sent a memorandum to Dornbush, Schwartz and Joseph, listing the agreed terms of the Transaction. He did not send the memorandum to any other members of the Benihana board. Schwartz did tell Becker, Sturges, Sano, and possibly Pine that BFC was the potential buyer. At its next meeting, held on May 6, 2004, the entire board was officially informed of BFC's involvement in the Transaction. Abdo made a presentation on behalf of BFC and then left the meeting. Joseph distributed an updated board book, which explained that Abdo had approached Morgan Joseph on behalf of BFC, and included the negotiated terms. The trial court found that the board was not informed that Abdo had negotiated the deal on behalf of BFC. But the board did know that Abdo was a principal of BFC. After discussion, the board reviewed and approved the Transaction, subject to the receipt of a fairness opinion.

On May 18, 2004, after he learned that Morgan Joseph was providing a fairness opinion, Schwartz publicly announced the stock issuance. Two days later, Aoki's counsel sent a letter asking the board to abandon the Transaction and pursue other, more favorable, financing alternatives. The letter expressed concern about the directors' conflicts, the dilutive effect of the stock issuance, and its "questionable legality." [...]The board then approved the Transaction. [...]

On June 8, 2004, Benihana and BFC executed the Stock Purchase Agreement. On June 11, 2004, the board met and approved resolutions ratifying the execution of the Stock Purchase Agreement and authorizing the stock issuance. [...]On July 2, 2004, BOT filed this action against all of Benihana's directors, except Kevin Aoki, alleging breaches of fiduciary duties; and against BFC, alleging that it aided and abetted the fiduciary violations. Three months later, as the parties were filing their pre-trial briefs, the board again reviewed the Transaction. After considering the allegations in the amended complaint, the board voted once more to approve it. [...]

A. Section 144(a)(1) Approval

Section 144 of the Delaware General Corporation Law provides a safe harbor for interested transactions, like this one, if "[t]he material facts as to the director's. . . relationship or interest and as to the contract or transaction are disclosed or are known to the board of directors ... and the board . . . in good faith authorizes the contract or transaction by the affirmative votes of a majority of the disinterested directors. . . ."[111] After approval by disinterested directors, courts review the interested transaction under the business judgment rule,[112] which "is a presumption that in making a business decision, the directors of a corporation acted on an informed basis, in good faith and in the honest belief that the action taken was in the best interest of the company."[113]

BOT argues that § 144(a)(1) is inapplicable because, when they approved the Transaction, the disinterested directors did not know that Abdo had negotiated the terms for BFC.[114] Abdo's role as negotiator is material, according to BOT, because Abdo had been given the confidential term sheet prepared by Joseph and knew which of those terms Benihana was prepared to give up during negotiations. We agree that the board needed to know about Abdo's involvement in order to make an informed decision. The record clearly [121] establishes, however, that the board possessed that material information when it approved the Transaction on May 6, 2004 and May 20, 2004.

Shortly before the May 6 meeting, Schwartz told Becker, Sturges and Sano that BFC was the proposed buyer. Then, at the meeting, Abdo made the presentation on behalf of BFC. Joseph's board book also explained that Abdo had made the initial contact that precipitated the negotiations. The board members knew that Abdo is a director, vice-chairman, and one of two people who control BFC. Thus, although no one ever said, "Abdo negotiated this deal for BFC," the directors understood that he was BFC's representative in the Transaction. As Pine testified, "whoever actually did the negotiating, [Abdo] as a principal would have to agree to it. So whether he sat in the room and negotiated it or he sat somewhere else and was brought the results of someone else's negotiation, he was the ultimate decision-maker."[115] Accordingly, we conclude that the disinterested directors possessed all the material information on Abdo's interest in the Transaction, and their approval at the May 6 and May 20 board meetings satisfies § 144(a)(1).[116]

B. Abdo's alleged fiduciary violation

BOT next argues that the Court of Chancery should have reviewed the Transaction under an entire fairness standard because Abdo breached his duty of loyalty when he used Benihana's confidential information to negotiate on behalf of BFC. This argument starts with a flawed premise. The record does not support BOT's contention that Abdo used any confidential information against Benihana. Even without Joseph's comments at the February 17 board meeting, Abdo knew the terms a buyer could expect to obtain in a deal like this. Moreover, as the trial court found, "the negotiations involved give and take on a number of points" and Benihana "ended up where [it] wanted to be" for the most important terms.[117] Abdo did not set the terms of the deal; he did not deceive the board; and he did not dominate or control the other directors' approval of the Transaction. In short, the record does not support the claim that Abdo breached his duty of loyalty.[118]

C. Dilution of BOT's voting power

Finally, BOT argues that the board's primary purpose in approving the Transaction was to dilute BOT's voting control. BOT points out that Schwartz was concerned about BOT's control in 2003 and even discussed with Dornbush the possibility of issuing a huge number of Class A shares. Then, despite the availability of other financing options, the board decided on a stock issuance, and agreed to give BFC "as if converted" voting rights. According to BOT, the trial court overlooked this powerful evidence of the board's improper purpose.

It is settled law that, "corporate action . . . may not be taken for the sole or [122] primary purpose of entrenchment."[119] Here, however, the trial court found that "the primary purpose of the . . . Transaction was to provide what the directors subjectively believed to be the best financing vehicle available for securing the necessary funds to pursue the agreed upon Construction and Renovation Plan for the Benihana restaurants."[120] That factual determination has ample record support, especially in light of the trial court's credibility determinations. Accordingly, we defer to the Court of Chancery's conclusion that the board's approval of the Transaction was a valid exercise of its business judgment, for a proper corporate purpose.

Conclusion

Based on the foregoing, the judgment of the Court of Chancery is affirmed.

[1] The directors at the time of the challenged transaction were: Dornbush, John E. Abdo, Norman Becker, Max Pine, Yoshihiro Sano, Joel Schwartz, Robert B. Sturges, Takanori Yoshimoto, and Kevin Aoki.

Fliegler v. Lawrence

4.3.4.3

Section 144 provides alternate methods to insulate interested director transactions from attack for voidness. In addition to seeking the approval of a majority of the disinterested directors, a board can seek the approval of the stockholders. Notice that the statute requires only that the challenged transaction is approved by a majority of the stockholders in order to gain the protection of the statutory safe harbor and not necessarily a majority of disinterested stockholders.

Remember the protections of § 144 extend only to the question of void or voidability of an interested director transaction and not further. One can see how there would be many situations where one might not want stockholder approval of an interested director transaction to do much more than simply rescue a transaction from voidness. Where a controlling stockholder approves a transaction with itself (as a director) we may be okay with that transaction not being void, but we might still want the interested director/stockholder to be required to prove the transaction is nevertheless entirely fair to the corporation.

The court in the following case, *Fliegler,* recognizes this problem and makes it clear that for directors who are seeking the additional protection of the business judgment presumption, they would have to do more than just comply with § 144(a)(2). For those directors, they will have to take the additional step of complying with the requirements of common law stockholder ratification doctrine and seek informed approval of a majority of disinterested stockholders.

FLIEGLER V. LAWRENCE

361 A.2d 218 (1976)

McNEILLY, Justice:

In this shareholder derivative action brought on behalf of Agau Mines, Inc., a Delaware corporation, (Agau) against its officers and directors and United States Antimony Corporation, a Montana corporation (USAC), we are asked to decide whether the individual defendants, in their capacity as directors and officers of both corporations, wrongfully usurped a corporate opportunity belonging to Agau, and whether all defendants wrongfully profited by causing Agau to exercise an option to purchase that opportunity. [...]

I

In November, 1969, defendant, John C. Lawrence (then president of Agau, a publicly held corporation engaged in a dual-phased gold and silver exploratory venture) in his individual capacity, acquired certain antimony properties under a lease-option for $60,000.[1-1]Lawrence offered to [220] transfer the properties, which were then "a raw prospect", to Agau, but after consulting with other members of Agau's board of directors, he and they agreed that the corporation's legal and financial position would not permit acquisition and development of the properties at that time. Thus, it was decided to transfer the properties to USAC, (a closely held corporation formed just for this purpose and a majority of whose stock was owned by the individual defendants) where capital necessary for development of the properties could be raised without risk to Agau through the sale of USAC stock; it was also decided to grant Agau a long-term option to acquire USAC if the properties proved to be of commercial value.

In January, 1970, the option agreement was executed by Agau and USAC. Upon its exercise and approval by Agau shareholders, Agau was to deliver 800,000 shares of its restricted investment stock for all authorized and issued shares of USAC. [...]

In July, 1970, the Agau board resolved to exercise the option, an action which was approved by majority vote of the shareholders in October, 1970. Subsequently, plaintiff instituted this suit on behalf of Agau to recover the 800,000 shares and for an accounting. [...]

III

Plaintiff contends that because the individual defendants personally profited through the use of Agau's resources, *viz.,* personnel (primarily Lawrence) to develop the USAC properties and stock purchase warrants to secure a $300,000. indebtedness (incurred by USAC because it could not raise sufficient capital through sale of stock), they must be compelled to account to Agau for that profit. This argument pre-supposes that defendants did in fact so misuse corporate assets; however, the record reveals substantial evidence to support the Vice-Chancellor's conclusion that there was no misuse of either Agau personnel or warrants. Issuance of the warrants in fact enhanced the value of Agau's option at a time when there was reason to believe that USAC's antimony properties had a "considerable potential", and plaintiff did not prove that alleged use of Agau's personnel and equipment was detrimental to the corporation.

Nevertheless, our inquiry cannot stop here, for it is clear that the individual defendants stood on both sides of the transaction in implementing and fixing the terms of the option agreement. [...]

A.

Preliminarily, defendants argue that they have been relieved of the burden of proving fairness by reason of shareholder ratification of the Board's decision to exercise the option. They rely on 8 Del.C. § 144(a)(2) and *Gottlieb v. Heyden Chemical Corp.,* Del.Supr., 33 Del.Ch. 177, 91 A. 2d 57 (1952).

In *Gottlieb,* this Court stated that shareholder ratification of an "interested transaction", although less than unanimous, shifts the burden of proof to an objecting shareholder to demonstrate that the terms are so unequal as to amount to a gift or waste of corporate assets. Also see *Saxe v. Brady,* 40 Del.Ch. 474, 184 A.2d 602 (1962). The Court explained:

> "[T]he entire atmosphere is freshened and a new set of rules invoked where formal approval has been given by a majority of independent, fully informed [share]holders." 91 A.2d at 59.

The purported ratification by the Agau shareholders would not affect the burden of proof in this case because the majority of shares voted in favor of exercising the option were cast by defendants in their capacity as Agau shareholders. Only about one-third of the "disinterested" shareholders voted, and we cannot assume that such non-voting shareholders either approved or disapproved. Under these circumstances, we cannot say that "the entire atmosphere has been freshened" and that departure from the objective fairness test is permissible. [...] In short, defendants have not established factually a basis for applying *Gottlieb.*

Nor do we believe the Legislature intended a contrary policy and rule to prevail by enacting 8 Del.C. § 144, which provides, in part:

(a) No contract or transaction between a corporation and 1 or more of its directors or officers, or between a corporation and any other corporation, partnership, association, or other organization in which 1 or more of its directors [222] or officers, are directors or officers, or have a financial interest, shall be void or voidable solely for this reason, or solely because the director or officer is present at or participates in the meeting of the board or committee which authorizes the contract or transaction, or solely because his or their votes are counted for such purpose, if:

[...]

(2) The material facts as his relationship or interest and as to the contract or transaction are disclosed or are known to the shareholders entitled to vote thereon, and the contract or transaction is specifically approved in good faith by vote of the shareholders; [...]

Defendants argue that the transaction here in question is protected by § 144(a)(2)[3] which, they contend, does not require that ratifying shareholders be "disinterested" or "independent"; nor, they argue, is there warrant for reading such a requirement into the statute. [...]We do not read the statute as providing the broad immunity for which defendants contend. It merely removes an "interested director" cloud when its terms are met and provides against invalidation of an agreement "solely" because such a director or officer is involved. Nothing in the statute sanctions unfairness to Agau or removes the transaction from judicial scrutiny.

Stockholder Ratification Doctrine   4.3.5

For anyone with more than a passing familiarity with the law of agency, stockholder ratification doctrine will sound very familiar. As you remember in the Restatement (3rd) of Agency, §8.06 conduct by an agent that would otherwise constitute a breach of a fiduciary duty does not constitute a breach of duty if the principal consents to the conduct, provided that the agent acts in good faith, discloses all material facts that the agent knows, has reason to know, or should know would reasonably affect the principal's judgment, and the agent otherwise deals fairly with the principal. Full and adequate disclosure of an agent's actions followed by knowing and uncoerced assent by the principal in effect cleanses the otherwise disloyal acts of an agent.

In the context of the corporate law, common law courts have adopted a very similar approach to the unauthorized acts of boards, or agents of the corporation. For example, self-dealing by a board will, upon a stockholder challenge, be subject to the stringent entire fairness standard with the board bearing the burden of proving that it dealt fairly with the corporation. However, where the material facts about those acts are fully disclosed to the stockholders and disinterested stockholders have an uncoerced opportunity to vote 'yay or nay' on those actions, board actions so approved by the disinterested stockholders will be granted the deference of business judgment rather than be subject to entire fairness review.

Although in a successful ratification case, the board is not required prove entire fairness, in order to establish that the ratification is effective, the board is required to bear the burden of proving that it disclosed to stockholders all the material facts related to the challenged transaction available to it at the time.

Once a board has successfully established that stockholder ratification the effect of such ratification is to shift the substantive test on judicial review of the act from one of fairness to one of "corporate waste".

The Cleansing Power of Disinterested Directors   4.3.5.1

The key to understanding the statutory safe harbor
afforded by Section 144(a)(1) is that where
disinterested directors are fully informed and approve an interested
director transaction that transaction will not be void or voidable

solely because of the director's interest, even if the number of disinterested directors who have approved the transaction are less than a majority of the board. Such transactions, however, are still subject to attack for lack of fairness.

A related question is what is the effect when a majority of the board of directors is made up of disinterested directors and they, with full information, approve an interested director transaction? Remember, because §141(a) vests the power to manage the corporation with the board. Consequently, a court will be hesitant place itself between the corporation and a statutorily authorized decisionmaking body. The fact that a majority of the board of directors is made up of neutral decisionmakers with no pecuniary interest in the challenged transaction will be critical for a court.

In general, where a board is composed of a majority of disinterested directors who approve a transaction involving an interested directors, so long as the interested director fully discloses her interest and a majority of the disinterested directors ratify the interested transaction, the decision will generally receive the benefit of the business judgment presumption. The presence of a neutral decisionmaker is decisive in that regard. "The Court will presume, therefore, that the vote of a disinterested director signals that the interested transaction furthers the best interests of the corporation despite the interest of one or more directors" (Cooke v Oolie (2000 WL 710199)).

Where a majority of the board is interested in the challenged transaction, there is no neutral decisionmaker for a court to look to. In that case, entire fairness will be the standard of review. The effect of compliance with Section 144(a)(1), even though the disinterested directors are less than a majority will be to shift the burden of proving entire fairness from the defendants to the plaintiffs who will bear a burden of demonstrating the transaction was unfair (Cooke v Oolie (2000 WL 710199)).

The cleansing power of disinterested and independent directors is clear, especially so when one begins to consider the effect of disinterested and independent directors in the demand futility context in derivative litigation. Consequently, corporations have powerful incentives to appoint independent directors to their boards of directors.

Contours of Section 144 and Stockholder Ratification

4.3.5.2

The common law doctrine of stockholder ratification is a close cousin of §144(a)(2). However, it is important to remember that the two, though structurally similar in some respects, are very different.

Consider how the common law doctrine of stockholder ratification interacts with the requirements of §144(a)(2). Section 144(a)(2) provides a statutory safe harbor from voidness challenges for interested director transactions when the transaction in question was approved by stockholders of the corporation. Having been cleansed for purposes of a voidness challenge, such transactions are nevertheless may still be vulnerable for loyalty transactions (ie. that they were not fair to the corporation).

The language of the statute, which permits an interested stockholder to vote in favor of an interested director transaction, presents an obstacle for relying on stockholder votes to do more than protection against voidness challenges. A statutory provision that permits an ostensibly bad actor to cleanse their own bad acts seems patently unreasonable. Consequently, §144(a)(2) cannot be relied on to do more than the statute permits.

Common law ratification, however, relies on disclosure to and approval of disinterested stockholders. The effect of which is to cleanse a transaction for purposes of loyalty challenges. If one analogizes back to principles of agency law, one sees the effect of disclosure and uncoerced approval by a principle of an agent's ostensibly bad acts cleanses such actions. The same is true of common law ratification. That is, though, different from the protection afforded by the §144 statutory safe harbor.

In *Lewis v Vogelstein*, 699 A.2d 327 (Del. Ch. 1997), then Chancellor Allen outlined the contours of stockholder ratification in the context of director compensation, a transaction where directors are obviously interested parties, as follows:

> What is the effect under Delaware corporation law of shareholder ratification of an interested transaction? ...
>
> In order to state my own understanding I first note that by shareholder ratification I do not refer to every instance in which shareholders vote affirmatively with respect to a question placed before them. I exclude from the question those instances in which shareholder votes are a necessary step in authorizing a transaction. Thus the law of ratification as here discussed has no direct bearing on shareholder action to amend a certificate of incorporation or bylaws. *Cf. Williams v. Geier*, Del.Supr., 671 A.2d 1368 (1996); nor does that law bear on shareholder votes necessary to authorize a merger, a sale of substantially all the corporation's assets, or to dissolve the enterprise. For analytical purposes one can set such cases aside.
>
> *1. Ratification generally:* I start with principles broader than those of corporation law. Ratification is a concept deriving from the law of agency which contemplates the *ex post* conferring upon or confirming of the legal authority of an agent in circumstances in which the agent had no authority or arguably had no authority. RESTATEMENT (SECOND) OF AGENCY § 82 (1958). To be effective, of course, the agent must fully disclose all relevant circumstances with respect to the transaction to the principal prior to the ratification. *See, e.g., Breen Air Freight Ltd. v. Air Cargo, Inc., et al.*, 470 F.2d 767, 773 (2d Cir.1972); RESTATEMENT (SECOND) OF AGENCY § 91 (1958). Beyond that, since the relationship between a principal and agent is fiduciary in character, the agent in seeking ratification must act not only with candor, but with loyalty. Thus an attempt to coerce the principal's consent improperly will invalidate the effectiveness of the ratification. RESTATEMENT (SECOND) OF AGENCY § 100 (1958).

Assuming that a ratification by an agent is validly obtained, what is its effect? One way of conceptualizing that effect is that it provides, after the fact, the grant of authority that may have been wanting at the time of the agent's act. Another might be to view the ratification as consent or as an estoppel by the principal to deny a lack of authority. *See* RESTATEMENT (SECOND) OF AGENCY § 103 (1958). In either event the effect of informed ratification is to validate or affirm the act of the agent as the act of the principal. *Id.* § 82.

Application of these general ratification principles to shareholder ratification is complicated by three other factors. First, most generally, in the case of shareholder ratification there is of course no single individual acting as principal, but rather a class or group of divergent individuals — the class of shareholders. This aggregate quality of the principal means that decisions to affirm or ratify an act will be subject to collective action disabilities; that some portion of the body doing the ratifying may in fact have conflicting interests in the transaction; and some dissenting members of the class may be able to assert more or less convincingly that the "will" of the principal is wrong, or even corrupt and ought not to be binding on the class. In the case of individual ratification these issues won't arise, assuming that the principal does not suffer from multiple personality disorder. Thus the collective nature of shareholder ratification makes it more likely that following a claimed shareholder ratification, nevertheless, there is a litigated claim on behalf of the principal that the agent lacked authority or breached its duty. The second, mildly complicating factor present in shareholder ratification is the fact that in corporation law the "ratification" that shareholders provide will often not be directed to lack of legal authority of an agent but will relate to the consistency of some authorized director action with the equitable duty of loyalty. Thus shareholder ratification sometimes acts not to confer legal authority — but as in this case — to affirm that action taken is consistent with shareholder interests. Third, when what is "ratified" is a director conflict transaction, the statutory law — in Delaware Section 144 of the Delaware General Corporation Law — may bear on the effect.

2. Shareholder ratification: These differences between shareholder ratification of director action and classic ratification by a single principal, do lead to a difference in the effect of a valid ratification in the shareholder context. The principal novelty added to ratification law generally by the shareholder context, is the idea — no doubt analogously present in other contexts in which common interests are held — that, in addition to a claim that ratification was defective because of incomplete information or coercion, shareholder ratification is subject to a claim by a member of the class that the ratification is ineffectual (1) because a majority of those affirming the transaction had a conflicting interest with respect to it or (2) because the transaction that is ratified constituted a corporate waste. As to the second of these, it has long been held that shareholders may not ratify a waste except by a unanimous vote. *Saxe v. Brady,*Del.Ch., 184 A.2d 602, 605 (1962). The idea behind this rule is apparently that a transaction that satisfies the high standard of waste constitutes a *gift* of corporate property and no one should be forced against their will to make a gift of their property. *In all events, informed, uncoerced, disinterested shareholder ratification of a transaction in which corporate directors have a material conflict of interest has the effect of protecting the transaction from judicial review except on the basis of waste.* (emphasis added)

In *Gantler v. Stephens* (965 A.2d 695)(2009), the Delaware Supreme provided some clarity on the question of shareholder ratification:

Under current Delaware case law, the scope and effect of the common law doctrine of shareholder ratification is unclear, making it difficult to apply that doctrine in a coherent manner. As the Court of Chancery has noted in *In re Wheelabrator Technologies, Inc., Shareholders Litigation:*

[The doctrine of ratification] might be thought to lack coherence because the decisions addressing the effect of shareholder

410

"ratification" have fragmented that subject into three distinct compartments,.... In its "classic" ... form, shareholder ratification describes the situation where shareholders approve board action that, legally speaking, could be accomplished without any shareholder approval.... "[C]lassic" ratification involves the voluntary addition of an independent layer of shareholder approval in circumstances where shareholder approval is not legally required. But "shareholder ratification" has also been used to describe the effect of an informed shareholder vote that was statutorily required for the transaction to have legal existence.... That [the Delaware courts] have used the same term is such highly diverse sets of factual circumstances, without regard to their possible functional differences, suggests that "shareholder ratification" has now acquired an expanded meaning intended to describe any approval of challenged board action by a fully informed vote of shareholders, irrespective of whether that shareholder vote is legally required for the transaction to attain legal existence.

To restore coherence and clarity to this area of our law, we hold that the scope of the shareholder ratification doctrine must be limited to its so-called "classic" form; that is, to circumstances where a fully informed shareholder vote approves director action that does *not* legally require shareholder approval in order to become legally effective. Moreover, the only director action or conduct that can be ratified is that which the shareholders are specifically asked to approve. With one exception, the "cleansing" effect of such a ratifying shareholder vote is to subject the challenged director action to business judgment review, as opposed to "extinguishing" the claim altogether (*i.e.,* obviating all judicial review of the challenged action).

Following *Gantler* and *Vogelstein*, it is clear that an *informed, uncoerced, vote of disinterested stockholders ratifying a transaction in which corporate directors have a material conflict of interest has the effect of providing the interested director transaction to protection of the business judgment presumption.* While such a transaction is still subject to possible attack, the directors' interest may not be the basis of a subsequent challenge.

The court in *Corwin* reaffirmed this basic teaching in the context of a post-merger trial for damages. Some commentators and defendants have attempted to extend *Corwin* further. However, the courts have pushed back. In *Massey Energy Company Derivative and Class Action Litigation* (2017), Chancellor Bouchard provided the following comment on the limits of the reach of *Corwin* and stockholder ratification:

> The policy underlying *Corwin,* to my mind, was never intended to serve as a massive eraser, exonerating corporate fiduciaries for any and all of their actions or inactions *preceding* (ed. emphasis added) their decision to undertake a transaction for which stockholder approval is obtained. Here, in voting on the Merger, the Massey stockholders were asked simply whether or not they wished to accept a specified amount of Alpha shares and cash in exchange for their Massey shares or, alternatively, to stay the course as stockholders of Massey as a standalone enterprise, which would have allowed plaintiffs to press derivative claims. Massey's stockholders were *not* asked in any direct or straightforward way to approve releasing defendants from any liability they may have to the Company for the years of alleged mismanagement that preceded the sale process. Indeed, the proxy statement for the Merger implied just the opposite in stating that control over the derivative claims likely would pass to Alpha as a result of the Merger. To top it off, if defendants' view of *Corwin* were correct, it would have the disconcerting and perverse effect of negating the value of the derivative claims that Alpha paid to acquire along with Massey's other assets.

> In short, in order to invoke the cleansing effect of a stockholder vote under *Corwin,* there logically must be a far more proximate relationship than exists here between the transaction or issue for which stockholder approval is sought and the nature of the claims to be "cleansed" as a result of a fully-informed vote.

Stockholder ratification will be limited strictly to the claims presented to stockholders. Absent a truly fully-informed vote, stockholders will not be deemed to have ratified director action and directors will not be absolved from wrongdoing.

In re Investors Bancorp, Inc. Stockholder Litigation 4.3.5.3

Because directors have a statutory right to set their own compensation (See DGCL §122(15) and §141(h)), director compensation plans are neither void nor voidable. However, the ability of boards to set their own compensation is not without limits. Director compensation is a quintessential "interested director" transaction. In these cases, directors are deciding the amounts and nature of their own compensation and naturally have at least implicit biases in favor of larger amounts. It is no surprise then that director decisions to set their own compensation are subject to entire fairness review upon a stockholder challenge.

In the case that follows, the Delaware Supreme Court addresses whether stockholder ratification in the form of fully-informed, disinterested stockholder approval of a compensation plan for non-employee directors affords the plan the protection of the business judgment presumption rather than the more exacting entire fairness standard. *Investors Bancorp* also provides a useful overview of the doctrinal development of stockholder ratification for non-employee director compensation.

Note that the discussion in *Investors Bancorp* relates to *director* compensation, not compensation of corporate *executives*. Decisions by the board of directors to compensate corporate executives, like the CEO and other C-level executives who are not simultaneously directors of the corporation, are typically treated like arms-length transactions and granted the protection of the business judgment presumption. Absent a successful attack under the waste standard, claims that the board violated their duty of loyalty to the corporation by approving *executive* compensation plans will typically fail.

IN RE INVESTORS BANCORP, INC. STOCKHOLDER LITIGATION
177 A.3d 1208

SEITZ, Justice.

In this appeal we consider the limits of the stockholder ratification defense when directors make equity awards to themselves under the general parameters of an equity incentive plan. In the absence of stockholder approval, if a stockholder properly challenges equity incentive plan awards the directors grant to themselves, the directors must prove that the awards are entirely fair to the corporation. But, when the stockholders have approved an equity incentive plan, the affirmative defense of stockholder ratification comes into play. Stated generally, stockholder ratification means a majority of fully informed, uncoerced, and disinterested stockholders approved board action, which, if challenged, typically leads to a deferential business judgment standard of review.

For equity incentive plans in which the award terms are fixed and the directors have no discretion how they allocate the awards, the stockholders know exactly what they are being asked to approve. But, other plans—like the equity incentive plan in this appeal—create a pool of equity awards that the directors can later award to themselves in amounts and on terms they decide. The Court of Chancery has recognized a ratification defense for such discretionary plans as long as the plan has "meaningful limits" on the awards directors can make to themselves.[1] If the discretionary plan does not contain meaningful limits, the awards, if challenged, are subject to an entire fairness standard of review.

Stockholder ratification serves an important purpose—directors can take self-interested action secure in the knowledge that the stockholders have expressed their approval. But, when directors make discretionary awards to themselves, that discretion must be exercised consistent with their fiduciary duties. Human nature being what it is,[2] self-interested discretionary acts by directors should in an appropriate case be subject to review by the Court of Chancery.

We balance the competing concerns—utility of the ratification defense and the need for judicial scrutiny of certain self-interested discretionary acts by directors—by focusing on the specificity of the acts submitted to the stockholders for approval. When the directors submit their specific compensation decisions for approval by fully informed, uncoerced, and disinterested stockholders, ratification is properly asserted as a defense in support of a motion to dismiss. The same applies for self-executing plans, meaning plans that make awards over time based on fixed criteria, with the specific amounts and terms approved by the stockholders. But, when stockholders have approved an equity incentive plan that gives the directors discretion to grant themselves awards within general parameters, and a stockholder properly alleges that the directors inequitably exercised that discretion, then the ratification defense is unavailable to dismiss the suit, and the directors will be required to prove the fairness of the awards to the corporation.

Here, the Equity Incentive Plan ("EIP") approved by the stockholders left it to the discretion of the directors to allocate up to 30% of all option or restricted stock shares available as awards to themselves. The plaintiffs have alleged facts leading to a pleading stage reasonable inference that the directors breached their fiduciary duties by awarding excessive equity awards to themselves under the EIP. Thus, a stockholder ratification defense is not available to dismiss the case, and the directors must demonstrate the fairness of the awards to the Company. We therefore reverse the Court of Chancery's decision dismissing the complaint and remand for further proceedings consistent with this opinion.

I.

According to the allegations of the complaint, which we must accept as true at this stage of the proceedings,[3] the plaintiffs are stockholders of Investors Bancorp, Inc. ("Investors Bancorp" or the "Company") and were stockholders at the time of the awards challenged in this case. The defendants fall into two groups—ten non-employee director defendants[4] and two executive director defendants.[5][...]

The board sets director compensation based on recommendations of the Compensation and Benefits Committee ("Committee"), composed of seven of the ten non-employee directors. In 2014, the non-employee directors were compensated by (i) a monthly cash retainer; (ii) cash awards for attending board and board committee meetings; and (iii) perquisites and personal benefits. [...]

Just a few months after setting the 2015 board compensation, in March, 2015, the board proposed the 2015 EIP. The EIP was intended to "provide additional incentives for [the Company's] officers, employees and directors to promote [the Company's] growth and performance and to further align their interests with those of [the Company's] stockholders . . . and give [the Company] the flexibility [needed] to continue to attract, motivate and retain highly qualified officers, employees and directors."[9]

The Company reserved 30,881,296 common shares for restricted stock awards, restricted stock units, incentive stock options, and non-qualified stock options for the Company's 1,800 officers, employees, non-employee directors, and service providers. The EIP has limits within each category. Of the total shares, a maximum of 17,646,455 can be issued for stock options or restricted stock awards and 13,234,841 for restricted stock units or performance shares. Those limits are further broken down for employee and non-employee directors:

• A maximum of 4,411,613 shares, in the aggregate (25% of the shares available for stock option awards), may be issued or delivered to any one employee pursuant to the exercise of stock options;

• A maximum of 3,308,710 shares, in the aggregate (25% of the shares available for restricted stock awards and restricted stock units), may be issued or delivered to any one employee as a restricted stock or restricted stock unit grant; and

• The maximum number of shares that may be issued or delivered to all non-employee directors, in the aggregate, pursuant to the exercise of stock options or grants of restricted stock or restricted stock units shall be 30% of all option or restricted stock shares available for awards, "all of which may be granted in any calendar year."[10]

According to the proxy sent to stockholders, "[t]he number, types and terms of awards to be made pursuant to the [EIP] are subject to the discretion of the Committee and have not been determined at this time, and will not be determined until subsequent to stockholder approval."[111] At the Company's June 9, 2015 annual meeting, 96.25% of the voting shares approved the EIP (79.1% of the total shares out-standing).[112] [...]

The board awarded themselves 7.8 million shares.[125] Non-employee directors each received 250,000 stock options—valued at $780,000—and 100,000 restricted shares—valued at $1,254,000; Cashill and Dittenhafer received 150,000 restricted shares—valued at $1,881,000—due to their years of service. The non-employee director awards totaled $21,594,000 and averaged $2,159,400. Peer companies' non-employee awards averaged $175,817. Cummings received 1,333,333 stock options and 1,000,000 restricted shares, valued at $16,699,999 and alleged to be 1,759% higher than the peer companies' average compensation for executive directors. Cama received 1,066,666 stock options and 600,000 restricted shares, valued at $13,359,998 and alleged 1216*1216 to be 2,571% higher than the peer companies' average. [...]

After the Company disclosed the awards, stockholders filed three separate complaints in the Court of Chancery alleging breaches of fiduciary duty by the directors for awarding themselves excessive compensation. Following the filing of a consolidated complaint, the defendants moved to dismiss under Court of Chancery Rule 12(b)(6) for failure to state a claim and under Court of Chancery Rule 23.1 for failure to make a demand before filing suit.

The Court of Chancery granted both motions and dismissed the plaintiffs' complaint.[127] Relying on the court's earlier decisions in In re 3COM Corp.[128] and Calma on Behalf of Citrix Systems, Inc. v. Templeton,[129] the court dismissed the complaint against the non-employee directors because the EIP contained "meaningful, specific limits on awards to all director beneficiaries" like the 3COM plan, as opposed to the broad-based plan in Citrix that contained a generic limit covering director and non-director beneficiaries.[130] The court also dismissed the claims directed to the executive directors because the plaintiffs failed to make a pre-suit demand on the board.

We review the Court of Chancery decision dismissing the complaint de novo.[31]

II.

Unless restricted by the certificate of incorporation or bylaws, Section 141(h) of Delaware General Corporation Law ("DGCL") authorizes the board "to fix the compensation of directors."[32] Although authorized to do so by statute, when the board fixes its compensation, it is self-interested in the decision because the directors are deciding how much they should reward themselves for board service.[33] If no other factors are involved, the board's decision will "lie outside the business judgment rule's presumptive protection, so that, where properly challenged, the receipt of self-determined benefits is subject to an affirmative showing that the compensation arrangements are fair to the corporation."[34] In other words, the entire fairness standard of review will apply.[35]

Other factors do sometimes come into play. When a fully informed, uncoerced, and disinterested majority of stockholders approve the board's authorized corporate action, the stockholders are said to have ratified the corporate act. Stockholder ratification of corporate acts applies in different corporate law settings.[36] Here, we address the affirmative defense of stockholder ratification of director self-compensation decisions.

A.

Early Supreme Court cases recognized a ratification defense by directors when reviewing their self-compensation decisions. In the 1952 decision Kerbs v. California Eastern Airways, Inc., a stockholder filed suit against the directors attacking a stock option and profit sharing plan on a number of grounds.[37] As to the stock option plan, 250,000 shares of the corporation's unissued stock were granted in specific amounts to named executives of the corporation at a $1 per share exercise price.[38] The profit sharing plan was based on a mathematical formula tied to the financial performance of the corporation.[39] Both plans were approved at a board meeting where five of the eight directors were beneficiaries of both plans.[140] The stockholders approved the plans.

Addressing the effect of stockholder approval of the stock option plan, our Court held that "ratification cures any voidable defect in the action of the [b]oard. Stockholder ratification of voidable acts of directors 1218*1218 is effective for all purposes unless the action of the directors constituted a gift of corporate assets to themselves or was ultra vires, illegal, or fraudulent."[141] As to the profit sharing plan, the Court viewed things differently because "the effectiveness of such ratification depends upon the type of notice sent to the stockholder and the explanation to them of the plan itself,"[142] and the record on appeal was insufficient to determine the adequacy of the disclosures.[143]

The stock option plan approved by the stockholders in Kerbs was self-executing, meaning once approved by the stockholders, implementing the awards required no discretion by the directors.[144] The Court addressed a similar dispute in a case decided the following day. In Gottlieb v. Heyden Chemical Corp.,[145] the restricted stock option plan granted specific company officers—six of whom were board members—present and future options to purchase fixed amounts of common stock at prices to be set by the board, subject to a price collar. The plan was contingent upon ratification by a majority of the stockholders.[146] In advance of the stockholder meeting, the board disclosed the names of the officers receiving the awards, the number of shares allocated to each, the price per share, and the schedule for future issuances.[147] The stockholders approved the plan.[148]

After initially denying the stockholder's challenge to the plan, on reargument, the Court noted the effect of stockholder ratification. For the current awards specifically approved by the stockholders:

> Where there is stockholder ratification,. . . the burden of proof is shifted to the objector. In such a case the objecting stockholder must convince the court that no person of ordinary sound business judgment would be expected to entertain the view that the consideration furnished by the individual directors is a fair exchange for the options conferred.[149]

But, for the options subject to future awards, the court explained that they were not ratified because the 25,500 shares had not been placed into any contracts prior to approval.[50] The stockholders only approved the allocation of shares "of a certain general pattern," but "nobody [knew] what all of the terms of these future contracts [would] be."[51] The Court concluded that ratification "cannot be taken to have approved specific bargains not yet proposed."[52] 1219*1219 Thus, after Kerbs and Gottlieb, directors could successfully assert the ratification defense when the stockholders were fully informed and approved stock option plans containing specific director awards. But the award of "specific bargains not yet proposed" could not be ratified by general stockholder approval of the compensation plan.[53]

Our Court has not considered ratification of director self-compensation decisions since Kerbs and Gottlieb. The Court of Chancery has, however, continued to develop this area of the law.

B.

Following the Supreme Court's lead recognizing the ratification defense only when specific acts are presented to the stockholders for approval, the Court of Chancery in Steiner v. Meyerson[54] and Lewis v. Vogelstein[55] recognized the directors' ratification defense when awards made to directors under equity compensation plans were specific as to amounts and value. In Steiner, the stock option plan granted each non-employee director "an option to purchase 25,000 shares upon election to the Telxon board, and an additional 10,000 shares on the anniversary of his election while he remains on the board."[56] In Lewis, the plan provided for two categories of director compensation: (i) one-time grants of 15,000 options per director; and (ii) annual grants of up to 10,000 options per director depending on length of board service.[57] The plans were self-executing, meaning that no further director action was required to implement the awards as they were earned. In both cases, the Court of Chancery held that the stockholders validly ratified the awards, and the standard of review following ratification was waste.[58]

Two Court of Chancery decisions following Steiner and Lewis addressed a twist in previous cases that bears directly on this appeal—the plans approved by the stockholders set upper limits on the amounts to be awarded, but allowed the directors to decide the specific awards or change the conditions of the awards after stockholder approval.[59] In In re 3COM Corp. Shareholders Litigation, the option grants were 1220*1220 based on "specific ceilings on the awarding of options each year" which "differ based on specific categories of service, such as service on a committee, position as a lead director, and chairing the [b]oard."[60] The plaintiff alleged in conclusory fashion that grants made by the board were "lavish and excessive compensation tantamount to a waste of corporate assets."[61] Because the board exercised its discretion within the specific limits approved by the stockholders, the Court of Chancery determined that the stockholder approval of the plan parameters extended to the specific awards made after plan approval.[62] Thus, the directors' post-approval compensation decisions were subject to the business judgment rule standard of review, requiring the directors to show waste.[63]

In Criden v. Steinberg, the Court of Chancery addressed a broad-based stock option plan that allowed the directors to re-price the options after stockholder approval of the plan.[64] The re-pricing decisions, although not submitted to the stockholders for approval, were subject to a business judgment standard of review.[65] According to the court, the stockholders approved a plan setting the re-pricing parameters, and the directors re-priced the options within those parameters.[66] Thus, the directors' decisions were reviewed under a business judgment rule standard of review.

After 3COM and Criden, the Court of Chancery decided Sample v. Morgan.[67] In Sample, the Court addressed two non-employee directors on the compensation committee who awarded 200,000 shares to the company's three employee directors under a management stock incentive plan.[68] A disinterested majority of Randall Bearings' stockholders had previously approved the plan, which authorized up to 200,000 shares, with no parameters on how the shares should be awarded. The court rejected a ratification defense and stated:

[T]he Delaware doctrine of ratification does not embrace a "blank check" theory. When uncoerced, fully informed, and disinterested stockholders approve a specific corporate action, the doctrine of ratification, in most situations, precludes claims for breach of fiduciary duty attacking that action. But the mere approval by stockholders of a request by directors for the authority to take action within broad parameters does not insulate all future action by the directors within those parameters from attack. Although the fact of stockholder approval might have some bearing on consideration of a fiduciary duty claim in that context, it does not, by itself, preclude such a claim. An essential aspect of our form of corporate law is the balance between law (in the form of statute and contract, including the contracts governing the internal affairs of corporations, such as charters and bylaws) and equity (in the form of concepts of fiduciary duty). Stockholders can entrust directors with broad legal authority precisely because they know that authority 1221*1221 must be exercised consistently with equitable principles of fiduciary duty. Therefore, the entrustment to the [compensation committee] of the authority to issue up to 200,000 shares to key employees under discretionary terms and conditions cannot reasonably be interpreted as a license for the [c]ommittee and other directors making proposals to it to do whatever they wished, unconstrained by equity. Rather, it is best understood as a decision by the stockholders to give the directors broad legal authority and to rely upon the policing of equity to ensure that authority would be utilized properly. For this reason alone, the directors' ratification argument fails.[69]

The court in Sample did not address either 3COM or Criden. But, in Seinfeld v. Slager,[70] the court addressed 3COM and a concern that recognizing ratification for plans approved by stockholders with only general parameters for making compensation awards provided insufficient protection from possible self-dealing. The plan in Seinfeld was a broad-based plan applying to directors, officers, and employees.[71] Unlike the plan in 3COM, where each category of beneficiaries had an upper limit on what they could receive, the

Seinfeld plan contained a single generic limit on awards, with no restrictions on how the awards could be distributed to the different classes of beneficiaries.[172] Rather than essentially approve a blank check, or in the Vice Chancellor's words—give the directors carte blanche—to make awards as the directors saw fit, the court required "some meaningful limit imposed by the stockholders on the [b]oard for the plan to be consecrated by 3COM and receive the blessing of the business judgment rule."[173] Thus, after Seinfeld, directors could retain the discretion to make awards after stockholder plan approval, but the plan had to contain meaningful limits on the awards the directors could make to themselves before ratification could be successfully asserted.

Finally, in Cambridge Retirement System v. Bosnjak, although the plan did not set forth the specific compensation awarded to the directors, the specific awards were submitted to the stockholders for approval.[174] Thus, the court found that the directors could assert a ratification defense.[175] And, in Calma on Behalf of Citrix Systems, Inc. v. Templeton, Chancellor Bouchard, after a thorough review of the case law, determined that directors could not assert a ratification defense when the incentive plan had generic limits on compensation for all the plan beneficiaries.[176] The court denied a ratification defense, holding "when the [b]oard sought stockholder approval of the broad parameters of the plan and the generic limits specified therein, Citrix stockholders were not asked to approve any action specific to 1222*1222 director compensation."[177]

III.

A.

As ratification has evolved for stockholder-approved equity incentive plans, the courts have recognized the defense in three situations—when stockholders approved the specific director awards; when the plan was self-executing, meaning the directors had no discretion when making the awards; or when directors exercised discretion and determined the amounts and terms of the awards after stockholder approval. The first two scenarios present no real problems. When stockholders know precisely what they are approving, ratification will generally apply. The rub comes, however, in the third scenario, when directors retain discretion to make awards under the general parameters of equity incentive plans. The defendants rely on 3COM and Criden, where the Court of Chancery recognized a stockholder ratification defense even though the directors' self-compensation awards were not submitted for stockholder approval.[78] As noted earlier, in 3COM, the Court of Chancery recognized ratification for director-specific compensation plans, where the plans contained specific limits for awards depending on factors set forth in the plan.[79] In Criden, the court upheld a ratification defense when the plan authorized the directors to re-price the options after stockholder approval.[80]

The court's decisions in 3COM and Criden opened the door to the difficulties raised in this appeal. After those decisions, the Court of Chancery had to square 3COM and Criden—and their expanded use of ratification for discretionary plans— with existing precedent, which only recognized ratification when stockholders approved the specific awards. The Court of Chancery tried to harmonize the decisions by requiring "meaningful limits" on the amounts directors could award to themselves.

We think, however, when it comes to the discretion directors exercise following stockholder approval of an equity incentive plan, ratification cannot be used to foreclose the Court of Chancery from reviewing those further discretionary actions when a breach of fiduciary duty claim has been properly alleged. As the Court of Chancery emphasized in Sample, using an expression coined many years ago, director action is "twice-tested," first for legal authorization, and second by equity.[81] When stockholders approve the general parameters of an equity compensation plan and 1223*1223 allow directors to exercise their "broad legal authority" under the plan, they do so "precisely because they know that authority must be exercised consistently with equitable principles of fiduciary duty."[82] The stockholders have granted the directors the legal authority to make awards. But, the directors' exercise of that authority must be done consistent with their fiduciary duties. Given that the actual awards are self-interested decisions not approved by the stockholders, if the directors acted inequitably when making the awards, their "inequitable action does not become permissible simply because it is legally possible"[183] under the general authority granted by the stockholders.

The Sample case underlines the need for continued equitable review of self-interested discretionary director self-compensation decisions. As noted before, the plaintiffs in Sample alleged that the board adopted "a self-dealing plan to entrench the Company under the then-current management and massively dilute the equity interests of the public holders to benefit management personally."[184] If ratification could be invoked at the outset, those breach of fiduciary duty allegations would be insulated from judicial review. Other cases reinforce the same point—when a stockholder properly alleges that the directors breached their fiduciary duties when exercising their discretion after stockholders approve the general parameters of an equity incentive plan, the directors should have to demonstrate that their self-interested actions were entirely fair to the company.[185]

B.

The Investors Bancorp EIP is a discretionary plan as described above. It covers about 1,800 officers, employees, non-employee directors, and service providers. Specific to the directors, the plan reserves 30,881,296 shares of common stock for restricted stock awards, restricted stock units, incentive stock options, and non-qualified stock options for the Company's officers, employees, non-employee directors, and service providers.[186] Of those reserved shares and other equity, the non-employee directors were entitled to up to 30% of all option and restricted stock shares, all of which could be granted in 1224*1224 any calendar year.[187] But, "[t]he number, types, and terms of the awards to be made pursuant to the [EIP] are subject to the discretion of the Committee and have not been determined at this time, and will not be determined until subsequent to stockholder approval."[188]

When submitted to the stockholders for approval, the stockholders were told that "[b]y approving the Plan, stockholders will give [the Company] the flexibility [it] need[s] to continue to attract, motivate and retain highly qualified officers, employees and directors by offering a competitive compensation program that is linked to the performance of [the Company's] common stock."[89] The complaint alleges that this representation was reasonably interpreted as forward-looking. In other words, by approving the EIP, stockholders understood that the directors would reward Company employees for future performance, not past services.

After stockholders approved the EIP, the board eventually approved just under half of the stock options available to the directors and nearly thirty percent of the shares available to the directors as restricted stock awards, based predominately on a five-year going forward vesting period. The plaintiffs argue that the directors breached their fiduciary duties by granting themselves these awards because they were unfair and excessive.[90] According to the plaintiffs, the stockholders were told the EIP would reward future performance, but the Board instead used the EIP awards to reward past efforts for the mutual-to-stock conversion—which the directors had already accounted for in determining their 2015 compensation packages.[91] Also, according to the plaintiffs, the rewards were inordinately higher than peer companies'. As alleged in the complaint, the Board paid each non-employee director more than $2,100,000 in 2015,[92] which "eclips[ed] director pay at every Wall Street firm."[93] This significantly exceeded the Company's non-employee director compensation in 2014, which ranged from $97,200 to $207,005.[94] It also far surpassed the $198,000 median pay at similarly sized companies and the $260,000 median pay at much larger companies.[95] And the awards were over twenty-three times more than the $87,556 median award granted to other companies' non-employee directors after mutual-to-stock conversions.[96]

In addition, according to the complaint, Cama and Cummings' compensation far exceeded their prior compensation and that of peer companies. Cummings' $20,006,957 total compensation in 2015 was 1225*1225 seven times more than his 2014 compensation package of $2,778,000.[97] And Cama's $15,318,257 compensation was nine times more than his 2014 compensation package of $1,665,794.[98] Cummings' $16,699,999 award was 3,683% higher than the median award other companies granted their CEOs after mutual-to-stock conversions. And Cama's $13,359,998 award was

5,384% higher than the median other companies granted their second-highest paid executives after the conversions.[99]

The plaintiffs have alleged facts leading to a pleading stage reasonable inference that the directors breached their fiduciary duties in making unfair and excessive discretionary awards to themselves after stockholder approval of the EIP. Because the stockholders did not ratify the specific awards the directors made under the EIP, the directors must demonstrate the fairness of the awards to the Company.

Duty of Good Faith 4.3.6

The ubiquity of exculpation provisions in charters as well as precedent like *Malpiede v. Townson* have made it extremely difficult – if not impossible – for shareholder plaintiffs to succeed on claims that simply allege violations of the duty of care. In response to foreclosing that litigation avenue, shareholder plaintiffs have brought other theories to court in attempts to generate monetary liability for otherwise disinterested directors when their decision-making process has fallen short of the mark. Duty of good faith claims are one such theory. In the good faith claims, plaintiffs argue that otherwise disinterested directors' inaction or decision-making was so poor such that it exceeds gross negligence – the standard of a duty of care claim – and rises to the level of a violation of the nonexculpable duty of good faith.

The object of these theories is to work around the limitations of exculpation provisions. To the extent they are successful, such theories might be able to generate monetary liability against disinterested directors. The Delaware Supreme Court took up these various theories of good faith in *In re Disney Stockholder Litigation* (2006). The court distilled the various theories of good faith put forward by plaintiffs as they attempted to generate monetary liability for directors. The court evaluated these various theories and provides us with guidance with respect to what makes up a valid good faith and what types of facts fall short.

In re Walt Disney Co. Derivative Litigation, 906 A. 2d 27 - Del: Supreme Court 2006

The precise question is whether the Chancellor's articulated standard for bad faith corporate fiduciary conduct — intentional dereliction of duty, a conscious disregard for one's responsibilities — is legally correct. In approaching that question, we note that the Chancellor characterized that definition as "an appropriate (although not the only) standard for determining whether fiduciaries have acted in good faith." That observation is accurate and helpful, because as a matter of simple logic, at least three different categories of fiduciary behavior are candidates for the "bad faith" pejorative label.

The first category involves so-called "subjective bad faith," that is, fiduciary conduct motivated by an actual intent to do harm. That such conduct constitutes classic, quintessential bad faith is a proposition so well accepted in the liturgy of fiduciary law that it borders on axiomatic. ...

The second category of conduct, which is at the opposite end of the spectrum, involves lack of due care — that is, fiduciary action taken solely by reason of gross negligence and without any malevolent intent. In this case, appellants assert claims of gross negligence to establish breaches not only of director due care but also of the directors' duty to act in good faith. Although the Chancellor found, and we agree, that the appellants failed to establish gross negligence, to afford guidance we address the issue of whether gross negligence (including a failure to inform one's self of available material facts), without more, can also constitute bad faith. The answer is clearly no. ...

That leaves the third category of fiduciary conduct, which falls in between the first two categories of (1) conduct motivated by subjective bad intent and (2) conduct resulting from gross negligence. This third category is what the Chancellor's definition of bad faith — intentional dereliction of duty, a conscious disregard for one's responsibilities — is intended to capture. The question is whether such misconduct is properly treated as a non-exculpable, non-indemnifiable violation of the fiduciary duty to act in good faith. In our view it must be, for at least two reasons.

First, the universe of fiduciary misconduct is not limited to either disloyalty in the classic sense (i.e., preferring the adverse self-interest of the fiduciary or of a related person to the interest of the corporation) or gross negligence. Cases have arisen where corporate directors have no conflicting self-interest in a decision, yet engage in misconduct that is more culpable than simple inattention or failure to be informed of all facts material to the decision. To protect the interests of the corporation and its shareholders, fiduciary conduct of this kind, which does not involve disloyalty (as traditionally defined) but is qualitatively more culpable than gross negligence, should be proscribed. A vehicle is needed to address such violations doctrinally, and that doctrinal vehicle is the duty to act in good faith. The Chancellor implicitly so recognized in his Opinion, where he identified different examples of bad faith as follows:

The good faith required of a corporate fiduciary includes not simply the duties of care and loyalty, in the narrow sense that I have discussed them above, but all actions required by a true faithfulness and devotion to the interests of the corporation and its shareholders. A failure to act in good faith may be shown, for instance, where the fiduciary intentionally acts with a purpose other than that of advancing the best interests of the corporation, where the fiduciary acts with the intent to violate applicable positive law, or where the fiduciary intentionally fails to act in the face of a known duty to act, demonstrating a conscious disregard for his duties. There may be other examples of bad faith yet to be proven or alleged, but these three are the most salient.

Those articulated examples of bad faith are not new to our jurisprudence. Indeed, they echo pronouncements our courts have made throughout the decades.

> *Second, the legislature has also recognized this intermediate
> category of fiduciary misconduct, which ranks between conduct
> involving subjective bad faith and gross negligence. Section
> 102(b)(7)(ii) of the DGCL expressly denies money damage
> exculpation for "acts or omissions not in good faith or which
> involve intentional misconduct or a knowing violation of law."
> By its very terms that provision distinguishes between
> "intentional misconduct" and a "knowing violation of law" (both
> examples of subjective bad faith) on the one hand, and "acts ...
> not in good faith," on the other. Because the statute exculpates
> directors only for conduct amounting to gross negligence, the
> statutory denial of exculpation for "acts ... not in good faith"
> must encompass the intermediate category of misconduct
> captured by the Chancellor's definition of bad faith.*

Following *Disney* there were three viable avenues for successful
good faith claims against disinterested directors: 1) where a director
intentionally acts with a purpose other than that of advancing the
best interests of the corporation; 2) where the fiduciary acts with the
intent to violate applicable positive law; and 3) where the fiduciary
intentionally fails to act in the face of a known duty to act,
demonstrating a conscious disregard for his duties. Of these, the
third, so-called oversight claims, have been the most hotly litigated.

Oversight Claims   4.3.6.1

Of the categories of good faith claims identified by
the Delaware Supreme Court in Disney, oversight
claims have received the most attention in recent
years, especially in the wake of the global financial
crisis of 2008. In *Caremark*, plaintiff stockholders argued that the
board violated its duty of good faith by failing in its obligation to
provide reasonable oversight of the corporation's activities, leading
to avoidable losses. In approving a settlement of the litigation, the
Chancery Court in *Caremark* formulated the following standard for
assessing the liability of directors where the directors are unaware of

employee misconduct that results in the corporation being held liable (i.e. oversight claims):

> Generally where a claim of directorial liability for corporate loss is predicated upon ignorance of liability creating activities within the corporation . . . only a sustained or systematic failure of the board to exercise oversight—such as an utter failure to attempt to assure a reasonable information and reporting system exists—will establish the lack of good faith that is a necessary condition to liability.
> - In re Caremark Inter'l S'holder Litigation, 698 A.2d 959 (1996).

Caremark articulates two categories of potentially successful oversight claims: first, where the directors utterly failed to implement any reporting or information system or controls thus blinding themselves to knowledge about the corporation's activities; or second, having implemented a system or controls, where the board consciously failed to monitor or oversee its operations thus disabling themselves from being informed of risks or problems requiring their attention.

Although *Caremark* oversight claims are extremely difficult to prevail, a recent line of cases suggests courts are open to entertaining arguments at least for purposes of demand futility under *Zuckerberg (Rales)* where the board of a corporation in a highly regulated industry fails to actively engage with business critical regulatory authorities.

IN RE CLOVIS ONCOLOGY, INC. DERIVATIVE LITIGATION.

SLIGHTS, Vice Chancellor.

Like many upstart biopharmaceutical companies, nominal defendant, Clovis Oncology, Inc. (or the "Company"), had one drug among its drugs under development, Rociletinib (or "Roci"), that was especially promising. Roci, a therapy for the treatment of lung cancer, performed well during the early stages of its clinical trial. But data from later stages of the trial revealed the drug likely would not be approved for market by the Food and Drug Administration ("FDA"). Plaintiffs, Clovis stockholders, allege members of the Clovis board of directors (the "Board") breached their fiduciary duties by failing to oversee the Roci clinical trial and then allowing the Company to mislead the market regarding the drug's efficacy.[1] These breaches, it is alleged, caused Roci to sustain corporate trauma in the form of a sudden and significant depression in market capitalization. Plaintiffs also allege that certain members of the Board and a member of senior management engaged in unlawful stock trades before the market was apprised of Roci's failure.[2]

Defendants have moved to dismiss each of Plaintiffs' derivative claims under Court of Chancery Rules 23.1 and 12(b)(6) for failure to plead demand futility with particularity and failure to state viable claims. As explained below, Plaintiffs have well-pled that Defendants face a substantial likelihood of liability under Caremark and our Supreme Court's recent explication of Caremark in Marchand v. Barnhill.[3] Clovis conducted its clinical trial of Roci subject to strict protocols and associated FDA regulations. Yet, assuming the pled facts are true, the Board ignored red flags that Clovis was not adhering to the clinical trial protocols, thereby placing FDA approval of the drug in jeopardy. With the trial's skewed results in hand, the Board then allowed the Company to deceive regulators and the market regarding the drug's efficacy.

As explained in Marchand, "to satisfy their duty of loyalty, directors must make a good faith effort to implement an oversight system and then monitor it."[4] This is especially so when a monoline company operates in a highly regulated industry.[5] Here, Plaintiffs have well-pled Roci was "intrinsically critical to the [C]ompany's business operation," yet the Board ignored multiple warning signs that management was inaccurately reporting Roci's efficacy before seeking confirmatory scans to corroborate Roci's cancer-fighting potency—violating both internal clinical trial protocols and associated FDA regulations.[6] In other words, Plaintiffs have well-pled a Caremark claim. [...]

I. FACTUAL BACKGROUND

A. Parties and Relevant Non-Parties

Nominal Defendant, Clovis, is a biopharmaceutical firm focused on acquiring, developing and commercializing cancer treatments.[12] During the Relevant Period,[13] Clovis had no drugs on the market but did have three drugs in development. Of these, Roci was the most promising.[14]

Plaintiffs bring this derivative action against all nine members of the Board (collectively, the "Board Defendants"), each of whom was a member of the Board during the Relevant Period.[15] Defendant, Erle Mast, is Clovis' former Executive Vice President and Chief Financial Officer ("CFO").[16] Defendants collectively owned upwards of 17.4% of the Company's stock.[17]

The Board has two relevant sub-committees. The Nominating and Corporate Governance Committee is charged with developing and overseeing the effectiveness of Clovis' legal, ethics and regulatory compliance matters.[18] The Audit Committee oversees typical audit functions and, importantly, reviews earnings reports with management before release to the market.[19]

Defendant, Brian G. Atwood, has served on the Board since Clovis' inception in 2009.[20] He served as a member of the Audit Committee and the Nominating and Corporate Governance Committee for fiscal years 2013-2015.[21] Atwood had previous experience as co-founder of a biotechnology company and as a managing director for a healthcare-focused venture capital firm.[22]

Defendant, M. James Barrett, Ph.D., has served on the Board since Clovis' inception.[23] He serves as Chairman of the Board and as Chairman of the Nominating and Corporate Governance Committee.[24] Additionally, Barrett has held positions as a general partner in a healthcare venture capital firm and as the chairman, CEO and founder of a medical technology company.[25]

Defendant, James Blair, Ph.D., has served on the Board since Clovis' inception.[26] He is a member of the Nominating and Corporate Governance Committee and serves as Chairman of the Compensation Committee.[27] Blair has over thirty years of experience as a general partner in a life sciences venture capital management company.[28] Some of his other experience includes serving on the boards of over 40 life science companies as well as the advisory board of the Department of Molecular Biology at Princeton University.[29]

Defendant, Keith Flaherty, M.D., has served on the Board since 2013.[30] He is a member of the Nominating and Corporate Governance Committee.[31] Additionally, Flaherty is an Associate Professor of Medicine at Harvard Medical School and has been a principal investigator for numerous first-in-human clinical trials with novel, targeted therapies.[32]

Defendant, Ginger Graham, has served on the Board since 2013.[33] She is a member of the Compensation Committee.[34] Graham has previous experience as the president and CEO of a biopharmaceutical company and has served on the boards of multiple healthcare firms.[35]

Defendant, Paul Klingenstein, has served on the Board since Clovis' inception.[36] He is a member of the Audit Committee.[37] Klingenstein has additional experience as a managing partner of a healthcare venture capital firm, which he formed in

1999.[38] And he has served on the boards of multiple pharmaceutical companies.[39]

Defendant, Patrick J. Mahaffy, is one of Clovis' co-founders and has been Clovis' CEO, President and a member of the Board since Clovis' inception.[40] Mahaffy previously served as the president and CEO of two biopharmaceutical companies—one of which he also founded.[41]

Defendant, Edward J. McKinley, has served on the Board since Clovis' inception.[42] He is a member of the Audit Committee.[43]

Defendant, Thorlef Spickschen, has served on the Board since Clovis' inception.[44] He is a member of the Compensation Committee.[45] Before joining Clovis, he served as the chairman of a publicly-traded biotechnology company, as well as Eli Lilly & Co.'s managing director for Germany and Central Europe.[46]

Defendant, Erle T. Mast, is a Clovis co-founder and served as Executive Vice President and CFO from the Company's inception in 2009 until his resignation in March 2016.[47] Mast was not a member of the Board during the Relevant Period.[48]

Non-party, Dr. Andrew Allen, served as Clovis' Chief Medical Officer ("CMO") during the Relevant Period.[49] Non-party, AstraZeneca PLC, is a pharmaceutical company based in the United Kingdom. AstraZeneca manufactures Tagrisso (described below), which would have directly competed with Roci had Roci made it to market.[50]

B. Clovis Initiates Roci's Clinical Trial

At the beginning of the Relevant Period, Clovis had no products on the market and generated no sales revenue.[51] Accordingly, Clovis "reli[ed] solely on investor capital for all [] operations."[52] The Company's prospects rested largely on one of its three developmental drugs, Roci, a cancer drug designed to treat a previously-untreatable type of lung cancer.[53] Because of the estimated $3 billion annual market for drugs of its type, Clovis expected Roci to generate large profits if Clovis could secure FDA approval for the drug and shepherd it to market.[54]

As the Roci clinical trial began, the Board knew time was of the essence. AstraZeneca's competing drug, Tagrisso, was also in the race for FDA approval.[55] Appreciating Roci's importance to Clovis' success, the Board was hyper-focused on the drug's development and clinical trial.[56] Indeed, it is alleged the Board Defendants "spent hours at Board meetings discussing [Roci]" and were "regularly apprised" of the drug's progress.[57]

To obtain FDA approval, new drugs like Roci and Tagrisso must prove their efficacy and safety in clinical trials.[58] Before commencing a clinical trial, the FDA requires a drug's sponsor to agree to certain standards that define how the trial will be conducted, how the trial data will be analyzed and, most relevant here, how success in the trial will be measured.[59] These agreed-upon standards become the "clinical trial protocol."[60] If the drug's sponsor fails to adhere to the clinical trial protocol, the FDA will not approve a new drug for market.[61]

Clovis named its Roci clinical trial "TIGER-X."[62] TIGER-X incorporated a standardized and well-known clinical trial protocol called "RECIST."[63] Clovis chose RECIST instead of a lesser-known or bespoke clinical trial protocol because RECIST "has become the most widely used system for assessing response in cancer clinical trials, and is the preferred and accepted system for use in new drug applications to regulatory agencies."[64] By selecting RECIST, Clovis was able to "give investors confidence in the Company's reported results" by facilitating "comparisons between [Roci] and competing therapies."[65]

One of RECIST's important functions is to establish the "criteria defining success" for the clinical trial.[66] This success-defining metric is called the objective response rate (or "ORR").[67] ORR measures the percentage of patients who experience meaningful tumor shrinkage when treated with the drug.[68] This metric is important both to the FDA in its approval process and to physicians in deciding whether to prescribe the drug.[69] Not surprisingly, then, the "[Board] was laser-focused on [Roci's] ORR."[70]

As Roci's clinical trial progressed, the Board knew investors would not view an ORR incorporating unconfirmed responses as "meaningful," nor would the FDA accept such results as "approvable."[71] Indeed, each of the Board Defendants appreciated the FDA "could only make its decision . . . to approve Roci based [] on confirmed responses."[72]

C. TIGER-X Trial's Undisclosed Failure to Follow RECIST Standards

Ostensibly intending to follow RECIST, the TIGER-X protocol specifically required and set out a schedule for confirmation scans.[73] And throughout the Relevant Period, Clovis' press releases, investor calls, Securities and Exchange Commission ("SEC") filings and statements to medical journals reinforced the belief that Clovis was reporting a confirmed ORR of about 60% "per RECIST."[74] Mindful of the race to market, Clovis' management consistently represented that Roci's ORR was at least as encouraging as Tagrisso's.[75]

Despite these public signals, as early as June 12, 2014, the Board received reports indicating Clovis was improperly calculating Roci's ORR.[76] Specifically, these reports suggested that, while the clinical trial protocol required Clovis to calculate ORR based only on confirmed responses, Clovis was actually calculating ORR, in part, based on unconfirmed responses.[77] For example, on June 12, 2014, the Board reviewed management's presentations from a May 31, 2014 medical conference (the "ASCO conference").[78] That data indicated Roci's ORR was "58 percent" (the "ASCO ORR").[79] At the same meeting, management told the Board the ASCO ORR would improve "as patients get to their second and third scans."[80] By definition, then, the ASCO ORR was partially based on unconfirmed results (i.e., it was not RECIST compliant).[81] Notwithstanding this revelation, the Board did nothing.

Mahaffy continued publicly to report Roci's ORR at 58% in investor calls,[82] and on August 7, 2014, Clovis issued a press release restating this inflated number.[83] Soon after, the Board viewed another report signaling that Clovis' management was calculating Roci's ORR with unconfirmed responses and that only "80% of unconfirmed [responses] convert to confirmed."[84]

On September 9, 2014, Clovis closed a critical $287 million private placement of convertible senior notes in order to finance ongoing operations.[85] The Board relied heavily upon the market's positive reaction to Roci's publicly reported ORR to make its case for further investment in the Company.[86]

As the Company was touting Roci's prospects, management gave a presentation to the Board explicitly comparing Roci's 63% mixed ORR to Tagrisso's confirmed 70%.[87] Another Board presentation from the same time period showed that management was reporting Roci's ORR using partially unconfirmed responses by noting that Roci's ORR was "*Unconfirmed."[88]

As TIGER-X progressed, Clovis' public statements regarding Roci remained upbeat. Roci was Clovis' champion and it was prepared to do battle with Tagrisso. On September 9, 2014, Mahaffy told a securities analyst that Roci and Tagrisso had "similar response rate[s]," and on November 18, 2014, Clovis issued a press release stating that Roci's ORR was 67%.[89]

The Board, however, continued to receive signals that management was not vigilantly following RECIST. On December 3, 2014, the Board reviewed a report stating, "in mid-March, we will have a response rate of less than 60% (could be less than 50%)."[90] The same report revealed the Company was waiting on "data maturity" and that at least some patients had not received a second scan at that time, indicating continued non-compliance with RECIST.[91]

With hands on their ears to muffle the alarms, on February 27, 2015, Defendants Mahaffy, Mast, Atwood, Barrett, Blair, Flaherty, Graham, Klingenstein, McKinley and Spickschen signed Clovis' 2014 Annual Report.[92] The report reaffirmed previous, inflated ORR reports and omitted that Clovis was relying on partially unconfirmed responses.[...]

Clovis officials met with the FDA regarding Roci's critical New Drug Application ("NDA").[98] The NDA filing necessarily included the

Company's disclosure of TIGER-X data for final FDA approval.[99] At the meeting, management reported an ORR of 50% without informing the FDA that this ORR included unconfirmed responses.[100] Notwithstanding its report to the FDA, management continued to report a 60% ORR in public statements.[101]

On June 19, 2015, Mahaffy, Mast and other members of senior management received "close to final" data from the TIGER-X trial.[102] The data showed an ORR of 45.1% for the 500mg dose (significantly lower than the 60% ORR the Company had been disclosing to the market).[103] Mahaffy wrote to another Clovis executive that the data "[s]eems worrying."[104] Three days later, on June 22, CMO Allen resigned without warning.[105] On July 7, Clovis' management received the "final" TIGER-X data showing that Roci's ORR was only 42%. [...]

The FDA requested additional data in support of the NDA in October 2015.[110] In response, Clovis disclosed that Roci's current confirmed ORR was between 28% and 34%.[111] At the same time, management presented a slide to the Board to illustrate how Roci was stacking up against Tagrisso.[112] The slide clearly showed an ORR of 46% that was "(Unconf + Conf)" while Tagrisso's ORR was "Confirmed."[113] Management advised the Board in connection with the NDA that "[w]e will cite the unconfirmed investigator assessed response rate of ~46%."[114] The public continued to hear a different story, however. For instance, a November 5, 2015 press release and earnings call announced third quarter results and cited presentations from medical conferences claiming Roci's ORR was 60%.[115]

D. The Fallout

The conflicting reports regarding Roci's ORR eventually prompted the FDA to ask questions and to call for a meeting with Clovis executives on November 9, 2015.[116] During the meeting, the FDA emphasized it would credit only confirmed responses on the NDA[117] and insisted Clovis comply with TIGER-X's stated protocol (which had explicitly incorporated RECIST).[118] Mahaffy updated the Board on this most recent FDA meeting the following week.[119]

The public was finally informed of Roci's true ORR when, on November 16, 2015, Clovis issued a press release stating the correct confirmed ORR was as low as 28-34%.[120] Clovis' stock price immediately dropped 70%, wiping out more than $1 billion in market capitalization.[121]

On April 8, 2016, the FDA voted to delay action on Clovis' NDA until the Company could provide concrete evidence of a risk/benefit profile meriting approval.[122] On this news, Clovis' stock price fell another 17%.[123] On May 5, 2016, Clovis withdrew its NDA for Roci and terminated enrollment in all ongoing Roci studies.[124]

G. Procedural Posture

On May 31, 2016 and December 15, 2016, Plaintiffs served the Company with demands to inspect books and records under 8 Del. C. § 220 in response to which they received approximately 3,000 pages of documents.[153] Plaintiffs filed their first complaint on March 23, 2017.[154] They amended the complaint on May 18, 2017.[155] Defendants moved to dismiss the first amended complaint under Court of Chancery Rules 23.1 and 12(b)(6) on August 1, 2017.[156] [...]

II. ANALYSIS

As for Count I, Plaintiffs have pled particularized facts that "create a reasonable doubt that, as of the time the complaint [was] filed, the board of directors could have properly exercised its independent and disinterested business judgment in responding to a demand."[165] Specifically, Plaintiffs have well-pled that the Board ignored red flags that the Company was violating—perhaps consciously violating— the RECIST protocol and then misleading the market and regulators regarding Roci's progress through the TIGER-X trial. Because Plaintiffs have pled particularized facts to support a reasonable inference the Board Defendants face a substantial likelihood of liability on Count I, Defendants' motion to dismiss Count I under Rule 23.1 must be denied. Having so concluded, a fortiori, I deny the Motion to Dismiss under Rule 12(b)(6) as well.[166] [...]

A. The Applicable Rule 23.1 Standard

There is no dispute that each of the Complaint's three counts purports to state a derivative claim.[167] As Justice Moore emphasized in his seminal Aronson decision, 8 Del. C. § 141(a) codifies a bedrock of Delaware corporate law—the board of directors, not stockholders, manages the business and affairs of the corporation, including the decision to cause the corporation to sue.[168] With this in mind, our law has established procedural imperatives to ensure that shareholders do not "imping[e] on the managerial freedom of directors."[169] To wrest control over the litigation asset away from the board of directors, the stockholder must demonstrate that demand on the board to pursue the claim would be futile such that the demand requirement should be excused.[170]

Plaintiffs acknowledge they did not make a pre-suit demand on the Board.[171] It is settled, therefore, that their Complaint must "comply with stringent requirements of factual particularity that differ substantially from the permissive notice pleadings" of Chancery Rule 8 in order to demonstrate that demand upon the Board would have been futile.[172] Where, as here, a plaintiff challenges board inaction—as opposed to a business decision of the Board—the court analyzes demand futility under the well-known and "well-balanced" Rales standard.[173] This standard requires plaintiffs to plead facts regarding demand futility with particularity but balances that requirement with a mandate that the court draw all reasonable inferences in the plaintiffs' favor.[174]

Demand futility turns on "whether the board that would be addressing the demand can impartially consider [the demand's] merits without being influenced by improper considerations."[175] Such improper influence arises if a majority of the board's members (i) are "compromised" because they face "a `substantial likelihood' of personal liability" with respect to at least one of the alleged claims or (ii) lack independence because they are beholden to an interested person.[176]

441

B. Plaintiffs Have Well-Pled the Board Faces a Substantial Likelihood of Liability Under Caremark (Count I)

The parties agree that Count I implicates Caremark, Stone v. Ritter and their progeny.[1177] These cases require well-pled allegations of bad faith to survive dismissal—i.e., allegations "the directors knew that they were not discharging their fiduciary obligations," a standard of wrongdoing "qualitatively different from, and more culpable than . . . gross negligence."[1178] Given this high bar, it is now indubitably understood, and oft-repeated, that a Caremark claim is among the hardest to plead and prove.[1179] At the pleadings stage, this means Plaintiffs must allege particularized facts that either (i) "the directors completely fail[ed] to implement any reporting or information system or controls, or . . . [(ii)] having implemented such a system or controls, consciously fail[ed] to monitor or oversee its operations thus disabling themselves from being informed of risks or problems requiring their attention."[1180] Implicit in these standards is the requirement that plaintiffs plead particular facts allowing a reasonable inference the directors acted with scienter, which "requires proof that a director acted inconsistent with his fiduciary duties and, most importantly, that the director knew he was so acting."[1181]

Caremark rests on the presumption that corporate fiduciaries are afforded "great discretion to design context- and industry-specific approaches tailored to their companies' businesses and resources."[1182] Indeed, "[b]usiness decision-makers must operate in the real world, with imperfect information, limited resources, and uncertain future. To impose liability on directors for making a `wrong' business decision would cripple their ability to earn returns for investors by taking business risks."[1183] But, as fiduciaries, corporate managers must be informed of, and oversee compliance with, the regulatory environments in which their businesses operate. In this regard, as relates to Caremark liability, it is appropriate to distinguish the board's oversight of the company's management of business risk that is inherent in its business plan from the board's oversight of the company's compliance with positive law—including regulatory mandates. As this Court recently noted, "[t]he legal academy has observed that Delaware courts are more inclined to find Caremark oversight liability at the board level when the company operates in the midst of obligations imposed upon it by positive law yet fails to implement compliance systems, or fails to monitor existing compliance systems, such that a violation of law, and resulting liability, occurs."[184]

Our Supreme Court's recent decision in Marchand v. Barnhill underscores the importance of the board's oversight function when the company is operating in the midst of "mission critical" regulatory compliance risk.[185] The regulatory compliance risk at issue in Marchand was food safety and the failure to manage it at the board level allegedly allowed Blue Bell Creameries to distribute mass quantities of ice cream tainted by listeria.[186] The Court held that Blue Bell's board had not made a "good faith effort to put in place a reasonable system of monitoring and reporting" when it left compliance with food safety mandates to management's discretion rather than implementing and then overseeing a more structured compliance system.[187]

As Marchand makes clear, when a company operates in an environment where externally imposed regulations govern its "mission critical" operations, the board's oversight function must be more rigorously exercised.[188] Key to the Supreme Court's analysis was the fact that food safety was the "most central safety and legal compliance issue facing the company."[189] To be sure, even in this context, Caremark does not demand omniscience. But it does demand a "good faith effort to implement an oversight system and then monitor it."[190] This entails a sensitivity to "compliance issue[s] intrinsically critical to the company[]."[191]

1. Caremark's First Prong

The so-called first prong of Caremark requires Plaintiffs to well-plead that the Board "completely fail[ed] to implement any reporting or information system or controls[.]"[192] But Plaintiffs acknowledge the Board's Nominating and Corporate Governance Committee was "specifically charged" with "provid[ing] general compliance oversight . . . with respect to . . . Federal health care program requirements and FDA requirements."[193] And they further acknowledge "[t]he Board . . . reviewed detailed information regarding [Roci's] TIGER-X trial at each Board meeting."[194] Given these acknowledged facts, it is difficult to conceive how Plaintiffs would prove the Board had no "reporting or information system or controls[.]"[195]

2. Caremark's Second Prong

Caremark's second prong is implicated when it is alleged the company implemented an oversight system but the board failed to "monitor it."[196] To state a claim under this prong, Plaintiffs must well-plead that a "red flag" of non-compliance waived before the Board Defendants but they chose to ignore it.[197] In this regard, the court must remain mindful that "red flags are only useful when they are either waived in one's face or displayed so that they are visible to the careful observer."[198] But, as Marchand makes clear, the careful observer is one whose gaze is fixed on the company's mission critical regulatory issues.[199] For Clovis, this was Roci's TIGER-X trial and the clinical trial protocols and related FDA regulations governing that study.

Plaintiffs have alleged particularized facts supporting reasonable inferences that: (i) the Board knew the TIGER-X protocol incorporated RECIST;[200] (ii) RECIST requires reporting only confirmed responses;[201] (iii) industry practice and FDA guidance require that the study managers report only confirmed responses;[202] (iv) management was publicly reporting unconfirmed responses to keep up with Tagrisso's response rate;[203] and (v) the Board knew management was incorrectly reporting responses but did nothing to address this fundamental departure from the RECIST protocol.[204] When Clovis' serial non-compliance with RECIST was finally revealed to the regulators, Roci was doomed.[205] And when the drug's failure was revealed to the market, Clovis' stock price tumbled.[206]

ORR was the crucible in which Roci's safety and efficacy were to be tested.[207] Roci was Clovis' mission critical product.[208] And the Board knew, upon completion of the TIGER-X trial, the FDA would consider only confirmed responses when determining whether to approve Roci's NDA per the agency's own regulations.[209] As pled, these regulations, and the reporting requirements of the RECIST protocol, were not nuanced.[210] The Board was comprised of experts and the RECIST criteria are well-known in the pharmaceutical industry.[211] Moreover, given the degree to which Clovis relied upon ORR when raising capital, it is reasonable to infer the Board would have understood the concept and would have appreciated the distinction between confirmed and unconfirmed responses.[212] The inference of Board knowledge is further enhanced by the fact the Board knew that even after FDA approval, physicians (i.e., future prescribers) would evaluate Roci based on its ORR.[213]

Defendants argue the FDA blessed Clovis' plan to report unconfirmed responses for "interim" results because Roci was on an accelerated approval track.[214] Additionally, Defendants claim FDA guidance was not as clear as the Complaint depicts.[215] But, again, that is not what the Complaint alleges.[216] Whether Plaintiffs' allegations hold up during discovery, at summary judgment or at trial remains to be seen.

Drawing all reasonable inferences in Plaintiffs' favor, I am satisfied they have well-pled that the Board consciously ignored red flags that revealed a mission critical failure to comply with the RECIST protocol and associated FDA regulations. Additionally, at this stage, Plaintiffs' allegation that this failure of oversight caused monetary and reputational harm to the Company is sufficient to provide a causal nexus between the breach of fiduciary duty and the corporate trauma.[217] Therefore, Defendants' motion to dismiss Count I (Plaintiffs' Caremark claim) under Rules 23.1 and 12(b)(6) must be denied.

Violations of the law and the duty of loyalty   4.3.7

Sometimes in the popular press or in the media
(movies, television, etc) you will see discussions
about how directors of the corporation might have a fiduciary

obligation to pursue corporate profits even if to do so requires the corporation to adopt a policy of violating the law. Nothing can be further from the truth. Delaware courts, as well as other state courts, have repeatedly and unequivocally ruled that directors who adopt corporate policies to violate the law are not acting in the best interests of the corporation and are therefore disloyal directors.

Given that certificates of incorporation limit the purpose of the corporation for "any lawful purpose for which a corporation may be organized." If a corporate board pursues as a corporate policy activities which are illegal or contrary to a positive law, then such acts are also *ultra vires*, or outside the scope of permitted activities for corporate activity.

In addition, directors are not exculpated from financial liability under §102(b)(7) for "acts or omissions not in good faith or which involve intentional misconduct or a knowing violation of the law." Consequently, a director who intentionally causes the firm to violate the law has violated their duty of good faith (i.e. loyalty) to the corporation and may be subject to financial liability.

TW Services v SWT Acquisition Corp

Chancellor Allen described the duty of loyalty as requiring directors to endeavor to "manage the corporation within the law, with due care and in a way intended to maximize the long run interests of shareholders."

TW Servs., Inc. v. SWT Acquisition Corp., C.A. Nos. 10427, 10298, 1989 WL 20290, at *7 (Del. Ch. Mar. 2, 1989)

Metro Commc'n Corp. BVI v. Advanced Mobilecomm Techs. Inc.

Holding that if directors engaged in unlawful bribery for the purpose of helping the corporation obtain governmental permits, they had violated their "duty of loyalty" and further stating that "[u]nder Delaware law, a fiduciary may not choose to manage an entity in an illegal fashion, even if the fiduciary believes that the illegal activity will result in profits for the entity."

Metro Commc'n Corp. BVI v. Advanced Mobilecomm Techs. Inc., 854 A.2d 121, 131, 163–64 (Del. Ch. 2004)

Guttman v. Huang

"[O]ne cannot act loyally as a corporate director by causing the corporation to violate the positive laws it is obliged to obey."

Guttman v. Huang, 823 A.2d 492, 506 (Del. Ch. 2003)

Miller v. Am. Tel. & Tel. Co.

"[D]irectors must be restrained from engaging in activities which are against public policy."

Miller v. Am. Tel. & Tel. Co., 507 F.2d 759, 762 (3d Cir. 1974)

Roth v. Robertson

"Where the directors and officers of a corporation engage in ultra vires transactions [illegal acts], and they cause loss to the corporation, they must be held jointly and severally liable for such damages."

Roth v. Robertson, 118 N.Y.S. 351, 353 (N.Y. Gen. Term 1909)

Desimone

"Directors "have no authority knowingly to cause the corporation to become a rogue, exposing the corporation to penalties from criminal and civil regulators."

Desimone, 924 A.2d at 934.

In addition to a fiduciary duty claim against the directors for knowingly causing the corporation to violate a positive law, upon an application by the state Department of Justice, Delaware courts can, and do, revoke the corporate charters of firms that have been involved in corporate criminal activity. For example, Backpage.com, LLC ran a notorious website that facilitated sex trafficking. In its November 2018 application for revocation, the Delaware Attorney General restated the Delaware corporate law's view on law breaking activities of corporations:

> Delaware law has never permitted or condoned the use of business entities formed under its laws for unlawful or nefarious purposes, and thus Defendants' guilty pleas are proof that Defendants, and their principals, have abused and misused not only Defendants' powers and privileges, but their very existences, in perhaps the most reprehensible manner possible. Having abandoned the responsibilities that come with status as Delaware limited liability companies, Defendants must be forever denied the rights and privileges that also come with that status, and their certificates of formation must therefore be canceled.

Denn v. Backpage.com (Nov. 2018)

Duty of Candor

The final fiduciary duty is the duty of candor or the duty of disclosure. Like good faith, the duty of candor is not an independent fiduciary duty, but rather - depending on the circumstances - a subsidiary element of the duty of loyalty or care. The duty of candor implicates a series of legal obligations under both state corporate law and Federal securities laws. The *Wayport* case that follows summarizes how the duty of candor is implicated depending on the circumstance.

4.3.8

In Re Wayport Inc. Litigation   4.3.8.1

Four varieties of "candor".

IN RE WAYPORT INC LITIGATION
Consol. C.A. No. 4167-VCL

LASTER, Vice Chancellor.

The plaintiffs sued for damages arising out of their sales of stock in
Wayport, Inc. ("Wayport" or the "Company"). Vice Chancellor
Lamb granted the defendants' motion to dismiss in part, and his
rulings represent law of the case. *See Latesco, L.P. v. Wayport, Inc.,*
2009 WL 2246793 (Del. Ch. July 24, 2009) (the "Dismissal
Opinion"). The litigation proceeded to trial against the remaining
defendants on claims for breach of fiduciary duty, aiding and
abetting a breach of fiduciary duty, common law fraud, and
equitable fraud. Judgment is entered in favor of plaintiff Brett
Stewart and against defendant Trellis Partners Opportunity Fund,
L.P. ("Trellis Opportunity Fund") in the amount of $470,000,
subject to an adjustment to be calculated by the parties in
accordance with this opinion, plus pre- and post-judgment interest at
the legal rate, compounded quarterly. Judgment otherwise is
entered against the plaintiffs and in favor of the defendants. [...]

N. The Plaintiffs Sue.

On November 17, 2008, Stewart filed this litigation. As amended,
his complaint contained seven counts:

- Count I—Breach of the fiduciary duty of disclosure;

- Count II—Breach of the fiduciary duty of loyalty;

- Count III—Common law fraud;

- Count IV—Civil conspiracy;

- Count V—Aiding and abetting a breach of fiduciary duty;

- Count VI—Unjust enrichment;

- Count VII—Breach of the implied covenant of good faith and fair dealing.

In the Dismissal Opinion, Vice Chancellor Lamb dismissed all claims with respect to any stock sales that took place before 2007. He also dismissed Counts I, IV, VI, and VII with respect to the 2007 stock sales. The motion to dismiss Counts II and III was denied as to defendants Wayport, Williams, Trellis, and NEA. The motion to dismiss Count V was denied as to Wayport. Dismissal Op. at *8-10.

After discovery, the plaintiffs moved to amend their complaint to add a claim for equitable fraud. Leave was granted on the grounds that all of the elements of equitable fraud are subsumed within the elements of common law fraud and therefore were already at issue in the case. *See* Ct. Ch. R. 15(a) ("leave [to amend] shall be freely given when justice so requires"); *Ikeda v. Molock,* 603 A.2d 785, 788 (Del. 1991) (finding reversible error and ordering new trial where trial court failed to permit amendment of the pleadings on the morning of trial); *see also Bellanca Corp. v. Bellanca,* 169 A.2d 620, 622 (Del. 1961) (affirming grant of leave to amend mid-trial under Ct. Ch. R. 15(b) where additional theory of liability did not require "additional evidence" and thereby posed "no possible prejudice"). [...]

A. The Claim For Breach Of Fiduciary Duty

The plaintiffs contended at trial that Trellis, NEA, Williams, and Wayport breached their fiduciary duties of loyalty. The plaintiffs did not carry their burden of proof, and judgment is entered in favor of the defendants on the fiduciary duty claim.

1. The Nature Of The Fiduciary Duty Claim

The plaintiffs contended that the defendants owed them fiduciary duties that included a duty to disclose material information when they purchased the plaintiffs' shares. Directors of a Delaware corporation owe two fiduciary duties: care and loyalty. *Stone ex rel. AmSouth Bancorporation v. Ritter,* 911 A.2d 362, 370 (Del. 2006). The "duty of disclosure is not an independent duty, but derives from the duties of care and loyalty." *Pfeffer v. Redstone,* 965 A.2d 676, 684 (Del. 2009) (internal quotation marks omitted). The duty of disclosure arises because of "the application in a specific context of the board's fiduciary duties . . . ." *Malpiede v. Townson,* 780 A.2d 1075, 1086 (Del. 2001). Its scope and requirements depend on context; the duty "does not exist in a vacuum." *Stroud v. Grace,* 606 A.2d 75, 85 (Del. 1992). When confronting a disclosure claim, a court therefore must engage in a contextual specific analysis to determine the source of the duty, its requirements, and any remedies for breach. *See* Lawrence A. Hamermesh, *Calling Off the Lynch Mob: The Corporate Director's Fiduciary Disclosure Duty,* 49 Vand. L. Rev. 1087, 1099 (1996). Governing principles have been developed for recurring scenarios, four of which are prominent.

The first recurring scenario is classic common law ratification, in which directors seek approval for a transaction that does not otherwise require a stockholder vote under the DGCL. *See Gantler v. Stephens,* 965 A.2d 695, 713 (Del. 2009) (describing ratification in its classic form); *id.* at 713 n.54 (distinguishing "the common law doctrine of shareholder ratification" from "the effect of an approving vote of disinterested shareholders" under 8 *Del. C.* § 144). If a director or officer has a personal interest in a transaction that conflicts with the interests of the corporation or its stockholders generally, and if the board of directors asks stockholders to ratify the transaction, then the directors have a duty "to disclose all facts that are material to the stockholders' consideration of the transaction and that are or can reasonably be obtained through their position as directors." Hamermesh, *supra,* at 1103. The failure to disclose material information in this context will eliminate any effect that a favorable stockholder vote otherwise might have for the validity of the transaction or for the applicable standard of review. *Id.; see Gantler,* 965 A.2d at 713 ("With one exception, the `cleansing' effect of such a ratifying shareholder vote is to subject the challenged director action to business judgment review, as opposed to `extinguishing' the claim altogether (*i.e.*, obviating all judicial review of the challenged action)."); *id.* at 713 n.54 ("The only species of claim that shareholder ratification can validly extinguish is a claim that the directors lacked the authority to take action that was later ratified. Nothing herein should be read as altering the well-established principle that void acts such as fraud, gift, waste and ultra vires acts cannot be ratified by a less than unanimous shareholder vote.").

A second and quite different scenario involves a request for stockholder action. When directors submit to the stockholders a transaction that requires stockholder approval (such as a merger, sale of assets, or charter amendment) or which requires a stockholder investment decision (such as tendering shares or making an appraisal election), but which is not otherwise an interested transaction, the directors have a duty to "exercise reasonable care to disclose all facts that are material to the stockholders' consideration of the transaction or matter and that are or can reasonably be obtained through their position as directors." Hamermesh, *supra,* at 1103; *see Stroud,* 606 A.2d at 84 ("[D]irectors of Delaware corporations [have] a fiduciary duty to disclose fully and fairly all material information within the board's control when it seeks shareholder action."). A failure to disclose material information in this context may warrant an injunction against, or rescission of, the transaction, but will not provide a basis for damages from defendant directors absent proof of (i) a culpable state of mind or non-exculpated gross negligence, (ii) reliance by the stockholders on the information that was not disclosed, and (iii) damages proximately caused by that failure. *See Loudon v. Archer-Daniels-Midland Co.,* 700 A.2d 135, 146-47 (Del. 1997).

A third scenario involves a corporate fiduciary who speaks outside of the context of soliciting or recommending stockholder action, such as through "public statements made to the market," "statements informing shareholders about the affairs of the corporation," or public filings required by the federal securities laws. *Malone v.*

Brincat, 722 A.2d 5, 11 (Del. 1998). In that context, directors owe a duty to stockholders not to speak falsely:

> Whenever directors communicate publicly or directly with shareholders about the corporation's affairs, with or without a request for shareholder action, directors have a fiduciary duty to shareholders to exercise due care, good faith and loyalty. It follows *a fortiori* that when directors communicate publicly or directly with shareholders about corporate matters the *sine qua non* of directors' fiduciary duty to shareholders is honesty.

Id. at 10. "[D]irectors who knowingly disseminate false information that results in corporate injury or damage to an individual stockholder violate their fiduciary duty, and may be held accountable in a manner appropriate to the circumstances." *Id.* at 9; *see id.* at 14 ("When the directors are not seeking shareholder action, but are deliberately misinforming shareholders about the business of the corporation, either directly or by a public statement, there is a violation of fiduciary duty."). Breach "may result in a derivative claim on behalf of the corporation," "a cause of action for damages," or "equitable relief . . . ." *Id.*

The fourth scenario arises when a corporate fiduciary buys shares directly from or sells shares directly to an existing outside stockholder. Hamermesh, *supra,* at 1103. Under the "special facts doctrine" adopted by the Delaware Supreme Court in *Lank v. Steiner,* 224 A.2d 242 (Del. 1966), a director has a fiduciary duty to disclose information in the context of a private stock sale "only when a director is possessed of special knowledge of future plans or secret resources and deliberately misleads a stockholder who is ignorant of them." *Id.* at 244. If this standard is met, a duty to speak exists, and the director's failure to disclose material information is evaluated within the framework of common law fraud. If the standard is not met, then the director does not have a duty to speak and is liable only to the same degree as a non-fiduciary would be. It bears emphasizing that the duties that exist in this context do not apply to purchases or sales in impersonal secondary markets. *See* Hamermesh, *supra,* at 1153 & n.296. Transactions in the public markets are distinctly different. *See, e.g., In re Am. Int'l Gp., Inc.,*

965 A.2d 763, 800 (Del. Ch. 2009), *aff'd,* 11 A.3d 228 (Del. 2011) (TABLE); *In re Oracle Corp.,* 867 A.2d 904, 932-33, 953 (Del. Ch. 2004), *aff'd,* 872 A.2d 960 (Del. 2005); *Guttman v. Huang,* 823 A.2d 492, 505 (Del. Ch. 2003).

The current case originally raised the second, third, and fourth scenarios, but only the fourth remains. Count I of the complaint was titled "Breach of Fiduciary Duty of Disclosure." Dkt. 25 at 20. At the motion to dismiss stage, it was understood to invoke the second scenario, *viz.,* the duty of disclosure in the context of a request for stockholder action. Vice Chancellor Lamb dismissed Count I on the grounds that "a call for an individual stockholder to sell his shares does not, without more, qualify as a call for stockholder action." Dismissal Op. at *6 n.18.

Count II of the complaint was titled "Breach of Fiduciary Duty of Loyalty." Dkt. 25 at 21. At the motion to dismiss stage, it was understood to invoke both the third scenario (the duty under *Malone* not to engage in deliberate falsehoods) and the fourth scenario (the duty to speak that a fiduciary may have in the context of a direct purchase of shares from a stockholder). As to the former, Vice Chancellor Lamb recognized that the "corporation and its officers and directors are, of course, subject to the underlying duty of loyalty not to make false statements or otherwise materially misrepresent the facts in such a way as to defraud the stockholder in any such negotiation [over the purchase of shares]." Dismissal Op. at *6 n.19 (citing *Malone,* 722 A.2d at 10). He held, however, that the complaint pled "no facts whatsoever to suggest that the company, or its directors or officers, made any knowingly false statements . . . ." *Id.* He therefore dismissed Count II as to the Company and the director defendants, effectively disposing of the *Malone* claim. As to the latter, Vice Chancellor Lamb denied the motion to dismiss, holding that Count II implicated the "normal standard of fraud, *as applied to transactions between corporate insiders . . . .*" Dismissal Op. at *5 (emphasis added). In a footnote, Vice Chancellor Lamb contrasted this variety of fraud with "the affirmative-misrepresentation or intentional concealment species of fraud (that is, the forms of fraud that do not require a duty to speak)" that applies to non-fiduciaries. *Id.* at *5 n.17. This remaining aspect of Count II was litigated and tried. [...]

Corporate Waste   5

Although we all think we know what a waste is, the
concept of corporate waste has a very specific
meaning. As a legal standard, corporate waste claims
are – along with good faith claims – among some of
the hardest claims for plaintiffs to succeed on. Chancellor Allen
observed that a successful waste claim is much like the Loch Ness
monster:

"[T]he waste theory represents a theoretical exception to the
statement very rarely encountered in the world of real transactions.
There surely are cases of fraud; of unfair self dealing and, much
more rarely negligence. But rarest of all — and indeed like Nessie
[of Loch Ness fame], possibly non existent — would be the case of
disinterested business people making non fraudulent deals (non-
negligently) that meet the legal standard of waste!" (Steiner v.
Meyerson, Del. Ch., C.A. No. 13139, Allen, C. (July 18, 1995),
Mem. Op. at 2, 1995 WL 441999.)

The judicial standard for determination of corporate waste is well
developed. A waste entails an exchange of corporate assets for
consideration so disproportionately small as to lie beyond the range
at which any reasonable person might be willing to trade. Most often
the claim is associated with a transfer of corporate assets that serves
no corporate purpose; or for which no consideration at all is
received. Such a transfer is in effect a gift. If, however, there is *any*
substantial consideration received by the corporation, and if there is
a *good faith judgment* that in the circumstances the transaction is
worthwhile, there should be no finding of waste, even if the fact
finder would conclude *ex post* that the transaction was unreasonably
risky. Courts are ill-fitted to attempt to weigh the "adequacy" of
consideration under the waste standard or, *ex post,* to judge
appropriate degrees of business risk (Lewis v. Vogelstein, 699 A. 2d
327, 336 (1997).

Nevertheless, corporate waste claims are not uncommon. In recent
years, plaintiffs have brought many corporate waste claims against
boards for their executive compensation practices. Few – if any – of
these claims are ever successful.

In Re The Goldman Sachs Group, Inc. Shareholder   5.1
Litigation

In recent years executive compensation has soared
to almost unimaginable levels. It is not uncommon to see headlines
about an executive being paid multiple million dollars a year to run
a failing business. You have probably seen headlines like those and
thought to yourself: "What a waste." You wouldn't be alone.

Following the financial crisis of 2008 a number of very high profile
cases were brought on behalf of stockholders against boards alleging
among other things that the compensation schemes deployed by
boards amounted to a "corporate waste" and that they even created
incentives that encouraged excessive risk-taking, bringing the entire
economy to the brink of collapse. Goldman Sachs, the case that
follows, is an example of such a case. The court is asked to rule on
whether the executive compensation plan approved by the board
amounted to a "corporate waste". As you will see this standard is
very difficult to meet.

IN RE THE GOLDMAN SACHS GROUP, INC.
SHAREHOLDER LITIGATION
Court of Chancery of Delaware (2011)

GLASSCOCK, Vice Chancellor.

The Plaintiffs allege that under this compensation structure,
Goldman's employees would attempt to maximize short-term
profits, thus increasing their bonuses at the expense of stockholders'
interests. The Plaintiffs contend that Goldman's employees would
do this by engaging in highly risky trading practices and by over-

leveraging the company's assets. If these practices turned a profit, Goldman's employees would receive a windfall; however, losses would fall on the stockholders.

The Plaintiffs allege that the Director Defendants breached their fiduciary duties by approving the compensation structure discussed above. Additionally, the Plaintiffs claim that the payments under this compensation structure constituted corporate waste. [...]

C. Compensation

Goldman employed a "pay for performance" philosophy linking the total compensation of its employees to the company's performance.[11] Goldman has used a Compensation Committee since at least 2006 to oversee the development and implementation of its compensation scheme.[12] The Compensation Committee was responsible for reviewing and approving the Goldman executives' annual compensation.[13] To fulfill their charge, the Compensation Committee consulted with senior management about management's projections of net revenues and the proper ratio of compensation and benefits expenses to net revenues (the "compensation ratio").[14] Additionally, the Compensation Committee compared Goldman's compensation ratio to that of Goldman's competitors such as Bear Stearns, Lehman Brothers, Merrill Lynch, and Morgan Stanley. The Compensation Committee would then approve a ratio and structure that Goldman would use to govern Goldman's compensation to its employees.[15]

The Plaintiffs allege that from 2007 through 2009, the Director Defendants approved a management-proposed compensation structure that caused management's interests to diverge from those of the stockholders.[16] According to the Plaintiffs, in each year since 2006 the Compensation Committee approved the management-determined compensation ratio, which governed "the total amount of funds available to compensate all employees including senior executives," without any analysis.[17] Although the total compensation paid by Goldman varied significantly each year, total compensation as a percentage of net revenue remained relatively constant.[18] Because management was awarded a relatively constant percentage of total revenue, management could maximize their compensation by increasing Goldman's total net revenue and total stockholder equity.[19] The Plaintiffs contend that this compensation structure led management to pursue a highly risky business strategy that emphasized short term profits in order to increase their yearly bonuses.[--]

E. The Plaintiffs' Claims

The Plaintiffs allege that the Director Defendants breached their fiduciary duties by [...] (2) committing waste by "approving a compensation ratio to Goldman employees in an amount so disproportionately large to the contribution of management, as opposed to capital as to be unconscionable."[50][...]

3. Waste

The Plaintiffs also contend that Goldman's compensation levels were unconscionable and constituted waste. To sustain their claim that demand would be futile, the Plaintiffs must raise a reasonable doubt that Goldman's compensation levels were the product of a valid business judgment. Specifically, to excuse demand on a waste claim, the Plaintiffs must plead particularized allegations that "overcome the general presumption of good faith by showing that the board's decision was so egregious or irrational that it could not have been based on a valid assessment of the corporation's best interests."[152]

"[W]aste entails an exchange of corporate assets for consideration so disproportionately small as to lie beyond the range at which any reasonable person might be willing to trade."[153] Accordingly, if "there is any *substantial* consideration received by the corporation, and if there is a *good faith judgment* that in the circumstances the transaction is worthwhile, there should be no finding of waste."[154] The reason being, "[c]ourts are ill-fitted to attempt to weigh the `adequacy' of consideration under the waste standard or, *ex post,* to judge appropriate degrees of business risk."[155] Because of this, "[i]t is the essence of business judgment for a board to determine if a particular individual warrant[s] large amounts of money."[1156]

The Plaintiffs' waste allegations revolve around three premises: that Goldman's pay per employee is significantly higher than its peers, that Goldman's compensation ratios should be compared to hedge funds and other shareholder funds to reflect Goldman's increasing reliance on proprietary trading as opposed to traditional investment banking services, and that Goldman's earnings and related compensation are only the result of risk taking.

The Plaintiffs consciously do not identify a particular individual or person who received excessive compensation, but instead focus on the average compensation received by each of Goldman's 31,000 employees.[1157] The Plaintiffs allege that "Goldman consistently allocated and distributed anywhere from two to six times the amounts that its peers distributed to each employee,"[1158] and the Plaintiffs provide comparisons of Goldman's average pay per employee to firms such as Morgan Stanley, Bear Stearns, Merrill Lynch, Citigroup, and Bank of America.[1159] The Plaintiffs note that these firms are investment banks, but do not provide any indication of why these firms are comparable to Goldman or their respective primary areas of business. The Plaintiffs do not compare trading segment to trading segment or any other similar metric. A broad assertion that Goldman's board devoted more resources to compensation than did other firms, standing alone, is not a particularized factual allegation creating a reasonable doubt that Goldman's compensation levels were the product of a valid business judgment.

The Plaintiffs urge that, in light of Goldman's increasing reliance on proprietary trading, Goldman's employees' compensation should be compared against a hedge fund or other shareholder fund.[1160] The Plaintiffs allege that Goldman's compensation scheme is equal to 2% of net assets and 45% of the net income produced, but a typical hedge fund is only awarded 2% of net assets and 20% of the net income produced.[1161] The Plaintiffs paradoxically assert that "no hedge fund manager may command compensation for managing assets at the annual rate of 2% of net assets and 45% of net revenues," but then immediately acknowledge that in fact there are hedge funds that have such compensation schemes.[162] It is apparent to me from the allegations of the complaint that while the majority of hedge funds may use a "2 and 20" compensation scheme, this is not the exclusive method used too set such compensation. Even if I were to conclude that a hedge fund or shareholder fund would be an appropriate yardstick with which to measure Goldman's compensation package and "even though the amounts paid to defendants exceeded the industry average," I fail to see a "shocking disparity" between the percentages that would render them "legally excessive."[163]

In the end, while the Goldman employees may not have been doing, in the words of the complaint and Defendant Blankfein, "God's Work,"[164] the complaint fails to present facts that demonstrate that the work done by Goldman's 31,000 employees was of such limited value to the corporation that no reasonable person in the directors' position would have approved their levels of compensation.[165] Absent such facts, these decisions are the province of the board of directors rather than the courts.[166] Without examining the payment to a specific individual, or group of individuals, and what was specifically done in exchange for that payment, I am unable to determine whether a transaction is "so one sided that no business person of ordinary, sound judgment could conclude that the corporation has received adequate consideration."[167]

The closest the Plaintiffs come to pleading waste with any factual particularity is in regards to the payment to the Trading and Principal Investment segment in 2008. The Plaintiffs allege that in 2008 "the Trading and Principal Investments segment produced $9.06 billion in net revenue, but, as a result of discretionary bonuses paid to employees, lost more than $2.7 billion for the [stockholders]."[168] The Plaintiffs' allegations, however, are insufficient to raise a reasonable doubt that Goldman's compensation levels in this segment were the product of a valid business judgment. As a strictly pedagogic exercise, imagine a situation where one half of the traders lost money, and the other half made the same amount of money, so that the firm broke even. Even if no bonus was awarded to the half that lost money, a rational manager would still want to award a bonus to the half that did make money in order to keep that talent from leaving. Since net trading gains were $0, these bonuses would cause a net loss, but there would not be a waste of corporate assets because there was adequate consideration for the bonuses. Without specific allegations of unconscionable transactions and details regarding who was paid and for what reasons they were paid, the Plaintiffs fail to adequately plead demand futility on the basis of waste.

Finally, the Plaintiffs herald the fact that during the sub-prime crisis the Director Defendants continued to allocate similar percentages of net revenue as compensation while the firm was engaged in risky transactions; however, "there should be no finding of waste, even if the fact finder would conclude *ex post* that the transaction was unreasonably risky. Any other rule would deter corporate boards from the optimal rational acceptance of risk."[169] Because this complaint lacks a particular pleading that an individual or group of individuals was engaged in transactions so unconscionable that no rational director could have compensated them, the Plaintiffs have failed to raise a reasonable doubt that the compensation decisions were not the product of a valid business judgment. [...]

Seinfeld v. Slager — 5.2

Stockholder challenges to excessive executive compensation packages are relatively common. For the most part, such challenges are extremely difficult for plaintiffs to win. In most instances, the executives' pay is approved by a disinterested board of directors. As you already know, a disinterested board making an informed decision will receive the protection of the business judgment presumption when the decision to pay an executive a large amount of money is challenged by stockholders. Because it is extremely difficult to plead demand futility in such cases, they are often characterized as "waste" claims in order to access *Aronson*'s second prong.

Some believe that boards have an obligation to minimize tax liability or to avoid paying taxes. Such a view has never been supported by any corporate law doctrine. Nevertheless, that fact does not stop some litigants from bringing challenges against board decisions with respect to tax strategy. Such challenges, assuming a disinterested and reasonably informed board are doomed for failure. Consequently, plaintiffs who bring such claims are left to characterize such claims as "waste" claims.

One area where plaintiffs are more successful is in claims against directors, rather than executives, for director compensation. Although directors are expressly authorized by statute to set their own pay (DGCL 141(h)), the levels of such pay can give courts pause. Plaintiffs are obviously more successful in such cases because by their nature, directors are interested parties in their own pay. Consequently, plaintiffs are much more likely to succeed in overcoming *Aronson*'s demand futility pleading burden.

In Seinfeld, the court deals with all three of these issues.

<u>SEINFELD v. SLAGER</u>
MEMORANDUM OPINION

GLASSCOCK, Vice Chancellor.

I. BACKGROUND

A. Parties

The Plaintiff, Frank David Seinfeld, is a stockholder of Republic Services, Inc. ("Republic" or the "Company"), who has held Republic stock during all relevant times.

Defendant Republic is a Delaware corporation that engages in waste hauling and waste disposal.[iii]

Defendants James E. O'Connor, Donald W. Slager, John W. Croghan, James W. Crownover, William J. Flynn, David I. Foley,

Michael Larson, Nolan Lehmann, W. Lee Nutter, Ramon A. Rodriguez, Allan Sorensen, John M. Trani, and Michael W. Wickham are members of Republic's board of directors (collectively, the "Defendant Directors"). [...]

II. STANDARDS OF REVIEW

The Defendants have moved to dismiss all claims under Court of Chancery Rule 12(b)(6) for failure to state a claim. Except for the excessive compensation claim, the Defendants have also moved to dismiss pursuant to Rule 23.1, on the basis that the Plaintiff has failed to make demand or plead particularized facts that demonstrate demand futility.

The Plaintiff alleges that demand is excused for all his claims because the challenged transactions were not the product of a valid exercise of business judgment. The Plaintiff also alleges that demand is futile because the Defendants were interested or lacked independence in the stock option claim and the excessive compensation claim. [...]

C. Demand Futility

The Plaintiff challenges affirmative decisions by Republic's board and has failed to make pre-suit demand; therefore, to show demand futility, under the well-known *Aronson* test, the Plaintiff must allege particularized facts that raise a reason to doubt that "(1) the directors are disinterested and independent [or] (2) the challenged transaction was otherwise the product of a valid exercise of business judgment."[112] Under the first prong of *Aronson,* a director is interested if he sits on both sides of a transaction or derives a benefit from a transaction that is not shared by the corporation or all stockholders generally.[113] A director is not interested merely because he is named as a defendant in a suit, and generally, an inference of financial interest is not imputed to a director solely because he receives customary compensation for his board service.[114] When addressing *Aronson*'s second prong, there is a presumption that the business judgment rule applies, and the plaintiff must rebut this presumption by pleading "particularized facts to create a reasonable doubt that either (1) the action was taken honestly and in good faith or (2) the board was adequately informed in making the decision."[15]

D. Waste

Demand may be excused under the second prong of *Aronson* if a plaintiff properly pleads a waste claim.[16] In a derivative suit, this Court analyzes each of the challenged transactions individually to determine demand futility.[17] The Plaintiff here alleges that he has adequately pled waste for each of his claims and that demand should be excused.

"[T]he doctrine of waste is a residual protection for stockholders that polices the outer boundaries of the broad field of discretion afforded directors by the business judgment rule."[18] As such, a plaintiff faces an uphill battle in bringing a waste claim, and a plaintiff "must allege particularized facts that lead to a reasonable inference that the director defendants authorized `an exchange that is so one sided that no business person of ordinary, sound judgment could conclude that the corporation has received adequate consideration.'"[19] "Where, however, the corporation has received `any substantial consideration' and where the board has made `a good faith judgment that in the circumstances the transaction was worthwhile,' a finding of waste is inappropriate, even if hindsight proves that the transaction may have been ill-advised."[20] This Court has described the waste standard as "an extreme test, very rarely satisfied by a shareholder plaintiff, because if under the circumstances any reasonable person might conclude that the deal made sense, then the judicial inquiry ends."[21] The rationale behind these stringent requirements is that "[c]ourts are ill-fitted to attempt to weigh the adequacy of consideration under the waste standard or, *ex post,* to judge the appropriate degrees of business risk."[22]

E. Taxes

467

The Plaintiff argues that demand should be excused under *Aronson*'s second prong on the ground that he has properly pleaded that the Defendants failed to minimize taxes. The Plaintiff appears to contend that there is an independent duty to minimize taxes, or alternatively that the failure to minimize taxes is *per se* a waste of corporate assets. The Plaintiff, however, does not point to any Delaware jurisprudence for this position; instead, the Plaintiff presents a smattering of inapposite cases from various other jurisdictions which I find logically unpersuasive.[23]

This Court has concluded that "there is no general fiduciary duty to minimize taxes."[24] There are a variety of reasons why a company may choose or not choose to take advantage of certain tax savings,[25] and generally a company's tax policy "typif[ies] an area of corporate decision-making best left to management's business judgment, so long as it is exercised in an appropriate fashion."[26] I am not foreclosing the theoretical possibility that under certain circumstances overpayment of taxes might be the result of a breach of a fiduciary duty.[27] I am simply noting that a decision to pursue or forgo tax savings is generally a business decision for the board of directors. Accordingly, despite the Plaintiff's contentions, Delaware law is clear that there is no separate duty to minimize taxes, and a failure to do so is not automatically a waste of corporate assets.

Using the above standards, I now address the Plaintiff's claims and the facts relevant thereto.

III. FACTS AND ANALYSIS

A. Past Consideration

Defendant O'Connor worked for Republic, serving as its CEO and a member of its board, for 10 years.[28] During this time, O'Connor was compensated for his services.[29] O'Connor signed an employment agreement (the "Employment Agreement") with the company, effective May 14, 2009, that provided him with retirement benefits such as a $10 million payment, health benefits, and stock options.[30] On June 24, 2010, the Company accepted O'Connor's retirement as CEO, to be effective on January 1, 2011;[131] however, the next day, on June 25, 2010, O'Connor signed a "Retirement Agreement" with the Company that provided him with a variety of retirement benefits in return for stated consideration, which included a release of claims and an assurance that his retirement occurred on "mutually acceptable terms."[132] One of the benefits conferred on O'Connor was a $1.8 million cash payment, given, according to the explicit terms of the Retirement Agreement, "to reward [O'Connor] for [his] long service to the Company."[133]

The Plaintiff contends that this $1.8 million payment was a gift constituting a waste of corporate assets. The Plaintiff alleges that the $1.8 million payment was not included in the May 14, 2009, employment agreement—and thus was not contractually required—and further argues that there is nothing in the expressed purpose of the payment—reward for service—indicating that the amount was reasonable in light of the services rendered.[134] The Plaintiff, therefore, asserts that this $1.8 million payment was retroactive compensation, constituting a gift or waste.[135] The Defendants point to the Retirement Agreement and argue that O'Connor provided consideration for the $1.8 million payment, and also point out that the Plaintiff has failed to allege that the $1.8 million payment was unreasonable in light of O'Connor's past service to the company.[136]

1. Payment for Services Already Rendered

Earlier decisions of Delaware courts held that payment for services previously rendered and compensated generally would constitute a waste of corporate assets.[139] This Court has recognized, however, that there may be many sufficient reasons for a board to award a severance or retirement bonus.[140] Accordingly, the Court has declined to substitute its judgment for that of the board, even absent a contractual basis for the bonus, where the retroactive payment was not unreasonable under the circumstances.[141][...]

In *Zucker v. Andreessen*, this Court recently addressed whether a generous severance package given to a departing executive in exchange for general releases constituted waste.[151] The plaintiff alleged that the company had no contractual obligation to provide the departing executive with a severance and the company could have avoided paying the executive severance because the company had grounds to terminate him for cause.[52] The *Zucker* court found that the general releases provided at least some consideration, that a portion of the severance pay awarded could represent reasonable compensation for past performance, and that an amicable severance of ties may have had some value.[53] The plaintiff, therefore, had not adequately pleaded that the severance package constituted waste, and the *Zucker* court dismissed the waste claim there under Rule 23.1.[54][...]

2. Past Consideration and Waste

Employment compensation decisions are core functions of a board of directors, and are protected, appropriately, by the business judgment rule.[55] A plaintiff, as here, alleging waste arising from the decision of an independent board concerning employee compensation has set himself a Herculean, and perhaps Sisyphean, task. "Where . . . the corporation has received `any substantial consideration' and where the board has made `a good faith judgment that in the circumstances the transaction was worthwhile,' a finding of waste is inappropriate, even if hindsight proves that the transaction may have been ill-advised."[56]

A board of directors may have a variety of reasons for awarding an executive bonuses for services already rendered. For instance, awarding retroactive compensation to an employee who stays with the company may encourage him to continue his employment.[57] In the case of a retiring employee, the award may serve as a signal to current and future employees that they, too, might receive extra compensation at the end of their tenure if they successfully serve their term. Other factors may also properly influence the board, including ensuring a smooth and harmonious transfer of power, securing a good relationship with the retiring employee, preventing future embarrassing disclosure and lawsuits, and so on. Therefore, an informed and disinterested decision whether or not to award an employee a reasonable bonus for services that have already been rendered, for which the employee has already been compensated, properly falls within a board's business judgment.

Looked at in this light, the question then becomes whether the Employment Agreement was a transaction so lacking in value to the Company that no reasonable director could have been in favor of it; in other words, was the transaction so one-sided that it amounted to waste. The fact that an employee has already been compensated for his work goes directly to whether compensation is reasonable and whether there is a rational basis for "directors to conclude that the amount and form of compensation is appropriate and likely to be beneficial for the company."[158] This fact alone, however, is not determinative. It is simply another, albeit important, factor to be considered.

The Retirement Agreement, considered as a whole, is clear from its explicit terms that it provided the cash bonus as part of a package intended to secure a general release, to provide continuity in the Board, and to ensure that O'Connor's separation from the Company was amicable.[160] It is clear, therefore, that there was some consideration for the benefits provided to O'Connor.[161]

Moreover, the Plaintiff fails to plead—let alone specifically allege— that the amount of the retirement bonus was unreasonable.[162] The Plaintiff only points to the Board's own description, in the Retirement Agreement itself, that the $1.8 million cash bonus was "to reward [O'Connor] for [his] long service to the Company."[163] The Plaintiff conflates "reward" with unreasonable gift. Most bonuses carry with them an aspect of reward for service, as the word bonus itself necessarily conveys. While the Plaintiff has adequately pleaded that the cash retirement bonus was not contractually required and was meant to, among other factors spelled out in the Retirement Agreement, reward O'Connor's service, he has failed to allege with particularity that the bonus was not made in good faith.

The Plaintiff's complaint is void of allegations which, if true, would lead to the conclusion that the retirement bonus, though retroactive and not required by prior contract, constituted waste. O'Connor had been CEO for ten years. He was Chairman of the Board of Directors. The Company had an interest in seeing that his separation was amicable, that he completed his term on the board, and that any potential sources of post-termination litigation were foreclosed, as well as in incentivizing O'Connor's successor and other employees. As part of his retirement package, the Board provided a cash bonus of $1.8 million. Is that bonus, in light of all the circumstances that were known to the board, "too much?" That is a core question for the Board of Directors. Because the Plaintiff has failed to plead with particularity facts that indicate that the amount of this bonus was unreasonable or that otherwise establish waste, the claim must be dismissed.

B. Incentive Award

In addition to challenging the $1.8 million payment to O'Connor, the Plaintiff attacks a $1.25 million incentive award also paid to O'Connor upon his retirement.[64] The Plaintiff contends that by paying O'Connor this award, Republic's compensation plan will be rendered non-tax-deductible.[65] The Plaintiff does not assert that the Defendant Directors were interested in the transaction; instead, the Plaintiff argues that demand is excused because the loss of this tax deduction constitutes a waste of company assets.[66]

1. The Taxman Cometh?

§ 162(m) provides that annual compensation in excess of $1 million is not tax-deductible unless the compensation is granted pursuant to a performance-based, stockholder-approved plan that contains pre-established, objective criteria. [...]

The Company has such a stockholder-approved compensation plan, the Executive Incentive Plan (the "EIP").[68] Under the EIP, the Company pays performance bonuses to participating employees for meeting or exceeding certain performance goals, as measured by the Company's financial results.[69-1]

O'Connor participated in the EIP in 2009 and 2010[75] and had an employment contract, effective February 21, 2007, which provided that the Company would pay him upon his retirement the "full target amount" of his performance bonuses, i.e., the amount he would have received if he had worked for the entire bonus period and achieved his performance goal, with no pro-rata reduction.[76] This contract provided, therefore, that O'Connor would receive "the full target amount" of his performance bonuses regardless of whether O'Connor actually met the performance goal or worked for the entire applicable period.[...]

The Plaintiff's waste claim is that, hypothetically, O'Connor's compensation scheme will lead to an unnecessary payment to the federal government in the future, in the form of a greater tax bill.[89] The Plaintiff's waste claim, concerning the Board's decision to award O'Connor the full target amount, is unusual because the alleged tax ramifications have not actually occurred and there is nothing in the record suggesting when, if ever, they will occur.

This argument is facially unsound. I find that the decision of an independent board to rely, in setting compensation, on a revenue ruling of the IRS, is within the business judgment of the board, and that the Plaintiff's waste claim arising from this decision must be dismissed.

C. Stock Plan Awards

The Company also compensates employees through its 2007 Stock Incentive Plan (the "Stock Plan"), which allows the Company to grant stock awards to its employees, officers, and directors.[95] The Stock Plan's stated purpose is to "enable the Company to attract, retain, reward and motivate" employees, officers, and directors, and to "incentivize them to expend maximum effort for the growth and success of the Company."[96] The Stock Plan is administered by a committee of non-employee members of the Board, or if no committee exists, by the Board itself (the "Committee");[97] however, "with respect to the grant of Awards to non-employee directors, the Committee shall be the Board."[...]

The Defendant Directors are participants in the Stock Plan, and pursuant to it have awarded themselves time-vesting restricted stock units.[107] In 2009, the Board gave each Defendant Director, except

O'Connor, restricted stock units worth $743,700.[1-] The Plaintiff alleges that the Defendant Directors' annual compensation far exceeds the compensation of directors by one of the Company's peers.[111]

Because the Defendant Directors awarded themselves these units, the Plaintiff asserts that they are interested in the transaction.[112] The Plaintiff contends that this compensation constitutes waste because the awards are unreasonable and are not tax-deductible.[1-]

In *In re 3COM Corp. Shareholders Litigation,* the plaintiff contended that members of 3COM's board violated their fiduciary duties and wasted corporate assets when they granted themselves stock options under 3COM's stockholder approved Director Stock Option Plan.[115] The *3COM* plaintiff asserted that because the directors granted themselves the options under this plan, this transaction was a self-interested one and the plaintiff's claim should be reviewed under the entire fairness standard.[116] Then-Vice Chancellor Steele found that corporate directors who "administer a stockholder approved director stock option plan are entitled to the protection of the business judgment rule, and in absence of waste, a total failure of consideration, they do not breach their duty of loyalty by acting consistently with the terms of the stockholder-approved plan."[117] The Vice Chancellor explained:

> I do not see this as a case of directors independently or unilaterally granting themselves stock options, but instead a case where stock options accrued to these directors under the terms of an established option plan with *sufficiently defined terms.* One cannot plausibly contend that the directors structured and implemented a self-interested transaction inconsistent with the interests of the corporation and its shareholders when the shareholders knowingly set the parameters of the Plan, approved it in advance, and the directors implemented the Plan according to its terms. Precedent in this Court clearly establishes that "self-interested" director transactions made under a stock option plan approved by the corporation's shareholders are entitled to the benefit of the business judgment rule.[118]

Here, even though the stockholders approved the plan, the Defendant Directors are interested in self-dealing transactions under the Stock Plan. The Stock Plan lacks sufficient definition to afford the Defendant Directors protection under the business judgment rule. The sufficiency of definition that anoints a stockholder-approved option or bonus plan with business judgment rule protection exists on a continuum. Though the stockholders approved this plan, there must be some *meaningful* limit imposed by the stockholders on the Board for the plan to be consecrated by *3COM* and receive the blessing of the business judgment rule, else the "sufficiently defined terms" language of *3COM* is rendered toothless. A stockholder-approved *carte blanche* to the directors is insufficient. The more definite a plan, the more likely that a board's compensation decision will be labeled disinterested and qualify for protection under the business judgment rule. If a board is free to use its absolute discretion under even a stockholder-approved plan, with little guidance as to the *total* pay that can be awarded, a board will ultimately have to show that the transaction is entirely fair.

In reading the Complaint and the Stock Plan, I find no effective limits on the total amount of pay that can be awarded through time-vesting restricted stock units. The plan before me confers on the Defendant Directors the theoretical ability to award themselves as much as tens of millions of dollars per year, with few limitations; therefore, I find that the Defendant Directors are interested in the decision to award themselves a substantial bonus. While the Defendant Directors may be able to show that the amounts they awarded themselves are entirely fair, their motion to dismiss must be denied with respect to this claim.

2. Time-Vesting Stock Options Granted to Employees

The Plaintiff's next claim addresses the Board's decision to award to employees certain forms of compensation instead of others. The Plaintiff alleges that while the Stock Plan allows the Board to grant both time-vesting and performance-vesting units, the Board breached its duties by only granting non-tax-deductible time-vesting options.[...]

The Plaintiff alleges that the Defendant Directors' choice to award only time-vesting stock units contravened the Stock Plan because granting time-vesting units did not sufficiently align the Covered Employees' interests with the stockholders' and did not incentivize the Covered Employees to expend "maximum efforts."[1122] The Plaintiff argues that the Defendant Directors breached their duty of loyalty by not following the terms of the Stock Plan. The Plaintiff also contends that the Defendant Directors' decision wasted corporate assets because the time-vesting units were not tax deductible.[1123] The Plaintiff, in support of his position, asserts that three of Republic's "peer group companies" award mainly performance-based stock compensation.[1124]

The Plaintiff is challenging quintessential Board decisions: how much to pay employees and how to allocate company assets efficiently.[1125] The Plaintiff's contention is that Republic could have received a lower tax bill, while achieving better results, if the Board had chosen performance-vesting units instead of time-vesting units. As discussed above, "there is no general fiduciary duty to minimize taxes,"[1126] and the fact that higher taxes were paid, without more, is insufficient to sustain a waste claim.

[...]

In other words, the Plaintiff mainly disagrees with a business decision by the Board; this disagreement does not state a cognizable claim.

Insider Trading 6

Anyone familiar with the law of agency will very
quickly understand why insider trading is so
troublesome. When an insider uses the information
of the corporation for their own benefit, the agent violates their duty
of loyalty to the corporation. Over the years, the jurisprudence of
insider trading has evolved to meet the changing landscape of the
marketplace. In the following cases we start with classical insider
trading theory and then progress to more modern evolutions
including liability for insider trading under Federal
misappropriation theory.

State-based liability 6.1

State-based insider trading liability takes the form a derivative action by stockholders against insiders. In such an action, the basic claim is that directors (or "insiders") used confidential information of the corporation for their own benefit and not for the benefit of the corporation. As a derivative action based, state-based insider trading liability is prosecuted by stockholders and not by state regulators or the SEC. *In re Oracle* as well as *Guttman v. Huang* from earlier in the semester are examples of stockholders bringing derivative suits against board members who have allegedly engaged in insider trading in the stock of the corporation. The claim in each of those cases was, in part, that the defendant directors violated their duty of the loyalty to the corporation by using the corporation's material, nonpublic information in order to trade stock in the corporation benefiting themselves.

State-based insider trading claims are also known as "*Brophy*" claims. A *Brophy* claim is a derivative claim against a director. Consistent with other derivative actions, the remedy, if any, is paid to the corporation in the form of disgorgement of profits. Because the state-based action is derivative, neither stockholders nor any governmental entity is entitled to receive any of the profits disgorged as a remedy. Those illicit profits are paid back to the corporation and are not paid as fines to the SEC or any other regulator. In addition, state-based insider trading liability is civil and not criminal.

Notice that the case that follows is a ruling on a special litigation committee's Rule 56 motion to dismiss. You have come across the special litigation committee in the context of derivative litigation before. Before ruling on the *Brophy* claim, the court applies the two-prong test from *Zapata* to the special litigation committee's effort to have the litigation dismissed.

Kahn v. KKR & Co.   6

                                                                .

                                                                1

                                                                .

                                                                1

KAHN v. KOLBERG KRAVIS ROBERTS & CO., L.P.
23 A.3d 831 (2011)

STEELE, Chief Justice:

The Appellants in this derivative action, Linda Kahn and Alan Spiegal, who are shareholders of Primedia, Inc., appeal the Court of Chancery's decision granting the Primedia Special Litigation Committee's Motion to Dismiss claims arising out of a series of alleged violations of fiduciary duty by defendants, Kohlberg, Kravis, Roberts & Co., Primedia, Inc., and other Primedia officers and directors. Because we do not agree with the Court of Chancery's interpretation of a *Brophy* claim as explained in *Pfeiffer,* we must reverse the Court of Chancery's judgment of dismissal and remand the case for further proceedings consistent with this Opinion.

I. FACTS AND PROCEDURAL HISTORY

The nominal defendant in this action is Primedia, Inc., (the Company) a Delaware corporation whose main executive offices are located in New York City. Primedia's business involves ownership of media properties and brands that "connect buyers and sellers through print publications, websites, events, newsletters, and video programs." [...]

Defendant below/appellee Kohlberg Kravis Roberts & Co. L.P. is an investment partnership that specializes in management buyouts of business entities. KKR indirectly controlled a majority of the common stock of Primedia. [...]

B. The Facts

On December 19, 2001, Primedia's board of directors approved a plan for Primedia to acquire up to $100 million dollars of its preferred shares, at 50% to 60% of redemption value, in exchange for common stock. As of December 19, 2001, KKR controlled approximately 60% of Primedia's outstanding stock and had three of its designees on Primedia's board. At the May 16, 2002 board meeting, Primedia's directors authorized an additional $100 million in buybacks of its preferred shares. On May 21, 2002, Primedia's KKR directors authored an advisory memo to KKR's Investment Committee and Portfolio Committee containing an update on Primedia's second quarter performance and advocating the purchase of Primedia's preferred shares. The May 21st memo contained nonpublic information about Primedia.

At some point in 2002, KKR sought from the Primedia board of directors permission for KKR to purchase Primedia's preferred shares, as long as Primedia was not purchasing those shares in the market. On July 2, 2002, Primedia director (and General Counsel) Beverley Chell circulated the unanimous written consent to the disinterested directors. After receiving advice from outside counsel, Chell circulated the written consent to Primedia's entire board on July 8, 2002. The written consent stated, in part, that KKR's purchase of up to $50 million in Primedia preferred stock was acceptable and not a usurpation of corporate opportunity. [...] On July 3, 2002, KKR formed ABRA III LLC as an investment vehicle to purchase Primedia's preferred shares, and ABRA began purchasing preferred shares on July 8, 2002. Between July 8 and November 5, 2002, KKR (through ABRA) purchased over $75 million of Primedia's preferred stock, an amount that exceeded the $50 million limit allowed by the written consent.

On September 26, 2002, Primedia's board of directors met and approved the sale of one of its biggest assets, the American Baby Group, for approximately $115 million in cash. Primedia did not publicly disclose the American Baby Group sale until November 4, 2002. Between September 26 and November 4, 2002, KKR spent $39 million[iii] to acquire Primedia's preferred stock. On November

5, 2002, Primedia's board of directors decided to explore repurchasing Primedia preferred shares. ABRA made its last purchase of Primedia's preferred shares on November 5, 2002.

C. The Procedural History

Plaintiffs originally filed the Derivative Action on November 29, 2005. Thereafter, they filed the First Amended and Consolidated Complaint on April 26, 2006. Defendants moved to dismiss and on September 25, 2006, the Court of Chancery denied the motion.[12] Primedia formed a Special Litigation [835] Committee, which comprised Primedia Directors Daniel Ciporin and Kevin Smith, each of whom joined the board of directors after commencement of the action. On July 13, 2007, the SLC moved to stay the action pending its investigation and report. The court granted the stay, and on February 28, 2008, the SLC submitted its report and moved to dismiss the action.

The First Amended Complaint alleged that redemptions of Primedia's D, F and H preferred stock (the cash-pay preferreds), and Series J paid-in-kind preferred stock in 2004-2005 were unfair to Primedia and resulted in the enrichment to KKR, at a cost to Primedia. [...]

The Second Amended Complaint alleged that KKR engineered Primedia's plans to restructure and redeem the preferred stock, and then formed ABRA "as a vehicle to buy the exact same Series D Stock, Series F Stock, and Series H Stock that were the subject of Primedia's buyback." The Second Amended Complaint also challenged the Board's written consent approval of ABRA's purchases.

On January 11, 2008, after the SLC's investigation concluded, plaintiffs presented a new claim to SLC's counsel. Plaintiffs claimed that the KKR defendants breached their fiduciary duty to the Company by purchasing the preferred stock at a time when they possessed material, non-public information. The allegations supporting the *Brophy* claim did not appear in the Second Amended Complaint, because the plaintiffs had purportedly uncovered the information while reviewing materials after they filed the Second Amended Complaint.[3]

On March 16, 2010, plaintiffs filed a Third Amended Complaint, which included the *Brophy* claim that KKR possessed material, non-public information. This latest complaint alleged that KKR knew that: (1) Primedia's earnings would be better than previously forecasted to the market, and (2) the Company anticipated at some point redeeming its outstanding preferred stock and KKR traded on this information during the period July 8 to November 5, 2002.

On June 14, 2010, the Court of Chancery heard oral argument and, ruling from the bench, granted the SLC's Motion to Dismiss. Kahn now appeals from that judgment. First, Kahn argues that the Court of Chancery erroneously held that disgorgement was not an available remedy for its *Brophy* claims, consistent with *Pfeiffer's* holding.[4] Second, Kahn contends the Court of Chancery erroneously concluded that the SLC had demonstrated the absence of any genuine issue of material fact regarding the thoroughness of its investigation or the reasonableness of its conclusions.

II. ANALYSIS

B. Brophy Does Not Require an Element of Harm to the Corporation Before Disgorgement is an Available Remedy and to the Extent Pfeiffer Conflicts With This Holding, It is Wrong.

We review a trial judge's legal conclusions *de novo.*[10] The Vice Chancellor's analysis focused on the SLC's investigation of three issues: (1) the *Brophy* claim based on the May 21st Insider Information Memo; (2) the *Brophy* claim based on the agreement to sell American Baby Group; and (3) the Breach of Contract Claim based on the backdated written consent and the $50 million restriction.[11] The Vice Chancellor applied the two-part *Zapata* standard to the SLC's motion to dismiss.[12] The first prong of the *Zapata* standard analyzes the independence and good faith of the committee members, the quality of its investigation and the reasonableness of its conclusions.[13] Under *Zapata's* first prong, the

Vice Chancellor found the SLC based its decision on an independently thorough investigation of the claims merits and a cost benefit analysis of pursuing the claims.[114] The Vice Chancellor found that the SLC met its burden under the first prong of *Zapata,* but rather than granting the motion to dismiss immediately, the Vice Chancellor addressed *Zapata's* discretionary second prong.[115]

Under *Zapata's* second prong, which is purely discretionary, the court looks at a claim that may be sustainable but that the SLC decided should not be pursued for other reasons.[116] The Court of [837] Chancery's function under *Zapata's* second prong is to "strik[e] a balance between `legitimate corporate claims' as expressed in the derivative shareholder suit and the corporation's best interest as ascertained by the Special Litigation Committee."[117] Here, the Vice Chancellor started from "the proposition that there is a *Brophy* claim [ ] that would blow by a motion to dismiss on failure to state a claim."[118] Then the Vice Chancellor held that under the law, as explained in *Pfeiffer v. Toll,* disgorgement is not an available remedy for most of the *Brophy* claims.[119] But, *Pfeiffer's* holding—which requires a plaintiff to show that the corporation suffered actual harm before bringing a *Brophy* claim—is not a correct statement of our law. To the extent *Pfeiffer v. Toll* conflicts with our current interpretation of *Brophy v. Cities Service Co., Pfeiffer* cannot be Delaware law.

In the venerable case of *Brophy v. Cities Service Co.,* one of the defendants was an employee who had acquired inside information that the corporate plaintiff was about to enter the market and purchase its own shares. Using this confidential information, the employee, who was not an officer, bought a large block of shares and, after the corporation's purchases had caused the price to rise, resold them at a profit.[120] Because the employee defendant occupied a position of trust and confidence within the plaintiff corporation, the court found his relationship analogous to that of a fiduciary.[121] The employee defendant argued that the plaintiff had failed to state a claim because "it [did] not appear that the corporation suffered any loss through his purchase of its stock."[122] The Court of Chancery expressly rejected that argument, stating that:

> In equity, when the breach of confidential relation by an
> employee is relied on and an accounting for any resulting profit
> is sought, loss to the corporation need not be charged in the
> complaint. . . . Public policy will not permit an employee
> occupying a position of trust and confidence toward his
> employer to abuse that relation to his own profit, regardless of
> whether his employer suffers a loss.[23]

Thus, actual harm to the corporation is not required for a plaintiff
to state a claim under *Brophy.* In *Brophy,* the court relied on the
principles of restitution and equity, citing the Restatement of the
Law of Restitution § 200, comment a, for the proposition that a
fiduciary cannot use confidential corporate information for his own
benefit.[24] As the court recognized in *Brophy,* [838] it is inequitable
to permit the fiduciary to profit from using confidential corporate
information. Even if the corporation did not suffer actual harm,
equity requires disgorgement of that profit.[25]

This Court has cited *Brophy* approvingly when discussing how the
duty of loyalty governs the misuse of confidential corporate
information by fiduciaries.[26] In *In re Oracle Corp. Deriv. Litig.,*[27]
we affirmed the Court of Chancery's articulation of the elements
essential for a plaintiff to prevail on a *Brophy* claim. The plaintiff
must show that: "1) the corporate fiduciary possessed material,
nonpublic company information; and 2) the corporate fiduciary
used that information improperly by making trades because she was
motivated, in whole or in part, by the substance of that
information."[28]

In *Pfeiffer v. Toll,* the plaintiff stockholder brought a derivative
action against the defendants, who were eight members of the Toll
Brothers' board of directors, to recover damages suffered by the
company from their alleged insider trading.[29] Pfeiffer claimed that
the defendants sold significant amounts of Toll Brothers stock from
December 2004 through September 2005 while in possession of
material, non-public information about Toll Brothers' future
prospects.[30] Specifically, Toll Brothers was projecting 20% growth
in net income for 2006 and 2007, and its stock price more than
doubled from December 2004 to July 2005. During this same

period, the director defendants allegedly sold 14 million shares of stock for over $615 million. Based on those sales, which were inconsistent with past trading patterns and were suspicious in their timing and amount, Pfeiffer asserted a derivative claim for breach of fiduciary duty under *Brophy*.

The defendants moved to dismiss the complaint, arguing, among other things, that *Brophy* is an outdated precedent in light of the federal securities laws, which govern insider trading claims. While on [839] one hand upholding *Brophy* as good law,[31] the Court of Chancery concluded that "[t]he purpose of a *Brophy* claim is to remedy harm to the corporation."[32] By focusing on that harm, it "disposes of the defendants' contentions that Brophy is a misguided vehicle for recovering the same trading losses that are addressed by the federal securities laws . . . [and] the contention that *Brophy* grants a remedy without underlying harm."[33] Next, the Vice Chancellor concluded that the harm to the corporation "is generally not measured by insider trading gains or reciprocal losses."[34] Citing to this Court's precedent on two occasions, the Vice Chancellor found that Delaware law "does not provide a class-wide remedy for market based-harm"[35] and "interpreting *Brophy* as a basis for recovering those measures of damages would conflict with [those holdings]."[36] Moreover, the court found that "disgorgement of insider trading profits. . . is also not the appropriate measure of damages because insiders who trade on an impersonal market typically are not engaging in the type of self-dealing transaction to which a disgorgement remedy historically applies."[37] The court also held that market trading "typically does not involve the usurpation of a corporate opportunity, where disgorgement has been the preferred remedy."[38]

To that end, the Vice Chancellor concluded that in the context of a *Brophy* claim, disgorgement is "theoretically available" in two circumstances: (1) "when a fiduciary engages directly in actual fraud and benefits from trading on the basis of the fraudulent information;" and (2) "if the insider used confidential corporate information to compete directly with the corporation."[39] *Brophy*, in the Vice Chancellor's view, was an example of the second circumstance where disgorgement is an [840] appropriate remedy.[40]

But, in most circumstances a corporation would only be able to recover for "actual harm causally related (in both the actual and proximate sense) to the breach of the duty of loyalty"—for example "costs and expenses for regulatory proceedings and internal investigations, fees paid to counsel and other professionals, fines paid to regulators, and judgments in litigation."[141]

We decline to adopt *Pfeiffer's* thoughtful, but unduly narrow, interpretation of *Brophy* and its progeny. We also disagree with the *Pfeiffer* court's conclusion that the purpose of *Brophy* is to "remedy harm to the corporation." In fact, *Brophy* explicitly held that the corporation did not need to suffer an actual loss for there to be a viable claim.[142] Importantly, *Brophy* focused on preventing a fiduciary wrongdoer from being unjustly enriched.[143] Moreover, we have found no cases requiring that the corporation suffer actual harm for a plaintiff to bring a *Brophy* claim.[144] To read *Brophy* as applying only where the corporation has suffered actual harm improperly limits its holding.

We decline to adopt Pfeiffer's interpretation that would limit the disgorgement remedy to a usurpation of corporate opportunity or cases where the insider used confidential corporate information to compete directly with the corporation. Brophy was not premised on either of those rationales. Rather, Brophy focused on the public policy of preventing unjust enrichment based on the misuse of confidential corporate information. Just as the *Brophy* court relied on the seminal decision in *Guth v. Loft,*[146] we also rely on the *Guth* court's rationale in this case, and refuse to restrict disgorgement in *Brophy* cases as *Pfeiffer* suggests.

The rule, inveterate and uncompromising in its rigidity, does not rest upon the narrow ground of injury or damage to the corporation resulting from a betrayal of confidence, but upon a broader foundation of a wise public policy that, for the purpose of removing all temptation, extinguishes all possibility of profit flowing from a breach of the confidence imposed by the fiduciary relation.[147]

Given *Guth's* eloquent articulation of Delaware's public policy and the fact that "Delaware law dictates that the scope of recovery for a breach of the duty of loyalty is not to be determined narrowly,"[148] we find no reasonable public policy ground to restrict the scope of disgorgement remedy in *Brophy* cases—irrespective of arguably parallel remedies grounded in federal securities law. [...]

Federal-based liability

6
.
2

In additional to state-based liability, traders trading on the basis of inside information may also be liable under the federal securities laws. Federal insider trading liability carries with it potentially both civil and criminal liability. Like state-based liability, federal liability for insider trading is derived from the common law. There is no federal statute that explicitly prohibits insider trading. Rather, courts have interpreted Section 10b of the Securities Act of 1934, the Act's anti-fraud provision, as prohibiting insider trading.

Rule 10b-5

6
.
2
.
1

§ 240.10b-5 Employment of manipulative and deceptive devices.

It shall be unlawful for any person, directly or indirectly, by the use of any means or instrumentality of interstate commerce, or of the mails or of any facility of any national securities exchange,

(a) To employ any device, scheme, or artifice to defraud,

(b) To make any untrue statement of a material fact or to omit to state a material fact necessary in order to make the statements made, in the light of the circumstances under which they were made, not misleading, or

(c) To engage in any act, practice, or course of business which operates or would operate as a fraud or deceit upon any person,

in connection with the purchase or sale of any security.

SEC v. Texas Gulf Sulphur Co.   6
.
 The following case, Texas Gulf Sulphur is an early   2
federal insider trading case. In TGS, the court starts ;
from the position that insiders, as fiduciaries, have   2
an obligation not to use the corporation's
information for their personal benefit. As fiduciaries, insiders have
an obligation to "disclose" the confidential inside information, or
"abstain from trading" while in possession of the corporation's
material, confidential inside information. Questions arise as to what
information is material and when is information no longer
confidential such that an insider may freely trade on it.

SEC V. TEXAS GULF SULPHUR CO.

401 F.2d 833 (1968)

THE FACTUAL SETTING

This action derives from the exploratory activities of TGS begun in
1957 on the Canadian Shield in eastern Canada. In March of 1959,
aerial geophysical surveys were conducted over more than 15,000
square miles of this area by a group led by defendant Mollison, a
mining engineer and a Vice President of TGS. The group included
defendant Holyk, TGS's chief geologist, defendant Clayton, an
electrical engineer and geophysicist, and defendant Darke, a
geologist. These operations resulted in the detection of numerous
anomalies, i. e., extraordinary variations in the conductivity of rocks,
one of which was on the Kidd 55 segment of land located near
Timmins, Ontario.

On October 29 and 30, 1963, Clayton conducted a ground
geophysical survey on the northeast portion of the Kidd 55 segment
which confirmed the presence of an anomaly and indicated the
necessity of diamond core drilling for further evaluation. Drilling of
the initial hole, K-55-1, at the strongest part of the anomaly was
commenced on November 8 and terminated on November 12 at a
depth of 655 feet. Visual estimates by Holyk of the core of K-55-1
indicated an average copper content of 1.15% and an average zinc
content of 8.64% over a length of 599 feet. This visual estimate

convinced TGS that it was desirable to acquire the remainder of the Kidd 55 segment, and in order to facilitate this acquisition TGS President Stephens instructed the exploration group to keep the results of K-55-1 confidential and undisclosed even as to other officers, directors, and employees of TGS. The hole was concealed and a barren core was intentionally drilled off the anomaly. Meanwhile, the core of K-55-1 had been shipped to Utah for chemical assay which, when received in early December, revealed an average mineral content of 1.18% copper, 8.26% zinc, and 3.94% ounces of silver per ton over a length of 602 feet. These results were so remarkable that neither Clayton, an experienced geophysicist, nor four other TGS expert witnesses, had ever seen or heard of a comparable initial exploratory drill hole in a base metal deposit. So, the trial court concluded, "There is no doubt that the drill core of K-55-1 was unusually [844] good and that it excited the interest and speculation of those who knew about it." Id. at 282. By March 27, 1964, TGS decided that the land acquisition program had advanced to such a point that the company might well resume drilling, and drilling was resumed on March 31.

During this period, from November 12, 1963 when K-55-1 was completed, to March 31, 1964 when drilling was resumed, certain of the individual defendants listed in fn. 2, supra, and persons listed in fn. 4, supra, said to have received "tips" from them, purchased TGS stock or calls thereon. Prior to these transactions these persons had owned 1135 shares of TGS stock and possessed no calls; thereafter they owned a total of 8235 shares and possessed 12,300 calls.

[...]

Meanwhile, rumors that a major ore strike was in the making had been circulating throughout Canada. On the morning of Saturday, April 11, Stephens at his home in Greenwich, Conn. read in the New York Herald Tribune and in the New York Times unauthorized reports of the TGS drilling which seemed to infer a rich strike from the fact that the drill cores had been flown to the United States for chemical assay. Stephens immediately contacted Fogarty at his [845] home in Rye, N. Y., who in turn telephoned and later that day visited Mollison at Mollison's home in Greenwich to obtain a current report and evaluation of the drilling progress.[21]

The following morning, Sunday, Fogarty again telephoned Mollison, inquiring whether Mollison had any further information and told him to return to Timmins with Holyk, the TGS Chief Geologist, as soon as possible "to move things along." With the aid of one Carroll, a public relations consultant, Fogarty drafted a press release designed to quell the rumors, which release, after having been channeled through Stephens and Huntington, a TGS attorney, was issued at 3:00 P. M. on Sunday, April 12, and which appeared in the morning newspapers of general circulation on Monday, April 13. It read in pertinent part as follows:

NEW YORK, April 12 — The following statement was made today by Dr. Charles F. Fogarty, executive vice president of Texas Gulf Sulphur Company, in regard to the company's drilling operations near Timmins, Ontario, Canada. Dr. Fogarty said:

"During the past few days, the exploration activities of Texas Gulf Sulphur in the area of Timmins, Ontario, have been widely reported in the press, coupled with rumors of a substantial copper discovery there. These reports exaggerate the scale of operations, and mention plans and statistics of size and grade of ore that are without factual basis and have evidently originated by speculation of people not connected with TGS.

"The facts are as follows. TGS has been exploring in the Timmins area for six years as part of its overall search in Canada and elsewhere for various minerals — lead, copper, zinc, etc. During the course of this work, in Timmins as well as in Eastern Canada, TGS has conducted exploration entirely on its own, without the participation by others. Numerous prospects have been investigated by geophysical means and a large number of selected ones have been core-drilled. These cores are sent to the United States for assay and detailed examination as a matter of routine and on advice of expert Canadian legal counsel. No inferences as to grade can be drawn from this procedure.

"Most of the areas drilled in Eastern Canada have revealed either barren pyrite or graphite without value; a few have resulted in discoveries of small or marginal sulphide ore bodies.

"Recent drilling on one property near Timmins has led to preliminary indications that more drilling would be required for proper evaluation of this prospect. The drilling done to date has not been conclusive, but the statements made by many outside quarters are unreliable and include information and figures that are not available to TGS.

"The work done to date has not been sufficient to reach definite conclusions and any statement as to size and grade of ore would be premature and possibly misleading. When we have progressed to the point where reasonable and logical conclusions can be made, TGS will issue a definite statement to its stockholders and to the public in order to clarify the Timmins project."

* * * * * *

The release purported to give the Timmins drilling results as of the release date, April 12. From Mollison Fogarty had been told of the developments through 7:00 P. M. on April 10, and of [846] the remarkable discoveries made up to that time, detailed supra, which discoveries, according to the calculations of the experts who testified for the SEC at the hearing, demonstrated that TGS had already discovered 6.2 to 8.3 million tons of proven ore having gross assay values from $26 to $29 per ton. TGS experts, on the other hand, denied at the hearing that proven or probable ore could have been calculated on April 11 or 12 because there was then no assurance of continuity in the mineralized zone.

The evidence as to the effect of this release on the investing public was equivocal and less than abundant. On April 13 the New York Herald Tribune in an article head-noted "Copper Rumor Deflated" quoted from the TGS release of April 12 and backtracked from its original April 11 report of a major strike but nevertheless inferred from the TGS release that "recent mineral exploratory activity near

Timmins, Ontario, has provided preliminary favorable results, sufficient at least to require a step-up in drilling operations." Some witnesses who testified at the hearing stated that they found the release encouraging. On the other hand, a Canadian mining security specialist, Roche, stated that "earlier in the week [before April 16] we had a Dow Jones saying that they [TGS] didn't have anything basically" and a TGS stock specialist for the Midwest Stock Exchange became concerned about his long position in the stock after reading the release. The trial court stated only that "While, in retrospect, the press release may appear gloomy or incomplete, this does not make it misleading or deceptive on the basis of the facts then known." Id. at 296.

Meanwhile, drilling operations continued. [...]

While drilling activity ensued to completion, TGC officials were taking steps toward ultimate disclosure of the discovery. On April 13, a previously-invited reporter for The Northern Miner, a Canadian mining industry journal, visited the drillsite, interviewed Mollison, Holyk and Darke, and prepared an article which confirmed a 10 million ton ore strike. This report, after having been submitted to Mollison and returned to the reporter unamended on April 15, was published in the April 16 issue. A statement relative to the extent of the discovery, in substantial part drafted by Mollison, was given to the Ontario Minister of Mines for release to the Canadian media. Mollison and Holyk expected it to be released over the airways at 11 P. M. on April 15th, but, for undisclosed reasons, it was not released until 9:40 A. M. on the 16th. An official detailed statement, announcing a strike of at least 25 million tons of ore, based on the drilling data set forth above, was read to representatives of American financial media from 10:00 A. M. to 10:10 or 10:15 A. M. on April 16, and appeared over Merrill Lynch's private wire at 10:29 A. M. and, somewhat later than [847] expected, over the Dow Jones ticker tape at 10:54 A. M.

Between the time the first press release was issued on April 12 and the dissemination of the TGS official announcement on the morning of April 16, the only defendants before us on appeal who engaged in market activity were Clayton and Crawford and TGS director Coates. Clayton ordered 200 shares of TGS stock through his Canadian broker on April 15 and the order was executed that day over the Midwest Stock Exchange. Crawford ordered 300 shares at midnight on the 15th and another 300 shares at 8:30 A. M. the next day, and these orders were executed over the Midwest Exchange in Chicago at its opening on April 16. Coates left the TGS press conference and called his broker son-in-law Haemisegger shortly before 10:20 A. M. on the 16th and ordered 2,000 shares of TGS for family trust accounts of which Coates was a trustee but not a beneficiary; Haemisegger executed this order over the New York and Midwest Exchanges, and he and his customers purchased 1500 additional shares.

During the period of drilling in Timmins, the market price of TGS stock fluctuated but steadily gained overall. On Friday, November 8, when the drilling began, the stock closed at 17 3/8 on Friday, November 15, after K-55-1 had been completed, it closed at 18. After a slight decline to 16 3/8 by Friday, November 22, the price rose to 20 7/8 by December 13, when the chemical assay results of K-55-1 were received, and closed at a high of 24 1/8 on February 21, the day after the stock options had been issued. It had reached a price of 26 by March 31, after the land acquisition program had been completed and drilling had been resumed, and continued to ascend to 30 1/8 by the close of trading on April 10, at which time the drilling progress up to then was evaluated for the April 12th press release. On April 13, the day on which the April 12 release was disseminated, TGS opened at 30 1/8, rose immediately to a high of 32 and gradually tapered off to close at 30 7/8. It closed at 30¼ the next day, and at 29 3/8 on April 15. On April 16, the day of the official announcement of the Timmins discovery, the price climbed to a high of 37 and closed at 36 3/8. By May 15, TGS stock was selling at 58¼.

I. THE INDIVIDUAL DEFENDANTS

A. *Introductory*

Rule 10b-5, 17 CFR 240.10b-5, on which this action is predicated, provides:

> It shall be unlawful for any person, directly or indirectly, by the use of any means or instrumentality of interstate commerce, or of the mails, or of any facility of any national securities exchange,
>
> (1) to employ any device, scheme, or artifice to defraud,
>
> (2) to make any untrue statement of a material fact or to omit to state a material fact necessary in order to make the statements made, in the light of the circumstances under which they were made, not misleading, or
>
> (3) to engage in any act, practice, or course of business which operates or would operate as a fraud or deceit upon any person,
>
> in connection with the purchase or sale of any security.

Rule 10b-5 was promulgated pursuant to the grant of authority given the SEC by Congress in Section 10(b) of the Securities Exchange Act of 1934 (15 U.S.C. § 78j(b).[1] The Act and the Rule apply to the transactions here, all of which were consummated on exchanges. [...]Whether predicated on traditional fiduciary concepts,[...] or on the "special facts" doctrine[...], the Rule is based in policy on the justifiable expectation of the securities marketplace that all investors trading on impersonal exchanges have relatively equal access to material information[...]. The essence of the Rule is that anyone who, trading for his own account in the securities of a corporation has "access, directly or indirectly, to information intended to be available only for a corporate purpose and not for the personal benefit of anyone" may not take "advantage of such information knowing it is unavailable to those with whom he is dealing," i. e., the investing public. Matter of Cady, Roberts & Co., 40 SEC 907, 912 (1961). Insiders, as directors or management officers are, of course, by this Rule, precluded from so unfairly dealing, but the Rule is also applicable to one possessing the information who may not be strictly termed an "insider" within the meaning of Sec. 16(b) of the Act.

Cady, Roberts, supra. Thus, anyone in possession of material inside information must either disclose it to the investing public, or, if he is disabled from disclosing it in order to protect a corporate confidence, or he chooses not to do so, must abstain from trading in or recommending the securities concerned while such inside information remains undisclosed. So, it is here no justification for insider activity that disclosure was forbidden by the legitimate corporate objective of acquiring options to purchase the land surrounding the exploration site; if the information was, as the SEC contends, material, its possessors should have kept out of the market until disclosure was accomplished. [...]

B. *Material Inside Information*

An insider is not, of course, always foreclosed from investing in his own company merely because he may be more familiar with company operations than are outside investors. An insider's duty to disclose information or his duty to abstain from dealing in his company's securities arises only in "those situations which are essentially extraordinary in nature and which are reasonably certain to have a substantial effect on the market price of the security if [the extraordinary situation is] disclosed." [...]

Nor is an insider obligated to confer upon outside investors the benefit of his superior financial or other expert analysis by disclosing his educated guesses or predictions. [...] The only regulatory objective is that access to material information be enjoyed equally, but this objective requires nothing more than the disclosure of basic facts so that outsiders may draw upon their own evaluative expertise in reaching their own investment decisions with knowledge equal to that of the insiders.

This is not to suggest, however, as did the trial court, that "the test of materiality must necessarily be a conservative one, particularly since many actions under Section 10(b) are brought on the basis of hindsight,"[...] in the sense that the materiality of facts is to be assessed solely by measuring the effect the knowledge of the facts would have upon prudent or conservative investors. [...] "The basic test of materiality * * * is whether a reasonable man would attach importance * * * in determining his choice of action in the transaction in question. [...] Such a fact is a material fact and must be effectively disclosed to the investing public prior to the commencement of insider trading in the corporation's securities. The speculators and chartists of Wall and Bay Streets are also "reasonable" investors entitled to the same legal protection afforded conservative traders.[10] Thus, material facts include not only information disclosing the earnings and distributions of a company but also those facts which affect the probable future of the company and those which may affect the desire of investors to buy, sell, or hold the company's securities.[...]

Our survey of the facts found below conclusively establishes that knowledge of the results of the discovery hole, K-55-1, would have been important to a reasonable investor and might have affected the price of the stock.[12] On April 16, The Northern Miner, a trade publication in wide circulation among mining stock specialists, called K-55-1, the discovery hole, "one of the most impressive drill holes completed in modern times."[13] Roche, a Canadian broker whose firm specialized in mining securities, characterized the [851] importance to investors of the results of K-55-1. He stated that the completion of "the first drill hole" with "a 600 foot drill core is very very significant * * * anything over 200 feet is considered very significant and 600 feet is just beyond your wildest imagination." He added, however, that it "is a natural thing to buy more stock once they give you the first drill hole." Additional testimony revealed that the prices of stocks of other companies, albeit less diversified, smaller firms, had increased substantially solely on the basis of the discovery of good anomalies or even because of the proximity of their lands to the situs of a potentially major strike.

Finally, a major factor in determining whether the K-55-1 discovery was a material fact is the importance attached to the drilling results by those who knew about it. In view of other unrelated recent developments favorably affecting TGS, participation by an informed person in a regular stock-purchase program, or even sporadic trading by an informed person, might lend only nominal support to the inference of the materiality of the K-55-1 discovery; nevertheless, the timing by those who knew of it of their stock purchases and their purchases of *short-term* calls — purchases in some cases by individuals who had never before purchased calls or even TGS stock — virtually compels the inference that the insiders were influenced by the drilling results. [...] No reason appears why outside investors, perhaps better acquainted with speculative modes of investment and with, in many cases, perhaps more capital at their disposal for intelligent speculation, would have been less influenced, and would not have been similarly motivated to invest if they had known what the insider investors knew about the K-55-1 discovery. [...]

The core of Rule 10b-5 is the implementation of the Congressional purpose that all investors should have equal access to the rewards of participation [852] in securities transactions. It was the intent of Congress that all members of the investing public should be subject to identical market risks, — which market risks include, of course the risk that one's evaluative capacity or one's capital available to put at risk may exceed another's capacity or capital. The insiders here were not trading on an equal footing with the outside investors. They alone were in a position to evaluate the probability and magnitude of what seemed from the outset to be a major ore strike; they alone could invest safely, secure in the expectation that the price of TGS stock would rise substantially in the event such a major strike should materialize, but would decline little, if at all, in the event of failure, for the public, ignorant at the outset of the favorable probabilities would likewise be unaware of the unproductive exploration, and the additional exploration costs would not significantly affect TGS market prices. Such inequities based upon unequal access to knowledge should not be shrugged off as inevitable in our way of life, or, in view of the congressional concern in the area, remain uncorrected.

We hold, therefore, that all transactions in TGS stock or calls by individuals apprised of the drilling results[14] of K-55-1 were made in violation of Rule 10b-5.[1-] The geologist Darke possessed undisclosed material information and traded in TGS securities. Therefore we reverse the dismissal of the action as to him and his personal transactions. [...]

With reference to Huntington, the trial court found that he "had no detailed knowledge as to the work" on the Kidd-55 segment, 258 F.Supp. 281. Nevertheless, the evidence shows that he knew about and participated in TGS's land acquisition program which followed the receipt of the K-55-1 drilling results, and that on February 26, 1964 he purchased 50 shares of TGS stock. Later, on March 16, he helped prepare a letter for Dr. Holyk's signature in which TGS made a substantial offer for lands near K-55-1, and on the same day he, who had never before purchased calls on any stock, purchased a call on 100 shares of TGS stock. We are satisfied that these purchases in February and March, coupled with his readily inferable and probably reliable, understanding of the highly favorable nature of preliminary operations on the Kidd segment, demonstrate that Huntington possessed material inside information such as to make his purchase violative of the Rule and the Act. [...]

Appellant Crawford, who ordered[127] the purchase of TGS stock shortly before the TGS April 16 official announcement, and defendant Coates, who placed orders with and communicated the news to his broker immediately after the official announcement was read at the TGS-called press conference, concede that they were in possession of material information. They contend, however, that their purchases were not proscribed purchases for the news had already been effectively disclosed. We disagree.

[...]16th, with instructions to buy at the opening of the Midwest Stock Exchange that morning. The trial court's finding that "he sought to, and did, `beat the news,'" 258 F.Supp. at 287, is well documented by the record. The rumors of a major ore strike which had been circulated in Canada and, to a lesser extent, in New York, had been disclaimed by the TGS press release of April 12, which significantly promised the public an official detailed announcement when possibilities had ripened into actualities. The abbreviated announcement to the Canadian press at 9:40 A.M. on the 16th by the Ontario Minister of Mines and the report carried by The Northern Miner, parts of which had sporadically reached New York on the morning of the 16th through reports from Canadian affiliates to a few New York investment firms, are assuredly not the equivalent of the official 10-15 minute announcement which was not released to the American financial press until after 10:00 A.M. Crawford's orders had been [854] placed before that. Before insiders may act upon material information, such information must have been effectively disclosed in a manner sufficient to insure its availability to the investing public. Particularly here, where a formal announcement to the entire financial news media had been promised in a prior official release known to the media, all insider activity must await dissemination of the promised official announcement.

Coates was absolved by the court below because his telephone order was placed shortly before 10:20 A.M. on April 16, which was after the announcement had been made even though the news could not be considered already a matter of public information. 258 F. Supp. at 288. This result seems to have been predicated upon a misinterpretation of dicta in *Cady, Roberts,* where the SEC instructed insiders to "keep out of the market until the established procedures for public release of the information are *carried out* instead of hastening to execute transactions in advance of, and in frustration of, the objectives of the release," 40 SEC at 915 (emphasis supplied). The reading of a news release, which prompted Coates into action, is merely the first step in the process of dissemination required for compliance with the regulatory objective of providing all investors with an equal opportunity to make informed investment judgments. Assuming that the contents of the official release could instantaneously be acted upon,[18] at the minimum Coates should have waited until the news could reasonably have been expected to appear over the media of widest circulation, the Dow Jones broad tape, rather than hastening to insure an advantage to himself and his broker son-in-law. [...]

Tipper/Tippee Liability   6.2.3

Remember, classical insider trading liability starts with an insider who violates their fiduciary duty to their principle by trading in their own company's stock while in possession of inside information.

What about liability for trading in situations where the trading doesn't involve an insider?

Tipping by insiders to outsiders is a direct challenge to the classical insider trading doctrine. Because the recipient of inside information does not have a fiduciary duty to the shareholders or the corporation, classical insider trading theory does not extend to recipients of inside information. Courts have responded to these situations by finding ways to extend liability to recipients of inside information, "tippees".

Dirks v. SEC

DIRKS V. SEC
103 S. Ct. 3255 (1983)

6
.
2
.
3
.
1

JUSTICE POWELL delivered the opinion
of the Court.

Petitioner Raymond Dirks received material nonpublic information from "insiders" of a corporation with which he had no connection. He disclosed this information to investors who relied on it in trading in the shares of the corporation. The question is whether Dirks violated the antifraud provisions of the federal securities laws by this disclosure. [...]

In 1973, Dirks was an officer of a New York broker-dealer firm who specialized in providing investment analysis of insurance company securities to institutional investors.[1] On [649] March 6, Dirks received information from Ronald Secrist, a former officer of Equity Funding of America. Secrist alleged that the assets of Equity Funding, a diversified corporation primarily engaged in selling life insurance and mutual funds, were vastly overstated as the result of fraudulent corporate practices. Secrist also stated that various regulatory agencies had failed to act on similar charges made by

Equity Funding employees. He urged Dirks to verify the fraud and disclose it publicly.

Dirks decided to investigate the allegations. He visited Equity Funding's headquarters in Los Angeles and interviewed several officers and employees of the corporation. The senior management denied any wrongdoing, but certain corporation employees corroborated the charges of fraud. Neither Dirks nor his firm owned or traded any Equity Funding stock, but throughout his investigation he openly discussed the information he had obtained with a number of clients and investors. Some of these persons sold their holdings of Equity Funding securities, including five investment advisers who liquidated holdings of more than $16 million.[2]

While Dirks was in Los Angeles, he was in touch regularly with William Blundell, the Wall Street Journal's Los Angeles bureau chief. Dirks urged Blundell to write a story on the fraud allegations. Blundell did not believe, however, that such a massive fraud could go undetected and declined to [650] write the story. He feared that publishing such damaging hearsay might be libelous.

During the 2-week period in which Dirks pursued his investigation and spread word of Secrist's charges, the price of Equity Funding stock fell from $26 per share to less than $15 per share. This led the New York Stock Exchange to halt trading on March 27. Shortly thereafter California insurance authorities impounded Equity Funding's records and uncovered evidence of the fraud. Only then did the Securities and Exchange Commission (SEC) file a complaint against Equity Funding[3] and only then, on April 2, did the Wall Street Journal publish a front-page story based largely on information assembled by Dirks. Equity Funding immediately went into receivership.[4]

The SEC began an investigation into Dirks' role in the exposure of the fraud. After a hearing by an Administrative Law Judge, the SEC found that Dirks had aided and abetted violations of [...] SEC Rule 10b-5, 17 CFR § 240.10b-5 (1983),[2] by repeating the allegations of fraud to members of the investment community who later sold their Equity Funding stock. The SEC concluded: "Where `tippees' —

regardless of their motivation or occupation — come into possession of material `corporate information that they know is confidential and know or should know came from a corporate insider,' they must either publicly disclose that information or refrain from trading." [...] Recognizing, however, that Dirks "played an important role in bringing [Equity Funding's] massive fraud [652] to light," 21 S. E. C. Docket, at 1412,[8] the SEC only censured him.[9] [...]

II

In the seminal case of *In re Cady, Roberts & Co.,* 40 S. E. C. 907 (1961), the SEC recognized that the common law in some jurisdictions imposes on "corporate `insiders,' particularly officers, directors, or controlling stockholders" an "affirmative duty of disclosure . . . when dealing in securities." *Id.,* at 911, and n. 13.[10] The SEC found that not only did breach of this common-law duty also establish the elements of a Rule 10b-5 violation,[11] but that individuals other than corporate insiders could be obligated either to disclose material nonpublic information[12] before trading or to abstain from trading altogether. *Id.,* at 912. In *Chiarella,* we accepted the two elements set out in *Cady, Roberts* for establishing a Rule 10b-5 violation: "(i) the existence of a relationship affording access to inside information intended to be available only for a corporate purpose, and (ii) the unfairness of allowing a corporate insider to take advantage of that information [654] by trading without disclosure." 445 U. S., at 227. In examining whether Chiarella had an obligation to disclose or abstain, the Court found that there is no general duty to disclose before trading on material nonpublic information,[13] and held that "a duty to disclose under § 10(b) does not arise from the mere possession of nonpublic market information." *Id.,* at 235. Such a duty arises rather from the existence of a fiduciary relationship. See *id.,* at 227-235.

Not "all breaches of fiduciary duty in connection with a securities transaction," however, come within the ambit of Rule 10b-5. *Santa Fe Industries, Inc.* v. *Green,* 430 U. S. 462, 472 (1977). There must also be "manipulation or deception." *Id.,* at 473. In an inside-trading case this fraud derives from the "inherent unfairness involved where one takes advantage" of "information intended to be available only for a corporate purpose and not for the personal benefit of anyone." [...] Thus, an insider will be liable under Rule 10b-5 for inside trading only where he fails to disclose material nonpublic information before trading on it and thus makes "secret profits." [...]

III

We were explicit in *Chiarella* in saying that there can be no duty to disclose where the person who has traded on inside information "was not [the corporation's] agent, . . . was not a fiduciary, [or] was not a person in whom the sellers [of the securities] had placed their trust and confidence." [...] Not to require such a fiduciary relationship, we recognized, would "depar[t] radically from the established doctrine that duty arises from a specific relationship between [655] two parties" and would amount to "recognizing a general duty between all participants in market transactions to forgo actions based on material, nonpublic information." [...]This requirement of a specific relationship between the shareholders and the individual trading on inside information has created analytical difficulties for the SEC and courts in policing tippees who trade on inside information. Unlike insiders who have independent fiduciary duties to both the corporation and its shareholders, the typical tippee has no such relationships.[14] In view of this absence, it has been unclear how a tippee acquires the *Cady, Roberts* duty to refrain from trading on inside information. [...]

In effect, the SEC's theory of tippee liability in both cases appears rooted in the idea that the antifraud provisions require equal information among all traders. This conflicts with the principle set forth in *Chiarella* that only some persons, under some circumstances, will be barred from trading while in possession of material nonpublic information.[16] Judge Wright correctly read our opinion in *Chiarella* as repudiating any notion that all traders must enjoy equal information before trading: "[T]he `information' theory is rejected. Because the disclose-or-refrain duty is extraordinary, it attaches only when a party has legal obligations other than a mere duty to comply with the general antifraud proscriptions in the federal securities laws." [...]We reaffirm today that "[a] duty [to disclose] [658] arises from the relationship between parties . . . and not merely from one's ability to acquire information because of his position in the market." [...]

B

The conclusion that recipients of inside information do not invariably acquire a duty to disclose or abstain does not mean that such tippees always are free to trade on the information. The need for a ban on some tippee trading is clear. Not only are insiders forbidden by their fiduciary relationship from personally using undisclosed corporate information to their advantage, but they also may not give such information to an outsider for the same improper purpose of exploiting the information for their personal gain. [...]As we noted in *Chiarella,* "[t]he tippee's obligation has been viewed as arising from his role as a participant after the fact in the insider's breach of a fiduciary duty." [...]

Thus, some tippees must assume an insider's duty to the shareholders not because they receive inside information, but rather because it has been made available to them *improperly.*[19] And for Rule 10b-5 purposes, the insider's disclosure is improper only where it would violate his *Cady, Roberts* duty. Thus, a tippee assumes a fiduciary duty to the shareholders of a corporation not to trade on material nonpublic information only when the insider has breached his fiduciary duty to the shareholders by disclosing the information to the tippee and the tippee knows or should know that there has been a breach.[20]

C

In determining whether a tippee is under an obligation to disclose or abstain, it thus is necessary to determine whether the insider's "tip" constituted a breach of the insider's fiduciary duty. All disclosures of confidential corporate information [662] are not inconsistent with the duty insiders owe to shareholders. In contrast to the extraordinary facts of this case, the more typical situation in which there will be a question whether disclosure violates the insider's *Cady, Roberts* duty is when insiders disclose information to analysts. [...]In some situations, the insider will act consistently with his fiduciary duty to shareholders, and yet release of the information may affect the market. For example, it may not be clear — either to the corporate insider or to the recipient analyst — whether the information will be viewed as material nonpublic information. Corporate officials may mistakenly think the information already has been disclosed or that it is not material enough to affect the market. Whether disclosure is a breach of duty therefore depends in large part on the purpose of the disclosure. This standard was identified by the SEC itself in *Cady, Roberts:* a purpose of the securities laws was to eliminate "use of inside information for personal advantage." [...]. Thus, the test is whether the insider personally will benefit, directly or indirectly, from his disclosure. Absent some personal gain, there has been no breach of duty to stockholders. And absent a breach by the insider, there is no derivative breach.[1-1]

But to determine whether the disclosure itself "deceive[s], manipulate[s], or defraud[s]" shareholders,[...] the initial inquiry is whether there has been a breach of duty by the insider. This requires courts to focus on objective criteria, *i. e.,* whether the insider receives a direct or indirect personal benefit from the disclosure, such as a pecuniary gain or a reputational benefit that will translate into future earnings. [...] Brudney, Insiders, Outsiders, and Informational Advantages Under the Federal Securities [664] Laws, 93 Harv. L. Rev. 322, 348 (1979) ("The theory . . . is that the insider, by giving the information out selectively, is in effect selling the information to its recipient for cash, reciprocal information, or other things of value for himself. . ."). There are objective facts and circumstances that often justify such an inference. For example, there may be a relationship between the insider and the recipient that suggests a *quid pro quo* from the latter, or an intention to benefit the particular recipient. The elements of fiduciary duty and exploitation of nonpublic information also exist when an insider makes a gift of confidential information to a trading relative or friend. The tip and trade resemble trading by the insider himself followed by a gift of the profits to the recipient.

Determining whether an insider personally benefits from a particular disclosure, a question of fact, will not always be easy for courts. But it is essential, we think, to have a guiding principle for those whose daily activities must be limited and instructed by the SEC's inside-trading rules, and we believe that there must be a breach of the insider's fiduciary duty before the tippee inherits the duty to disclose or abstain. In contrast, the rule adopted by the SEC in this case would have no limiting principle.[24]

IV

Under the inside-trading and tipping rules set forth above, we find that there was no actionable violation by Dirks.[25] It is undisputed that Dirks himself was a stranger to Equity Funding, with no pre-existing fiduciary duty to its shareholders.[26] He took no action, directly or indirectly, that induced the shareholders or officers of Equity Funding to repose trust or confidence in him. There was no expectation by Dirks' sources that he would keep their information in confidence. Nor did Dirks misappropriate or illegally obtain the information about Equity Funding. Unless the insiders breached their *Cady, Roberts* duty to shareholders in disclosing the nonpublic information to Dirks, he breached no duty when he passed it on to investors as well as to the Wall Street Journal.

[666] It is clear that neither Secrist nor the other Equity Funding employees violated their *Cady, Roberts* duty to the corporation's shareholders by providing information to Dirks.[27] [667] The tippers received no monetary or personal benefit for revealing Equity Funding's secrets, nor was their purpose to make a gift of valuable information to Dirks. As the facts of this case clearly indicate, the tippers were motivated by a desire to expose the fraud. [...] In the absence of a breach of duty to shareholders by the insiders, there was no derivative breach by Dirks. See n. 20, *supra.* Dirks therefore could not have been "a participant after the fact in [an] insider's breach of a fiduciary duty." *Chiarella,* 445 U. S., at 230, n. 12.

V

We conclude that Dirks, in the circumstances of this case, had no duty to abstain from use of the inside information that he obtained. The judgment of the Court of Appeals therefore is

Reversed.

SEC. v. Switzer   6.2.3.2

Not all tippees will be subject to liability for trading on a corporation's material, confidential inside information. In the case that follows, the court tests the limits of liability for tippees when the source has not violated their fiduciary duty when disclosing the information.

SEC V. SWITZER

590 F. Supp. 756 (W.D. of Ok)

SAFFELS, District Judge, Sitting by Designation.

This action brought by the Securities and Exchange Commission [hereinafter SEC] was tried to the court on March 19-22, 1984. It involved allegations of violations of Section 10(b) of the Securities Exchange Act of 1934 and violations of Commission Rule 10b-5. [...]

6. Barry L. Switzer resides at 2811 Castlewood Drive, Norman, Oklahoma (73070). At all times mentioned in the complaint, Switzer was the head football coach at the University of Oklahoma in Norman, Oklahoma. [...]

13. Texas International Company [hereinafter TIC] is a Delaware corporation with principal offices located in Oklahoma City, Oklahoma. At all times mentioned in the complaint, TIC was

engaged in, among other things, exploration for and development of oil and natural gas properties. At all times mentioned in the complaint, TIC's common stock was registered with the SEC pursuant to Section 12(b) of the Securities Exchange Act [15 U.S.C. 78*l*(b)] and was traded on the New York Stock Exchange, as well as other exchanges. On or about June 18, 1982, a wholly-owned subsidiary of TIC merged with Phoenix Resources Company [hereinafter Phoenix] and Phoenix became a wholly-owned subsidiary of TIC. At all times mentioned in the complaint prior to the merger, TIC owned in excess of fifty percent (50%) of the common stock of Phoenix, and, by reason of such ownership position, controlled Phoenix through election of three of the five members of the Phoenix Board of Directors.

[759] 14. Prior to the merger, Phoenix, the successor to King Resources Company, was a Maine corporation with principal offices located in Oklahoma City, Oklahoma. At all times mentioned in the complaint prior to the merger, Phoenix engaged in, among other things, exploration for and development of oil and natural gas properties. At all times mentioned in the complaint prior to the merger, Phoenix's common stock was registered with the SEC pursuant to Section 12(b) of the Securities Exchange Act [15 U.S.C. 78*l*(b)] and was traded in the Over-the-Counter securities market on the National Association of Securities Dealers Automated Quotation System. [...]

32. Barry Switzer is a well-recognized "celebrity" in Oklahoma and elsewhere. He has an interest in the oil and gas industry, as he is personally involved in various ventures within the industry.

33. Over the past several years, defendants Switzer, Kennedy, Deem, Smith, Hodges, Amyx and Hoover have acted together in varying combinations of persons (or in various groups of persons) in making investments. They have formed partnerships such as S & H Investments, Waverly Ltd., and Hodges, Amyx, Cross and Hodges, to assist them in their investment ventures. Often times, they trade on rumors or gossip they hear within the investing community. Profits and losses occurring as a result of stock investments made through these partnerships are shared by the members of the partnerships.

34. TIC had been considering various options for either consolidating or separating TIC and Phoenix for some time prior to its approaching Morgan Stanley on June 4 or 5, 1981. Rumors concerning these various options were circulating within the investing oil and gas community prior to June 4 or 5, 1981.

35. On June 6, 1981, four days prior to the public announcement concerning Phoenix, a state invitational secondary school track meet was held at John Jacobs Field on the University of Oklahoma campus. The track meet was a day long event. Several hundred spectators attended, including Barry Switzer, who arrived at the meet between 10:00 and 10:30 a.m. to watch his son compete, and George and Linda Platt, who arrived between 9:00 and 10:00 a.m. to watch their son compete. Soon after Switzer's arrival at the track meet, he and G. Platt recognized and greeted each other. Neither Switzer nor G. Platt knew that the other would be attending the meet.

36. G. Platt was a supporter of Oklahoma University football and had met Switzer at a few social engagements prior to June of 1981. TIC was a sponsor of Switzer's football show, "Play Back." G. Platt had had season tickets to the OU football games for approximately five years. G. Platt had obtained autographs from Switzer for G. Platt's minor children, and had had his secretary telephone Switzer to request that his season tickets be upgraded. Upgrading of tickets was extended as a courtesy by Switzer to many season ticket holders. On at least two occasions Switzer had phoned G. Platt requesting continued sponsorship by TIC of Switzer's football television program. These calls were made at the urging of Tom Goodgame, General Manager of the television station which then produced "Play Back." As of June 5, 1981, Switzer knew that G. Platt was Chairman of the Board of TIC and further knew that TIC was a substantial shareholder of Phoenix because Switzer was a stockholder in TIC and thereby knew Phoenix was a subsidiary.

37. Neither G. Platt nor his wife Linda are particularly impressed by Switzer. They view him as "just a nice fellow."

38. Upon first greeting each other at the track meet, G. Platt and Switzer exchanged pleasantries. Switzer then departed and continued on through the bleachers.

39. Throughout the course of the day, G. Platt and Linda Platt generally remained in one place in the bleachers. Switzer, however, throughout the day moved around a great deal, at times speaking with his son or other participants and their families, signing autographs and watching the different events on the field. While moving about, Switzer joined the Platts to visit with them about three to five times. During these visits Switzer and the Platts talked about their sons' participation in the meet, the oil and gas business, the economy, football and their respective personal investments.

40. G. Platt and Switzer did not have any conversations regarding Phoenix or Morgan Stanley, nor did they have any conversations regarding any mergers, acquisitions, take-overs or possible liquidations of Phoenix in which Morgan Stanley would play a part. G. Platt did not make [762] any stock recommendations to Switzer, nor did he intentionally communicate material, non-public corporate information to Switzer about Phoenix during their conversations at the track meet. The information that Switzer heard at the track meet about Phoenix was overheard and was not the result of an intentional disclosure by G. Platt.

41. Sometime in the afternoon, after his last conversation with G. Platt, Switzer laid down on a row of bleachers behind the Platts to sunbathe while waiting for his son's next event. While Switzer was sunbathing, he overheard G. Platt talking to his wife about his trip to New York the prior day. In that conversation, G. Platt mentioned Morgan Stanley and his desire to dispose of or liquidate Phoenix. G. Platt further talked about several companies bidding on Phoenix. Switzer also overheard that an announcement of a "possible" liquidation of Phoenix might occur the following Thursday. Switzer remained on the bleachers behind the Platts for approximately twenty minutes then got up and continued to move about.

42. At this time Switzer had no knowledge as to whether the information he had overheard was confidential.

43. G. Platt was not conscious of Switzer's presence on the bleachers behind him that day, nor that Switzer had overheard any conversation.

44. G. Platt had returned home late the previous day from his meetings in New York, and his wife was to leave town for an entire week on the following day. Having minor children, it is the Platts' common practice to try to arrange for G. Platt to be at home when his wife is out of town. The day of the track meet provided the Platts with an opportunity to discuss their respective plans for the up-coming week. During this discussion, G. Platt's prior business activities in New York and its resultant obligations and appointments were mentioned. In addition, when G. Platt appears distracted, it is not uncommon for his wife to inquire of him what is on his mind. On these occasions, he will talk to her about his problems, even though she does not have an understanding of nor interest in business matters. On the day of the track meet, Phoenix was weighing upon the mind of G. Platt, as it had been for the past several years, prompting G. Platt to talk to his wife about it.

45. On June 6, 1981, after the track meet, Switzer returned home and looked up the price of Phoenix in the paper. He then had dinner with Sedwyn Kennedy, a close friend of both his and defendant Lee Allan Smith. In the past, they had all made investments through their partnership, SKS. Switzer told Kennedy he had overheard a conversation about the possible liquidation of Phoenix and that it would probably occur or be announced the next Thursday. Switzer told him the source was a gentlemen who was an executive with TIC. Switzer did not tell Kennedy the man was G. Platt. Switzer and Kennedy are close friends and have known each other since 1966.

46. By the end of the evening, Switzer and Kennedy had each expressed an intention to purchase Phoenix stock. [...]

48. On or about Monday, June 8, 1981, Kennedy purchased five thousand (5,000) shares of Phoenix stock at Forty-Two and 75/100 Dollars ($42.75) per share through the S&H Investments account; and on or about Tuesday, June 9, 1981, after further discussions with Deem, Kennedy purchased an additional one thousand (1,000)

shares of Phoenix at Forty-Nine Dollars ($49) per share. (See stipulated fact No. 15, *supra.*)

49. On Sunday, June 7, 1981, Switzer called Lee Allan Smith, a close friend with whom he had previously entered joint investments. [763] Switzer told Smith that he had been at a track meet on Saturday and had overheard some information regarding the possible liquidation or buy-out of Phoenix. Switzer attributed the information to "someone who should know," and said that he had overheard that Morgan Stanley was involved and that something could happen by Thursday of the following week. Switzer and Smith decided to approach Harold Hodges and Robert Hoover about providing the capital for buying some Phoenix stock with them because Smith and Switzer had insufficient available cash at that time to purchase a significant number of shares on their own. Hodges, Smith and Switzer were personal friends through participation in community and charitable activities in Oklahoma City. Hoover has known Smith for thirty years and has been a personal friend of both Smith and Switzer. [...]

61. G. Platt did not share in the profits made through the transactions in Phoenix stock by Switzer, Kennedy, Deem, Smith, Hodges, Amyx and Hoover, nor did he receive any other financial benefit as a result of those transactions.

62. G. Platt did not receive any direct or indirect pecuniary gain nor any reputational benefit likely to translate into future earnings due to Switzer's inadvertent receipt of the information regarding Phoenix.

63. G. Platt did not make any gift to Switzer at this time, nor has he ever made a gift to Switzer.

64. Neither Switzer, Kennedy, Smith, Deem, Hodges, Amyx nor Hoover has ever been employed by or been an officer or director of Phoenix or TIC, nor have any of these defendants ever had any business relationship with Phoenix or with G. Platt personally. None of these defendants is a relative or personal friend of G. Platt.

65. None of the defendants had a relationship of trust and confidence with Phoenix, its shareholders or G. Platt. [...]

3. It is undisputed that G. Platt was an insider in regard to both TIC and Phoenix as of June 6, 1981.

4. Switzer, Kennedy, Deem, Smith, Hodges, Amyx and Hoover were not insiders of Phoenix. None of them had any fiduciary duty to the stockholders of TIC or Phoenix by virtue of their positions. None of them were employed by Phoenix, nor did they have any position of trust or confidence with Phoenix. These defendants were strangers to Phoenix and had no preexisting fiduciary duties to the shareholders of Phoenix. In its recent opinion of *Dirks v. Securities Exchange Commission,* 463 U.S. 646, 103 S.Ct. 3255, 77 L.Ed.2d 911 (1983), the United States Supreme Court addressed tippee liability. The court pointed out that, unlike insiders who have independent fiduciary duties to both the corporation and its shareholders, the typical tippee has no such fiduciary relationship. In view of the absence of this fiduciary relationship, the court notes it has been unclear how a tippee acquires the *Cady, Roberts* duty to disclose or refrain from trading on inside information first stated in *In re Cady, Roberts & Co.,* 40 S.E.C. 907 (1961). Although the SEC, in *Dirks,* urged the court to accept what has become known as the "information" theory, which in essence states that anyone knowingly receiving non-public, material information acquires an insider fiduciary duty to disclose or abstain from trading, the court rejected this theory as they had in *Chiarella v. United States,* 445 U.S. 222, 100 S.Ct. 1108, 63 L.Ed.2d 348 (1980). The court in *Dirks* stated: "We reaffirm today that `[a] duty [to disclose] arises from the relationship between parties ... and not merely from one's ability to acquire information because of his position in the market.'" *Dirks,* 103 S.Ct. at 3263, quoting from *Chiarella v. United States,* 445 U.S. at 232-33, n. 14, 100 S.Ct. at 1116 n. 14. The court further stated in *Dirks:* "As we emphasized in *Chiarella,* mere possession of non-public information does not give rise to a duty to disclose or abstain; only a specific relationship does that. And we do not believe that the mere receipt of information from an insider creates such a special relationship between the tippee and the corporation's shareholders." 103 S.Ct. at 3262, n. 15.

6. Essentially, in *Dirks* the court found that the *Cady, Roberts* duty of a tippee "to disclose or abstain" is *derivative* from that of the insider's duty. The court stated:

> ... [S]ome tippees must assume an insider's duty to the shareholders not because they receive inside information, but rather because it has been made available to them *improperly.* And for Rule 10b-5 purposes, the insider's disclosure is improper only where it would violate his *Cady, Roberts* duty. Thus, a tippee assumes a fiduciary duty to the shareholders of a corporation not to trade on material nonpublic information only when the insider has breached his fiduciary duty to the shareholders by disclosing the information to the tippee and the tippee knows or should know that there has been a breach. As Commissioner Smith perceptively observed in *Investors Management Co.:* `[T]ippee responsibility must be related back to insider responsibility by a necessary finding that the tippee knew the information was given to him in breach of a duty by a person having a special relationship to the issuer not to disclose the information .... `44 S.E.C., at 651 (concurring in the result). Tipping thus properly is viewed only as a means of indirectly violating [766] the *Cady, Roberts* disclose-or-abstain rule.

Dirks v. S.E.C [...]

7. Thus, only when a disclosure is made for an "improper purpose" will such a "tip" constitute a breach of an insider's duty, and only when there has been a breach of an insider's duty which the "tipee" knew or should have known constituted such a breach will there be "tippee" liability sufficient to constitute a violation of § 10(b) and Commission Rule 10b-5.

8. In *Dirks,* the court held that a disclosure is made for an "improper purpose" when an insider personally will benefit, directly or indirectly, from his disclosure. That court stated: "Absent some personal gain, there has been no breach of duty to stockholders. And absent a breach by the insider [to his stockholders], there is no derivative breach [by the tippee]. *Dirks,* 103 S.Ct. at 3265.

9. G. Platt did not breach a fiduciary duty to stockholders of Phoenix for purposes of Rule 10b-5 liability nor § 10(b) liability, when he disclosed to his wife at the track meet of June 6, 1981, that there was going to be a possible liquidation of Phoenix.

10. This information was given to Mrs. Platt by G. Platt for the purpose of informing her of his up-coming business schedule so that arrangements for child care could be made.

11. The information was inadvertently overheard by Switzer at the track meet.

12. Rule 10b-5 does not bar trading on the basis of information inadvertently revealed by an insider. [...]

14. G. Platt did not personally benefit, directly or indirectly, monetarily or otherwise from the inadvertent disclosure.

15. As noted above, *Dirks* set forth a two-prong test for purposes of determining whether a tippee has acquired a fiduciary duty. First, it must be shown that an insider breached a fiduciary duty to the shareholders by disclosing inside information; and, second, it must be shown that the tippee knew or should have known that there had been a breach by the insider. *Dirks,* 103 S.Ct. at 3264.

16. G. Platt did not breach a duty to the shareholders of Phoenix, and thus plaintiff failed to meet its burden of proof as to the first prong established in *Dirks.* Since G. Platt did not breach a fiduciary duty to Phoenix shareholders, Switzer did not acquire nor assume a fiduciary duty to Phoenix's shareholders, and because Switzer did not acquire a fiduciary duty to Phoenix shareholders, any information he passed on to defendants Smith, Hodges, Amyx, Hoover, Kennedy and Deem was not in violation of Rule 10b-5. [...]

On the basis of the above findings of fact and conclusions of law, the court orders judgment in favor of defendants.

A note on US v Newman   6.2.3.3

The classic tipper-tippee scenario in insider trading
prosecutions involves a corporate insider who, in
exchange for a personal benefit, discloses material nonpublic
information to an outsider, who then later trades in reliance on this
inside information. For many years, courts leaned on increasingly
vague assertions of "personal benefit" received by tippers to assign
criminal liability to remote tippees. In some cases, courts have been
willing to "daisy chain" to recipients of inside information who are
extremely remote from the original source.

In *United States v. Newman* the Second Circuit reduced the
criminal liability of remote tippees by holding that a tippee cannot
be criminally convicted unless the tippee "knows of the personal
benefit received by the insider in exchange for the disclosure." In
addition, *Newman* held the "personal benefit" received by the
tipper "must be of some consequence" and must be a true *quid pro
quo*, rejecting the notion that mere friendship and association could
meet this requirement.

From the *Newman* opinion:

> [T]he Government presented evidence that a group of financial
> analysts exchanged information they obtained from company
> insiders, both directly and more often indirectly. Specifically,
> the Government alleged that these analysts received information
> from insiders at Dell and NVIDIA disclosing those companies'
> earnings numbers before they were publicly released in Dell's
> May 2008 and August 2008 earnings announcements and
> NVIDIA's May 2008 earnings announcement. These analysts
> then passed the inside information to their portfolio managers,
> including Newman and Chiasson, who, in turn, executed trades
> in Dell and NVIDIA stock, earning approximately $4 million
> and $68 million, respectively, in profits for their respective
> funds.
>
> Newman and Chiasson were several steps removed from the
> corporate insiders and there was no evidence that either was
> aware of the source of the inside information. With respect to

the Dell tipping chain, the evidence established that Rob Ray of Dell's investor relations department tipped information regarding Dell's consolidated earnings numbers to Sandy Goyal, an analyst at Neuberger Berman. Goyal in turn gave the information to Diamondback analyst Jesse Tortora. Tortora in turn relayed the information to his manager Newman as well as to other analysts including Level Global analyst Spyridon "Sam" Adondakis. Adondakis then passed along the Dell information to Chiasson, making Newman and Chiasson three and four levels removed from the inside tipper, respectively. ...

Newman and Chiasson moved for a judgment of acquittal pursuant to Federal Rule of Criminal Procedure 29. They argued that there was no evidence that the corporate insiders provided inside information in exchange for a personal benefit which is required to establish tipper liability under *Dirks v. S.E.C.,*463 U.S. 646, 103 S.Ct. 3255, 77 L.Ed.2d 911 (1983). Because a tippee's liability derives from the liability of the tipper, Newman and Chiasson argued that they could not be found guilty of insider trading. Newman and Chiasson also argued that, even if the corporate insiders had received a personal benefit in exchange for the inside information, there was no evidence that they knew about any such benefit. Absent such knowledge, appellants argued, they were not aware of, or participants in, the tippers' fraudulent breaches of fiduciary duties to Dell or NVIDIA, and could not be convicted of insider trading under *Dirks.* ...

In light of *Dirks,* we find no support for the Government's contention that knowledge of a breach of the duty of confidentiality without knowledge of the personal benefit is sufficient to impose criminal liability. Although the Government might like the law to be different, nothing in the law requires a symmetry of information in the nation's securities markets. The Supreme Court explicitly repudiated this premise not only in*Dirks,* but in a predecessor case, *Chiarella v. United States.* In *Chiarella,* the Supreme Court rejected this Circuit's conclusion that "the federal securities laws have created a system providing equal access to information necessary for reasoned and intelligent investment decisions.... because [material non-public] information gives certain buyers or sellers an unfair advantage over less informed buyers and sellers." 445 U.S. at 232, 100 S.Ct. 1108. The Supreme Court emphasized that "[t]his reasoning suffers from [a] defect.... [because] not every instance of financial unfairness constitutes fraudulent activity under § 10(b)." *Id. See also United States v. Chestman,* 947 F.2d 551, 578 (2d Cir. 1991) (Winter, J., concurring) ("[The policy rationale [for prohibiting insider trading] stops well short of prohibiting all trading on material nonpublic information. Efficient capital markets depend on the protection of property rights in information. However, they also require that persons who acquire and act on information about companies be able to profit from the information they generate....")]. Thus, in both *Chiarella* and *Dirks,* the Supreme Court affirmatively established that insider trading liability is based on breaches of fiduciary duty, not on informational asymmetries. This is a critical limitation on insider trading liability that protects a corporation's interests in confidentiality while promoting efficiency in the nation's securities markets.

As noted above, *Dirks* clearly defines a breach of fiduciary duty as a breach of the duty of confidentiality in exchange for a personal benefit. ... Accordingly, we conclude that a tippee's knowledge of the insider's breach necessarily requires knowledge that the insider disclosed confidential information in exchange for personal benefit. In reaching this conclusion, we join every other district court to our knowledge—apart from Judge Sullivan—that has confronted this question. ...

Our conclusion also comports with well-settled principles of substantive criminal law. As the Supreme Court explained in *Staples v. United States,* under the common law, *mens rea,* which requires that the defendant know the facts that make his conduct illegal, is a necessary element in every crime. Such a requirement is particularly appropriate in insider trading cases where we have acknowledged "it is easy to imagine a ... trader who receives a tip and is unaware that his conduct was illegal and therefore wrongful." *United States v. Kaiser.* This is also a statutory requirement, because only "willful" violations are subject to criminal provision. *See United States v. Temple* ("`Willful' repeatedly has been defined in the criminal context as intentional, purposeful, and voluntary, as distinguished from accidental or negligent").

In sum, we hold that to sustain an insider trading conviction against a tippee, the Government must prove each of the following elements beyond a reasonable doubt: that (1) the corporate insider was entrusted with a fiduciary duty; (2) the corporate insider breached his fiduciary duty by (a) disclosing confidential information to a tippee (b) in exchange for a personal benefit; (3) the tippee knew of the tipper's breach, that is, he knew the information was confidential and divulged for personal benefit; and (4) the tippee still used that information to trade in a security or tip another individual for personal benefit.

Misappropriation Theory

Classical insider trading theory generates liability for insiders. However, classical insider trading theory has an obvious limitation. Under the classical theory of insider trading, there is no liability if the insider uses the material inside information of the corporation to trade in the stock of ANOTHER corporation and not the corporation to which the insider has a fiduciary duty. However, clearly, there are lots of situations where corporations have inside information that could affect the stock price of another corporation. If insiders could trade without fear of liability because the inside information is about a company to whom the insider owes no duty, that would be a problem.

The following cases lay out the courts' response to the limitations of the classical insider trading theory while holding on to its fiduciary duty core.

U.S. v. O'Hagan   6.2.4.1

UNITED STATES v. O'HAGAN
117 S. Ct. 2199 (1997)

Justice Ginsburg, delivered the opinion of the Court.

I

Respondent James Herman O'Hagan was a partner in the law firm
of Dorsey & Whitney in Minneapolis, Minnesota. In July 1988,
Grand Metropolitan PLC (Grand Met), a company based in
London, England, retained Dorsey & Whitney as local counsel to
represent Grand Met regarding a potential tender offer for the
common stock of the Pillsbury Company, headquartered in
Minneapolis. Both Grand Met and Dorsey & Whitney took
precautions to protect the confidentiality of Grand Met's tender
offer plans. O'Hagan did no work on the Grand Met representation.
[...]

On August 18, 1988, while Dorsey & Whitney was still representing
Grand Met, O'Hagan began purchasing call options for Pillsbury
stock. Each option gave him the right to purchase 100 shares of
Pillsbury stock by a specified date in September 1988. Later in
August and in September, O'Hagan made additional purchases of
Pillsbury call options. By the end of September, he owned 2,500
unexpired Pillsbury options, apparently more than any other
individual investor.[...]When Grand Met announced its tender
offer in October, the price of Pillsbury stock rose to nearly $60 per
share. O'Hagan then sold his Pillsbury call options and common
stock, making a profit of more than $4.3 million.

The Securities and Exchange Commission (SEC or Commission)
initiated an investigation into O'Hagan's transactions, culminating in
a 57-count indictment. The indictment alleged that O'Hagan

defrauded his law firm and its client, Grand Met, by using for his own trading purposes material, nonpublic information regarding Grand Met's planned tender offer. *Id.,* at 8.[2] According to the indictment, O'Hagan used the profits he gained through this trading to conceal his previous embezzlement and conversion of unrelated client trust funds. [...]

A

In pertinent part, § 10(b) of the Exchange Act provides:

> "It shall be unlawful for any person, directly or indirectly, by the use of any means or instrumentality of interstate commerce or of the mails, or of any facility of any national securities exchange—

. . . . .

> "(b) To use or employ, in connection with the purchase or sale of any security registered on a national securities exchange or any security not so registered, any manipulative or deceptive device or contrivance in contravention of such rules and regulations as the [Securities and Exchange] Commission may prescribe as necessary or appropriate in the public interest or for the protection of investors." 15 U. S. C. § 78j(b). [651] The statute thus proscribes (1) using any deceptive device (2) in connection with the purchase or sale of securities, in contravention of rules prescribed by the Commission. The provision, as written, does not confine its coverage to deception of a purchaser or seller of securities, see *United States* v. *Newman,* 664 F. 2d 12, 17 (CA2 1981); rather, the statute reaches any deceptive device used "in connection with the purchase or sale of any security."

Pursuant to its § 10(b) rulemaking authority, the Commission has adopted Rule 10b–5, which, as relevant here, provides:

"It shall be unlawful for any person, directly or indirectly, by the use of any means or instrumentality of interstate commerce, or of the mails or of any facility of any national securities exchange,

"(a) To employ any device, scheme, or artifice to defraud, [or]

. . . . .

"(c) To engage in any act, practice, or course of business which operates or would operate as a fraud or deceit upon any person, "in connection with the purchase or sale of any security." 17 CFR § 240.10b—5 (1996).

Liability under Rule 10b—5, our precedent indicates, does not extend beyond conduct encompassed by § 10(b)'s prohibition. [...]

Under the "traditional" or "classical theory" of insider trading liability, § 10(b) and Rule 10b—5 are violated when a corporate insider trades in the securities of his corporation [652] on the basis of material, nonpublic information. Trading on such information qualifies as a "deceptive device" under § 10(b), we have affirmed, because "a relationship of trust and confidence [exists] between the shareholders of a corporation and those insiders who have obtained confidential information by reason of their position with that corporation." *Chiarella* v. *United States,* 445 U. S. 222, 228 (1980). That relationship, we recognized, "gives rise to a duty to disclose [or to abstain from trading] because of the `necessity of preventing a corporate insider from . . . tak[ing] unfair advantage of . . . uninformed . . . stockholders.' " *Id.,* at 228-229 (citation omitted). The classical theory applies not only to officers, directors, and other permanent insiders of a corporation, but also to attorneys, accountants, consultants, and others who temporarily become fiduciaries of a corporation. See *Dirks* v. *SEC,* 463 U. S. 646, 655, n. 14 (1983).

The "misappropriation theory" holds that a person commits fraud "in connection with" a securities transaction, and thereby violates § 10(b) and Rule 10b—5, when he misappropriates confidential information for securities trading purposes, in breach of a duty owed to the source of the information. See Brief for United States

14. Under this theory, a fiduciary's undisclosed, self-serving use of a principal's information to purchase or sell securities, in breach of a duty of loyalty and confidentiality, defrauds the principal of the exclusive use of that information. In lieu of premising liability on a fiduciary relationship between company insider and purchaser or seller of the company's stock, the misappropriation theory premises liability on a fiduciary-turned-trader's deception of those who entrusted him with access to confidential information.

The two theories are complementary, each addressing efforts to capitalize on nonpublic information through the purchase or sale of securities. The classical theory targets a corporate insider's breach of duty to shareholders with whom the insider transacts; the misappropriation theory outlaws [653] trading on the basis of nonpublic information by a corporate "outsider" in breach of a duty owed not to a trading party, but to the source of the information. The misappropriation theory is thus designed to "protec[t] the integrity of the securities markets against abuses by `outsiders' to a corporation who have access to confidential information that will affect th[e] corporation's security price when revealed, but who owe no fiduciary or other duty to that corporation's shareholders." [...]

Deception through nondisclosure is central to the theory of liability for which the Government seeks recognition. As counsel for the Government stated in explanation of the theory at oral argument: "To satisfy the common law rule that a trustee may not use the property that [has] been entrusted [to] him, there would have to be consent. To satisfy the requirement of the Securities Act that there be no deception, there would only have to be disclosure."[...]

The misappropriation theory advanced by the Government is consistent with *Santa Fe Industries, Inc.* v. *Green,* 430 U. S. 462 (1977), a decision underscoring that § 10(b) is not an all-purpose breach of fiduciary duty ban; rather, it trains on conduct involving manipulation or deception. See *id.,* at 473-476. In contrast to the Government's allegations in this case, in *Santa Fe Industries,* all pertinent facts were disclosed by the persons charged with violating § 10(b) and Rule 10b—5, see *id.,* at 474; therefore, there was no deception through nondisclosure to which liability under those provisions could attach, see *id.,* at 476. Similarly, full disclosure forecloses liability under the misappropriation theory: Because the deception essential to the misappropriation theory involves feigning fidelity to the source of information, if the fiduciary discloses to the source that he plans to trade on the nonpublic information, there is no "deceptive device" and thus no § 10(b) violation—although the fiduciary-turnedtrader may remain liable under state law for breach of a duty of loyalty.[181]

We turn next to the § 10(b) requirement that the misappropriator's deceptive use of information be "in connection with [656] the purchase or sale of [a] security." This element is satisfied because the fiduciary's fraud is consummated, not when the fiduciary gains the confidential information, but when, without disclosure to his principal, he uses the information to purchase or sell securities. [...] A misappropriator who trades on the basis of material, nonpublic information, in short, gains his advantageous market position through deception; he deceives the source of the information and simultaneously harms members of the investing public. [...]

The misappropriation theory targets information of a sort that misappropriators ordinarily capitalize upon to gain norisk profits through the purchase or sale of securities. Should a misappropriator put such information to other use, the statute's prohibition would not be implicated. The theory does not catch all conceivable forms of fraud involving confidential information; rather, it catches fraudulent means of capitalizing on such information through securities transactions. [...]

The misappropriation theory comports with § 10(b)'s language, which requires deception "in connection with the purchase or sale of any security," not deception of an identifiable purchaser or seller. The theory is also well tuned to an animating purpose of the Exchange Act: to insure honest securities markets and thereby promote investor confidence. See 45 Fed. Reg. 60412 (1980) (trading on misappropriated information "undermines the integrity of, and investor confidence in, the securities markets"). Although informational disparity is inevitable in the securities markets, investors likely would hesitate to venture their capital in a market where trading based on misappropriated nonpublic information is unchecked by law. An investor's informational disadvantage vis-à-vis a misappropriator with material, nonpublic information [659] stems from contrivance, not luck; it is a disadvantage that cannot be overcome with research or skill. [...]

In sum, considering the inhibiting impact on market participation of trading on misappropriated information, and the congressional purposes underlying § 10(b), it makes scant sense to hold a lawyer like O'Hagan a § 10(b) violator if he works for a law firm representing the target of a tender offer, but not if he works for a law firm representing the bidder. The text of the statute requires no such result.[10] The misappropriation at issue here was properly made the subject of a § 10(b) charge because it meets the statutory requirement that there be "deceptive" conduct "in connection with" securities transactions. [...]

The judgment of the Court of Appeals for the Eighth Circuit is reversed, and the case is remanded for further proceedings consistent with this opinion.

It is so ordered.

Rule 10b5-2 Duties of trust or confidence 6.2.4.2

In a situation where a party receives confidential, inside information from a close family member, confidant or some other person where there is an existing duty of trust or confidence, the person who receives the information is under the same obligation as the source when it comes to trading.

Although the duties of trust or confidence can be found in the caselaw, when those duties arise remains sufficiently vague. In order to clarify duties of trust or confidence, the SEC adopted Rule 10b5-2, which attempts to outline common situations where a duty of trust or confidence can be presumed for purposes of insider trading liability.

Such situations include when the party receiving the information explicitly agrees to enter into a relationship of trust or confidence by, for example, signing a confidentiality agreement. Alternatively, where the recipient and the source of the information has a history of sharing confidences. Or, finally, where the recipient and the source of the information have a familial relationship.

Where a recipient trades on information and breaches their duty of trust or confidence to the source, the recipient has breached a duty sufficient to generate liability under the laws of insider trading.

Preliminary Note to § 240.10b5-2:

This section provides a non-exclusive definition of circumstances in which a person has a duty of trust or confidence for purposes of the "misappropriation" theory of insider trading under Section 10(b) of the Act and Rule 10b-5. The law of insider trading is otherwise defined by judicial opinions construing Rule 10b-5, and Rule 10b5-2 does not modify the scope of insider trading law in any other respect.

(a) *Scope of Rule.* This section shall apply to any violation of Section 10(b) of the Act (15 U.S.C. 78j(b)) and § 240.10b-5 thereunder that is based on the purchase or sale of securities on the basis of, or the communication of, material nonpublic information misappropriated in breach of a duty of trust or confidence.

(b) *Enumerated "duties of trust or confidence."* For purposes of this section, a "duty of trust or confidence" exists in the following circumstances, among others:

(1) Whenever a person agrees to maintain information in confidence;

(2) Whenever the person communicating the material nonpublic information and the person to whom it is communicated have a history, pattern, or practice of sharing confidences, such that the recipient of the information knows or reasonably should know that the person communicating the material nonpublic information expects that the recipient will maintain its confidentiality; or

(3) Whenever a person receives or obtains material nonpublic information from his or her spouse, parent, child, or sibling; *provided,* however, that the person receiving or obtaining the information may demonstrate that no duty of trust or confidence existed with respect to the information, by establishing that he or she neither knew nor reasonably should have known that the person who was the source of the information expected that the person would keep the information confidential, because of the parties' history, pattern, or practice of sharing and maintaining confidences, and because there was no agreement or understanding to maintain the confidentiality of the information.

Securities & Exchange Commission v. Cuban   **6.2.4.3**

SEC v. CUBAN
620 F.3d 551 (2010)

PATRICK E. HIGGINBOTHAM, Circuit Judge:

This case raises questions of the scope of liability under the misappropriation theory of insider trading. Taking a different view from our able district court brother of the allegations of the complaint, we are persuaded that the case should not have been dismissed under Fed.R.Civ.P. 9(b) and 12 and must proceed to discovery.

Mark Cuban is a well known entrepreneur and current owner of the Dallas Mavericks and Landmark theaters, among other businesses. The SEC brought this suit against Cuban alleging he violated Section 17(a) of the Securities Act of 1933, Section 10(b) of the Securities Exchange Act of 1934, and Rule 10b-5 by trading in Mamma.com stock in breach of his duty to the CEO and Mamma.com — amounting to insider trading under the misappropriation theory of liability. The core allegation is that Cuban received confidential information from the CEO of Mamma.com, a Canadian search engine company in which Cuban was a large minority stakeholder, agreed to keep the information confidential, and acknowledged he could not trade on the information. The SEC alleges that, armed with the inside information regarding a private investment of public equity (PIPE) offering, Cuban sold his stake in the company in an effort to avoid losses from the inevitable fall in Mamma.com's share price when the offering was announced.

[...]

The SEC alleges that Cuban's trading constituted insider trading and violated Section 10(b) of the Securities Exchange Act. Section 10(b) makes it

> unlawful for any person, directly or indirectly, by the use of any means or instrumentality of interstate commerce or of the mails, or of any facility of any national securities exchange ... [t]o use or employ, in connection with the purchase or sale of any security ... any manipulative or deceptive device or contrivance in contravention of such rules and regulations as the Commission may prescribe as necessary or appropriate in the public interest or for the protection of investors.

Pursuant to this section, the SEC promulgated Rule 10b-5, which makes it unlawful to

> (a) To employ any device, scheme, or artifice to defraud,

> (b) To make any untrue statement of a material fact or to omit to state a material fact necessary in order to make the statements made, in the light of the circumstances under which they were made, not misleading, or

> (c) To engage in any act, practice, or course of business which operates or would operate as a fraud or deceit upon any person, in connection with the purchase or sale of any security.

The Supreme Court has interpreted section 10(b) to prohibit insider trading under two complementary theories, the "classical theory" and the "misappropriation theory."

The classical theory of insider trading prohibits a "corporate insider" from trading on material nonpublic information obtained from his position within the corporation without disclosing the information. According to this theory, there exists "a relationship of trust and confidence between the shareholders of a corporation and those insiders who have obtained confidential information by reason of their position with that corporation." Trading on such confidential information qualifies as a "deceptive device" under section 10(b) because by using that information for his own personal benefit, the corporate insider breaches his duty to the shareholders. The corporate insider is under a duty to "disclose or abstain" — he must tell the shareholders of his knowledge and intention to trade or abstain from trading altogether.

There are at least two important variations of the classical theory of insider trading. The first is that even an individual who does not qualify as a traditional insider may become a "temporary insider" if by entering "into a special confidential relationship in the conduct of the business of the enterprise [they] are given access to information solely for corporate purposes." Thus underwriters, accountants, lawyers, or consultants are all considered corporate insiders when by virtue of their professional relationship with the corporation they are given access to confidential information. The second variation is that an individual who receives information from a corporate insider may be, but is not always, prohibited from trading on that information as a tippee. "[T]he tippee's duty to disclose or abstain is derivative from that of the insider's duty" and the tippee's obligation arises "from his role as a participant after the fact in the insider's breach of a fiduciary duty." Crucially, "a tippee assumes a fiduciary duty to the shareholders of a corporation not to trade on material nonpublic information only when the insider has breached his fiduciary duty to the shareholders by disclosing the information to the tippee and the tip-pee knows or should know there has been a breach." The insider breaches his fiduciary duty when he receives a "direct or indirect personal benefit from the disclosure."

Both the temporary-insider and tippee twists on the classical theory retain its core principle that the duty to disclose or abstain is derived from the corporate insider's duty to his shareholders. The misappropriation theory does not rest on this duty. It rather holds that a person violates section 10(b) "when he misappropriates confidential information for securities trading purposes, in breach of a duty owed to the source of the information." The Supreme Court first adopted this theory in *United States v. O'Hagan.* There, a lawyer traded the securities of a company his client was targeting for a takeover. O'Hagan could not be liable under the classical theory as he owed no duty to the shareholders of the target company. Nevertheless, the court found O'Hagan violated section 10(b). The Court held that in trading the target company's securities, *O'Hagan* misappropriated the confidential information regarding the planned corporate takeover, breaching "a duty of trust and confidence" he owed to his law firm and client. Trading on such information "involves feigning fidelity to the source of information and thus utilizes a 'deceptive device' as required by section 10(b)." The Court stated that while there is "no general duty between all participants in market transactions to forgo actions based on material nonpublic information," the breach of a duty to the source of the information is sufficient to give rise to insider trading liability.

While *O'Hagan* did not set the contours of a relationship of "trust and confidence" giving rise to the duty to disclose or abstain and misappropriation liability, we are tasked to determine whether Cuban had such a relationship with Mamma.com. The SEC seeks to rely on Rule 10b5 − 2(b)(1), which states that a person has "a duty of trust and confidence" for purposes of misappropriation liability when that person "agrees to maintain information in confidence." In dismissing the case, the district court read the complaint to allege that Cuban agreed not to disclose any confidential information but did not agree not to trade, that such a confidentiality agreement was insufficient to create a duty to disclose or abstain from trading under the misappropriation theory, and that the SEC overstepped its authority under section 10(b) in issuing Rule 10b5 − 2(b)(1). We differ from the district court in reading the complaint and need not reach the latter issues.

The complaint alleges that, in March 2004, Cuban acquired 600,000 shares, a 6.3% stake, of Mamma.com. Later that spring, Mamma.com decided to raise capital through a PIPE offering on the advice of the investment bank Merriman Curhan Ford & Co. At the end of June, at Merriman's suggestion, Mamma.com decided to invite Cuban to participate in the PIPE offering. "The CEO was instructed to contact Cuban and to preface the conversation by informing Cuban that he had confidential information to convey to him in order to make sure that Cuban understood — before the information was conveyed to him — that he would have to keep the information confidential."

After getting in touch with Cuban on June 28, Mamma.com's CEO told Cuban he had confidential information for him and Cuban agreed to keep whatever information the CEO shared confidential. The CEO then told Cuban about the PIPE offering. Cuban became very upset "and said, among other things, that he did not like PIPEs because they dilute the existing shareholders." "At the end of the call, Cuban told the CEO 'Well, now I'm screwed. I can't sell.' "

The CEO told the company's executive chairman about the conversation with Cuban. The executive chairman sent an email to the other Mamma.com board members updating them on the PIPE offering. The executive chairman included:

> Today, after much discussion, [the CEO] spoke to Mark Cuban about this equity raise and whether or not he would be interested in participating. As anticipated he initially "flew off the handle" and said he would sell his shares (recognizing that he was not able to do anything until we announce the equity) but then asked to see the terms and conditions which we have arranged for him to receive from one of the participating investor groups with which he has dealt in the past.

The CEO then sent Cuban a follow up email, writing " '[i]f you want more details about the private placement please contact ... [Merriman].' "

Cuban called the Merriman representative and they spoke for eight minutes. "During that call, the salesman supplied Cuban with additional confidential details about the PIPE. In response to Cuban's questions, the salesman told him that the PIPE was being sold at a discount to the market price and that the offering included other incentives for the PIPE investors." It is a plausible inference that Cuban learned the off-market prices available to him and other PIPE participants.

With that information and one minute after speaking with the Merriman representative, Cuban called his broker and instructed him to sell his entire stake in the company. Cuban sold 10,000 shares during the evening of June 28, 2004, and the remainder during regular trading the next day.

That day, the executive chairman sent another email to the board, updating them on the previous day's discussions with Cuban, stating " 'we did speak to Mark Cuban ([the CEO] and, subsequently, our investment banker) to find out if he had any interest in participating to the extent of maintaining his interest. His answers were: he would not invest, he does not want the company to make acquisitions, he will sell his shares which he can not do until after we announce.' "

After the markets closed on June 29, Mamma.com announced the PIPE offering. The next day, Mammaxom's stock price fell 8.5% and continued to decline over the next week, eventually closing down 39% from the June 29 closing price. By selling his shares when he did, Cuban avoided over $750,000 in losses. Cuban notified the SEC that he had sold his stake in the company and publicly stated that he sold his shares because Mamma.com "was conducting a PIPE, which issued shares at a discount to the prevailing market price and also would have caused his ownership position to be diluted."

In reading the complaint to allege only an agreement of confidentiality, the court held that Cuban's statement that he was "screwed" because he "[could not] sell" "appears to express his belief, at least at that time, that it would be illegal for him to sell his Mamma.com shares based on the information the CEO provided." But the court stated that this statement "cannot reasonably be understood as an agreement not to sell based on the information." The court found "the complaint asserts no facts that reasonably suggest that the CEO intended to obtain from Cuban an agreement to refrain from trading on the information as opposed to an agreement merely to keep it confidential." Finally, the court stated that "the CEO's expectation that Cuban would not sell was also insufficient" to allege any further agreement.

Reading the complaint in the light most favorable to the SEC, we reach a different conclusion. In isolation, the statement "Well, now I'm screwed. I can't sell" can plausibly be read to express Cuban's view that learning the confidences regarding the PIPE forbade his selling his stock before the offering but to express no agreement not to do so. However, after Cuban expressed the view that he could not sell to the CEO, he gained access to the confidences of the PIPE offering. According to the complaint's recounting of the executive chairman's email to the board, during his short conversation with the CEO regarding the planned PIPE offering, Cuban requested the terms and conditions of the offering. Based on this request, the CEO sent Cuban a follow up email providing the contact information for Merriman. Cuban called the salesman, who told Cuban "that the PIPE was being sold at a discount to the market price and that the offering included other incentives for the PIPE investors." Only after Cuban reached out to obtain this additional information, following the statement of his understanding that he could not sell, did Cuban contact his broker and sell his stake in the company.

The allegations, taken in their entirety, provide more than a plausible basis to find that the understanding between the CEO and Cuban was that he was not to trade, that it was more than a simple confidentiality agreement. By contacting the sales representative to obtain the pricing information, Cuban was able to evaluate his potential losses or gains from his decision to either participate or refrain from participating in the PIPE offering. It is at least plausible that each of the parties understood, if only implicitly, that Mamma.com would only provide the terms and conditions of the offering to Cuban for the purpose of evaluating whether he would participate in the offering, and that Cuban could not use the information for his own personal benefit. It would require additional facts that have not been put before us for us to conclude that the parties could not plausibly have reached this shared understanding. Under Cuban's reading, he was allowed to trade on the information but prohibited from telling others — in effect providing him an exclusive license to trade on the material nonpublic information. Perhaps this was the understanding, or perhaps Cuban mislead the CEO regarding the timing of his sale in order to obtain a confidential look at the details of the PIPE. We say only that on this factually sparse record, it is at least equally plausible that all sides understood there was to be no trading before the PIPE. That both Cuban and the CEO expressed the belief that Cuban could not trade appears to reinforce the plausibility of this reading.

Given the paucity of jurisprudence on the question of what constitutes a relationship of "trust and confidence" and the inherently fact-bound nature of determining whether such a duty exists, we decline to first determine or place our thumb on the scale in the district court's determination of its presence or to now draw the contours of any liability that it might bring, including the force of Rule 10b5-2(b)(1). Rather, we VACATE the judgment dismissing the case and REMAND to the court of first instance for further proceedings including discovery, consideration of summary judgment, and trial, if reached.

SEC v. Dorozhko   6.2.4.4

Like tipper/tippee liability, there are limits to use of misappropriation theory. In Dorozhko, the Second Circuit extends misappropriation theory in a novel way. Dorozhko involves a Ukrainian hacker who steals inside information and then trades on it. The lack of a fiduciary relationship to the source of the information should mean there is no liability under misappropriation theory. However, here the court agrees with the SEC's theory and extends liability but in a novel way, suggesting that fiduciary relationships are not actually required in order to establish liability under 10b-5.

SEC v. DOROZHKO
574 F.3d 42 (2009)

JOSÉ A. CABRANES, Circuit Judge:

We are asked to consider whether, in a civil enforcement lawsuit brought by the United States Securities and Exchange Commission ("SEC") under Section 10(b) [44] of the Securities Exchange Act of 1934 ("Section 10(b)"), computer hacking may be "deceptive" where the hacker did not breach a fiduciary duty in fraudulently obtaining material, nonpublic information used in connection with the purchase or sale of securities. For the reasons stated herein, we answer the question in the affirmative. [...]

In early October 2007, defendant Oleksandr Dorozhko, a Ukranian national and resident, opened an online trading account with Interactive Brokers LLC ("Interactive Brokers") and deposited $42,500 into that account. At about the same time, IMS Health, Inc. ("IMS") announced that it would release its third-quarter earnings during an analyst conference call scheduled for October 17, 2007 at 5 p.m.—that is, after the close of the securities markets in New York City. IMS had hired Thomson Financial, Inc. ("Thomson") to provide investor relations and web-hosting services, which included managing the online release of IMS's earnings reports.

Beginning at 8:06 a.m. on October 17, and continuing several times during the morning and early afternoon, an anonymous computer hacker attempted to gain access to the IMS earnings report by hacking into a secure server at Thomson prior to the report's official release. At 2:15 p.m.—minutes after Thomson actually received the IMS data—that hacker successfully located and downloaded the IMS data from Thomson's secure server.

Beginning at 2:52 p.m., defendant—who had not previously used his Interactive Brokers account to trade—purchased $41,670.90 worth of IMS "put" options that would expire on October 25 and 30, 2007.[iii] These purchases represented approximately 90% of all purchases of "put" options for IMS stock for the six weeks prior to October 17. In purchasing these options, which the SEC describes as "extremely risky," defendant was betting that IMS's stock price would decline precipitously (within a two-day expiration period) and significantly (by greater than 20%). [...]

At 4:33 p.m.—slightly ahead of the analyst call—IMS announced that its earnings per share were 28% below "Street" expectations, *i.e.,* the expectations of many Wall Street analysts. When the market opened the next morning, October 18, at 9:30 a.m., IMS's stock price sank approximately 28% almost immediately—from $29.56 to $21.20 per share. Within six minutes of the market opening, defendant had sold all of his IMS options, realizing a net profit of $286,456.59 overnight.

Interactive Brokers noticed the irregular trading activity and referred the matter to the SEC, which now alleges that defendant was the hacker.[...] On October 29, 2007, the SEC sought and received from the United States District Court for the Southern District of New York (Naomi Reice Buchwald, *Judge*) a temporary restraining order freezing the proceeds of the "put" option transactions in defendant's brokerage [45] account. [...]

On January 8, 2008, in a thoughtful and careful opinion, the District Court denied the SEC's request for a preliminary injunction because the SEC had not shown a likelihood of success. Specifically, the District Court ruled that computer hacking was not "deceptive" within the meaning of Section 10(b) as defined by the Supreme Court. According to the District Court, "a breach of a fiduciary duty of disclosure is a required element of any ` deceptive' device under § 10b." [...] The District Court reasoned that since defendant was a corporate outsider with no special relationship to IMS or Thomson, he owed no fiduciary duty to either. Although computer hacking might be fraudulent and might violate a number of federal and state criminal statutes, the District Court concluded that this behavior did not violate Section 10(b) without an accompanying breach of a fiduciary duty.

[...] On appeal, the SEC maintains its theory that the fraud in this case consists of defendant's alleged computer hacking, which involves various misrepresentations. The SEC does not argue that defendant breached any fiduciary duties as part of his scheme. In this critical regard, we recognize that the SEC's claim against defendant—a corporate outsider who owed no fiduciary duties to the source of the information—is not based on either of the two generally accepted theories of insider trading. *See United States v. Cusimano,* 123 F.3d 83, 87 (2d Cir.1997) (distinguishing "the traditional theory of insider trading, under which a corporate insider trades in the securities of his own corporation on the basis of material, non-public information," from "the misappropriation theory, [under which] § 10(b) and Rule 10b-5 are violated whenever a person trades while in knowing possession of material, non-public information that has been gained in violation of a fiduciary duty to its source"). The SEC's claim is nonetheless based on a claim of fraud, and we turn our attention to whether this fraud is "deceptive" within the meaning of Section 10(b). [...]

"Section 10(b) prohibits the use or employ, in connection with the purchase or sale of any security . . ., [of] any manipulative or deceptive device or contrivance in contravention of such rules and regulations as the [SEC] may prescribe." 15 U.S.C. § 78j(b)[2] The instant case requires us to [46] decide whether the "device" in this case— computer hacking—could be "deceptive."[3]

In construing the text of any federal statute, we first consider the precedents that bind us as an intermediate appellate court—namely, the holdings of the Supreme Court and those of prior panels of this Court, which provide definitive interpretations of otherwise ambiguous language. Insofar as those precedents fail to resolve an apparent ambiguity, we examine the text of the statute itself, interpreting provisions in light of their ordinary meaning and their contextual setting. [...]

The District Court determined that the Supreme Court has interpreted the "deceptive" element of Section 10(b) to require a breach of a fiduciary duty.[...] ("[T]he Supreme Court has in a number of opinions carefully established that the essential component of a § 10(b) violation is a breach of a fiduciary duty to disclose or abstain that coincides with a securities transaction."). The District Court reached this conclusion by relying principally on

537

three Supreme Court opinions: *Chiarella v. United States,* 445 U.S. 222, 100 S.Ct. 1108, 63 L.Ed.2d 348 (1980), *United States v. O'Hagan,* 521 U.S. 642, 117 S.Ct. 2199, 138 L.Ed.2d 724 (1997), and *SEC v. Zandford,* 535 U.S. 813, 122 S.Ct. 1899, 153 L.Ed.2d 1 (2002). We consider each of these cases in turn.

In *Chiarella,* the defendant was employed by a financial printer and used information passing through his office to trade securities offered by acquiring and target companies. In a criminal prosecution, [47] the government alleged that the defendant committed fraud by not disclosing to the market that he was trading on the basis of material, nonpublic information. The Supreme Court held that defendant's "silence," or nondisclosure, was not fraud because he was under no obligation to disclose his knowledge of inside information. "When an allegation of fraud is based upon nondisclosure, there can be no fraud absent a duty to speak. We hold that a duty to disclose under § 10(b) does not arise from the mere possession of nonpublic market information." 445 U.S. at 235, 100 S.Ct. 1108; *see also United States v. Chestman,* 947 F.2d 551, 575 (2d Cir. 1991) (Winter, *J.,* concurring in part and dissenting in part) (stating that, after *Chiarella,* "silence cannot constitute a fraud absent a duty to speak owed to those who are injured"). Justice Blackmun, joined by Justice Marshall, dissented. In their view, stealing information from an employer was fraudulent within the meaning of Section 10(b) because the statute was designed as a "catchall" provision to protect investors from unknown risks. *Id.* at 246, 100 S.Ct. 1108 (Blackmun, *J.,* dissenting). According to Justice Blackmun, the majority had "confine[d]" the meaning of fraud "by imposition of a requirement of a `special relationship' akin to fiduciary duty before the statute gives rise to a duty to disclose or to abstain from trading upon material, nonpublic information." *Id.*[1]

In *O'Hagan,* the defendant was an attorney who traded in securities based on material, nonpublic information regarding his firm's clients. As in *Chiarella,* the government alleged that the defendant had committed fraud through "silence" because the defendant had a duty to disclose to the source of the information (his client) that he would trade on the information. The Supreme Court agreed, noting that "[d]eception through nondisclosure is central to the theory of liability for which the Government seeks recognition." 521 U.S. at 654, 117 S.Ct. 2199. "[I]f the fiduciary discloses to the source that he plans to trade on the nonpublic information, there is no `deceptive device' and thus no § 10(b) violation—although the fiduciary-turned-trader may remain liable under state law for breach of a duty of loyalty." *Id.* at 655, 117 S.Ct. 2199.

In *Zandford,* the defendant was a securities broker who traded under a client's account and transferred the proceeds to his own account. The Fourth Circuit held that the defendant's fraud was not "in connection with" the purchase or sale of a security because it was mere theft that happened to involve securities, rather than true securities fraud. The Supreme Court reversed in a unanimous opinion, observing that Section 10(b) "should be construed not technically and restrictively, but flexibly to effectuate its remedial purposes." 535 U.S. at 819, 122 S.Ct. 1899. Although the Court warned that not "every common-law fraud that happens to involve securities [is] a violation of § 10(b)," *id.* at 820, 122 S.Ct. 1899, the defendant's scheme was a single plan to deceive, rather than a series of independent frauds, and was therefore "in connection with" the purchase or sale of a security, *id.* at 825, 122 S.Ct. 1899. In a final footnote, the Court offered the following observation: "[I]f the [48] broker told his client he was stealing the client's assets, that breach of fiduciary duty might be in connection with a sale of securities, but it would not involve a deceptive device or fraud." 535 U.S. at 825 n. 4, 122 S.Ct. 1899. In the instant case, the District Court interpreted the *Zandford* footnote as an "explicit[ ] acknowledg[ment] that Zandford would not be liable under § 10(b) if he *had* disclosed to Wood that he was planning to steal his money." *Dorozhko,* 606 F.Supp.2d at 338.

The District Court concluded that in *Chiarella, O'Hagan,* and *Zandford,* the Supreme Court developed a requirement that any "deceptive device" requires a breach of a fiduciary duty. In applying that interpretation to the instant case, the District Court ruled that "[a]lthough [defendant] may have broken the law, he is not liable in a civil action under § 10(b) because he owed no fiduciary or similar duty either to the source of his information or to those he transacted with in the market." [...]At least one of our sister circuits has made the same observation relying on the same precedent. [...]

In our view, none of the Supreme Court opinions relied upon by the District Court—much less the sum of all three opinions — establishes a fiduciary-duty requirement as an element of every violation of Section 10(b). In *Chiarella, O'Hagan,* and *Zandford,* the theory of fraud was silence or nondisclosure, not an affirmative misrepresentation. The Supreme Court held that remaining silent was actionable only where there was a duty to speak, arising from a fiduciary relationship. In *Chiarella,* the Supreme Court held that there was no deception in an employee's silence because he did not have duty to speak. [...]In *O'Hagan,* an attorney who traded on client secrets had a fiduciary duty to inform his firm that he was trading on the basis of the confidential information. [...]Even in *Zandford,* which dealt principally with the statutory requirement that a deceptive device be used "in connection with" the purchase or sale of a security, the defendant's fraud consisted of not telling his brokerage client—to whom he owed a fiduciary duty—that he was stealing assets from the account. [...]

Chiarella, O'Hagan, and *Zandford* all stand for the proposition that nondisclosure in breach of a fiduciary duty "satisfies § 10(b)'s requirement . . . [of] a `deceptive device or contrivance,'" [...] However, what is sufficient is not always what is necessary, and none of the Supreme Court opinions considered by the District Court *require* a fiduciary relationship as an element of an actionable securities claim under Section 10(b). [...] Even if a person does not have a fiduciary duty to "disclose or abstain from trading," there is nonetheless an affirmative obligation in commercial dealings not to mislead. [...]

In this case, the SEC has not alleged that defendant fraudulently remained silent in the face of a "duty to disclose or abstain" from trading. Rather, the SEC argues that defendant affirmatively misrepresented himself in order to gain access to material, nonpublic information, which he then used to trade. We are aware of no precedent of the Supreme Court or our Court that forecloses or prohibits the SEC's straightforward theory of fraud.[6] Absent a controlling precedent that "deceptive" has a more limited meaning than its ordinary meaning, we see no reason to complicate the enforcement of Section 10(b) by divining new requirements. In reaching this conclusion, we are mindful of the Supreme Court's oft-repeated instruction that Section 10(b) "should be construed not technically and restrictively, but flexibly to effectuate its remedial purposes." [...]

In its ordinary meaning, "deceptive" covers a wide spectrum of conduct involving cheating or trading in falsehoods. *See* Webster's International Dictionary[...]. In light of this ordinary meaning, it is not at all surprising that Rule 10b-5 equates "deceit" with "fraud." [...]

The District Court—summarizing the SEC's allegations—described the computer hacking in this case as "employ[ing] electronic means to trick, circumvent, or bypass computer security in order to gain unauthorized access to computer systems, networks, and information . . . and to steal such data." [...]On appeal, the SEC adds a further gloss, arguing that, in general, "[computer [51] h]ackers either (1) `engage in false identification and masquerade as another user[']. . . or (2) `exploit a weakness in [an electronic] code within a program to cause the program to malfunction in a way that grants the user greater privileges.'" [...] In our view, misrepresenting one's identity in order to gain access to information that is otherwise off limits, and then stealing that information is plainly "deceptive" within the ordinary meaning of the word. It is unclear, however, that exploiting a weakness in an electronic code to gain unauthorized access is "deceptive," rather than being mere theft. Accordingly, depending on how the hacker gained access, it seems to us entirely possible that computer hacking could be, by definition, a "deceptive device or contrivance" that is prohibited by Section 10(b) and Rule 10b-5.

[...]Having established that the SEC need not demonstrate a breach of fiduciary duty, we now remand to the District Court to consider, in the first instance, whether the computer hacking in this case involved a fraudulent misrepresentation that was "deceptive" within the ordinary meaning of Section 10(b). [...]

Theories of liability v. extending liability   6.2.4.5

There are two basic theories of liability with respect
to insider trading liability: classical theory and
misappropriation theory. Classical theory creates liability when the
insider trades in her own company's stock while in posession of
material nonpublic information. Misappropriation theory creates
liability when the insider trades in the stock of a company to whom
she owes no fiduciary duty.

Tipper/tippee theories and 10b5-2 are not independent theories of
liability. Rather, they simply extend classical or misappropriation
liability to traders who might otherwise not face liability because
they lack a fiduciary connection to the source of the material
nonpublic information.

Takeovers   7

The merger transaction is probably one of the most
significant events possible in the life of a
corporation. Because mergers are so important to
the corporation, they can be regulated quite closely.
Although the corporate law typically grants great deference to the
decisions of boards of directors, when boards take actions in the
context of pursuing a sale or defending against an unwanted offer,
courts are more apt to enquire into process relied on by the board.
In the following sections we explore both the mechanics of the
merger transaction as well as the fiduciary duties of directors in the
merger scenario.

Statutory Mergers   **7.1**

The statutory merger is the building block of all
M&A activity. The provisions that follow provide an
outline for the mechanics of the statutory merger
transaction. Although the statutory mergers described in Section
251 involve two Delaware corporations, statutory mergers under
other provisions of the code permit mergers between corporations
and other business forms, including business forms from other
states. The mechanics of those transactions are not substantially
dissimilar from the process outlined in Section 251 below.

DGCL Sec 251   7
                                                          .
                                                          1
                                                          .
                                                          1

§ 251. Merger or consolidation of domestic corporations.

(a) Any 2 or more corporations existing under the laws of this State
may merge into a single corporation, which may be any 1 of the
constituent corporations or may consolidate into a new corporation
formed by the consolidation, pursuant to an agreement of merger or
consolidation, as the case may be, complying and approved in
accordance with this section.

(b) The board of directors of each corporation which desires to
merge or consolidate shall adopt a resolution approving an
agreement of merger or consolidation and declaring its advisability.
The agreement shall state:

(1) The terms and conditions of the merger or consolidation;

(2) The mode of carrying the same into effect;

(3) In the case of a merger, such amendments or changes in the certificate of incorporation of the surviving corporation as are desired to be effected by the merger (which amendments or changes may amend and restate the certificate of incorporation of the surviving corporation in its entirety), or, if no such amendments or changes are desired, a statement that the certificate of incorporation of the surviving corporation shall be its certificate of incorporation;

(4) In the case of a consolidation, that the certificate of incorporation of the resulting corporation shall be as is set forth in an attachment to the agreement;

(5) The manner, if any, of converting the shares of each of the constituent corporations into shares or other securities of the corporation surviving or resulting from the merger or consolidation, or of cancelling some or all of such shares, and, if any shares of any of the constituent corporations are not to remain outstanding, to be converted solely into shares or other securities of the surviving or resulting corporation or to be cancelled, the cash, property, rights or securities of any other corporation or entity which the holders of such shares are to receive in exchange for, or upon conversion of such shares and the surrender of any certificates evidencing them, which cash, property, rights or securities of any other corporation or entity may be in addition to or in lieu of shares or other securities of the surviving or resulting corporation; and

(6) Such other details or provisions as are deemed desirable, including, without limiting the generality of the foregoing, a provision for the payment of cash in lieu of the issuance or recognition of fractional shares, interests or rights, or for any other arrangement with respect thereto, consistent with § 155 of this title.
[...]

(c) The agreement required by subsection (b) of this section shall be submitted to the stockholders of each constituent corporation at an annual or special meeting for the purpose of acting on the agreement. Due notice of the time, place and purpose of the meeting shall be mailed to each holder of stock, whether voting or nonvoting, of the corporation at the stockholder's address as it appears on the records of the corporation, at least 20 days prior to the date of the meeting. The notice shall contain a copy of the agreement or a brief summary thereof. At the meeting, the agreement shall be considered and a vote taken for its adoption or rejection. If a majority of the outstanding stock of the corporation entitled to vote thereon shall be voted for the adoption of the agreement, that fact shall be certified on the agreement by the secretary or assistant secretary of the corporation, provided that such certification on the agreement shall not be required if a certificate of merger or consolidation is filed in lieu of filing the agreement. If the agreement shall be so adopted and certified by each constituent corporation, it shall then be filed and shall become effective, in accordance with § 103 of this title. In lieu of filing the agreement of merger or consolidation required by this section, the surviving or resulting corporation may file a certificate of merger or consolidation, executed in accordance with § 103 of this title, which states:

(1) The name and state of incorporation of each of the constituent corporations;

(2) That an agreement of merger or consolidation has been approved, adopted, executed and acknowledged by each of the constituent corporations in accordance with this section;

(3) The name of the surviving or resulting corporation;

(4) In the case of a merger, such amendments or changes in the certificate of incorporation of the surviving corporation as are desired to be effected by the merger (which amendments or changes may amend and restate the certificate of incorporation of the surviving corporation in its entirety), or, if no such amendments or changes are desired, a statement that the certificate of incorporation of the surviving corporation shall be its certificate of incorporation;

(5) In the case of a consolidation, that the certificate of incorporation of the resulting corporation shall be as set forth in an attachment to the certificate;

(6) That the executed agreement of consolidation or merger is on file at an office of the surviving corporation, stating the address thereof; and

(7) That a copy of the agreement of consolidation or merger will be furnished by the surviving corporation, on request and without cost, to any stockholder of any constituent corporation.

(d) Any agreement of merger or consolidation may contain a provision that at any time prior to the time that the agreement (or a certificate in lieu thereof) filed with the Secretary of State becomes effective in accordance with § 103 of this title, the agreement may be terminated by the board of directors of any constituent corporation notwithstanding approval of the agreement by the stockholders of all or any of the constituent corporations; in the event the agreement of merger or consolidation is terminated after the filing of the agreement (or a certificate in lieu thereof) with the Secretary of State but before the agreement (or a certificate in lieu thereof) has become effective, a certificate of termination or merger or consolidation shall be filed in accordance with § 103 of this title. [...]

(e) In the case of a merger, the certificate of incorporation of the surviving corporation shall automatically be amended to the extent, if any, that changes in the certificate of incorporation are set forth in the agreement of merger.

(f) Notwithstanding the requirements of subsection (c) of this section, unless required by its certificate of incorporation, no vote of stockholders of a constituent corporation surviving a merger shall be necessary to authorize a merger if (1) the agreement of merger does not amend in any respect the certificate of incorporation of such constituent corporation, (2) each share of stock of such constituent corporation outstanding immediately prior to the effective date of the merger is to be an identical outstanding or treasury share of the surviving corporation after the effective date of the merger, and (3) either no shares of common stock of the surviving corporation and no shares, securities or obligations convertible into such stock are to be issued or delivered under the plan of merger, or the authorized unissued shares or the treasury shares of common stock of the surviving corporation to be issued or delivered under the plan of merger plus those initially issuable upon conversion of any other shares, securities or obligations to be issued or delivered under such plan do not exceed 20% of the shares of common stock of such constituent corporation outstanding immediately prior to the effective date of the merger. No vote of stockholders of a constituent corporation shall be necessary to authorize a merger or consolidation if no shares of the stock of such corporation shall have been issued prior to the adoption by the board of directors of the resolution approving the agreement of merger or consolidation. If an agreement of merger is adopted by the constituent corporation surviving the merger, by action of its board of directors and without any vote of its stockholders pursuant to this subsection, the secretary or assistant secretary of that corporation shall certify on the agreement that the agreement has been adopted pursuant to this subsection and, (1) if it has been adopted pursuant to the first sentence of this subsection, that the conditions specified in that sentence have been satisfied, or (2) if it has been adopted pursuant to the second sentence of this subsection, that no shares of stock of such corporation were issued prior to the adoption by the board of directors of the resolution approving the agreement of merger or consolidation, provided that such certification on the agreement shall not be required if a certificate of merger or consolidation is filed in lieu of filing the agreement. The agreement so adopted and certified shall then be filed and shall become effective, in accordance with § 103 of this title. Such filing shall constitute a representation by the person who executes the agreement that the facts stated in the certificate remain true immediately prior to such filing.

Board Obligations in the Takeover Context 7.2

Decisions whether or not to sell the corporation are like other business decisions taken by the board. Absent special circumstances such decisions are going to be subject to the business judgment presumption. The cases that follow some of these special circumstances are present.

These cases involve fact scenarios where the board adopts defenses to fend off an unwanted buyer, or when the board of its own accord decides to engage in a sale of control of the corporation, or when the board takes an action that might interfere with stockholders' voting rights. Each of these situations will engender additional judicial scrutiny before they are let to stand.

The courts have developed the intermediate standard to assist the courts in determining whether in these specific factual scenarios the court should deploy the business judgment presumption or whether the actions of the board should be subject to the more intensive entire fairness scrutiny. It is important to remember that Delaware's intermediate standard is a preliminary inquiry and not a liability inducing standard. Rather than create new "duties" or obligations, the intermediate standard provides courts a framework for analysing otherwise permissable board decisions in order to evaluate both the motive and means of the board's decisionmaking process. To the extent the board is able to demonstrate proper motive and means, then courts will defer the board's business judgment. However, if the decisionmaking process appears to be improperly motivated or relies on draconian means, then the board's decisionmaking process will be subject to entire fairness review.

Unocal Corp. v. Mesa Petroleum Co.   7.2.1

Board decisions typically receive the deferential presumption of business judgment. However, in some sets of facts it may be difficult to ascertain immediately whether actions taken by the board are in fact acts taken by a fully informed, disinterested board acting in the best interests of the corporation or if they are acting to entrench themselves and not in the best interests of the corporation.

For example, when a board unilaterally adopts defensive measures in response to a perceived threat to its corporate policy or effectiveness, that decision might be motivated by a desire to protect the corporation from some outside threat (best case scenario) or it could also be motivated by a desire to entrench disloyal managers (worst case scenario).

In such situations, those board decisions will be subject to a preliminary review (the intermediate standard) before the court determines whether to subject those decisions to deferential business judgment or the more exacting entire fairness standard. The nature of this review is an inquiry into the motivations behind board actions and then a determination about the reasonableness of the means adopted by the board. In testing the motive and means of the board, the burden is on the board to show that it was properly motivated and that the means it adopted were reasonable.

To the extent the board is able to establish it was properly motivated and acted reasonably, the board's actions will receive the presumption of business judgment. On the other hand, if the board was not properly motivated or if the defensive measures adopted by the board are not reasonable, the board's decision will be subject to entire fairness review. Because entire fairness review places such a heavy burden on defendants, resolution of the preliminary inquiry laid out in *Unocal* will often be outcome determinative.

UNOCAL CORP. V. MESA PETROLEUM
493 A.2d 946 (1985)

MOORE, Justice.

We confront an issue of first impression in Delaware — the validity of a corporation's self-tender for its own shares which excludes from participation a stockholder making a hostile tender offer for the company's stock. [...]

On April 8, 1985, Mesa, the owner of approximately 13% of Unocal's stock, commenced a two-tier "front loaded" cash tender offer for 64 million shares, or approximately 37%, of Unocal's outstanding stock at a price of $54 per share. The "back-end" was designed to eliminate the remaining publicly held shares by an exchange of securities purportedly worth $54 per share. However, pursuant to an order entered by the United States District Court for the Central District of California on April 26, 1985, Mesa issued a supplemental proxy statement to Unocal's stockholders disclosing that the securities offered in the second-step merger would be highly subordinated, and that Unocal's capitalization would differ significantly from its present [950] structure. Unocal has rather aptly termed such securities "junk bonds".[3]

Unocal's board consists of eight independent outside directors and six insiders. It met on April 13, 1985, to consider the Mesa tender offer. Thirteen directors were present, and the meeting lasted nine and one-half hours. The directors were given no agenda or written materials prior to the session. However, detailed presentations were made by legal counsel regarding the board's obligations under both Delaware corporate law and the federal securities laws. The board then received a presentation from Peter Sachs on behalf of Goldman Sachs & Co. (Goldman Sachs) and Dillon, Read & Co. (Dillon Read) discussing the bases for their opinions that the Mesa proposal was wholly inadequate. Mr. Sachs opined that the minimum cash value that could be expected from a sale or orderly liquidation for 100% of Unocal's stock was in excess of $60 per share. [...]

Mr. Sachs also presented various defensive strategies available to the board if it concluded that Mesa's two-step tender offer was inadequate and should be opposed. One of the devices outlined was a self-tender by Unocal for its own stock with a reasonable price range of $70 to $75 per share. The cost of such a proposal would cause the company to incur $6.1-6.5 billion of additional debt, and a presentation was made informing the board of Unocal's ability to handle it. The directors were told that the primary effect of this obligation would be to reduce exploratory drilling, but that the company would nonetheless remain a viable entity.

The eight outside directors, comprising a clear majority of the thirteen members present, then met separately with Unocal's financial advisors and attorneys. Thereafter, they unanimously agreed to advise the board that it should reject Mesa's tender offer as inadequate, and that Unocal should pursue a self-tender to provide the stockholders with a fairly priced alternative to the Mesa proposal. The board then reconvened and unanimously adopted a resolution rejecting as grossly inadequate Mesa's tender offer. Despite the nine and one-half hour length of the meeting, no formal decision was made on the proposed defensive self-tender.

On April 15, the board met again with four of the directors present by telephone [951] and one member still absent.[4] This session lasted two hours. Unocal's Vice President of Finance and its Assistant General Counsel made a detailed presentation of the proposed terms of the exchange offer. A price range between $70 and $80 per share was considered, and ultimately the directors agreed upon $72. The board was also advised about the debt securities that would be issued, and the necessity of placing restrictive covenants upon certain corporate activities until the obligations were paid. The board's decisions were made in reliance on the advice of its investment bankers, including the terms and conditions upon which the securities were to be issued. Based upon this advice, and the board's own deliberations, the directors unanimously approved the exchange offer. Their resolution provided that if Mesa acquired 64 million shares of Unocal stock through its own offer (the Mesa Purchase Condition), Unocal would buy the remaining 49% outstanding for an exchange of debt securities having an aggregate par value of $72 per share. [...]

Unocal's exchange offer was commenced on April 17, 1985, and Mesa promptly challenged it by filing this suit in the Court of Chancery. On April 22, the Unocal board met again and was advised by Goldman Sachs and Dillon Read to waive the Mesa Purchase Condition as to 50 million shares. This recommendation was in response to a perceived concern of the shareholders that, if shares were tendered to Unocal, no shares would be purchased by either offeror. The directors were also advised that they should tender their own Unocal stock into the exchange offer as a mark of their confidence in it.

Another focus of the board was the Mesa exclusion. Legal counsel advised that under Delaware law Mesa could only be excluded for what the directors reasonably believed to be a valid corporate purpose. The directors' discussion centered on the objective of adequately compensating shareholders at the "back-end" of Mesa's proposal, which the latter would finance with "junk bonds". To include Mesa would defeat that goal, because under the proration aspect of the exchange offer (49%) every Mesa share accepted by Unocal would displace one held by another stockholder. Further, if Mesa were permitted to tender to Unocal, the latter would in effect be financing Mesa's own inadequate proposal. [...]

On April 29, 1985, the Vice Chancellor temporarily restrained Unocal from proceeding with the exchange offer unless it included Mesa. [...]

Unocal immediately sought certification of an interlocutory appeal to this Court pursuant to Supreme Court Rule 42(b). [...]

On May 13, 1985 the Court of Chancery certified this interlocutory appeal to us as a question of first impression, and we accepted it on May 14. The entire matter was scheduled on an expedited basis.[5]

II.

The issues we address involve these fundamental questions: Did the Unocal board have the power and duty to oppose a takeover threat it reasonably perceived to be harmful to the corporate enterprise, and if so, is its action here entitled to the protection of the business judgment rule?

Mesa contends that the discriminatory exchange offer violates the fiduciary duties Unocal owes it. Mesa argues that because of the Mesa exclusion the business judgment rule is inapplicable, because the directors by tendering their own shares will derive a financial benefit that is not available to *all* Unocal stockholders. Thus, it is Mesa's ultimate contention that Unocal cannot establish that the exchange offer is fair to *all* shareholders, and argues that the Court of Chancery was correct in concluding that Unocal was unable to meet this burden.

Unocal answers that it does not owe a duty of "fairness" to Mesa, given the facts here. Specifically, Unocal contends that its board of directors reasonably and in good faith concluded that Mesa's $54 two-tier tender offer was coercive and inadequate, and that Mesa sought selective treatment for itself. Furthermore, Unocal argues that the board's approval of the exchange offer was made in good faith, on an informed basis, and in the exercise of due care. Under these circumstances, Unocal contends that its directors properly employed this device to protect the company and its stockholders from Mesa's harmful tactics.

III.

We begin with the basic issue of the power of a board of directors of a Delaware corporation to adopt a defensive measure of this type. Absent such authority, all other questions are moot. Neither issues of fairness nor business judgment are pertinent without the basic underpinning of a board's legal power to act.

The board has a large reservoir of authority upon which to draw. Its duties and responsibilities proceed from the inherent powers conferred by 8 *Del.C.* § 141(a), respecting management of the corporation's "business and affairs".[6] Additionally, the powers here being exercised derive from 8 *Del.C.* § 160(a), conferring broad authority upon a corporation to deal in its own stock.[7] From this it is now well established that in the acquisition of its shares a [954] Delaware corporation may deal selectively with its stockholders, provided the directors have not acted out of a sole or primary purpose to entrench themselves in office. [...]

Finally, the board's power to act derives from its fundamental duty and obligation to protect the corporate enterprise, which includes stockholders, from harm reasonably perceived, irrespective of its source. [...] Thus, we are satisfied that in the broad context of corporate governance, including issues of fundamental corporate change, a board of directors is not a passive instrumentality.[8]

Given the foregoing principles, we turn to the standards by which director action is to be measured. In *Pogostin v. Rice*[...], we held

that the business judgment rule, including the standards by which
director conduct is judged, is applicable in the context of a takeover.
[...]The business judgment rule is a "presumption that in making a
business decision the directors of a corporation acted on an
informed basis, in good faith and in the honest belief that the action
taken was in the best interests of the company." *Aronson v. Lewis*[
...]. A hallmark of the business judgment rule is that a court will not
substitute its judgment for that of the board if the latter's decision
can be "attributed to any rational business purpose." *Sinclair Oil
Corp. v. Levien*[...].

When a board addresses a pending takeover bid it has an obligation
to determine whether the offer is in the best interests of the
corporation and its shareholders. In that respect a board's duty is no
different from any other responsibility it shoulders, and its decisions
should be no less entitled to the respect they otherwise would be
accorded in the realm of business judgment.[9]*See also Johnson v.
Trueblood,* 629 F.2d 287, 292-293 (3d Cir.1980). There are,
however, certain caveats to a proper exercise of this function.
Because of the omnipresent specter that a board may be acting
primarily in its own interests, rather than those of the corporation
and its shareholders, there is an enhanced duty which calls for
judicial examination at the threshold before the protections of the
business judgment rule may be conferred. [...]

In the face of this inherent conflict directors must show that they
had reasonable grounds for believing that a danger to corporate
policy and effectiveness existed because of another person's stock
ownership. [...] However, they satisfy that burden "by showing good
faith and reasonable investigation...." [...] Furthermore, such proof
is materially enhanced, as here, by the approval of a board
comprised of a majority of outside independent directors who have
acted in accordance with the foregoing standards. [...]

IV.

A.

In the board's exercise of corporate power to forestall a takeover bid our analysis begins with the basic principle that corporate directors have a fiduciary duty to act in the best interests of the corporation's stockholders. [...] As we have noted, their duty of care extends to protecting the corporation and its owners from perceived harm whether a threat originates from third parties or other shareholders.[10] But such powers are not absolute. A corporation does not have unbridled discretion to defeat any perceived threat by any Draconian means available.

The restriction placed upon a selective stock repurchase is that the directors may not have acted solely or primarily out of a desire to perpetuate themselves in office. [...]The standard of proof [...]is designed to ensure that a defensive measure to thwart or impede a takeover is indeed motivated by a good faith concern for the welfare of the corporation and its stockholders, which in all circumstances must be free of any fraud or other misconduct. [...] However, this does not end the inquiry.

B.

A further aspect is the element of balance. If a defensive measure is to come within the ambit of the business judgment rule, it must be reasonable in relation to the threat posed. This entails an analysis by the directors of the nature of the takeover bid and its effect on the corporate enterprise. Examples of such concerns may include: inadequacy of the price offered, nature and timing of the offer, questions of illegality, the impact on "constituencies" other than shareholders (i.e., creditors, customers, employees, and perhaps even the community generally), the risk of nonconsummation, and the quality of securities being offered in the exchange. *See* Lipton and Brownstein, *Takeover Responses and Directors' Responsibilities: An Update,* p. 7, ABA National Institute on the Dynamics of Corporate Control (December 8, 1983). While not a controlling factor, it also seems to us that a board may reasonably consider the basic stockholder [956] interests at stake, including those of short term speculators, whose actions may have fueled the coercive aspect of the offer at the expense of the long term investor.[111] Here, the threat posed was viewed by the Unocal board as a grossly inadequate two-tier coercive tender offer coupled with the threat of greenmail.

Specifically, the Unocal directors had concluded that the value of Unocal was substantially above the $54 per share offered in cash at the front end. Furthermore, they determined that the subordinated securities to be exchanged in Mesa's announced squeeze out of the remaining shareholders in the "back-end" merger were "junk bonds" worth far less than $54. It is now well recognized that such offers are a classic coercive measure designed to stampede shareholders into tendering at the first tier, even if the price is inadequate, out of fear of what they will receive at the back end of the transaction.[112] Wholly beyond the coercive aspect of an inadequate two-tier tender offer, the threat was posed by a corporate raider with a national reputation as a "greenmailer".[113]

In adopting the selective exchange offer, the board stated that its objective was either to defeat the inadequate Mesa offer or, should the offer still succeed, provide the 49% of its stockholders, who would otherwise be forced to accept "junk bonds", with $72 worth of senior debt. We find that both purposes are valid.

However, such efforts would have been thwarted by Mesa's participation in the exchange offer. First, if Mesa could tender its shares, Unocal would effectively be subsidizing the former's continuing effort to buy Unocal stock at $54 per share. Second, Mesa could not, by definition, fit within the class of shareholders being protected from its own coercive and inadequate tender offer.

Thus, we are satisfied that the selective exchange offer is reasonably related to the threats posed. [...]

V.

Mesa contends that it is unlawful, and the trial court agreed, for a corporation to discriminate in this fashion against one shareholder. It argues correctly that no case has ever sanctioned a device that precludes a raider from sharing in a benefit available to all other stockholders. However, as we have noted earlier, the principle of selective stock repurchases by a Delaware corporation is neither unknown nor unauthorized. *Cheff v. Mathes,* 199 A.2d at 554; *Bennett v. Propp,* 187 A.2d at 408; *Martin v. American Potash & Chemical Corporation,* 92 A.2d at 302; *Kaplan v. Goldsamt,* 380 A.2d at 568-569; *Kors v. Carey,* 158 A.2d at 140-141; 8 *Del. C.* § 160. The only difference is that heretofore the approved transaction was the payment of "greenmail" to a raider or dissident posing a threat to the corporate enterprise. All other stockholders were denied such favored treatment, and given Mesa's past history of greenmail, its claims here are rather ironic.

However, our corporate law is not static. It must grow and develop in response to, indeed in anticipation of, evolving concepts and needs. Merely because the General Corporation Law is silent as to a specific matter does not mean that it is prohibited. [...]

More recently, as the sophistication of both raiders and targets has developed, a host of other defensive measures to counter such ever mounting threats has evolved and received judicial sanction. These include defensive charter amendments and other devices bearing some rather exotic, but apt, names: Crown Jewel, White Knight, Pac Man, and Golden Parachute. Each has highly selective features, the object of which is to deter or defeat the raider.

Thus, while the exchange offer is a form of selective treatment, given the nature of the threat posed here the response is neither unlawful nor unreasonable. If the board of directors is disinterested, has acted in good faith and with due care, its decision in the absence of an abuse of discretion will be upheld as a proper exercise of business judgment.

[...]

VI.

In conclusion, there was directorial power to oppose the Mesa tender offer, and to undertake a selective stock exchange made in good faith and upon a reasonable investigation pursuant to a clear duty to protect the corporate enterprise. Further, the selective stock repurchase plan chosen by Unocal is reasonable in relation to the threat that the board rationally and reasonably believed was posed by Mesa's inadequate and coercive two-tier tender offer. Under those circumstances the board's action is entitled to be measured by the standards of the business judgment rule. Thus, unless it is shown by a preponderance of the evidence that the directors' decisions were primarily based on perpetuating themselves in office, or some other breach of fiduciary duty such as fraud, overreaching, lack of good faith, or being uninformed, a Court will not substitute its judgment for that of the board. [...]

Revlon, Inc. v. MacAndrews & Forbes Holdings, Inc.   7.2.2

When a board, under Unocal, is asked to justify its decision to adopt defensive measures by identifying some threat to the corporation or corporate policy, the board generally has broad discretion in identifying the threat. The court in Unocal noted that boards may be permitted to consider "the impact on "constituencies" other than shareholders (i.e., creditors, customers, employees, and perhaps even the community generally)". That is to say, the board is permitted to take a long term view and consider the potential impact of a threat on the many constituencies that the corporation requires over the long term.

Revlon provides us with an alternative application of *Unocal*s intermediate standard. In situations like *Revlon* where the board has decided of its own accord to look to the short term by engaging in a sale of control of the corporation, then the board may no longer consider long term constituencies. When the board has focused on the short term, then the only cogniziable threat to corporate policy are those that affect value in the short term. If a board in a *Revlon*-like situation adopts defenses, it will have to justify them as reasonable in relation to the threat posed to the corporation in the short run.

In the *Revlon* opinion that follows notice how the court applies *Unocal*s intermediate standard before and after a break up of the corporation becomes imminent.

REVLON, INC. V MACANDREWS & FORBES HOLDING
506 A.2d 173 (1985)

MOORE, Justice:

The prelude to this controversy began in June 1985, when Ronald O. Perelman, chairman of the board and chief executive officer of Pantry Pride, met with his counterpart at Revlon, Michel C. Bergerac, to discuss a friendly acquisition of Revlon by Pantry Pride. Perelman suggested a price in the range of $40-50 per share, but the meeting ended with Bergerac dismissing those figures as considerably below Revlon's intrinsic value. All subsequent Pantry Pride overtures were rebuffed, perhaps in part based on Mr. Bergerac's strong personal antipathy to Mr. Perelman.

Thus, on August 14, Pantry Pride's board authorized Perelman to acquire Revlon, either through negotiation in the $42-$43 per share range, or by making a hostile tender offer at $45. Perelman then met with Bergerac and outlined Pantry Pride's alternate approaches. Bergerac remained adamantly opposed to such schemes and conditioned any further discussions of the matter on Pantry Pride executing a standstill agreement prohibiting it from acquiring Revlon without the latter's prior approval.

On August 19, the Revlon board met specially to consider the impending threat of a hostile bid by Pantry Pride.[3] At the meeting, Lazard Freres, Revlon's investment [177] banker, advised the directors that $45 per share was a grossly inadequate price for the company. Felix Rohatyn and William Loomis of Lazard Freres explained to the board that Pantry Pride's financial strategy for acquiring Revlon would be through "junk bond" financing followed by a break-up of Revlon and the disposition of its assets. With proper timing, according to the experts, such transactions could produce a return to Pantry Pride of $60 to $70 per share, while a sale of the company as a whole would be in the "mid 50" dollar range. Martin Lipton, special counsel for Revlon, recommended two defensive measures: first, that the company repurchase up to 5 million of its nearly 30 million outstanding shares; and second, that it adopt a Note Purchase Rights Plan. Under this plan, each Revlon shareholder would receive as a dividend one Note Purchase Right (the Rights) for each share of common stock, with the Rights entitling the holder to exchange one common share for a $65 principal Revlon note at 12% interest with a one-year maturity. The Rights would become effective whenever anyone acquired beneficial ownership of 20% or more of Revlon's shares, unless the purchaser acquired all the company's stock for cash at $65 or more per share. In addition, the Rights would not be available to the acquiror, and prior to the 20% triggering event the Revlon board could redeem the rights for 10 cents each. Both proposals were unanimously adopted.

Pantry Pride made its first hostile move on August 23 with a cash tender offer for any and all shares of Revlon at $47.50 per common share and $26.67 per preferred share, subject to (1) Pantry Pride's obtaining financing for the purchase, and (2) the Rights being redeemed, rescinded or voided.

The Revlon board met again on August 26. The directors advised the stockholders to reject the offer. Further defensive measures also were planned. On August 29, Revlon commenced its own offer for up to 10 million shares, exchanging for each share of common stock tendered one Senior Subordinated Note (the Notes) of $47.50 principal at 11.75% interest, due 1995, and one-tenth of a share of $9.00 Cumulative Convertible Exchangeable Preferred Stock valued at $100 per share. Lazard Freres opined that the notes would trade at their face value on a fully distributed basis.[11] Revlon stockholders tendered 87 percent of the outstanding shares (approximately 33 million), and the company accepted the full 10 million shares on a pro rata basis. The new Notes contained covenants which limited Revlon's ability to incur additional debt, sell assets, or pay dividends unless otherwise approved by the "independent" (nonmanagement) members of the board.

At this point, both the Rights and the Note covenants stymied Pantry Pride's attempted takeover. The next move came on September 16, when Pantry Pride announced a new tender offer at $42 per share, conditioned upon receiving at least 90% of the outstanding stock. [...]While this offer was lower on its face than the earlier $47.50 proposal, Revlon's investment banker, Lazard Freres, described the two bids as essentially equal in view of the completed exchange offer.

The Revlon board held a regularly scheduled meeting on September 24. The directors rejected the latest Pantry Pride offer and authorized management to negotiate with other parties interested in acquiring Revlon. Pantry Pride remained determined in its efforts and continued to make cash bids for the company, offering $50 per share on September 27, and raising its bid to $53 on October 1, and then to $56.25 on October 7.

In the meantime, Revlon's negotiations with Forstmann [...] had produced results. [...]the directors unanimously agreed to a leveraged buyout by Forstmann. The terms of this accord were as follows: each stockholder would get $56 cash per share; management would purchase stock in the new company by the exercise of their Revlon "golden parachutes";[5] Forstmann would assume Revlon's $475 million debt incurred by the issuance of the Notes; and Revlon would redeem the Rights and waive the Notes covenants for Forstmann or in connection with any other offer superior to Forstmann's. The board did not actually remove the covenants at the October 3 meeting, because Forstmann then lacked a firm commitment on its financing, but accepted the Forstmann capital structure, and indicated that the outside directors would waive the covenants in due course. Part of Forstmann's plan was to sell Revlon's Norcliff Thayer and Reheis divisions to American Home Products for $335 million. Before the merger, Revlon was to sell its cosmetics and fragrance division to Adler & Shaykin for $905 million. These transactions would facilitate the purchase by Forstmann or any other acquiror of Revlon.

When the merger, and thus the waiver of the Notes covenants, was announced, the market value of these securities began to fall. [...]One director later reported (at the October 12 meeting) a "deluge" of telephone calls from irate noteholders, and on October 10 the Wall Street Journal reported threats of litigation by these creditors.

Pantry Pride countered with a new proposal on October 7, raising its $53 offer to $56.25, subject to nullification of the Rights, a waiver of the Notes covenants, and the election of three Pantry Pride directors to the Revlon board. [...] Pantry Pride announced that it would engage in fractional bidding and top any Forstmann offer by a slightly higher one. It is also significant that Forstmann, to Pantry Pride's exclusion, had been made privy to certain Revlon financial data. Thus, the parties were not negotiating on equal terms.

[...] privately armed with Revlon data, Forstmann met on October 11 with Revlon's special counsel and investment banker. On October 12, Forstmann made a new $57.25 per share offer, based on several conditions.[6] The principal demand was a lock-up option to purchase Revlon's Vision Care and National Health Laboratories divisions for $525 million, some $100-$175 million below the value ascribed to them by Lazard Freres, if another acquiror got 40% of Revlon's shares. Revlon also was required to accept a no-shop provision. The Rights and Notes covenants had to be removed as in the October 3 agreement. There would be a $25 million cancellation fee to be placed in escrow, and released to Forstmann if the new agreement terminated or if another acquiror got more than 19.9% of Revlon's stock. Finally, there would be no participation by Revlon management in the merger. In return, Forstmann agreed to support the par value [179] of the Notes, which had faltered in the market, by an exchange of new notes. Forstmann also demanded immediate acceptance of its offer, or it would be withdrawn. The board unanimously approved Forstmann's proposal because: (1) it was for a higher price than the Pantry Pride bid, (2) it protected the noteholders, and (3) Forstmann's financing was firmly in place.[7] The board further agreed to redeem the rights and waive the covenants on the preferred stock in response to any offer above $57 cash per share. The covenants were waived, contingent upon receipt of an investment banking opinion that the Notes would trade near par value once the offer was consummated.

Pantry Pride, which had initially sought injunctive relief from the Rights plan on August 22, filed an amended complaint on October

14 challenging the lock-up, the cancellation fee, and the exercise of the Rights and the Notes covenants. Pantry Pride also sought a temporary restraining order to prevent Revlon from placing any assets in escrow or transferring them to Forstmann. Moreover, on October 22, Pantry Pride again raised its bid, with a cash offer of $58 per share conditioned upon nullification of the Rights, waiver of the covenants, and an injunction of the Forstmann lock-up. [...]

The ultimate responsibility for managing the business and affairs of a corporation falls on its board of directors. 8 *Del.C.* § 141(a).[8] In discharging this function the directors owe fiduciary duties of care and loyalty to the corporation and its shareholders. [...]These principles apply with equal force when a board approves a corporate merger pursuant to 8 *Del.C.* § 251(b);[9] *Smith v. Van Gorkom,* Del.Supr., 488 A.2d 858, 873 (1985); and of course they are the bedrock of our law regarding corporate takeover issues. [...]While the business judgment rule may be applicable to the actions of corporate directors responding to takeover threats, the principles upon which it is founded — care, loyalty and independence — must first be satisfied.[10] *Aronson v. Lewis,* 473 A.2d at 812.

If the business judgment rule applies, there is a "presumption that in making a business decision the directors of a corporation acted on an informed basis, in good faith and in the honest belief that the action taken was in the best interests of the company." [...]However, when a board implements anti-takeover measures there arises "the omnipresent specter that a board may be acting primarily in its own interests, rather than those of the corporation and its shareholders ..." [...]This potential for conflict places upon the directors the burden of proving that they had reasonable grounds for believing there was a danger to corporate policy and effectiveness, a burden satisfied by a showing of good faith and reasonable investigation. *Id.* at 955. In addition, the directors must analyze the nature of the takeover and its effect on the corporation in order to ensure balance — that the responsive action taken is reasonable in relation to the threat posed. [...]

The first relevant defensive measure adopted by the Revlon board was the Rights Plan, which would be considered a "poison pill" in the current language of corporate takeovers — a plan by which shareholders receive the right to be bought out by the corporation at a substantial premium on the occurrence of a stated triggering event. [...] the board clearly had the power to adopt the measure. [...]Thus, the focus becomes one of reasonableness and purpose.

The Revlon board approved the Rights Plan in the face of an impending hostile takeover bid by Pantry Pride at $45 per share, a price which Revlon reasonably concluded was grossly inadequate. [...] In adopting the Plan, the board protected the shareholders from a hostile takeover at a price below the company's intrinsic value, while retaining sufficient flexibility to address any proposal deemed to be in the stockholders' best interests.

To that extent the board acted in good faith and upon reasonable investigation. Under the circumstances it cannot be said that the Rights Plan as employed was unreasonable, considering the threat posed. Indeed, the Plan was a factor in causing Pantry Pride to raise its bids from a low of $42 to an eventual high of $58. At the time of its adoption the Rights Plan afforded a measure of protection consistent with the directors' fiduciary duty in facing a takeover threat perceived as detrimental to corporate interests.[...]Far from being a "show-stopper," as the plaintiffs had contended in *Moran,* the measure spurred the bidding to new heights, a proper result of its implementation. [...]

Although we consider adoption of the Plan to have been valid under the circumstances, its continued usefulness was rendered moot by the directors' actions on October 3 and October 12. At the October 3 meeting the board redeemed the Rights conditioned upon consummation of a merger with Forstmann, but further acknowledged that they would also be redeemed to facilitate any more favorable offer. On October 12, the board unanimously passed a resolution redeeming the Rights in connection with any cash proposal of $57.25 or more per share. Because all the pertinent offers eventually equalled or surpassed that amount, the Rights clearly were no longer any impediment in the contest for Revlon. This mooted any question of their propriety under *Unocal.* [...]

The second defensive measure adopted by Revlon to thwart a Pantry Pride takeover was the company's own exchange offer for 10 million of its shares. [...]

The Revlon directors concluded that Pantry Pride's $47.50 offer was grossly inadequate. In that regard the board acted in good faith, and on an informed basis, with reasonable grounds to believe that there existed a harmful threat to the corporate enterprise. The adoption of a defensive measure, reasonable in relation to the threat posed, was proper and fully accorded with the powers, duties, and responsibilities conferred upon directors under our law. [...]

However, when Pantry Pride increased its offer to $50 per share, and then to $53, it became apparent to all that the break-up of the company was inevitable. The Revlon board's authorization permitting management to negotiate a merger or buyout with a third party was a recognition that the company was for sale. The duty of the board had thus changed from the preservation of Revlon as a corporate entity to the maximization of the company's value at a sale for the stockholders' benefit. This significantly altered the board's responsibilities under the *Unocal* standards. It no longer faced threats to corporate policy and effectiveness, or to the stockholders' interests, from a grossly inadequate bid. The whole question of defensive measures became moot. The directors' role changed from defenders of the corporate bastion to auctioneers charged with getting the best price for the stockholders at a sale of the company. [...]

This brings us to the lock-up with Forstmann and its emphasis on shoring up the sagging market value of the Notes in the face of threatened litigation by their holders. Such a focus was inconsistent with the changed concept of the directors' responsibilities at this stage of the developments. [...]

The original threat posed by Pantry Pride — the break-up of the company — had become a reality which even the directors embraced. Selective dealing to fend off a hostile but determined bidder was no longer a proper objective. Instead, obtaining the highest price for the benefit of the stockholders should have been the central theme guiding director action. Thus, the Revlon board could not make the requisite showing of good faith by preferring the noteholders and ignoring its duty of loyalty to the shareholders. The rights of the former already were fixed by contract. [...] The noteholders required no further protection, and when the Revlon board entered into an auction-ending lock-up agreement with Forstmann on the basis of impermissible considerations at the expense of the shareholders, the directors breached their primary duty of loyalty.

The Revlon board argued that it acted in good faith in protecting the noteholders because *Unocal* permits consideration of other corporate constituencies. [...] However, such concern for non-stockholder interests is inappropriate when an auction among active bidders is in progress, and the object no longer is to protect or maintain the corporate enterprise but to sell it to the highest bidder. [...]

V.

In conclusion, the Revlon board was confronted with a situation not uncommon in the current wave of corporate takeovers. A hostile and determined bidder sought the company at a price the board was convinced was inadequate. The initial defensive tactics worked to the benefit of the shareholders, and thus the board was able to sustain its *Unocal* burdens in justifying those measures. However, in granting an asset option lock-up to Forstmann, we must conclude that under all the circumstances the directors allowed considerations other than the maximization of shareholder profit to affect their judgment, and followed a course that ended the auction for Revlon, absent court intervention, to the ultimate detriment of its shareholders. No such defensive measure can be sustained when it represents a breach of the directors' fundamental duty of care. *See Smith v. Van Gorkom,* Del.Supr., 488 A.2d 858, 874 (1985). In that context the board's action is not entitled to the deference accorded it by the business judgment rule. [...]

PARAMOUNT COMM., INC. V. TIME, INC.
571 A.2d 1140 (1989)

HORSEY, Justice:

Paramount Communications, Inc. ("Paramount") [...] filed suits in the Delaware Court of Chancery seeking a preliminary injunction to halt Time's tender offer for 51% of Warner Communication, Inc.'s ("Warner") outstanding shares at $70 cash per share. [...]

Shareholder Plaintiffs also assert a claim based on *Revlon v. MacAndrews & Forbes Holdings, Inc.,* Del.Supr., 506 A.2d 173 (1986). They argue that the original Time-Warner merger agreement of March 4, 1989 resulted in a change of control which effectively put Time up for sale, thereby triggering *Revlon* duties. Those plaintiffs argue that Time's board breached its *Revlon* duties by failing, in the face of the change of control, to maximize shareholder value in the immediate term.

Applying our standard of review, we affirm the Chancellor's ultimate finding and conclusion under *Unocal.* We find that Paramount's tender offer was reasonably perceived by Time's board to pose a threat to Time and that the Time board's "response" to that threat was, under the circumstances, reasonable and proportionate. Applying *Unocal,* we reject the argument that the only corporate threat posed by an all-shares, all-cash tender offer is the possibility of inadequate value.

We also find that Time's board did not by entering into its initial merger agreement with Warner come under a *Revlon* duty either to auction the company or to maximize short-term shareholder value, notwithstanding the unequal share exchange. Therefore, the Time board's original plan of merger with Warner was subject only to a business judgment rule analysis. *See Smith v. Van Gorkom,* Del.Supr., 488 A.2d 858, 873-74 (1985).[2]

Time is a Delaware corporation with its principal offices in New York City. Time's traditional business is publication of magazines and books; however, Time also provides pay television programming through its Home Box Office, Inc. and Cinemax subsidiaries. In addition, Time owns and operates cable television franchises through its subsidiary, American Television and Communication Corporation. During the relevant time period, Time's board consisted of sixteen directors. Twelve of the directors were "outside," nonemployee directors. Four of the directors were also officers of the company. [...]

As early as 1983 and 1984, Time's executive board began considering expanding Time's operations into the entertainment industry. [...]This expansion, as the Chancellor noted, was predicated upon two considerations: first, Time's desire to have greater control, in terms of quality and price, over the film products delivered by way of its cable network and franchises; and second, Time's concern over the increasing globalization of the world economy. Some of Time's outside directors, especially Luce and Temple, had opposed this move as a threat to the editorial integrity and journalistic focus of Time.[4] Despite this concern, the board recognized that a [1144] vertically integrated video enterprise to complement Time's existing HBO and cable networks would better enable it to compete on a global basis. [...]

The board's consensus was that a merger of Time and Warner was feasible, but only if Time controlled the board of the resulting corporation and thereby preserved a management committed to Time's journalistic integrity. To accomplish this goal, the board stressed the importance of carefully defining in advance the corporate governance provisions that would control the resulting entity. Some board members expressed concern over whether such a business combination would place Time *"in play."* The board discussed the wisdom of adopting further defensive measures to lessen such a possibility.[5] [...]

From the outset, Time's board favored an all-cash or cash and securities acquisition of Warner as the basis for consolidation. [...] Warner insisted on a stock swap in order to preserve its shareholders' equity in the resulting corporation. Time's officers, on the other hand, made it abundantly clear that Time would be the acquiring corporation and that Time would control the resulting board. Time refused to permit itself to be cast as the "acquired" company.

Negotiations ended when the parties reached an impasse. Time's board refused to compromise on its position on corporate governance. Time, and particularly its outside directors, viewed the corporate governance provisions as critical for preserving the "Time Culture" through a pro-Time management at the top. [...]

Warner and Time resumed negotiations in January 1989. The catalyst for the resumption of talks was a private dinner between Steve Ross and Time outside director, Michael Dingman. Dingman was able to convince Ross that the transitional nature of the proposed co-CEO arrangement did not reflect a lack of confidence in Ross. Ross agreed that this course was best for the company and a meeting between Ross and Munro resulted. Ross agreed to retire in five years and let Nicholas succeed him. Negotiations resumed and many of the details of the original stock-for-stock exchange agreement remained [1146] intact. [...]

The parties ultimately agreed upon an exchange rate favoring Warner of .465. On that basis, Warner stockholders would have owned approximately 62%[7] of the common stock of Time-Warner.

On March 3, 1989, Time's board, with all but one director in attendance, met and unanimously approved the stock-for-stock merger with Warner. Warner's board likewise approved the merger. The agreement called for Warner to be merged into a wholly-owned Time subsidiary with Warner becoming the surviving corporation. The common stock of Warner would then be converted into common stock of Time at the agreed upon ratio. Thereafter, the name of Time would be changed to Time-Warner, Inc.

The rules of the New York Stock Exchange required that Time's issuance of shares to effectuate the merger be approved by a vote of

Time's stockholders. The Delaware General Corporation Law required approval of the merger by a majority of the Warner stockholders. Delaware law did not require any vote by Time stockholders. [...]

At its March 3, 1989 meeting, Time's board adopted several defensive tactics. Time entered an automatic share exchange agreement with Warner. Time would receive 17,292,747 shares of Warner's outstanding common stock (9.4%) and Warner would receive 7,080,016 shares of Time's outstanding common stock (11.1%). Either party could trigger the exchange. Time sought out and paid for "confidence" letters from various banks with which it did business. In these letters, the banks promised not to finance any third-party attempt to acquire Time. Time argues these agreements served only to preserve the confidential relationship between itself and the banks. The Chancellor found these agreements to be inconsequential and futile attempts to "dry up" money for a hostile takeover. Time also agreed to a "no-shop" clause, preventing Time from considering any other consolidation proposal, thus relinquishing [1147] its power to consider other proposals, regardless of their merits. Time did so at Warner's insistence. Warner did not want to be left "on the auction block" for an unfriendly suitor, if Time were to withdraw from the deal. [...]

Time representatives lauded the lack of debt to the United States Senate and to the President of the United States. Public reaction to the announcement of the merger was positive. Time-Warner would be a media colossus with international scope. The board scheduled the stockholder vote for June 23; and a May 1 record date was set. On May 24, 1989, Time sent out extensive proxy statements to the stockholders regarding the approval vote on the merger. In the meantime, with the merger proceeding without impediment, the special committee had concluded, shortly after its creation, that it was not necessary either to retain independent consultants, legal or financial, or even to meet. Time's board was unanimously in favor of the proposed merger with Warner; and, by the end of May, the Time-Warner merger appeared to be an accomplished fact.

On June 7, 1989, these wishful assumptions were shattered by Paramount's surprising announcement of its all-cash offer to purchase all outstanding shares of Time for $175 per share. The following day, June 8, the trading price of Time's stock rose from $126 to $170 per share. Paramount's offer was said to be "fully negotiable."[8]

Time found Paramount's "fully negotiable" offer to be in fact subject to at least three conditions. First, Time had to terminate its merger agreement and stock exchange agreement with Warner, and remove certain other of its defensive devices, including the redemption of Time's shareholder rights. Second, Paramount had to obtain the required cable franchise transfers from Time in a fashion acceptable to Paramount in its sole discretion. Finally, the offer depended upon a judicial determination that section 203 of the General Corporate Law of Delaware (The Delaware Anti-Takeover Statute) was inapplicable to any Time-Paramount merger. [...]

On June 8, 1989, Time formally responded to Paramount's offer. Time's chairman and CEO, J. Richard Munro, sent an aggressively worded letter to Paramount's CEO, Martin Davis. Munro's letter attacked Davis' personal integrity and called Paramount's offer "smoke and mirrors." [...]

Over the following eight days, Time's board met three times to discuss Paramount's $175 offer. The board viewed Paramount's offer as inadequate and concluded that its proposed merger with Warner was the better course of action. [...]

In June, Time's board of directors met several times. [...]

At these June meetings, certain Time directors expressed their concern that Time stockholders would not comprehend the long-term benefits of the Warner merger. Large quantities of Time shares were held by institutional investors. The board feared that even though there appeared to be wide support for the Warner transaction, Paramount's cash premium would be a tempting prospect to these investors. [...]

Time's board decided to recast its consolidation with Warner into an outright cash and securities acquisition of Warner by Time; and Time so informed Warner. Time accordingly restructured its proposal to acquire Warner as follows: Time would make an

immediate all-cash offer for 51% of Warner's outstanding stock at
$70 per share. The remaining 49% would be purchased at some
later date for a mixture of cash and securities worth $70 per share.
To provide the funds required for its outright acquisition of
Warner, Time would assume 7-10 billion dollars worth of debt, thus
eliminating one of the principal transaction-related benefits of the
original merger agreement. Nine billion dollars of the total purchase
price would be allocated to the purchase of Warner's goodwill. [...]

On June 23, 1989, Paramount raised its all-cash offer to buy Time's
outstanding stock to $200 per share. Paramount still professed that
all aspects of the offer were negotiable. Time's board met on June
26, 1989 and formally rejected Paramount's $200 per share second
offer. The board reiterated its belief that, despite the $25 increase,
the offer was still inadequate. The Time board maintained that the
Warner transaction offered a greater long-term value for the
stockholders and, unlike Paramount's offer, did not pose a threat to
Time's survival and its "culture." Paramount then filed this action in
the Court of Chancery.

II

The Shareholder Plaintiffs first assert a *Revlon* claim. They contend
that the March 4 Time-Warner agreement effectively put Time up
for sale, triggering *Revlon* duties, requiring Time's board to enhance
short-term shareholder value and to treat all other interested
acquirors on an equal basis. The Shareholder Plaintiffs base this
argument on two facts: (i) the ultimate Time-Warner exchange ratio
of .465 favoring Warner, resulting in Warner shareholders' receipt
of 62% of the combined company; and (ii) the subjective intent of
Time's directors as evidenced in their statements that the market
might perceive the Time-Warner merger as putting Time up "for
sale" and their adoption of various defensive measures. [...]

The Court of Chancery posed the pivotal question presented by this
case to be: Under what circumstances must a board of directors
abandon an in-place plan of corporate development in order to
provide its shareholders with the option to elect and realize an
immediate control premium? As applied to this case, the question

becomes: Did Time's board, having developed a strategic plan of global expansion to be launched through a business combination with Warner, come under a fiduciary duty to jettison its plan and put the corporation's [1150] future in the hands of its shareholders?

While we affirm the result reached by the Chancellor, we think it unwise to place undue emphasis upon long-term versus short-term corporate strategy. Two key predicates underpin our analysis. First, Delaware law imposes on a board of directors the duty to manage the business and affairs of the corporation. 8 *Del.C.* § 141(a). This broad mandate includes a conferred authority to set a corporate course of action, including time frame, designed to enhance corporate profitability. Thus, the question of "long-term" versus "short-term" values is largely irrelevant because directors, generally, are obliged to chart a course for a corporation which is in its best interests without regard to a fixed investment horizon. Second, absent a limited set of circumstances as defined under *Revlon,* a board of directors, while always required to act in an informed manner, is not under any *per se* duty to maximize shareholder value in the short term, even in the context of a takeover.[1121] In our view, the pivotal question presented by this case is: "Did Time, by entering into the proposed merger with Warner, put itself up for sale?" A resolution of that issue through application of *Revlon* has a significant bearing upon the resolution of the derivative *Unocal* issue.

A.

We first take up plaintiffs' principal *Revlon* argument, summarized above. In rejecting this argument, the Chancellor found the original Time-Warner merger agreement not to constitute a "change of control" and concluded that the transaction did not trigger *Revlon* duties. The Chancellor's conclusion is premised on a finding that "[b]efore the merger agreement was signed, control of the corporation existed in a fluid aggregation of unaffiliated shareholders representing a voting majority — in other words, in the market." The Chancellor's findings of fact are supported by the record and his conclusion is correct as a matter of law. However, we premise our rejection of plaintiffs' *Revlon* claim on different grounds, namely, the absence of any substantial evidence to conclude that Time's board, in negotiating with Warner, made the dissolution or break-up of the corporate entity inevitable, as was the case in *Revlon.*

Under Delaware law there are, generally speaking and without excluding other possibilities, two circumstances which may implicate *Revlon* duties. The first, and clearer one, is when a corporation initiates an active bidding process seeking to sell itself or to effect a business reorganization involving a clear break-up of the company. *See, e.g., Mills Acquisition Co. v. Macmillan, Inc,* Del.Supr., 559 A.2d 1261 (1988). However, *Revlon* duties may also be triggered where, in response to a bidder's offer, a target abandons its long-term strategy and seeks an alternative transaction involving the breakup of the company.[~]If, however, the board's reaction to a hostile tender offer is found to constitute only a defensive response and not an abandonment of the corporation's continued existence, *Revlon* duties are not triggered, though *Unocal* [1151] duties attach.[~1]

Plaintiffs rely on the subjective intent of Time's board of directors and principally upon certain board members' expressions of concern that the Warner transaction *might* be viewed as effectively putting Time up for sale. [...]

We agree with the Chancellor that such evidence is entirely insufficient to invoke *Revlon* duties; and we decline to extend *Revlon*'s application to corporate transactions simply because they might be construed as putting a corporation either "in play" or "up for sale." *See Citron v. Fairchild Camera,* Del.Supr., 569 A.2d 53, (1989); *Macmillan,* 559 A.2d at 1285 n. 35. The adoption of structural safety devices alone does not trigger *Revlon.*[15] Rather, as the Chancellor stated, such devices are properly subject to a *Unocal* analysis.

Finally, we do not find in Time's recasting of its merger agreement with Warner from a share exchange to a share purchase a basis to conclude that Time had either abandoned its strategic plan or made a sale of Time inevitable.[16] The Chancellor found that although the merged Time-Warner company would be large (with a value approaching approximately $30 billion), recent takeover cases have proven that acquisition of the combined company might nonetheless be possible. [...] The legal consequence is that *Unocal* alone applies to determine whether the business judgment rule attaches to the revised agreement. [...]

In *Unocal,* we held that before the business judgment rule is applied to a board's adoption of a defensive measure, the burden will lie with the board to prove (a) reasonable grounds for believing that a danger to corporate policy and effectiveness existed; and (b) that the defensive measure adopted was reasonable in relation to the threat posed. *Unocal,* 493 A.2d 946. Directors satisfy the first part of the *Unocal* test by demonstrating good faith and reasonable investigation. We have repeatedly stated that the refusal to entertain an offer may comport with a valid exercise of a board's business judgment. [...]

Thus, Paramount would have us hold that only if the value of Paramount's offer were determined to be clearly inferior to the value created by management's plan to merge with Warner could the offer be viewed — objectively — as a threat.

Implicit in the plaintiffs' argument is the view that a hostile tender offer can pose only two types of threats: the threat of coercion that results from a two-tier offer promising unequal treatment for nontendering shareholders; and the threat of inadequate value from an all-shares, all-cash offer at a price below what a target board [1153] in good faith deems to be the present value of its shares. *See, e.g., Interco*[...]. Since Paramount's offer was all-cash, the only conceivable "threat," plaintiffs argue, was inadequate value.[17] We disapprove of such a narrow and rigid construction of *Unocal,* for the reasons which follow.

Plaintiffs' position represents a fundamental misconception of our standard of review under *Unocal* principally because it would involve the court in substituting its judgment as to what is a "better" deal for that of a corporation's board of directors. To the extent that the Court of Chancery has recently done so in certain of its opinions, we hereby reject such approach as not in keeping with a

proper *Unocal* analysis. *See, e.g., Interco,* 551 A.2d 787, and its
progeny; *but see TW Services, Inc. v. SWT Acquisition Corp.,*
Del.Ch., C.A. No. 1047, Allen, C. 1989 WL 20290 (March 2,
1989).

The usefulness of *Unocal* as an analytical tool is precisely its
flexibility in the face of a variety of fact scenarios. *Unocal* is not
intended as an abstract standard; neither is it a structured and
mechanistic procedure of appraisal. Thus, we have said that
directors may consider, when evaluating the threat posed by a
takeover bid, the "inadequacy of the price offered, nature and timing
of the offer, questions of illegality, the impact on `constituencies'
other than shareholders ... the risk of nonconsummation, and the
quality of securities being offered in the exchange." [...]The open-
ended analysis mandated by *Unocal* is not intended to lead to a
simple mathematical exercise[...]. To engage in such an exercise is
a distortion of the *Unocal* process and, in particular, the application
of the second part of *Unocal*'s test, discussed below.

In this case, the Time board reasonably determined that inadequate
value was not the only legally cognizable threat that Paramount's all-
cash, all-shares offer could present. Time's board concluded that
Paramount's eleventh hour offer posed other threats. One concern
was that Time shareholders might elect to tender into Paramount's
cash offer in ignorance or a mistaken belief of the strategic benefit
which a business combination with Warner might produce. [...]

We turn to the second part of the *Unocal* analysis. [...]

Paramount argues that, assuming its tender offer posed a threat,
Time's response was unreasonable in precluding Time's
shareholders from accepting the tender offer or receiving a control
premium in the immediately foreseeable future. Once again, the
contention stems, we believe, from a fundamental misunderstanding
of where the power of corporate governance lies. Delaware law
confers the management of the corporate enterprise to the
stockholders' duly elected board representatives. 8 *Del.C.* § 141(a).
The fiduciary duty to manage a corporate enterprise includes the
selection of a time frame for achievement of corporate goals. That
duty may not be delegated to the stockholders. [...] Directors are

not obliged to abandon a deliberately conceived corporate plan for a short-term shareholder profit unless there is clearly no basis to sustain the corporate strategy. [...]

We have found that even in light of a valid threat, management actions that are coercive in nature or force upon shareholders a management-sponsored alternative to a hostile offer may be struck down as unreasonable and non-proportionate responses. [...]

Here, on the record facts, the Chancellor found that Time's responsive action to Paramount's tender offer was not aimed at [1155] "cramming down" on its shareholders a management-sponsored alternative, but rather had as its goal the carrying forward of a pre-existing transaction in an altered form.[19] Thus, the response was reasonably related to the threat. The Chancellor noted that the revised agreement and its accompanying safety devices did not preclude Paramount from making an offer for the combined Time-Warner company or from changing the conditions of its offer so as not to make the offer dependent upon the nullification of the Time-Warner agreement. Thus, the response was proportionate. [...]

Paramount Communications, Inc. v. QVC Network, Inc. [24]

The court in QVC returns to the question of application of the intermediate standard under Revlon. Ultimately, QVC will become a very important case in the development and application of the Revlon standard. In QVC, the court makes it clear that Revlon is not about a new standard of review but rather, akin to Unocal, it is an inquiry into the motive and means of the board.

If the board's motive is impaired by conflicts of interest, or if the board's means in defending its decision merge with a preferred party are draconian, the court will apply the entire fairness standard to a review of that decision. If not, then the a board's decision to engage in a sale of control transaction will get the presumption of business judgment, even if that decision is not perfect or, in hindsight, appears unwise.

PARAMOUNT COMM., INC. V. QVC NETWORK, INC.
637 A.2d 34 (1993)

VEASEY, Chief Justice.

In this appeal we review an order of the Court of Chancery dated November 24, 1993 (the "November 24 Order"), preliminarily enjoining certain defensive measures designed to facilitate a so-called strategic alliance between Viacom Inc. ("Viacom") and Paramount Communications Inc. ("Paramount") approved by the board of directors of Paramount (the "Paramount Board" or the "Paramount directors") and to thwart an unsolicited, more valuable, tender offer by QVC Network Inc. ("QVC"). In affirming, we hold that the sale of control in this case, which is at the heart of the proposed strategic alliance, implicates enhanced judicial scrutiny of the conduct of the Paramount Board under *Unocal Corp. v. Mesa Petroleum Co.,* Del. Supr., 493 A.2d 946 (1985), and *Revlon, Inc. v. MacAndrews & Forbes Holdings, Inc.,* Del.Supr., 506 A.2d 173 (1986). We further hold that the conduct of the Paramount Board was not reasonable as to process or result.

I. FACTS

Paramount is a Delaware corporation with its principal offices in New York City. Approximately 118 million shares of Paramount's common stock are outstanding and traded on the New York Stock Exchange. The majority of Paramount's stock is publicly held by numerous unaffiliated investors. Paramount owns and operates a diverse group of entertainment businesses, including motion picture and television studios, book publishers, professional sports teams, and amusement parks. [...]

Viacom is a Delaware corporation with its headquarters in Massachusetts. Viacom is controlled by Sumner M. Redstone ("Redstone"), its Chairman and Chief Executive Officer, who owns indirectly approximately 85.2 percent of Viacom's voting Class A stock and approximately 69.2 percent of Viacom's nonvoting Class B stock through National Amusements, Inc. ("NAI"), an entity 91.7 percent owned by Redstone. [...]

QVC is a Delaware corporation with its headquarters in West Chester, Pennsylvania. QVC has several large stockholders, including Liberty Media Corporation, Comcast Corporation, Advance Publications, Inc., and Cox Enterprises Inc. Barry Diller ("Diller"), the Chairman and Chief Executive Officer of QVC, is also a substantial stockholder. [...]

Beginning in the late 1980s, Paramount investigated the possibility of acquiring or merging with other companies in the entertainment, media, or communications industry. Paramount considered such transactions to be desirable, and perhaps necessary, in order to keep pace with competitors in the rapidly evolving field of entertainment and communications. Consistent with its goal of strategic expansion, Paramount made a tender offer for Time Inc. in 1989, but was ultimately unsuccessful. *See Paramount Communications, Inc. v. Time Inc.,* Del. Supr., 571 A.2d 1140 (1990) ("*Time-Warner*").

Although Paramount had considered a possible combination of Paramount and Viacom as early as 1990, recent efforts to explore such a transaction began at a dinner meeting between Redstone and Davis on April 20, 1993. [...]

It was tentatively agreed that Davis would be the chief executive officer and Redstone would be the controlling stockholder of the combined company, but the parties could not reach agreement on the merger price and the terms of a stock option to be granted to Viacom. With respect to price, Viacom offered a package of cash and stock (primarily Viacom Class B nonvoting stock) with a market value of approximately $61 per share, but Paramount wanted at least $70 per share.

Shortly after negotiations broke down in July 1993, two notable events occurred. First, Davis apparently learned of QVC's potential interest in Paramount, and told Diller over lunch on July 21, 1993, that Paramount was not for sale. Second, the market value of Viacom's Class B nonvoting stock increased from $46.875 on July 6 to $57.25 on August 20. QVC claims (and Viacom disputes) that this price increase was caused by open market purchases of such stock by Redstone or entities controlled by him.

[39] On August 20, 1993, discussions between Paramount and Viacom resumed when Greenhill arranged another meeting between Davis and Redstone. After a short hiatus, the parties negotiated in earnest in early September, and performed due diligence with the assistance of their financial advisors, Lazard Freres & Co. ("Lazard") for Paramount and Smith Barney for Viacom. On September 9, 1993, the Paramount Board was informed about the status of the negotiations and was provided information by Lazard, including an analysis of the proposed transaction.

On September 12, 1993, the Paramount Board met again and unanimously approved the Original Merger Agreement whereby Paramount would merge with and into Viacom. The terms of the merger provided that each share of Paramount common stock would be converted into 0.10 shares of Viacom Class A voting stock, 0.90 shares of Viacom Class B nonvoting stock, and $9.10 in cash. In addition, the Paramount Board agreed to amend its "poison pill" Rights Agreement to exempt the proposed merger with Viacom. The Original Merger Agreement also contained several provisions designed to make it more difficult for a potential competing bid to succeed. We focus, as did the Court of Chancery, on three of these defensive provisions: a "no-shop" provision (the "No-Shop Provision"), the Termination Fee, and the Stock Option Agreement.

First, under the No-Shop Provision, the Paramount Board agreed that Paramount would not solicit, encourage, discuss, negotiate, or endorse any competing transaction unless: (a) a third party "makes an unsolicited written, bona fide proposal, which is not subject to any material contingencies relating to financing"; and (b) the Paramount Board determines that discussions or negotiations with the third party are necessary for the Paramount Board to comply with its fiduciary duties.

Second, under the Termination Fee provision, Viacom would receive a $100 million termination fee if: (a) Paramount terminated the Original Merger Agreement because of a competing transaction; (b) Paramount's stockholders did not approve the merger; or (c) the Paramount Board recommended a competing transaction.

The third and most significant deterrent device was the Stock Option Agreement, which granted to Viacom an option to purchase approximately 19.9 percent (23,699,000 shares) of Paramount's outstanding common stock at $69.14 per share if any of the triggering events for the Termination Fee occurred. In addition to the customary terms that are normally associated with a stock option, the Stock Option Agreement contained two provisions that were both unusual and highly beneficial to Viacom: (a) Viacom was permitted to pay for the shares with a senior subordinated note of questionable marketability instead of cash, thereby avoiding the need to raise the $1.6 billion purchase price (the "Note Feature"); and (b) Viacom could elect to require Paramount to pay Viacom in cash a sum equal to the difference between the purchase price and the market price of Paramount's stock (the "Put Feature"). Because the Stock Option Agreement was not "capped" to limit its maximum dollar value, it had the potential to reach (and in this case did reach) unreasonable levels.

After the execution of the Original Merger Agreement and the Stock Option Agreement on September 12, 1993, Paramount and Viacom announced their proposed merger. In a number of public statements, the parties indicated that the pending transaction was a virtual certainty. Redstone described it as a "marriage" that would "never be torn asunder" and stated that only a "nuclear attack" could break the deal. Redstone also called Diller and John Malone of Tele-Communications Inc., a major stockholder of QVC, to dissuade them from making a competing bid.

Despite these attempts to discourage a competing bid, Diller sent a letter to Davis on September 20, 1993, proposing a merger in which QVC would acquire Paramount for approximately $80 per share, consisting of 0.893 shares of QVC common stock and $30 in cash. [...]

On October 21, 1993, QVC filed this action and publicly announced an $80 cash tender offer for 51 percent of Paramount's outstanding shares (the "QVC tender offer"). Each remaining share of Paramount common stock would be converted into 1.42857 shares of QVC common stock in a second-step merger. The tender offer was conditioned on, among other things, the invalidation of the Stock Option Agreement, which was worth over $200 million by that point.[5] QVC contends that it had to commence a tender offer because of the slow pace of the merger discussions and the need to begin seeking clearance under federal antitrust laws.

Confronted by QVC's hostile bid, which on its face offered over $10 per share more than the consideration provided by the Original Merger Agreement, Viacom realized that it would need to raise its bid in order to remain competitive. Within hours after QVC's tender offer was announced, Viacom entered into discussions with Paramount concerning a revised transaction. These discussions led to serious negotiations concerning a comprehensive amendment to the original Paramount-Viacom transaction. In effect, the opportunity for a "new deal" with Viacom was at hand for the Paramount Board. With the QVC hostile bid offering greater value to the Paramount stockholders, the Paramount Board had considerable leverage with Viacom.

At a special meeting on October 24, 1993, the Paramount Board approved the Amended Merger Agreement and an amendment to the Stock Option Agreement. The Amended Merger Agreement was, however, essentially the same as the Original Merger Agreement, except that it included a few new provisions. One provision related to an $80 per share cash tender offer by Viacom for 51 percent of Paramount's stock, and another changed the merger consideration so that each share of Paramount would be converted into 0.20408 shares of Viacom Class A voting stock, 1.08317 shares of Viacom Class B nonvoting stock, and 0.20408 shares of a new series of Viacom convertible preferred stock. The Amended Merger Agreement also added a provision giving Paramount the right not to amend its Rights Agreement to exempt

Viacom if the Paramount Board determined that such an amendment would be inconsistent with its fiduciary duties because another offer constituted a "better alternative."[16] Finally, the Paramount Board was given the power to terminate the Amended Merger Agreement if it withdrew its recommendation of the Viacom transaction or recommended a competing transaction.

Although the Amended Merger Agreement offered more consideration to the Paramount stockholders and somewhat more flexibility to the Paramount Board than did the Original Merger Agreement, the defensive measures designed to make a competing bid more difficult were not removed or modified. [41] In particular, there is no evidence in the record that Paramount sought to use its newly-acquired leverage to eliminate or modify the No-Shop Provision, the Termination Fee, or the Stock Option Agreement when the subject of amending the Original Merger Agreement was on the table. [...]

On November 6, 1993, Viacom unilaterally raised its tender offer price to $85 per share in cash and offered a comparable increase in the value of the securities being proposed in the second-step merger. [...]

QVC responded to Viacom's higher bid on November 12 by increasing its tender offer to $90 per share and by increasing the securities for its second-step merger by a similar amount. [...]

At its meeting on November 15, 1993, the Paramount Board determined that the new QVC offer was not in the best interests of the stockholders. The purported basis for this conclusion was that QVC's bid was excessively conditional. The Paramount Board did not communicate with QVC regarding the status of the conditions because it believed that the No-Shop Provision prevented such communication in the absence of firm financing. Several Paramount directors also testified that they believed the Viacom transaction would be more advantageous to Paramount's future business prospects than a QVC transaction.[17] Although a number of materials were distributed to the Paramount Board describing the Viacom and QVC transactions, the only quantitative analysis of the consideration to be received by the stockholders under each proposal was based on then-current market prices of the securities involved, not on the anticipated value of such securities at the time when the stockholders would receive them.[8]

The preliminary injunction hearing in this case took place on November 16, 1993. On November 19, Diller wrote to the Paramount Board to inform it that QVC had obtained financing commitments for its tender offer and that there was no antitrust obstacle to the offer. [...]

II. APPLICABLE PRINCIPLES OF ESTABLISHED DELAWARE LAW

The General Corporation Law of the State of Delaware (the "General Corporation Law") and the decisions of this Court have repeatedly recognized the fundamental principle that the management of the business and affairs of a Delaware corporation is entrusted to its directors, who are the duly elected and authorized representatives of the [42] stockholders. 8 *Del.C.* § 141(a); *Aronson v. Lewis,* Del.Supr., 473 A.2d 805, 811-12 (1984); *Pogostin v. Rice,* Del.Supr., 480 A.2d 619, 624 (1984). Under normal circumstances, neither the courts nor the stockholders should interfere with the managerial decisions of the directors. The business judgment rule embodies the deference to which such decisions are entitled. [...]

Nevertheless, there are rare situations which mandate that a court take a more direct and active role in overseeing the decisions made and actions taken by directors. In these situations, a court subjects the directors' conduct to enhanced scrutiny to ensure that it is reasonable.[9] The decisions of this Court have clearly established the circumstances where such enhanced scrutiny will be applied. *E.g., Unocal,* 493 A.2d 946; *Moran v. Household Int'l, Inc.,* Del.Supr., 500 A.2d 1346 (1985); *Revlon,* 506 A.2d 173; *Mills Acquisition Co. v. Macmillan, Inc.,* Del.Supr., 559 A.2d 1261 (1989); *Gilbert v. El Paso Co.,* Del.Supr., 575 A.2d 1131 (1990). The case at bar implicates two such circumstances: (1) the approval of a transaction resulting in a sale of control, and (2) the adoption of defensive measures in response to a threat to corporate control.

A. The Significance of a Sale or Change[10] of Control

When a majority of a corporation's voting shares are acquired by a single person or entity, or by a cohesive group acting together, there is a significant diminution in the voting power of those who thereby become minority stockholders. Under the statutory framework of the General Corporation Law, many of the most fundamental corporate changes can be implemented only if they are approved by a majority vote of the stockholders. [...]

In the absence of devices protecting the minority stockholders,[11] stockholder votes are likely to become mere formalities where there is a majority stockholder. [...] Absent effective protective provisions, minority stockholders must rely for protection solely on the fiduciary duties owed to them by the directors and the majority stockholder, since the minority stockholders have lost the power to influence corporate direction through the ballot. The acquisition of majority status and the consequent privilege of exerting the powers of majority ownership come at a price. That price is usually a control premium which recognizes not only the value of a control block of shares, but also compensates the minority stockholders for their resulting loss of voting power.

In the case before us, the public stockholders (in the aggregate) currently own a majority of Paramount's voting stock. Control of the corporation is not vested in a single person, entity, or group, but vested in the fluid aggregation of unaffiliated stockholders. In the event the Paramount-Viacom transaction is consummated, the public stockholders will receive cash and a minority equity voting position in the surviving corporation. Following such consummation, there will be a controlling stockholder who will have the voting power to: (a) elect directors; (b) cause a break-up of the corporation; (c) merge it with another company; (d) cash-out the public stockholders; (e) amend the certificate of incorporation; (f) sell all or substantially all of the corporate assets; or (g) otherwise alter materially the nature of the corporation and the public stockholders' interests. Irrespective of the present Paramount Board's vision of a long-term strategic alliance with Viacom, the proposed sale of control would provide the new controlling stockholder with the power to alter that vision.

Because of the intended sale of control, the Paramount-Viacom transaction has economic consequences of considerable significance to the Paramount stockholders. Once control has shifted, the current Paramount stockholders will have no leverage in the future to demand another control premium. As a result, the Paramount stockholders are entitled to receive, and should receive, a control premium and/or protective devices of significant value. There being no such protective provisions in the Viacom-Paramount transaction, the Paramount directors had an obligation to take the maximum advantage of the current opportunity to realize for the stockholders the best value reasonably available.

B. The Obligations of Directors in a Sale or Change of Control Transaction

The consequences of a sale of control impose special obligations on the directors of a corporation.[13] In particular, they have the obligation of acting reasonably to seek the transaction offering the best value reasonably available to the stockholders. The courts will apply enhanced scrutiny to ensure that the directors have acted reasonably. [...]

In the sale of control context, the directors must focus on one primary objective — to secure the transaction offering the best value reasonably available for the stockholders — and they must exercise their fiduciary duties to further that end. [...]

Barkan teaches some of the methods by which a board can fulfill its obligation to seek the best value reasonably available to the stockholders. [...]These methods are designed to determine the existence and viability of possible alternatives. They include conducting an auction, canvassing the market, etc. Delaware law recognizes that there is "no single blueprint" that directors must follow. [...]

In determining which alternative provides the best value for the stockholders, a board of directors is not limited to considering only the amount of cash involved, and is not required to ignore totally its view of the future value of a strategic alliance. *See Macmillan, 559* A.2d at 1282 n. 29. Instead, the directors should analyze the entire situation and evaluate in a disciplined manner the consideration being offered. Where stock or other non-cash consideration is involved, the board should try to quantify its value, if feasible, to achieve an objective comparison of the alternatives.[14] In addition, the board may assess a variety of practical considerations relating to each alternative, including:

> [an offer's] fairness and feasibility; the proposed or actual financing for the offer, and the consequences of that financing; questions of illegality; ... the risk of nonconsum[m]ation;... the bidder's identity, prior background and other business venture experiences; and the bidder's business plans for the corporation and their effects on stockholder interests.

[...]While the assessment of these factors may be complex, [45] the board's goal is straightforward: Having informed themselves of all material information reasonably available, the directors must decide which alternative is most likely to offer the best value reasonably available to the stockholders.

C. Enhanced Judicial Scrutiny of a Sale or Change of Control Transaction

Board action in the circumstances presented here is subject to enhanced scrutiny. Such scrutiny is mandated by: (a) the threatened diminution of the current stockholders' voting power; (b) the fact that an asset belonging to public stockholders (a control premium) is being sold and may never be available again; and (c) the traditional concern of Delaware courts for actions which impair or impede stockholder voting rights (see *supra* note 11). In *Macmillan,* this Court held:

> When *Revlon* duties devolve upon directors, this Court will continue to exact an enhanced judicial scrutiny at the threshold,

as in *Unocal,* before the normal presumptions of the business judgment rule will apply.[15]

559 A.2d at 1288. The *Macmillan* decision articulates a specific two-part test for analyzing board action where competing bidders are not treated equally:[16]

> In the face of disparate treatment, the trial court must first examine whether the directors properly perceived that shareholder interests were enhanced. In any event the board's action must be reasonable in relation to the advantage sought to be achieved, or conversely, to the threat which a particular bid allegedly poses to stockholder interests.

[...]

The key features of an enhanced scrutiny test are: (a) a judicial determination regarding the adequacy of the decisionmaking process employed by the directors, including the information on which the directors based their decision; and (b) a judicial examination of the reasonableness of the directors' action in light of the circumstances then existing. The directors have the burden of proving that they were adequately informed and acted reasonably.

Although an enhanced scrutiny test involves a review of the reasonableness of the substantive merits of a board's actions,[17] a court should not ignore the complexity of the directors' task in a sale of control. There are many business and financial considerations implicated in investigating and selecting the best value reasonably available. The board of directors is the corporate decisionmaking body best equipped to make these judgments. Accordingly, a court applying enhanced judicial scrutiny should be deciding whether the directors made a reasonable decision, not a perfect decision. If a board selected one of several reasonable alternatives, a court should not second-guess that choice even though it might have decided otherwise or subsequent events may have cast doubt on the board's determination. Thus, courts will not substitute their business judgment for that of the directors, but will determine if the directors' decision was, on balance, within a range of reasonableness. [...]

D. Revlon and Time-Warner Distinguished

The Paramount defendants and Viacom assert that the fiduciary obligations and the enhanced judicial scrutiny discussed above are not implicated in this case in the absence of a "break-up" of the corporation, and that the order granting the preliminary injunction should be reversed. This argument is based on their erroneous interpretation of our decisions in *Revlon* and *Time-Warner*.

In *Revlon,* we reviewed the actions of the board of directors of Revlon, Inc. ("Revlon"), which had rebuffed the overtures of Pantry Pride, Inc. and had instead entered into an agreement with Forstmann Little & Co. ("Forstmann") providing for the acquisition of 100 percent of Revlon's outstanding stock by Forstmann and the subsequent break-up of Revlon. Based on the facts and circumstances present in *Revlon,* we held that "[t]he directors' role changed from defenders of the corporate bastion to auctioneers charged with getting the best price for the stockholders at a sale of the company." 506 A.2d at 182. We further held that "when a board ends an intense bidding contest on an insubstantial basis, ... [that] action cannot withstand the enhanced scrutiny which *Unocal* requires of director conduct." *Id.* at 184.

It is true that one of the circumstances bearing on these holdings was the fact that "the break-up of the company . . . had become a reality which even the directors embraced." *Id.* at 182. It does not follow, however, that a "break-up" must be present and "inevitable" before directors are subject to enhanced judicial scrutiny and are required to pursue a transaction that is calculated to produce the best value reasonably available to the stockholders. In fact, we stated in *Revlon* that "when bidders make relatively similar offers, or dissolution of the company becomes inevitable, the directors cannot fulfill their enhanced *Unocal* duties by playing favorites with the contending factions." *Id.* at 184 (emphasis added). *Revlon* thus does not hold that an inevitable dissolution or "break-up" is necessary.

The decisions of this Court following *Revlon* reinforced the applicability of enhanced scrutiny and the directors' obligation to seek the best value reasonably available for the stockholders where there is a pending sale of control, regardless of whether or not there is to be a break-up of the corporation. In *Macmillan,* this Court held:

> We stated in *Revlon,* and again here, that in a sale of corporate control the responsibility of the directors is to get the highest value reasonably attainable for the shareholders.

559 A.2d at 1288 (emphasis added). In *Barkan,* we observed further:

> We believe that the general principles announced in *Revlon,* in *Unocal Corp. v. Mesa Petroleum Co.,* Del.Supr., 493 A.2d 946 (1985), and in *Moran v. Household International, Inc.,* Del.Supr., 500 A.2d 1346 (1985) govern this case and every case in which a fundamental change of corporate control occurs or is contemplated.

567 A.2d at 1286 (emphasis added).

Although *Macmillan* and *Barkan* are clear in holding that a change of control imposes on directors the obligation to obtain the best value reasonably available to the stockholders, the Paramount defendants have interpreted our decision in *Time-Warner* as requiring a corporate break-up in order for that obligation to apply. The facts in *Time-Warner,* however, were quite different from the facts of this case, and refute Paramount's position here. In *Time-Warner,* the Chancellor held that there was no change of control in the original stock-for-stock merger between Time and Warner because Time would be owned by a fluid aggregation of unaffiliated stockholders both before and after the merger:

> If the appropriate inquiry is whether a change in control is contemplated, the answer must be sought in the specific circumstances surrounding the transaction. Surely under some circumstances a stock for stock merger could reflect a transfer of corporate control. That would, for example, plainly be the case here if Warner were a private company. But where, as [47] here, the shares of both constituent corporations are widely held, corporate control can be expected to remain unaffected by a stock for stock merger. This in my judgment was the situation

591

with respect to the original merger agreement. When the specifics of that situation are reviewed, it is seen that, aside from legal technicalities and aside from arrangements thought to enhance the prospect for the ultimate succession of [Nicholas J. Nicholas, Jr., president of Time], neither corporation could be said to be acquiring the other. Control of both remained in a large, fluid, changeable and changing market.

The existence of a control block of stock in the hands of a single shareholder or a group with loyalty to each other does have real consequences to the financial value of "minority" stock. The law offers some protection to such shares through the imposition of a fiduciary duty upon controlling shareholders. But here, effectuation of the merger would not have subjected Time shareholders to the risks and consequences of holders of minority shares. This is a reflection of the fact that no control passed to anyone in the transaction contemplated. The shareholders of Time would have "suffered" dilution, of course, but they would suffer the same type of dilution upon the public distribution of new stock.

Paramount Communications Inc. v. Time Inc., Del.Ch., No. 10866, 1989 WL 79880, Allen, C. (July 17, 1989), reprinted at 15 Del.J.Corp.L. 700, 739 (emphasis added). Moreover, the transaction actually consummated in *Time-Warner* was not a merger, as originally planned, but a sale of Warner's stock to Time.

In our affirmance of the Court of Chancery's well-reasoned decision, this Court held that "The Chancellor's findings of fact are supported by the record and his conclusion is correct as a matter of law." 571 A.2d at 1150 (emphasis added). Nevertheless, the Paramount defendants here have argued that a break-up is a requirement and have focused on the following language in our *Time-Warner* decision:

However, we premise our rejection of plaintiffs' *Revlon* claim on different grounds, namely, the absence of any substantial evidence to conclude that Time's board, in negotiating with

Warner, made the dissolution or break-up of the corporate entity inevitable, as was the case in *Revlon.*

Under Delaware law there are, generally speaking and without excluding other possibilities, two circumstances which may implicate *Revlon* duties. The first, and clearer one, is when a corporation initiates an active bidding process seeking to sell itself or to effect a business reorganization involving a clear break-up of the company. However, *Revlon* duties may also be triggered where, in response to a bidder's offer, a target abandons its long-term strategy and seeks an alternative transaction involving the breakup of the company.

Id. at 1150 (emphasis added) (citation and footnote omitted).

The Paramount defendants have misread the holding of *Time-Warner.* Contrary to their argument, our decision in *Time-Warner* expressly states that the two general scenarios discussed in the above-quoted paragraph are not the only instances where "*Revlon* duties" may be implicated. The Paramount defendants' argument totally ignores the phrase "without excluding other possibilities." Moreover, the instant case is clearly within the first general scenario set forth in *Time-Warner.* The Paramount Board, albeit unintentionally, had "initiate[d] an active bidding process seeking to sell itself" by agreeing to sell control of the corporation to Viacom in circumstances where another potential acquiror (QVC) was equally interested in being a bidder.

The Paramount defendants' position that both a change of control and a break-up are required must be rejected. Such a holding would unduly restrict the application of *Revlon,* is inconsistent with this Court's decisions in *Barkan* and *Macmillan,* and has no basis in policy. There are few events that have a more significant impact on the stockholders than a sale of control or a corporate breakup. Each event represents a fundamental [48] (and perhaps irrevocable) change in the nature of the corporate enterprise from a practical standpoint. It is the significance of each of these events that justifies: (a) focusing on the directors' obligation to seek the best value reasonably available to the stockholders; and (b) requiring a close scrutiny of board action which could be contrary to the stockholders' interests.

Accordingly, when a corporation undertakes a transaction which will cause: (a) a change in corporate control; or (b) a breakup of the corporate entity, the directors' obligation is to seek the best value reasonably available to the stockholders. This obligation arises because the effect of the Viacom-Paramount transaction, if consummated, is to shift control of Paramount from the public stockholders to a controlling stockholder, Viacom. Neither *Time-Warner* nor any other decision of this Court holds that a "break-up" of the company is essential to give rise to this obligation where there is a sale of control.

III. BREACH OF FIDUCIARY DUTIES BY PARAMOUNT BOARD

We now turn to duties of the Paramount Board under the facts of this case and our conclusions as to the breaches of those duties which warrant injunctive relief.

A. The Specific Obligations of the Paramount Board

Under the facts of this case, the Paramount directors had the obligation: (a) to be diligent and vigilant in examining critically the Paramount-Viacom transaction and the QVC tender offers; (b) to act in good faith; (c) to obtain, and act with due care on, all material information reasonably available, including information necessary to compare the two offers to determine which of these transactions, or an alternative course of action, would provide the best value reasonably available to the stockholders; and (d) to negotiate actively and in good faith with both Viacom and QVC to that end.

Having decided to sell control of the corporation, the Paramount directors were required to evaluate critically whether or not all material aspects of the Paramount-Viacom transaction (separately and in the aggregate) were reasonable and in the best interests of the Paramount stockholders in light of current circumstances, including:

the change of control premium, the Stock Option Agreement, the Termination Fee, the coercive nature of both the Viacom and QVC tender offers,[118] the No-Shop Provision, and the proposed disparate use of the Rights Agreement as to the Viacom and QVC tender offers, respectively.

These obligations necessarily implicated various issues, including the questions of whether or not those provisions and other aspects of the Paramount-Viacom transaction (separately and in the aggregate): (a) adversely affected the value provided to the Paramount stockholders; (b) inhibited or encouraged alternative bids; (c) were enforceable contractual obligations in light of the directors' fiduciary duties; and (d) in the end would advance or retard the Paramount directors' obligation to secure for the Paramount stockholders the best value reasonably available under the circumstances.

The Paramount defendants contend that they were precluded by certain contractual provisions, including the No-Shop Provision, from negotiating with QVC or seeking alternatives. Such provisions, whether or not they are presumptively valid in the abstract, may not validly define or limit the directors' fiduciary duties under Delaware law or prevent the Paramount directors from carrying out their fiduciary duties under Delaware law. To the extent such provisions are inconsistent with those duties, they are invalid and unenforceable. *See Revlon*, 506 A.2d at 184-85.

Since the Paramount directors had already decided to sell control, they had an obligation [49] to continue their search for the best value reasonably available to the stockholders. This continuing obligation included the responsibility, at the October 24 board meeting and thereafter, to evaluate critically both the QVC tender offers and the Paramount-Viacom transaction to determine if: (a) the QVC tender offer was, or would continue to be, conditional; (b) the QVC tender offer could be improved; (c) the Viacom tender offer or other aspects of the Paramount-Viacom transaction could be improved; (d) each of the respective offers would be reasonably likely to come to closure, and under what circumstances; (e) other material information was reasonably available for consideration by the Paramount directors; (f) there were viable and realistic alternative courses of action; and (g) the timing constraints could be managed so the directors could consider these matters carefully and deliberately.

B. The Breaches of Fiduciary Duty by the Paramount Board

The Paramount directors made the decision on September 12, 1993, that, in their judgment, a strategic merger with Viacom on the economic terms of the Original Merger Agreement was in the best interests of Paramount and its stockholders. Those terms provided a modest change of control premium to the stockholders. The directors also decided at that time that it was appropriate to agree to certain defensive measures (the Stock Option Agreement, the Termination Fee, and the No-Shop Provision) insisted upon by Viacom as part of that economic transaction. Those defensive measures, coupled with the sale of control and subsequent disparate treatment of competing bidders, implicated the judicial scrutiny of *Unocal, Revlon, Macmillan,* and their progeny. We conclude that the Paramount directors' process was not reasonable, and the result achieved for the stockholders was not reasonable under the circumstances.

When entering into the Original Merger Agreement, and thereafter, the Paramount Board clearly gave insufficient attention to the potential consequences of the defensive measures demanded by Viacom. The Stock Option Agreement had a number of unusual and potentially "draconian"[19] provisions, including the Note Feature and the Put Feature. Furthermore, the Termination Fee, whether or not unreasonable by itself, clearly made Paramount less attractive to other bidders, when coupled with the Stock Option Agreement. Finally, the No-Shop Provision inhibited the Paramount Board's ability to negotiate with other potential bidders, particularly QVC which had already expressed an interest in Paramount.[20]

Throughout the applicable time period, and especially from the first QVC merger proposal on September 20 through the Paramount Board meeting on November 15, QVC's interest in Paramount provided the opportunity for the Paramount Board to seek significantly higher value for the Paramount stockholders than that being offered by Viacom. QVC persistently demonstrated its intention to meet and exceed the Viacom offers, and [50] frequently expressed its willingness to negotiate possible further increases.

The Paramount directors had the opportunity in the October 23-24 time frame, when the Original Merger Agreement was renegotiated, to take appropriate action to modify the improper defensive measures as well as to improve the economic terms of the Paramount-Viacom transaction. Under the circumstances existing at that time, it should have been clear to the Paramount Board that the Stock Option Agreement, coupled with the Termination Fee and the No-Shop Clause, were impeding the realization of the best value reasonably available to the Paramount stockholders. Nevertheless, the Paramount Board made no effort to eliminate or modify these counterproductive devices, and instead continued to cling to its vision of a strategic alliance with Viacom. Moreover, based on advice from the Paramount management, the Paramount directors considered the QVC offer to be "conditional" and asserted that they were precluded by the No-Shop Provision from seeking more information from, or negotiating with, QVC.

By November 12, 1993, the value of the revised QVC offer on its face exceeded that of the Viacom offer by over $1 billion at then current values. This significant disparity of value cannot be justified on the basis of the directors' vision of future strategy, primarily because the change of control would supplant the authority of the current Paramount Board to continue to hold and implement their strategic vision in any meaningful way. Moreover, their uninformed process had deprived their strategic vision of much of its credibility. See Van Gorkom, 488 A.2d at 872; Cede v. Technicolor, 634 A.2d at 367; Hanson Trust PLC v. ML SCM Acquisition Inc., 2d Cir., 781 F.2d 264, 274 (1986).

When the Paramount directors met on November 15 to consider QVC's increased tender offer, they remained prisoners of their own misconceptions and missed opportunities to eliminate the restrictions they had imposed on themselves. Yet, it was not "too late" to reconsider negotiating with QVC. The circumstances existing on November 15 made it clear that the defensive measures, taken as a whole, were problematic: (a) the No-Shop Provision could not define or limit their fiduciary duties; (b) the Stock Option Agreement had become "draconian"; and (c) the Termination Fee, in context with all the circumstances, was similarly deterring the realization of possibly higher bids. Nevertheless, the Paramount directors remained paralyzed by their uninformed belief that the QVC offer was "illusory." This final opportunity to negotiate on the stockholders' behalf and to fulfill their obligation to seek the best value reasonably available was thereby squandered.[211]

IV. VIACOM'S CLAIM OF VESTED CONTRACT RIGHTS

Viacom argues that it had certain "vested" contract rights with respect to the No-Shop Provision and the Stock Option Agreement.[221] In effect, Viacom's argument is that the Paramount directors could enter into an agreement in violation of their fiduciary duties and then render Paramount, and ultimately its stockholders, liable for failing to carry out an agreement in violation of those duties. Viacom's protestations about vested rights are without merit. This Court has found that those defensive measures were improperly designed to deter potential bidders, and that [51] such measures do not meet the reasonableness test to which they must be subjected. They are consequently invalid and unenforceable under the facts of this case.

The No-Shop Provision could not validly define or limit the fiduciary duties of the Paramount directors. To the extent that a contract, or a provision thereof, purports to require a board to act or not act in such a fashion as to limit the exercise of fiduciary duties, it is invalid and unenforceable. *Cf. Wilmington Trust v. Coulter,* 200 A.2d at 452-54. Despite the arguments of Paramount and Viacom to the contrary, the Paramount directors could not contract away their fiduciary obligations. Since the No-Shop Provision was invalid, Viacom never had any vested contract rights in the provision.

As discussed previously, the Stock Option Agreement contained several "draconian" aspects, including the Note Feature and the Put Feature. While we have held that lock-up options are not *per se* illegal, *see Revlon,* 506 A.2d at 183, no options with similar features have ever been upheld by this Court. Under the circumstances of this case, the Stock Option Agreement clearly is invalid. Accordingly, Viacom never had any vested contract rights in that Agreement.

Viacom, a sophisticated party with experienced legal and financial advisors, knew of (and in fact demanded) the unreasonable features of the Stock Option Agreement. It cannot be now heard to argue that it obtained vested contract rights by negotiating and obtaining contractual provisions from a board acting in violation of its fiduciary duties. As the Nebraska Supreme Court said in rejecting a similar argument in *ConAgra, Inc. v. Cargill, Inc.,* 222 Neb. 136, 382 N.W.2d 576, 587-88 (1986), "To so hold, it would seem, would be to get the shareholders coming and going." Likewise, we reject Viacom's arguments and hold that its fate must rise or fall, and in this instance fall, with the determination that the actions of the Paramount Board were invalid.

V. CONCLUSION

The realization of the best value reasonably available to the stockholders became the Paramount directors' primary obligation under these facts in light of the change of control. That obligation was not satisfied, and the Paramount Board's process was deficient. The directors' initial hope and expectation for a strategic alliance with Viacom was allowed to dominate their decisionmaking process to the point where the arsenal of defensive measures established at the outset was perpetuated (not modified or eliminated) when the situation was dramatically altered. QVC's unsolicited bid presented the opportunity for significantly greater value for the stockholders and enhanced negotiating leverage for the directors. Rather than seizing those opportunities, the Paramount directors chose to wall themselves off from material information which was reasonably available and to hide behind the defensive measures as a rationalization for refusing to negotiate with QVC or seeking other alternatives. Their view of the strategic alliance likewise became an empty rationalization as the opportunities for higher value for the stockholders continued to develop.

It is the nature of the judicial process that we decide only the case before us — a case which, on its facts, is clearly controlled by established Delaware law. Here, the proposed change of control and the implications thereof were crystal clear. In other cases they may be less clear. The holding of this case on its facts, coupled with the holdings of the principal cases discussed herein where the issue of sale of control is implicated, should provide a workable precedent against which to measure future cases. [...]

Appendix: Corporate Documents 8

 Below you will find the current Certificates of
Incorporation for Meta Platforms as well as United Holdings. Meta,
as you will likely know, used to be known as Facebook, Inc. The
current certificate was amended in October 2021 to change the
name of the corporation from Facebook to Meta Platforms. In all
other respects, the certificate is the same as the previous certificate
for Facebook. Meta relies on a dual-class stock structure to ensure
that Mark Zuckerberg is able to maintain control of the company.

United Airlines Holding, Inc. is the parent company of United
Airlines. United Airlines Holding was formed in 2010 with the
merger of United and Continental Airlines. The United-
Continental merger was a "merger of equals" relying on a holding
company strategy to accomplish the transaction. United Airlines
Holding also relies on a multiclass share structure, with a special
class of shares for United pilots. In addition, federal law prohibits
foreign control of domestic airlines, consequently, you will find
restrictions on the transfer of United stock in the certificate.

Amended & Restated Certificate of Incorporation of 8
Meta Platforms, Inc.

1

Facebook, Inc.

AMENDED & RESTATED CERTIFICATE OF INCORPORATION

Facebook, Inc., a Delaware corporation, hereby certifies as follows.

1. The name of the corporation is Facebook, Inc. The date of filing its original Certificate of Incorporation with the Secretary of State was July 29, 2004, under the name TheFacebook, Inc.

2. The Amended & Restated Certificate of Incorporation of the corporation attached hereto as Exhibit A, which is incorporated herein by this reference, and which restates, integrates and further amends provisions of the Certificate of Incorporation of this corporation as heretofore amended and/or restated, has been duly adopted by the corporation's Board of Directors and by the stockholders in accordance with Sections 242 and 245 of the General Corporation Law of the State of Delaware.

3. The Amended & Restated Certificate of Incorporation shall be effective on the date of filing with the Secretary of State of Delaware.

4. The text of the Restated Certificate of Incorporation is hereby amended and restated in its entirety to read as Exhibit A hereto.

IN WITNESS WHEREOF, this corporation has caused this Amended & Restated Certificate of Incorporation to be signed by its duly authorized officer and the foregoing facts stated herein are true and correct.

Date: October 2, 2019   Facebook, Inc.

                                                            By:

                                                            /s/ Mark Zuckerberg

        Chief Executive Officer

EXHIBIT A

META PLATFORMS, INC.

AMENDED & RESTATED CERTIFICATE OF INCORPORATION

ARTICLE I: NAME

The name of the corporation is Meta Platforms, Inc.

ARTICLE II: AGENT FOR SERVICE OF PROCESS

The address of the corporation's registered office in the State of Delaware is 251 Little Falls Drive, Wilmington, New Castle County, 19808. The name of the registered agent of the corporation at that address is Corporation Service Company.

ARTICLE III: PURPOSE

The purpose of the corporation is to engage in any lawful act or activity for which corporations may be organized under the General Corporation Law of the State of Delaware (" *General Corporation Law*").

ARTICLE IV: AUTHORIZED STOCK

1. **Total Authorized.**

The total number of shares of all classes of capital stock that the corporation has authority to issue is 9,241,000,000 shares, consisting of: 5,000,000,000 shares of Class A Common Stock, $0.000006 par value per share (" *Class A Common Stock*"), 4,141,000,000 shares of Class B Common Stock, $0.000006 par value per share (" *Class B Common Stock*" and together with the Class A Common Stock, the " *Common Stock*") and 100,000,000 shares of Preferred Stock, $0.000006 par value per share. The number of authorized shares of Class A Common Stock or Class B Common Stock may be increased or decreased (but not below the number of shares thereof then outstanding) by the affirmative vote of the holders of capital stock representing a majority of the voting power of all the then-outstanding shares of capital stock of the corporation entitled to vote thereon, irrespective of the provisions of Section 242(b)(2) of the General Corporation Law.

2.   **Designation of Additional Shares**

2.1. The Board of Directors is authorized, subject to any limitations prescribed by the laws of the State of Delaware, by resolution or resolutions, to provide for the issuance of the shares of Preferred Stock in one or more series, and, by filing a certificate of designation pursuant to the applicable law of the State of Delaware ("*Certificate of Designation*"), to establish from time to time the number of shares to be included in each such series, to fix the designation, powers (including voting powers), preferences and relative, participating, optional or other rights, if any, of the shares of each such series and any qualifications, limitations or restrictions thereof, and to increase (but not above the total number of authorized shares of such class) or decrease (but not below the number of shares of such series then outstanding) the number of shares of any such series. The number of authorized shares of Preferred Stock may also be increased or decreased (but not below the number of shares thereof then outstanding) by the affirmative vote of the holders of a majority of the voting power of all the then-outstanding shares of capital stock of the corporation entitled to vote thereon, without a separate vote of the holders of the Preferred Stock or any series thereof, irrespective of the provisions of Section 242(b)(2) of the General Corporation Law, unless a vote of any such holders is required pursuant to the terms of any Certificate of Designation designating a series of Preferred Stock.

2.2. Except as otherwise expressly provided in any Certificate of Designation designating any series of Preferred Stock pursuant to the foregoing provisions of this ARTICLE IV, any new series of Preferred Stock may be designated, fixed and determined as provided herein by the Board of Directors without approval of the holders of Common Stock or the holders of Preferred Stock, or any series thereof, and any such new series may have powers, preferences and rights, including, without limitation, voting powers, dividend rights, liquidation rights, redemption rights and conversion rights, senior to, junior to or pari passu with the rights of the Common Stock, the Preferred Stock, or any future class or series of Preferred Stock or Common Stock.

3. **Rights of Class A Common Stock and Class B Common Stock.**

3.1. Equal Status. Except as otherwise provided in this Restated Certificate of Incorporation or required by applicable law, shares of Class A Common Stock and Class B Common Stock shall have the same rights and powers, rank equally (including as to dividends and distributions, and upon any liquidation, dissolution or winding up of the corporation), share ratably and be identical in all respects and as to all matters.

3.2. Voting Rights. Except as otherwise expressly provided by this Restated Certificate of Incorporation or as provided by law, the holders of shares of Class A Common Stock and Class B Common Stock shall (a) at all times vote together as a single class on all matters (including the election of directors) submitted to a vote or for the consent (if action by written consent of the stockholders is permitted at such time under this Restated Certificate of Incorporation) of the stockholders of the corporation, (b) be entitled to notice of any stockholders' meeting in accordance with the Bylaws of the corporation and (c) be entitled to vote upon such matters and in such manner as may be provided by applicable law. Except as otherwise expressly provided herein or required by applicable law, each holder of Class A Common Stock shall have the right to one (1) vote per share of Class A Common Stock held of record by such holder and each holder of Class B Common Stock shall have the right to ten (10) votes per share of Class B Common Stock held of record by such holder.

3.3. Dividend and Distribution Rights. Shares of Class A Common Stock and Class B Common Stock shall be treated equally, identically and ratably, on a per share basis, with respect to any dividends or distributions as may be declared and paid from time to time by the Board of Directors out of any assets of the corporation legally available therefor; provided, however, that in the event a dividend is paid in the form of shares of Class A Common Stock or

Class B Common Stock (or rights to acquire such shares), then holders of Class A Common Stock shall receive shares of Class A Common Stock (or rights to acquire such shares, as the case may be) and holders of Class B Common Stock shall receive shares of Class B Common Stock (or rights to acquire such shares, as the case may be), with holders of shares of Class A Common Stock and Class B Common Stock receiving, on a per share basis, an identical number of shares of Class A Common Stock or Class B Common Stock, as applicable. Notwithstanding the foregoing, the Board of Directors may pay or make a disparate dividend or distribution per share of Class A Common Stock or Class B Common Stock (whether in the amount of such dividend or distribution payable per share, the form in which such dividend or distribution is payable, the timing of the payment, or otherwise) if such disparate dividend or distribution is approved in advance by the affirmative vote (or written consent if action by written consent of stockholders is permitted at such time under this Restated Certificate of Incorporation) of the holders of a majority of the outstanding shares of Class A Common Stock and Class B Common Stock, each voting separately as a class.

3.4. <u>Subdivisions Combinations or Reclassifications</u>. Shares of Class A Common Stock or Class B Common Stock may not be subdivided, combined or reclassified unless the shares of the other class are concurrently therewith proportionately subdivided, combined or reclassified in a manner that maintains the same proportionate equity ownership between the holders of the outstanding Class A Common Stock and Class B Common Stock on the record date for such subdivision, combination or reclassification; provided, however, that shares of one such class may be subdivided, combined or reclassified in a different or disproportionate manner if such subdivision, combination or reclassification is approved in advance by the affirmative vote (or written consent if action by written consent of stockholders is permitted at such time under this Restated Certificate of Incorporation) of the holders of a majority of the outstanding shares of Class A Common Stock and Class B Common Stock, each voting separately as a class.

3.5. <u>Liquidation, Dissolution or Winding Up</u>. Subject to the preferential or other rights of any holders of Preferred Stock then outstanding, upon the dissolution, liquidation or winding up of the corporation, whether voluntary or involuntary, holders of Class A Common Stock and Class B Common Stock will be entitled to receive ratably all assets of the corporation available for distribution to its stockholders unless disparate or different treatment of the shares of each such class with respect to distributions upon any such liquidation, dissolution or winding up is approved in advance by the affirmative vote (or written consent if action by written consent of stockholders is permitted at such time under this Restated Certificate of Incorporation) of the holders of a majority of the outstanding shares of Class A Common Stock and Class B Common Stock, each voting separately as a class.

3.6. <u>Merger or Consolidation</u>. In the case of any distribution or payment in respect of the shares of Class A Common Stock or Class B Common Stock upon the consolidation or merger of the Corporation with or into any other entity, or in the case of any other transaction having an effect on stockholders substantially similar to that resulting from a consolidation or merger, such distribution or payment shall be made ratably on a per share basis among the holders of the Class A Common Stock and Class B Common Stock as a single class; provided, however, that shares of one such class may receive different or disproportionate distributions or payments in connection with such merger, consolidation or other transaction if (i) the only difference in the per share distribution to the holders of the Class A Common Stock and Class B Common Stock is that any securities distributed to the holder of a share Class B Common Stock have ten times the voting power of any securities distributed to the holder of a share of Class A Common Stock, or (ii) such merger, consolidation or other transaction is approved by the affirmative vote (or written consent if action by written consent of stockholders is permitted at such time under this Restated Certificate of Incorporation) of the holders of a majority of the outstanding shares of Class A Common Stock and Class B Common Stock, each voting separately as a class.

3.7. <u>Change of Control Class B Vote</u>. Until the first date on which the outstanding shares of Class B Common Stock represent less than thirty-five percent (35%) of the total voting power of the then outstanding shares of the corporation then entitled to vote generally in the election of directors, the corporation shall not consummate a Change in Control Transaction (as defined in Section 4 of this ARTICLE IV) without first obtaining the affirmative vote (or written consent if action by written consent of stockholders is permitted at such time under this Restated Certificate of Incorporation) of the holders of a majority of the then outstanding shares of Class B Common Stock, voting as a separate class, in addition to any other vote required by applicable law, this Restated Certificate of Incorporation or the Bylaws.

3.8. <u>Conversion of Class B Common Stock</u>.

(a) <u>Voluntary Conversion</u>. Each share of Class B Common Stock shall be convertible into one (1) fully paid and nonassessable share of Class A Common Stock at the option of the holder thereof at any time upon written notice to the corporation. Before any holder of Class B Common Stock shall be entitled to voluntarily convert any shares of such Class B Common Stock, such holder shall surrender the certificate or certificates therefor (if any), duly endorsed, at the principal corporate office of the corporation or of any transfer agent for the Class B Common Stock, and shall give written notice to the corporation at its principal corporate office, of the election to convert the same and shall state therein the name or names (i) in which the certificate or certificates representing the shares of Class A Common Stock into which the shares of Class B Common Stock are so converted are to be issued if such shares are certificated or (ii) in which such shares are to be registered in book entry if such shares are uncertificated. The corporation shall, as soon as practicable thereafter, issue and deliver at such office to such holder of Class B Common Stock, or to the nominee or nominees of such holder, a certificate or certificates representing the number of shares of Class A Common Stock to which such holder shall be entitled as aforesaid (if such shares are certificated) or, if such shares are uncertificated, register such shares in book-entry form. Such conversion shall be deemed to have been made immediately prior

609

to the close of business on the date of such surrender of the shares
of Class B Common Stock to be converted following or
contemporaneously with the written notice of such holder's election
to convert required by this Section 3.8(a), and the person or persons
entitled to receive the shares of Class A Common Stock issuable
upon such conversion shall be treated for all purposes as the record
holder or holders of such shares of Class A Common Stock as of
such date. Each share of Class B Common Stock that is converted
pursuant to this Section 3.8(a) shall be retired by the corporation
and shall not be available for reissuance.

(b) <u>Automatic Conversion</u>. (i) Each share of Class B Common Stock
shall be automatically, without further action by the holder thereof,
converted into one (1) fully paid and nonassessable share of Class A
Common Stock, upon the occurrence of a Transfer (as defined in
Section 4 of this ARTICLE IV), other than a Permitted Transfer (as
defined in Section 4 of this ARTICLE IV), of such share of Class B
Common Stock and (ii) all shares of Class B Common Stock shall
be automatically, without further action by any holder thereof,
converted into an identical number of shares of Class A Common
Stock at such date and time, or the occurrence of an event, specified
by the affirmative vote (or written consent if action by written
consent of stockholders is permitted at such time under this
Restated Certificate of Incorporation) of the holders of a majority of
the then outstanding shares Class B Common Stock, voting as a
separate class (the occurrence of an event described in clause (i) or
(ii) of this Section 3.8(b), a "*Conversion Event*"). Each outstanding
stock certificate that, immediately prior to a Conversion Event,
represented one or more shares of Class B Common Stock subject
to such Conversion Event shall, upon such Conversion Event, be
deemed to represent an equal number of shares of Class A
Common Stock, without the need for surrender or exchange
thereof. The corporation shall, upon the request of any holder
whose shares of Class B Common Stock have been converted into
shares of Class A Common Stock as a result of a Conversion Event
and upon surrender by such holder to the corporation of the
outstanding certificate(s) formerly representing such holder's shares
of Class B Common Stock (if any), issue and deliver to such holder
certificate(s) representing the shares of Class A Common Stock into

which such holder's shares of Class B Common Stock were converted as a result of such Conversion Event (if such shares are certificated) or, if such shares are uncertificated, register such shares in book-entry form. Each share of Class B Common Stock that is converted pursuant to this Section 3.8(b) of ARTICLE IV shall thereupon be retired by the corporation and shall not be available for reissuance.

(c) The corporation may, from time to time, establish such policies and procedures, not in violation of applicable law or the other provisions of this Restated Certificate, relating to the conversion of the Class B Common Stock into Class A Common Stock, as it may deem necessary or advisable in connection therewith. If the corporation has reason to believe that a Transfer giving rise to a conversion of shares of Class B Common Stock into Class A Common Stock has occurred but has not theretofore been reflected on the books of the corporation, the corporation may request that the holder of such shares furnish affidavits or other evidence to the corporation as the corporation deems necessary to determine whether a conversion of shares of Class B Common Stock to Class A Common Stock has occurred, and if such holder does not within ten (10) days after the date of such request furnish sufficient evidence to the corporation (in the manner provided in the request) to enable the corporation to determine that no such conversion has occurred, any such shares of Class B Common Stock, to the extent not previously converted, shall be automatically converted into shares of Class A Common Stock and the same shall thereupon be registered on the books and records of the corporation. In connection with any action of stockholders taken at a meeting or by written consent (if action by written consent of stockholders is permitted at such time under this Restated Certificate of Incorporation), the stock ledger of the corporation shall be presumptive evidence as to who are the stockholders entitled to vote in person or by proxy at any meeting of stockholders or in connection with any such written consent and the class or classes or series of shares held by each such stockholder and the number of shares of each class or classes or series held by such stockholder.

3.9. <u>Reservation of Stock</u>. The corporation shall at all times reserve and keep available out of its authorized but unissued shares of Class A Common Stock, solely for the purpose of effecting the conversion of the shares of Class B Common Stock, such number of shares of Class A Common Stock as shall from time to time be sufficient to effect the conversion of all outstanding shares of Class B Common Stock into shares of Class A Common Stock.

3.10. <u>Protective Provision</u>. The corporation shall not, whether by merger, consolidation or otherwise, amend, alter, repeal or waive Sections 3 or 4 of this Article IV (or adopt any provision inconsistent therewith), without first obtaining the affirmative vote (or written consent if action by written consent of stockholders is permitted at such time under this Restated Certificate of Incorporation) of the holders of a majority of the then outstanding shares of Class B Common Stock, voting as a separate class, in addition to any other vote required by applicable law, this Restated Certificate of Incorporation or the Bylaws.

4. **Definitions**. For purposes of this Restated Certificate of Incorporation:

4.1. "<u>Change in Control Transaction</u>" means the occurrence of any of the following events:

(a) the sale, lease, exchange, encumbrance or other disposition (other than licenses that do not constitute an effective disposition of all or substantially all of the assets of the corporation and its subsidiaries taken as a whole, and the grant of security interests in the ordinary course of business) by the corporation of all or substantially all of the corporation's assets; or

(b) the merger or consolidation of the corporation with or into any other entity, other than a merger or consolidation that would result in the Class B Common Stock of the corporation outstanding immediately prior thereto continuing to represent (either by remaining outstanding or by being converted into voting securities of the surviving entity or its sole parent entity) more than fifty percent (50%) of the total voting power represented by the voting securities of the corporation or such surviving entity or its sole parent entity outstanding immediately after such merger or consolidation.

4.2. "<u>Charitable Trust</u>" means a trust that is exempt from taxation under Section 501(c)(3) of the United States Internal Revenue Code of 1986, as amended (or any successor provision thereto) (whether a determination letter with respect to such exemption is issued before, at or after the Covered Security Date), and further includes any successor entity that is exempt from taxation under Section 501(c)(3) (or any successor provision thereto) upon a conversion of, or transfer of all or substantially all of the assets of, a Charitable Trust to such successor entity (whether a determination letter with respect to such successor's exemption is issued before, at or after the conversion date).

4.3. "<u>Covered Security Date</u>" means May 14, 2012.

4.4. "Family Member" shall mean with respect to any natural person who is a Qualified Stockholder, the spouse, parents, grandparents, lineal descendants, siblings and lineal descendants of siblings of such Qualified Stockholder. Lineal descendants shall include adopted persons, but only so long as they are adopted during minority.

4.5. "<u>Qualified Stockholder</u>" shall mean (a) the registered holder of a share of Class B Common Stock as of the Covered Security Date; (b) the initial registered holder of any shares of Class B Common Stock that are originally issued by the corporation after the Covered Security Date pursuant to the exercise or conversion of options or warrants or settlement of restricted stock units (RSUs) that, in each case, are outstanding as of the Covered Security Date; (c) each natural person who Transferred shares of or equity awards for Class B Common Stock (including any option or warrant exercisable or convertible into or any RSU that can be settled in shares of Class B Common Stock) to a Permitted Entity that is or becomes a Qualified Stockholder pursuant to subclauses (a) or (b) of this Section 4.5; and (d) a Permitted Transferee.

4.6. "<u>Parent</u>" of an entity shall mean any entity that directly or indirectly owns or controls a majority of the voting power of the voting securities of such entity.

4.7. "Permitted Entity" shall mean with respect to a Qualified Stockholder (a) a Permitted Trust solely for the benefit of (i) such Qualified Stockholder, (ii) one or more Family Members of such Qualified Stockholder, (iii) any other Permitted Entity of such Qualified Stockholder and/or (iv) any entity that is described in Sections 501(c)(3), 170(b)(1)(A), 170(c), 2055(a) or 2522(a) of the United States Internal Revenue Code of 1986, as amended (or any successor provision thereto), (b) any general partnership, limited partnership, limited liability company, corporation or other entity exclusively owned by (i) such Qualified Stockholder, (ii) one or more Family Members of such Qualified Stockholder and/or (iii) any other Permitted Entity of such Qualified Stockholder, (c) any Charitable Trust created by a Qualified Stockholder, which Charitable Trust was (x) validly created and (y) a registered holder of shares of capital stock of the corporation, in each case prior to the Covered Security Date (whether or not it continuously holds such shares of capital stock or any other shares of capital stock of the corporation at all times before or after the Covered Security Date), (d) the personal representative of the estate of a Qualified Stockholder upon the death of such Qualified Stockholder solely to the extent the executor is acting in the capacity as personal representative of such estate, (e) a revocable living trust, which revocable living trust is itself both a Permitted Trust and a Qualified Stockholder, during the lifetime of the natural person grantor of such trust, or (f) a revocable living trust, which revocable living trust is itself both a Permitted Trust and a Qualified Stockholder, following the death of the natural person grantor of such trust, solely to the extent that such shares are held in such trust pending distribution to the beneficiaries designated in such trust. Except as explicitly provided for herein, a Permitted Entity of a Qualified Stockholder shall not cease to be a Permitted Entity of that Qualified Stockholder solely by reason of the death of that Qualified Stockholder.

4.8. "Permitted Transfer" shall mean, and be restricted to, any Transfer of a share of Class B Common Stock:

(a) by a Qualified Stockholder (or the estate of a deceased Qualified Stockholder) to (i) one or more Family Members of such Qualified

Stockholder, or (ii) any Permitted Entity of such Qualified Stockholder; or (iii) to such Qualified Stockholder's revocable living trust, which revocable living trust is itself both a Permitted Trust and a Qualified Stockholder;

(b) by a Permitted Entity of a Qualified Stockholder to (i) such Qualified Stockholder or one or more Family Members of such Qualified Stockholder, or (ii) any other Permitted Entity of such Qualified Stockholder; or

(c) by a Qualified Stockholder that is a natural person or revocable living trust to an entity that is exempt from taxation under Section 501(c)(3) of the United States Internal Revenue Code of 1986, as amended (or any successor provision thereto) (a "501(c)(3) Organization") or an entity that is exempt from taxation under Section 501(c)(3) and described in Section 509(a)(3) of United States Internal Revenue Code of 1986, as amended (or any successor provision thereto) (a "Supporting Organization"), as well as any Transfer by a 501(c)(3) Organization to a Supporting Organization of which such 501(c)(3) Organization (x) is a supported organization (within the meaning of Section 509(f)(3) of the United States Internal Revenue Code of 1986, as amended (or any successor provision thereto)), and (y) has the power to appoint a majority of the board of directors, provided that such 501(c)(3) Organization or such Supporting Organization irrevocably elects, no later than the time such share of Class B Common Stock is Transferred to it, that such share of Class B Common Stock shall automatically be converted into Class A Common Stock upon the death of such Qualified Stockholder or the natural person grantor of such Qualified Stockholder.

4.9. "Permitted Transferee" shall mean a transferee of shares of Class B Common Stock received in a Transfer that constitutes a Permitted Transfer.

4.10. "Permitted Trust" shall mean a bona fide trust where each trustee is (a) a Qualified Stockholder, (b) a Family Member of a Qualified Stockholder, (c) a professional in the business of providing trustee services, including private professional fiduciaries, trust companies and bank trust departments, or (d) solely in the case

615

of any such trust established by a natural person grantor prior to the Covered Security Date, any other bona fide trustee.

4.11. "Transfer" of a share of Class B Common Stock shall mean, directly or indirectly, any sale, assignment, transfer, conveyance, hypothecation or other transfer or disposition of such share or any legal or beneficial interest in such share, whether or not for value and whether voluntary or involuntary or by operation of law (including by merger, consolidation or otherwise), including, without limitation, a transfer of a share of Class B Common Stock to a broker or other nominee (regardless of whether there is a corresponding change in beneficial ownership), or the transfer of, or entering into a binding agreement with respect to, Voting Control (as defined below) over such share by proxy or otherwise. A "Transfer" shall also be deemed to have occurred with respect to a share of Class B Common Stock beneficially held by (i) an entity that is a Permitted Entity, if there occurs any act or circumstance that causes such entity to no longer be a Permitted Entity or (ii) an entity that is a Qualified Stockholder, if there occurs a Transfer on a cumulative basis, from and after the Covered Security Date, of a majority of the voting power of the voting securities of such entity or any direct or indirect Parent of such entity, other than a Transfer to parties that are, as of the Covered Security Date, holders of voting securities of any such entity or Parent of such entity. Notwithstanding the foregoing, the following shall not be considered a "Transfer" within the meaning of this ARTICLE IV:

(a) the granting of a revocable proxy to officers or directors of the corporation at the request of the Board of Directors in connection with actions to be taken at an annual or special meeting of stockholders or in connection with any action by written consent of the stockholders solicited by the Board of Directors (if action by written consent of stockholders is permitted at such time under this Restated Certificate of Incorporation);

(b) entering into a voting trust, agreement or arrangement (with or without granting a proxy) solely with stockholders who are holders of Class B Common Stock, which voting trust, agreement or arrangement (i) is disclosed either in a Schedule 13D filed with the Securities and Exchange Commission or in writing to the Secretary of the corporation, (ii) either has a term not exceeding one (1) year or is terminable by the holder of the shares subject thereto at any time and (iii) does not involve any payment of cash, securities, property or other consideration to the holder of the shares subject thereto other than the mutual promise to vote shares in a designated manner;

(c) the pledge of shares of Class B Common Stock by a stockholder that creates a mere security interest in such shares pursuant to a bona fide loan or indebtedness transaction for so long as such stockholder continues to exercise Voting Control over such pledged shares; provided, however, that a foreclosure on such shares or other similar action by the pledgee shall constitute a "Transfer" unless such foreclosure or similar action qualifies as a "Permitted Transfer" at such time; or

(d) any change in the trustees or the person(s) and/or entity(ies) having or exercising Voting Control over shares of Class B Common Stock (i) of a Charitable Trust that qualifies as a Permitted Entity pursuant to ARTICLE IV, Section 4.7 above, or (ii) of a Permitted Entity provided that following such change such Permitted Entity continues to be a Permitted Entity pursuant to ARTICLE IV, Section 4.7 above.

4.12. "Voting Control" shall mean, with respect to a share of Class B Common Stock, the power (whether exclusive or shared) to vote or direct the voting of such share by proxy, voting agreement or otherwise.

4.13. "Voting Threshold Date" shall mean 5:00 p.m. (Eastern Time) on the first day falling on or after the date on which the outstanding shares of Class B Common Stock represent less than a majority of the total voting power of the then outstanding shares of the corporation then entitled to vote generally in the election of directors.

ARTICLE V: AMENDMENT OF BYLAWS

The Board of Directors of the corporation shall have the power to adopt, amend or repeal the Bylaws of the corporation. Any adoption, amendment or repeal of the Bylaws of the corporation by the Board of Directors shall require the approval of a majority of the Whole Board. For purposes of this Restated Certificate of Incorporation, the term "**Whole Board**" shall mean the total number of authorized directors whether or not there exist any vacancies in previously authorized directorships. The stockholders shall also have power to adopt, amend or repeal the Bylaws of the corporation. Prior to the Voting Threshold Date, in addition to any vote of the holders of any class or series of stock of the corporation required by applicable law or by this Restated Certificate of Incorporation (including any Preferred Stock issued pursuant to a Certificate of Designation), such adoption, amendment or repeal of the Bylaws of the corporation by the stockholders shall require the affirmative vote of a majority in voting power of all of the then outstanding shares of capital stock of the corporation entitled to vote generally in the election of directors, voting together as a single class. From and after the Voting Threshold Date, in addition to any vote of the holders of any class or series of stock of the corporation required by applicable law or by this Restated Certificate of Incorporation (including any Preferred Stock issued pursuant to a Certificate of Designation), such adoption, amendment or repeal of the Bylaws of the corporation by the stockholders shall require the affirmative vote of the holders of at least two-thirds of the voting power of all of the then-outstanding shares of the capital stock of the corporation entitled to vote generally in the election of directors, voting together as a single class.

ARTICLE VI: MATTERS RELATING TO THE BOARD OF DIRECTORS

1. **Director Powers.** The business and affairs of the corporation shall be managed by or under the direction of the Board of Directors. In addition to the powers and authority expressly conferred upon them by statute or by this Restated Certificate of Incorporation or the Bylaws of the corporation, the directors are hereby empowered to exercise all such powers and do all such acts and things as may be exercised or done by the corporation.

2. **Number of Directors.** Subject to the rights of the holders of any series of Preferred Stock to elect additional directors

under specified circumstances, the number of directors shall be fixed from time to time exclusively by resolution adopted by a majority of the Whole Board.

3. **Classified Board.** Subject to the rights of the holders of any series of Preferred Stock to elect additional directors under specified circumstances, immediately following the Voting Threshold Date, the directors shall be divided, with respect to the time for which they severally hold office, into three classes designated as Class I, Class II and Class III, respectively (the "*Classified Board*"). The Board of Directors may assign members of the Board of Directors in office immediately prior to the Classified Board becoming effective to the several classes of the Classified Board, which assignments shall become effective at the same time the Classified Board becomes effective. Directors shall be assigned to each class in accordance with a resolution or resolutions adopted by a majority of the Board of Directors, with the number of directors in each class to be divided as nearly equal as reasonably possible. The initial term of office of the Class I directors shall expire at the corporation's first annual meeting of stockholders following the date on which the Classified Board becomes effective, the initial term of office of the Class II directors shall expire at the corporation's second annual meeting of stockholders following the date on which the Classified Board becomes effective, and the initial term of office of the Class III directors shall expire at the corporation's third annual meeting of stockholders following the date on which the Classified Board becomes effective. At each annual meeting of stockholders following the date on which the Classified Board becomes effective, directors elected to succeed those directors of the class whose terms then expire shall be elected for a term of office to expire at the third succeeding annual meeting of stockholders after their election.

4. **Term and Removal.**

(a) Each director shall hold office until such director's successor is elected and qualified, or until such director's earlier death, resignation or removal. Any director may resign at any time upon notice to the corporation given in writing or by any electronic transmission permitted in the corporation's Bylaws or in accordance with applicable law. No decrease in the number of directors constituting the Whole Board shall shorten the term of any incumbent director.

(b) Notwithstanding anything in this Section 4 of this ARTICLE VI to the contrary, subject to the rights of the holders of any series of Preferred Stock with respect to directors elected thereby, from and after the effectiveness of the Classified Board, no director may be removed except for cause and only by the affirmative vote of the holders of at least a majority of the voting power of the then-outstanding shares of capital stock of the corporation then entitled to vote at an election of directors voting together as a single class.

(c) For so long as the Federal Trade Commission's Order Modifying Prior Decision and Order in Docket No. C-4365, dated as of April 27, 2020 (the "*Order*"), remains in effect, (i) no director serving on the Independent Privacy Committee, as that term is defined in the Order (any such director, a "*Privacy Committee Delegate*"), shall be removed solely for reasons related to actions taken in good faith in furtherance of such Privacy Committee Delegate's duties as a member of the Independent Privacy Committee as set forth in the Order (a "*Privacy Reason*"), except by the affirmative vote of the holders of at least two-thirds of the voting power of the then-outstanding shares of the capital stock of the corporation entitled to vote generally in the election of directors, voting together as a single class, and (ii) no Privacy Committee Delegate shall be removed for reasons other than a Privacy Reason with the intent to circumvent the requirements of clause (i) above, except by the affirmative vote of the holders of at least two-thirds of the voting power of the then-outstanding shares of the capital stock of the corporation entitled to vote generally in the election of directors, voting together as a single class.

5. **Board Vacancies**. Subject to the rights of the holders of any series of Preferred Stock to elect directors under specified circumstances, from and after the effectiveness of the Classified Board, any vacancy occurring in the Board of

Directors for any cause, and any newly created directorship resulting from any increase in the authorized number of directors, shall (unless (a) the Board of Directors determines by resolution that any such vacancy or newly created directorship shall be filled by the stockholders or (b) otherwise required by applicable law) be filled only by the affirmative vote of a majority of the directors then in office, even if less than a quorum, or by a sole remaining director, and not by the stockholders. Any director elected in accordance with the preceding sentence shall hold office for a term expiring at the annual meeting of stockholders at which the term of office of the class to which the director has been elected expires or until such director's successor shall have been duly elected and qualified.

6. **Vote by Ballot.** Election of directors need not be by written ballot.

ARTICLE VII: DIRECTOR LIABILITY; INDEMNIFICATION

1. **Limitation of Liability.** To the fullest extent permitted by law, no director of the corporation shall be personally liable to the corporation or its stockholders for monetary damages for breach of fiduciary duty as a director. Without limiting the effect of the preceding sentence, if the General Corporation Law is hereafter amended to authorize the further elimination or limitation of the liability of a director, then the liability of a director of the corporation shall be eliminated or limited to the fullest extent permitted by the General Corporation Law, as so amended.

2. **Indemnification.** The corporation shall indemnify to the fullest extent permitted by law any person made or threatened to be made a party to an action or proceeding, whether criminal, civil, administrative or investigative, by reason of the fact that he, his testator or intestate is or was a director or officer of the corporation or any predecessor of the Corporation, or serves or served at any other enterprise

as a director or officer at the request of the corporation or any predecessor to the corporation.

3. **Change in Rights.** Neither any amendment nor repeal of this ARTICLE VII, nor the adoption of any provision of this Restated Certificate of Incorporation inconsistent with this ARTICLE VII, shall eliminate or reduce the effect of this Article VII in respect of any matter occurring, or any action or proceeding accruing or arising or that, but for this Article VII, would accrue or arise, prior to such amendment, repeal or adoption of an inconsistent provision.

ARTICLE VIII: MATTERS RELATING TO STOCKHOLDERS

1. **No Action by Written Consent of Stockholders.** Subject to the rights of the holders of any series of Preferred Stock with respect to actions by the holders of shares of such series, from and after the Voting Threshold Date, (a) no action shall be taken by the stockholders of the corporation except at a duly called annual or special meeting of stockholders and (b) no action shall be taken by the stockholders of the corporation by written consent.

2. **Special Meeting of Stockholders.** Subject to the rights of the holders of any series of Preferred Stock with respect to actions by the holders of shares of such series, special meetings of the stockholders of the corporation may be called only by the Board of Directors acting pursuant to a resolution adopted by a majority of the Whole Board, the Chief Executive Officer, President or the Chairperson of the Board, and may not be called by any other person or persons. Business transacted at special meetings of stockholders shall be confined to the purpose or purposes stated in the notice of meeting.

3. **Advance Notice of Stockholder Nominations.** Advance notice of stockholder nominations for the election of directors of the corporation and of business to be brought by stockholders before any meeting of stockholders of the

corporation shall be given in the manner provided in the Bylaws of the corporation.

4.   **Business Combinations.** The corporation elects not to be governed by Section 203 of the General Corporation Law.

ARTICLE IX: CHOICE OF FORUM

Unless the corporation consents in writing to the selection of an alternative forum, the Court of Chancery of the State of Delaware shall, to the fullest extent permitted by law, be the sole and exclusive forum for (1) any derivative action or proceeding brought on behalf of the corporation, (2) any action asserting a claim of breach of a fiduciary duty owed by, or other wrongdoing by, any director, officer, employee or agent of the corporation to the corporation or the corporation's stockholders, (3) any action asserting a claim arising pursuant to any provision of the General Corporation Law or the corporation's Restated Certificate of Incorporation or Bylaws, (4) any action to interpret, apply, enforce or determine the validity of the corporation's Restated Certificate of Incorporation or Bylaws or (5) any action asserting a claim governed by the internal affairs doctrine, in each such case subject to said Court of Chancery having personal jurisdiction over the indispensable parties named as defendants therein. Any person or entity purchasing or otherwise acquiring any interest in shares of capital stock of the corporation shall be deemed to have notice of and consented to the provisions of this ARTICLE IX.

ARTICLE X: AMENDMENT OF RESTATED CERTIFICATE OF INCORPORATION

The corporation reserves the right to amend or repeal any provision contained in this Restated Certificate of Incorporation in the manner prescribed by the laws of the State of Delaware and all rights conferred upon stockholders are granted subject to this reservation; provided, however, that, notwithstanding any other provision of this Restated Certificate of Incorporation or any provision of applicable law that might otherwise permit a lesser vote or no vote, but in addition to any vote of the holders of any class or series of the capital stock of this corporation required by applicable law or by this Restated Certificate of Incorporation, from and after the Voting Threshold Date, any amendment to or repeal of this ARTICLE X or ARTICLE V, ARTICLE VI, ARTICLE VII, ARTICLE VIII or ARTICLE IX of this Restated Certificate of Incorporation (or the adoption of any provision inconsistent therewith) shall require the affirmative vote of the holders of at least two-thirds of the voting power of the then outstanding shares of capital stock of the corporation entitled to vote generally in the election of directors, voting together as a single class.

* * * * * * * * * * *

AMENDED AND RESTATED CERTIFICATE

OF INCORPORATION OF UNITED CONTINENTAL HOLDINGS, INC.

The present name of the corporation is United Continental Holdings, Inc. (the "Corporation"). The Corporation was incorporated under the name "UAL, Inc." by the filing of its original Certificate of Incorporation with the Secretary of State of the State of Delaware on December 30, 1968. This Amended and Restated Certificate of Incorporation of the Corporation (this "Restated Certificate"), which restates and integrates and also further amends the provisions of the Corporation's Restated Certificate of Incorporation, was duly adopted in accordance with the provisions of Sections 242 and 245 of the General Corporation Law of the State of Delaware. The Restated Certificate of Incorporation of the Corporation is hereby amended, integrated and restated to read in its entirety as follows:

ARTICLE FIRST. The name of the Corporation is UNITED AIRLINES HOLDINGS, INC.

ARTICLE SECOND. The registered office of the Corporation in the State of Delaware is located at Corporation Trust Center, 1209 Orange Street, in the City of Wilmington, County of New Castle, Delaware 19801. The name of its registered agent at such address is The Corporation Trust Company.

ARTICLE THIRD. The purpose of the Corporation is to engage in any lawful act or activity for which corporations may be organized under the General Corporation Law of the State of Delaware (the "GCL").

ARTICLE FOURTH. The total number of shares of capital stock of all classes of which the Corporation shall have authority to issue is 1,250,000,002, divided into four classes, as follows: 250,000,000 shares of Preferred Stock, without par value (hereinafter referred to as "Serial Preferred Stock"), one (1) share of Class Pilot MEC Junior Preferred Stock, par value $0.01 per share (the "Class Pilot MEC Preferred Stock"), one (1) share of Class IAM Junior Preferred Stock, par value $0.01 per share (the "Class IAM Preferred Stock" and, together with the Serial Preferred Stock and the Class Pilot MEC Preferred Stock, the "Preferred Stock"), and 1,000,000,000 shares of Common Stock, par value $0.01 per share (the "Common Stock").

PART I

Serial Preferred Stock

The board of directors of the Corporation (the "Board of Directors") is expressly authorized, without any vote or other action by the stockholders and subject to limitations prescribed by law, to adopt, from time to time, a resolution or resolutions providing for the issue of Serial Preferred Stock in one or more series, to fix the number of shares in each such series and to fix the designations and the powers, preferences and relative, participating, optional or other special rights, and the qualifications, limitations and restrictions thereof, of each such series. The authority of the Board of Directors with respect to each such series shall include a determination of the following (which may vary as between the different series of Serial Preferred Stock):

(a) The number of shares constituting the series and the distinctive designation of the series;

(b) The dividend rate on the shares of the series, the conditions and dates upon which dividends thereon shall be payable, the extent, if any, to which dividends thereon shall be cumulative, and the relative rights of preference, if any, of payment of dividends thereon;

(c) Whether or not the shares of the series are redeemable and, if redeemable, the time or times during which they shall be redeemable and the amount per share payable on redemption thereof, which amount may, but need not, vary according to the time and circumstances of such redemption;

(d) The amount payable in respect of the shares of the series, in the event of any liquidation, dissolution or winding up of the Corporation, which amount may, but need not, vary according to the time or circumstances of such action, and the relative rights of preference, if any, of payment of such amount;

(e) Any requirement as to a sinking fund for the shares of the series, or any requirement as to the redemption, purchase or other retirement by the Corporation of the shares of the series;

(f) The right, if any, to exchange or convert shares of the series into other securities or property, and the rate or basis, time, manner and condition of exchange or conversion;

(g) The voting rights, if any, to which the holders of shares of the series shall be entitled in addition to the voting rights provided by law; and

(h) Any other term, condition or provision with respect to the series not inconsistent with the provisions of this Article Fourth, Part I or any resolution adopted by the Board of Directors pursuant thereto.

PART II

Class Pilot MEC Junior Preferred Stock

Unless otherwise indicated, any reference in this Article Fourth, Part II to "Section," "subsection," "paragraph," "subparagraph," or "clause" shall refer to a Section, subsection, paragraph, subparagraph or clause in this Article Fourth, Part II.

Section 1. *Issuance; Restrictions on Transfer.* The share of Class Pilot MEC Preferred Stock shall be issued only to, and shall be held only by, (i) the United Airlines Pilots Master Executive Council (the "MEC") of the Air Line Pilots Association, International ("ALPA") pursuant to ALPA's authority as the collective bargaining representative for the crafts or class of pilots employed by United Air Lines, Inc. ("United OpCo") or (ii) a duly authorized agent acting for the benefit of the MEC. Any purported sale, transfer, pledge or other disposition (a "transfer") of the share of Class Pilot MEC Preferred Stock to any person, other than a successor to the MEC by merger or reorganization of ALPA (in any such case, an "ALPA Successor"), or a duly authorized agent acting for the benefit of ALPA or an ALPA Successor, shall be null and void and of no force and effect. Upon any purported transfer of the share of Class Pilot MEC Preferred Stock by the holder thereof other than as expressly permitted above, and without any further action by the Corporation, such holder or any other person or entity, such share shall, to the extent of funds legally available therefor and subject to the other provisions of this Restated Certificate, be automatically redeemed by the Corporation in accordance with Subsection 9.2 hereof, and thereupon such share shall no longer be deemed outstanding, and neither such holder nor any purported transferee thereof shall have in respect thereof any of the voting powers, preferences or relative, participating, optional or special rights ascribed to the share of Class Pilot MEC Preferred Stock hereunder, but rather such holder thereafter shall only be entitled to receive the amount payable upon redemption in accordance with Section 9. The certificate representing the share of Class Pilot MEC Preferred Stock shall be legended to reflect the restrictions on transfer and automatic redemption provided for herein.

Section 2. *Definitions*. For purposes of this Article Fourth, Part II, the following terms shall have the meanings indicated:

2.1 *"Affiliate"* shall have the meaning defined in Rule 12b-2 under the Exchange Act.

2.2 *"Board of Directors"* shall mean the board of directors of the Corporation or any committee thereof authorized by such board of directors to perform any of its responsibilities with respect to the Class Pilot MEC Preferred Stock.

2.3 *"Business Day"* shall mean any day other than a Saturday, Sunday or a day on which state or federally chartered banking institutions in New York, New York are not required to be open.

2.4 *"Exchange Act"* means the Securities Exchange Act of 1934, as amended, or any successor act thereto.

2.5 *"set apart for payment"* shall be deemed to include, without any action other than the following, the recording by the Corporation in its accounting ledgers of any accounting or bookkeeping entry which indicates, pursuant to a declaration of dividends or other distribution by the Board of Directors, the allocation of funds to be so paid on any series or class of capital stock of the Corporation; provided, however, that if any funds for any class or series of stock of the Corporation ranking on a parity with or junior to the Class Pilot MEC Preferred Stock as to distributions upon liquidation, dissolution or winding up of the Corporation are placed in a separate account of the Corporation or delivered to a disbursing, paying or other similar agent, then "set apart for payment" with respect to the Class Pilot MEC Preferred Stock shall mean, with respect to such distributions, placing such funds in a separate account or delivering such funds to a disbursing, paying or other similar agent.

2.6 *"Transfer Agent"* means the Corporation or such agent or agents of the Corporation as may be designated from

629

time to time by the Board of Directors as the transfer agent for the Class Pilot MEC Preferred Stock.

Section 3. *Dividends.* The holder of the share of Class Pilot MEC Preferred Stock as such shall not be entitled to receive any dividends or other distributions (except as provided in Section 4).

Section 4. *Payments upon Liquidation.*

4.1 In the event of any voluntary or involuntary liquidation, dissolution or winding up of the Corporation, before any payment or distribution of the assets of the Corporation (whether capital or surplus) shall be made to or set apart for payment to the holders of any class or series of stock of the Corporation that ranks junior to the Class Pilot MEC Preferred Stock as to amounts distributable upon liquidation, dissolution or winding up of the Corporation, the holder of the share of Class Pilot MEC Preferred Stock shall be entitled to receive $0.01 for the share of Class Pilot MEC Preferred Stock (the "MEC Liquidation Preference"), but such holder shall not be entitled to any further payment. If, upon any liquidation, dissolution or winding up of the Corporation, the assets of the Corporation, or proceeds thereof, distributable to the holder of the share of Class Pilot MEC Preferred Stock shall be insufficient to pay in full the MEC Liquidation Preference and the liquidation preference on all other shares of any class or series of stock of the Corporation that ranks on a parity with the Class Pilot MEC Preferred Stock as to amounts distributable upon liquidation, dissolution or winding up of the Corporation, then such assets, or the proceeds thereof, shall be distributed among the holder of the share of Class Pilot MEC Preferred Stock and any such other parity stock ratably in accordance with the respective amounts that would be payable on such share of Class Pilot MEC Preferred Stock and any such other parity stock if all amounts payable thereon were paid in full. For the purposes of this Section 4, (i) a consolidation or merger of the Corporation with or into one or more corporations, or (ii) a sale, lease, exchange or transfer of all or substantially all of the Corporation's assets, shall not be deemed to be a liquidation, dissolution or winding up, voluntary or involuntary, of the Corporation.

4.2 Subject to the rights of the holders of shares of any series or class of stock ranking prior to or on a parity with the Class Pilot MEC Preferred Stock as to amounts distributable upon liquidation, dissolution or winding up of the Corporation, after payment shall have been made to the holder of the share of Class Pilot MEC Preferred Stock, as and to the fullest extent provided in this Section 4, any series or class of stock of the Corporation that ranks junior to the Class Pilot MEC Preferred Stock as to amounts distributable upon liquidation, dissolution or winding up of the Corporation, shall, subject to the respective terms and provisions (if any) applying thereto, be entitled to receive any and all assets remaining to be paid or distributed, and the holder of the share of Class Pilot MEC Preferred Stock shall not be entitled to share therein.

Section 5. *Shares to be Retired.* The share of Class Pilot MEC Preferred Stock which shall have been issued and reacquired in any manner (other than redemption pursuant to Section 9.1) by the Corporation shall be retired and restored to the status of an authorized but unissued share of Class Pilot MEC Preferred Stock and, in the event of the redemption of such share pursuant to Section 9.1 hereof, shall not be reissued.

Section 6. *Ranking.*

6.1 Any class or series of stock of the Corporation shall be deemed to rank:

(a) prior to the Class Pilot MEC Preferred Stock as to the distribution of assets upon liquidation, dissolution or winding up, if the holders of such class or series shall be entitled to the receipt of amounts distributable upon liquidation, dissolution or winding up in preference or priority to the holder of Class Pilot MEC Preferred Stock;

(b) on a parity with the Class Pilot MEC Preferred Stock as to the distribution of assets upon liquidation, dissolution or winding up, whether or not the liquidation prices per share thereof be different from those of the Class Pilot MEC Preferred Stock, if the holders of such class or series and the Class Pilot MEC Preferred Stock shall be entitled to the receipt of amounts distributable upon liquidation, dissolution or winding up in proportion to their respective liquidation preferences, without preference or priority one over the other; and

(c) junior to the Class Pilot MEC Preferred Stock, as to the distribution of assets upon liquidation, dissolution or winding up, if the holder of Class Pilot MEC Preferred Stock shall be entitled to the receipt of amounts distributable upon liquidation, dissolution or winding up in preference or priority to the holders of shares of such class or series.

6.2 The Class IAM Preferred Stock shall be deemed to rank on a parity with the Class Pilot MEC Preferred Stock as to amounts distributable upon liquidation, dissolution or winding up. The Common Stock shall each be deemed to rank junior to the Class Pilot MEC Preferred Stock as to amounts distributable upon liquidation, dissolution or winding up.

Section 7. *Consolidation, Merger, etc.*

7.1 In case the Corporation enters into any consolidation, merger, share exchange or similar transaction, however named, involving the Corporation or its subsidiary, United

OpCo (or any successor to all or substantially all the assets or business of United OpCo), pursuant to which the outstanding shares of Common Stock are to be exchanged for or changed, reclassified or converted into securities of any successor or resulting or other company (including the Corporation), or cash or other property (each of the foregoing transactions is referred to herein as a "Merger Transaction"), proper provision shall be made so that, upon consummation of such transaction, the share of Class Pilot MEC Preferred Stock shall be converted, reclassified or changed into or exchanged for preferred stock of such successor or resulting or other company having, in respect of such company, the same powers, preferences and relative, participating, optional or other special rights (including the rights provided by this Section 7), and the qualifications, limitations or restrictions thereof, that the Class Pilot MEC Preferred Stock had, in respect of the Corporation, immediately prior to such transaction; specifically including, without limitation, the right, until the ALPA Termination Date (as defined in Section 8.1 below), to elect one member of the board of directors (or similar governing body) of such company.

7.2 In case the Corporation shall enter into any agreement providing for any Merger Transaction, then the Corporation shall as soon as practicable thereafter (and in any event at least fifteen (15) Business Days before consummation of such transaction) give notice of such agreement and the material terms thereof to the holder of the share of Class Pilot MEC Preferred Stock. The Corporation shall not consummate any such Merger Transaction unless all of the terms of this Section 7 and Section 8 have been complied with.

Section 8. *Voting*. The holder of the share of Class Pilot MEC Preferred Stock shall have the following voting rights:

8.1 Until such time (the "ALPA Termination Date") as (i) there are no longer any persons represented by ALPA (or any ALPA Successor) employed by the Corporation or any of its Affiliates or (ii) the collective bargaining agreement between the Corporation or any of its Affiliates and ALPA has been amended by the parties thereto so that such agreement no longer provides that ALPA has the right to appoint a director of the Corporation, the holder of the share of Class Pilot MEC Preferred Stock shall have the right (a) voting as a separate class, to (1) elect one director to the Board of Directors at each annual meeting of stockholders for a term of office to expire at the succeeding annual meeting of stockholders, (2) remove such director with or without cause and (3) fill any vacancies in such directorship resulting from death, resignation, disqualification, removal or other cause, and (b) voting together as a single class with the holders of Common Stock and the holders of such other classes or series of stock that vote together with the Common Stock as a single class, to vote on all matters submitted to a vote of the holders of Common Stock of the Corporation (other than the election of Directors), except as otherwise required by law.

8.2 The affirmative vote of the holder of the share of Class Pilot MEC Preferred Stock, voting as a separate class, shall be necessary for authorizing, effecting or validating the amendment, alteration or repeal (including any amendment, alteration or repeal by operation of merger or consolidation) of any of the provisions of this Restated Certificate or of any certificate amendatory thereof or supplemental thereto (including any Certificate of Designation, Preferences and Rights or any similar document relating to any series of Serial Preferred Stock) which would adversely affect the powers, preferences or special rights of the Class Pilot MEC Preferred Stock.

8.3 For purposes of the foregoing provisions of Sections 8.1 and 8.2, the share of Class Pilot MEC Preferred Stock shall have one (1) vote.

Section 9. *Redemption.*

9.1 The share of Class Pilot MEC Preferred Stock shall, to the extent of funds legally available therefor and subject to the other provisions of this Restated Certificate, be automatically redeemed on the ALPA Termination Date, at a price of $0.01 per share, as provided herein below. As promptly as reasonably possible following the occurrence of the ALPA Termination Date, the Corporation shall give notice thereof and of the redemption under this Section 9 to the record holder of the Class Pilot MEC Preferred Stock. From and after the redemption provided for in this Section 9.1, all rights of the holder of the Class Pilot MEC Preferred Stock as such, except the right to receive the redemption price of such share upon the surrender of the certificate formerly representing the same, shall cease and terminate and such share shall not thereafter be deemed to be outstanding for any purpose whatsoever.

9.2 The share of Class Pilot MEC Preferred Stock shall, to the extent of funds legally available therefor and subject to the other provisions of this Restated Certificate, be automatically redeemed upon any purported transfer thereof other than as expressly permitted under Section 1.2. The redemption price to be paid in connection with any redemption shall be $0.01 per share of Class Pilot MEC Preferred Stock. Upon any such redemption, all rights of the holder of Class Pilot MEC Preferred Stock as such, except the right to receive the redemption price of such share upon the surrender of the certificate formerly representing the same, shall cease and terminate and such share shall not thereafter be deemed to be outstanding for any purpose whatsoever.

9.3 The holder of the share of Class Pilot MEC Preferred Stock so redeemed pursuant to Section 9.1 or 9.2 shall present and surrender the certificate formerly representing such share to the Corporation and thereupon the redemption price of such share shall be paid to or on the order of the person whose name appears on such certificate as the owner thereof and the surrendered certificate shall be cancelled.

Section 10. *Record Holders.* The Corporation and the Transfer Agent (if other than the Corporation) may deem and treat the record holder of the share of Class Pilot MEC Preferred Stock as the true and lawful owner thereof for all purposes, and, except as otherwise provided by law, neither the Corporation nor the Transfer Agent shall be affected by any notice to the contrary.

PART III

Class IAM Junior Preferred Stock

Unless otherwise indicated, any reference in this Article Fourth, Part III to "Section," "subsection," "paragraph," "subparagraph," or "clause" shall refer to a Section, subsection, paragraph, subparagraph or clause in this Article Fourth, Part III.

Section 1. *Issuance; Restrictions on Transfer.* The share of Class IAM Preferred Stock shall be issued only to, and shall be held only by, (i) the International Association of Machinists and Aerospace Workers (the "IAM") pursuant to the IAM's authority as the collective bargaining representative for certain crafts or classes of public contact employees, ramp and stores employees, food service and security officer employees, Mileage Plus public contact employees, fleet technical instructors and related and maintenance instructor employees employed by United OpCo or (ii) a duly authorized agent acting for the benefit of the IAM. Any purported sale, transfer, pledge or other disposition (hereinafter a "transfer") of the share of Class

IAM Preferred Stock to any person, other than a successor to the IAM by merger or reorganization of the IAM (in any such case, an "IAM Successor"), or a duly authorized agent acting for the benefit of the IAM or an IAM Successor, shall be null and void and of no force and effect. Upon any purported transfer of the share of Class IAM Preferred Stock by the holder thereof other than as expressly permitted above, and without any further action by the Corporation, such holder or any other person or entity, such share shall, to the extent of funds legally available therefor and subject to the other provisions of this Restated Certificate, be automatically redeemed by the Corporation in accordance with Subsection 9.2 hereof, and thereupon such share shall no longer be deemed outstanding, and neither such holder nor any purported transferee thereof shall have in respect thereof any of the voting powers, preferences or relative, participating, optional or special rights ascribed to the share of Class IAM Preferred Stock hereunder, but rather such holder thereafter shall only be entitled to receive the amount payable upon redemption in accordance with Section 9. The certificate representing the share of Class IAM Preferred Stock shall be legended to reflect the restrictions on transfer and automatic redemption provided for herein.

Section 2. *Definitions.* For purposes of this Article Fourth, Part III, the following terms shall have the meanings indicated:

2.1 "*Affiliate*" shall have the meaning defined in Rule 12b-2 under the Exchange Act.

2.2 "*Board of Directors*" shall mean the board of directors of the Corporation or any committee thereof authorized by such board of directors to perform any of its responsibilities with respect to the Class IAM Preferred Stock.

2.3 "*Business Day*" shall mean any day other than a Saturday, Sunday or a day on which state or federally chartered banking institutions in New York, New York are not required to be open.

2.4 *"Exchange Act"* means the Securities Exchange Act of 1934, as amended, or any successor act thereto.

2.5 *"set apart for payment"* shall be deemed to include, without any action other than the following, the recording by the Corporation in its accounting ledgers of any accounting or bookkeeping entry which indicates, pursuant to a declaration of dividends or other distribution by the Board of Directors, the allocation of funds to be so paid on any series or class of capital stock of the Corporation; provided, however, that if any funds for any class or series of stock of the Corporation ranking on a parity with or junior to the Class IAM Preferred Stock as to distributions upon liquidation, dissolution or winding up of the Corporation are placed in a separate account of the Corporation or delivered to a disbursing, paying or other similar agent, then "set apart for payment" with respect to the Class IAM Preferred Stock shall mean, with respect to such distributions, placing such funds in a separate account or delivering such funds to a disbursing, paying or other similar agent.

2.6 *"Transfer Agent"* means the Corporation or such agent or agents of the Corporation as may be designated from time to time by the Board of Directors as the transfer agent for the Class IAM Preferred Stock.

Section 3. *Dividends.* The holder of the share of Class IAM Preferred Stock as such shall not be entitled to receive any dividends or other distributions (except as provided in Section 4).

Section 4. *Payments upon Liquidation.*

4.1 In the event of any voluntary or involuntary liquidation, dissolution or winding up of the Corporation, before any payment or distribution of the assets of the Corporation (whether capital or surplus) shall be made to or set apart for payment to the holders of any class or series of stock of the Corporation that ranks junior to the Class IAM Preferred Stock as to amounts distributable upon liquidation, dissolution or winding up of the Corporation, the holder of the share of Class IAM Preferred Stock shall be entitled to receive $0.01 for the share of Class IAM Preferred Stock (the "IAM Liquidation Preference"), but such holder shall not be entitled to any

further payment. If, upon any liquidation, dissolution or winding up of the Corporation, the assets of the Corporation, or proceeds thereof, distributable to the holder of the share of Class IAM Preferred Stock shall be insufficient to pay in full the IAM Liquidation Preference and the liquidation preference on all other shares of any class or series of stock of the Corporation that ranks on a parity with the Class IAM Preferred Stock as to amounts distributable upon liquidation, dissolution or winding up of the Corporation, then such assets, or the proceeds thereof, shall be distributed among the holder of the share of Class IAM Preferred Stock and any such other parity stock ratably in accordance with the respective amounts that would be payable on such share of Class IAM Preferred Stock and any such other parity stock if all amounts payable thereon were paid in full. For the purposes of this Section 4, (i) a consolidation or merger of the Corporation with or into one or more corporations, or (ii) a sale, lease, exchange or transfer of all or substantially all of the Corporation's assets, shall not be deemed to be a liquidation, dissolution or winding up, voluntary or involuntary, of the Corporation.

4.2 Subject to the rights of the holders of shares of any series or class of stock ranking prior to or on a parity with the Class IAM Preferred Stock as to amounts distributable upon liquidation, dissolution or winding up of the

Corporation, after payment shall have been made to the holder of the share of Class IAM Preferred Stock, as and to the fullest extent provided in this Section 4, any series or class of stock of the Corporation that ranks junior to the Class IAM Preferred Stock as to amounts distributable upon liquidation, dissolution or winding up of the Corporation, shall, subject to the respective terms and provisions (if any) applying thereto, be entitled to receive any and all assets remaining to be paid or distributed, and the holder of the share of Class IAM Preferred Stock shall not be entitled to share therein.

Section 5. *Shares to be Retired.* The share of Class IAM Preferred Stock which shall have been issued and reacquired in any manner (other than redemption pursuant to Section 9.1) by the Corporation shall be retired and restored to the status of an authorized but unissued share of Class IAM Preferred Stock and, in the event of the redemption of such share pursuant to Section 9.1 hereof, shall not be reissued.

Section 6. *Ranking.*

6.1 Any class or series of stock of the Corporation shall be deemed to rank:

(a) prior to the Class IAM Preferred Stock as to the distribution of assets upon liquidation, dissolution or winding up, if the holders of such class or series shall be entitled to the receipt of amounts distributable upon liquidation, dissolution or winding up in preference or priority to the holder of Class IAM Preferred Stock;

(b) on a parity with the Class IAM Preferred Stock as to the distribution of assets upon liquidation, dissolution or winding up, whether or not the liquidation prices per share thereof be different from those of the Class IAM Preferred

Stock, if the holders of such class or series and the Class
IAM Preferred Stock shall be entitled to the receipt of
amounts distributable upon liquidation, dissolution or
winding up in proportion to their respective liquidation
preferences, without preference or priority one over the
other; and (c) junior to the Class IAM Preferred Stock, as to
the distribution of assets upon liquidation, dissolution or
winding up, if the holder of Class IAM Preferred Stock shall
be entitled to the receipt of amounts distributable upon
liquidation, dissolution or winding up in preference or
priority to the holders of shares of such class or series.

6.2 The Class Pilot MEC Preferred Stock shall be deemed
to rank on a parity with the Class IAM Preferred Stock as to
amounts distributable upon liquidation, dissolution or
winding up. The Common Stock shall be deemed to rank
junior to the Class IAM Preferred Stock as to amounts
distributable upon liquidation, dissolution or winding up.

Section 7. *Consolidation, Merger, etc.*

7.1 In case the Corporation enters into any consolidation,
merger, share exchange or similar transaction, however
named, involving the Corporation or its subsidiary, United
OpCo (or any successor to all or substantially all the assets
or business of United OpCo), pursuant to which the
outstanding shares of Common Stock are to be exchanged
for or changed, reclassified or converted into securities of
any successor or resulting or other company (including the
Corporation), or cash or other property (each of the
foregoing transactions is referred to herein as a "Merger
Transaction"), proper provision shall be made so that, upon
consummation of such transaction, the share of Class IAM
Preferred Stock shall be converted, reclassified or changed
into or exchanged for preferred stock of such successor or
resulting or other company having, in respect of such
company, the same powers, preferences and relative,
participating, optional or other special rights (including the

rights provided by this Section 7), and the qualifications, limitations or restrictions thereof, that the Class IAM Preferred Stock had, in respect of the Corporation, immediately prior to such transaction; specifically including, without limitation, the right, until the IAM Termination Date (as defined in Section 8.1 below), to elect one member of the board of directors (or similar governing body) of such company.

7.2 In case the Corporation shall enter into any agreement providing for any Merger Transaction, then the Corporation shall as soon as practicable thereafter (and in any event at least fifteen (15) Business Days before consummation of such transaction) give notice of such agreement and the material terms thereof to the holder of the share of Class IAM Preferred Stock. The Corporation shall not consummate any such Merger Transaction unless all of the terms of this Section 7 and Section 8 have been complied with.

Section 8. *Voting.* The holder of the share of Class IAM Preferred Stock shall have the following voting rights:

8.1 Until such time (the "IAM Termination Date") as (i) there are no longer any persons represented by the IAM (or any IAM Successor) employed by the Corporation or any of its Affiliates or (ii) the letter agreement between the Corporation and the IAM, dated as of May 1, 2003, no longer provides that the IAM has the right to appoint a director of the Corporation, the holder of the share of Class IAM Preferred Stock shall have the right (a) voting as a separate class, to (1) elect one director to the Board of Directors at each annual meeting of stockholders for a term of office to expire at the succeeding annual meeting of stockholders, (2) remove such director with or without cause and (3) fill any vacancies in such directorship resulting from death, resignation, disqualification, removal or other cause, and (b) voting together as a single class with the holders of

Common Stock and the holders of such other classes or series of stock that vote together with the Common Stock as a single class, to vote on all matters submitted to a vote of the holders of Common Stock of the Corporation (other than the election of Directors), except as otherwise required by law.

8.2 The affirmative vote of the holder of the share of Class IAM Preferred Stock, voting as a separate class, shall be necessary for authorizing, effecting or validating the amendment, alteration or repeal (including any amendment, alteration or repeal by operation of merger or consolidation) of any of the provisions of this Restated Certificate or of any certificate amendatory thereof or supplemental thereto (including any Certificate of Designation, Preferences and Rights or any similar document relating to any series of Serial Preferred Stock) which would adversely affect the powers, preferences or special rights of the Class IAM Preferred Stock.

8.3 For purposes of the foregoing provisions of Sections 8.1 and 8.2, the share of Class IAM Preferred Stock shall have one (1) vote.

Section 9. *Redemption.*

9.1 The share of Class IAM Preferred Stock shall, to the extent of funds legally available therefor and subject to the other provisions of this Restated Certificate, be automatically redeemed on the IAM Termination Date, at a price of $0.01 per share, as provided herein below. As promptly as reasonably possible following the occurrence of the IAM Termination Date, the Corporation shall give notice thereof and of the redemption under this Section 9 to the record holder of the Class IAM Preferred Stock. From and after the redemption provided for in this Section 9.1, all rights of the holder of the Class IAM Preferred Stock as such, except the right to receive the redemption price of such share upon the surrender of the certificate formerly representing the same, shall cease and terminate and such share shall not thereafter be deemed to be outstanding for any purpose whatsoever.

9.2 The share of Class IAM Preferred Stock shall, to the extent of funds legally available therefor and subject to the other provisions of this Restated Certificate, be automatically redeemed upon any purported transfer thereof other than as expressly permitted under Section 1.2. The redemption price to be paid in connection with any redemption shall be $0.01 per share of Class IAM Preferred Stock. Upon any such redemption, all rights of the holder of Class IAM Preferred Stock as such, except the right to receive the redemption price of such share upon the surrender of the certificate formerly representing the same, shall cease and terminate and such share shall not thereafter be deemed to be outstanding for any purpose whatsoever.

9.3 The holder of the share of Class IAM Preferred Stock so redeemed pursuant to Sections 9.1 or 9.2 shall present and surrender the certificate formerly representing such share to the Corporation and thereupon the redemption price of such share shall be paid to or on the order of the person whose name appears on such certificate as the owner thereof and the surrendered certificate shall be cancelled.

Section 10. *Record Holders.* The Corporation and the Transfer Agent (if other than the Corporation) may deem and treat the record holder of the share of Class IAM Preferred Stock as the true and lawful owner thereof for all purposes, and, except as otherwise provided by law, neither the Corporation nor the Transfer Agent shall be affected by any notice to the contrary.

PART IV

Common Stock

Unless otherwise indicated, any reference in this Article Fourth, Part IV to "Section," "subsection," "paragraph," "subparagraph," or "clause" shall refer to a Section, subsection, paragraph, subparagraph or clause in this Article Fourth, Part IV.

Section 1. *Dividends.* Subject to any rights to receive dividends to which the holders of the shares of any other class or series of stock may be entitled, the holders of shares of Common Stock shall be entitled to receive dividends, if and when declared payable from time to time by the Board of Directors, from any funds legally available therefor.

Section 2. *Liquidation.* In the event of any dissolution, liquidation or winding up of the Corporation, whether voluntary or involuntary, after there shall have been paid to the holders of shares of any other class or series of stock ranking prior to the Common Stock in respect thereof the full amounts to which they shall be entitled, and subject to any rights of the holders of any other class or series of stock to participate therein, the holders of the then outstanding shares of Common Stock shall be entitled to receive, pro rata, any remaining assets of the Corporation available for distribution to its stockholders. Subject to the foregoing, the Board of Directors may distribute in kind to the holders of the shares of Common Stock such remaining assets of the Corporation, or may sell, transfer or otherwise dispose of all or any part of such remaining assets to any other corporation, trust or other entity and receive payment therefor in cash, stock or obligations of such other corporation, trust or entity or any combination thereof, and may sell all or any part of the consideration so received, and may distribute the consideration so received or any balance thereof in kind to holders of the shares of Common Stock. The voluntary sale, conveyance, lease, exchange or transfer of all or substantially all the property or assets of the

Corporation (unless in connection therewith the dissolution, liquidation or winding up of the Corporation is specifically approved), or the merger or consolidation of the Corporation into or with any other corporation, or the merger of any other corporation into it, or any purchase or redemption of shares of stock of the Corporation of any class, shall not be deemed to be a dissolution, liquidation or winding up of the corporation for the purpose of this Section 2.

Section 3. *Voting.* Except as provided by law or this Restated Certificate, each outstanding share of Common Stock of the Corporation shall entitle the holder thereof to one vote on each matter submitted to a vote at a meeting of stockholders.

PART V

Section 1. *No Preemptive Rights.* Except as otherwise provided herein, no holder of stock of the Corporation of any class shall have any preemptive, preferential or other right to purchase or subscribe for any shares of stock, whether now or hereafter authorized, of the Corporation of any class, or any obligations convertible into, or any options or warrants to purchase, any shares of stock, whether now or hereafter authorized, of the Corporation of any class, other than such, if any, as the Board of Directors may from time to time determine, and at such price as the Board of Directors may from time to time fix; and any shares of stock or any obligations, options or warrants which the Board of Directors may determine to offer for subscription to holders of any shares of stock of the Corporation may, as the Board of Directors shall determine, be offered to holders of shares of stock of the Corporation of any class or classes or series, and if offered to holders of shares of stock of more than one class or series, in such proportions as between such classes and series as the Board of Directors may determine.

Section 2. *Non-Citizen Voting Limitation.* All (x) capital stock of, or other equity interests in, the Corporation, (y) securities convertible into or exchangeable for shares of capital stock, voting securities or other equity interests in the Corporation, and (z) options, warrants or other rights to acquire the securities described in clauses (x) and (y), whether fixed or contingent, matured or unmatured, contractual, legal, equitable or otherwise (collectively, "Equity Securities") shall be subject to the following limitations:

(a) Non-Citizen Voting Limitation. In no event shall the total number of shares of Equity Securities held by all persons who fail to qualify as a "citizen of the United States," as the term is used in Section 40102(a)(15) of Title 49 of the United States Code, in any similar legislation of the United States enacted in substitution or replacement therefor, and as interpreted by the Department of Transportation, be entitled to be more than 24.9% (or such other maximum percentage as such Section or substitute or replacement legislation shall hereafter provide) of the aggregate votes of all outstanding Equity Securities of the Corporation (the "Cap Amount").

(b) Allocation of Cap Amounts. The restrictions imposed by the Cap Amount shall be applied pro rata among the holders of Equity Securities who fail to qualify as "citizens of the United States" based on the number of votes the underlying securities are entitled to.

(c) Each certificate or other representative document for Equity Securities (including each such certificate or representative document for Equity Securities issued upon any permitted transfer of Equity Securities) shall contain a legend in substantially the following form:

"The **[type of Equity Securities]** represented by this **[certificate/representative document]** are subject to voting restrictions with respect to **[shares/warrants, etc.]** held by persons or entities that fail to qualify as "citizens of the United States" as the term is defined used in Section 40102(a)(15) of Title 49 of the United States Code. Such voting restrictions are contained in the Restated Certificate of United Airlines Holdings, Inc., as the same may be amended or restated from time to time. A complete and correct copy of the Restated Certificate shall be furnished free of charge to the holder of such shares of **[type of Equity Securities]** upon written request to the Secretary of United Airlines Holdings, Inc."

Section 3. *Restrictions on Issuance of Securities.* (a) The Corporation shall not issue nonvoting equity securities to the extent prohibited by Section 1123(a)(6) of the United States Bankruptcy Code for so long as such Section is in effect and applicable to the Corporation.

(b) Except as required by law or as approved by the stockholders, the Corporation shall not issue Serial Preferred Stock pursuant to Article Fourth, Part I with voting rights (unless such Serial Preferred Stock is convertible into Common Stock, in which case such Serial Preferred Stock may vote with the Common Stock on an as-converted basis).

Section 4. *Stockholder Action.* Any action required or permitted to be taken by the stockholders of the Corporation must be effected at a duly called annual or special meeting of such stockholders and may not be effected by any consent in writing by such stockholders.

Section 5. *5% Ownership Limit.*

5.1 For purposes of Sections 5, 6 and 7, the following terms shall have the meanings indicated (and any references to any portions of Treasury Regulation § 1.382-2T shall include any successor provisions):

"*5% Transaction*" means any Transfer of Corporation Securities described in clause (y) or (z) of paragraph 5.2, subject to the provision of such paragraph 5.2.

An "*Affiliate*" of any Person means any other Person, that, directly or indirectly through one or more intermediaries, controls or is controlled by, or is under common control with, such Person; and, for the purposes of this definition only, "control" (including the terms "controlling", "controlled by" and "under common control with") means the possession, direct or indirect, of the power to direct or cause the direction of the management, policies or activities of a Person whether through the ownership of securities, by contract or agency or otherwise.

"*Associate*" has the meaning ascribed to such term in Rule 12b-2 under the Exchange Act.

A Person will be deemed the "*Beneficial Owner*" of, and will be deemed to "*Beneficially Own*," and will be deemed to have "*Beneficial Ownership*" of:

(a) any securities that such Person or any of such Person's Affiliates or Associates is deemed to "Beneficially Own" within the meaning of Rule 13d-3 under the Exchange Act, and any securities deposited into a trust established by or on behalf of the Person or any of its Affiliates or Associates, the sole beneficiaries of which are the shareholders of the Person;

(b) any securities (the "Underlying Securities") that such Person or any of such Person's Affiliates or Associates has the right to acquire (whether such right is exercisable immediately or only after the passage of time) pursuant to any agreement, arrangement or understanding (written or oral), or upon the exercise of conversion rights, exchange rights, rights, warrants or options, or otherwise (it being understood that such Person will also be deemed to be the

Beneficial Owner of the securities convertible into or exchangeable for the Underlying Securities); and

(c) any securities Beneficially Owned by persons that are part of a "group" (within the meaning of Rule 13d-5(b) under the Exchange Act) with such Person. For purposes of calculating the percentage of Voting Securities that are Beneficially Owned by any Person, such calculation will be made based on the aggregate number of issued and outstanding securities at the time of such calculation, but will not include in the denominator any such securities issuable upon any options, warrants or other securities that are exercisable for such securities.

"*Code*" means the Internal Revenue Code of 1986, as amended.

"*Corporation Securities*" means (i) shares of Common Stock, (ii) shares of Preferred Stock (other than preferred stock described in Section 1504(a)(4) of the Code), (iii) warrants, rights, or options (including options within the meaning of Treasury Regulation § 1.382-2T(h)(4)(v)) to purchase stock of the Corporation, and (iv) any other interest that would be treated as "stock" of the Corporation pursuant to Treasury Regulation § 1.382-2T(f)(18).

"*Effective Date*" means February 1, 2006.

"*Exchange Act*" means the Securities Exchange Act of 1934, as amended, or any successor act thereto.

"*Five-Percent Shareholder*" means a Person or group of Persons that is identified as a "5-percent shareholder" of the Corporation pursuant to Treasury Regulation § 1.382-2T(g).

"*Percentage Stock Ownership*" means the percentage Stock Ownership interest as determined in accordance with Treasury Regulation § 1.382-2T(g), (h), (j) and (k).

"*Person*" means any individual, firm, corporation or other legal entity, and includes any successor (by merger or otherwise) of such entity.

"*Prohibited Transfer*" means any purported Transfer of Corporation Securities to the extent that such Transfer is prohibited and/or void under this Section 5.

"*Tax Benefit*" means the net operating loss carryovers, capital loss carryovers, general business credit carryovers, alternative minimum tax credit carryovers and foreign tax credit carryovers, as well as any loss or deduction attributable to a "net unrealized built-in loss" within the meaning of Section 382, of the Corporation or any direct or indirect subsidiary thereof.

"*Transfer*" means, with respect to any person other than the Corporation, any direct or indirect sale, transfer, assignment, conveyance, pledge or other disposition, other than a sale, transfer, assignment, conveyance, pledge or other disposition to a wholly owned subsidiary of the transferor, or, if the transferor is wholly owned by a Person, to a wholly owned subsidiary of such Person. A Transfer also shall include the creation or grant of an option (including an option within the meaning of Treasury Regulation § 1.382-2T(h)(4)(v)).

"*Voting Securities*" means all securities that by their terms are entitled to vote generally in the election of directors of the Corporation (without giving effect to any contractual limitations on voting).

5.2 Any attempted Transfer of Corporation Securities prior to the earliest of (A) February 1, 2014, or such later date as may be approved by the Board of Directors, (B) the repeal, amendment or modification of Section 382 of the Code (and any comparable successor provision) ("Section 382") in such a way as to render the restrictions imposed by Section 382 no longer applicable to the Corporation, (C) the beginning of a taxable year of the Corporation (or any successor thereof) in which no Tax Benefits are available, and (D) the date on which the limitation amount imposed by Section 382 in the event of an ownership change of the Corporation, as defined in Section 382, would not be materially less than the net operating loss carryforward or net unrealized built-in loss of the Corporation (the "Restriction Release Date"), or any attempted Transfer of Corporation Securities pursuant to an agreement entered into prior to the Restriction Release Date, shall be prohibited and void ab initio so far as it purports to transfer ownership or rights in respect of such stock to the Purported Transferee (y) if the transferor is a Five-Percent Shareholder or (z) to the extent that, as a result of such Transfer (or any series of Transfers of which such Transfer is a part), either (1) any Person or group of Persons shall become a Five-Percent Shareholder other than by reason of Treasury Regulation Section 1.382-2T(j)(3) or any successor to such regulation or (2) the Percentage Stock Ownership interest in the Corporation of any Five-Percent Shareholder shall be increased; provided, that this paragraph 5.2 shall not apply to, nor shall any other provision in this Restated Certificate prohibit, restrict or limit in any way, (i) the issuance of Corporation Securities by the Corporation in accordance with the Second Amended Joint Plan of Reorganization of the Corporation dated January 20, 2006 (the "Chapter 11 Plan") or (ii) the issuance of Corporation Securities by the Corporation pursuant to the Agreement and Plan of Merger among UAL Corporation, Continental Airlines, Inc. and JT Merger Sub Inc. dated as of May 2, 2010, but not any subsequent transfer of such Corporation Securities.

5.3 The restrictions set forth in paragraph 5.2 shall not apply to an attempted Transfer that is a 5% Transaction if the transferor or the transferee obtains the prior written approval of the Board of Directors or a duly authorized committee thereof.

As a condition to granting its approval pursuant to this paragraph 5.3, the Board of Directors may, in its discretion, require (at the expense of the transferor and/or transferee) an opinion of counsel selected by the Board of Directors that the Transfer shall not result in the application of any

Section 382 limitation on the use of the Tax Benefits. The Board of Directors may exercise the authority granted by this Section 5 through duly authorized officers or agents of the Corporation.

5.4 Each certificate representing shares of Corporation Securities issued prior to the Restriction Release Date shall contain the legend set forth on <u>Exhibit A</u> hereto, evidencing the restrictions set forth in this Section 5 and Sections 6 and 7.

Section 6. *Treatment of Excess Securities.*

6.1 No employee or agent of the Corporation shall record any Prohibited Transfer, and the purported transferee of such a Prohibited Transfer (the "Purported Transferee") shall not be recognized as a stockholder of the Corporation for any purpose whatsoever in respect of the Corporation Securities which are the subject of the Prohibited Transfer (the "Excess Securities"). Until the Excess Securities are acquired by another Person in a Transfer that is not a Prohibited Transfer, the Purported Transferee shall not be entitled with respect to such Excess Securities to any rights of stockholders of the Corporation, including, without limitation, the right to vote such Excess Securities and to receive dividends or distributions, whether liquidating or otherwise, in respect thereof, if any; provided, however, that the Transferor of such Excess Securities shall not be required to disgorge, and shall be permitted to retain for its own account, any proceeds of such Transfer, and shall have no further rights, responsibilities, obligations or liabilities with respect to such Excess Securities, if such Transfer was a Prohibited Transfer pursuant to Section 5.2(z). Once the Excess Securities have been acquired in a Transfer that is not a Prohibited Transfer, the Corporation Securities shall cease to be Excess Securities. For this purpose, any transfer of Excess Securities not in accordance with the provisions of this Section 6 shall also be a Prohibited Transfer.

6.2 If the Board of Directors determines that a Transfer of Corporation Securities constitutes a Prohibited Transfer then, upon written demand by the Corporation, the Purported Transferee shall transfer or cause to be transferred any certificate or other evidence of ownership of the Excess Securities within the Purported Transferee's possession or control, together with any dividends or other distributions that were received by the Purported Transferee from the Corporation with respect to the Excess Securities ("Prohibited Distributions"), to an agent designated by the Board of Directors (the "Agent"). The Agent shall thereupon sell to a buyer or buyers, which may include the Corporation, the Excess Securities transferred to it in one or more arm's-length transactions (over the New York Stock Exchange or other national securities exchange on which the Corporation Securities may be traded, if possible, or otherwise privately); provided, however, that the Agent shall effect such sale or sales in an orderly fashion and shall not be required to effect any such sale within any specific time frame if, in the Agent's discretion, such sale or sales would disrupt the market for the Corporation Securities or otherwise would adversely affect the value of the Corporation Securities. If the Purported Transferee has resold the Excess Securities before receiving the Corporation's demand to surrender Excess Securities to the Agent, the Purported Transferee shall be deemed to have sold the Excess Securities for the Agent, and shall be required to transfer to the Agent any Prohibited Distributions and proceeds of such sale, except to the extent that the Corporation grants written permission to the Purported Transferee to retain a portion of such sales proceeds not exceeding the amount that the Purported Transferee would have received from the Agent pursuant to Section 6.3 if the Agent rather than the Purported Transferee had resold the Excess Securities.

6.3 The Agent shall apply any proceeds of a sale by it of Excess Securities and, if the Purported Transferee had previously resold the Excess Securities, any amounts

received by it from a Purported Transferee as follows: (x)
first, such amounts shall be paid to the Agent to the extent
necessary to cover its costs and expenses incurred in
connection with its duties hereunder; (y) second, any
remaining amounts shall be paid to the Purported
Transferee, up to the amount paid by the Purported
Transferee for the Excess Securities (or the fair market
value, (1) calculated on the basis of the closing market price
for the Corporation Securities on the day before the
Prohibited Transfer, (2) if the Corporation Securities are
not listed or admitted to trading on any stock exchange but
are traded in the over-the-counter market, calculated based
upon the difference between the highest bid and lowest
asked prices, as such prices are reported by the National
Association of Securities Dealers through its NASDAQ
system or any successor system on the day before the
Prohibited Transfer or, if none, on the last preceding day
for which such quotations exist, or (3) if the Corporation
Securities are neither listed nor admitted to trading on any
stock exchange nor traded in the over-the-counter market,
then as determined in good faith by the Board of Directors,
of the Excess Securities at the time of the Prohibited
Transfer to the Purported Transferee by gift, inheritance, or
similar Transfer), which amount (or fair market value) shall
be determined at the discretion of the Board of Directors;
and (z) third, any remaining amounts, subject to the
limitations imposed by the following proviso, shall be paid
to one or more organizations qualifying under Section
501(c)(3) of the Code (or any comparable successor
provision) ("Section 501(c)(3)") selected by the Board of
Directors; provided, however, that if the Excess Securities
(including any Excess Securities arising from a previous
Prohibited Transfer not sold by the Agent in a prior sale or
sales), represent a 5% or greater Percentage Stock
Ownership in any class of Corporation Securities, then any
such remaining amounts to the extent attributable to the
disposition of the portion of such Excess Securities
exceeding a 4.99% Percentage Stock Ownership interest in

such class shall be paid to two or more organizations qualifying under Section 501(c)(3) selected by the Board of Directors. The recourse of any Purported Transferee in respect of any Prohibited Transfer shall be limited to the amount payable to the Purported Transferee pursuant to clause (y) of the preceding sentence. In no event shall the proceeds of any sale of Excess Securities pursuant to this Section 6 inure to the benefit of the Corporation.

6.4 If the Purported Transferee fails to surrender the Excess Securities or the proceeds of a sale thereof to the Agent within thirty days from the date on which the Corporation makes a written demand pursuant to Section 6.2, then the Corporation shall use its best efforts to enforce the provisions hereof, including the institution of legal proceedings to compel the surrender.

6.5 The Corporation shall make the written demand described in Section 6.2 within thirty days of the date on which the Board of Directors determines that the attempted Transfer would result in Excess Securities; provided, however, that if the Corporation makes such demand at a later date, the provisions of Sections 5 and 6 shall apply nonetheless.

Section 7. *Board Authority.*

The Board of Directors shall have the power to determine all matters necessary for assessing compliance with Sections 5 and 6, including, without limitation, (A) the identification of Five-Percent Shareholders, (B) whether a Transfer is a 5% Transaction or a Prohibited Transfer, (C) the Percentage Stock Ownership in the Corporation of any Five-Percent Shareholder, (D) whether an instrument constitutes a Corporation Security, (E) the amount (or fair market value) due to a Purported Transferee pursuant to clause (y) of Section 6.3, and (F) any other matters which the Board of Directors determines to be relevant; and the good faith determination of the Board of Directors on such matters shall be conclusive and binding for all the purposes of Sections 5 and 6.

ARTICLE FIFTH.

Unless otherwise indicated, any reference in this Article Fifth to "Section," "subsection," "paragraph," "subparagraph," or "clause" shall refer to a Section, subsection, paragraph, subparagraph or clause in this Article Fifth.

Section 1. *Definitions.* As used in this Restated Certificate, the following terms shall have the following meanings:

1.1 *"Chief Executive Officer"* means the Chief Executive Officer of the Corporation.

1.2 *"Director"* means a director of the Corporation.

1.3 *"Exchange Act"* means the Securities Exchange Act of 1934, as amended, or any successor act thereto.

1.4 *"GCL"* means the General Corporation Law of the State of Delaware, as amended from time to time.

1.5 *"Person"* means any individual, corporation, limited liability company, association, partnership, joint venture, trust or unincorporated organization, or a governmental entity or any department, agency or political subdivision thereof.

1.6 *"Restated Bylaws"* means the Amended and Restated Bylaws of the Corporation, as amended from time to time.

1.7 *"Stockholders"* means the stockholders of the Corporation.

Section 2. *Directors.*

2.1 *General Powers.* Except as otherwise provided in this Restated Certificate, the business and affairs of the

Corporation shall be managed by or under the direction of the Board of Directors. The Board of Directors may adopt such rules and regulations, not inconsistent with this Restated Certificate, the Restated Bylaws or applicable law, as it may deem proper for the conduct of its meetings and the management of the Corporation. In addition to the powers conferred expressly by this Restated Certificate and the Restated Bylaws, the Board of Directors may exercise all powers and perform all acts that are not required, by this Restated Certificate, the Restated Bylaws or applicable law, to be exercised or performed by the Stockholders.

2.2 *Number.* Except as otherwise provided for or fixed by or pursuant to the provisions of Article Fourth hereof relating to the rights of the holders of any class or series of stock to elect Directors and take certain actions with respect to such elected Directors, the number of Directors shall be fixed from time to time exclusively pursuant to a resolution of the Board of Directors (but shall not be fewer than five).

2.3 *Term of Office.* Except as otherwise provided in this Restated Certificate, each Director shall hold office until the next annual meeting of Stockholders and until his or her successor is elected and qualified, subject to such Director's earlier death, resignation or removal.

2.4 *Resignation of Directors.* Any Director may resign at any time upon written notice to the Corporation.

2.5 *Voting by Directors.* Subject to any greater or additional vote of the Board or of any class of Directors required by law, by this Restated Certificate or the Restated Bylaws, an act of the Board shall require the affirmative vote of at least a majority of the votes entitled to be cast by the Directors present at a meeting of the Board at which a quorum is present. Each Director shall have one vote.

Section 3. *Special Voting Provisions.*

3.1 *Election of Directors.* Notwithstanding any other provision of this Restated Certificate, and except as otherwise required by law, whenever the holders of one or more series of Preferred Stock shall have the right, voting separately as a class, to elect one or more Directors, the term of office, the filling of vacancies, the removal from office and other features of such directorships shall be governed by the terms of this Restated Certificate or the resolution or resolutions of the Board of Directors establishing such series of Preferred Stock. During any period when the holders of any series of Preferred Stock (other than the Class Pilot MEC Preferred Stock and the Class IAM Preferred Stock) have the right to elect additional Directors as provided for or fixed by or pursuant to the provisions of Article Fourth hereof, then upon commencement and for the duration of the period during which such right continues: (i) the then otherwise total authorized number of Directors of the Corporation shall automatically be increased by such specified number of Directors, and the holders of such Preferred Stock shall be entitled to elect the additional Directors so provided for or fixed by or pursuant to said provisions, and (ii) each such additional Director shall serve until such office terminates pursuant to said provisions, whichever occurs earlier, subject to his or her earlier death, disqualification, resignation or removal. Except as otherwise provided by the Board of Directors in the resolution or resolutions establishing a series of Preferred Stock, whenever the holders of any series of Preferred Stock having a right to elect additional Directors are divested of such right pursuant to the provisions of such series of Preferred Stock, the terms of office of all such additional Directors elected by the holders of such series of Preferred Stock, or selected to fill any vacancies resulting from the death, resignation, disqualification or removal of such additional Directors, shall forthwith terminate and the total authorized number of Directors of the Corporation shall be reduced accordingly.

3.2 *Amendment to the Restated Bylaws.* The Board of
Directors is expressly authorized to make, alter, amend or
repeal the Restated Bylaws, and to adopt new bylaws;
provided, however, that (i) prior to the Chairman
Succession Date (as defined in the Restated Bylaws), the
Board of Directors shall not be permitted to alter, amend or
repeal Section 5.5(c), Section 5.14, the last sentence of
Section 5.6 or the proviso to Section 8.1 and (ii) no bylaws
hereafter adopted shall invalidate any prior act of the Board
of Directors that would have been valid if such bylaws had
not been adopted.

ARTICLE SIXTH.

(a) A director of the Corporation shall not be personally
liable to the Corporation or its stockholders for monetary
damages for breach of fiduciary duty as a director, except
for liability (i) for any breach of the director's duty of loyalty
to the Corporation or its stockholders, (ii) for acts or
omissions not in good faith or which involve intentional
misconduct or a knowing violation of law, (iii) under Section
174 of the GCL, or (iv) for any transaction from which the
director derived an improper personal benefit.

(b) Each person who was or is made a party or is threatened
to be made a party or is involved in any threatened, pending
or completed action, suit or proceeding, whether civil,
criminal, administrative or investigative (hereinafter a
"proceeding"), by reason of the fact that he or she, or a
person of whom he or she is the legal representative, is or
was a director or officer of the Corporation or is or was
serving at the request of the Corporation as a director,
officer or employee of another corporation or of a
partnership, joint venture, trust or other enterprise,
including service with respect to employee benefit plans,
whether the basis of such proceeding is alleged action in an
official capacity as a director or officer or in any other
capacity while serving as a director, officer or employee

shall be indemnified and held harmless by the Corporation to the fullest extent authorized by the GCL, as the same exists or may hereafter be amended (but, in the case of any such amendment, only to the extent that such amendment permits the Corporation to provide broader indemnification rights than said law permitted the Corporation to provide prior to such amendment), against all expense, liability and loss (including attorneys' fees, judgments, fines, ERISA excise taxes or penalties and amounts paid or to be paid in settlement) actually and reasonably incurred or suffered by such person in connection therewith. Such indemnification shall continue as to a person who has ceased to be a director or officer and shall inure to the benefit of his or her heirs, executors and administrators; provided, however, that, except as provided in paragraph (c) hereof, the Corporation shall indemnify any such person seeking indemnification in connection with a proceeding (or part thereof) initiated by such person only if such proceeding (or part thereof) was authorized by the Board of Directors. Notwithstanding anything to the contrary herein, the Corporation shall not be obligated to indemnify a director or officer for costs and expenses relating to proceedings (or any part thereof) instituted against the Corporation by such director or officer (other than proceedings pursuant to which such director or officer is seeking to enforce such director's or officer's indemnification rights hereunder). The right to indemnification conferred in this Article Sixth with respect to directors and officers shall be a contract right and shall include the right to be paid by the Corporation the expenses incurred in defending any such proceeding in advance of its final disposition; provided, however, that, if the GCL requires, the payment of such expense incurred by a director or officer in his or her capacity as a director or officer (and not in any other capacity in which service was or is rendered by such person while a director or officer, including, without limitation, service to an employee benefit plan) in advance of the final disposition of a proceeding, shall be made only upon delivery to the Corporation of an undertaking, by or on behalf of such director or officer, to repay all amounts so advanced if it shall ultimately be determined that such director or officer is not entitled to be indemnified under this Article Sixth or otherwise. The Corporation may provide indemnification to employees (other than officers) and agents of the Corporation with the same scope and effect as the foregoing indemnification of directors and officers to the extent (i) permitted by the laws of the State of Delaware as from time to time in effect, and (ii) authorized in the sole discretion any of the Chief Executive Officer, the President, the Chief Financial Officer or the General Counsel of the Corporation; provided, however, that any such indemnification shall not constitute a contract right for any such employee or agent.

(c) If a claim under paragraph (b) of this Article Sixth is not paid in full by the Corporation within thirty days after a written claim has been received by the Corporation, the claimant may at any time thereafter bring suit against the Corporation to recover the unpaid amount of the claim and, if successful in whole or in part, the claimant shall be entitled to be paid also the expense of prosecuting such claim. It shall be a defense to any such action (other than an action brought to enforce a claim for expenses incurred in defending any proceeding in advance of its final disposition where the required undertaking, if any is required, has been tendered to the Corporation) that the claimant has not met the standards of conduct which make it permissible under the GCL for the Corporation to indemnify the claimant for the amount claimed, but the burden of proving such defense shall be on the Corporation. Neither the failure of the Corporation (including its Board of Directors, independent legal counsel, or its stockholders) to have made a determination prior to the commencement of such action that indemnification of the claimant is proper in the circumstances because he or she has met the applicable standard of conduct set forth in the GCL, nor an actual determination by the Corporation (including its Board of Directors, independent legal counsel, or its stockholders) that the claimant has not met such applicable standard of conduct, shall be a defense to the action or create a presumption that the claimant has not met the applicable standard of conduct.

(d) The right to indemnification and the payment of expenses incurred in defending a proceeding in advance of its final disposition conferred in this Article Sixth shall not be exclusive of any other right which any person may have or hereafter acquire under any statute, provision of this Restated Certificate, by-law, agreement, vote of stockholders or disinterested directors or otherwise.

(e) The Corporation may maintain insurance, at its expense, to protect itself and any director, officer, employee or agent of the Corporation or another corporation, partnership, joint venture, trust or other enterprise against any such expense, liability or loss, whether or not the Corporation would have the power to indemnify such person against such expense, liability or loss under the GCL.

ARTICLE SEVENTH.

Except as expressly provided in this Restated Certificate, the Corporation reserves the right to amend, alter, change or repeal any provision contained in this Restated Certificate, in the manner now or hereafter prescribed by the laws of Delaware and this Restated Certificate, and all rights and powers conferred herein upon stockholders and directors are granted subject to this reservation.

IN WITNESS WHEREOF, the Corporation has caused this Amended and Restated Certificate of Incorporation to be executed by its duly authorized officer on this 27th day of June, 2019.

UNITED CONTINENTAL HOLDINGS, INC.

By: /s/ Jennifer L. Kraft

Name: Jennifer L. Kraft
Title: Vice President and
                         Secretary

Made in United States
North Haven, CT
01 September 2023

40985659R00370